Management Control Systems

MANAGEMENT CONTROL SYSTEMS

Cases and Readings

BY

ROBERT N. ANTHONY

While serving as Ross Graham Walker Professor of Management Controls
(since appointed Assistant Secretary of Defense [Comptroller])

JOHN DEARDEN

Professor of Business Administration

AND

RICHARD F. VANCIL

Associate Professor of Business Administration

All of the Graduate School of Business Administration,
Harvard University

1965

RICHARD D. IRWIN, INC.

Homewood, Illinois

First Printing, December, 1965
Second Printing, May, 1966
Third Printing, January, 1967
Fourth Printing, December, 1967
Fifth Printing, April, 1968
Sixth Printing, December, 1968
Seventh Printing, June, 1969
Eighth Printing, October, 1969
Ninth Printing, April, 1970

Library of Congress Catalog Card No. 65–27842

PRINTED IN THE UNITED STATES OF AMERICA

PREFACE

This book is concerned with management control. Management control is the process by which managers assure that resources are obtained and used effectively and efficiently in the accomplishment of an organization's objectives.

The area within management control that has been developed furthest is the control of production costs. Standard costs and flexible budgets have been used effectively for a considerable period of time. Because this area is dealt with extensively by other authors, this book deliberately has little material on this area. Instead its focus is on those areas of management control that are less developed. Some of these areas are just beginning to emerge as fields for serious study. In particular, this book is principally concerned with the control of managed costs, with profit centers, and with capital acquisitions.

The book is designed for a one-semester course, for students who have had a course in management accounting and who wish to study management control in greater depth. (In fact, most of the material in the book is currently being used in a second-year course in the Control Field at the Harvard Business School.) None of the readings and few of the cases require a detailed knowledge of accounting or finance. Many of the cases have been used successfully in management education courses where many of the participants have had no formal accounting courses.

All of the cases in the book have been used at the Harvard Business School. Many have also been used at other institutions. All have been selected for their interest and educational value as a basis for class discussion. They are not necessarily intended to illustrate either correct or incorrect handling of management problems. As in all cases of this type, there are no right answers. The educational value of the cases comes from the practice the student receives in analyzing management control problems and in discussing and defending his analysis before the class.

Acknowledgments

The course from which the material in this book was drawn was originally developed at the Harvard Business School by Professor Ross G. Walker. We wish to acknowledge his pioneering work in the development of both the concepts underlying the course, and the methods of teaching these concepts. Subsequently the course was taught by Russell H. Hassler, now Financial Vice President of Hawaiian Electric Company, Ltd., and by

Neil E. Harlan, now Vice President–Finance, Anderson, Clayton & Company. Their contribution in developing the course is sincerely acknowledged.

Specific cases were contributed to this book by Professors E. P. Learned, E. Raymond Corey, David F. Hawkins, and Erich A. Helfert at the Harvard Business School, and by Dean Glenn D. Overman of Arizona State University, Professor William Rotch of the University of Virginia, and Professor E. L. Swearingen of Oklahoma State University. Their permission to include their cases in this collection are appreciated. In addition, we wish to acknowledge the assistance provided us over the past few years by our research assistants: L. Paul Berman, Robert H. Caplan, James S. Hekimian, John Mauriel, F. Warren McFarlan, Chei-Min Paik, and Jack L. Treynor. Misses Marian V. Sears and Carol Peterson were invaluable in editing and supervising the preparation of various stages of the manuscript, and their assistance is gratefully acknowledged.

Except where otherwise noted, all cases in this book are copyrighted by the President and Fellows of Harvard College, and we appreciate their permission to reproduce them here. We owe an even greater debt to the many businessmen who cooperated with us in the preparation of these cases, and to the administration of the Harvard Business School for supporting our efforts in case collection and the development of this course.

ROBERT N. ANTHONY
JOHN DEARDEN
RICHARD F. VANCIL

HARVARD UNIVERSITY
September 1, 1965

Case material of the Harvard Graduate School of Business Administration is made possible by the co-operation of business firms who may wish to remain anonymous by having names, quantities and other identifying details disguised while maintaining basic relationships. Cases are prepared as the basis for class discussion rather than to illustrate either effective or ineffective handling of administrative situations.

TABLE OF CONTENTS

Chapter One

CHARACTERISTICS OF MANAGEMENT CONTROL SYSTEMS

By Robert N. Anthony*

Since dogs and humans are both mammals, some generalizations that apply to one species also apply to the other. It is for this reason that some new surgical techniques can be tested on dogs before being risked on humans. But dogs and humans differ, and unless these differences are recognized, generalizations that are valid for one species may be erroneously applied to the other. For example, canine behavior can be largely explained in terms of reflexes, but human behavior is much more complicated. Similarly, some generalizations can be made about the whole planning and control process in a business; however, there actually are several quite different types of planning and control processes, and mistakes may be made if a generalization (principle, rule, technique) valid for one type is applied to the other.

This note suggests a classification of the main topics or "species" that come within the broad term Planning and Control Systems as well as the distinguishing characteristics of each topic. It is hoped that such a classification will lead to a sorting out and sharpening of principles and techniques applicable to each species. The particular classification chosen has been arrived at after careful analysis of how well various alternatives match statements made in the literature and, more important, what is found in practice. It is, however, tentative. Better schemes may well be developed, and we expose this one primarily in the hope that discussion of it will lead to agreement

* Based on research sponsored by the Division of Research at Harvard Business School. See R. N. Anthony, *Planning and Control Systems: A Framework for Analysis* (Boston: Division of Research, Harvard Business School, 1965).

on *some* scheme, not necessarily this one. The classification is discussed in more detail in my book, *Planning and Control Systems: A Framework for Analysis*.

In this note, we shall focus on a process labeled management control. We shall describe its main characteristics, and distinguish it from other processes labeled strategic planning, operational control, financial accounting, and information handling. Obviously, we do not assert that these processes can be separated by sharply defined boundaries; one shades into another. Strategic planning sets the guidelines for management control, and management control sets the guidelines for operational control. The complete management function involves an integration of all these processes, and the processes are complementary. We do assert that the processes are sufficiently distinct so that those who design and use planning and control systems will make expensive errors if they fail to take into account both the common characteristics of a process and the differences between processes. This note describes these similarities and differences and points out some of the errors made when they are not recognized.

MANAGEMENT CONTROL

Management control is the process by which managers assure that resources are obtained and used effectively and efficiently in the accomplishment of the organization's objectives.

Management control is a process carried on within the framework established by strategic planning. Objectives, facilities, organization, and financial factors are more or less accepted as givens. Decisions about next year's budget, for example, are constrained within policies and guidelines prescribed by top management. The management control process is intended to make possible the achievement of planned objectives as effectively and efficiently as possible within these givens.

The purpose of a management control system is to encourage managers to take actions that are in the best interests of the company. Technically, this purpose can be described as *goal congruence*. For many reasons, perfect goal congruence is not achievable; the most we can realistically aim for is a minimum amount of conflict between individual goals and corporate goals. Clearly, if the system increases this conflict—as happens when a certain course of action makes the reported performance of an individual appear better, even though it is detrimental to the best interests of the company—something is wrong with the system. For example, if the system is structured so that a certain course of action increases the reported profits of a division and at the same time lessens the profits of the company as a whole, there is something wrong. Psychological considerations are dominant in management control. Activities such as communicating, persuading, exhorting, inspiring, and criticizing are an important part of the process.

Ordinarily, a management control system is a *total* system in the sense that it embraces all aspects of the company's operation. It needs to be a total system because an important management function is to assure that all parts of the operation are in balance with one another; and in order to examine balance, management needs information about each of the parts.

With rare exceptions, the management control system is built around a financial structure; that is, resources and outputs are expressed in monetary units. Money is the only common denominator by means of which the heterogeneous elements of output and resources (e.g., hours of labor, type of labor, quantity and quality of material, amount and kind of products produced) can be combined and compared. Although the financial structure is usually the central focus, nonmonetary measures such as time, number of persons, and reject and spoilage rates are also important parts of the system.)

The management control process tends to be rhythmic; it follows a definite pattern and timetable, month after month and year after year. In budgetary control, which is an important part of the management control process, certain steps are taken in a prescribed sequence and at certain dates each year: dissemination of guidelines, preparation of original estimates, transmission of these estimates up through the several echelons in the organization, review of these estimates, final approval by top management, dissemination back through the organization, operation, reporting, and the appraisal of performance. The procedure to be followed at each step in this process, the dates when the steps are to be completed, and even the forms to be used can be, and often are, set forth in a manual.

A management control system is, or should be, a coordinated, integrated system; that is, although data collected for one purpose may differ from those collected for another purpose, these data should be reconcilable with one another. In a sense, the management control system is a *single* system, but it is perhaps more accurate to think of it as a set of interlocking subsystems. In many organizations, for example, three types of cost information are needed for management control: (1) costs by responsibility centers, used for planning and controlling the activities of responsible supervisors; (2) full program costs, used for pricing and other operating decisions in normal circumstances; (3) direct program costs, used for pricing and other operating decisions in special circumstances, such as when management wishes to utilize idle capacity. ("Program" is here used for any activity in which the organization engages. In industrial companies, programs consist of products or product lines, and "product costs" can be substituted in the above statements.)

Line managers are the focal points in management control. They are the persons whose judgments are incorporated in the approval plans, and they are the persons who must influence others and whose performance is measured. Staff people collect, summarize, and present information that is useful in the process, and they make calculations that translate management judgments into the format of the system. Such a staff may be large in numbers; indeed, the control department is often the largest staff department in a company. However, the significant decisions are made by the line managers, not by the staff.

STRATEGIC PLANNING

Strategic planning is the process of deciding on the objectives of the organization, on changes in these objectives, on the resources used to attain these objectives, and on the policies that are to govern the acquisition, use, and disposition of these resources.

The word strategy is used here in its usual sense of deciding on how to combine and employ resources. Thus, strategic planning is a process having to do with the formulation of long-range, strategic, policy-type plans that change the character or direction of the organization. In an industrial company, this includes planning that affects the objectives of the company; policies of all types (including policies as to management control and other processes); the acquisition and disposition of major facilities, divisions, or subsidiaries; the markets to be served and distribution channels for serving them; the organization structure (as distinguished from individual personnel actions); research and development of new product lines (as distinguished from modifications in existing products and product changes within existing lines); sources of new permanent capital, dividend policy, and so on. Strategic planning decisions affect the physical, financial, and organizational framework within which operations are carried on. Briefly, here are some ways in which the strategic planning process differs from the management control process.

A strategic plan usually relates to some part of the organization, rather than to the totality; the concept of a master planner who constantly keeps all parts of the organization at some coordinated optimum is a nice concept, but an unrealistic one. Life is too complicated for any human, or computer, to do this.

Strategic planning is essentially *irregular*. Problems, opportunities, and bright ideas do not arise according to some set timetable, and they have to be dealt with whenever they happen to be perceived. The appropriate analytical techniques depend on the nature of the problem being analyzed, and no overall approach (such as a mathematical model) has been developed that is of much help in analyzing all types of strategic problems. Indeed, an overemphasis on a systematic approach is quite likely to stifle the essential element of creativity. In strategic planning, management works now on one problem, now on another, according to the needs and opportunities of the moment.

The estimates used in strategic planning are intended to show the *expected* results of the plan. They are neutral and impersonal. By contrast, the management control process and the data used in it are intended to influence managers to take actions that will lead to *desired* results. Thus, in connection with management control it is appropriate to discuss how tight an operating budget should be. Should the goals be set so high that only an outstanding manager can achieve them, or should they be set so that they are attainable by the average manager? At what level does frustration inhibit a manager's best efforts? Does an attainable budget lead to complacency? And so on. In strategic planning, the question to be asked about the figures is simply: Is this the most reasonable estimate that can be made?

Strategic planning relies heavily on external information—that is, on data collected from outside the company, such as market analyses, estimates of costs and other factors involved in building a plant in a new locality, technological developments, and so on. When data from the normal information system are used, they usually must be recast to fit the needs of the problem being anaylzed. For example, current operating costs that are collected for measuring performance and for making pricing and other operating decisions usually must be restructured before they are useful in deciding whether to close down the plant. Another characteristic of the relevant information is that much of it is imprecise. The strategic planner estimates what will probably happen, often over a rather long time period. These estimates are likely to have a high degree of uncertainty, and they must be treated accordingly.

In the management control process, the communication of objectives, policies, guidelines, decisions, and results throughout the organization is extremely important. In the strategic planning process, communication is much simpler and involves relatively few persons; indeed, the need for secrecy often requires that steps be taken to inhibit communication. (Wide communication of the decisions that result from strategic planning is obviously important; this is part of the management control process.) Strategic planning is essentially applied economics, whereas management control is essentially applied social psychology.

Both management control and strategic planning involve top management, but middle managers (i.e., operating management) typically have a much more important role in management control than in strategic planning. Middle managers usually are not major participants in the strategic planning process and sometimes are not even aware that a plan is being considered. Many operating executives are by temperament not very good at strategic planning. Also, the pressures of current activities usually do not allow them to devote the necessary time to such work. Currently, there is a tendency in companies to set up separate staffs to gather the facts and make the analyses that provide the background material for strategic decisions. These and other differences between management control and strategic planning are summarized in Exhibit 1.

Strategic planning and management control activities tend to conflict with one another in some respects. The time that management spends in thinking about the future is taken from time that it could otherwise use in controlling current operations, so in this indirect way strategic planning can hurt current performance. And, of course, the reverse also is true. More directly, many actions that are taken for long-run, strategic reasons make current profits smaller than they otherwise would be. Research and some types of advertising expenditures are obvious examples. The problem of striking the right balance between strategic and operating considerations is one of the central problems in the whole management process.

Consequences of Confusion

Following are statements illustrating some of the consequences of failing to make a distinction between strategic planning and management control.

"We should set up a long-range planning procedure and work out a systematized way of considering *all* our plans, similar to the way we construct next year's budget." A long-range plan shows the estimated consequences over the next several years of strategic decisions already taken. It is part of the management control process. Although it provides a useful background for considering strategic proposals, it is not strategic planning. Strategic proposals should be made whenever the opportunity or the need is perceived in a form that best presents the arguments.

"The only relevant costs are incremental costs; pay no attention to fixed or sunk costs." This is so in strategic planning, but operating managers are often motivated in the wrong direction if their decisions are based on incremental costs—for example, in intracompany transactions.

"We may be selling Plant X someday. We should therefore set up the operating reports so that management will have at its fingertips the information it will need when it is deciding this question. For example, we should show inventory and fixed assets at their current market value." Operating reports should be designed to assist in the management of current operations. Special compilations of data are needed for such major, non routine actions as the sale of a plant. Collection of such data routinely is both too expensive and likely to impede sound operating decisions.

"Our ultimate goal is an all-purpose control system—integrated data processing—so that management will have all the data it needs for whatever problem it decides to tackle. We should collect data in elemental building blocks that can be combined in various ways to answer all conceivable questions." This is an impossible goal. Each strategic proposal requires that the data be assembled in the way that best fits the requirements of that proposal. No one can foresee all the possibilities. The building block idea is sound within limits, but the limits are not so broad that all problems are encompassed.

"All levels of management should participate in planning." All levels of management should participate in the planning part of the management control process, but operating managers typically do not have the time, the inclination, or the analytical bent that is required for formulating strategic plans. Furthermore, such plans often must be kept highly secret.

Exhibit 1

SOME DISTINCTIONS BETWEEN STRATEGIC PLANNING AND MANAGEMENT CONTROL

Characteristic	*Strategic Planning*	*Management Control*
Focus of plans	On one aspect at a time	On whole organization
Complexities	Many variables	Less complex
Degree of structure	Unstructured and irregular; each problem different	Rhythmic; prescribed procedures
Nature of information	Tailor-made for the problem; more external and predictive; less accurate	Integrated; more internal and historical; more accurate
Communication of information	Relatively simple	Relatively difficult
Purpose of estimates	Show expected results	Lead to desired results
Persons primarily involved	Staff and top management	Line and top management
Number of persons involved	Small	Large
Mental activity	Creative; analytical	Administrative; persuasive
Source discipline	Economics	Social psychology
Planning and control	Planning dominant, but some control	Emphasis on both planning and control
Time horizon	Tends to be long	Tends to be short
End result	Policies and precedents	Action within policies and precedents
Appraisal of the job done	Extremely difficult	Much less difficult

OPERATIONAL CONTROL

Operational control is the process of assuring that specific tasks are carried out effectively and efficiently.

As the definition suggests, the focus of operational control is on individual tasks or transactions: scheduling and controlling individual jobs through a shop, as contrasted with measuring the performance of the shop as a whole; procuring specific items for inventory, as contrasted with the management of inventory as a whole; specific personnel actions, as contrasted with personnel management; and so on.

The definition does not suggest another characteristic that applies to most activities that are subject to operational control, namely, that these activities are capable of being programmed. In order to explain what these activities are, we need first to develop the concept of outputs and inputs.

Outputs are the products, services, or other effects created by an organization. *Inputs* are the resources the organization consumes. Every organization has, or at least is intended to have, outputs, even though they may not be readily measurable or even clearly definable; that is, every organization does something, and that something is its output. In a business, outputs are goods, services, and other intangibles. In a school, the output is education; in a hospital, patient care; in a law office, advice and counsel; in a government, public service or defense posture. Similarly, the inputs may range from easily valued items, such as purchased parts, to such intangible items as executive thought.

Moreover, every unit within an organization has outputs. In the case of factories, the output is a product. In all other units—personnel, transportation, sales, engineering, administration, and so on—it is a service. Since these services are often not priced, the amounts are difficult to measure. Nevertheless, the outputs exist.

One of the important management tasks in an organization is to seek the *optimum* relationship between outputs and inputs. In many situations, it is rarely if ever possible to determine the optimum relationship between outputs and inputs objectively; instead, the choice of a relationship is a matter of subjective judgment. This is true because there is no scientific or objective way of determining how output will be affected by changes in inputs. How much should a company spend for advertising? Are additional fire trucks, or schoolteachers, or policemen worth their cost? Informed people will disagree on the answers to questions of this type.

The term managed costs is descriptive of the type of inputs for which an objective decision cannot be made as to the optimum quantity to be employed. An important management control function is to make judgments as to the "right" amount of managed costs in a given set of circumstances. These are, by definition, subjective judgments, and such judgments fall within the management control process.

In other situations, there is at least the possibility that an optimum relationship between outputs and inputs can be found. It is unrealistic to imply that this relationship ever can be determined in an absolute sense, inasmuch as new and better ways of doing things are constantly being developed; therefore, a more realistic meaning of optimum is this: The optimum is that combination of resources, out of all *known* combinations, that will produce the desired output at the lowest cost. If the optimum input-output relationship for a given activity can be predetermined, then the inputs that should be employed in a given set of circumstances can be described and reduced to rules; that is, they can be programmed.

An an example of an activity to which operational control is applicable, consider the inventory area. If the demand for an item, the cost of storing it, its production cost and production time, and the loss involved in not filling an order are known, then the optimum inventory level and the optimum production or procurement schedule can be calculated. Even if these factors cannot be known with certainty (as, of course, is the case with all future events), sound estimates nevertheless can be made, inventory levels and production or procurement schedules based on these estimates can be calculated, and reasonable men will agree with the results of these calculations.

An inventory control system using rules derived from such calculations is an example of operational control.

By contrast, consider the legal department of a company. No device can measure the quality, or even the quantity, of the legal service that constitutes the output of this department. No formula can show the amount of service the department should render or the optimum amount of costs that should be incurred. Impressions as to the "right" amount of service, the "right" amount of cost, and the "right" relationship between the service actually rendered and the cost actually incurred are strictly subjective. They are judgments made by management. If persons disagree on these judgments, there is no objective way of resolving the disagreement. Yet the legal department, as a part of the whole organization, must be controlled; the chief counsel must operate within the framework of policies prescribed by top management. The type of control necessary in this situation is management control.

Examples of activities that are susceptible to operational control are automated plants, such as cement plants, oil refineries, and power generating stations; the directly productive operations of most manufacturing plants, but often not the indirect, overhead items; production scheduling; inventory control; the order-taking type of selling activity; and order processing, premium billing, payroll accounting, check handling, and similar paperwork activities.

Examples of activities for which management control is necessary are the total operation of most manufacturing plants, which includes such judgment inputs as indirect labor, employees' benefit and welfare programs, safety activities, training, and supervision; most advertising, sales promotion, pricing, selling (as distinguished from order-taking), and similar marketing activities; most aspects of finance; most aspects of research, development, and design; the work of staff units of all types; and the activities of top management.

The control appropriate for the whole of any unit that carries on both programmed and nonprogrammed types of activities is management control. Thus, the control of one division of a company is management control. The control of the whole accounting department is management control, even though operational control is appropriate for certain aspects of the work, such as posting and check writing.

Some people believe that the distinction between the two classes of activities described above is merely one of degree rather than of kind; they say that all we are doing is distinguishing between situations in which control is easy and those in which control is difficult. We think the distinction is more fundamental, and hope this will be apparent from the following brief list of characteristics that distinguish management control from operational control.

Management control covers the whole of an organization. Each operational control procedure is restricted to a subunit, often a narrowly circumscribed activity. Just as management control occurs within a set of policies derived from strategic planning, so operational control occurs within a set of well-defined procedures and rules derived from management control.

Control is more difficult in management control than in operational control because of the absence of a scientific standard with which actual performance can be compared. A good operational control system can provide a much higher degree of assurance that actions are proceeding as desired than can a management control system.

An operational control system is a *rational* system; that is, the action to be taken is decided by a set of logical rules. These rules may or may not cover all aspects of a given problem. Situations not covered by the rules are designated as exceptions and are resolved by human judgment. Other than these exceptions, application of the rules is automatic. The rules in principle can be programmed into a computer, and the choice between using a computer and using a human being depends primarily on the relative cost of each method.

In management control, psychological considerations are dominant. The management control system at most assists those who take action; it does not directly or by itself result in action without human intervention. By contrast, the end product of an inventory control system can be an order, such as a decision to replenish a certain inventory item, and this order may be based entirely on calculations from formulas incorporated in the system. (The formulas were devised by human beings, but this is a management control process, not an operational control process.)

In a consideration of operational control, analogies with mechanical, electrical, and hydraulic systems are reasonable and useful, and such terms as feedback, network balancing, optimization, and so on are relevant. It is perfectly appropriate, for example, to view an operational control system as analogous to a thermostat which turns the furnace on and off according to its perception of changes in temperature. These analogies do not work well as models for management control systems, however, because the success of these systems is highly dependent on their impact on people, and people are not like thermostats or furnaces; one can't light a fire under a human being simply by turning up a thermostat.

The management control system is ordinarily built around a financial structure, whereas operational control data are often nonmonetary. They may be expressed in terms of man-hours, number of items, pounds of waste, and so on. Since each operational control procedure is designed for a limited area of application, it is feasible to use the basis of measurement that is most appropriate for that area.

Data in an operational control system are often in real time (i.e., they are reported as the event is occurring) and relate to individual events, whereas data in a management control system are often retrospective and summarize many separate events. Computer specialists who do not make such a distinction dream about a system that will display to the management the current status of every individual activity in the organization. Although this *could* be done, it *should not* be done; management does not want such detail. Management does not need to know the time at which lot No. 1007 was transferred from station 27 to station 28; rather, it needs to know only that the process is, or is not, proceeding as planned, and if not, where the trouble lies.

Similarly, operational control uses exact data, whereas management control needs only approximations. Material is ordered and scheduled in specific quantities, employers are paid the exact amount due them, but data on management control reports need contain only two or three significant digits and are therefore rounded to thousands of dollars, to millions of dollars, or even (in the U.S. government) to billions of dollars.

An operational control system requires a mathematical model of the operation. Although it may not always be expressed explicitly in mathematical notation, a decision rule states that given certain values for parameters a, $b, \ldots n$, action X is to be taken. Models are not so important in management control. In a sense, a budget and a PERT network are models associated with the management control process, but they are not the essence of the process.

The formal management control *system* is only a part of the management control *process*, actually a relatively unimportant part. The system can help motivate the manager to make decisions that are in the best interests of the organization, and the system can provide information that aids the manager in making these decisions; but many other stimuli are involved in motivating the manager, and good information does not automatically produce good decisions. The success or failure of the management control process depends on the personal characteristics of the manager—his judgment, his knowledge, his ability to influence others.

In operational control, the system itself is relatively more important. Except in fully automated operations, it is an exaggeration to say that the system *is* the process, but it is not much of an exaggeration. An operational control system ordinarily states what action should be taken; it makes the decisions. As with any operation, management vigilance is required to detect an unforeseen foul-up in the operation or a change in the conditions on which the technique is predicated, and to initiate the necessary corrective action. And management will be seeking ways to improve the technique. In general, however, the degree of management involvement in operational control is small, whereas in management control it is large.

As new techniques are developed, there is a tendency for more and more activities to become susceptible to operational control. In the factory, the production schedule that was formerly set according to the foreman's intuition is now derived by linear programming. And although not very long ago it was believed that operational control was appropriate only for factory operations, we now see models and formulas being used for certain marketing decisions, such as planning salesmen's calls and planning direct-mail advertising. This shift probably will continue; it is a large part of what people have in mind when they say, "management is becoming increasingly scientific."

Consequences of Confusion

Following are statements illustrating the consequences of failing to make a distinction between management control and operational control.

"Computers will make middle management obsolete." Although computers can replace human beings in operational control, they are not a substitute for the human judgment that is an essential part of the management control process.

"Business should develop a management control system like the SAGE and SAC control systems that work so well for the military." The military systems mentioned are operational control systems. They are not related to the management control problem in the military, let alone that in business.

"The way to improve the management control process is to develop better management decision rules." This implies that mathematics, rather than human beings, is the essence of management control.

"Transfer prices should be calculated centrally." This gives no recognition to the importance of negotiation and the exercise of judgment by divisional managers in many situations.

"If you follow the planning and control techniques described in this book, your profits are a near predictable certainty." This, from an advertisement for a well-known book, implies that the technique, rather than the quality of management, is the principal determinant of success.

FINANCIAL ACCOUNTING

Financial accounting is the process of reporting financial information about the organization to the outside world.

The purpose of financial accounting is to provide financial information about a business or other organization to outside parties—investors, lending agencies, regulatory bodies, and the public. The reader should be entitled to assume that the information is presented "in accordance with generally accepted accounting principles." An important criterion in devising these principles is that of objectivity; that is, it is considered essential that financial statement data be predominantly derived from objective evidence, rather than the subjective, and hence unverifiable, judgments of management.

Management accounting is the term used for the type of accounting done in connection with the processes already described—strategic planning, management control, and operational control. Management accounting differs from financial accounting in that it is not bound by the generally accepted principles of financial accounting. In devising its management accounting structure, management may prescribe whatever rules it finds useful, without regard to whether these are consistent with generally accepted principles.

Even so, the management accounting structure will resemble the financial accounting structure in most respects, both because the principles useful in reporting to outside parties are often equally useful in reporting to management and because the internally generated data are the raw material for the published financial statements, which makes it desirable to have the differences kept to a minimum.

Consequences of Confusion

Following are statements illustrating the consequences of confusing management accounting and financial accounting.

"Management makes judgments regarding fixed assets on the basis of estimates of the present value of their future earnings; therefore, fixed assets should be valued in this way on published balance sheets." Regardless of how useful such estimates may be to management, this principle is inappropriate for financial accounting because of the impossibility of obtaining objective estimates of present values.

"In measuring divisional return on investment, fixed assets should be shown at their balance sheet amounts." This is the opposite of the above error. The criterion for management accounting is this: What method will encourage division managers to make the best decisions regarding the acquisition, utilization, and disposition of fixed assets? The way in which assets are shown on the published balance sheet is not governing.

"Direct costing is not permitted under generally accepted accounting principles; therefore, we shouldn't use direct costing in our management system." Again, financial accounting principles are not governing in management accounting.

"Information that is useful to management is also useful to investors; therefore, there should be no difference between management accounting and financial accounting." This statement implies incorrectly that the objectivity criterion is of no consequence.

INFORMATION HANDLING

Information handling is the process of collecting, manipulating, and transmitting information, whatever its use is to be.

Space permits only a brief mention of this process here. Clearly, there is much that can be said about the most efficient ways of collecting and transmitting information without reference to the use that is to be made of it. Such generalizations range all the way from the statement, "manual copying should be avoided," up through matters relating to the design and programming of computer systems. In recent years, systems specialists, computer specialists, forms designers, and others have developed an expertise that they can apply to a wide variety of problems in any of the areas already discussed. It is this expertise that constitutes the subject matter which is here labeled information handling.

SUMMARY

We have described several subsystems that come under the general heading, "planning and control systems." Although related to one another, they have different purposes and different characteristics; different ways of thinking about each of them are therefore required. Generalizations about the whole area are, if valid, so vague as not to be useful. By contrast, useful generalizations, principles, and techniques, can be developed for each of the subsystems. Mistakes are made when those valid for one subsystem are applied to another.

Chapter Two

ORGANIZATIONAL RELATIONSHIPS

This is not a book on controllership. Although the controller has primary responsibility for the design of a management control system and some responsibility for its operation, he has other responsibilities that are not related to the management control system and, hence, are outside the scope of this book. The cases in this section focus on the role of the controller in connection with the management control system.

Three main questions are raised in these cases:

1. What is the proper division of responsibility between the controller and line managers? In part, the division of responsibilities in a given company is a reflection of tradition in that company, and in part it is a reflection of personalities. There may be, however, some generalizations that are relevant for most situations.
2. What parts of the planning and control process should be the responsibility of the controller, and what parts should be the responsibility of other staff departments? The Hutter Company case raises this question.
3. What should be the relationship between the divisional controller and his divisional manager on the one hand and the corporate controller on the other? This perplexing question is raised both in the Hutter Company and Rendell Company cases.

Reading 2-1

The Disintegration of an Information System

By Neil Milroy*

Although accounting is usually regarded as having a restraining influence on wasteful practices, it is sometimes disturbing to find that a limited concept of its function in corporate life is often directly responsible for one of the most insidious causes of waste in many companies: inadequate business information.

Today's profit squeeze has prompted many business executives to seek various means to improve revenue and to cut production and administrative costs. These attempts are normally carried on along organizational lines as each major activity is scrutinized for improvement. This "functional" approach usually fails to fully recognize the inadequacy of the information process, however, as it is seen only in segmented form.

Problems Compounded

It is surprising that many companies, while taking great pains to improve manufacturing technology and marketing effort, disregard the information process almost entirely. This is particularly serious when one considers the many corporate problems that are greatly compounded, though perhaps not uniquely caused, by the lack, inaccuracy, or excessive handling and interpretation of information. Consider for example:

Overinvestment in inventories
Excessive overhead costs

* A principal with P. S. Ross & Partners, Montreal, Canada. Reproduced by permission from *Canadian Chartered Accountant,* May, 1963.

"Panic" material buying or financing
Unproductive selling expenses
Low labor productivity
Rising clerical costs
Poor communications
Prematurely obsolete equipment
Ill-advised business decisions

The need for information to minimize the effect of these and other problems has stimulated many attempts to improve the process. Mechanized and electronic data processing techniques have been developed at a remarkable rate. Systems and methods improvements have been introduced. In addition, specialized departments have been created to analyze and interpret business information. In many situations, however, such measures provide merely patchwork improvements on a fundamentally unsound process and the problem of information inadequacy persists.

Since the extent of the waste can mean the difference between success or failure for many companies, it would be advantageous for many to reappraise their information systems objectively to determine whether or not they are wasting hard-earned profits by neglecting the application of the accounting function in its widest sense.

To illustrate the problems of information inadequacy, their development and possible means of solution, let us consider the following case—a hypothetical one, perhaps, but only so in the aggregate and in the sequence of events. The detail occurs too often in industry to be imaginary.

A company's development will be traced briefly through various stages of growth and each stage will be related to the information system employed to satisfy its evolving needs. Although these stages might span a period of several years, their characteristics can be seen in varying degrees and in different combinations in industries today.

STAGE 1

Accounting Meets All Internal Information Needs

A small business enterprise made and sold its products in a comparatively captive market. The owner-manager supervised the production force directly, and sold through local merchants.

Its information system, adapted to support the company's expansion borrowing, was maintained by one bookkeeper and consisted only of basic books of account, monthly and annual financial statements (for treasury and tax purposes), and an informal system based on the owner's direct supervision and intimate knowledge of the current production and marketing cycles. It was basic. Minimum manufacturing and sales information was supplied by the formal accounting system, and the need for further detail was obviated by the owner's informal information feedback.

STAGE 2

Accounting Is Expanded to Meet External Demands

Faced with increased product demand, the company required further expansion capital. The owner-manager floated a stock issue, although continuing to run a "one-man show."

Since information was required by the company's new shareholders, the investing public, legislation, and external auditors, and since (at this stage) the internal requirements were few, the satisfaction of external demands received greater emphasis in the accounting system (Chart 1).

Chart 1

ACCOUNTING MEETS ALL FORMAL NEEDS

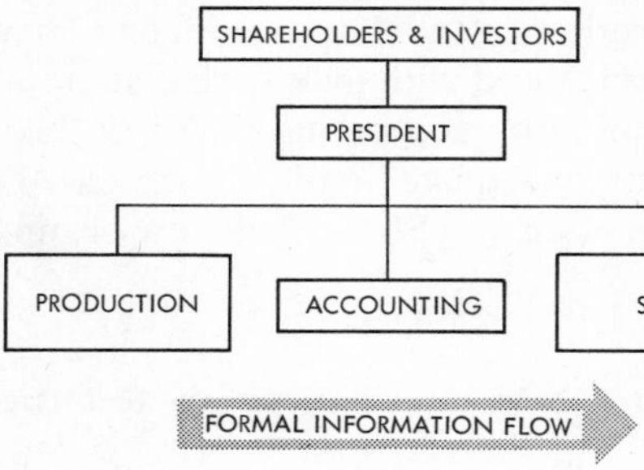

These demands, though basic, were not easily satisfied. The company hired a qualified accountant to discharge the responsibilities created by the increased external demands.

At this stage in the company's development, financial accounting constituted a corporate information system, to the extent that formal data and reports were required. No matter how complex the operations, under the existing organizational and personnel circumstances, the financial accounting system was considered quite adequate by all concerned.

The owner-manager-president, however, began to feel the strain of pressures imposed by his booming enterprise. He therefore delegated the responsibility for the two main functions of production and sales to two senior executives, and he himself retained control of product research and public relations.

His directives were quite specific. He charged the production vice president with the achievement of two basic objectives: increased production efficiency, and effective use of production facilities.

The sales vice president was charged with: improving sales volume, and improving the percentage return on sales.

These over-all responsibilities dictated the provision of specific information for each vice president, without which neither the scope of their undertakings nor the channelling of effort could be defined. This information was basic, not specialized or requiring outside sources. It did require, however, detailed analysis of sales performance and costs, modification of the data-accumulating procedures and considerable clerical effort. Their information needs also included the establishment of valid standards and the subsequent comparison of actual performance against these.

The accountant's training might have suggested the adoption of a standard cost accounting system and use of high speed data processing equipment, as well as a radical revision of the existing accounting system. However, circumstances conspired against him. A reluctance to accept standards in the valuation of inventories, the apparent high cost of data processing equipment, and the inertia of an accounting system that had proved satisfactory for years, all prevented—or at least seriously delayed—the necessary action.

The needs for information relentlessly continued. They were even desperate. The accountant was faced with mounting daily routine demands and countless technicalities raised by accounting theorists. The achievements of the system became further inadequate despite his increased efforts. Whatever the reasons, the transformation into State 3 had now begun.

STAGE 3

Separate Information Systems Created to Fill the Vacuum

Attempts by the vice presidents to obtain the statistics vital to the fulfillment of their duties were politely but firmly given second priority to financial requirements.

The production vice president could not fathom why the system was unable to use his valid standards for both assessment of operating efficiencies and valuation of inventories. Finally he developed his own system to improve performance. It assigned attainable efficiency standards and measured performance against them.

The sales vice president was forced to take a similar expedient course, creating his own sales statistics and analysis department. Even if the statistics had been produced originally, they would have contained marketing inaccuracies caused by untimely raising of invoices, lack of indication of sales territories, and so on.

The creation of separate information systems, though not serious at this point, was rationalized by all concerned as providing essential specialized information service. It was argued that there was no duplication and that each one was designed according to particular functional needs. This information system might be illustrated as in Chart 2. Again, only total production and sales information is incorporated into the official accounting system.

Despite arguments in favor of information specialization, however, it should be noted that all departments were deriving their basic historical data from the same sources and, further, that all these data were finding ultimate expression in financial statement terms.

The president began asking searching questions arising, ironically, out of the information supplied by the separate systems.

"Which products are yielding highest returns?"

"Why are we still in that unprofitable market?"

"Why is our gross profit down despite increased sales?"

"Why are our profits down in spite of supposedly lower unit production costs?"

Chart 2

SEPARATE SYSTEMS FILL INFORMATION VACUUM

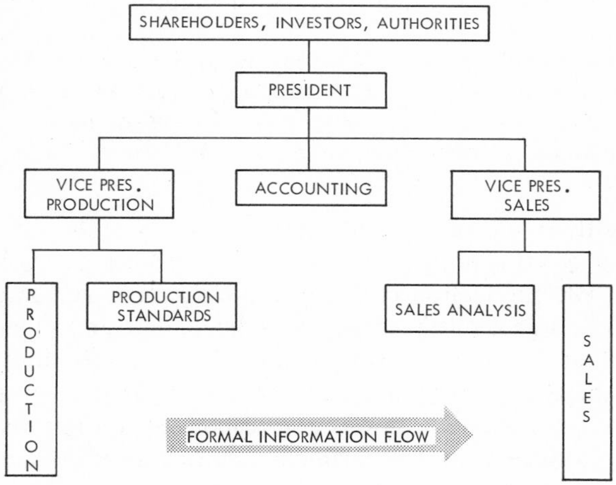

The answers could not be readily supplied. No single information system was equipped to do so. The systems were incomplete and contained arbitrary allocations of overhead costs that clouded the pertinent information required to provide answers to specific questions.

While modern accounting techniques using a marginal or direct costing approach could have readily provided greater insight into the nature and behaviour of costs, such improvements had not been made due to many technicalities of an accounting nature. The accounting system, though accurately reporting results for financial purposes, fell more and more into operating disuse. More detailed and time-consuming analyses were developed by all information systems to provide answers to the president's questions. As this process continued, the metamorphosis into Stage 4 was accelerated.

STAGE 4

Duplication and Confusion Result in Disintegration

In this atmosphere of narrow information systems (which were, in effect, designed to satisfy specific requirements to the exclusion of others), the disintegration process became serious because the company experienced the following wastes, over and above the increase in clerical costs:

1. Duplication in information coverage as each system used and interpreted the same data to suit its own needs.
2. Breakdown in corporate communications as fundamentally identical information was distorted by different interpretations.
3. Executive and management confusion as the decision-making process was complicated by the need to evaluate conflicting information supplied by different sources.
4. Waste of specialized talents as some (whose aims in corporate life were the development, manufacture, or sale of products) were dissipating these skills by the need to administer what amounted to accounting routines.
5. Inefficient data processing as no one system was large enough to justify the best equipment.

These costly results of the inefficient information system were overlooked while the various functions expanded to provide for their evolving information needs. The production division, requiring more accurate estimates of sales demands, organized a planning department over and above its standards and scheduling or "control" departments. The sales division, charged with the responsibility of moving the inventories, organized an inventory control section. And since the division was also responsible for improving the return on sales, a product control department was organized to support selective selling decisions with detailed product-cost studies.

Disintegration of the information system (see Chart 3) had, of course, been developing for some time but it became a confirmed reality when the president never accepted information without a nagging doubt.

Belated Salvaging Attempt

The president then made, in effect, a belated attempt to salvage what was left of the information system. He authorized the appointment of an analyst in the accounting department whose primary function was to restore some order to the information chaos. Our analyst, however, became another member of the accounting department which, under the circumstances, was of little help to either production or sales vice presidents. The financial accounting system merely became more refined and the degree of "accuracy" increased but still within the same framework.

The production vice president still maintained his own standards. Admittedly they were not accurate, as variances always existed, but how much more accurate were the "actual" costs which contained prorations, allocations, deferments, accruals and certain "adjustments for tax purposes"?

Chart 3

DUPLICATION AND CONFUSION OF CONFLICTING INFORMATION

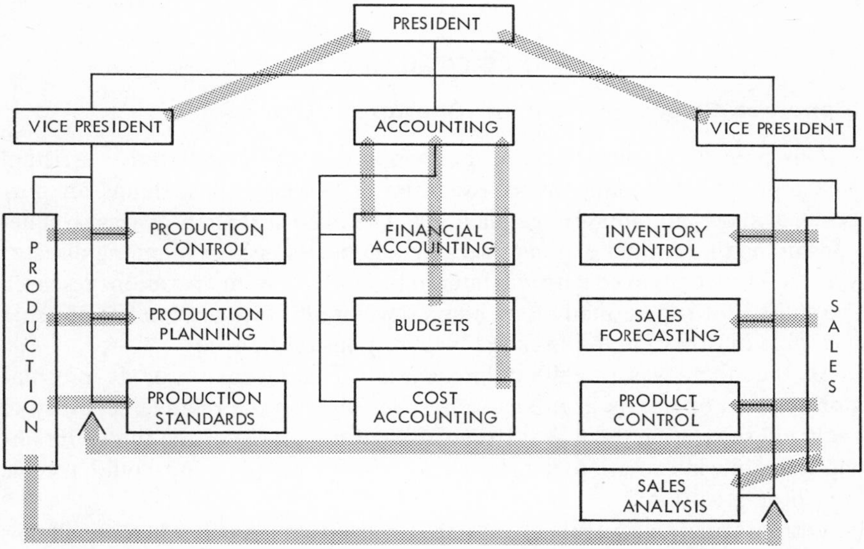

The sales vice president continued to rearrange figures (instead of developing new business) because he had to prove to the president that market "X" was providing some return, in spite of indications to the contrary by the company's absorption costing system.

Again the president tried. A controller was hired and the accountant was made treasurer to handle the task of providing shareholders and income tax authorities with "consistent" accounts.

The controller assessed the situation as chaotic and hired a systems man and a data processing expert with all the necessary tools. These were all justified to the president on the basis of accounting needs and were intended to improve the accounting function even further.

The systems man devoted much time to streamlining accounting routines, forms and reports. Improved reports appeared containing an even greater degree of accuracy than before. Available time on the data processing equipment was used "productively" to analyse items of cost of relatively little consequence (such as postage and telephone costs) and even to calculate the cost of each mechanized application.

Some attempts were made to provide for the company's need to plan its activities and to subsequently assess its actual performance against those plans. Corporate budgeting and basic control accounting were developed, but these potentially valuable control tools were weakened by their adherence to financial accounting principles.

The ultimate in specialized information refinement was being reached, but the fundamental problem had remained unchanged in nature and had greatly expanded in degree and cost. The situation was now ready for the development of Stage 5.

STAGE 5

Elaborate Structure Built on Shattered Foundation

Our president, aging rapidly, then employed an administrative assistant whose primary function was to assist him in analyzing past trends for purposes of short- and long-range planning. The historical analysis was so time-consuming that formal planning became a hopeless task. A planning director was therefore employed who was later to be assisted by an operations research specialist. Both spent many long hours developing ways and means of using available information to discharge their responsibilities.

By then there was a wealth of information. There were five or six information systems operating at full capacity. Deciding on the relative accuracy of each and separating the wheat from the chaff took most of the time. Obtaining valuable information for decision-making and planning could receive very little attention.

Our information system can perhaps be illustrated, again schematically, as in Chart 4.

The interaction of all these new information requirements resulted in the progressive refinement of each system. The whole process could have been written off to the pains of evolution and the strong features of each system could have been salvaged. The situation could have been salvaged, in fact, at any of the previous stages, although at successively increased cost. Unfortunately, our company selected another approach.

STAGE 6

The Final Bitter Irony

Having allowed the information "system" to develop haphazardly into such a time-consuming, confusing and costly monster, the president was advised that confusion would be minimized by the use of written instructions.

Accordingly, a paralyzing blow was struck. The chaos was reduced to standard procedures (which had to be observed and could not be changed except after careful consideration and approval by a procedures committee).

Chart 4

FUNDAMENTAL ERROR COMPOUNDED INTO CHAOS

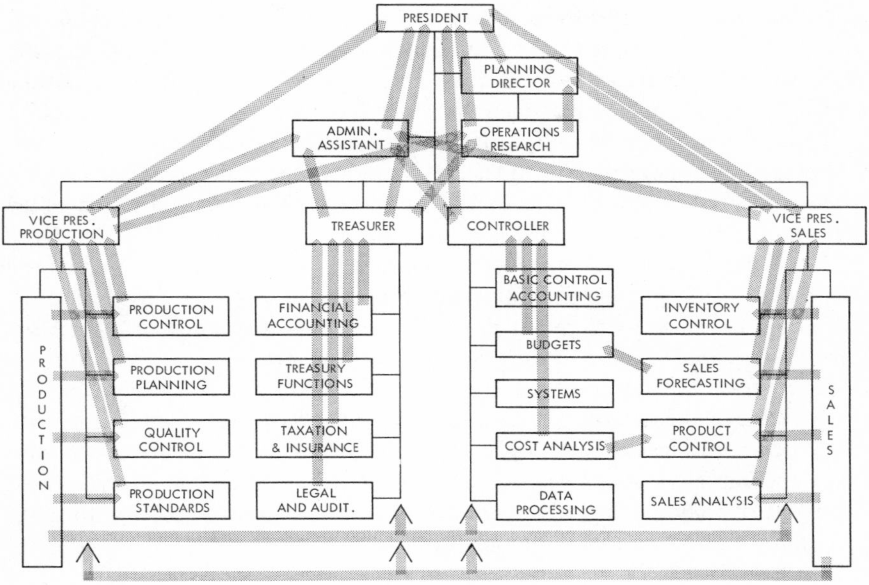

The laudable purpose was to ensure that current procedures were not amended unless all those affected approved of, or made due allowances for, the change. The effect, however, was to introduce an inflexibility that defied any attempts to centralize the information system. The creeping paralysis continued as more current procedures were reduced to writing and as more proposed changes were added to the agenda for the procedures committee. Nevertheless, the company earned some profits, not because of the system but in spite of it.

The company took many actions that were, in themselves, worthwhile. They were well intentioned and, in theory (as often in practice), desirable. To draw a contrary conclusion is not the intention. Neither should it be concluded that the personnel employed were unnecessary, that their potential value was not significant, nor that they acted irrationally. All the positions created and the departments organized could have provided the company with extremely valuable service had they been supported by an adequate information system. In this situation, however, their efforts were, to a greater or lesser extent, wasted and unproductive.

STAGE 7

Restoration of Order

The difficulties of restoring order were, at this stage, very great and the cost of remedial action significant. Many personnel relationships had been formed and many practices and procedures developed. Highly refined and specialized techniques imposed further difficulties in co-ordinating and integrating the information requirements.

However, the president was sufficiently aware of the costs, both hidden and measurable, of dissipated skills, inefficient information processing and the many losses attributable to inadequate information, that he resolved to take drastic action. He further reasoned that since the restoration program required was complex, the opportunities for savings must be substantial.

Fortunately, there was no question of redundant staff, as all specialists hired could be effectively used, so that support for the program was enlisted with relative ease, once the information chaos was understood.

The objectives of the improvement program seemed clear: to reduce the wastes and inefficiencies inherent in the system; and to provide for future information needs so as *to avoid the recurrence of the situation in which the information needs exceeded the capacity (both quantitative and qualitative) of the information system.*

To achieve these objectives a thorough review of the organization's information needs was carried out, giving thought to the organization structure and the company's objectives. Although it became apparent that some reassignment of major delegated responsibilities was necessary, the restoration program included the following major phases:

1. Centralization of information processing under one senior executive responsible for the co-ordination of all planning activities, actual performance measurement and evaluation (including external reporting) and the development of control practices and systems. He was also responsible for the constant appraisal of new data processing techniques vis à vis the anticipated further evolution of information needs. This centralization (along the lines suggested schematically in Chart 5) was based on the premise that the processing of data is in itself a specialized function that should not be shared by the users of such information. Centralization was further justified by the economics of data processing equipment.

2. An accelerated mechanization program to handle, initially, all basic information and paperwork routines, thus freeing accounting personnel to develop new systems and methods. In evaluating the feasibility of data processing equipment, however, allowance was made for all justifiable corporate information requirements and for their anticipated expansion.

3. The design and implementation of modern management accounting techniques as most of the company's information requirements could be satisfied by such methods. These included flexible budgetary control, refined sales forecasting, improved capital expenditure evaluation, inventory planning, marginal or direct costing and integrated profit planning, to mention only a few aspects of modern management accounting.

4. An advanced training program for all senior accounting personnel to enable them to appreciate the information needs of operating executives and anticipate improved control requirements. This phase included the hiring of competent

Chart 5

INTEGRATED INFORMATION SYSTEM RESTORES ORDER

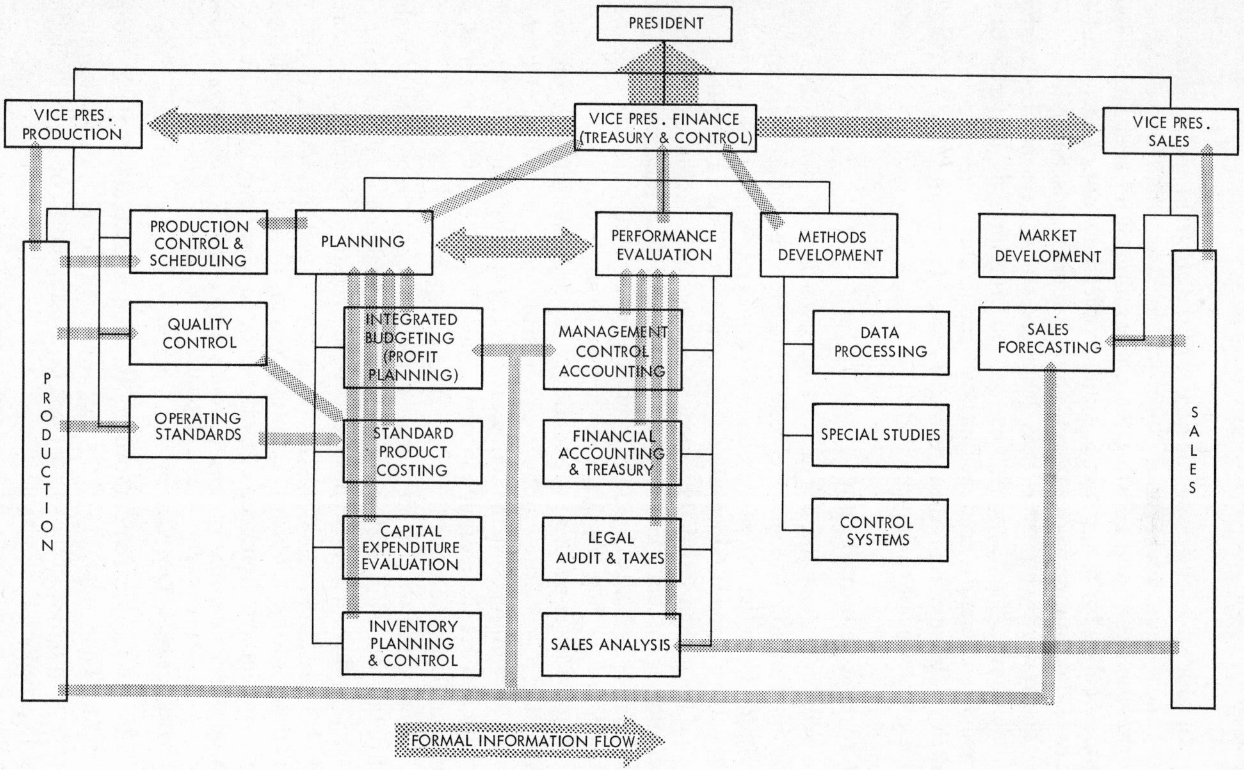

accountants, as the company had learned that limiting the accounting staff had been shortsighted, as evidenced by the duplicate information systems.

In addition to these specific phases of the program, management was faced with the monumental task of objectively assessing the relative urgency of information needs and enlisting the cooperation of all staff levels. This reappraisal called for tact, patience, and an objectivity not often prevailing when day-to-day administrative responsibilities must be discharged.

The rewards, however, have been great and have not been affected by unpleasant staff reductions. The revision program was, by virtue of its complexity, sufficiently gradual that staff reductions were achieved by normal attrition. In any event, the rewards in terms of over-all efficiency far exceeded considerations of savings in staff costs.

The Fundamental Flaw

Whatever the series of circumstances was that led to the disintegration of the information system, one conclusion emerges clearly: its disintegration resulted from the *inability of the accounting system to provide vital information*. Furthermore, since all requirements specified or implied in this case could have been satisfied by modern management accounting techniques, the accounting system's inability was in turn due to a fundamental flaw that is sufficiently prevalent in today's industry to warrant some concern: *the limited concept of the function of accounting in corporate life*.

The wider concept of accounting as a corporate information and control system receives little emphasis considering its implications. Unfortunately, many accounting systems today are limited to a treasury or "custodial" capacity and, as such, often contribute directly to the development of separate information systems with all their attendant wastes.

Greatly improved modern management accounting, coupled with the speed of data processing equipment, permits the application of the wider concept. The existence of inadequate business information, therefore, is increasingly unjustifiable. The modern accountant appreciates this and is aware, perhaps painfully, of the need for accounting systems to be constantly adapted to suit evolving information needs. In other words, in spite of all the improvements made, *the accounting systems of today may be grossly inadequate tomorrow*.

Complacence Too Costly

Few companies can afford to be complacent about their information systems. The symptoms of disintegration can be seen all too frequently and the consequences of the disease can be too serious to be stoically and erroneously accepted as inevitable.

The necessary reviews of information requirements and the methods used to satisfy them deserve top-management action to avoid the natural functional biases that might prejudice subsequent revision programs. Company concepts of the function of accounting in corporate life should also be reviewed to ensure that its major purpose is to provide information in its broadest sense.

To do anything less can be extremely shortsighted. The cost of information inadequacy or of separate information systems can greatly exceed that of modernizing the information systems and the supporting organizations. Furthermore, the benefits are likely to continue long after the pains of critical reappraisal and revision are forgotten.

Reading 2-2

Decentralization—A Managerial Philosophy

By Ralph J. Cordiner*

Every company should be managed in accordance with some workable, ethically responsible philosophy of management. That is, the managers of the company should be in general agreement on a set of underlying principles that will guide their work in providing leadership for the company.

For some companies, the set of principles that guide the managers may be tacitly understood, without ever being presented systematically. They may be part of the company's tradition or may even reflect the personal philosophy of the chief executive.

While General Electric's present philosophy of management has had a long evolution in Company tradition and reflects the personalities of its great leaders in years gone by, considerable effort has been devoted in the past ten years to "thinking through" and presenting this managerial philosophy in a systematic way.

In this lecture, I should like to discuss the results of these studies: the philosophy of decentralization, and how it has been applied by General Electric in building an organization structure to meet the challenges of an expanding economy.

At the very outset, let me make clear that I am not selling our particular approach to organizing and managing as a solution for the problems of other companies. If I have any thesis, it is that each company should study, for itself, the particular conditions that will determine its future, and out of such

---

* President, General Electric Company. A talk in the McKinsey Foundation Lecture Series given at the Graduate School of Business, Columbia University, in 1956. Reprinted from *New Frontiers for Professional Managers*, by Ralph J. Cordiner. Copyright © 1956 by the Trustees of Columbia University in the City of New York. Used by permission of McGraw-Hill Company.

detailed study should evolve a philosophy and structure that is fully appropriate for an individual company. The patterns of organization with which I shall deal are General Electric's solutions to General Electric's problems, and may or may not be applicable elsewhere.

. . . . .

Decentralization has different meanings for different people. The decision to decentralize General Electric did not mean that it was decided to "break up the Company" into smaller pieces. This would be self-defeating, because it would lose to the public and to the Company those advantages that are the distinctive contribution of large enterprises: the ability to serve as a source of major innovations in the nation's economic life, creating new products, new industries, new employment, and new outlets for smaller businesses; the ability to energize the flow of mass production and mass distribution; and the ability to provide a broad range of advanced technical capacity in order to produce the more complex products and systems of our times.

In General Electric, decentralization is a way of preserving and enhancing these contributions of the large enterprise, and at the same time achieving the flexibility and the "human touch" that are popularly associated with—though not always attained by—small organizations.

Under this concept, we have undertaken decentralization not only according to products, geography, and functional types of work. The most important aspect of the Company's philosophy is thorough decentralization of the responsibility and authority for making business decisions.

Here is the underlying logic. The share owners, through their Board of Directors, delegate to the President responsibility for the conduct of the whole business. The responsibility carries with it all the authority required to get the work done, except such authorities as are specifically withheld by the Board and the share owners. The total responsibility also carries with it full accountability for results. General Electric may be unique in that the Board of Directors has issued a position guide for the President, stating in detail his responsibility, authority, and accountability.

Now, the President is of course unable to do all the work himself, and so he delegates the responsibility for portions of the total work through organization channels to individuals who have the talents and knowledge required to do it. This is done by planning and building the work of the Company into an organization structure which consists of all the necessary positions and components required to do all the work in the most effective and efficient manner.

Each employee thus takes on responsibility for some part of the over-all Company work. Along with this responsibility, each position naturally carries with it full accountability for measured results, and all the necessary authority required for the position except those authorities that are specifically stated as withheld. Therefore each employee of the Company has, in his position, full responsibility, authority, and accountability for a certain defined body of work and teamwork. Through teamwork he recognizes his relationships to the other employees who perform a share of the total work of the Company.

With this philosophy, General Electric achieves a community of purpose between leaders and their associates, and is able to attain that voluntary integration which is the hallmark of a free and decentralized enterprise.

In such compressed statement, this management philosophy may sound somewhat obscure, but its practical result is to put the responsibility for making business decisions not with a few top executives, but with the individual managerial and functional employees who have the most immediately applicable information required to make sound decisions and take prompt action. When such responsibility—along with commensurate authority and accountability—has been delegated according to a carefully planned organization of work, then each individual in the Company has a challenging and dignified position which will bring out his full resources and enthusiastic cooperation. . . .

TEN GUIDING PRINCIPLES

Since philosophy is, by definition, a system of first principles, I should like to list for you ten principles which express General Electric's philosophy of decentralization.

1. Decentralization places authority to make decisions at points as near as possible to where actions take place.
2. Decentralization is likely to get best over-all results by getting greatest and most directly applicable knowledge and most timely understanding actually into play on the greatest number of decisions.
3. Decentralization will work if real authority is delegated; and not if details then have to be reported, or, worse yet, if they have to be "checked" first.
4. Decentralization requires confidence that associates in decentralized positions will have the capacity to make sound decisions in the majority of cases; and such confidence starts at the executive level. Unless the President and all the other Officers have a deep personal conviction and an active desire to decentralize full decision-making responsibility and authority, actual decentralization will never take place. The Officers must set an example in the art of full delegation.
5. Decentralization requires understanding that the main role of staff or services is the rendering of assistance and advice to line operators through a relatively few experienced people, so that those making decisions can themselves make them correctly.
6. Decentralization requires realization that the natural aggregate of many individually sound decisions will be better for the business and for the public than centrally planned and controlled decisions.
7. Decentralization rests on the need to have general business objectives, organization structure, relationships, policies, and measurements known, understood, and followed; but realizing that definition of policies does not necessarily mean uniformity of methods of executing such policies in decentralized operations.

8. Decentralization can be achieved only when higher executives realize that authority genuinely delegated to lower echelons cannot, in fact, also be retained by them. We have, today, Officers and Managers who still believe in decentralization down to themselves and no further. By paying lip-service to decentralization, but actually reviewing detailed work and decisions and continually "second-guessing" their associates, such Officers keep their organization in confusion and prevent the growth of self-reliant men.

9. Decentralization will work only if responsibility commensurate with decision-making authority is truly accepted and exercised at all levels.

10. Decentralization requires personnel policies based on measured performance, enforced standards, rewards for good performance, and removal for incapacity or poor performance.

DESIGNING ORGANIZATIONAL STRUCTURE

Now, given this philosophy, how can it be expressed in an organization structure suitable to the General Electric Company? In our experience, the following work must be done to attain a sound, flexible, and dynamic organization structure:

1. Determine the objectives, and the policies, programs, plans, and schedules that will best achieve these objectives; for the Company as a whole and, in turn, for each component of the business.
2. Determine the work to be done to achieve these objectives, under such guiding policies.
3. Divide and classify or group related work into a simple, logical, understandable, and comprehensive organization structure.
4. Assign essential work clearly and definitely to the various components and positions in the organization structure.
5. Determine the requirements and qualifications of personnel to occupy such positions.
6. Staff the organization with persons who meet these qualifications.
7. Establish methods and procedures which will help to achieve the objectives of the organization.

This is the procedure which has been followed in carrying out General Electric's current decentralization program, which had its beginnings in studies started in 1943, and went into the actual application phase in February, 1951. As you can imagine, the entire process involves a tremendous amount of self-analysis and education throughout the organization. Not only new ideas, but new attitudes need to be developed and accepted. Many former positions and organizations need to be discontinued, and many new and responsible positions and components are created. Persons may feel, under such changing circumstances, that their careers and livelihoods are threatened, so that they may be inclined to the suspicious, or at least over-cautious, until the new philosophy has been thoroughly assimilated, refined, and established. Timing is of the utmost importance, and I personally felt in

1951 that five years would be required to evolve the new structure and have it implemented with understanding and enthusiasm. The program appears to be just about on schedule.

Through all these difficult conditions, the General Electric men and women have performed with admirable wisdom and maturity, maintaining the momentum of progress in serving their customers while absorbing this latest phase in the Company's evolution. The work of organization is never done, and the structure has to be continuously adapted to new and anticipated conditions. Nevertheless, it is safe to say that the new type of decentralized organization structure has been substantially established and manned, with outstanding personnel, products, and facilities to make it effective. The results, in terms of better values for customers and better earnings for share owners and employees, are reflected in the Company's statement for the first quarter of 1956, which shows an increase of 14% in sales and 30% in orders, over the first quarter of 1955.

GENERAL ELECTRIC'S OBJECTIVES

. . . The first step in organization is to sharpen up the objectives of the Company as a whole, to provide a framework for the objectives of each organization component and each position in the Company.

These Company objectives have been subjected to deep study, and are still undergoing review by managers throughout the organization. At present, they are ten in number and broad in character, and they are reflected in the Company's organization structure. Briefly summarized, General Electric's objectives are as follows:

1. To carry on a diversified, growing, and profitable worldwide manufacturing business in electrical apparatus, appliances, and supplies, and in related materials, products, systems, and services for industry, commerce, agriculture, government, the community, and the home.
2. To lead in research in all fields of science and all areas of work relating to the business in order to assure a constant flow of new knowledge that will make real the Company theme, "Progress Is Our Most Important Product."
3. To operate each decentralized business venture to achieve its own customer acceptance and profitable results, by taking the appropriate business risks.
4. To design, make, and market all Company products and services with good quality and with inherent customer value, at fair, competitive prices.
5. To build public confidence and friendly feeling for products and services bearing the Company's name and brands.
6. To provide good jobs, wages, working conditions, work satisfactions, stability of employment, and opportunities for advancement for employees, in return for their loyalty, initiative, skill, care, effort, attendance, and teamwork.
7. To manage the human and material resources of the enterprise for continuity and flow of progress, growth, profit, and public service in accordance with the principles of decentralization, sound organization structure, and professional management.

8. To attract and retain investor capital through attractive returns as a continuing incentive for wide investor participation and support.

9. To cooperate with suppliers, distributors, retailers, contractors, and others who facilitate the production, distribution, installation, and servicing of Company products and systems.

10. To meet the Company's social, civic, and economic responsibilities with imagination and with voluntary action which will merit the understanding and support of all concerned among the public.

To the casual reader or listener, these broad objectives may sound vague and obvious, but thoughtful study will reveal that each of them represents a number of deliberate and important managerial decisions. They provide a direct expression of the Company's ethical standards, its managerial philosophy, and its continuing purposes—in a form which makes them understandable and acceptable, after study, to every member of the organization.

GENERAL ELECTRIC'S ORGANIZATION STRUCTURE

In order to achieve these objectives on a continuing and profitable basis, an improved organization structure was devised in accordance with the principles of decentralization. This structure and the reasons for it are outlined in considerable detail in a paper I presented before the American Management Association in June, 1952, but here we shall sketch only the main outline of the structure.

The organization of General Electric is essentially a three-part structure which carefully distinguishes between Operating work, Services work, and Executive work.

THE OPERATING COMPONENTS

First let us consider the Operating work. Today, General Electric's products are engineered, manufactured, and marketed by nearly a hundred decentralized Operating Departments, each of them bearing full operating responsibility and authority for the Company's success and profitability in a particular product or service field. The special skills and knowledge required for each operating business are thus brought to bear by a local business managerial team which can concentrate on the opportunities of a specific product or marketing area. Through these integrated managerial teams, each with a specific profit-and-loss responsibility for the operation of a defined business, we achieve the flexibility, drive, and the "human touch" that comes from direct participation in the daily problems of a business.

To demonstrate that the responsibility, authority, and accountability of these Operating Departments is real, not window dressing, consider their pricing authority. The price of a product can be raised or lowered by the managers of the Department producing it, with only voluntary responsibility on their part to give sensible consideration to the impact of such price changes on other Company products. In one area of General Electric products, the major appliances such as refrigerators, ranges, and home laundry equipment, there are two Divisions competing directly with each other. The Hotpoint Division in Chicago and the Major Appliance and Television Receiver Division in Louisville have different facilities, different product designs, different distribution, and different prices. They compete at the market place very aggressively, and, incidentally, very profitably. Other Departments compete with each other by presenting different types of products that perform essentially the same function. For example, there is the competition between electronic tubes and transistors, or between room air conditioners and central air conditioning.

As further evidence of the freedom provided by decentralization to the Operating Departments, consider the fact that the operating budget of the General Electric Company is not a document prepared by the Executive Offices in New York. It is an addition of the budgets prepared by the Operating Department General Managers, with the concurrence of the Division General Managers and Group Executives. These budgets include planned sales volume, product development plans, expenditures for plant and equipment, market targets, turnover of investment, net earnings, projected organization structure, and other related items. . . .

At the present time the Company has nearly 100 manufacturing Operating Departments, plus a number of sales and service business departments. For purposes of management, these departments are grouped into 21 Operating Divisions. Each division might be described as a family of businesses; for example, the Turbine Division consists of the Gas Turbine Department, the Large Steam Turbine Generator Department, the Medium Steam Turbine, Generator, and Gear Department, the Small Turbine Department, and the Foundry Department.

After he has proven his capacity to be an Officer, the General Manager of a Division is usually elected a Vice President of the Company. Most of the Division General Manager's time is devoted to long-range planning for the Division as a part of the over-all Company, while operating responsibilities for the specific businesses are clearly delegated to the Department General Managers.

To assure that the Operating Departments and their customers will receive the full benefit of the Company's broad resources in knowledge and risk-taking capacity, two other types of work are provided for in the Company's over-all organization structure: Services work and Executive work.

THE SERVICES

The functional services are components at the corporate level, staffed with the Company's most experienced personnel in the major business functions: accounting, engineering, legal and corporate, management consultation, manufacturing, marketing, public and employee relations, treasury, and research. It is important to note that, in contrast with the powerful Operating authority wielded by headquarters functional Executives under the earlier centralized structure, these Services people have no authority whatsoever over the Operating Departments and Divisions, except the authority of knowledge. They have, instead, two Company-wide responsibilities: to do research, teaching, and long-range guidance in personnel development in their functional field; and to do such functional operating work for the Company as a whole as can best be done at the corporate level. . . .

THE EXECUTIVES

Leadership and long-range planning for the Company as a whole constitute the Executive classification of work in the Company structure. To understand this Executive aspect of the General Electric organization, it is important to understand two unusual organizational devices: The President's Office and the Executive Office.

The President's Office is a group of Executives who share the work of the President. In addition to the President, it includes the Chairman of the Board, and five Executive Vice Presidents. The Chairman of the Board, in addition to the duties assigned him directly by the Board, represents the President in such areas as financial affairs, public and governmental liaison, and international matters, and each of the Executive Vice Presidents represents the President in relationships with a specific group of Operating Divisions. This unique organizational device was created in recognition of the fact that no one man would have the time and knowledge required to provide effective Executive leadership for the variety of businesses in a Company as large and as diversified as General Electric. Thus each Executive Vice President serves as the President in a defined Operating area, without in any sense relieving the President of the ultimate responsibility placed upon him by the Board of Directors for the success of the enterprise as a whole.

The Executive Vice Presidents, in General Electric, are true Executives. That is, they have been freed of Operating responsibility and administrative details so that they can devote their time to long range planning, appraisal of current performance, bringing divisional objectives and plans into a working pattern with over-all Company needs, and making sure of the needed continuity of competent managerial and other personel in the decentralized businesses.

These seven members of the President's Office, together with the nine Company Officers in charge of the Services, form what is known as the Executive Office. These Senior Officers deliberately set aside about 20% of their time to serve, not as Executives for their particular area of Operations or Services, but as a well-balanced group of general Executives who advise the President on matters that concern all functions and all operations—in other words, the Company as a whole. In this way the Executive Office provides a melding of extensive business judgment and advanced functional knowledge to help the President plan the Company's management, growth, and course ten or more years ahead.

There you have the organizational structure of the General Electric Company: a three-part structure consisting of the Executives, who provide leadership and long-range planning for the Company as a whole; the Services, which provide leadership and advanced research in each functional field; and the Operating components, which have decentralized responsibility for the success, growth, and competitive profitability of the Company's diverse Operating businesses.

A significant feature of this organization is that it has no place for assistants, "assistants-to," or "administrative assistants." It is our firm belief that such titles or positions create confusion as to responsibility, authority, and accountability, and tend to retard the growth of men and the Company. If a position is too big for one person and appears to require assistants, then the work should be divided up and reorganized into as many positions as are required to do the work efficiently. Each position in the Company should be able to "stand on its own," with a specifically defined area of responsibility, authority, and accountability.

Likewise, General Electric structure has no place for committees as decision-making bodies. It is my feeling that a committee moves at the speed of its least informed member, and too often is used as a way of sharing irresponsibility. Before decentralization, an official tried to get on a great number of committees. He would lead a very calm, safe, orderly life. Not much would happen, but nothing would ever happen to him.

Today, a committee may be helpful as an advisory group, and indeed the Executive Office of the General Electric Company meets twice monthly as an Advisory Council for the President. In any such arrangement, however, it must be made abundantly clear that the authority for any particular decision lies with the responsible individual, even if he makes it while sitting with the other Council members.

Such a deliberate avoidance of assistants and decision-making committees is directly in keeping with the decentralization philosophy, which requires full delegation of responsibility, authority, and accountability to the person who is best qualified to make the decisions for a certain area of work. . . .

A PHILOSOPHY OF FREEDOM

What I have said of decentralization as a philosophy applies with equal force to any large organization of free human beings, whether it be a government, a university, a union, or a business. Decentralization is a creative response to the challenges of our time, a way of preserving and enhancing the competitive enterprise system as it evolves into the new forms that have been so aptly named the "people's capitalism."

The economy of the United States, and its position as a world power, make large enterprises both an irreversible fact and an actual necessity for economic and national security reasons. Any attendant perils lie not in bigness itself, but in the way the energies of large organizations are organized and managed. Centralized administration of large institutions of any kind can lead to irresponsibility, shortsightedness, inefficiency, and the abuse of power—but this need not happen under wise and self-disciplined guidance. Responsible decentralization—as a philosophy—makes it possible to provide at once the big results that come from big enterprises, with the human freedom that comes from respecting the competence and dignity of every individual in the enterprise.

General Electric's particular form of decentralization may or may not be applicable elsewhere, but it is built firmly on the chosen philosophy that recognizes the dignity and capacity of the individual human being, and recognizes his responsibility and authority for making the decisions that count. This philosophy, I deeply urge, must prevail if freedom is to survive in the world.

Case 2-1

Hutter Company

BACKGROUND

The Hutter Company was founded during World War I to make parts for military aircraft engines. During the period from 1921 to 1938, several young men who shared the adventurous spirit of the founders joined the company. These men developed new products which were expected to appeal to automobile manufacturers and air transport companies. In addition, they worked on other products in cooperation with the Army Air Corps and Army and Navy Ordnance. These government agencies, however, had small appropriations for such work during this period, and little money was available in the company itself, with the result that many items got no farther than the drawingboard stage, only a few were perfected to experimental state, and fewer still were marketed, and those only in small volume. Partly in order to save money for developmental work and partly because the small scale of operation did not require elaborate controls, the company had kept at an irreducible minimum the expenses for cost accounting systems, operating statistics, budget procedures, and the like.

After Munich, the tempo changed for the Hutter Company. Armament orders from both Europe and the United States increased the sales of the company. The inherent value of the past development work in its relation to the war became evident, and the directors decided to expand on a large scale. This action required new financing. To assist in this undertaking, the directors elected Daniel Hall as chairman of the board.

Under the pressure of the defense and war programs, the Hutter Company grew rapidly. It increased the number of plants from two to fifteen, and old plants were expanded. The personnel employed increased more than fortyfold. Old management was spread thin, promotions were rapid, and many new employees at all levels of management and supervision had to be recruited from nonwar industries. The chairman and the president both agreed that it took from December, 1940, to April, 1944, for the full expansion to bear fruit. It was in April, 1944, that production reached its peak. By that time, organizational relationships were reasonably well established and most of the bugs were out of both products and organization. In the opinion of several vice-presidents, most employees were proud of results to date, even though they were somewhat weary from the stresses and strains of organization and reorganization at various levels.

MANAGEMENT

The management personnel affected by the problem presented herewith are shown in the organization chart in Exhibit 1. Additional information about them follows.

Exhibit 1

ORGANIZATION CHART

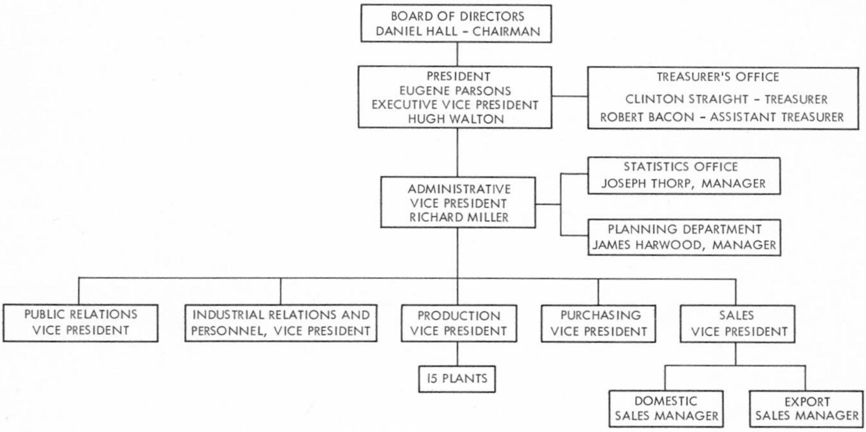

Daniel Hall, chairman of the board, had long been a stockholder and director of the company. He was a close personal friend of Eugene Parsons, the president, as well as of several of the vice-presidents; in World War I he had served in the army with some of them. He had retired from his banking connections and joined the Hutter Company on a full-time basis in 1940. According to Parsons and several of the vice-presidents, Hall, who was fifty, had a striking personality. His associates admired his keen mind, his capacity to penetrate to fundamental problems and issues promptly and effectively, and his willingness to back with all his resourcefulness and wholehearted support any idea that appeared to make the company function more effectively. He was respected by everyone, and though his suggestions were never taken as orders—except when so worded—nearly all executive personnel weighted heavily any comments or suggestions from Hall because their experience with, and analysis of, his suggestions so often verified his wisdom. Hall's activities in connection with his position as chairman of the board included public relations, relations with the government on financing of expansion, review of general policy matters with the president, monthly review of operating results, and corporate financial problems.

Eugene Parsons, president, had been associated with the Hutter Company from the beginning. According to Hall, Parsons had imagination and was quick to grasp new scientific ideas as well as to see their long-run implications to the technology of the company and the industry. He was an innovator. Some said he liked to play with new gadgets. Parsons' ideas often were far ahead of those of his vice-presidents. They thought some of his ideas fantastic, and his ever-present drive to force them to convert ideas into real products—tested in use in "much too short" spans of time—often irritated them. If the organization really tried to make a product or change a process, and failed, Parsons was willing to face the facts and give it up, turning to some other solution. As a result of this drive and determination to get the job done, the impossible often was accomplished—sometimes, to be sure, at the cost of a subordinate who did not make good. According to Hall, many of the vice-presidents were afraid of Parsons. Nevertheless, most of the time Parsons expressed himself in a quite friendly manner. This characteristic, added to the satisfaction that arises in an organization from accomplishing the seemingly impossible, brought considerable personal loyalty and affection to Parsons from his vice-presidents and subordinate executives.

Hugh Walton, executive vice-president, assisted Parsons and acted for him in his absence. Walton followed operating details more closely than Parsons, thus freeing Parsons for broad policy-making functions. He was a man of about fifty who had wide experience within the Hutter Company. He had grown up in the production end of the business, having been manager of one of the domestic plants. At one time, he was in charge of the export department and he also had served for a brief period as vice-president in charge of production. His versatility was indicated by the fact that he also had been in charge of public relations just before his election to the post of executive vice-president. He was particularly adept at maintaining good public relations for the company. Some people, however, questioned whether he really had as much ability as his position implied.

Clinton Straight, treasurer, was a wealthy man of fifty. Having married well and invested and speculated successfully, he was proposing to retire to his country estate after the war and engage in the breeding of race horses. The treasurer's office was charged with the supervision and administration of all budget and financial functions. It was expected (*a*) to outline a financial program that would enable the company to carry out its current marketing and production plans and to finance its longer-term capital requirements; (*b*) to prescribe the kind of budgeting and accounting organizations needed in the various offices and plants, and to outline systems, methods, procedures, and necessary financial reports required of all parts of the company; (*c*) to conduct supervisory activities for compliance with the above-mentioned methods and policies; (*d*) to direct the audit functions of the company.

Straight believed in decentralization and claimed that he practiced it. He established a financial office under a manager in each plant as well as in the export and sales departments. These managers were under the line control of the head of the department or plant they served, and they provided the managers and other executives thereof with such reports as were requested. The organizations under these plant or department finance managers recorded expenses in accordance with a home office manual of expense classifications, and they related these expenses to major budget classifications or capital appropriations approved by the board and the president. Furthermore, when requested by plant managers or department heads, the managers kept cost accounts and made cost analyses. There was no uniform cost system employed in all plants. In Straight's opinion, he did not interfere with the operation of the finance office in each plant or department. He was satisfied that the procedures and methods prescribed by his office insured that all cash, incoming and outgoing, was properly accounted for and protected.

Richard Miller, administrative vice-president, was a likeable man of fifty-five who had been with the company for twenty-five years. He relied on the vice-presidents below him to take the initiative in drawing up policy proposals and preparing operating plans. He reviewed their proposals to make sure they had been broadly considered; for instance, when the vice-president in charge of sales proposed a plan for the modification, elimination, or addition of a new product, he checked to determine whether the effect on production, purchasing, personnel, and public relations had been adequately studied. Much of his time was given to verification of such facts and to conferences with vice-presidents or their representatives to resolve differences of opinion. After Miller's review of major plans and proposals, Executive Vice-President Walton, or President Parsons took the necessary action to approve or revise plans, after which the domestic plants, sales, and export departments proceeded to operate accordingly. Interested vice-presidents or department heads were supposed to review their operations and the operations of the domestic plants and sales departments, and to prepare summaries of results for Miller.

Joseph Thorp was manager of the statistical office. As the expansion program progressed, the top officers realized that the intimate and first-hand personal knowledge of operations and people that had been an important element in their control of the company when it operated on a small scale would diminish as the scale of operations expanded. They therefore decided to expand a small statistics section in the production department into a statistical office serving all parts of the company. The new office reported to

Miller, the administrative vice-president. This department was placed at a high level in the organization for the purpose of conveying to all executives an appreciation of its importance to top management. This department was to render service to all executives and departments, and, at the same time, it was not to be subordinated to the interests of any one department.

The manager was told to collect, revise, and consolidate the operating facts originating at the lowest levels of operation into summaries and analyses appropriate for each of the levels of supervision. Like many other such ventures, this office was faced immediately with nonstandard statistics, different definitions and classifications, and some personal opposition, at both high and lower levels of management, to the notion of standardization, summarization, and comparison of the operating statistics of separate plants or departments.

Thorp was an aggressive leader. He induced the management to establish similar functional offices in each plant and department, and he assisted these units in the procurement of qualified personnel. Thorp indoctrinated the men at plant levels with his philosophy of service to management and urged them to become aggressive leaders in their own organizations. These men were on the staffs of department heads or plant managers from whom they received orders and to whom they tried to sell a more effective use of statistics by management.

In Hall's opinion, it was at least a year and a half after the statistical office was established before major resistance to its efforts by executives and supervisors was overcome. Supervisors, at plant levels, tended to resent "home office interference" in management methods. They did not like to be told what reports to use; they were not sure whether the reports were to help them or to highlight their deficiencies. Both at the home office and in the plants there was an initial resentment by line officers who objected to being told by staff officers what facts they should use and how they should interpret these facts in carrying out their own defined responsibilities. Whenever explosions on such questions got as far as Hall, he nearly always supported Thorp and his assistants.

James Harwood, manager of the planning department, had an expertly trained staff. They endeavored to cooperate with all home office departments in the solution of operating and planning problems. The aim of the planning department was to help the organization as a whole to succeed. During the expansion, there had been serious breakdowns in coordination among functional departments such as sales, production, purchasing, finance, and personnel; and schedules of operations were not sufficiently well synchronized. Therefore, late in the expansion program the planning department was established to insure that the various aspects of the expansion program were coordinated and properly scheduled, and that all departments and plants kept in step on the same sales program. When this program was revised as a result of changes in the orders of the government or industrial customers, this department was expected to watch the follow-up of these changes in the operating plans of the company.

THE CURRENT PROBLEM

In November, 1945, Hall was examining certain preliminary budgets for the year 1946. He was very much dissatisfied with them. They seemed too large, not particularly well founded on realistic operating plans, and apparently "costed" on fallacious cost data. Consequently, he prepared the following memorandum.

As a result of the end of the war with Japan and the cancellation of government contracts, we have entered the cycle of sharp contraction, of reduction of expenditures, and of competition of departments or projects for the limited funds and personnel we can now make available. Our business increased in complexity during the war, and the outlook is for greater complexity in peace. We are requiring a selectivity of product projects more accurate than ever before and a more intense follow-up of the application of limited funds to such projects. In short, we must be sure that every dollar allocated to a capital expenditure goes to the most needed project, and we must get a full dollar's worth as well out of every dollar expended in the current operating program. This requirement calls for the best business management, not only to provide basic facts for policy decisions but also to follow through on such matters.

Sound practice requires the Hutter Company to further develop a plan that can provide organized and completely coordinated operating and capital expenditure budgets. This plan will require an organization that has a thorough knowledge of the facts from a practical and analytical, and not a bookkeeping, angle. We have made much progress during the war in adjusting our business methods to those of a larger scale organization by adding the statistics office and the planning department. We need to further improve our expense controls and cost accounting procedures, and we should make much more careful analyses of needs than we were able to during the war period. I believe the solution of this major problem lies in the merger of the office of the treasurer with the two other departments mentioned to form a new unit, office of the treasurer and controller, to be headed by a vice-president. In my opinion, this new office should report directly to either the president or the executive vice-president.

The general functions of the new office would include the following duties: (*a*) to organize and unify the operating plans of the various departments and factories into a single master budget program; (*b*) before submitting that program to the president and the board of directors for approval, to check the phrasing of the various parts of the operating budget; (*c*) to analyze current actual performance against the scheduled standards of performance used in the preparation of the budget; (*d*) to perform functions similar to *a*, *b*, and *c* for capital expenditures; (*e*) to make continuous studies in cooperation with departmental and factory agencies with respect to operating standards; (*f*) after approval by the board of the master budgets, to allocate funds among various activities and supervise the accounting and auditing systems in connection therewith.

In my opinion, the steps outlined above should result in a more orderly development of our budgets and make possible more expert and persuasive presentation to the board of directors. Some saving may be anticipated from the simple combination of such functions.

Hall was planning an extended trip combining some vacation with visits to certain key plants. Before leaving, he had an informal talk with Parsons about his proposal. He gave Parsons the written memorandum because, he said, "it gives a succinct statement of my views on an important problem." Parsons told Hall that he was in general agreement with him and suggested that Hall's memorandum be given to Walton, executive vice-president, for further review, analysis, and ultimate comment.

Walton received Hall's memorandum from Parsons with considerable misgiving. He was not sure what it was intended to convey. He realized that Parsons, who had not analyzed the matter at all, was favorably disposed to Hall's suggestion. Miller, the administrative vice-president, also thought it was worthy of careful study. Later in the day, Walton was in Hall's office and Hall asked, "What do you think of my memorandum?" Walton replied, "Your memorandum places too much emphasis on planning and coordination and builds up the position of the proposed new vice-president so much that I can't see why I'm needed in the company anymore."

Walton sent copies of Hall's memorandum to the administrative vice-president and to the other vice-presidents shown on the home office organization chart, and asked for their comments. Each of them expressed a desire to study the matter further and made no additional comments either for or against the project. Thus, the matter came back to Walton for further action. He appointed a special committee consisting of representatives from the office of each vice-president, and included, in addition, representatives of the treasurer's office, the planning department, and the statistics office. After a month's study, this group turned in a report considered wholly unsatisfactory by Walton. The group had not made a penetrating analysis of the proposal, and obviously did not want to get into organization politics, with which this project apparently was being tarred. A period of two months had elapsed since Hall made his proposal to Parsons. Both Hall and Parsons were asking Walton what results he had obtained and what his final recommendation was going to be.

Walton felt that he had to reach some kind of conclusion. He called on Barton James to write a report on the situation, recommending to what extent, if any, Hall's recommendation should be accepted, and indicating what steps should be taken to make any of James's proposals effective.

STUDY BY BARTON JAMES

Barton James was well known to many of the Hutter Company officers. He had been loaned to the company during the war to assist it in its expansion program. He was a close personal friend of several members of management, and his views had always been given consideration by them.

James hesitated to accept Walton's request to write such a report. He was of the opinion that writing reports on this type of problem was not a particularly good use of time; if he were working within the organization, he thought, he could help resolve issues such as those stated in Hall's memorandum, but he had little faith in outside suggestions on inside problems. A number of executives spoke to him about undertaking the assignment, and expressed their confidence in his unbiased judgment. Walton asked the president of James's company to lend him for a short period to the Hutter Company. Reluctantly, James accepted the job.

CONFERENCES

This section is a brief account of his conferences prior to the time he wrote his report.

Conference with Hugh Walton

After accepting the assignment, James had a brief conference with Walton to talk about budget planning. Neither wanted to become very specific at this point, but they agreed that Hall and Parsons probably would be satisfied with a statement of the process, which can be described in a general way as follows:

The vice-president in charge of sales, working with the other functional vice-presidents and with the export sales department and the domestic sales manager, should approve each year an estimate of sales by products. After approval or revision of this estimate, all master plans were to be based upon it. A finance committee of the board of directors, working closely with the vice-president in charge of sales, the vice-president in charge of production, the vice-president in charge of purchasing, and the treasurer, might set inventory limits on various types of finished goods and work in process. Efforts should be made to schedule production throughout the year on as even a basis as possible, giving due weight to variations in sales and allowed variation in inventory limits for various seasons of the year.

The principal job of the treasurer's enlarged department would be to see that the master plan so generally conceived was worked out on a broad basis at the home office level and on a more detailed basis in the departments and plants. Thus, estimated deliveries from production and some corresponding factor for sales departments would become the basis of properly time-phrased requirements for personnel, raw materials, purchased parts, and other services required in the sales, production, and office organizations. Presumably, the volume flowing through a department would be the basis upon which budgets were determined. To the estimated volumes by time periods, cost factors and purchase prices could be applied to arrive at financial estimates. This process required good planning of flows and presumed the knowledge and use of good operating standards.

Conference with Clinton Straight

Straight emphasized in his interview that he was planning to retire within a month and was therefore not a candidate for the enlarged position of treasurer and controller with the title of vice-president. He stated that he could not honestly recommend Bacon, the assistant treasurer, for the vice-presidency, but he did feel that Bacon was a worthy successor for the limited functions of the present treasurer's office.

He thought that during his period of service with the company he had established a basically sound underlying internal auditing, accounting, and financial organization. He did not believe in prescribing systems for department heads and managers. That is why he had long favored decentralization of control. His internal audit organization checked on the adequacy of the procedures set up by the department and plant managers for safeguarding and recording assets, as well as on the observance of these procedures and others that the home office had to announce on a company-wide basis. In carrying out the budget functions assigned to his office, he had taken a relatively passive interest. He assumed that the figures presented to him for budget purposes by the plant managers were based on sound data for volume requirements and unit cost. It was with this view that Hall apparently expressed disagreement. Nevertheless, Straight doubted the wisdom of expanding the treasurer's organization by merger, because it would upset existing relationships and would, in his opinion, inevitably lead to increasing the control of the home office over the subordinate department heads and plant managers. This possibility he regarded as a mistake, and he was certain, moreover, that the old-timers who held these positions would vigorously oppose such encroachment on their authority and responsibility. He thought that if Hall's proposal meant the top management was not satisfied with the domestic sales manager and the domestic plant managers they could solve the problem better by getting new managers than by complicating the control and organization setups.

Conference with Robert Bacon

James found that Bacon also doubted the wisdom of a merger of the three offices, but for entirely different reasons. He felt that the aggressive efforts of the statistics office had caused friction, and joining up with such an office would tend to weaken his own prospective influence within the Hutter Company. He was convinced, however, that there was need for better management on the part of the heads of domestic plants, the domestic sales manager, the various vice-presidents, and their supporting staffs. In Bacon's opinion, these men had all the facts they now needed from the three offices separately organized. The problem was to get them to use the facts they had. Too many of the executives, in his opinion, were men of the old school who did not realize that times and the scale of company operations had changed.

When asked who in the company would take the leadership in improving the capabilities of the executives, he had no answer. He more or less implied that it was the problem of Miller, the administrative vice-president, and Walton, the executive vice-president. He pointed out, without being asked, that Miller was quite good in listening to and seeking out facts for reaching company decisions but that Walton was notorious for making policy and operating decisions on insufficient facts and without adequate consultation with the vice-presidents.

Conference with Joseph Thorp

When James called on Thorp, the manager of the statistics office, he found an enthusiastic supporter of Hall's proposal. Thorp thought the move should be made at once. He had no desire to be the head man, and he thought it most inadvisable to set up the three offices as separate entities within the new vice-president's office. He wanted to start reorganizing from the bottom, and suggested the possibility of organizing within the new office divisions such as budget planning, budget analysis—that is, comparison of actual expenditures versus budget—funds control, statistical analysis, a planning section, and the like. He thought the organization should report to the administrative vice-president instead of to the executive vice-president. He favored organizing corresponding offices in the domestic sales department, the export department, and the various plants; and he wanted the home office to have complete technical supervision over these offices, their general procedures, and certain standard reports required by the home office. These offices should, he thought, be under the line supervision of the particular plant or department, but personnel would be selected and trained by the home office organization. He believed that merging the three offices and reorganizing the office internally would give the managers at lower levels in the organization, as well as top management, a more lucid picture of the operating results and problems of the company. It would be easier for such a technical organization to cooperate with the methods men in the plants and the office managers of other departments in working out and checking on standards of performance. The general pattern of tight control from top down to the lower levels of organization, implicit in the views of the head of this department, was in sharp contrast to the views of the treasurer.

Conference with James Harwood

Harwood concurred in some of the statements made by the treasurer and the assistant treasurer. He felt that there was a great need for better coordination and financial planning, and thought also that it was necessary to develop better methods both in the factory and in the offices, and to tighten standards of performance. He agreed with Bacon on the old-fashioned approach of many of the department heads or plant managers and some of the home office staff. He had grave doubts whether any improvement could be made, but thought the plan was worth a trial. He realized that he had no chance of becoming the new vice-president in charge of the office of treasurer and controller.

He urged James to point out in his report the importance of the right kind of person for that position. He had in mind one of the abler managers of one of the domestic plants, Stanley Poole. Poole had served in the sales department as a young man and had served in the export department in Asia. At one point, he had been an assistant to the vice-president in charge of sales in the home office, and at present he was manager of one of the larger domestic plants. Harwood admitted that Poole might not regard as a promotion the change from the line control of a plant to a staff position in top management. However, Poole was considered very loyal to the organization. Moreover, he prepared excellent plans for operations and usually submitted good budgets as well. He had a broad conception of policy matters, and he knew how to dig into detail when that sort of work was required. He was also a man with whom Harwood would like to work. James thought that Harwood meant by this statement that he would like to be the principal assistant to Poole in case Poole were made vice-president.

Conference with Richard Miller

During the readjustment period, Miller had had so much trouble getting coordinated plans from his vice-presidents, department heads, and plant managers that he was automatically for the proposal and felt that it would assist him greatly in carrying out his responsibilities. He suggested that the job of top management was simply too great for the four men now charged with it and that they needed the expert assistance of the enlarged office of treasurer and controller. He suggested the possibility that the general collection of reports and facts from subordinate plants or departments might be accomplished without merger by the statistics office, now under his control, and that the analytical functions of that office might be combined with those of the planning department and the treasurer's office to form the new organization. He urged that the new office report directly to the executive vice-president and not to him. He believed an assignment of the enlarged office to the executive vice-president would increase its importance in the home office, in the minds of managers of the domestic plants, and of the domestic sales manager.

Other Conferences

James also talked to the vice-president in charge of sales and the vice-president in charge of production. These interviews served only to confirm his opinion that as long as the functions of treasurer and controller were conducted in a manner to asssist vice-presidents and the plant and department managers in the operation of the business, any plan would be acceptable. However, if the proposed plan was designed to tighten controls on these officers and to lead to any diminution in their authority or policy-making responsibility, they were likely to be against it.

The vice-president in charge of production suggested that the size of the proposed organization might be reduced if the treasurer's general functions were not included in the enlarged office. He proposed, as an alternative, taking the budget and accounting functions out of the treasurer's office and setting them up in a separate controller's office. Under his plan, the treasurer would not report to the president and the executive vice-president, but would be on a par with the other vice-presidents reporting to the administrative vice-president. The treasurer's activities would consist largely of responsibility for funds and investments. It seemed to be a matter of indifference to the production vice-president whether the proposed controller's department should report directly to the executive vice-president or to the administrative vice-president, which would place him on a par with the other vice-presidents. Under the production vice-president's plan, the controller would be on control matters the principal adviser or assistant to top management and would have responsibility for the coordinated preparation of budgets throughout the company. The controller would be in charge of the development of standardized systems of accounts, budgetary procedures, uniform statistics, cost accounts, and the like. By prescribing the minimum essentials for accounting and statistical systems and procedures, he would provide the basis for uniform records on which depended analyses, comparisons between plants, and summarization of results.

The vice-president in charge of sales raised in his interview a question regarding the advisability of making too drastic a change in the existing organization during a period when outside events beyond the control of the company were themselves far-reaching in character and upsetting as well.

From other talks with more than one vice-president, James learned that the company was pretty well organized as it was, and that with the reduced pressure on executives as a result of the end of the war there should be opportunity for better coordination of activities and for better planning, budgeting, and setting of standards. In their opinions, recognition of the need for information for making decisions and willingness to use it were probably as essential as any changes in organization. They pointed out, without prompting from anyone, that both the president and particularly the executive vice-president were sometimes remiss in not using the available facts. They could see some slight margin of advantage in favor of the production vice-president's suggested modification of Hall's proposal, because of the complete unification under the controller of the budget, comparison, and coordination functions. Nevertheless they seriously doubted the wisdom of establishing the proposed office unless the president and executive vice-president were willing to do two things: (1) assign competent personnel to the office and (2) be informed regularly by it of the progress of the company and of any problems revealed by analyses of operations. They stated that

James's report would be genuinely incomplete if he failed to discuss this matter. They argued, further, that James was risking his reputation if he failed to point out the extent to which the two considerations mentioned above affected the ultimate success of Hall's proposal or any modification thereof.

TENTATIVE CONCLUSIONS

After completing these interviews and before writing this report, James went away feeling that he had a choice among the following possibilities: (1) maintenance of the status quo, (2) complete endorsement of Hall's proposal, (3) some modification of Hall's proposal in accordance with suggestions made by different officers, or (4) presentation of an entirely new plan. In view of the time when his initial report was due and the complicated political situation within the organization, he ruled out the fourth possibility.

QUESTIONS

1. What is your recommendation with respect to the new office proposed by Mr. Hall?
2. If the new office is set up, who should head it?

Case 2–2

Rendell Company

Fred Bevins, controller of the Rendell Company, was concerned about the organizational status of his divisional controllers. In 1959, and for many years previously, the divisional controllers reported to the general managers of their divisions. Although Mr. Bevins knew this to be the general practice in many other divisionally organized companies, he was not entirely satisfied with it. His interest in making a change was stimulated by a description of organizational responsibilities given him by the controller of the Martex Corporation.

The Rendell Company had seven operating divisions; the smallest had $10 million in annual sales, and the largest over $100 million. Each division was responsible for both the manufacturing and the marketing of a distinct product line. Some parts and components were transferred between divisions, but the volume of such interdivisional business was not large.

The company had been in business and profitable for over fifty years. In the early 1950's, although it continued to make profits, its rate of growth slowed considerably. James Hodgkin, later the president, was hired in 1954 by the directors because of their concern about this situation. His first position was controller. He became executive vice-president in 1957 and president in 1958. Mr. Bevins joined the company as assistant controller in 1955, when he was thirty-three years old. He became controller in 1957.

In 1954, the corporate control organization was primarily responsible for (1) financial accounting, (2) internal auditing, and (3) analysis of capital budgeting requests. A budgetary control system was in existence, but the reports prepared under this system were submitted to the top management group directly by the operating divisions, with little analysis by the corporate control organization.

Mr. Hodgkin, as controller, thought it essential that the corporate control organization play a more active role in the process of establishing budgets and analyzing performance. He personally took an active role in reviewing budgets and studying divisional performance reports, and hired several young analysts to assist him. Mr. Bevins continued to move in the same direction after his promotion to controller. By 1959, the corporate organization was beginning to be well enough staffed so that it could, and did, give careful attention to the information submitted by the divisions.

Divisional controllers reported directly to the divisional general managers, but the corporate controller always was consulted prior to the appointment of a new division controller, and he also was consulted in connection with salary increases for divisional controllers. The corporate controller specified the accounting system to which the divisions were expected to conform, and the general procedures they were to follow in connection with budgeting and reporting performance. It was clearly understood, however, that budgets and performance reports coming from a division were the responsibility of that division's general manager, with the divisional controller acting as his staff assistant in the preparation of these documents. For example, the divisional general manager personally discussed his budget with top management prior to its approval, and although the divisional controller usually was present at these meetings to give information on technical points, his role was strictly that of a staff man.

Most of the divisional controllers had worked for Rendell for 10 years or more. Usually, they worked up through various positions in the controller organization, either at headquarters, in their division, or both. Two of the divisional controllers were in their early thirties, however, and had only a few years' experience in the headquarters controller organization before being made, first, divisional assistant controller and then divisional controller.

Mr. Bevins foresaw increasing difficulties with this relationship as the corporation introduced more modern control techniques. For one thing, he thought the existing relationship between himself and the divisional controllers was not so close that he could urge the development and use of new techniques as rapidly as he wished. More important, he thought that he was not getting adequate information about what was actually happening in the divisions. The divisional controllers' primary loyalty was to his division manager, and it was unreasonable to expect that he would give Mr. Bevins frank, unbiased reports. For example, Mr. Bevins was quite sure that some fat was hidden in the divisional expense budgets, and that the divisional controllers had a pretty good idea as to where it was. In short, he thought he would get a much better idea of what was going on in the divisions if reports on divisional activities came directly from controllers working for him rather than for the divisional manager.

Mr. Bevins was therefore especially interested in the controller organization at the Martex Company as he learned about it from E. F. Ingraham, the Martex controller, when he visited that company.

Until his visit to Martex, Mr. Bevins had not discussed the organization problem with anyone. Shortly thereafter, he gave William Harrigan, his assistant controller, a memorandum describing his visit (see the appendix) and asked for Mr. Harrigan's reaction. Mr. Harrigan had been with Rendell for 25 years, and had been a divisional controller before going to headquarters in 1956. Mr. Bevins respected his knowledge of the company and his opinion on organizational matters. Mr. Harrigan was accustomed to speaking frankly with Mr. Bevins. The gist of his comments follows.

I don't think the Martex plan would work with us; in fact, I am not even sure it works at Martex in the way suggested by the job descriptions and organization charts.

Before coming to headquarters, I had five years' experience as a divisional controller. When I took that job, I was told by the corporate controller and by my general manager that my function was to help the general manager every way I could. This is the way I operated. My people got together a lot of the information that was helpful in preparing the divisional budget, but the final product represented the thinking and decisions of my general manager, and he was the person who sold it to top management. I always went with him to the budget meetings, and he often asked me to explain some of the figures. When the monthly reports were prepared, I usually went over them, looking for danger signals, and then took them in to the general manager. He might agree with me, or he might spot other things that needed looking into. In either case, he usually was the one to put the heat on the operating organization, not me.

We did have some problems. The worst, and this happened several times a year, was when someone from the corporate controller's office would telephone and ask questions such as, "Do you think your division could get along all right if we cut $X out of the advertising budget?" Or, "Do you really believe that the cost savings estimate on this equipment request is realistic?" Usually, I was in complete agreement with the data in question and defended them as best I could. Once in a while, however, I might privately disagree with the "official" figures, but I tried not to say so.

Questions of this sort really should be asked of the general manager, not of me. I realize that the head office people probably didn't think the question was important enough to warrant bothering the general manager, and in many cases they were right. The line is a fine one.

This business of the division controller's being an "unbiased source of information" sounds fine when you word it that way, but another way to say it is that he is a front office spy, and that doesn't sound so good. It would indeed make our life easier if we could count on the divisional controllers to give us the real lowdown on what is going on. But if this is to be their position, then we can't expect that the general manager will continue to treat his controller as a trusted assistant. Either the general manager will find somebody else to take over this work unofficially, or it won't get done.

I think we are better off the way we are. Sure, the budgets will have some fat in them, and not all the bad situations will be highlighted in the operating reports, and this makes our job more difficult. But I'd rather have this than the alternative. If we used the Martex method (or, rather, what they claim is their method), we can be sure that the divisional controller will no longer be a member of the management team. They'll isolate him as much as they can, and the control function in the division will suffer.

QUESTIONS

1. What is the organizational philosophy of Martex with respect to the controller function? What do you think of it? Should Rendell adopt this philosophy?
2. To whom should the divisional controllers report in the Rendell Company? Why?
3. What should be the relationship between the corporate controller and the divisional controllers? What steps would you take to establish this relationship on a sound footing?
4. Would you recommend any major changes in the basic responsibilities of either the corporate controller or the divisional controller?

Appendix

Notes on Martex Controller Organization

Mr. Ingraham, the corporate controller, reports directly to the president and has reporting to him all division controllers and other accounting, data processing, and analysis groups. The Martex Company's organization charts and descriptions of responsibility are included herein (Exhibits 1, 2, 3, and 4), and indicate the structure and function of the organization.

The controller's organization is charged with the responsibility of establishing cost and profit standards in the corporation and of taking appropriate action to see that these standards are attained. It reviews all research projects, and assigns names and numbers to them in order to coordinate research activities in the various divisions and their central research. The organization also handles all matters involving cost and profit estimates.

The present size of divisional controllers' staffs ranges from three to twenty-two. Division controllers are not involved in preparing division profit and loss statements; these are prepared by a separate group for all divisions and the corporation.

LINE-STAFF RELATIONSHIPS

A division manager has no staff of his own, not even a personal assistant. He receives staff assistance from two sources.

First, he has some people assigned to him from the general staff—typically, a controller, an engineer, and a purchasing agent.

All division management and all the corporate staff are located in the corporate headquarters building. However, the "assigned staff" are located physically with their staff colleagues; for example, a divisional controller and his assistants are located in the controller's section of the building, not near his divisional manager's office.

Second, the division can call on the central staff to the extent that the manager wishes. The divisions are charged for these services on the basis of service rendered. The central staff units are listed in the General Staff Services box of Exhibit 2.

DIVISION MANAGER-CONTROLLER RELATIONSHIP

The success of the Martex controller organization and its relations with divisional managers appears to be largely the result of managers' and controllers' having grown up with the arrangement and accepting it long before they arrived at their managerial positions.

Some additional factors that appear to contribute to their successful relationship are the following:

1. A uniform and centralized accounting system.
2. Predetermined financial objectives for each division.
   a. Growth in dollar sales.
   b. A specified rate of profit as a percent of sales.
3. Profit sharing by managers and controllers.

ACCOUNTING SYSTEM

The controller's division has complete control of the accounting system. It determines how and what accounts will be kept. The controller's division has developed an accounting system that is the same for all divisions. Mr. Ingraham pointed out that no division had a system perfectly tailored to its needs, but he believes that the disadvantages to the divisions were more than offset by having a system uniform over all divisions and understood by all concerned. Mr. Ingraham indicated it was likely that if Martex divisions were free to establish their own accounting systems, every division would have a different one within two years, and interpretation by corporate management would be difficult, if possible at all.

The accounting system appears to provide a common basis for all divisional financial reports and analyses, and it aids in maintaining the bond of confidence between division managers and controllers.

DIVISION OBJECTIVES

The corporation has established two financial objectives for each division. These are (*a*) growth in dollar sales, (*b*) a specified rate of profit as a percent of sales.

These objectives are determined in advance by recommendations of the controller's division with the advice and counsel of divisional managers. The objectives are long-range in nature; the target profit rate has been changed only three times since 1935.

The particular percentage of sales selected as the target profit rate is based on several factors, among which are (1) the patentability of products, (2) a desired rate of return on investment, (3) the industry's margin of profit, and (4) the industry's rate of return on investment. These factors and others determine the profit rate finally selected.

Within limits, attainment of these financial objectives represents the primary task required of division general managers by corporate management.

PROFIT SHARING

Divisional managers receive about 75 percent of their total compensation from profit sharing and stock options. Divisional controllers receive about 25 percent of their compensation from profit sharing—half from a share in divisional profits, and the other half from corporate profits.

DIVISION MANAGERS' VIEW OF THE SYSTEM

Mr. Ingraham indicated that divisional managers like to have divisional controllers report to the corporate controller because (1) it gives them an unbiased partner armed with relevant information, (2) the controller is in a better position to do the analysis needed for decision-making, and (3) when cost reports are issued there is little or no argument about them among affected parties.

Exhibit 1

POSITION DESCRIPTIONS FROM THE MARTEX MANAGEMENT GUIDEBOOK

Controller

The trend of modern business management is to change the basic concept of the controller's position from that of an administrative function concerned largely with accounting detail to that of an important position in management as it relates to the control of costs and the profitable operation of the business as a whole.

The more our business becomes diversified with operations scattered throughout the U.S.A., the greater is the need for an officer to whom the president delegates

Exhibit 1—Continued

authority with respect to those factors affecting costs and profits in the same manner as he may delegate authority to others in strong staff positions.

In our vertical type of organization there is great need for an appointed officer whose responsibility it is to establish budgetary standards of operations and objective per cent of profit on sales targets for each of the operating divisions and domestic subsidiaries. He shall also establish budgetary standards of operation for staff functions in line with divisional and over-all company profit objectives. When the standard of operations or profit target is not attained, the controller has the right and the responsibility within his delegated authority to question the failure and recommend changes to accomplish the desired result.

The controller shall work with the various divisions of the company through divisional controllers assigned to each major operating division and staff function. It is not intended that the controller take the initiative away from the division managers, since the responsibility for efficient operations and profits are assumed by the managers. However, the controller and his staff should have the right and the responsibility to expect certain operating results from the division head, and when a difference of opinion occurs as to the reasonableness of the demand for results, the matter should then be referred by either party to the president.

Along with the foregoing, the following responsibilities are an essential part of the position and apply to the corporation and its subsidiaries:

1. The installation and supervision of all accounting records.
2. The preparation, supervision, and interpretation of all divisional and product profit and loss statements, operating statements, and cost reports, including reports of costs of production, research, distribution, and administration.
3. The supervision of taking and costing of all physical inventories.
4. The preparation and interpretation of all operating statistics and reports, including interpretation of charts and graphs, for use by Management Committees and the board of directors.
5. The preparation, as budget director, in conjunction with staff officers and heads of divisions and subsidiaries, of an annual budget covering all operations for submission to the president prior to the beginning of the fiscal year.
6. The initiation, preparation, and issuance of standard practice regulations and the coordination of systems, including clerical and office methods relating to all operating accounting procedures.
7. Membership of the controller or his designated representative in all division and subsidiary Management Committees.

He shall be responsible for the selection, training, development, and promotion of qualified personnel for his organization and their compensation within established company policy. He shall submit to the president an organization plan for accomplishing desired objectives.

The controller may delegate to members of his organization certain of his responsibilities, but in so doing he does not relinquish his over-all responsibility or accountability for results.

Treasurer and Assistant Treasurers

Subject to the rules and regulations of the Finance Committee, the treasurer is the chief financial officer and generally his functions include control of corporate funds and attending to the financial affairs of the corporation and its domestic and foreign subsidiaries wherever located. More specifically the duties and responsibilities are as follows:

Banking: He shall have custody of and be responsible for all money and securities and shall deposit in the name of the corporation in such depositories as are approved by the president all funds coming into his possession for the company account.

Exhibit 1—Continued

Credits and Collections: He shall have supervision over all cashiers, cash receipts, and collection records and accounts receivable ledgers. He shall initiate and approve all credit policies and procedures.

Disbursements: He shall authorize disbursements of any kind by signature on checks. This includes direct supervision over accounts payable and payroll departments and indirect supervision over all receiving departments for the purpose of checking on the accuracy of invoices presented for payment. He shall maintain adequate records of authorized appropriations and also determine that all financial transactions covered by minutes of Management and Executive Committees and the board of directors are properly executed and recorded.

General Financial Reports: He shall prepare and supervise all general accounting records. He shall prepare and interpret all general financial statements, including the preparation of the quarterly and annual reports for mailing to stockholders. This also includes the preparation and approval of the regulations on standard practices required to assure compliance with orders or regulations issued by duly constituted governmental agencies and stock exchanges.

He shall supervise the continuous audit (including internal controls) of all accounts and records and shall supervise the audit and procedures of Certified Public Accountants.

Taxes: He shall supervise the preparation and filing of all tax returns and shall have supervision of all matters relating to taxes and shall refer to the general counsel all such matters requiring interpretation of tax laws and regulations.

Insurance Property Records: He shall supervise the purchase and placing of insurance of any kind including the insurance required in connection with employee benefits. He shall be responsible for recommending adequate coverage for all ascertainable risks and shall maintain such records as to avoid any possibility that various hazards are not being properly insured. He shall maintain adequate property records and valuations for insurance and other purposes and, if necessary, employ appraisal experts to assist in determining such valuations and records.

Loans: He shall approve all loans and advances made to employees within limits prescribed by the Executive Committee.

Investments: As funds are available beyond normal requirements, he shall recommend suitable investments to the Finance Committee. He shall have custody of securities so acquired and shall use the safekeeping facilities of the banks for that purpose. As securities are added or removed from such vaults or facilities, he shall be accompanied by an authorized officer of the Corporation.

Office Management: He will be responsible for the coordination of all office management functions throughout the company and its domestic subsidiaries.

Financial Planning: He shall initiate and prepare current and long-range cash forecasts, particularly as such forecasts are needed for financing programs to meet anticipated cash requirements for future growth and expansion. He shall arrange to meet sinking fund requirements for all outstanding debenture bonds and preferred stock and shall anticipate such requirements whenever possible.

He shall have such other powers and shall perform such other duties as may be assigned to him by the board of directors and the president.

The treasurer shall be responsible for the selection, training, development, and promotion of qualified personnel for his organization and their compensation within established company policy. It is expected that since he will have to delegate many of the duties and responsibilities enumerated above, he shall confer with and submit to the president an organization plan and chart.

The treasurer may delegate to members of his organization certain of his responsibilities together with appropriate authority for fulfillment; however, in so doing he does not relinquish his over-all responsibility or accountability for results.

The treasurer is a member of the Finance, Retirement, and Inventory Review Committees.

Exhibit 2

MARTEX CORPORATION

Organization Chart, Division A, January 1, 1959

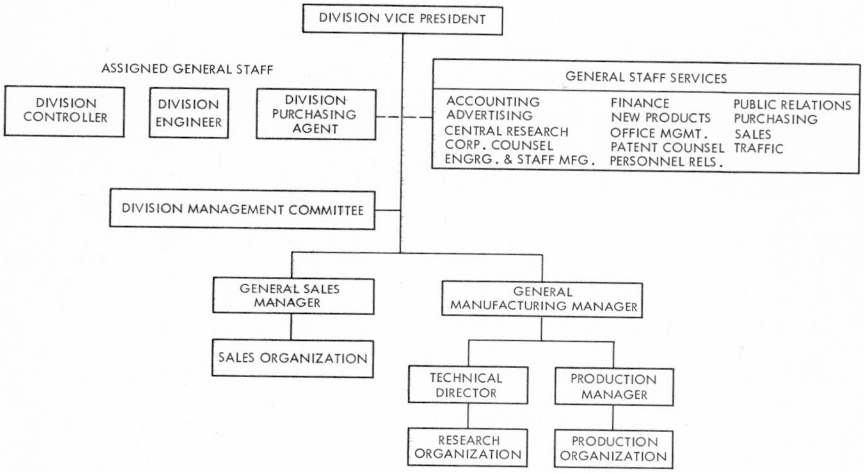

NOTE: Various levels on the chart do not necessarily indicate relative importance of positions.

Exhibit 3

MARTEX CORPORATION

Organization Chart of Controller's Division, January 1, 1959

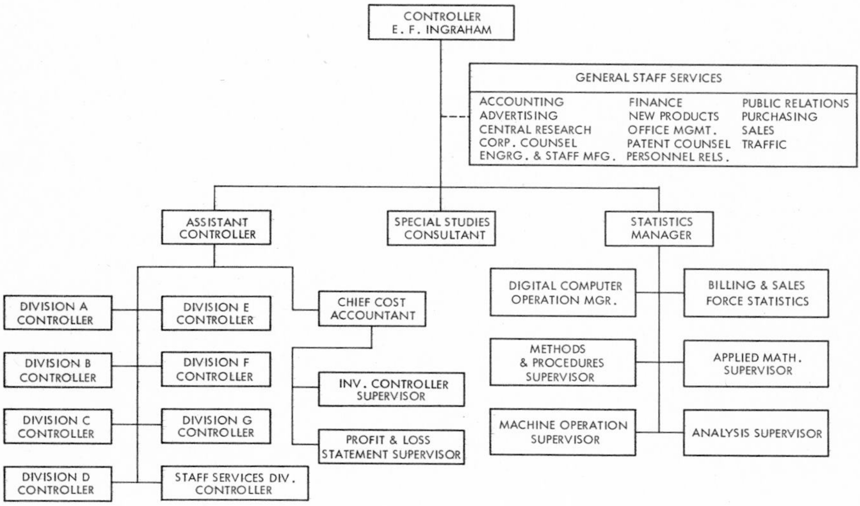

Exhibit 4

MARTEX CORPORATION

Organization Chart of Treasurer's Division, August 1, 1959

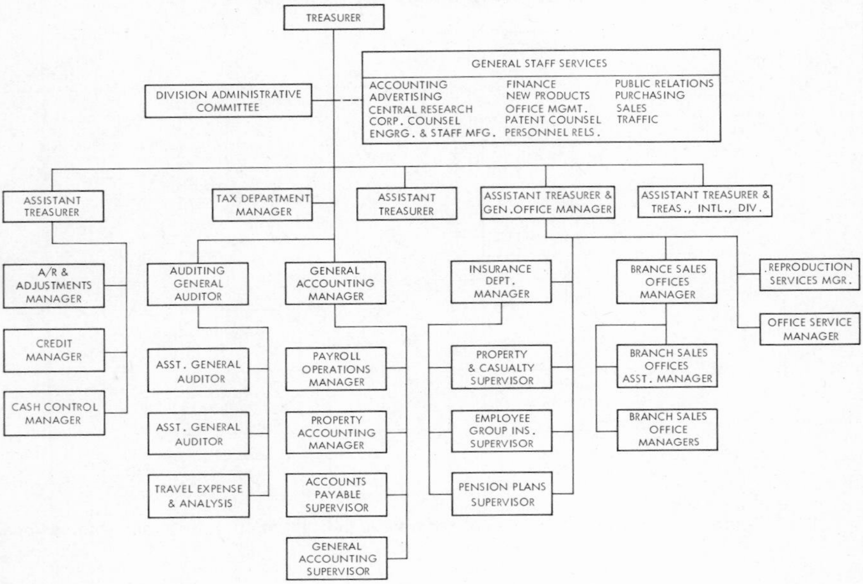

NOTE: Various levels on the chart do not necessarily indicate relative importance of positions.

Chapter Three

RELATING THE SYSTEM TO ORGANIZATIONAL OBJECTIVES

A management control system is one of the major tools used in guiding a company toward the achievement of its objectives. Thus, in the broadest sense, the management control system is an implementing device. If the system is to be effective, therefore, an important first step in designing it is to prepare an explicit statement of the goals and objectives of the enterprise. When an explicit statement cannot be elicited, the systems designer must infer, as best he can from the words and deeds of the management, what the objectives actually are.

The *determination* of company objectives is a matter for top management; it involves a complex set of interrelated considerations and subjective evaluations. This topic is beyond the scope of this book. We are, however, vitally interested in knowing what a company's objectives are so that we may tailor the control system to fit them. It is dangerous to attempt to generalize about corporate objectives, but one statement can be safely made: They are complex. The convenient assumption that corporations are striving toward the single goal of profit maximization is certainly too oversimplified to be operationally useful in a practical business setting. Most corporations, like most people, are multivalued creatures; they are striving to achieve some mix of goals (economic wealth, social or political power, prestige, etc.). On the other hand, most corporations do place great emphasis on the achievement of economic goals. Even so, many hard decisions must be made concerning the trade-off of a certain amount of profit this year for the expectation of even more profit in the future.

A common weakness of many management control systems is an overemphasis on current profit performance. It is relatively easy to improve this year's profit result by curtailing research or advertising expenditures, deferring maintenance, skimping on product quality, and so forth. A control system that relies too heavily on current profit performance encourages such actions by division managers.

There are two primary ways to counteract the tendency of a control system to become overly concerned with current profits. One way is to have the statement of objectives reflect management's interest in the accomplishment of goals other than mere profits. An explicit statement that current profitability is only one of several goals is helpful in keeping the importance of profits in a broader perspective. The other way involves careful systems design, particularly in the definitions used in the measurement of profit, to insure the highest possible degree of consistency between the profit figure and the achievement of corporate goals. The cases in this chapter illustrate these two approaches. Because of the importance of the second approach, and its susceptibility to an analytical framework, many of the cases in subsequent chapters are relevant to it.

Reading 3-1

The Accomplishment of Purpose: Organizational Processes and Behavior

By Edmund P. Learned, C. Roland Christensen, Kenneth R. Andrews, and William D. Guth*

Our study of strategy has brought us to the prescription that organizational structure must follow strategy if implementation is to be effective. We have seen that structural design involves inevitably (1) a suitable specialization of task, (2) a parallel provision for coordination, and (3) information systems for meeting the requirement that specialists be well informed and their work coordinated. We have seen that a variety of structures may be suitable to a strategy so long as the performance influenced by structural characteristics is not diverted from strategic ends.

We turn now from structural considerations to other influences upon organizational behavior. A logical structure does not insure effective organized effort any more than a high degree of technical skill in individual members insures achievements of organizational purposes. We suggest the following proposition for testing in your analysis of cases: *Organizational performance is effective to the extent that (in an atmosphere deliberately created to encourage the development of required skills and to provide the satisfactions of personal progress) individual energy is successfully directed toward organizational goals.* Convergence of energy upon purpose is made effective by individual and group commitment to purpose.

Man-made and natural organizational *systems* and *processes* are available

---

* From *Business Policy: Text and Cases* (Homewood, Ill.: Richard D. Irwin, Inc., 1965).

to influence individual development and performance. In any organization the system which relates specific influences upon behavior to each other (so as to constitute an ultimate impact upon behavior) is made up of some six elements: (1) standards, (2) measures, (3) incentives, (4) rewards, (5) penalties, and (6) controls. The distinguishing characteristic of a system, of course, is the interaction of its elements. This interdependence will vary from organization to organization and from situation to situation and cannot always be observed, controlled, or completely analyzed.

The familiar processes which bear on performance are (1) measurement, (2) evaluation, (3) motivation, (4) control, and (5) individual development. The most important aspect of a process is the speed and direction of its forward motion and the nature of its side effects. So far as the uniqueness of each company situation allows, we shall look at combinations of these organizational systems and processes in the following order:

1. The establishment of standards and measurement of performance.
2. The administration of motivation and incentive systems.
3. The operation of systems of restraint and control.
4. The recruitment and development of management.

These processes have been studied in detail by specialists of several kinds. We shall not attempt to extract all the wisdom or expose all the folly which, over the years, has accumulated in the study of human relations and organizational behavior. We are now concerned, as always, with the limited but important ways in which specialized bodies of knowledge can be put to use in the implementation of strategy. The idea of strategy will dominate our approach to the internal organizational systems which animate structure, just as it dominated our discussion of the factors that determine structure itself. It may be desirable to point out that our aim is not to coerce and manipulate unwilling individuals. It is instead to support and direct individuals who are at least assenting to or, more desirably, committed to organizational goals. Commitment to purpose remains in our scheme of things the overriding necessary condition of effective accomplishment.

ESTABLISHMENT OF STANDARDS AND MEASUREMENT OF PERFORMANCE

If progress toward goals is to be supervised at all, it will have to be observed and measured. If it is to be measured, whether quantitatively or qualitatively, there must be some idea of where an organization is compared to where it ought to be. To state where an organization ought to be is to set a standard. A standard takes shape as a projection of hoped-for or budgeted performance. As time passes, positive and negative variances between budgeted and actual performance are recorded. This comparison makes possible, although it does not necessarily justify, relating incentives and controls to performance as measured against standards. . . .

It is virtually impossible to make meaningful generalizations about how proper standards might be set in particular companies. It can be said, however, that in any organization the over-all strategy can be translated into more or less detailed future plans (the detail becoming less predictable as the time span grows longer), which permits comparison of actual with predicted performance. . . . Whether standards are being set at exactly the proper level is less significant than the fact that an effort is being made to raise them steadily as organizational power and resources increase. External events may, however, invalidate predictions. It must be recognized that for good reasons as well as bad, standards are not always attainable. Hence the need for skill in variable budgeting.

By far the most important problem of measurement is that increased interest in the measurement of performance against standards brings increased danger that the executive evaluation program may encourage performance which detracts from rather than supports the overall strategy.

The temptation to use measurement primarily for the purpose of judging executive performance is acute. The desire to put management responsibility in the ablest hands leads to comparing managers in terms of results. Failure to meet a standard leads naturally to the assignment of blame to persons. The general manager's most urgent duty is to see that planned results are indeed accomplished. Such pressure, unfortunately, may lead to exaggerated respect for specific measures and for the short-run results they quantify, and thus to ultimate misevaluation of performance.

The problems of measurement cluster about the fallacy of the single criterion.[1] When any single measure like return on investment, for example, is used to determine the compensation, promotion, or reassignment of a manager, the resultant behavior will often lead to unplanned and undesired outcomes. No single measure can encompass the total contribution of an individual either to immediate and longer-term results or to the efforts of others. The sensitivity of individuals to evaluation leads them to produce the performance that will measure up in terms of the criterion rather than in terms of more important purposes. Since managers respond to the measures management actually takes to reward performance, mere verbal exhortations to behave in the manner required by long-range strategy carry no weight, and cannot be relied upon to preclude undesirable actions encouraged by a poorly designed measurement and reward system.

---

[1] See John Dearden's "Limits on Decentralized Profit Responsibility" and "Mirage of Profit Decentralization" in E. P. Learned, F. J. Aguilar, and R. C. K. Valtz, *European Problems in General Management,* pp. 570–97. These articles first appeared in the *Harvard Business Review,* July–August 1962, pp. 81–89; and November–December 1962, pp. 140–54.

Faith in the efficacy of a standard measure like return on investment can reach extreme proportions, especially among men to whom the idea of strategy is apparently unfamiliar. Thus a visiting top manager from a major automobile manufacturer told a class that the National Finance Company[2] could solve its apparently bothersome problem of designing an effective relationship between the home office and the branches by giving the branch managers a great deal of autonomy and then judging their performance solely on the basis of return on the capital employed by each. A student who was not convinced answered this argument as follows:

> Although this solution to the branch-home office relations problem had merit, it overlooked the fact that the company was dependent for a great deal of its capital on bankers who evaluated the company on bases other than return on investment. If the proposed solution was accepted, the branch manager might increase his return on investment by allowing his delinquency percentage to rise. Rising delinquency percentages might cause the bankers to withhold new credit from the company. The condition could therefore arise in which the branch manager, though carrying out policies which make his performance appear good under the evaluation system being used, would actually be acting in a manner destructive to the welfare of the company as a whole.[3]

Instances in which performance is measured in terms of just one figure or ratio are so numerous as to suggest that the pursuit of quantification and measurement as such has overshadowed the real goal of management evaluation. If we return to our original hypothesis that profit and return on investment are terms that can be usefully employed to denote the results to be sought by business, but are too general to characterize its distinctive mission or purpose, then we must say that short-term profitability is not by itself an adequate measure of managerial performance. Return on investment, when used alone, is another dangerous criterion, since it can lead businessmen to postpone needed product research or the modernization of facilities in the interest of keeping down the investment on the basis of which their performance is measured. Certainly we must conclude that evaluation of performance must not be focused exclusively upon the criterion of short-run profitability or any other single standard which may cause managers to act contrary to the long-range interests of the company as a whole.

As you discuss the cases that follow, you will be concerned with developing more adequate criteria. Our concern for strategy naturally leads us to suggest that the management evaluation system which plays so great a part in influencing management performance must employ a number of criteria, some of which are subjective and thus difficult to quantify. It is easy to argue that subjective judgments are unfair. But use of a harmful or irrelevant

---

[2] E. P. Learned, C. R. Christensen, and K. R. Andrews, *Problems of General Management* (Homewood, Ill.: Richard D. Irwin, Inc., 1961), pp. 277–376.

[3] David J. Dunn, "Evaluation of Performance" (unpublished student paper), reproduced by permission.

criterion just because it lends itself to quantification is a poor exchange for alleged objectivity.

Against multiple criteria, it may be argued that they restrict the freedom of the profit-center manager to produce the results required through any means he elects. This may of course be true, but the manager who does not want his methods to be subject to scrutiny does not want to be judged. Accountants, sometimes indifferent to the imperfections of their figures and the artificiality of their conventions, do not always make clear the true meaning of an annual profit figure or the extent to which a sharp rise from one year to the next may reflect the failure to make investments needed to sustain the future of a product line.

If multiple criteria are to be used, it is not enough for top management simply to announce that short-term profitability and return on investment are only two measures among many—including responsibility to society—by which executives are going to be judged. Such an announcement did not prevent violation of the antitrust laws by managers in the electrical industry, who believed it was more important for them to produce the expected profit than to inform their superiors that the basis for conducting business both honestly and profitably had disappeared. To give subordinates freedom to exercise judgment and simultaneously to demand profitability produces an enormous pressure which cannot be effectively controlled by endless talk about tying rewards to factors other than profit.

The tragedy of men, honorable in other ways, working for seniors who were apparently unaware of price-fixing practices, should dramatize one serious predicament of the profit-center form of organization, where, characteristically, management expects to solve the problems of evaluation by decentralizing freedom of decision to subordinates, so long as profit objectives are met. Decentralization seems sometimes to serve as a cloak for nonsupervision, except for the control implicit in the superficial measure of profitability. It would appear to preclude accurate evaluation, and the use of multiple criteria may indeed make a full measure of decentralization inappropriate.

To delegate authority to profit centers and to base evaluation upon proper performance must not mean that the profit center's strategic decisions are left unsupervised. *Even under decentralization, top management must remain familiar with divisional substrategy, with the fortunes—good and bad—that attend implementation, and with the problems involved in attempting to achieve budgeted performance.* The true function of measurement is to increase perception of the problems limiting achievement. If an individual sees where he stands in meeting a schedule, he may be led to inquire why he is not somewhere else. If this kind of question is not asked, the answer is not proffered. An effective system of evaluation must include information which will allow top management to understand the problems faced by subordinates in achieving the results for which they are held responsible. And certainly if evaluation is to be comprehensive enough to avoid the distortions cited thus far, immediate results will not be the only object of evaluation. The effectiveness with which problems are handled along the way will be evaluated, even though this judgment, like most of the important decisions of management, must remain subjective.

The formula of evaluation most consistent with the concept of strategy that is outlined in these notes is what is called "management by objectives." Instead of simply evaluating "traits," like some of the older appraisal systems, this process entails at all levels of management a meeting between subordinate and superior to agree on the achievements which the subordinate will try to accomplish during the forthcoming period. The subordinate's suggested objectives are modified if, after discussion, they appear either impracticable or understated. They are checked for the contribution they will make to the larger strategy of which they must be a part. They are designed to include quantitatively nonmeasurable items as well as items budgeted in the formal short-term and long-range plans. The problems of successfully designing such a system are easier to see than to solve. Nonetheless, an acceptance of the imperfections and inexactness of such a system, plus a shared interest in the problems to be overcome in serving strategy, make possible a kind of communication which cannot be replaced by the application of a single criterion. Certainly, it is the quality of his objectives and of his attempts to overcome obstacles posed by circumstance and by competition that is the most important thing to measure about a manager's performance.

Reading 3-2

An Industry View of Budgeting

By Robert W. Lewis*

Since General Electric's approach to budgeting is strongly influenced by our organization and management policies, it might be helpful to review very briefly General Electric's organization structure.

Under our policy of decentralized management, there have been established over one hundred product departments as the basic operating components of the Company. For reporting purposes, a number of these departments with similar market or product responsibilities are organized into a Division, which, in turn, is assigned to one of the four operating groups—Apparatus and Industrial; Consumer Products; Electronic, Atomic and Defense Systems; and International. Each Division is headed by a General Manager who may also be a Vice-President. The Groups are headed by a Vice-President who is also an Executive Officer of the Company reporting directly to the President. Neither the Group Executives nor the Division General Managers have any staff.

In addition to the operating organization, we have what we call Services components whose basic assignments are to carry on research work in their functional specialties and to provide expert technical service to the Product Departments, the Division Managers and Group Executives. The Services Officers in charge of these functional activities report to the Chairman of the Board. One of the Services Officers is the Comptroller, who is in charge of Accounting Services, of which Measurements Service is a part.

The over-all operation of each product department is guided by a General Manager who has reporting to him five functional managers—the Man-

---

* General Manager, Switchgear Department, General Electric Company. Reproduced by permission from *The Journal of Accountancy*, December, 1959.

agers of Marketing, Engineering, Manufacturing, Finance, and Relations—and a Legal Counsel. Through his functional managers, the General Manager is responsible for the development and design of the department's products; their manufacture; marketing the products; employee and community relations activities; and the financial work, including the preparation of budgets and forecasts.

DEFINITION OF BUDGETING

In most large companies, I am sure that budgeting is in the category of a household word. It is familiar to almost everyone but I suspect that it means different things to different people, depending upon their personal experiences and the point of view from which they make their observations. For example, some consider budgets to be a control tool to aid them in keeping track of their particular operation; some consider them to be devices strictly for the boss's use in holding people's feet to the fire; and still others look upon them as an annual game to be played with the accountants, to be forgotten once the numbers have been agreed upon.

From talking to others and reading the rather voluminous literature in the field, it is evident to me that there are at least three different ways in which people view budgets.

Two of them go back a number of years to the point in time when budgeting was thought of only in terms of expense control. One of these might be described as the appropriation type budget, which places a top limit on the amount of money that can be expended on a given activity or project—expenditures in excess of the ceiling amount require supplemental approval. Close relatives of this type of budget in General Electric are plant and equipment appropriations, product development or tooling authorizations, and advertising budgets.

The second type of expense control budget is the so-called flexible expense budget. Familiar versions of flexible budgets are the so-called "fixed-variable" budgets and "step" budgets used for many years in controlling manufacturing expenses. Both involve the establishment of varying expense allowances within the range of volume or activity levels at which the component expects to be operating during the budget period.

Subsequently a third viewpoint of budgeting came into being, encompassing elements of the first two but adding new dimensions. Under this viewpoint, a budget is defined as the expression, in financial and other appropriate terms, of an integrated plan of operation for a specified period of time, usually one year. It includes, therefore, not only expense budgets but such budgets as sales, production, material, labor, and plant and equipment. More importantly, the interaction of all the individual programs is reflected in a statement of profit or loss, a balance sheet, and a statement of the source and use of funds or cash flow for the business.

It is this broader concept that I have in mind in this paper.

PURPOSES OF BUDGETING

One of the comments frequently heard about budgeting is that it is not worth the time or effort, because a month or two after a lot of blood, sweat, and hours have been put into its preparation, it is useless, since actual conditions are so much at variance with those anticipated at the time the budget was prepared. A comment such as this indicates a need for a clearer understanding of the purpose of budgeting.

These purposes can be classified into four principal categories, not necessarily sequential:

1. The first of these is the part the budgeting process plays in integrating the activities of the various functions. It provides a means, for example, to assure that marketing is planning to sell the same products in the same quantities as manufacturing is planning to produce; that new designs coming out of engineering are properly integrated into marketing and manufacturing plans; that personnel requirements are capable of being met; and that investment requirements are not unreasonable.

2. A related purpose of the budgeting process is to provide a communications device through which all employees can see how their activities contribute to the intermediate goals of their functions and to the goals of the over-all business.

3. Another significant purpose of budgeting is to encourage consideration of profit planning. It necessitates establishing profit objectives, putting dollar signs on all the proposed activities of the business, and deciding on the allocation of resources which represents the best balance at a point in time.

4. The fourth major purpose of budgeting is to provide a means of measuring accomplishment against goals and how actual income and expense compare with planned amounts. In this respect, the budget is an instrument of self-control. To be most effective, it requires that variance between actual and budgeted performance be investigated to determine whether the original plan was sound and corrective action should be taken to get back to it, or whether the plan should be revised because of substantial changes in conditions.

With the foregoing purposes of budgeting in mind, we can now proceed to consideration of the basic principles underlying a sound budgeting program.

It is difficult to talk about principles of budgeting (or any other aspect of budgeting) without becoming involved quite quickly in a discussion of *business* planning. This follows, of course, from the definition of a budget as an integrated plan of operation.

In this context, there are three fundamental principles that must be followed in developing a sound budget:

1. The plan which the final budget is purported to represent should evolve from careful consideration and evaluation of alternative courses of action. The planning underlying any industrial budget is predicated on sets of assumptions—assumptions with respect to such factors as economic climate, competitive strategy, markets, changes in price and cost levels, probability of technical or manu-

facturing difficulties, introduction of new products, expenditure levels for new plant and equipment, major rearrangement programs, and product research and development activities. Obviously, plans based on one set of assumptions versus another set can yield radically different results and the planning process in part consists of weighing the various alternatives and arriving at an educated judgment as to what is most appropriate under the circumstances. Analyzing and pricing alternate plans in this orderly fashion and documenting the assumption in specific terms are of value in that:

a. The very process of weighing alternatives tends to result in a more thoughtful and realistic plan; and
b. If the analysis is done properly, alternative plans are available to be put into effect quickly in the event that conditions assumed under the primary plan do not materialize. In other words, the planning is done in advance in an atmosphere of reason, rather than on a crash basis in an atmosphere of crisis.

2. The selected plan for the business should be supported by documented plans in each of the functions. These sub-plans should spell out the contributions which the functions must make if the over-all business goals are to be achieved. In addition, they should identify the specific programs by which the functional goals are to be achieved, the assumptions made in establishing the program, the timetable of accomplishment, and the estimated cost. The documentation of assumptions underlying the business plan and the functional plans is particularly important. A written record of this kind of information will provide a basis for later determining whether variations from the plan are the result of unforeseeable changes, lack of essential business intelligence sources, a poorly conceived plan, or poor execution of the plan. This knowledge is essential if we are to improve our budgeting skills.

3. The budget should be geared to organizational philosophy and structure. If the budget is defined as the expression of an integrated plan of operation, it follows that the people who prepare the plans must also prepare the budget. To put it another way, if we want to practice our decentralization philosophy—which says we define the job, give a man responsibility and authority to do it, and hold him accountable for the results—the man to whom an activity has been assigned ought to be the one who prepares the budget for that activity. If he is to be held accountable for accomplishing specified results, he ought to have something to say about what he has to spend to get them. All the managerial or supervisory people, starting with the first level of the organization structure, should be participants in the budget program.

It is not my intent to imply that each manager should automatically be given a blank check to carry out all the programs he considers to be desirable. Until the millenium arrives, it will continue to be necessary to modify the budgets for individual activities in order to achieve a desired goal for the over-all business.

GENERAL ELECTRIC'S BUDGET PROGRAM

General Electric's budgeting program is initiated by having each department prepare in September, in October, and again in November, "order of magnitude" estimates of the following year's operating results, based on a series of alternative plans—selected by the departments—which are considered to be reasonable possibilities for the budget year. To aid in understanding the various alternates, the departments are asked to spell out the assumptions underlying each of the alternative estimates of operating results. In addition, they are requested to indicate a tentative selection of the single set of conditions considered most likely to occur and thus to represent the operating goals around which the budget might be developed.

In presenting these data, the departments indicate the estimated dollar size of the markets in which they will participate, their anticipated share, orders and unfilled order position at the end of the year, sales, profitability and cash flow, capacity data and plant investment expenditures, and number of employees.

In addition to encouraging the departments to weigh alternatives and thus follow an orderly process of thought and planning in developing their budgets, there are other reasons for our adoption of this three-step preliminary estimate procedure. One is that it is a way for the departments to give the Executive Officers a "feel" of the thinking supporting the broad planning. But more importantly, perhaps, it provides a mechanism through which the Executive Officers can reach agreement with the departments as to whether tentatively selected volume and profit levels are within acceptable order of magnitude limits. One of the difficulties encountered in past years was that the departments froze on sales and profit objectives early in the fall and proceeded to finalize detailed budgets throughout the organization, only to find out in the latter part of December, when the final budgets were submitted, that sales or profit or both were not acceptable. Our present procedure provides a way for circumventing this difficulity.

Effectively, then, as a result of this procedure there is evolved a tentative broad plan for the department on which agreement has been reached as to the order of magnitude of sales and production volume, market position, profitability, and investment. The next step involves completing the specific functional programs, detailed as to accomplishments, timing, and cost, designed to achieve the goals. In formulating these subsidiary programs and budgets, it is important that all levels of supervision participate. I have been led by my operating associates to believe that, in general, their departments do practice the principle of participation and that budget preparation is a co-operative affair, even though the blood may flow freely in the give and take process which yields the final department budget.

FORM OF FINAL BUDGET

The final budget is submitted through channels during the latter part of December. One of the activities of my group is to develop the form and content of the exhibits which the departments use in presenting their plans for review by the Executive Officers.

In developing the budget exhibits, we keep striving to minimize the amount of detail and to concentrate on the broad aspects of the plan. As a matter of information, our 1959 program called for the submission of six exhibits:

1. A Summary of Operations presented on a responsibility reporting basis, together with summary data on orders received, cash flow, average number of employees, and utilization of capacity;

2. An analysis of variance in profits between the current and budget year, identifying the changes attributable to selling prices, sales volume, product mix, material prices, salaries and wage rates, and so on;

3. A statement of profitability, market position, and product leadership by product line or classification;

4. The budget of plant investment expenditures showing details of those requiring approval by the Board of Directors or Executive Officers and classifying the total budgeted expenditures by amounts to be spent for profit improvement projects, expansion of capacity on current products, additional capacity for new products, laboratory facilities, and so on;

5. A cash flow budget, showing changes in major balance sheet classifications, expenditures for plant and equipment, depreciation, and income for the period—in other words, the principal items accounting for the generation or use of funds;

6. A new exhibit which called for the departments to recommend the continuing profitability standards which they considered appropriate for the kinds of businesses they are in, the bases supporting the selection of the standards, and the strategy and timetable for achieving the standards if they still lay in the future.

The exhibits change from year to year because we are continually seeking to develop new techniques of presenting the budget which will stimulate the thinking both of the individuals who prepare them and the people who appraise them.

The value of budgets—or of any business measurements, for that matter—is directly related to the degree to which managers utilize them to pinpoint areas of weakness and then devise and execute programs to overcome those weaknesses. Thus, for a budget program to be effective, there must be a reporting system which incorporates a comparison of actual performance with budgeted performance.

Just as the preparation of the budget should be consistent with organizational philosophy and structure, so should the reporting practices. If the preparation of the budget is decentralized, so that the individuals responsible for given activities from the first level up participate in its formulation, it follows logically that the reporting system should be designed to feed back performance data and comparisons with budget on the same basis. This is the concept of *responsibility reporting*. Stated briefly, the premise underlying this concept is that costs should be accumulated and reported in accordance with the delegation of responsibility and accountability. Costs by *element* are reported only to the first level of supervision and succeeding higher levels of management receive only the *total* costs incurred by the preceding component. Thus, the attention of managers above the first level is directed to appraisal of the over-all job rather than to analysis of details.

This does not mean, of course, that additional information, in whatever detail is required, will not be available. In the event that a manager wishes to obtain more data on a particular area because he feels it needs his personal attention, the information can be supplied. But it is apparent that if we are to realize the benefits of the responsibility reporting concept, such actions must be on an *exception basis*, rather than a matter of routine.

Needless to say, for the responsibility reporting system to be truly effective, the responsibility for all cost items must be specifically assigned. The existence of pooled costs for which accountability is left in mid-air tends to defeat the purpose of the system. By the same token it is imperative that the managers at each level appraise regularly the over-all performance of reporting components in terms of the *value of accomplishment* versus total cost. I think that sometimes we fall into the trap of assuming that simply because a functional component stays within its expense budget, it is doing a fine job. I would be the last to decry the desirability of staying within expense budgets, but it is even more important that we get value received for the cost we incur. I sometimes feel that we put the cart before the horse in our approach to appraising a project or activity. By this I mean we tend to concentrate on the cost before we have satisfied ourselves as to the value of doing the job in the first place.

It is my hope that by adopting responsibility reporting and minimizing the amount of detail that he must digest, the manager will be able to spend much more time in first appraising the value of specific programs and then in determining whether he received the value he paid for. Instead of a manager's spending his personal time analyzing the details of activities for which he has delegated responsibility, he should look to the man to whom the responsibility has been assigned, to communicate to him where he stands and the facts regarding deviations from planned performance.

Properly used, the responsibility reporting system will enhance the decentralization philosophy. It will develop better managers, place stress on the value and achievement of goals as well as on control of costs, and produce improved profitability.

I shall not dwell on the mechanics of the reporting system because the number, kind, and frequency will vary from department to department, depending on the type of business and the individual desires and needs of the people who will use the reports. As a minimum, there will be monthly reports reflecting actual versus budgeted results in terms of the statement of profit or loss, balance sheet, and statement of cash flow, as well as subsidiary reports on such items as sales, production, functional and sub-functional expenses, and inventory and receivables turnover.

PROBLEMS IN BUDGETING

While there are a number of items that fall into this category, the ones which deserve special mention can be phrased in terms of the following question:

1. Should a department have two budgets—an "optimistic" one for local use and a "conservative" one for use by highel level management?
2. Is a budget a guarantee of performance?
3. Should the budget be revised during the year?

While these questions are based upon our own experience and thus are oriented to a highly decentralized organization, I believe that parallel situations exist wherever there is a budget and more than one person is involved.

CONSERVATISM VERSUS OPTIMISM

The first question—"should a department have two budgets?"—is exemplified by the practice in some businesses of preparing a conservative or "safe" budget for submission to the Executive Office and a second, tougher budget for use within the department itself.

The surface justification for submitting a lower budget to the Executive Office is that it provides a sounder basis for general company planning, particularly with respect to the availability of cash. The reasoning is that, if everyone submits an optimistic budget, it is likely that many departments will miss their budgets and, as a result, the Company will always be falling short of its budgeted goals. I need not point out that there are probably *other* reasons for the suggestion that conservative or safe budgets should be submitted to the Executive Office. The truth of the matter is that the manager who misses a budget by having better results than were budgeted is frowned upon less than he who misses it in the other direction—that of having poorer results than budgeted.

I have heard it said that there are two theories of budgeting—conservative budgeting which is likely to produce easily achieved goals, and "reach" budgeting which incorporates difficult goals unlikely of attainment. I think that the classification of budgets into conservative and "reach" or optimistic is an oversimplification. To be sure, these represent the two extremes and there will probably always be some practitioners of the two philosophies. But there are many others who approach a budget not from the point of view of its being a sure thing or strictly an incentive gimmick, but rather from the point of view that it should express management's best judgment as to what is *most likely to occur* during the budget period, barring unforeseen circumstances or events beyond their control. What is most likely to occur is quite different from what you would *like* to see happen—the hope approach—or what you are *sure* can happen—the safe approach.

Let me hasten to add that in advocating the "most likely to occur" approach, I do not intend to imply that the budget should have no provision for reach—we do not wish to encourage planning for inefficiency. But the determination of the proper element of reach requires a rigorous appraisal of what kind of job has been done in the past in achieving "reach" objectives and a thorough evaluation of the specific programs underlying predicted improvements in performance. I do not deny the difficulty of achieving this particular state of Utopia, but we have to face up to the problem.

BUDGET—GUARANTEE OF PERFORMANCE

A question which is closely related to conservative versus optimistic budgeting concerns the way in which the budget should be viewed in measuring performance. Should it be considered as a guarantee of performance? Does meeting or exceeding the budget automatically indicate that a good job has been done and does missing it indicate poor performance?

I think we have to recognize that despite our best efforts to do an accurate planning and budgeting job, there will always be changes in conditions beyond the control of a department which will result in failure to attain budgeted volume and profitability goals. The bottom falls out of the economy, there are strikes at a major supplier's or major customer's plant, there is a long siege of unseasonably cold weather—any of these kinds of things may occur and have a substantial impact on operating results. Under these circumstances, it seems manifestly unfair to hold a manager accountable for his original budgeted results. But let us suppose that the changes in condition were favorable to the business—maybe there was a major technological breakthrough, or there was a sudden change for the better in the economy beyond what could reasonably be expected, or there was an exceptional demand for a product which heretofore had been slow in gaining customer acceptance. Under these conditions, in what way should the original budgeted results be used in appraising performance?

Perhaps what this suggests is that from the standpoint of using the budget to appraise performance, the fact that actual results are better, equal to, or worse than the budget is not conclusive evidence of the quality of the managerial job. To get at this, it is necessary to analyze the factors underlying the end results. Were there substantial changes in environment, both favorable and unfavorable, which had an important effect on actual results? Were they controllable or uncontrollable? How effective was the action taken in moving up on the controllable items? How were reductions in costs and expenses achieved—by sound management of expenses or by elimination of essential forward-looking programs? Appraisal of performance against budget requires good judgment.

If we prefer not to get involved in this kind of analysis—which admittedly is difficult and time consuming—and elect instead to look upon the results reflected in the budget as an absolute commitment, it is likely that the question of conservative versus optimistic budgets will be quickly resolved. It would be reasonable to expect that ultra conservatism would become the order of the day and that the budget might become such a sacred cow that it would force managers into making wrong decisions in order not to violate it. To state it simply, the danger in going too far down the "conservative" road or the "guarantee of performance" road is the destruction of the budget as a useful managing tool.

SHOULD THE BUDGET BE REVISED?

The third aspect of budgeting practice which is subject to debate concerns the question as to whether the budget should be revised when it becomes evident that the sales budget on which the expense and income levels were predicated cannot be achieved.

I would suggest that the opinions expressed on this question are likely to differ depending upon the screen through which it is viewed. For example, if you are an operating Department General Manager and your level of operations is substantially below that contemplated by the budget, you are quite likely to say that the fixed budget is useless from the standpoint of investment and expense control and besides you are weary of having to explain every month on your operations report to the Executive Office that you are missing your profit budget because volume is off. What you would prefer to have the boss understand is that your variable expenses are under control and that your profitability represents good performance for the volume level at which you are operating. To accomplish this, you would be greatly in favor of revising your budget and having your performance compared with the new budget.

But let us look at the problem as the President of the Company might look at it. Based on what the individual departments say they can achieve, he presents a budget to the Board of Directors, specifying that, as a Company, we propose to achieve certain specific goals. When the year gets under way and it turns out that the departments are failing to meet their sales and earnings goals, he is not as interested in explanations as to how tough things are as he is in inspiring the operating managers to come as close to their original profitability budgets as they possibly can, without curtailing essential long range activities. Thus his purpose is better served by retaining the original budget and using it to remind managers that they should not be complacent about the performance of their departments.

Of course, if these conditions were reversed—that is, if a department were operating at a higher level than the budget contemplated, the views of the General Manager and President would likely be reversed also. The General Manager would not be particularly anxious to have the budgeted goals increased while the Company President would probably be pointing out that with the additional sales, profits should be substantially higher and maybe the budget ought to be revised upward.

What this adds up to is that each of the two practices—adhering to a fixed budget or changing during the budget period—has advantages and disadvantages. As a practical matter, we use both in General Electric Company. On total Company financial statements and in reports of Company operations to the Board of Directors, performance comparisons are made with the original budget which is not changed during the year. Within many of the departments, however, when the volume bases contemplated by the fixed budget become unrealistic for purposes of expense control, there is brought into play a form of variable or step budget applicable to the volume range being experienced.

In order to keep members of the Executive Office informed of the departments' latest thinking as to how future operations will vary from the fixed budget, we use a procedure under which each month the departments submit an estimate of operating results for the next month and the remainder of the calendar year. In preparing these estimates, the departments take account of factors that were not foreseen in their original planning, recognize changes in timing that may have occurred since the original budget was prepared, and adjust for changes in the economic climate.

As part of this "forward look" procedure, the departments prepare a *Review and Estimate of Operations* each month, a portion of which is devoted to an analysis explaining variance between actual or forecast income and budgeted income. This provides an opportunity for the departments to explain the effect on profitability of volume changes, selling price changes, changes in material and labor levels, and any other significant factors affecting their operations.

In summary, it is our conviction that in industry, budgeting is a highly useful device serving varied managerial needs. At the same time, we should understand that the quality of a budget and its degree of usefulness are highly dependent upon the quality of planning and the skill with which the budget is administered.

Case 3–1

General Motors Corporation*

In an article in the *NACA Bulletin*, January 1, 1927, Albert Bradley described the pricing policy of General Motors Corporation. At that time, Mr. Bradley was general assistant treasurer; subsequently, he became vice-president, executive vice-president, and chairman of the board. There is reason to believe that current policy is substantially the same as that described in the 1927 statement. The following description consists principally of excerpts from Mr. Bradley's article.

GENERAL POLICY

Return on investment is the basis of the General Motors policy in regard to the pricing of product. The fundamental consideration is the average return over a protracted period of time, not the specific rate of return over any particular year or short period of time. This long-term rate of return on investment represents the official viewpoint as to the highest average rate of return that can be expected consistent with a healthy growth of the business, and may be referred to as the economic return attainable. The adjudged necessary rate of return on capital will vary as between separate lines of industry as a result of differences in their economic situations; and within each industry there will be important differences in return on capital resulting primarily from the relatively greater efficiency of certain producers.

The fundamental policy in regard to pricing product and expansion of the business also necessitates an official viewpoint as to the normal average rate of plant operation. This relationship between assumed normal average rate of operation and practical annual capacity is known as standard volume.

The fundamental price policy is completely expressed in the conception of standard volume and economic return attainable. For example, if it is the accepted policy that standard volume represents 80 percent of practical an-

* This case was prepared from published material.

nual capacity, and that an average of 20 percent per annum must be earned on the operating capital, it becomes possible to determine the standard price of a product—that is, that price which with plants operating at 80 percent of capacity will produce an annual return of 20 percent on the investment.

STANDARD VOLUME

Costs of production and distribution per unit of product vary with fluctuation in volume because of the fixed or nonvariable nature of some of the expense items. Productive materials and productive labor may be considered costs which are 100 percent variable, since within reasonable limits the aggregate varies directly with volume, and the cost per unit of product therefore remains uniform.

Among the items classified as manufacturing expense or burden there exist varying degrees of fluctuation with volume, owing to their greater or lesser degree of variability. Among the absolutely fixed items are such expenses as depreciation and taxes, which may be referred to as 100 percent fixed, since within the limits of plant capacity the aggregate will not change, but the amount per unit of product will vary in inverse ratio to the output.

Another group of items may be classified as 100 percent variable, such as inspection and material handling; the amount per unit of product is unaffected by volume. Between the classes of 100 percent fixed and 100 percent variable is a large group of expense items that are partially variable, such as light, heat, power, and salaries.

In General Motors Corporation, standard burden rates are developed for each burden center, so that there will be included in costs a reasonable average allowance for manufacturing expense. In order to establish this rate, it is first necessary to obtain an expression of the estimated normal average rate of plant operation.

Rate of plant operation is affected by such factors as general business conditions, extent of seasonal fluctuation is sales likely within years of large volume, policy with respect to seasonal accumulation of finished and/or semifinished product for the purpose of leveling the production curve, necessity or desirability of maintaining excess plant capacity for emergency use, and many others. Each of these factors should be carefully considered by a manufacturer in the determination of size of a new plant to be constructed, and before making additions to existing plants, in order that there may be a logical relationship between assumed normal average rate of plant operation and practical annual capacity. The percentage accepted by General Motors Corporation as its policy in regard to the relationship between assumed normal rate of plant operation and practical annual capacity is referred to as standard volume.

Having determined the degree of variability of manufacturing expense, the established total expense at the standard volume rate of operations can be estimated. A *standard burden rate* is then developed which represents the proper absorption of burden in costs at standard volume. In periods of low volume, the unabsorbed manufacturing expense is charged directly against profits as unabsorbed burden, while in periods of high volume, the overabsorbed manufacturing expense is credited to profits, as overabsorbed burden.

RETURN ON INVESTMENT

Factory costs and commercial expenses for the most part represent outlays by the manufacturer during the accounting period. An exception is depreciation of capital assets which have a greater length of life than the accounting period. To allow for this element of cost, there is included an allowance for depreciation in the burden rates used in compiling costs. Before an enterprise can be considered successful and worthy of continuation or expansion, however, still another element of cost must be reckoned with. This is the cost of capital, including an allowance for profit.

Thus, the calculation of standard prices of products necessitates the establishment of standards of capital requirement as well as expense factors, representative of the normal average operating condition. The standard for capital employed in fixed assets is expressed as a percentage of factory cost, and the standards for working capital are expressed in part as a percentage of sales, and in part as a percentage of factory cost.

The calculation of the standard allowance for fixed investment is illustrated by the following example.

Investment in plant and other fixed assets	$15,000,000
Practical annual capacity	50,000 units
Standard volume, per cent of practical annual capacity	80 %
Standard volume equivalent (50,000 × 80%)	40,000 units
Factory cost per unit at standard volume	$1,000
Annual factory cost of production at standard volume (40,000 × $1,000)	$40,000,000
Standard factor for fixed investment (ratio of investment to annual factory cost of production; $15,000,000 ÷ $40,000,000)	0.375

The amount tied up in working capital items should be directly proportional to the volume of business. For example, raw materials on hand should be in direct proportion to the manufacturing requirements—so many days' supply of this material, so many days' supply of that material, and so on—depending on the condition and location of sources of supply, transportation conditions, etc. Work in process should be in direct proportion to the requirements of finished production, since it is dependent on the length of time required for the material to pass from the raw to the finished state, and the amount of labor and other charges to be absorbed in the process. Finished product should be in direct proportion to sales requirements. Accounts receivable should be in direct proportion to sales, being dependent on terms of payment and efficiency of collections.

THE STANDARD PRICE

These elements are combined to construct the standard price as shown in Exhibit 1. Note that the economic return attainable (20 percent in the illustration) and the standard volume (80 percent in the illustration) are long-run figures and are rarely changed;[1] the other elements of the price are based on current estimates.

Exhibit 1

ILLUSTRATION OF METHOD OF DETERMINATION OF STANDARD PRICE

	In Relation to	*Turnover Per Year*	*Ratio to Sales Annual Basis*	*Ratio to Factory Cost Annual Basis*
Cash	Sales	20 times	0.050	—
Drafts and accounts receivable	Sales	10 times	0.100	—
Raw material and work in process	Factory cost	6 times	—	0.16⅔
Finished product	Factory cost	12 times	—	0.08⅓
Gross working capital			0.150	0.250
Fixed investment			—	0.375
Total investment			0.150	0.625
Economic return attainable, 20%			—	—
Multiplying the investment ratio by this, the necessary net profit margin is arrived at			0.030	0.125
Standard allowance for commercial expenses, 7%			0.070	—
Gross margin over factory cost			0.100	0.125
			a	*b*

$$\text{Selling price, as a ratio to factory cost} = \frac{1 + b}{1 - a} = \frac{1 + 0.125}{1 - 0.100} = 1.250$$

If standard cost = \$1,000
Then standard price = \$1,000 × 1.250 = \$1,250

---

[1] A Brookings Institution Survey reported that the principal pricing goal of General Motors Corporation in the 1950's was 20 percent on investment after taxes. See Lanzillotti, "Pricing Objectives in Large Companies," *American Economic Review*, December, 1958.

DIFFERENCES AMONG PRODUCTS

Responsibility for investment must be considered in calculating the standard price of each product as well as in calculating the overall price for all products, since products with identical accounting costs may be responsible for investments that vary greatly. In the illustration given below, a uniform standard selling price of $1,250 was determined. Let us now suppose that this organization makes and sells two products, A and B, with equal manufacturing costs of $1,000 per unit and equal working capital requirements, and that 20,000 units of each product are produced. However, an analysis of fixed investment indicates that $10 million is applicable to product A, while only $5 million of fixed investment is applicable to product B. Each product must earn 20 percent on its investment in order to satisfy the standard condition. Exhibit 2 illustrates the determination of the standard price for product A and product B.

From this analysis of investment, it becomes apparent that product A, which has the heavier fixed investment, should sell for $1,278, while product B should sell for only $1,222, in order to produce a return of 20 percent on the investment. Were both products sold for the composite average standard price of $1,250, then product A would not be bearing its share of the investment burden, while product B would be correspondingly overpriced.

Differences in working capital requirements as between different products may also be important due to differences in manufacturing methods, sales terms, merchandising policies, etc. The inventory turnover rate of one line of products sold by a division of General Motors Corporation may be six times a year, while inventory applicable to another line of products is turned over thirty times a year. In the second case, the inventory investment required per dollar cost of sales is only one-fifth of that required in the case of the product with the slower turnover. Just as there are differences in capital requirements as between different classes of product, so may the standard requirements for the same class of product require modification from time to time due to permanent changes in manufacturing processes, in location of sources of supply, more efficient scheduling and handling of materials, etc.

The importance of this improvement to the buyer of General Motors products may be appreciated from the following example. The total inventory investment for the 12 months ended September 30, 1926, would have averaged $182,490,000 if the turnover rate of 1923 (the best performance prior to 1925) had not been bettered, or an excess of $74,367,000 over the actual average investment. In other words, General Motors would have been compelled to charge $14,873,000 more for its products during this 12-month period than was actually charged if prices had been established to yield, say, 20 percent on the operating capital required.

Exhibit 2

VARIANCES IN STANDARD PRICE DUE TO VARIANCES IN RATE OF CAPITAL TURNOVER

	Product A		Product B		Total Product (A plus B)	
	Ratio to Sales Annual Basis	*Ratio to Factory Cost Annual Basis*	*Ratio to Sales Annual Basis*	*Ratio to Factory Cost Annual Basis*	*Ratio to Sales Annual Basis*	*Ratio to Factory Cost Annual Basis*
Gross working capital	0.150	0.250	0.150	0.250	0.150	0.250
Fixed investment	—	0.500	—	0.250	—	0.375
Total investment	0.150	0.750	0.150	0.500	0.150	0.625
Economic return attainable, 20%	—	—	—	—	—	—
Multiplying the investment ratio by this, the necessary net profit margin is arrived at	0.030	0.150	0.030	0.100	0.030	0.125
Standard allowance for commercial expenses, 7%	0.070	—	0.070	—	0.070	—
Gross margin over factory cost	0.100	0.150	0.100	0.100	0.100	0.125
	a	*b*	*a*	*b*	*a*	*b*
Selling price, as a ratio to Factory cost $= \frac{1+b}{1-a}$	$\frac{1.+0.150}{1.-0.100}$	$= 1.278$	$\frac{1.+0.100}{1.-0.100}$	$= 1.222$	$\frac{1.+0.125}{1.-0.100}$	$= 1.250$
If standard cost equals		$1,000		$1,000		$1,000
Then standard price equals		$1,278		$1,222		$1,250

CONCLUSION

The analysis as to the degree of variability of manufacturing and commercial expenses with increases or decreases in volume of output, and the establishment of "standards" for the various investment items, makes it possible not only to develop "Standard Prices," but also to forecast, with much greater accuracy than otherwise would be possible, the capital requirements, profits, and return on capital at the different rates of operation, which may result from seasonal conditions or from changes in the general business situation. Moreover, whenever it is necessary to calculate in advance the final effect on net profits of proposed increases or decreases in price, with their resulting changes in volume of output, consideration of the real economics of the situation is facilitated by the availability of reliable basic data.

It should be emphasized that the basic pricing policy stated in terms of the economic return attainable is a policy, and it does not absolutely dictate the specific price. At times, the actual price may be above, and at other times below, the standard price. The standard price calculation affords a means not only of interpreting actual or proposed prices in relation to the established policy, but at the same time affords a practical demonstration as to whether the policy itself is sound. If the prevailing price of product is found to be at variance with the standard price other than to the extent due to temporary causes, it follows that prices should be adjusted; or else, in the event of conditions being such that prices cannot be brought into line with the standard price, the conclusion is necessarily drawn that the terms of the expressed policy must be modified.[2]

QUESTIONS

1. An article in the *Wall Street Journal*, December 10, 1957, gave estimates of cost figures in "an imaginary car-making division in the Ford-Chevrolet-Plymouth field." Most of the data given below are derived from that article. Using these data, compute the standard price. Working capital ratios are not given; assume that they are the same as those in Exhibit 1.

Investment in plant and other fixed assets	$600,000,000
Required return on investment	30% before income taxes
Practical annual capacity	1,250,000
Standard volume—assume	80%

[2] This paragraph is taken from an article by Donaldson Brown, then vice-president, finance, General Motors Corporation, in *Management and Administration*, March, 1924.

Factory cost per unit:	
Outside purchases of parts	$ 500*
Parts manufactured inside	600*
Assembly labor	75
Burden	125
Total	$1,300

* Each of these items includes $50 of labor costs.

"Commercial cost," corresponding to the 7 percent in Exhibit 1, is added as a dollar amount, and includes the following:

Inbound and outbound freight	$ 85
Tooling and engineering	50
Sales and advertising	50
Administrative and miscellaneous	50
Warranty (repairs within guarantee)	15
Total	$ 250

Therefore, the 7 percent commercial allowance in Exhibit 1 should be eliminated, and in its place $250 should be added to the price as computed from the formula.

2. What would happen to profits and return on investment before taxes in a year in which volume was only 60 percent of capacity? What would happen in a year in which volume was 100 percent of capacity? Assume that nonvariable costs included in the $1,550 unit cost above are $350 million; i.e., variable costs are $1,550 − $350 = $1,200. In both situations, assume that cars were sold at the standard price established in Question 1, since the standard price is not changed to reflect annual changes in volume.

3. Is this policy good for General Motors? Is it good for America?

Case 3-2

General Electric Company

The General Electric Company is a large, multilocation corporation engaged in the manufacture and marketing of a wide variety of electrical and allied products. In 1964, there were almost 400 separate product lines and over three million catalog items. Sales volume in that year totaled $4,941 million, and net income was $237 million. Total employment was about 262,000.

Early in the 1950's, General Electric initiated an extensive decentralization of authority and responsibility for the operations of the company. The basic unit of organization became the product department. As of 1964, there were over 100 of these departments.

The company recognized that if this decentralization was to be fully effective it would need an improved system of management control. It also recognized that any improved system of control would require better measures of performance. To meet this need, the company established a measurements project and created a special organizational unit to carry out this project. This case summarizes the main features of this project, with particular emphasis on measuring performance of the operating (i.e., product) departments.

THE MEASUREMENTS PROJECT

The measurements project was established in 1952. Responsibility for the project was assigned to accounting services, one of the corporate func-

---

NOTE: With the exception of the statistical information and publicly known facts presented in the introduction of this case, the sources for the facts making up the body of this case are William T. Jerome, III, *Executive Control—The Catalyst* (New York: John Wiley & Sons, Inc., 1961), pp. 217–37; and Robert W. Lewis, "Measuring, Reporting and Appraising Results of Operations with Reference to Goals, Plans and Budgets," *Planning, Managing and Measuring the Business,* A Case Study of Management Planning and Control at General Electric Company (New York: Controllership Foundation, Inc., 1955).

tional services divisions. A permanent organizational unit, initially called measurements service, was set up to carry out this project.

An early step in the measurements project was the development of a set of principles by which the project was to be governed. Five such principles were formulated:

1. Measurements were to be designed to measure the performance of *organizational components*, rather than of *managers*.
2. Measurements were to involve common *indexes* of performance, but not common *standards* of performance. (For example, rate of return on investment might be the index of performance common to all product departments, but the standard in terms of this index might be 12 percent for one department and 25 percent for another.)
3. Measurements were to be designed as aids to judgment in appraisal of performance, and not to supplant judgment.
4. Measurements were to give proper weight to future performance as well as current performance, in order to facilitate the maintenance of a balance between the long run and the near term.
5. Measurements were to be selected so as to facilitate constructive action, not to restrict such action.

The overall measurements project was divided into three major subprojects:

1. Operational measurements of the results of a product department.
2. Functional measurements of the work of engineering, manufacturing, marketing finance, employee and plant community relations, and legal components of the organization.
3. Measurements of the work of managing as such—planning, organizing, integrating, and measuring itself.

The first step in the subproject on operational measurements was to develop an answer to the following question:

> What are the specific areas for which measurements should be designed, bearing in mind that sound measurements of overall performance require a proper balance among the various functions and among the aspects (planning, organizing, for example) of managing?[1]

In seeking an answer to this question, the organization made a careful analysis of the nature and purposes of the basic kinds of work performed by each functional unit with the purpose of singling out those functional objectives that were of sufficient importance to the welfare of the business[2] as a whole, to be termed "key result areas."

---

[1] Lewis, *op. cit.*, p 30.

[2] The word "business" is used here to refer to a product department, not to the whole company.

THE KEY RESULT AREAS

In order to determine whether an area tentatively identified according to the preceding analytical framework was sufficiently basic to qualify as a key result area, the organization established a criterion in the form of the following test question:

> Will continued failure in this area prevent the attainment of management's responsibility for advancing General Electric as a leader in a strong, competitive economy, even though results in all other key areas are good?[3]

As an outcome of analysis and application of this test, eight key result areas were decided on. These were as follows:

1. Profitability.
2. Market position.
3. Productivity.
4. Product leadership.
5. Personnel development.
6. Employee attitudes.
7. Public responsibility.
8. Balance between short-range and long-range goals.

Each of these key result areas is described below.

Profitability

The key index used by General Electric to measure profitability was "dollars of residual income." Residual income was defined as net profit after taxes, less a capital charge. The capital charge was a certain percentage (say, 6 percent) of the net assets assigned to the department; it corresponded to an imputed interest charge. The criteria formulated to guide the development of a satisfactory measure of profitability were expressed as follows:

1. An index that recognized the contribution of capital investment to profits.
2. An index that recognized what human work and effort contribute to profits.
3. An index that recognized the "corporate facts of life" (e.g., one consistent with General Electric's needs and organizational objectives).
4. An index that served to make the operating decisions of individual managers in the company's best interests.

In the process of selecting and developing a measure of profitability, the measurements organization considered several more conventional indices, including rate of return on investment, ratio of profit to sales, and ratio of profit to value added. A weakness of these ratios or indices was stated in this way:

---

[3] *Ibid.*, p. 30.

. . . the acid test of an index should be its effectiveness in guiding decentralized management to make decisions in the best interests of the company overall, since operating managers' efforts naturally will be to improve the performance of their businesses in terms of the index used for evaluation. This test points up the particular weakness of rate of return and of other ratio indexes, such as per cent profit to sales. This weakness is the tendency to encourage concentration on improvement of the *ratios* rather than on improvement in *dollar* profits. Specifically, the business with the better results in terms of the ratios will tend to make decisions based on the effect the decisions will have on the particular business's current *ratio* without consideration of the *dollar* profits involved. This tends to retard incentive to growth and expansion because it dampens the incentive of the more profitable businesses to grow.[4]

Market Position

Performance in this key result area was measured in terms of the share of the market obtained during a given measurement period. The measurement was expressed as a percentage of available business in the market. Market, as used in this sense, was expressed in dollars or units, kilowatt-ampere, or other meaningful terms.

The first major consideration in designing market position measurements is a determination of what constitutes a product line and what constitutes the market for each product line of a business. A product line may be defined as a grouping of products in accordance with the purposes they serve or the essential wants they satisfy. The definition is somewhat misleading in that a product line may be a broad classification, such as clocks, or it may be a narrow classification, such as alarm clocks, kitchen clocks, or mantel clocks. In addition, product lines may overlap so that a particular product could be included in several product lines. Hence, the actual grouping of products by product lines must be accurately identified.

There may be wide variations in the interpretation of what constitutes the market for a given product line. Therefore, it is important that for each of their lines, our product departments identify such things as:

1. Whether the market includes not only directly competing products but also indirectly competing products (electric ranges versus electric ranges; electric ranges versus all types of ranges—electric, gas, oil, and others).
2. Whether the market includes sales by all domestic competitors or only those reporting to trade associations.
3. Whether the market includes imports, if foreign sellers are competing in the domestic market.
4. Whether the market includes export sales.
5. Whether the market includes captive sales.
6. Whether the market is considered to be represented by sales to distributors, or to retailers, or to ultimate users.

---

[4] *Ibid.,* p. 32.

In other words, in establishing measurements of market position there should be a clear understanding of precisely what comprises the product line and what comprises the market. The purpose of having sharp definitions of these two items is, of course, to avoid being misled into thinking we are doing better than we actually are simply because of failure to identify the nature and extent of our competition.[5]

Productivity

Although the concept of productivity is a relatively simple one—a relationship of output of goods and services to the resources consumed in their production—this concept proved a difficult one to make operational as a measure of performance. For the national economy as a whole, it has been the practice to look at productivity simply in terms of the amount of output per unit of labor input. In any given firm, however, labor is only one of the factors contributing to output. Therefore, the company sought to develop an index that would accomplish two things: (1) broaden the input base so as to recognize that capital as well as labor contributed to improvements in productivity, and (2) eliminate from the measure those improvements contributed by suppliers of materials.

On the output side of the productivity ratio, the company considered several refinements of sales billed. One such refinement was the use of value added (e.g., sales billed less the cost of goods or services acquired outside the company). On the input side, the company considered payroll dollars plus depreciation dollars. Payroll dollars were employed as the variable, rather than labor hours, so as to give effect to differences in the labor skills employed. The inclusion of depreciation charges constituted an attempt to include the consumption of capital resources. All factors were to be readjusted for changes in the price level, so that changes in the resulting ratio would more nearly reflect real changes in productivity.

Product Leadership

Product leadership was defined as "the ability of a business to lead its industry in originating or applying the most advanced scientific and technical knowledge in the engineering, manufacturing and marketing fields to the development of new products and to improvements in the quality or value of existing products."[6] To make this definition operational, procedures were established for appraising periodically the products of each department. These appraisals were directed at providing answers to the following questions:

1. How did each product compare with competition and with company standards?
2. Where within the company was the research conducted upon which the product was based?

---

[5] *Ibid.*, p. 33.
[6] *Ibid.*, pp. 35–36.

3. Who first introduced the basic product and subsequent improvements, General Electric or a competitor?

The appraisal procedures were based largely on qualitative rather than quantitative considerations. Appraisals were made by appropriate experts from the areas of engineering, marketing, accounting, and manufacturing. In general, these experts were located within the product department for which the appraisal was to be made. Standard forms were employed so as to facilitate as high a degree of consistency as possible. The trends revealed by these appraisals over a period of time were considered to be as significant as the specific information revealed by an appraisal for a particular period.

Personnel Development

For the purposes of measurement, personnel development was defined as "the systematic training of managers and specialists to fill present and future needs of the company, to provide for further individual growth and retirements and to facilitate corporate growth and expansion."[7] Management of General Electric defined personnel development as including "programs in each field of functional endeavor, such as engineering, manufacturing, marketing and finance, and broad programs aimed at developing an understanding of the principles of managing. Such programs must be designed to provide a continuous flow of potentially promotable employees in sufficient numbers to permit proper selection and development of individuals for each position. And, at the same time, these programs must encourage competition and initiative for further individual growth."[8]

Three steps were involved in the measurement of performance in this key result area. (1) The basic soundness of the various programs or techniques being sponsored by a product department for the development of its employees was appraised. (2) An inventory was taken of the available supply of trained men, as well as their qualifications, for the key positions that must eventually be filled within the department. (3) The effectiveness with which the department executed its personnel development programs was evaluated.

The first step consisted of judgments regarding the adequacy of the following elements in the development process.

Recruitment. How good a job was being done in the selection of candidates for the development process?

On-the-job training. What programs were available for training candidates, for providing information and knowledge about both general company matters and job particulars, and for advanced training for those who had been on the job for a while?

Review and counsel. Was there any provision for periodically reviewing the

---

[7] *Ibid.*, p. 37.
[8] *Ibid.*

performance of the men, for discussing with an individual the caliber of his work, for providing help and consultation, and for identifying especially promising talent?

Placement. What was being done to see that recruits were placed in jobs commensurate with their interests and abilities, that the more promising were rotated, and that promotions came to those who merited them?

The second step was accomplished with the aid of manning tables and related inventorying procedures. These procedures were directed primarily at determining the training background of each man in the inventory; i.e., graduates of company-sponsored programs, those hired from outside the company, and those who attained their positions without the benefit of a company-sponsored program.

The investigating group used two statistical measures in carrying out the third step. The first of these was the ratio of the number of men promoted (both within department and through transfer to another department) in a given period (usually a year) to the total number of men regarded as "promotable" during the same period. The second measure was tied in with the personnel rating procedure employed throughout the company. At the conclusion of each performance review cycle, the rating forms for a particular department were analyzed to determine the proportions of employees whose performance was considered to be (*a*) improving, (*b*) unchanged, and (*c*) deteriorating.

Employee Attitudes

For purposes of developing measurements of performance in this key area, the group defined an attitude as "a generalized point of view towards objects, events or persons which might serve to influence future behavior." It used two basic approaches to the measurement of attitudes. The first involved the use of statistical indicators, such as turnover rate, absenteeism, number of grievances, lateness, and accident experience. The second approach involved a periodic survey of employees through questionnaires.

Several shortcomings were recognized in the first approach. (1) The statistical indicators provided little or no information about underlying causes. (2) In general, the indicators told of trouble only after the harm had been done. (3) Because these indicators were traditionally associated with the personnel functions, managers tended to minimize their importance or else place responsibility for improvement on the personnel function. (4) Unfavorable trends in certain of these indicators might be due to external factors (e.g., short labor supply) rather than to some shortcomings of management.

The attitude survey made use of a standardized questionnaire designed to reveal the attitudes of employees in a number of broad areas. The survey was administered at intervals of about eighteen months. Results for each attitude area were tabulated in terms of proportion of responses that were favorable. Tabulations were made by work groups and not by individual employees; this practice helped protect the anonymity of responses, and thus the validity of the surveys.

Public Responsibility

This key result area evolved from General Electric's recognition of its obligation to conduct itself as a good citizen within society, complying faithfully with the laws and ethics governing business conduct. The company believed its progress required not only an active recognition of the broad public interest, but also a responsiveness to certain special publics who had a stake in the success of the business—namely, shareowners, customers, employees, vendors, dealers and distributors, the plant community, educational institutions, and government.

While the responsibility to certain publics such as shareowners, educational institutions, and the federal government could best be measured from an overall company viewpoint rather than departmentally, nevertheless, the actions taken by a product department (including the individual acts of employees of that department) could have an important impact on the whole company's reputation as a good corporate citizen. Accordingly, the company attempted to assure wholehearted observance of the legal and ethical standards of business by insisting that all managerial and professional employees at least once a year conduct periodical surveys of the activities of those who reported to them with respect to antitrust compliance, conflict of interest, and other areas of business practice. These matters were discussed with each individual, who then signed a statement affirming his understanding and compliance.

Other measurements related to the effectiveness of department action in strengthening the company's reputation and business relationships. With respect to fulfilling obligations to customers, it was determined that the previously mentioned product leadership and market position areas were the best indicators. For the remaining publics, the following measures were recommended.

Shareowners. The total shares of General Electric Company stock were to be "allocated" to the various operating components that were assigned responsibility for preserving and enhancing "their portion" of the shareowners' investment in the company.

Vendors, Dealers, and Distributors. Suppliers of raw materials and parts were to be surveyed periodically to determine their appraisal of the department's practices in conducting its business as compared with the practices of others who bought from them. Dealers and distributors were likewise to be interviewed from time to time to measure whether these important relationships were being responsibly maintained.

Plant Community. Again, comprehensive reaction surveys were to be used, aimed at identifying the impact of the actions of a product department on the individuals who made up the community. These reactions disclosed by the opinion surveys were to be supplemented by use of trends developed from various types of data such as community wage rates, number of employment applications received, volume of purchases made locally, contributions to local charities, and participation in civic, church, and business organizations.

Balance between Short-Range and Long-Range Goals

This factor was set out separately as a key result area in order to emphasize the importance of the long-term survival and growth of the company. Short-range goals and performance had to be balanced against the need for satisfactory performance five, ten, fifteen years in the future, since undue pressure for current profits could, in effect, borrow from the future.

Various means were employed to experiment with suggested measures in this key result area. However, it is important to note that when the eight key result areas were established, each of the first seven had both short-range and long-range dimensions. The eighth area, balance between short-range and long-range goals, had been specifically identified to make sure that the long-range health of the company would not be sacrificed for short-term gains. The plans, goals, and actions in each of the other areas were, therefore, to be appraised in terms of both their short-term and their long-term implications.

During the period after the measurements project was established in 1952, deep research work was carried on to establish the specific measurements in each of the eight key result areas. Before communicating these measures to the product departments, the investigators reviewed the recommendations in each area with operating personnel and with officers, for their comments, suggestions, and final approval.

The company's business planning, budgeting, and forecasting program incorporated the use of selected key result areas in (1) reviewing the recent history and current status, (2) setting standards for each department, (3) planning to achieve the standards, and (4) periodic reporting and measurement of accomplishment. Since the first four key result areas lent themselves readily to numerical evaluations, they were a part of the planning, budgeting, forecasting, reporting, and measuring system. Building on this experience in using the key result areas to plan and measure performance, management at the General Electric Company made the search for effective business measurements a continuing, evolutionary process.

QUESTIONS

1. For the purpose described, how should profitability be defined? The definition should be specific enough so that a quantitative measure can be constructed from it.

2. What, if anything, do the factors other than profitability add to the proposed measurement system? Isn't the impact of the other factors reflected in the profitability measure if it is properly constructed?

Case 3–3

Carver Candy Company

A year after Carver Candy Company adopted, in 1959, the so-called "direct costing" method of accounting, its controller, Mr. Hohl, was, in general, satisfied with the way the system was working out. He was convinced that the new accounting system, by providing useful information needed for overall profit planning and control, had greatly helped the management in its effort to pull the company out of the recent period of approximately level annual sales and low or nonexistent profits.

INTRODUCTION OF DIRECT COSTING

Carver Candy Company was a long-established, medium-size manufacturer of candy products. In 1958, a new management team was organized to revitalize the company under the leadership of Mr. Dewey, the newly elected president. Mr. Hohl was brought in as a member of this team. He immediately recognized the inadequacy and even misleading nature of the existing accounting system. In his opinion, although any accounting system ought to serve at least three purposes—(1) to facilitate cost control, (2) to supply management with quantitative data timely and relevant for intelligent profit planning, and (3) to produce reports to stockholders, government and other outside agencies—the old Carver system had done reasonable justice only to the third. In order to serve the other two purposes effectively, he believed, the whole accounting system had to be reorganized around the concept of direct costing. With encouragement from Mr. Dodd, executive vice-president, and on approval by Mr. Herold, treasurer, Mr. Hohl put the new system into effect in the summer of 1959. The following sections of the case are based on his explanation of the procedures and his appraisal as to how the system met the needs of management.

Direct Costing Procedure

Direct costing is a method of recording and reporting cost data which distinguishes between period and direct elements of cost. Period costs are those costs that tend to remain constant over a given period of time independent of fluctuations in production or sales volume within the period. Insurance, depreciation, administrative expenses, factory supervisory salaries, and property taxes are of this nature. Direct costs, on the other hand, are those costs that tend to increase or decrease as production or sales volume moves up or down. Costs of raw materials, operating labor, certain factory overhead, and sales commissions vary directly with volume and belong to this category.

Under the new procedure of direct costing, Carver classified all its cost and expense items into these two categories, as they were initially collected for various cost centers; the segregation was maintained in the preparation of reports for internal control. Products were charged only with direct costs, and all period costs, whether manufacturing or not, were written off in the period incurred. No attempt was made to allocate period costs to products as under the old system, except for the preparation of external reports.

Exhibits 1 and 2 are sample forms of reports prepared for internal purposes under the direct costing system. Exhibit 1, Product Family Report, showed, in total and for each of the four product families, revenue, direct costs, and merchandising contribution or margin which was the difference between them. No period costs appeared on this report. Exhibit 2 was Consolidated Income Statement for all products. From the "total merchandising contribution" of all product families, there was deducted all period costs to arrive at the net operating income of the company.

Benefit in Cost Control

In Mr. Hohl's opinion, period costs are the responsibility of top management, while the responsibility for control of direct costs rests at a lower level of management—principally, foremen. Thus, the distinction between period costs and direct costs corresponded closely to that between controllable and noncontrollable costs, which was essential for effective cost control. Assuming no change in selling price, the amount and percentage of the merchandising contribution for an individual product was a direct indication of efficiency with which the product was manufactured, since changes in merchandising contribution reflected changes in controllable costs. The isolation of period costs in the reports to the top management stressed the nature and importance of the fixity of these costs and thus facilitated their control. Budgeting was the primary tool for controlling these period costs.

Benefits in Profit Planning

In Mr. Hohl's opinion, better understanding of the distinctly different behavior of direct and period costs in response to changes in sales and production volume made it easier to prepare reasonably accurate budgets of costs and profits. The analysis of profit–cost–volume relationships was no longer obscured or confused by the fluctuating unit product cost, which was unavoidable under the old absorption accounting system.

Exhibit 1

PRODUCT FAMILY REPORT FOR JUNE, 1960

	Total		Product Families							
			A		B		C		D	
	Amount	%	Amount	%	Amount	%	Amount	%	Amount	%
Gross sales	$1,199,800	100.0	$540,100	100.0	$143,800	100.0	$407,600	100.0	$108,300	100.0
Less: Allowances:										
Freight	84,800	7.0	37,800	7.0	9,900	6.9	29,400	7.2	7,700	7.1
Cash discount	21,400	1.8	10,200	1.9	2,200	1.5	7,400	1.8	1,600	1.5
Returns	5,700	0.5	1,100	0.2	2,200	1.5	2,000	0.5	400	0.4
General	6,900	0.6	3,800	0.7	800	0.6	1,600	0.4	700	0.6
Total Allowances	$ 118,800	9.9	$ 52,900	9.8	$ 15,100	10.5	$ 40,400	9.9	$ 10,400	9.6
Net sales	$1,081,000	90.1	$487,200	90.2	$128,700	89.5	$367,200	90.1	$ 97,900	90.4
Less: Direct cost of sales:										
Standard manufacturing costs	$ 706,200	58.9	$308,900	57.2	$ 81,000	56.3	$251,500	61.7	$ 64,800	59.8
Material variances	(5,700)	(0.5)	(4,800)	(0.9)	1,500	1.1	(2,000)	(0.5)	(400)	(0.3)
Labor and burden variances	11,000	0.9	3,800	0.7	3,600	2.5	3,600	0.9	—	—
Total direct manufacturing costs	$ 711,500	59.3	$307,900	57.0	$ 86,100	59.9	$253,100	62.1	$ 64,400	59.5
Direct warehouse and shipping costs	7,100	0.6	3,200	0.6	1,300	0.9	2,000	0.5	600	0.5
Direct selling costs	39,200	3.3	18,900	3.5	6,200	4.3	11,000	2.7	3,100	2.9
Total Direct Costs	$ 757,800	63.2	$330,000	61.1	$ 93,600	65.1	$266,100	65.3	$ 68,100	62.9
Merchandising contribution	$ 323,200	26.9	$157,200	29.1	$ 35,100	24.4	$101,100	24.8	$ 29,800	27.5

Exhibit 2

CONSOLIDATED INCOME STATEMENT FOR JUNE, 1960

Item	*Budget* Amount	*Budget* %	*Performance* Amount	*Performance* %
Gross sales	$1,386,000	100.0	$1,199,800	100.0
Less: Allowances:				
Freight	81,800	5.9	84,800	7.0
Cash discount	22,200	1.6	21,400	1.8
Returns	5,500	0.4	5,700	0.5
General	8,300	0.6	6,900	0.6
Total allowances	$ 117,800	8.5	$ 118,800	9.9
Net sales	$1,268,200	91.5	$1,081,000	90.1
Less: Direct cost of sales:				
Standard manufacturing costs	805,300	58.1	706,200	58.9
Material variances	—	—	(5,700)	(0.5)
Labor and burden variances	6,900	0.5	11,000	0.9
Total direct manufacturing costs	$ 812,200	58.6	$ 711,500	59.3
Direct warehouse and shipping costs	12,500	0.9	7,100	0.6
Direct selling costs	43,000	3.1	39,200	3.3
Total direct costs	$ 867,700	62.6	$ 757,800	63.2
Merchandising contribution	400,500	28.9	323,200	26.9
Less: Period costs:				
Manufacturing division	62,000		58,700	
Marketing division	53,600		52,000	
Financial division	27,800		27,100	
Purchasing division	4,100		4,000	
Personnel division	5,300		6,200	
President's office	11,000		10,400	
Advertising	89,300		92,500	
Depreciation	54,700		54,100	
State and local taxes	7,800		6,100	
Interest	5,000		4,400	
Total period costs	$ 320,600	23.1	$ 315,500	26.3
Net operating income	$ 79,900	5.8	$ 7,700	0.6
Other income or (expense)	600	—	1,800	0.2
Total Net Income	$ 80,500	5.8	$ 9,500	0.8

At the time direct costing was introduced, Carver had about 700 individual items in production, grouped into four broad product families. Although management suspected that some items were not profitable enough to justify their continued production, the old accounting reports, which included an arbitrary allocation of fixed costs to products, did not provide a ready basis for deciding which items to drop or, conversely, which items warranted special selling effort because of their attractive margins. The new procedure enabled management to identify a number of low-profit items; consequently, in the first year the line was reduced to 400 items. The practice was that any item with a low merchandising contribution was investigated. "Low" was defined as a merchandising contribution of less than $4,000 per annum and/or less than 25 percent of sales revenue. Such items were referred to the product line committee, consisting of executive vice-president, treasurer, production manager, marketing manager, purchasing manager, and controller, who decided whether their continued production was warranted. Unless selling price could be raised without much anticipated sacrifice in sales volume, or unless direct costs could be reduced substantially through increased efficiency or change in raw material composition, there was thought to be little justification for keeping them in the line, except possibly for items that brought some sales benefits to other products in the line.

When considering the addition of a new product, a calculation of its expected merchandising contribution in dollars and percentage gave a starting point for an intelligent decision. Here, also, the $4,000 and 25 percent merchandising contribution was the minimum requirement.

Theoretically, since any merchandising contribution, however small, represented a contribution to the recovery of period costs, the minimum acceptable selling price for an item was equal to an amount slightly above its direct cost. It could, therefore, be argued that with such a low minimum, sales people would be tempted to set selling prices too low. Mr. Hohl thought this danger was avoided by entrusting to the product line committee the authority for establishing and changing prices. Prices were set only after a careful consideration of all relevant factors such as cost, demand, competition, and customer relations. In addition, the $4,000 or 25 percent minimum rule was a safeguard against setting prices too low.

The $4,000 or 25 percent criterion was admittedly somewhat arbitrary. It was considered as furnishing an adequate cushion for any one, or combination, of the following factors:

1. The classification of direct and period costs was not exactly black and white; some arbitrary demarcation was unavoidable, particularly in classifying so-called "semi-variable" costs. Conservatism and long-run considerations therefore dictated that for deciding which items to drop or which items to add the acceptable minimum should be adjusted upward from the bare minimum of direct costs.

2. Adding or dropping a product item involved increase or decrease in certain period costs such as promotion and product design and engineering costs. No product could be said to be on its own feet until such costs were covered. The $4,000 or 25 percent adjusted for this factor.

3. Most important of all, since management-supervision capacity was limited, management's attention was not without an element of opportunity cost. The $4,000 or 25 percent represented, at least partly, this opportunity cost. Products unable to meet the requirement were regarded as not deserving of management's attention.

Specific example of how the new accounting aided management was in connection with establishment of the sales promotion policy for 1960; effort for additional sales was concentrated more on product family A than on product family C. The logic of the policy was obvious to the management once it concluded that the significant difference between merchandising contributions of the two product families in 1959 would be continued in 1960. Exhibit 3 shows a 29 percent contribution for A and 25 percent for C for the month of June, 1960. A dollar increase in sales of A would therefore contribute four cents more to the recovery of period costs than would the same increase in the sales of C.

Exhibit 3

SUMMARY OF SALES AND CONTRIBUTIONS BY PRODUCT FAMILIES FOR JUNE, 1960

Product Family	*Dollar Sales*	*Percent of Total*	*Merchandising Margin ($)*	*Merchandising Margin (%)*
A	$ 540,100	45.0%	$157,200	29.1%
B	143,800	12.0	35,100	24.4
C	407,600	34.0	101,100	24.8
D	108,300	9.0	29,800	27.5
Total	$1,199,800	100.0	$323,200	26.9

External Reporting

The new system did not apply to external reports. For reports to stockholders, tax authorities, and other governmental agencies, inventory values were adjusted to include fixed manufacturing costs. As a matter of fact, the board of directors periodically received from the treasurer a condensed income statement in the form of Exhibit 4, which showed this inventory adjustment and the net income calculated under the conventional system of absorption accounting.

Exhibit 4

CONDENSED INCOME STATEMENT FOR JUNE, 1960

Gross sales	$1,199,800	100.0%
Less: Allowances	118,800	9.9
Net sales	$1,081,000	90.1
Less: Direct cost of sales	757,800	63.2
Merchandising contribution	$ 323,200	26.9
Less: Period costs	315,500	26.3
Net operating income	$ 7,700	0.6
Other income or (expense)	1,800	0.2
Net income, direct cost basis	$ 9,500	0.8
Inventory adjustment to absorption	2,000	
Net income before taxes	$ 7,500	
Provision for taxes	4,100	
Net income after taxes	$ 3,400	

Summary of Controller's Appraisal

Pleased as he was with Carver's new accounting system, Mr. Hohl did not regard it as a cure-all. He recognized that direct costing did not eliminate the necessity of exercising sound judgment in using accounting data; the method merely reflected more closely the thinking of management in planning and control, making it easier for users to understand the reports. He also admitted that an intelligently designed and utilized conventional absorption accounting system could serve the same purposes as direct costing in that supplementary analyses for specific purposes could always be prepared from the accounting data. However, he thought that many people, including even accountants, are often puzzled by the fluctuations of unit cost with changing volume and the fluctuations of income when sales and production volumes of a period do not coincide, which is characteristic of conventional accounting.

TROUBLE

By the summer of 1960, Mr. Hohl was almost sure that everyone in the organization was happy with the direct cost system. However, in August, 1960, he had a long discussion with Mr. Herold, the treasurer, which raised some doubts in his mind. Mr. Herold had been with the company for over thirty years; his opinions were therefore based on long experience.

Mr. Herold suggested that the product line committee reexamine the policy that promotion of product family A be given priority over that of product family C. The substance of his reasoning is given below.

June 1960 was typical in that product family A had a substantially greater merchandising contribution than product family C. (See Exhibit 3.) Apparently, for the same dollar sales, A is more profitable than C. This inference, however, is incorrect, for ultimate profitability cannot be determined until meaningfully allocable fixed costs are taken into account. Under the old accounting procedure, depreciation of roughly $50,000 for the month of June, 1960, would have been allocated to the four product families as follows:

ALLOCATION OF DEPRECIATION

Product Family	*A*		*B*	*C*		*D*
Sales	$540,000		$144,000	$408,000		$108,000
Merchandising margin......	157,000	29%	35,000	101,000	25%	30,000
Depreciation	27,000		7,000	9,000		7,000
Margin after depreciation...	$130,000	24%	$ 28,000	$ 92,000	23%	$ 23,000

Apportionment of depreciation shifts the relative profitability of A and C; A is now only one percentage point ahead of C. This shift occurs because the ratio of direct cost to equipment use is different between the product families—in other words, because the manufacturing process is more mechanized for A than for C.

Depreciation of equipment is a fixed cost in the short run, but becomes variable if enough time is allowed. This fact becomes obvious when volume increases: Owing to the concentrated promotion, sales of A has been increasing at such a rate that soon the present equipment capacity for the production of A will become inadequate. Either additional equipment must be acquired or a new shift added, and either alternative will entail a jump in fixed costs.

The promotional cost itself, which we treat as a period cost, must also be taken into account. In June, 1960, out of the total advertising and other promotional period cost of $120,000, $66,000 was directly identifiable with product families and can be charged to them as follows:

ALLOCATION OF ADVERTISING AND PROMOTION COSTS

Product Family	*A*		*B*	*C*		*D*
Margin after depreciation......	$130,000	24%	$28,000	$92,000	23%	$23,000
Advertising and promotion	37,000		4,000	19,000		6,000
Margin	$ 93,000	17%	$24,000	$73,000	18%	$17,000
Sales per promotion dollar.....	$15			$22		

The adjusted margin of C becomes superior to that of A, after charging each with its direct advertising and other promotional expenses. Note also that a dollar expended on promotion of A brings in $15 of sales, while for C one dollar generates $22. This suggests that greater and greater effort is needed to obtain a dollar increase in sales as the level of sales moves up, and that A has possibly reached a saturation point. Talk with the sales people convinces me that an incremental advertising dollar spent for C will induce more sales than for A.

On the basis of the above analysis, I think we should reverse the present policy, and this leads me to wonder whether the direct costing system is causing us to make mistakes that we could avoid by returning to the conventional absorption costing.

QUESTION

Consider the advantages and limitations of a direct costing system for management control. One of the questions to be resolved is: Assuming that some version of full costs must be collected for financial accounting purposes, can a full cost system be made as useful as a direct cost system by the proper classification of accounts?

Chapter Four

KEY VARIABLES

The designer of a management control system must work within the confines of three major constraints. The first two of these, discussed in Chapters 1 and 2, are the objectives of the corporation and the organization structure it has adopted to achieve these objectives. The third, and equally important, consideration concerns the economics of the business itself. Here, the systems designer's job is especially difficult; he must gain a sufficient understanding of how the business operates to be able to design a flow of information that will promptly and accurately reflect how internal actions and external forces have affected the progress of the company toward its goals.

Why should a hotel chain have a management control system different from that of a magazine publisher? The two companies might have similar objectives within their respective industries, and their organization structures might be similar in the sense that they follow a natural, functional division of the work to be done. The overriding difference is that the two corporations seek to make profits in radically different ways. The control system must be tailored to the specific industry in which the company operates, it must identify the "critical success factors" that should receive careful and continuous management attention if the company is to be successful, and it must highlight these key variables in reports to all levels of management.

Summary measures of performance, such as profit or return on investment, may be good overall indicators that something is going wrong, but managers must also know *what* is going wrong, *why* it is going wrong, and *who* is responsible.

One way to isolate the key management variables is to look at the raison d'être of the industry itself, and that of the specific firm within the industry. A useful question is: Why, in a free-enterprise economy, should this company be able to operate at a profit? A hardheaded rethinking of this fundamental question should lead to a careful spelling-out of just what functions the company is performing that its customers are willing to pay for. Further thought should then be devoted to the question of what advantages this company has over its competitors. Then, finally, it may be possible to pinpoint those activities that need to be done particularly well if the company is to continue to be, or to become, successful.

Another approach that may be useful is to examine the way in which decisions are made. What decisions does management regard as major ones? What are the factors that management is concerned about in making these decisions? And specifically, for many types of intangible, discretionary expenditures, what will be the source of revenue from which the company will recover this cost and earn a profit? Questions such as these should also eventually lead to the identification of those elements critical to the success of a company in a competitive environment.

This analytical task is difficult and challenging, but the rewards, in terms of a useful control system that is really helpful to management in achieving the corporate goals, are commensurate. The cases in this chapter are aimed at providing some practice in key variable analysis, and in subsequent chapters the student will find that identifying these variables is a useful starting point for his evaluation of a company's control system.

Reading 4-1

Management Information Crisis

By D. Ronald Daniel*

In late 1960 a large defense contractor became concerned over a major project that was slipping badly. After 15 months costs were running far above the estimate and the job was behind schedule. A top-level executive, assigned as program manager to salvage the project, found he had no way of pinpointing what parts of the system were causing the trouble, why costs were so high, and which subcontractors were not performing.

Recently an American electronics company revamped its organizational structure. To compete more aggressively in international markets, management appointed "area managers" with operating responsibility—e.g., in Latin America, Western Europe, and the Far East. After nine months it was apparent that the new plan was not coming up to expectations. On checking with three newly created area managers, the company heard each say, in effect:

"In half of the countries in my area the political situation is in flux, and I can't anticipate what's going to happen next."

"I'm still trying to find out whether our operating costs in Austria are reasonable."

"I don't know where in South America we're making a profit."

A small but highly successful consumer products company recently followed the lead of its larger competitors by establishing product-manager positions. Although outstanding men were placed in the new jobs, an air of

---

* Associated with the management consulting firm of McKinsey & Company, Inc. From the *Harvard Business Review,* September–October, 1961. Reproduced by permission of *Harvard Business Review.*

general confusion soon developed, and the product managers began to show signs of frustration. After much study it became apparent that an important cause of the trouble was that no one had determined what kind of information the product managers would need in order to perform their new functions.

In retrospect it is obvious that these three companies were plagued by a common problem: inadequate management information. The data were inadequate, not in the sense of there not being enough, but in terms of relevancy for setting objectives, for shaping alternative strategies, for making decisions, and for measuring results against planned goals.

ASSESSING THE GAP

In each company the origin of the problem lay in the gap between a static information system and a changing organization structure. This difficulty is not new or uncommon. There is hardly a major company in the United States whose plan of organization has not been changed and rechanged since World War II. And with revised structures have come new jobs, new responsibilities, new decision-making authorities, and reshaped reporting relationships. All of these factors combine to create new demands for information—information that is usually missing in existing systems. As a result, many leading companies are suffering a major information crisis—often without fully realizing it.

Far-Reaching Trends

Some idea of the scope of this problem can be gained by reviewing the intensity of the three major causes of recent organization changes in American business:

Growth—Since 1945 the Gross National Product has risen 135%. In specific industries the growth rate has been even greater. Plastic production, for example, tripled between 1948 and 1958; electronics sales nearly quadrupled in the decade from 1950 to 1960. Many individual companies have shown even more startling growth. This growth, in turn, has fostered organizational change:

Divisions have been created and decentralization has been encouraged.

Greater precision in defining line-staff relationships has been necessitated.

Organization structures that were once adequate for $50-million businesses have proved unworkable for $500-million enterprises.

Diversification—Merger and acquisition have accounted for the growth of many large organizations. For these companies, the task of finding, evaluating, and consummating diversification deals—and assimilating newly acquired products and businesses—has required continuous organizational adjustment. Some corporations have diversified by developing new product lines to satisfy shifting market requirements; some have used other means.

But always the effect has been the same: different organization structures for parts of or perhaps for the entire enterprise.

International operations—There has been a threefold increase in the value of United States investments abroad since World War II. Major companies that once regarded foreign markets as minor sources of incremental profits, or as markets for surplus production, now look overseas for the bulk of their future profits and growth. They are setting up manufacturing and research as well as marketing organizations in foreign countries. Consequently, we are growing used to seeing a company's "export department" evolve into the "international division," and national companies grow into world-wide enterprises. All this calls for extensive modifications of organization structure.

The impact of any one of the above factors alone would be sufficient to create great change in an enterprise, but consider that in many cases at least two, and sometimes all three, have been at work. It is easy to see why so many company organization structures do become unstable and how this creates a management information problem large enough to hamper some firms and nearly paralyze others.

Linking Systems and Needs

Organization structure and information requirements are inextricably linked. In order to translate a statement of his duties into action, an executive must receive and use information. Information in this case is not just the accounting system and the forms and reports it produces. It includes *all* the data and intelligence—financial and nonfinancial—that are really needed to plan, operate, and control a particular enterprise. This embraces external information such as economic and political factors and data on competitive activity.

When viewed in this light, the impact of organization structure on needs for management information becomes apparent. The trouble is that in most companies it is virtually taken for granted that the information necessary for performance of a manager's duties flows naturally to the job. To a certain extent this is so. For example, internally generated information—especially accounting information—does tend to flow easily to the job or can be made to do so. Also, in companies doing business in only one industry and having a small, closely knit management group much vital interdepartmental and general information is conveyed by frequent face-to-face contact and coordination among executives. Economic and competitive information from outside is similarly transmitted, the bulk of it coming into the concern informally. Further, through trade contacts, general reading, and occasional special studies, executives toss bits of information into the common pool and draw from it as well.

The point is, however, that while such an informal system can work well for small and medium-size companies in simple and relatively static industries, it becomes inadequate when companies grow larger and especially when they spread over several industries, areas, and countries. At this point, most large companies have found that information has to be conveyed in a formal manner and less and less through direct observation.

Unfortunately, management often loses sight of the seemingly obvious and simple relationship between organization structure and information needs. Companies very seldom follow up on reorganizations with penetrating reappraisals of their information systems, and managers given new responsibilities and decision-making authority often do not receive all the information they require.

Causes of Confusion

The cornerstone for building a compact, useful management information system is the determination of each executive's information needs. This requires a clear grasp of the individual's role in the organization—his responsibilities, his authorities, and his relationships with other executives. The task is then to—

Design a network of procedures that will process raw data in such a way as to generate the information required for management use.

Implement such procedures in actual practice.

Such action steps, while demanding and time-consuming, have proved to be far less difficult than the creative and conceptual first step of defining information requirements. Seldom is the open approach of asking an executive what information he requires successful. For one thing he may find it difficult to be articulate because the organization structure of his company is not clearly defined.

Further, and more important, there is a widespread tendency among operating executives to think of information exclusively in terms of their companies' accounting systems and the reports thus generated. This way of thinking can be a serious deterrent because:

(1) Many conventional accounting reports cause confusion in the minds of nonfinancially trained executives. Take, for example, the profit-and-loss statement, with its arbitrary treatment of inventories, depreciation, allocated overhead expenses, and the like, or the statistical sales report, which is often a 40-page, untitled, machine-prepared tabulation of sales to individual customers. Such reports have made an indelible impression on managers' thinking, coloring their understanding and expectations of reports in general.

(2) By its very nature traditional accounting fails to highlight many important aspects of business operations. Accounting systems often are designed primarily to meet SEC, Internal Revenue, and other statutory requirements—requirements that, more often than not, fail to correspond to management's information needs. Accounting describes the past in dollars, usually without discriminating between the critical and noncritical elements of a business—the elements that control competitive success in a particular industry and the elements that do not.

(3) Accounting reports generally describe what has happened inside a company. Just consider what this approach omits:

Information about the future.

Data expressed in nonfinancial terms—e.g., share of market, productivity, quality levels, adequacy of customer service, and so on.

Information dealing with external conditions as they might bear on a particular company's operations.

Yet all of these items are essential to the intelligent managing of a business.

PLANNING NEEDS DEFINED

The key to the development of a dynamic and usable system of management information is to move beyond the limits of classical accounting reports and to conceive of information as it relates to two vital elements of the management process—planning and control. In the pages to follow I shall focus largely on the planning aspect.

We hear more these days about new techniques for inventory, cost, and other types of control, but information systems for business planning still represent a relatively unexplored horizon.

Planning, as used in this article, means: setting objectives, formulating strategy, and deciding among alternative investments or courses of action. This definition can be applied to an entire company, an integrated division, or a single operating department.

As Exhibit 1 shows, the information required to do planning of this kind is of three basic types:

1. *Environmental information*—Describes the social, political, and economic aspects of the climate in which a business operates or may operate in the future.
2. *Competitive information*—Explains the past performance, programs, and plans of competing companies.
3. *Internal information*—Indicates a company's own strengths and weaknesses.

Now let us consider each of these categories in some detail.

Environmental Information

The environmental data category is one of the least formalized and hence least used parts of a management information system in most companies. Specific examples of the data included in this category are:

Population—current levels, growth trends, age distribution, geographical distribution, effect on unemployment.

Price levels—retail, wholesale, commodities, government regulation.

Transportation—availability, costs, competition, regulation.

Foreign trade—balance of payments, exchange rates, convertibility.

Labor force—skills, availability, wages, turnover, unions.

Exhibit 1

ANATOMY OF MANAGEMENT INFORMATION

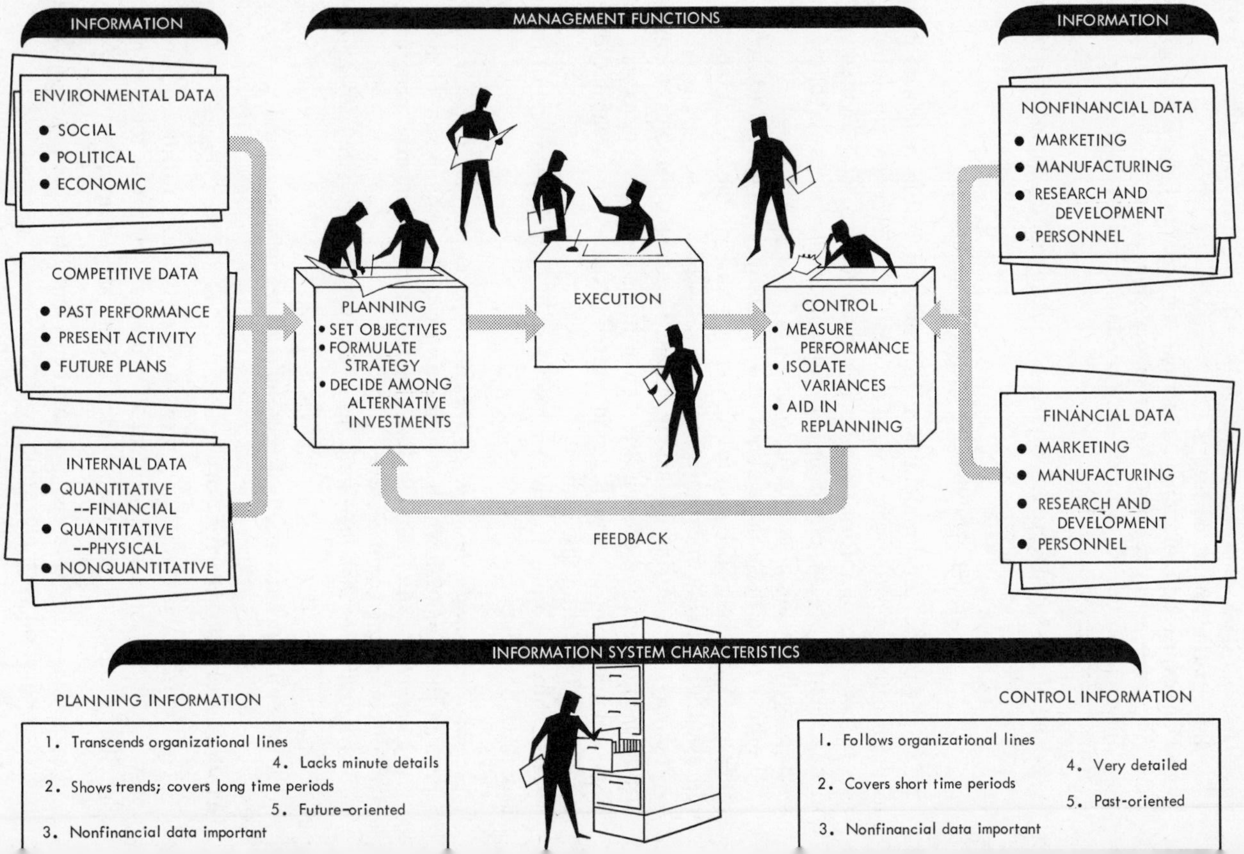
INFORMATION
ENVIRONMENTAL DATA
● SOCIAL
● POLITICAL
● ECONOMIC
COMPETITIVE DATA
● PAST PERFORMANCE
● PRESENT ACTIVITY
● FUTURE PLANS
INTERNAL DATA
● QUANTITATIVE --FINANCIAL
● QUANTITATIVE --PHYSICAL
● NONQUANTITATIVE
MANAGEMENT FUNCTIONS
PLANNING
• SET OBJECTIVES
• FORMULATE STRATEGY
• DECIDE AMONG ALTERNATIVE INVESTMENTS
EXECUTION
CONTROL
• MEASURE PERFORMANCE
• ISOLATE VARIANCES
• AID IN REPLANNING
FEEDBACK
INFORMATION
NONFINANCIAL DATA
● MARKETING
● MANUFACTURING
● RESEARCH AND DEVELOPMENT
● PERSONNEL
FINANCIAL DATA
● MARKETING
● MANUFACTURING
● RESEARCH AND DEVELOPMENT
● PERSONNEL
INFORMATION SYSTEM CHARACTERISTICS
PLANNING INFORMATION
1. Transcends organizational lines
2. Shows trends; covers long time periods
3. Nonfinancial data important
4. Lacks minute details
5. Future-oriented
CONTROL INFORMATION
1. Follows organizational lines
2. Covers short time periods
3. Nonfinancial data important
4. Very detailed
5. Past-oriented

To this list a company operating internationally would add another item—systematic collection and interpretation, on a country-by-country basis, of information on political and economic conditions in the foreign areas where business is being done. Here is an example of what can be accomplished:

A well-established international corporation with a highly sophisticated management makes a three-pronged effort to get data on local political and economic conditions. (a) There is a small but highly competent and well-paid four-man staff at corporate headquarters which travels extensively and publishes, using its own observations plus a variety of other sources, a weekly commentary on world events as they relate to the company. (b) This corporation has trained all its country managers to be keen observers of their local scene and to report their interpretive comments to headquarters regularly. (c) There is a little-talked-about group of "intelligence agents" who are not on the company's official payroll but are nevertheless paid for the information they pass along.

Certainly, not every organization has to go to these ends to keep itself informed of the situation in which it operates. However, those organizations that ignore environmental data or that leave its collection to the informal devices of individual executives are inviting trouble. Those companies that are knowledgeable concerning their environment are almost always in tune with the times and ahead of their competition. To illustrate:

(1) Good intelligence on the sociological changes taking place in the United States led several heavy manufacturing companies to enter the "leisure time" field with a great deal of success.

(2) Insight into the possible impact of foreign labor costs on parts of the electronics industry caused some U.S. corporations to acquire their own manufacturing facilities abroad. As a result, the firms were able not only to protect their domestic markets but also to open up profitable operations overseas.

(3) Knowledge of trends in age distribution in the United States added to an awareness of the rate of change of scientific learning provides ample proof for some firms of the desirability of being in the educational publishing field in the next decade.

To be of real use, environmental data must indicate trends; population figures, balance-of-payment data, or political shifts are of little significance when shown for one period because they don't help management make *analytical* interpretations.

The collection and transmission of good environmental data are often problematical. Even in the United States some kinds of information are not readily available and must be pieced together from several sources or acquired *sub rosa* from officially inaccessible sources. Transmitting environmental data, particularly political information, is so awkward that sometimes the data collector must sit down personally with those who need to know the information.

In sum, environmental data are an aspect of planning information that requires more attention and warrants formalization, especially in large geographically dispersed companies. The emergence of the corporate economics department is one development that could lead to better results in this area, but it is my impression that so far the progress of the units has been uneven.

Competitive Information

Data on competition comprise the second category of planning information. There are three important types to consider:

1. *Past performance*—This includes information on the profitability, return on investment, share of market, and so forth of competing companies. Such information is primarily useful in identifying one's competitors. It also is one benchmark when setting company objectives.
2. *Present activity*—This category covers new product introductions, management changes, price strategy, and so on—all current developments. Good intelligence on such matters can materially influence a company's planning; for example, it may lead to accelerating research programs, modifying advertising strategy, or switching distribution channels. The implication here is not that a company's plans should always be defensive and prompted by a competitor's moves but simply that anything important a competitor does should be recognized and factored into the planning process.
3. *Future plans*—This includes information on acquisition intentions, facility plans, and research and development efforts.

Competitive information, like environmental data, is an infrequently formalized part of a company's total information system. And so there seldom is a concerted effort to collect this kind of material, to process it, and to report it to management regularly. But some interesting exceptions to this general lack of concern exist:

Oil companies have long employed "scouts" in their land departments. These men report on acreage purchases, drilling results, and other competitive activity that may be pertinent to the future actions of their own company.

Business machine companies have "competitive equipment evaluation personnel" who continually assess the technical features of competitors' hardware.

Retail organizations employ "comparison shoppers" who appraise the prices and quality of merchandise in competitive stores.

Commercial intelligence departments are appearing more and more on corporate organization charts. An excerpt from the charter of one such group states its basic responsibility thus:

"To seek out, collect, evaluate, and report information covering the past performance and future plans of competitors in such a manner that the information will have potential utility in strategic and operational planning of the corporation. This means that in addition to reporting factual information, emphasis should be on determining the implications of such information for the corporation."

Internal Information

The third and final basic category of planning information is made up of internal data. As it relates to the total planning process, internal data are aimed at identifying a company's strengths and weaknesses—the characteristics that, when viewed in the perspective of the general business environment and in the light of competitive activity, should help management to shape its future plans. It is useful to think of internal data as being of three types:

1. *Quantitative-financial*—e.g., sales, costs, and cost behavior relative to volume changes.
2. *Quantitative-physical*—e.g., share of market, productivity, delivery performance, and manpower resources.
3. *Nonquantitative*—e.g., community standing and labor relations.

In reporting internal data, a company's information system must be discriminating and selective. It should focus on "success factors." In most industries there are usually three to six factors that determine success; these key jobs must be done exceedingly well for a company to be successful. Here are some examples from several major industries:

In the automobile industry, styling, an efficient dealer organization, and tight control of manufacturing costs are paramount.

In food processing, new product development, good distribution, and effective advertising are the major success factors.

In life insurance, the development of agency management personnel, effective control of clerical personnel, and innovation in creating new types of policies spell the difference.

The companies which have achieved the greatest advances in information analysis have consistently been those which have developed systems that have (a) been selective and (b) focused on the company's strengths and weaknesses with respect to its acknowledged success factors. By doing this, the managements have generated the kind of information that is most useful in capitalizing on strengths and correcting weaknesses. To illustrate:

An oil company devised a system of regularly reporting its "finding" costs—those costs incurred in exploring for new reserves of oil divided by the number of barrels of oil found. When this ratio trended upward beyond an established point, it was a signal to the company's management to consider the acquisition of other oil companies (together with their proved reserves) as a less expensive alternative to finding oil through its own exploratory efforts.

In the minds of most executives the accounting system exists primarily to meet the company's internal data needs; yet this is often an unreasonable and unfulfilled expectation. Accounting reports rarely focus on success factors that are nonfinancial in nature. Moreover, accounting practices with respect to allocation of expenses, transfer prices, and the like, often tend to obscure rather than clarify the underlying strengths and weaknesses of a company. This inadequacy should not be surprising since the *raison d'être* of many accounting systems is not to facilitate planning but rather to ensure the fulfillment of management's responsibility to the stockholders, the government, and other groups.

TAILORING THE REQUIREMENTS

If a company is to have a comprehensive, integrated system of information to support its planning process, it will need a set of management reports that regularly covers the three basic categories of planning data—i.e., environmental, competitive, and internal. The amount of data required in each area will naturally vary from company to company and will depend on such factors as the nature of the industry, the size and operating territory of the company, and the acceptance by management of planning as an essential function. However, it is important in every case for management to *formalize* and *regularize* the collection, transmission, processing, and presentation of planning information; the data are too vital to be ignored or taken care of by occasional "special studies." It is no accident that many of the most successful companies in this country are characterized by well-developed planning information systems.

Many companies have found that the most effective approach to determining requirements for planning information, whether it be for one executive or an entire company, is to relate the three types of planning data described earlier to the steps in the planning process—i.e., setting objectives, developing strategy, and deciding among alternative investments. Thus, one asks himself questions like these:

What political data are needed to set reasonable objectives for this company?

What sociological and economic data about the areas in which this company operates are needed to formulate new product strategy?

What competitive intelligence is necessary to develop share-of-market objectives?

What internal cost information is needed to choose between alternative facility locations?

Contrast with Control

In Exhibit 1 I have listed the five principal characteristics of planning data compared with the characteristics of control data. Note that in all but one case (nonfinancial information) they are different. It is most important to keep these differences in mind, lest the "fuel" for the planning system be confused with the "fuel" for the control system, and vice versa. Hence, I should like to emphasize the contrasts here:

1. *Coverage*—Good planning information is not compartmentalized by functions. Indeed, it seeks to transcend the divisions that exist in a company and to provide the basis on which *integrated* plans can be made. In contrast, control information hews closely to organizational lines so that it can be used to measure performance and help in holding specific managers more accountable.

2. *Length of time*—Planning information covers fairly long periods of time—months and years rather than days and weeks—and deals with trends. Thus, although it should be regularly prepared, it is not developed as frequently as control information.

3. *Degree of detail*—Excessive detail is the quicksand of intelligent planning. Unlike control, where precision and minute care do have a place, planning (and particularly long-range planning) focuses on the major outlines of the situation ahead. In the words of two authorities, L. Eugene Root and George A. Steiner, "The further out in time the planning, the less certain one can be about the precision of numbers. As a basic principle in planning it is understood that, in the longer range, details merge into trends and patterns."[1]

4. *Orientation*—Planning information should provide insights into the future. Control information shows past results and the reasons for them.

FUTURE DEVELOPMENTS

The heightened interest of management in its information crisis is already unmistakable. Dean Stanley F. Teele of the Harvard Business School, writing on the process of change in the years ahead, states, "I think the capacity to manage knowledge will be still more important to the manager. . . . The manager will need to increase his skill in deciding what knowledge he needs."[2]

Ralph Cordiner of General Electric Company in his book, *New Frontiers for Professional Managers,* writes:

> "It is an immense problem to organize and communicate the information required to operate a large, decentralized organization. . . .
>
> "What is required . . . is a . . . penetrating and orderly study of the business in its entirety to discover what specific information is needed at each particular position in view of the decisions to be made there. . . ."[3]

Invariably, increasing attention of leaders in education and industry precedes and prepares the way for frontal attacks on business problems. In many organizations the initial reaction to the management information problem is first evidenced by a concern over "the flood of paper work." Eventually, the problem itself is recognized—i.e., the need to define concisely the information required for intelligent planning and control of a business.

---

1 "The Lockheed Aircraft Corporation Master Plan," in *Long-Range Planning for Management,* edited by David W. Ewing (New York, Harper & Brothers, 1958), p. 151.

2 "Your Job and Mine," *The Harvard Business School Bulletin,* August 1960, p. 8.

3 New York, McGraw-Hill Book Company, Inc., 1956, p. 102.

Following this awakening interest in business information problems, we are likely to see the acceleration of two developments already in view: (a) improved techniques relating to the creation and operation of total information systems, and (b) new organizational approaches to resolving information problems.

Improved Techniques

While the crisis in management information has been growing, tools that may be useful in its solution have been under development. For example, the evolution of electronic data-processing systems, the development of supporting communications networks, and the formulation of rigorous mathematical solutions to business problems have provided potentially valuable tools to help management attack its information problems. Specifically, progress on three fronts is an encouraging indication that this kind of approach will prove increasingly fruitful:

(1) Managements of most companies are far more conversant with both the capabilities and the limitations of computer systems than they were five years ago. This growing understanding has done much to separate fact from fancy. One key result should be the increasing application of electronic data-processing concepts to the more critical, less routine problems of business.

(2) Computer manufacturers and communications companies are learning the worth of their products. They show signs of recognizing that it is not hardware but an information system which is extremely valuable in helping to solve management's problems.

(3) Significant improvements have been made in the techniques of harnessing computers. Advances in automatic programing and developments in creating a common business language are gratifying evidence that the gap is being narrowed between the technical potential of the hardware and management's ability to exploit it.

Organizational Moves

The development of new organizational approaches is less obvious. Earlier in this article I noted that: (a) progress in the systematic collection and reporting of information dealing with a company's environment or with its competitive situation has been slow, and (b) traditional accounting reports are often inadequate in providing the data needed for business planning. These conditions may result from a very basic cause; namely, that most organization structures do not pin down the responsibility for management information systems and tie it to specific executive positions. Controllers and other financial officers usually have been assigned responsibility for *accounting* information—but this, of course, does not meet the total need.

Nowhere has the absence of one person having specific and *total* responsibility for management information systems had a more telling effect than in defense contractor companies. In such organizations the usual information problems have been compounded by the rapid rate of technological advance and its attendant effect upon product obsolescence, and also by the requirement for "concurrency," which means that a single product or product complex is developed, tested, produced, and installed simultaneously. Under these conditions, some companies have been nearly paralyzed by too much of the wrong information.

Having recognized this problem, several corporations have attacked it by creating full-time management information departments. These groups are responsible for:

1. Identifying the information needs for all levels of management for both planning and control purposes. As prerequisites to this responsibility it is necessary to (a) define the authority and duties of each manager and (b) determine the factors that really contribute to competitive success in the particular business in question.
2. Developing the necessary systems to fulfill these information needs.
3. Operating the data-processing equipment necessary to generate the information which is required.

To some extent these departments, reporting high in the corporate structure, have impinged on responsibilities traditionally assigned to the accounting organization since they are concerned with financial as well as nonfinancial information. But to me this overlapping is inevitable, particularly in companies where the financial function operates under a narrow perspective and a preoccupation with accountancy. The age of the information specialist is nearing, and its arrival is inextricably tied in with the emergence of some of the newer tools of our management sciences. This notion is not far removed from the concept of Harold J. Leavitt and Thomas L. Whisler, who foresee the evolution of information technology and the creation of a "programing elite."[4]

CONCLUSION

The day when management information departments are as common as controller's departments is still years away. But this should not rule out concerted efforts to improve a company's information system. In fact, I would expect many broad-gauged controller's organizations to assume the initiative in their companies for such programs.

To this end, the nine questions listed in Exhibit 2 are for the executive to ask himself as a guide to assessing the improvement potential in his organization's planning information. If the answers to these questions tend to be negative, the chances are strong that changes are in order.

The impact of the information crisis on the executive will be significant. To an increasing extent, a manager's effectiveness will hinge on the quality

[4] "Management in the 1980's" HBR November–December 1958, p. 41.

Exhibit 2

HOW GOOD IS YOUR PLANNING INFORMATION?

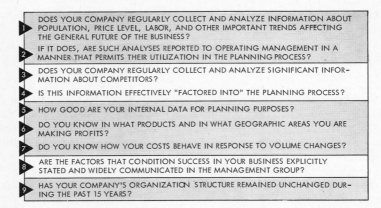

1. DOES YOUR COMPANY REGULARLY COLLECT AND ANALYZE INFORMATION ABOUT POPULATION, PRICE LEVEL, LABOR, AND OTHER IMPORTANT TRENDS AFFECTING THE GENERAL FUTURE OF THE BUSINESS?
2. IF IT DOES, ARE SUCH ANALYSES REPORTED TO OPERATING MANAGEMENT IN A MANNER THAT PERMITS THEIR UTILIZATION IN THE PLANNING PROCESS?
3. DOES YOUR COMPANY REGULARLY COLLECT AND ANALYZE SIGNIFICANT INFORMATION ABOUT COMPETITORS?
4. IS THIS INFORMATION EFFECTIVELY "FACTORED INTO" THE PLANNING PROCESS?
5. HOW GOOD ARE YOUR INTERNAL DATA FOR PLANNING PURPOSES?
6. DO YOU KNOW IN WHAT PRODUCTS AND IN WHAT GEOGRAPHIC AREAS YOU ARE MAKING PROFITS?
7. DO YOU KNOW HOW YOUR COSTS BEHAVE IN RESPONSE TO VOLUME CHANGES?
8. ARE THE FACTORS THAT CONDITION SUCCESS IN YOUR BUSINESS EXPLICITLY STATED AND WIDELY COMMUNICATED IN THE MANAGEMENT GROUP?
9. HAS YOUR COMPANY'S ORGANIZATION STRUCTURE REMAINED UNCHANGED DURING THE PAST 15 YEARS?

and completeness of the facts that flow to him and on his skill in using them. With technology changing at a rapid rate, with the time dimension becoming increasingly critical, and with organizations becoming larger, more diversified in product lines, and more dispersed geographically, it is inevitable that executives will rely more and more on formally presented information in managing their businesses.

What is more, some organizations are concluding that the easiest and most effective way to influence executive action is to control the flow of information into managerial positions. This notion holds that the discipline of information can be a potent factor in determining just what an executive can and cannot do—what decisions he can make, what plans he can draw up, what corrective steps he can take.

To the extent that this is true, information systems may be increasingly used to mold and shape executive behavior. Better data handling might well become a substitute for much of the laborious shuffling and reshuffling of positions and lines of authority that now goes on. Most reorganizations seek to alter the way certain managers or groups of managers operate. But simply drawing new organization charts and rewriting job descriptions seldom ensure the implementation of new concepts and relationships. The timing, content, and format of the information provided to management, however, *can* be a strong influence in bringing about such purposeful change.

Thus, developments in management information systems will affect the executive in two ways. Not only will the new concepts influence what he is able to do, but they will to a great extent control how well he is able to do it.

Case 4–1

The Atlantic Monthly Company (A)

Late in January, 1964, Donald B. Snyder, since 1933 the publisher of *The Atlantic Monthly* magazine, was preparing a report for the company's board of directors. For many years it had been Mr. Snyder's practice to submit a comprehensive report for discussion at the January board meeting; the report served as the primary basis on which the board reviewed the performance of the magazine during the preceding calendar year. Mr. Snyder thought his 1964 report was particularly important because: (1) he was planning to retire later that year, and he wanted to make a careful assessment of the recent progress of the magazine and its current situation at the time he turned his job over to his successor; and (2) the 1963 operating results provided the first real opportunity to review the effect of the price increase he had made in 1962. Mr. Snyder was convinced that the price increase had been a wise decision, but he thought it would be useful for the board to review the results of that action.

HISTORY OF THE ATLANTIC

The Atlantic Monthly, a magazine published in Boston, Massachusetts, was founded in 1857 by a group of distinguished New England literary and political leaders. The original prospectus of the magazine stated that its aim was "to concentrate the efforts of the best writers upon literature and politics, under the light of the highest morals." In 1957, this editorial policy was reaffirmed by the editor, Edward A. Weeks, in his introduction to the 100th anniversary issue.

The aims of the magazine were clearly defined in the first issue. It was to be primarily an American undertaking. "The publishers wish to say," so runs the prospectus, "that while native writers will receive the most solid encouragement, and will be mainly relied on to fill the pages of the *Atlantic*, they will not hesitate to draw from the foreign sources at their command, as occasion may require, relying rather on the competency of an author to treat a particular subject, than on any other claim whatever." In this way they hoped to make their periodical "welcome wherever the English tongue is spoken or read." We have from the first relied upon "the competency" of our authors; we have not tried to water down what they wrote but have given them the latitude to express conflicting and at times highly controversial opinions, for we still believe, as did our founders, that the free competition of ideas has made this country what it is.

"In Politics," so runs our charter, "the *Atlantic* will be the organ of no party or clique, but will honestly endeavor to be the exponent of what its conductors believe to be the American idea. . . . It will not rank itself with any sect of anties, but with that body of men which is in favor of Freedom, National Progress, and Honor, whether public or private." To the founders the Union was sacred, and ever since the Reconstruction we have held to the pledge that the magazine would be nonpartisan. At the time of national elections, as tempers have risen, we have had to resist the pressure of well-meaning friends who would have us become a Republican or a Democratic organ. Our refusal to do so has sometimes cost us readers and advertising, but we believe that it has increased our sense of responsibility and our value.[1]

From the very beginning, the *Atlantic* was a critical success, enjoying an increasing reputation for publishing excellent literary essays and critiques, high-quality fiction and poetry, and provocative political and topical articles. Financially, however, the Atlantic's success as a self-supporting commercial venture was somewhat less consistent. For the first 51 years of its existence, the *Atlantic* was published as an auxiliary activity by a variety of book publishing companies; the publishing rights changed hands seven times during these years. In 1908, the magazine became an independent enterprise when Ellery Sedgwick formed The Atlantic Monthly Company and purchased the magazine from Houghton Mifflin Company. During the first 15 years under Mr. Sedgwick's direction, the circulation of the *Atlantic* increased from less than 40,000 copies per issue to more than 125,000 copies.

The depression years of the 1930's affected the *Atlantic* as it did many other businesses; circulation dropped from 126,000 in 1930 to 101,000 in 1935. In 1938, Mr. Sedgwick sold his stock in the company to Richard E. Danielson. Under the new owner, Mr. Weeks, who had joined the organization in 1924 as associate editor, continued as editor, and Mr. Snyder remained as publisher; the positions were still held by these two men in 1964.

The *Atlantic*'s progress during the years 1950 to 1963 is documented in Exhibits 1, 2, and 3. Exhibit 1 presents comparative statistical data for the *Atlantic* and its most direct competitor, *Harper's Magazine*. Total average paid circulation of the *Atlantic* increased from 102,000 in 1940, to 170,000 in 1950, and 269,000 in 1963. The volume of advertising carried by the magazine also increased substantially during this period. Exhibit 2 presents

---

[1] *The Atlantic Monthly,* Vol. 200 (November, 1957), pp. 37–38.

Exhibit 1

COMPARATIVE STATISTICS FOR THE ATLANTIC MONTHLY AND HARPER'S MAGAZINE, SELECTED YEARS, 1950 TO 1963

		1963	*1962*	*1961*	*1960*	*1955*	*1950*
Average monthly paid circulation (calendar year):							
Subscriptions	*The Atlantic*	219,186	223,791	227,165	220,729	165,800	138,000
	Harper's	220,540	234,076	212,471	186,905	151,800	126,000
Newsstand	*The Atlantic*	49,413	50,196	54,764	44,505	42,500	31,500
	Harper's	49,388	52,427	52,426	52,086	36,900	35,300
Total	*The Atlantic*	268,599	273,987	281,929	265,234	208,300	169,500
	Harper's	269,928	286,503	264,897	238,991	188,700	161,300
Regular prices on December 31:							
One year subscription	*The Atlantic*	$8.50	$8.50	$7.50	$7.50	$6.00	$6.00
	Harper's	7.00	7.00	6.00	6.00	6.00	5.00
Single copy	*The Atlantic*	.75	.75	.60	.60	.50	.50
	Harper's	.60	.60	.60	.60	.50	.50
Advertising volume (calendar year):							
Pages	*The Atlantic*	620	491	481	535	341	239
	Harper's	569	468	460	509	314	326
Gross revenue	*The Atlantic*	$1,562,798	$1,206,867	$1,135,432	$1,181,815	$481,804	$237,759
	Harper's	1,448,168	1,165,542	1,012,613	1,046,262	369,808	350,207

SOURCES: Audit Bureau of Circulation, Standard Rate and Data Service, and Publishers Information Bureau.

Exhibit 2

COMPARATIVE STATEMENTS OF OPERATIONS

1959–63

	Twelve Months Ended April 30				
	1963	*1962*	*1961*	*1960*	*1959*
Operating revenues:					
Subscriptions earned	$1,080,349	$1,058,565	$1,036,243	$1,026,410	$1,004,694
Newsstand sales	249,716	240,350	194,564	202,659	204,024
Advertising sales	1,024,067	856,387	932,404	745,356	587,735
Total	$2,354,132	$2,155,302	$2,163,211	$1,974,425	$1,796,453
Operating expenses:					
Paper and paper handling	$ 367,501	$ 362,804	$ 358,997	$ 307,406	$ 282,685
Printing	348,887	331,360	302,121	257,486	225,837
Mailing	158,497	151,035	138,435	120,077	102,222
Subscription promotion	437,754	408,154	405,149	351,155	326,516
Subscription fulfillment	117,580	117,615	113,046	112,704	113,292
Manuscripts	136,662	131,226	106,825	102,376	101,595
Other editorial costs	169,985	157,963	168,414	146,608	137,147
Newsstand promotion	29,211	31,941	35,086	29,081	21,863
Advertising promotion	367,632	329,927	341,767	306,847	243,650
General and administration	128,906	136,895	122,036	116,263	115,577
Total	$2,262,615	$2,158,920	$2,091,876	$1,850,003	$1,670,384
Operating profit before taxes	$ 91,517	$ (3,618)	$ 71,335	$ 124,422	$ 126,069

income statements for The Atlantic Monthly Company for the five years, 1959 to 1963.

Excerpts from the balance sheet of The Atlantic Monthly Company are presented in Exhibit 3. The major liability shown on Exhibit 3 was for unearned magazine subscriptions. Subscriptions were sold at a variety of prices; the regular prices were 12 issues for $8.50, 24 issues for $16.00, and 36 issues for $23.00. In addition, trial subscriptions were sold on special offers, such as 8 issues for $2.84 or 12 issues for $4.50. The subscription price was collected or billed at the time the subscription was entered, but recognition of the revenue from the subscription was spread pro rata over the number of

Exhibit 3

CONDENSED BALANCE SHEET
April 30, 1963

ASSETS		
Current Assets:		
Cash and investments*		$ 251,416
Accounts receivable		
Advertisers	$108,715	
Subscribers	51,020	
Other	10,832	
Reserve for uncollected accounts	(3,000)	167,567
Inventories		
Paper	$102,513	
Manuscripts	39,647	
Other	13,991	156,151
Advances to authors		18,186
Prepaid expenses		21,981
Total Current Assets		$ 615,301
Fixed Assets:		
Office equipment and leasehold improvements (net)		60,839
Sundry assets		32,754
Intangible Assets:		
Deferred circulation costs		391,313
Total Assets		$1,100,207
LIABILITIES AND CAPITAL		
Current Liabilities:		
Accounts payable		$ 110,624
Accrued federal income tax		87,000
Other accruals		39,939
Total Current Liabilities		$ 237,563
Deferred Credits to Future Operations:		
Unearned magazine subscriptions	$784,916	
Deferred federal income tax	77,727	862,643
Capital stock and retained earnings*		1
Total Liabilities and Capital		$1,100,207

* Certain asset and liability accounts not pertaining to magazine operations have been eliminated, and the balances of the cash and investments and capital stock and retained earnings accounts have been modified in order to avoid the disclosure of confidential information.

issues to be delivered. The subscription liability account thus represented the revenue to be recognized in the future based upon (1) the number of copies to be delivered in the future and (2) the revenue per copy on those copies. As a practical matter, calculation of the liability was made at the end of each fiscal year. The new "revenue per copy" rate was a weighted average of (1) the unit revenue of the beginning "inventory" of the subscription liability account plus (2) the unit revenue for new subscriptions sold during the year. The subscription revenue recognized during the year was equal to the number of copies sold times the revenue per copy. In effect, therefore, the averaging procedure used in accounting for subscription revenue smoothed out the impact of changes in subscription prices and changes in the mix (trials vs. long renewals) of subscriptions sold.

In a similar manner, the expenses incurred in selling subscriptions were deferred at the time the subscription was sold and charged against income as the subscription was delivered. These deferred circulation costs amounted to $391,313 on April 30, 1963. For purposes of computing federal income taxes, however, magazine publishers had been permitted, since 1957, to deduct circulation promotion expenses in the year in which the expenses were incurred, and the *Atlantic* followed this procedure in computing its tax liability. As a result, the *Atlantic*'s balance sheet also contained a figure for deferred federal income tax. This liability account arose because the company's accountants had provided for estimated income tax expense based on the profit as reported to stockholders each year; the actual income tax liability had been less than this estimate because taxable profits were reduced by the full write-off of circulation promotion costs. The difference between taxable profits and profits reported to stockholders during the years 1957–63 amounted to about $150,000, the amount by which deferred circulation costs had increased during the period. When the tax law was changed in 1957, deferred circulation costs amounted by about $240,000. These costs were written off for tax purposes, and the resulting tax refund of approximately $120,000 was credited directly to retained earnings, because "it was the opinion of the management that the level of annual expenditures for subscription procurement achieved by 1957 constituted a plateau from which the company could not conceivably retreat."[2]

THE PRICE INCREASE IN 1962

According to Mr. Snyder, the *Atlantic* had raised its newsstand and subsubscription prices in 1962 because

> . . . our profit margin became too thin. Profits, which were satisfactory in 1959 and 1960, dropped significantly in 1961 and continued to drop in 1962. The reasons for the decline were complex; a combination of increases in our

[2] 1960 Annual Report of The Atlantic Monthly Company.

production costs and some decline in the editorial appeal of our product. Then, in January 1962, the House of Representatives passed a bill drastically raising postal rates on second-class and third-class mailings. We didn't wait for the bill to be acted on by the Senate; we raised our prices effective with the March 1962 issue. Fortunately, the Senate scaled down the postal rate increases, but we needed the higher price anyway.

Exhibits 4, 5, and 6 present detailed statistical data for The Atlantic Monthly Company for the years 1959 to 1963. Mr. Snyder's comments about these data and some of the developments reflected by these data are quoted below.

Number of Pages. We didn't feel that we could raise our prices unless we simultaneously offered a bigger and better magazine. The result was our *Atlantic* "Extra," a regular monthly supplement which explores an important topic in some depth. In the old days, our "saddle" (the main block of editorial material, which contained no advertising) was usually 44 pages per issue, with the exception of three "Supplement" issues that might contain an 88-page saddle. Now our policy is to have 12- or 16-page "Extras" in nine issues and a 32- or 48-page "Supplement" in the other three, in addition to our 44 pages of regular text. The net effect has been to increase the quantity of saddle text annually by about 100 pages or so.

During the last few years we have also seen a steady increase in the number of pages of editorial material printed as regular features by our "departments." Our readership surveys show that our *Atlantic* "Reports" on political developments around the world are important to a large percentage of our subscribers, and we've also increased the space devoted to "Accent on Living" and "Pleasures and Places." The department text is interspersed through the advertising sections that precede and follow the saddle and, to some extent at least, the increase in department text was necessary in order to space out the increased number of advertising pages we've been running. But department text is not "filler" in any sense of the word; it must make our total editorial package more attractive or we won't print it. In other words, more advertising gives us an opportunity to run more pages of department text, and we try to use the opportunity to make the *Atlantic* an even better magazine.

Paper and Printing Costs. Contrary to the practices of most magazines, we keep a careful breakdown of our costs as between text pages and advertising pages. We find that advertising pages are considerably more expensive to manufacture because the use of color requires a heavier paper as well as higher printing costs. In general, the costs for paper and printing have been creeping up for several years, although the trend took a breather in 1963. We began using a slightly lighter, and therefore, less expensive paper stock in the fall of 1961 in an attempt to hold our costs down. And, of course, the increase in printing costs has been mitigated to some extent as we have been able to spread our fixed costs for plates and set-up over an increasing number of copies printed.

Mailing and Distribution Costs. In a similar fashion, we separate the costs of distribution as between text pages and advertising pages. For copies mailed to subscribers this breakdown reflects the differences in postal rates: editorial

Exhibit 4. MANUFACTURING AND DISTRIBUTION COSTS, 1959–63

		Lines Used in Computations	*12 Months Ended April 30* 1963	1962	1961	1960	1959
1	*Number of pages printed during year:*						
2	Saddle text		834	782	729	685	740
3	Department text		336	330	306	300	262
4	Paid advertising		584	498	567	507	429
5	Other advertising		32	31	24	46	31
6	Total		1,786	1,641	1,626	1,538	1,462
7							
8	*Number of copies printed per issue*	23 + 29	327,905	329,653	323,483	313,675	310,705
9							
10	*Paper cost for the 12 months:*						
11	Text pages		$230,026	$233,580	$216,634	$189,100	$187,235
12	Cost per M pages	11 ÷ [(2+3) × 8]	.600	.637	.647	.612	.601
13	Advertising pages		137,475	129,224	142,363	118,306	95,450
14	Cost per M pages	13 ÷ [(4+5) × 8]	.681	.741	.745	.682	.668
15							
16	*Printing cost for the 12 months:*						
17	Text pages		$180,276	$174,469	$152,699	$138,953	$135,639
18	Cost per M impressions	17 ÷ [(2+3) × 8]	.470	.476	.456	.450	.436
19	Advertising pages		168,611	156,891	149,422	118,533	90,198
20	Cost per M impressions	19 ÷ [(4+5) × 8]	.835	.900	.782	.683	.631
21							
22	*Mailing subscriber copies:*						
23	No. of copies mailed (12-mo. average)		235,707	244,414	244,588	233,929	229,385
24	Cost of mailing text pages		$ 57,656	$ 57,110	$ 47,892	$ 43,248	$ 38,318
25	Cost per subscription year	24 ÷ 23	.245	.234	.196	.185	.167
26	Cost per M text pages	25 ÷ (2+3)	.209	.210	.189	.188	.167
27							
28	*Newsstand distribution costs:*						
29	No. of copies distributed (12-mo. average)		92,198	85,239	78,895	79,746	81,320
30	Cost of shipping text pages		$ 25,990	$ 23,123	$ 19,296	$ 18,239	$ 16,171
31	Cost per 12 copies	30 ÷ 29	.282	.271	.245	.229	.199
32	Cost per M text pages	31 ÷ (2+3)	.241	.244	.237	.232	.199
33							
34	*Advertising distribution costs:*						
35	Cost of mailing and shipping advertising pages		$ 74,851	$ 70,802	$ 71,247	$ 58,590	$ 47,733
36	Cost per M pages	35 ÷ [(4+5) × 8]	.371	.406	.372	[illegible]	[illegible]

Exhibit 5

EDITORIAL AND ADVERTISING STATISTICS

1959–63

		Lines Used in Computations	12 Months Ended April 30				
			1963	*1962*	*1961*	*1960*	*1959*
1	*Number of pages printed during year:*						
2	Saddle text		834	782	729	685	740
3	Department text		336	330	306	300	262
4	Paid advertising		584	498	567	507	429
5	Other advertising		32	31	24	46	31
6	Total		1,786	1,641	1,626	1,538	1,462
7							
8	*Editorial costs for 12 months:*						
9	Cost of manuscripts		$ 136,662	$131,226	$106,825	$102,376	$101,595
10	Cost/page of saddle text	9 ÷ 2	164	168	147	149	137
11	Cost/page of total text	9 ÷ (2+3)	117	118	103	104	101
12	Salaries and overhead costs		169,985	157,693	168,414	146,608	137,147
13	Total editorial costs	9 + 12	306,647	288,919	275,239	248,984	238,742
14	Cost/page of text	13 ÷ (2+3)	262	260	266	253	238
15							
16	*Advertising revenue and expense:*						
17	Total advertising revenue		$1,024,067	$856,387	$932,404	$745,356	$587,735
18	Average revenue/page	17 ÷ 4	1,754	1,720	1,644	1,470	1,370
19	Average paid circulation/issue		271,471	277,824	271,924	265,420	261,002
20	Average revenue/page/M paid	18 ÷ 19	$ 6.46	$ 6.19	$ 6.05	$ 5.54	$ 5.25
21	Commissions to *Harper's–Atlantic*		320,054	284,841	296,528	274,740	227,182
22	Cost/page of advertising sold	21 ÷ 4	548	572	523	542	530
23	Percent of advertising revenue	21 ÷ 17	31.3%	33.3%	31.8%	36.9%	38.7%
24	Other promotion costs						
25	Cash discounts (2%)		$ 19,668	$ 16,579	$ 18,749	$ 14,106	$ 11,269
26	Salaries and overhead		27,910	28,507	26,490	18,001	5,199
27	Total promotion costs	21 + 25 + 26	367,632	329,927	341,767	306,847	243,650
28	Cost/page of advertising sold	27 ÷ 4	630	663	603	605	568
29	Percent of advertising revenue	27 ÷ 17	35.9%	38.5%	36.7%	41.2%	41.5%

Exhibit 6. CIRCULATION STATISTICS, 1959–63

		Lines Used in Computations	12 Months Ended April 30: 1963	1962	1961	1960	1959
1	*Newsstand circulation:*						
2	Cover price at year end		$ .75	$ .75	$ .60*	$ .60*	$ .60*
3	Distribution/issue (12-mo. average)		92,198	85,239	78,895	79,746	81,320
4	Sales/issue		52,230	52,893	46,557	45,438	47,390
5	Net revenue during year†		$ 249,716	$ 240,350	$ 194,564	$ 202,659	$ 204,024
6	Average revenue/12 copies sold	5 ÷ 4	4.78	4.54	4.18	4.46	4.31
7							
8	*Subscription circulation:*						
9	One year regular rate at year end		$ 8.50	$ 8.50	$ 7.50	$ 7.50	$ 7.50
10	Paid circulation/issue (12-mo. average)		219,241	224,931	225,367	219,982	213,612
11	Subscription revenue recognized during year		$1,080,349	$1,058,565	$1,036,243	$1,026,410	$1,004,694
12	Average revenue/subscription year	11 ÷ 10	4.93	4.71	4.60	4.67	4.70
13							
14	*Combined circulation:*						
15	Total circulation revenue	5 + 11	$1,330,065	$1,298,915	$1,230,807	$1,229,069	$1,208,718
16	Paid circulation/issue (12-mo. average)	4 + 10	271,471	277,824	271,924	265,420	261,002
17	Average revenue/12 copies sold	15 ÷ 16	$ 4.90	$ 4.68	$ 4.53	$ 4.63	$ 4.63
18							
19	*Subscription promotion costs:*						
20	Promotion costs written off		$ 437,754	$ 408,154	$ 405,149	$ 351,155	$ 326,516
21	Costs/subscription year (paid)	20 ÷ 10	2.00	1.81	1.80	1.60	1.53
22							
23	*Subscription fulfillment costs:*						
24	Total fulfillment costs		$ 117,580	$ 117,615	$ 113,046	$ 112,704	$ 113,292
25	Costs/subscription year (paid)	24 ÷ 10	.54	.52	.50	.51	.53
26							
27	*Newsstand promotion activities:*						
28	Total promotion costs		$ 29,211	$ 31,941	$ 35,086	$ 29,081	$ 21,863
29	Promotion costs/12 copies sold	28 ÷ 4	.56	.60	.75	.64	.46
30							
31	*Net circulation revenue:*						
32	Newsstand net revenue	5 − 28	$ 220,505	$ 208,409	$ 159,478	$ 173,578	$ 182,161
33	Net/12 copies sold	32 ÷ 4	4.22	3.94	3.43	3.82	3.84
34	Subscription net revenue	11 − (24 + 20)	525,015	532,796	518,048	562,551	564,886
35	Net/subscription year (paid)	34 ÷ 10	2.39	2.38	2.30	2.56	2.64

* One issue during the year carried a cover price of $1.00.

material may be mailed anywhere in the country for 2½ cents per pound; advertising material is figured on a postal zone basis and ranges from 5 cents per pound for a Boston address to 14 cents per pound for the West Coast. The shipping costs on newsstand copies are a straight charge based on weight without regard to the type of material, so we merely prorate those costs between edit and advertising.

Editorial Costs. Although editorial costs are only a fraction of our costs for manufacturing and distribution, they are our most important product cost. The *Atlantic* is an editor's magazine, by which I mean that it is editorial judgment which really determines the success of the magazine. Without attractive material we would have neither readers nor the advertisers that pursue them. Over the years, I've worked closely with Ted Weeks, continually trying to assess the effectiveness of our editorial policies in attracting and holding readers. The job is a lot tougher than just trying to figure out what the readers want; a good editor is always a step or two ahead of his audience, giving them what they want before they even know they want it.

I'm not really concerned that our editorial costs have risen steadily over the last several years. The important thing is that, month after month, we're publishing an increasingly better magazine.

Advertising Revenue. Perhaps the most dramatic change in our business in the last few years is the growing recognition by advertisers of the efficiency with which a small magazine such as the *Atlantic* reaches an important and influential group of readers. We really don't compete with television and the mass magazines for the advertiser's dollar; rather, we compete with other media for our reader's leisure time. It's because we've won that battle that the advertisers are turning to our pages as a way of communicating with our selective, thoughtful subscribers.

Here's a summary of our advertising rates during the last several years:

Rate card	#32	#31	#30	#29	#28
Effective date	Sept. 1963	July 1960	Jan. 1959	May 1958	Jan. 1954
Guaranteed paid circulation	262,500	255,000	240,000	215,000	200,000
Cost of one insertion:					
Black and white page	$2,275	$2,100	$1,950	$1,750	$1,500
Four color page	3,525	3,250	2,925	2,650	2,200
Cost per thousand circulation for black and white page	$8.67	$8.24	$8.13	$8.14	$7.50

Actually, our rates involve a complex series of discounts based on the size and frequency of the insertion, and we have a special rate card for book publishers. On card #31, for example, the one-time rate for a black and white page was $2,100 for a general advertiser, but only $1,400 for a book publisher. These rates dropped to $1,890 and $1,260 if the advertiser made 12 insertions in any 12-month period. From these gross rates, the advertising agency deducts a 15% commission, and the revenue shown in our books is the 85% that they remit to us. The increase in revenue in the last few years is primarily due to (1) selling more pages of advertising, and (2) realizing more revenue per page as a result of more color ads and selling a higher percentage of our space at the general rate rather than the book publisher's rate. We raised our guarantee again, effective in September 1963, to 262,500. Based on that increase, and the fact that advertisers are increasingly aware of the selectivity of our audience, our new rate card shows an average page-rate increase of about eight per cent.

Advertising Promotion Expenses. We discovered an interesting thing in a major readership survey done back in the early 1950's: very few people read both *Harper's* and the *Atlantic* in any one month. Both magazines are edited for essentially the same audience, and there's a lot of switching back and forth by these readers, but very little direct overlap at any one point of time. The upshot of this fact was that we got together with *Harper's* to form the Harper-Atlantic Sales Company to sell advertising in both magazines. Up to that time we'd each had our own sales force, with all the duplication of effort that involved. Now we each own 50% of the sales company, and it's run on essentially a break-even basis.

This new sales approach has worked out exceedingly well. It's both more efficient in terms of calling on advertisers, as well as giving us a bigger package to sell. We find that an increasing number of advertisers are running the same insertion in both magazines the same month, and we offer a special 10% discount on the combined package. In terms of costs, we've really benefited from the economies of scale during the last few years. Each magazine pays a commission to the sales company based on the net revenue produced. The commission rates are on a declining scale based on the volume of net revenue billed by each magazine. Currently, the rates begin at 40% and drop to a low of 17% on billings in excess of $1,000,000 per year. We crossed that magic line for the first time in 1963.

Newsstand Circulation. Our newsstand distribution is handled by Curtis Circulation Company, the same firm that distributes *Saturday Evening Post*, *Look*, *The New Yorker*, and many other magazines. Newsstand sales are important to the *Atlantic*; they're an important segment of our total circulation, and the net revenue from newsstand sales is substantially higher than the net revenue from subscriptions.

Our volume on the newsstand has held up well in the face of the price increase, in part because we've increased the number of copies we're distributing. We used to distribute about 80,000 copies of each issue, but the average was over 92,000 in fiscal 1963 and is currently running higher than that. These extra copies have increased our exposure in terms of the number of newsstands where we're offered. Of course, when you put two copies on a marginal newsstand and only sell one, the efficiency of your total newsstand distribution drops. But single copy sales are a good way to broaden our readership base. For the same reason, most of our newsstand promotion costs, typically small ads in newspapers and other media, are aimed at college towns where we think our natural market is concentrated.

Subscription Circulation. The trickiest part of this business, without a doubt, is subscription circulation. There's nothing quite as comforting to a publisher as as a nice solid core of dedicated subscribers—and the *Atlantic* has it. A high percentage of our regular subscribers renew year after year. These renewals, which are mostly at regular rates, yield over $7.00 of revenue for 12 copies, and it only costs us about $1.00 for mailing and so forth to sell the renewal. Clearly, this is the most profitable source of circulation we have.

The problem is that since about 30% of our regular subscribers don't renew each year, we have to go out and sell new subscriptions in sizeable quantities. To make the job easier, we offer trial subscriptions at half price, although we worry about making our regular subscribers unhappy when we ask them to pay full price. In 1963 we decided to start going to the considerable expense of "unduplicating" our trial offer mailing lists, just to make sure that a current subscriber wasn't tempted to throw away our renewal notice and enter a new trial at half the price. So, the way it works out, we feel lucky if the revenue from a new trial subscription is enough to cover the costs of selling the trial. The thing that makes it worthwhile is that many trial subscribers are converted to regular subscribers when it comes time to renew.

In addition to subscription promotion costs, we have a considerable expense in "fulfilling" a subscription, a term used in the trade to refer to the cost of keeping the mailing list of subscribers up-to-date, processing changes of address and so forth. Taking everything together, subscription circulation involves a lot of costs in order to build, maintain, and serve that core of subscribers we want. The profitability of this type of circulation really depends on the renewal experience we enjoy both on our trial subscribers and on our regulars. And the renewal rates, of course, are a reflection of how well our readers like our editorial product.

QUESTIONS

1. Using data in the case for fiscal years ended April 30, try to isolate the reasons for the profit increase between 1962 and 1963. Specifically, try to deal with the following items:

   a) The *net* effect on profit of selling more advertising.

   b) The *net* effect on profit of increasing the price of the magazine.

   c) The *net* effect on profit of reducing the total paid circulation from 277,824 to 271,471.

NOTE: Unit costs, ratios, and percentages are presented in Exhibits 4 to 6. Not all these calculations are necessarily relevant, nor are these necessarily the only relevant calculations.

2. Think about how you might go about designing a model of a magazine publishing company. Ideally, such a model, when supplied with the input data for any particular year, would yield an approximation of the profit or loss for that year. What problems do you see in working out such a model? What would be the value, if any, to the management of The Atlantic Monthly Company of having such a model?

Case 4-2

The Atlantic Monthly Company (B)

In February, 1964, Donald B. Snyder, publisher of *The Atlantic Monthly* magazine, was reviewing his plans for circulation promotion during the months ahead. Tentative results of the January, 1964, direct-mail campaign for new trial subscriptions indicated a substantial improvement over previous years, and Mr. Snyder was trying to determine how, if at all, these new data should influence his future actions. Background data about *The Atlantic Monthly*, its editorial policies, and publishing performance for 1959 to 1963 are presented in the A case of this series.

THE SUBSCRIPTION CYCLE

Approximately four-fifths of the *Atlantic*'s paid circulation was sent by mail to subscribers who had contracted to receive a series of several monthly issues. The group of *Atlantic* subscribers was constantly changing, and this cycle is illustrated in Exhibits 1 and 2, Stencil List Reports prepared for Mr. Snyder each month. Exhibit 1 is a comparison of the calendar years 1961 and 1962; Exhibit 2 compares 1962 and 1963. The explanations below are in terms of the 1961 figures, but the same cycle was at work in the subsequent years.

During 1961, the *Atlantic*'s paid circulation delivered by mail averaged 224,136 copies per issue. The stencil list of subscribers had 184,884 names at the beginning of the year, and 187,731 names at the end of the year. In addition to stencil list subscribers, there were two other categories of mail-delivered circulation: (1) classroom copies used in high schools and colleges and (2) subscriptions sold by a contract agent. For Mr. Snyder's purpose of reviewing the operations of the circulation department, these two categories of circulation were excluded from the stencil list because neither category was expected to generate a significant number of renewals. Classroom copies were promoted directly to teachers, but the students changed every year, and renewals (in terms of names on the stencil list) could not be computed meaningfully.

The contract agent promoted subscriptions to the *Atlantic* as one of a group of magazines on which direct-mail customers were offered a substantial discount for entering several simultaneous subscriptions. The renewal rate on these subscriptions had historically been so low that the *Atlantic* made no serious effort to get these subscribers to renew.

The stencil list subscribers were divided into two categories for record-keeping and analytical purposes: (1) the long-term list of subscriptions entered at regular rates (including gift subscriptions offered at a $1.00 a year discount) and (2) the list of trial subscribers. Changes in the long-term list during 1961 occurred as follows. Of the 132,000 names on the list at the start of the year, 5,000 canceled their subscriptions (and received a pro rata refund) before expiration. Of the remaining 127,000 names, 10,000 subscriptions were not scheduled to expire during 1961; the original terms of these subscriptions exceeded one year. Thus, the long-term list on January 1, 1961, contained 117,000 names scheduled to expire during the year. Of these, 71,000 renewed their subscriptions (actually, 62.13 percent of those expiring[1]); the other 46,000 did not renew and were dropped (after a grace period of a month or two) from the subscriber list.

Total deductions from the stencil list in 1961 amounted to 51,000 names. Of these, 43,000 were replaced from two main sources: (1) 25,000 new long-term subscriptions were sold during the year, the bulk by catalog agents engaged in personal selling either door-to-door or by telephone; and (2) 18,000 trial subscribers who had originally responded to the *Atlantic*'s direct-mail promotion were converted to long-term subscribers by renewing their subscriptions at regular rates at the end of the initial trial period.

Exhibit 3 recapitulates the sale of subscriptions in 1961 and 1963. Of the 89,000 renewal subscriptions sold in 1961, 18,000 were first renewals of the trial subscribers who had been converted to regular status, and the other 71,000 were second or subsequent renewals of long-term stencil list subscribers. About 23,000 of these renewals were sold by catalog agents who had sold the original subscription. The *Atlantic* attempted to secure the renewals by mail, but many agents also maintained records of their expires and solicited the renewal. The renewal percentage in Exhibit 1 was computed without regard to whether the renewal was sold by the *Atlantic* directly or by a catalog agent.

---

1 Figures quoted in this and the following three paragraphs are approximations. The actual record-keeping by The Atlantic Monthly Company was done in terms of groups of expires, and the cutoff dates used in cumulating the data for preparing Exhibits 1 and 2 did not coincide exactly with the cutoff dates used in preparing Exhibits 3 and 4.

Exhibit 1

ATLANTIC MONTHLY MAGAZINE

Stencil List Report, 1961–62

12 Months of the ATLANTIC through (December 31)	1961	1962	PLUS OR MINUS
STENCIL LIST - "As the Year Began"			
Long Term List (Regulars & Gifts)	131, 527	123, 218	
Trial Subscribers	53, 357	64, 513	
Total Stencils	184, 884	187, 731	
WHAT HAPPENED TO THE "LONG TERM LIST" DURING THE 12 MONTHS ENDING (December 31)			
Long Terms & Gifts Renewed @	62. 13%	59. 67%	
Trials "Converted to Longs" @	25. 81%	20. 36%	
Long Terms & Gifts "Not Renewing" were	(45, 865)	(40, 417)	
Long Terms & Gifts Canceled were	(5, 036)	(5, 684)	
Total "Longs" Lost	(50, 901)	(46, 101)	
New "Long Terms & Gifts" Sold were	24, 871	24, 244	
Trials "Converted to Longs" were	17, 721	21, 847	
Total "Longs" Added	42, 592	46, 091	
Net Gain or Loss in the "Long Term List" during the 12 months ending (December 31)	(8, 309)	(10)	
STENCIL LIST - "As the Year Ended"			
Long Term List (Regulars & Gifts)	123, 218	123, 208	
Trial Subscribers	64, 513	53, 688	
Total Stencils (as of December 31)	187, 731	176, 896	
NET NEWSSALE (12 Months Ending December 31)			
Total Copies Shipped to Curtis	1, 010, 074	975, 492	
Total Copies Sold	650, 733	593, 571	
% of Sale	64. 4%	60. 85%	
Total Copies Returned	359, 341	381, 921	
AVERAGE A B C DELIVERY (12 Months Ending December 31)			
Mail Delivery - Monthly Average	224, 136	219, 918	
Net Newssale - Monthly Average	54, 228	48, 696	
A B C Average - 12 Months	278, 364	268, 614	

Exhibit 2

ATLANTIC MONTHLY MAGAZINE

Stencil List Report, 1962–63

12 Months of the ATLANTIC through (December 31)	1962	1963	PLUS OR MINUS
STENCIL LIST - "As the Year Began"			
Long Term List (Regulars & Gifts)	123,218	123,208	
Trial Subscribers	64,513	53,688	
Total Stencils	187,731	176,896	
WHAT HAPPENED TO THE "LONG TERM LIST" DURING THE 12 MONTHS ENDING (Dec. 31)			
Long Terms & Gifts Renewed @	59.67%	64.44%	
Trials "Converted to Longs" @	20.36%	25.60%	
Long Terms & Gifts "Not Renewing" were	(40,417)	(39,193)	
Long Terms & Gifts Cancelled were	(5,684)	(5,954)	
Total "Longs" Lost	(46,101)	(45,147)	
New "Long Terms & Gifts" Sold were	24,244	26,211	
Trials "Converted to Longs" were	21,847	18,058	
Total "Longs" Added	46,091	44,269	
Net Gain or Loss in the "Long Term List" during the 12 months ending (Dec. 31)	(10)	(878)	
STENCIL LIST - "As the Year Ended"			
Long Term List (Regulars & Gifts)	123,208	122,330	
Trial Subscribers	53,688	49,236	
Total Stencils (as of Dec. 31)	176,896	171,566	
NET NEWSSALE (12 Months Ending Dec. 31)			
Total Copies Shipped to Curtis	975,492	1,300,727	+325,235
Total Copies Sold	593,571	578,341	-(15,230)
% of Sale	60.85%	44.46%	-(16.39%)
Total Copies Returned	381,921	722,386	+340,465
AVERAGE A B C DELIVERY (12 Months Ending Dec. 31)			
Mail Delivery - Monthly Average	219,918	217,935	-(1983)
Net Newssale - Monthly Average	48,696	48,195	-(501)
A B C Average - 12 Months	268,614	266,130	-(2484)

The percentage of conversions reported in Exhibit 1 was based on the expiration of trial subscriptions that had originally been sold by the *Atlantic*'s direct-mail promotion; the trials sold by the catalog agent were not included in the stencil list accounting. At the beginning of 1961, the *Atlantic* was mailing copies to 53,000 stencil list trial subscribers, all of whose subscriptions were scheduled to expire during the year. In the early months of 1961 (as shown in Exhibit 4), 26,000 new short-term trial subscriptions were sold. Of these 79,000 trials that expired during 1961, 18,000 (25.81 percent) renewed their subscriptions at the regular rates. In addition, 65,000 new trials were sold during 1961 and were scheduled to expire in 1962.

Reviewing the figures on Exhibits 1 and 2, Mr. Snyder said:

> The drop in both renewal percentages in 1962 was very serious, but our 1963 results show that the trend has been more than reversed in our favor. The main value of the renewal percentage figures is as an indication of the continuing editorial appeal of the *Atlantic*. By good promotion, we may be able to sell someone a trial subscription, but after he's read it for several months, his decision to renew or not depends solely on how well he's liked what he's read. Some part of the 1962 decline may have been due to the price increase, but I doubt if it had much effect on our long-term subscribers because we gave them a special offer to renew in advance at the old prices. Really, the 1962 figures are so hard to evaluate that I've quit trying to make any sense out of them.

SUBSCRIPTION PROMOTION COSTS

The costs of selling new subscriptions for the *Atlantic* amounted to over $400,000 a year. An analysis of subscription promotion costs for the calendar years 1961 and 1963 is presented in Exhibit 3. For three reasons, the cost and revenue data here presented do not agree with similar data presented in the A case. First, the A case data were for fiscal years ending April 30, rather than calendar years. Second, in 1963, the *Atlantic* spent approximately $35,000 to screen its rented mailing lists before using them in its solicitation of trial subscriptions. Mr. Snyder called this process "unduplicating" the lists, and explained: "We eliminated the names of our regular subscribers from these lists so that they wouldn't be tempted to enter a new subscription at half price rather than renewing at the regular price. This cost is not included in these figures (Exhibit 3) because I can't figure out whether to allocate it to the cost of new subscriptions or to renewals." Finally, and perhaps the most important reason for the difference in promotion results reported in these two cases, the A case data were taken from the accounting records and reflect the *Atlantic*'s policies for recognizing subscription revenue and expense; the data in Exhibit 3 represent revenues actually collected (or billed) and expenses actually paid (or incurred) during the year.

The subscription promotion expenses given in Exhibit 3 include all expenses directly identifiable with specific subscription promotion campaigns.

	Total	Sources of Subscriptions: Direct Mail and N/S Inserts	Classroom	Catalog Agents	Contract Agents	Miscellaneous
12 Months Ended December 31, 1961						
Renewal subscriptions, number of orders	88,516	65,430		23,086		
Number of subscription years sold	105,937	76,711		29,226		
Total revenue	$599,793	$497,214		$102,579		
Revenue/subscription year	5.66	6.48		3.51		
Promotion costs	64,527	63,484		1,043		
Cost/subscription year	.61	.83		.04		
Net revenue	535,266	433,730		101,536		
Net/subscription year	5.05	5.65		3.47		
New subscriptions, number of orders	180,918	82,161	57,825	17,952	18,416	4,564
Number of subscription years sold	126,331	68,988	22,448	17,980	12,277	4,638
Total revenue	$456,286	$269,567	$86,257	$ 65,724	$ 6,656	$28,082
Revenue/subscription year	3.61	3.91	3.84	3.66	.54	6.05
Promotion costs	290,212	276,624	11,952	807	829	—
Cost/subscription year	2.30	4.01	.53	.04	.07	—
Net revenue	166,074	(7,057)	74,305	64,917	5,827	28,082
Net/subscription year	1.31	(.10)	3.31	3.61	.47	6.05
12 Months Ended December 31, 1963						
Renewal subscriptions, number of orders	89,559	67,110		22,449		
Number of subscription years sold	105,218	76,823		28,395		
Total revenue	$662,232	$543,244		$118,988		
Revenue/subscription year	6.29	7.07		4.19		
Promotion costs	74,069	73,254		815		
Cost/subscription year	.70	.95		.03		
Net revenue	588,163	469,990		118,173		
Net/subscription year	5.59	6.12		4.16		
New subscriptions, number of orders	170,876	61,609	55,626	20,371	27,997	5,273
Number of subscription years sold	117,091	49,957	22,664	20,402	18,665	5,403
Total revenue	$457,039	$224,170	$97,906	$ 88,780	$ 9,478	$36,705
Revenue/subscription year	3.90	4.49	4.32	4.35	.51	6.79
Promotion costs	224,008	205,867	16,400	733	1,008	—
Cost/subscription year	1.91	4.12	.72	.04	.05	—
Net revenue	233,031	18,303	81,506	88,047	8,470	36,705
Net/subscription year	1.99	.37	3.60	4.32	.45	6.79

In addition, for salaries, billing, and so forth, the *Atlantic* incurred overhead expenses of $108,215 in 1961 and $129,490 in 1963.

Reviewing the data in Exhibit 3, Mr. Snyder made the following comments:

There are tremendous differences in the profitability of various sources of subscriptions. Looking at the 1961 figures, for example, we netted $3.31 per 12 copies on classroom business, $3.61 from catalog agents, only 47¢ from our contract agent, and we lost 10¢ on the new trials that we sold by direct mail. These figures don't tell the whole story, though, because the real profit lies in renewal subscriptions. We don't get any renewals to speak of from contract agent business, and the renewals on classroom and catalog agents yield about the same net revenue as new subscriptions from those sources. But the renewals that we get on the trials that we sell are quite a different story. Even though only 20 to 30% of these trials renew, the net revenue per sub-year was $5.65 in 1961 and $6.12 last year. And, of course, once we've converted a trial into a regular subscriber, we know that 60 to 70% of them will continue to renew year after year.

The only way, therefore, to compare our contract agent business with direct mail trials is to take a long-run look at things. We may actually be better off to take an out-of-the-pocket loss on a trial in order to get a series of profitable renewals, than we are to take a nominal cash profit on each subscription sold by the contract agent. In fact, the challenge of circulation management is to continually adjust the mix of circulation sources used in such a way that we're using the most profitable combination at any one point in time.

Our circulation picture improved considerably in 1963 as compared to 1961. The average net revenue on new subs rose from $1.31 to $1.99. This improvement can be traced to three factors: (1) the higher subscription price resulted in more revenue per 12 copies; (2) We increased the use of the contract agent and cut back on the sale of trials by direct mail; and (3) We reduced the number of new subscriptions sold during the year, making up part of this drop by increasing our newsstand sale and part of it by reducing our bonus of paid circulation over the guarantee.

We have found, over the years, that the best time to mount a direct mail campaign is in the fall, when people are faced with the prospect of the long winter nights ahead, and in January. We do our biggest "cold" mailing right after Labor Day, offering a one year subscription at half-price. On the cold mailing in January, we offer eight issues at a cut rate so that those trials also expire in the fall when it's easier to get the first, crucial renewal. Our fall mailing is always more profitable because we get about the same percentage response but collect 50% more revenue from the 12-month trial.

This tabulation (Exhibit 4), summarizes the results of our January mailing for the last several years. Back in 1961, the losses on this source of business became so substantial that we decided to cut back our mailings. The primary advantage of mailing only a million and a quarter pieces, rather than two million, is that we can select only the better mailing lists; the lists that historically have been reasonably successful for us. Cutting back in this way raised our percentage response from 1.27% to 1.64% and cut the cost of getting a sub by nearly a third.

Exhibit 4

COMPARATIVE COSTS AND RESULTS OF COLD MAILINGS

January 1961 through 1964

	Estimated 1964	*1963*	*1962*	*1961*
Number of direct-mail pieces mailed	1,295,000	1,121,323	1,278,614	2,055,121
Trial subscription offered:				
Rate for 8 months	$ 2.84	$ 2.84	$ 2.50	$ 2.50
Number of orders received	32,800	24,115	21,011	26,053
Percentage response	2.53%	2.15%	1.64%	1.27%
Number of subscription years sold	21,866	16,077	14,007	17,369
Cost of direct-mail promotion	$78,000	$71,853	$68,190	$117,525
Per order received	2.38	2.98	3.25	4.51
Per subscription year sold	3.57	4.47	4.87	6.77
Subscription revenue per subscription year	$ 4.26	$ 4.26	$ 3.75	$ 3.75
Net revenue or (loss) per subscription year	$ .69	$ (.21)	$ (1.12)	$ (3.02)

It's harder to compare 1963 to 1962 because the price of our eight-month offer was 34¢ higher. In spite of the price increase, the response to our mailing rose again. Now, we have tentative results of the mailing we made last month, and it's clear that we've scored another major gain. For the first time in several years we show a profit on our January trials, and this is most welcome. This success, of course, raises some questions of its own. In 1962 and 1963, we increased our use of the contract agent by increasing the percentage that we paid for its promoting the *Atlantic*. The agency offers an 8-month, half-price subscription and charges us a commission based on the revenue it collects. In 1961, with a $2.50 offer, we were netting only 32¢, really 47¢ on a sub-year basis, or about 13% of the price paid by the subscriber. We sweetened the agent's commission at the time we raised our subscription prices, so that in 1963, we only netted 34¢ on a $2.84 subscription. Actually, the agency would like to sell a lot more subscriptions for us on the terms of the current arrangement, but we've been limiting the amount of business we'll take from them. In fact, it might be more profitable for us to stop using the agency at all.

Another thing we did beginning in 1963 was to increase our newsstand distribution substantially. We did this to counteract the effect of the increase in cover price, and I'm sure our newsstand sale would have declined in 1963 if we hadn't done it. But overdistribution is costly too, and I think this policy needs to be reconsidered in the light of the January mailing results.

Really, these are just the same questions that I have to deal with all the time. Broadly speaking, the problem is one of circulation management, and I'm just glad that I have a fine editorial package and a strong market demand facing me as I tackle the problem this year.

QUESTIONS

1. On the assumption that Mr. Snyder has the following alternatives to consider for the fall of 1964, which source of paid circulation (within the existing base of guaranteed circulation) would be more profitable for The Atlantic Monthly Company?

   a) Continue the policy of newsstand overdistribution. Assume that of the extra 20,000 copies distributed each month only 6,000 copies will be sold.

   b) Eliminate overdistribution and increase the September cold mailing to yield an extra 6,000 trial subscriptions. Assume that these subscriptions would yield $4.50 of revenue, would renew the first time at 20 percent, and then would continue to renew at 65 percent. In order to secure these new trials, however, the number of mailing lists used would have to be increased, and the total promotion costs for the fall mailing would be higher by $30,000.

2. What procedure do you recommend to Mr. Snyder for dealing with his continuing problem of securing the optimal circulation mix?

3. Do you think it would be profitable for the *Atlantic* to raise its total circulation if that action was coupled with an increase in the circulation guarantee? Assuming that the circulation guarantee was raised from 262,500 to 275,000, the advertising page rate was raised by 5 percent, and new paid circulation of 13,000 was provided, find the best combination of the following courses of action:

   a) Continue the present policy of newsstand overdistribution.

   b) Increase the use of the contract agency.

   c) Sell 6,000 new trial subs on the terms described in 1(*b*), above.

   d) Sell 13,000 new trials as described, except that the increase in the fall promotion budget would be $72,000.

Case 4-3

The Atlantic Monthly Company (C)

On January 25, 1964, Donald B. Snyder, publisher of *The Atlantic Monthly* magazine, submitted a report (see the appendix) to the board of directors of The Atlantic Monthly Company. Background information about the magazine, including a statement of the purpose of Mr. Snyder's January report, is presented in the A case in this series.

QUESTIONS

1. Evaluate the "early warning system" developed by Mr. Snyder. Does his report in Exhibit 2 provide the directors with the data they need to evaluate the performance of the magazine? If you were a director of the company, what additional information would you like to have? Why?
2. What is the value of the cash basis figures in Mr. Snyder's report? Why are these figures different from the accrued basis figures? Which figures are the more useful for what purposes?
3. Do you see any conflict between the accounting procedures used to determine periodic profit and the data needed by management for control (decision-making, evaluation) purposes? How, if at all, can (should?) these conflicts be resolved?

Appendix

Report of Donald B. Snyder to the Directors

January 25, 1964

To the Atlantic Directors:

In recent years I have provided the Directors with two annual reports. One has come along in January to set forth the Company's position on a *Cash Basis* at the end of the twelve calendar months ending December 31. Then, a second report in June, to analyze the Company's *Accrued Basis Operations* for the fiscal year ending April 30.

Herewith my *Cash Basis* report for the calendar year through December 31, 1963. Since this is the last annual Cash Basis report I shall be sending you, I am gratified that the report for 1963 is a good one. Over the past ten calendar years the Company has *more than doubled* its Gross Cash Receipts to an all-time high in 1963 of $2,667,596, as follows:

Calendar	*Gross Cash Income from All Sources*	*Number of ABC Magazine Customers*
1954	$1,240,318	205,582
1955	1,248,191	208,302
1956	1,428,812	211,360
1957	2,015,864	252,078
1958	1,898,750	258,097
1959	2,041,600	264,304
1960	2,149,129	270,809
1961	2,279,351	281,929
1962	2,453,688	273,987
1963	2,667,596	270,942 EST
10-Year Increase	115%	32%

How Have We Used the Above Increments?

To begin with, a considerable part of our gain in cash income from one year to the next has been earmarked to cover the additional cost of producing "increased physical volume." More Advertising income has meant more advertising pages to manufacture; more Subscription and Newsstand income has meant that our print order in 1963 had to be substantially larger than it was in 1954. When a magazine grows you can't avoid paying the printer and papermaker proportionately more. In addition, during the past ten years every magazine (and the ATLANTIC is no exception) has had to *gross substantially more* just to absorb the *inflationary price increases* in the three major items of magazine expense—namely, the cost of paper, printing, and postage—both 2nd Class and 3rd Class.

But, in spite of the inflationary pressures which have beset all forms of publishing enterprise during the past ten years, and after absorbing substantial "cost of living" pay increases, various bonus distributions to key people, and additional salaries for numerous additions to the staff of both the Magazine and the Press, we have managed to retain a sufficient balance out of our ten-year Increase in the Gross to accomplish the following:

1. We have enhanced the ATLANTIC physically—more text pages, a better grade of paper, better printing, better covers, and more illustrations, many in four colors.
2. We have financed a 30% increase in the number of ATLANTIC reader-customers—ABC.
3. We have contributed our share of the capital and commissions required to establish Harper-Atlantic Sales as a successful going concern.
4. And most important of all, we have rebuilt the ATLANTIC's operating capital to a point where it is no longer necessary for us to borrow bank money to finance the dry summer months. On January 1, 1954, the Company faced the new year with only $136,859 in the Working Balance. On January 1, 1964 (ten years later) our Working Balance for the new year we have just entered stood at $503,303.

On the small sheet attached (Exhibit 1) I have detailed the Cash Basis figures for the four calendar years, 1960, 1961, 1962, 1963.

Why Have Accrued Basis Figures?

Good *Cash Basis* figures are conclusive evidence that our policies and practices in the *immediately preceding years* were reasonably correct and have paid off. But unfortunately, *Cash Basis* figures for any given year (say 1963) are a poor criterion or predictor for the *years which lie immediately ahead.* Why is this true? Because *Cash Basis* figures deal in crude totals only! The danger is that *Cash Basis* figures may on occasion conceal subtle shifts in *Unit Cost Relationships* which start as a cloud on the horizon and gradu-

Exhibit 1

CASH BASIS FIGURES BY CALENDAR YEARS

January 1 through December 31, 1960–63

	1960	*1961*	*1962*	*1963*
Cash received from subscriptions	$1,036,636	$1,013,820	$1,154,298	$1,042,817
" " " advertising	868,236	849,859	916,302	1,149,724
" " " net newssale	189,150	228,104	220,396	274,224
" " " Reader's Digest	10,000	26,630	12,500	12,500
" " " interest	11,329	4,783	3,495	7,232
" " " non-magazine operations (net)	33,778	156,155	146,697	181,099
Total Cash Received	$2,149,129	$2,279,351	$2,453,688	$2,667,596

A.M.C. working balance as of December 31	*1960*	*1961*	*1962*	*1963*
1. Cash and investment (less reserves for taxes)	$ 260,639	$ 269,526	$ 296,942	$ 308,617
2. Paper inventory (at cost)	94,915	114,767	105,848	119,833
3. Circulation inventory and prepaid expense	89,030	67,559	89,491	74,853
Total "Working Balance" December 31	$ 444,584	$ 451,852	$ 492,281	$ 503,303

ally develop into a full-blown twister; witness the S.E.P.! Every magazine publisher needs "an early warning system." The ATLANTIC's radar screen is the *Accrued Basis Analysis of Unit Costs and Unit Receipts,* which we now maintain as a running 12-month calculation. These are the figures on which my second report to the Directors is based—the report you will be receiving in late June of this year. Query: Can we afford to wait that long?

It now appears that certain adverse trends which cropped up in the Accrued Basis Analysis at the end of 1961, and again at the end of Fiscal '63 (i.e., last June) are still running against us. I have, therefore, felt I should provide you with an interim *Accrued Basis Analysis,* computed for the 12 issues through December 1963, and comparable figures for the 12 issues at the *old price level* through December 1961. These are the figures on the large sheet attached, Exhibit 2.

Here are my Comments on Subscription Sales!

1. Every magazine in good times or bad must be able to recruit *new readers* via trial subscriptions or newsstand sales at unit costs which are not prohibitively high.

2. By 1961 our unit cost for subscriber procurement had reached the all-time high of $1.96 per 12 copies sold for subscription delivery. (See Column for 1961.)

3. Since the cash we received from subscribers in 1961 was at the rate of $4.56 per 12 copies sold and would not support a procurement cost of $1.96, we elected to increase our masthead price during the spring and summer of 1962.

4. Figures for Calendar 1962 are a mishmash; partly at the old rates, partly at the new rates. They are, therefore, invalid for purposes of comparative analysis, and I have omitted them.

5. However, by comparing the 12 issues through December 1963 (column 2) with the 12 issues through December 1961 (column 1) we can now begin to see how we are coming out. The "cost to procure readers" has cointinued to rise; it is now $2.14 per 12 copies sold.

6. *In mitigation* we should remember that 1963 was the first year in which we "unduped" our circular mailings at an average unit cost of about 19¢ per 12 copies sold.

7. *Moreover,* in 1963, *what we gained in receipts* from the sale of 12 subscription copies, or 41¢, *more than offset the increases in what we spent,* including unduplication and procurement expense. On balance, we bettered our performance by 12¢ per subscription year in 1963, or about $24,000 better off in the aggregate.

8. *But in spite* of our somewhat improved subscription balance in 1963, two facts stand out: (1) we spent more than ever, unitwise, in 1963 to find and hold subscribers, and (2) the number of subscribers in 1963 was 3% less than the number of subscribers in 1961.

Comments on Newsstand Sales

9. What happened to Newsstand Sales in 1963 must be analyzed in the light of what we set out to do; namely to *increase single-copy sales* and thereby *reduce*

Exhibit 2

INCOME AND EXPENSE

12 Months Ending December 1961, 1963

		1961		1963		PLUS OR MINUS
3 INCOME ACCOUNTS		12 Months Dollars Total	Per 12 Copies Sold	12 Months Dollars Total	Per 12 Copies Sold	Per 12 Copies Sold
SUBSCRIBER INCOME (12 Months ending November 30)		$1,020,436	$4.56	$1,089,340	$4.97	+ 41¢
Production of Subscriber Edition	(Paper:	$ 161,718	$ .72	$ 156,284	$ .71	
	(Printing:	117,879	.525	121,438	.56	
	(Mailing:	51,143	.23	57,461	.26	
Cost of Subscription Procurement		437,612	1.952	468,599	2.14	+ 18¢
Cost of Subscription Fulfillment		111,566	.50	121,409	.55	
	Total Spent	$ 879,918	$3.93	$ 925,191	$4.22	
BALANCE LEFT FROM SUBSCRIBER INCOME		$ 140,518	$ .63	$ 164,149	$ .75	+ 12¢
	Pages of Text Published	1043.3		1166.5		
NEWSSTAND INCOME (12 Months ending November 30)		$ 235,355	$4.30	$ 227,937	$4.75	+ 45¢
Production of Newsstand Edition	(Paper:	$ 59,900	$1.10	$ 71,648	$1.49	
	(Printing:	43,875	.80	55,966	1.17	
	(Shipping:	21,809	.40	29,196	.61	
Cost of Newsstand Sales		35,764	.65	38,092	.79	
	Total Spent	$ 161,348	$2.95	$ 194,902	$4.06	
BALANCE LEFT FROM NEWSSTAND INCOME		$ 74,007	$1.35	$ 33,035	$ .69	-(66¢)
ADVERTISING INCOME (12 Months ending November 30)		$ 861,717	$3.10	$1,184,633	$4.45	+$1.35
Cost of Advertising Sales		$ 326,799	$1.17	$ 416,735	$1.57	
Cost of Advertising Manufacture		285,695	1.03	349,556	1.31	
Cost of Advertising Mailing & Shipping		71,340	.26	88,394	.33	
	Total Spent	$ 683,834	$2.46	$ 854,685	$3.21	
BALANCE LEFT FROM ADVERTISING SALES		$ 177,883	$ .64	$ 329,948	$1.24	+ 60¢
	% Left	20.64%		27.9%		
	Pages of Paid Adv.	505.9		651.1		
BALANCE LEFT - ALL 3 INCOME ACCOUNTS		$ 392,408	$1.41	$ 527,132	$1.97	+ 56¢
Spent to Provide Text Content		$ 279,254	$1.00	$ 310,592	$1.16	+ 16¢
Undivided Payroll & Overhead		110,899	.39	105,695	.40	+ 1¢
A. M. MAGAZINE - Before Taxes, Pensions & Dividends		$ 2,255	$ .02	$ 110,845	$ .41	+ 39¢

Circulation Figures	1961	1963
Average Paid Stencil Delivery	223,735	218,000 EST
Average Net Newssale	54,783	48,000 EST
Average News Copies Returned	(29,414)	(59,000) EST

the pressure to sell Trial Subscriptions, on which we incur an initial cash loss.

10. With this in mind, we increased our average newsstand distribution from 85,000 copies per month in 1961 to an average of 107,000 copies per month in 1963.

11. *Result:* We averaged to sell 6,700 fewer copies per month in 1963 than we sold in 1961, although there were 22,000 more copies per month on display in 1963, backed up by substantial promotion in college and university towns, which we did not have in 1961.

12. *Query:* How many copies would we have sold on the average per month in 1963 had we not *over-distributed* and provided extra Newsstand promotion?

13. *My guess:* Less than 45,000 copies!

Comments on Advertising Sales

14. In 1961, the Net Profit we derived from the sale to advertisers of *one ABC unit* (either from subscribers or from single-copy sales) was at the rate of 64¢ per 12 consecutive issues of the magazine.

15. In 1963, the comparable Net Profit per ABC unit of 12 consecutive paid copies delivered was $1.24—a net gain of 60¢ in our profit per reader per year from Advertising Sales.

16. Total Net Profit from Advertising Sales in 1963 was at an all-time high of $329,948. This is $152,065 more than the comparable total for 1961, or almost twice as much as in 1961.

17. *Hence*, it is correct to state that the gratifying improvement in the Magazine's Net Profit before Taxes, Pensions and Dividends in 1963 (see the bottom line) was due entirely to the big jump in net profits from Advertising Sales.

18. *Even so*, the fact remains that "reader dollars" provided *more than 50%* of the wherewithal to operate the ATLANTIC in 1963.

In 1963

Gross Reader Dollars (Subs. & News)	$1,317,277	= 52.7%
Gross Advertiser Dollars	1,184,633	= 47.3%
Total Magazine Gross	$2,501,910	= 100%

19. *Moreover*, without "readers" there can be no "advertising profit"!

20. How to "attract and hold" ATLANTIC readers is now, and always has been, the crux of our problem.

D.B.S.

Case 4-4

National Tractor and Equipment Company

National Tractor and Equipment Company, Inc., was a manufacturer of a number of products, including a wide line of farm tractors. Tractors were divided into several fairly well-defined types, according to their capacity, and National manufactured tractors of each type. This case deals with one of these types, here referred to as type X.

Fixed costs represented a relatively large share of total costs at National, and, therefore, achieving a strong sales position was an important means of reducing unit costs and improving profits. Consequently, a major objective of the company was to be the sales leader in each of the several types. If National was not the leader during a particular year, its goal was to surpass whoever was the leader. If National was the leader, its goal was to maintain the size of its lead.

The company had experienced a rather erratic showing in sales of type X tractors over the previous several years. Though National had been the sales leader in four of the previous six years (1955–60), its lead in 1958 and 1959 had been slim, and in 1960 its chief competitor took over first place. Meanwhile, profits of this division of its business had fluctuated widely. Accordingly, early in 1961 the controller's department made a sales analysis of the type X tractor division.

William Lawrence, who was given the job of making the analysis, decided to use the approach the controller had used for other analyses. Usually, these analyses started with a comparison of actual costs or actual profit with some bench mark, such as the budget or the figures for some prior year when performance was satisfactory. The analyst then sought to isolate and quantify the various causes of the difference between actual and the standard applied in that particular case.

In the case of tractors, since management's objective was to surpass the sales leader, unit sales of the leading competitor—here called competitor A—seemed to be the most logical standard. Competitor A had sold 13,449 type X tractors in 1960, compared with 10,356 for National—a deficiency of 3,093. (A copy of Mr. Lawrence's analysis as presented to management appears as an appendix to this case.)

Mr. Lawrence began his analysis by looking at the profits and return on assets of the type X tractor division. Both had improved significantly over the 1958 and 1959 levels. However, in 1960 National dropped from the first-place sales position it had held during 1958 and 1959, and this was of grave concern to management. Furthermore, its market share had decreased from 25.0 percent to 23.5 percent. Both of its major competitors had increased their market shares, and competitor A had outsold National for the first time in five years.

Mr. Lawrence next prepared the sales portion of the table that appears as Exhibit 1 in the appendix. This table compares sales of type X tractors by National and competitor A for the preceding three years, 1958–60. The major task, then—and this was the crux of the analysis—was to identify and analyze those factors that accounted for the volume difference in each of the three years.

After he had completed this initial analysis, Mr. Lawrence, representing the controller's department, met with representatives of the sales department and the product development department. Together, they discussed the various factors that might have accounted for the volume differences in each of the three years under review. Using their collective judgments and estimates, they broke down the volume difference into as many specific factors as they could agree on. All the remaining factors, they decided, must have accounted for the remaining difference, although they could not agree on the proportions; so they gave the total under other factors.

The first matter that Mr. Lawrence called to the attention of this group was that a major fire in one of competitor A's plants in the latter part of 1959 had severely limited production. He had compiled monthly production estimates for competitor A for 1959 and the two prior years. He then had gathered estimates of industry sales during those years and developed certain relationships that seemed to him to hold among estimated monthly sales, actual monthly sales, and actual monthly production for 1957 and 1958 by competitor A. When he applied these relationships to 1959, it seemed evident to him that competitor A had produced significantly fewer type X tractors than it normally would have during the months when its plant was shut down.

Mr. Lawrence then had looked at sales patterns during 1957 and 1958, so that he could make an estimate of how much this lost production had resulted in a shifting of demand from 1959 to 1960; he tried to estimate how many competitor A customers for type X tractors delayed purchase of a new type X tractor from 1959 to 1960 because of the fire. In addition to research with the data available in his office, Mr. Lawrence traveled around the country and talked to distributors and dealers. He became convinced that a large number of potential purchasers of tractors actually had deferred their purchases of new type X tractors. Some of competitor A's dealers had had no type X tractors in stock in the latter part of 1959 because of the fire, and others had had only a limited supply.

On the basis of Mr. Lawrence's analysis and the collective judgments of the other members, the group agreed that the fire caused a shift of 1,500 of competitor A's tractor sales from 1959 to 1960. This shift was recorded as a minus factor in 1960 and a plus factor in 1959.

Sales of type X tractors to government agencies was another factor studied by this group. Since government sales figures were published, the group ascertained that National outsold competitor A by 138 units. Government sales depended almost entirely on price; therefore, this was the type of business a tractor manufacturer could "buy," depending on how badly he wanted it.

Mr. Lawrence had done a considerable amount of research into the advantage that competitor A enjoyed because of its larger owner body.[1] National's owner body had always been smaller than competitor A's, but National had made sizable gains since 1952. There was a tendency for the owner of a tractor to buy the same make when he purchased a new tractor; thus, competitor A enjoyed an advantage. Mr. Lawrence wanted to know *how much* this advantage was. An annual survey made by the trade association of the industry indicated the behavior of a representative sample of buyers of new type X tractors. This survey indicated that owners of competitor A's tractors were more loyal than were National tractor owners (see page 160). Using these survey results, Mr. Lawrence was able to calculate the advantage to competitor A of its larger owner body. Although only the calculations for 1960 are shown, he applied the same methodology to 1958 and 1959. Members of the group were impressed with this analysis and agreed to accept Mr. Lawrence's figures—a net advantage of 700 units for competitor A in 1960.

The next factor he analyzed was product differences. National did not have so varied a product line as did competitor A. Because of this, National dealers were at a competitive disadvantage for certain models of type X tractors. The group was able to agree on the approximate extent of this disadvantage.

The last main heading for variances listed in Exhibit 1 was other factors, which the group thought accounted for the remaining difference between National's sales and competitor A's sales. Mr. Lawrence had prepared a thorough analysis of these factors, too. For example, he had heard that competitor A built a more efficient and more durable type X tractor. He tried

[1] Owner body is the number of tractors in the hand of owners.

to quantify the effect of these variables by use of the data shown on pages 159 and 161. He also requisitioned five National type X tractors and five competitor A type X tractors, and arranged to have these tractors tested at National's experimental farm to determine their operating characteristics, including power, performance, durability, reliability, and economy. Mr. Lawrence himself actually drove some of these tractors. He also inspected each tractor and its performance at the end of the testing period.

The group could not agree, however, on the quantitative effect on sales volume of these factors or of the remaining factors listed under other. Therefore, they were represented by one figure. The total variance of all the factors affecting market penetration, of course, equaled the difference in sales between National and competitor A.

QUESTIONS

1. Are analyses of this type within the proper scope of a controller's function?
2. Can you suggest a better way of making the analysis?
3. What action, if any, should be taken on the basis of this study?

Appendix

National Tractor and Equipment Company

An Analysis of Type X Tractors

Prepared by the Controller's Department

PROFITS, ASSETS, AND AFTER-TAX RETURNS

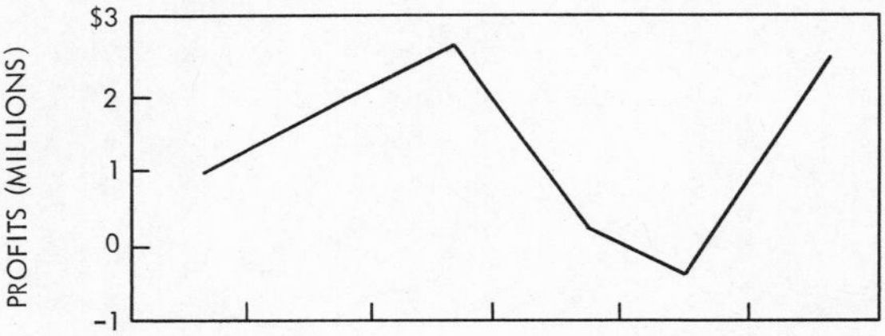

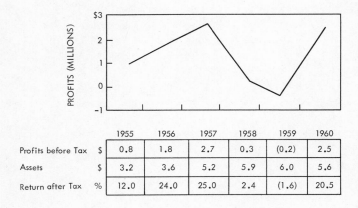

		1955	1956	1957	1958	1959	1960
Profits before Tax	$	0.8	1.8	2.7	0.3	(0.2)	2.5
Assets	$	3.2	3.6	5.2	5.9	6.0	5.6
Return after Tax	%	12.0	24.0	25.0	2.4	(1.6)	20.5

This chart depicts National's profits, assets, and return on assets for the years 1955–60. Profits have ranged from a high of $2.7 million in 1957 to a loss of $200,000 in 1959, and a profit of $2.5 million in 1960. Return on assets employed in 1960 was 20.5 percent after taxes.

MARKET PENETRATION VERSUS COMPETITION

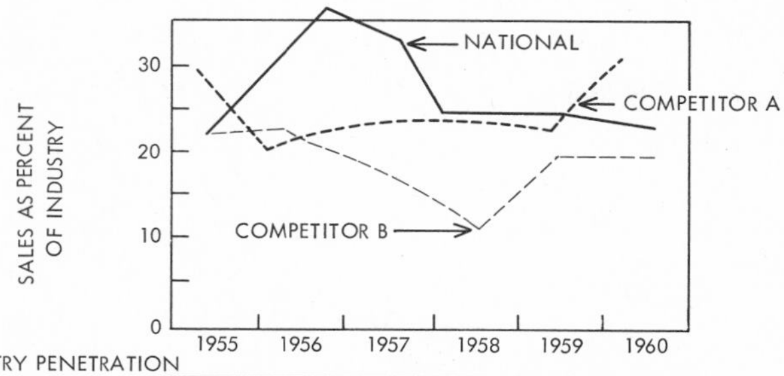

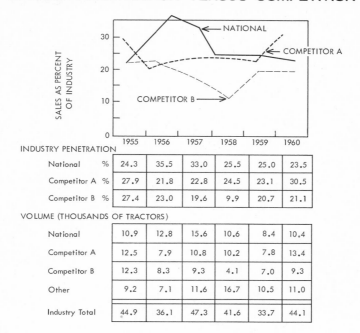

INDUSTRY PENETRATION

	1955	1956	1957	1958	1959	1960
National %	24.3	35.5	33.0	25.5	25.0	23.5
Competitor A %	27.9	21.8	22.8	24.5	23.1	30.5
Competitor B %	27.4	23.0	19.6	9.9	20.7	21.1

VOLUME (THOUSANDS OF TRACTORS)

	1955	1956	1957	1958	1959	1960
National	10.9	12.8	15.6	10.6	8.4	10.4
Competitor A	12.5	7.9	10.8	10.2	7.8	13.4
Competitor B	12.3	8.3	9.3	4.1	7.0	9.3
Other	9.2	7.1	11.6	16.7	10.5	11.0
Industry Total	44.9	36.1	47.3	41.6	33.7	44.1

This chart shows National's penetration of the domestic market for type X tractors from 1955–60, compared with its two major competitors.

National's penetration rose from 24.3 percent in 1955 to a peak of 35.5 percent in 1956. In 1960, National's penetration was 23.5 percent. Competitor A's penetration, which was 27.9 percent in 1955, fell to a low of 21.8 percent in 1956, and then increased to 30.5 percent in 1960. In four out of the last six years, National outsold competitor A in the type X tractor market. Competitor B's penetration moved from 27.5 percent in 1955 to 23.0 percent in 1956, but declined to 9.9 percent in 1958, rising to 21.0 percent in 1960.

Exhibit 1 sets forth those factors that account for the difference in market penetration between National and competitor A—its chief competitor in the type X tractor market. The upper portion of the table compares National's and competitor A's sales during the years 1958–60. The lower portion of the table shows the various factors that account for the differences between National's and competitor A's share of the market in each of these years. National's volume was 10,611 units in 1958, compared to competitor A's 10,246. In 1960, National's volume was 10,356 units, representing a market penetration of 23.5 percent, compared with A's volume of 13,449 units and 30.5 percent of the market. In 1960, National was outsold by 3,093 units.

Exhibit 1

SALES OF TYPE X TRACTORS AND FACTORS AFFECTING MARKET PENETRATION

National versus Competitor A, 1958 to 1960

	Jan.–Dec. 1958		*Jan.–Dec. 1959*		*Jan.–Dec. 1960*	
	Units	*% of Market**	*Units*	*% of Market**	*Units*	*% of Market**
Sales:						
National	10,611	25.5%	8,431	25.0%	10,356	23.5%
Competitor A	10,246	24.5	7,828	23.1	13,449	30.5
National over/(under) A	365	1.0%	603	1.9%	(3,093)	(7.0%)
Factors affecting market penetration:						
Effect of major fire at one of competitor A's plants	—	—	1,500	4.5	(1,500)	(3.4)
Sales to government agencies	(3)	—	321	1.0	138	0.3
Competitor A's advantage in size of owner body	(850)	(2.0)	(660)	(1.9)	(700)	(1.6)
Product differences	(269)	(0.6)	(1,071)	(3.2)	(1,986)	(4.5)
Other factors:						
Customer attitudes toward National: Operating cost; Durability and quality; National's price position; National's distribution system; Sales administration; Other factors	1,487	3.6	513	1.5	955	2.2
Total Variance	365	1.0%	603	1.9%	(3,093)	(7.0%)

* These percentages were calculated from the rounded numbers given on the preceding page; if calculated from the exact number of units, they would be somewhat different.

Turning to the specific factors that account for this volume difference, we have estimated that the effect of a major fire at one of competitor A's plants in the last half of 1959, which halted production for nearly five months, resulted in a deferral of demand for 1,500 of its type X tractors from 1959 to 1960. This estimate is based on our knowledge of competitor A's output in 1959 compared with other years, and represents our best estimate as to what sales might have been without the fire. In 1960, these 1,500 units represented 3.4 percent of market penetration. In 1960, National sold 138 more units to government agencies, equivalent to 0.3 percent of market penetration. We shall examine the effect on our market penetration of differences in the size of our respective owner bodies in subsequent tables.

The product differences result from gaps in our product line that prevent National from entering certain segments of the type X tractor market, thereby providing competitor A with a clear product advantage. For example, competitor A offers a larger variety of attachments and related equipment which increase the number of different jobs its tractor can perform. We have estimated, for each year, the net market advantage accruing to competitor A because of its broader product line.

Other factors, whose effects cannot be measured quantitatively, are summarized at the bottom of the table, including customer attitudes toward National with respect to operating cost, durability, quality, and similar factors. In 1960, these other factors, in total, represented a net advantage to National of 955 units, or 2.2 percent of market penetration.

BASIS FOR ESTIMATED ADVANTAGE TO COMPETITOR A OF OWNER BODY

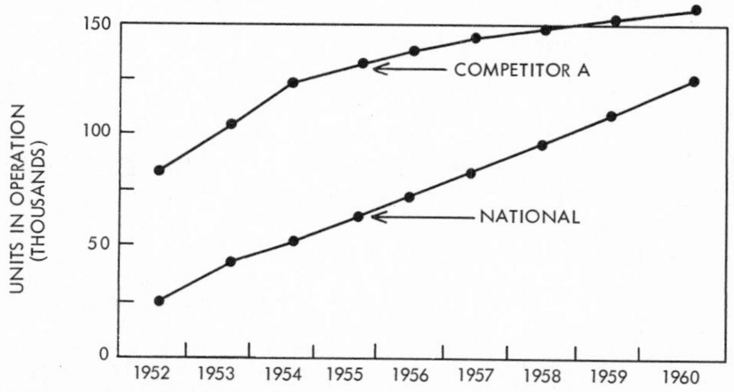

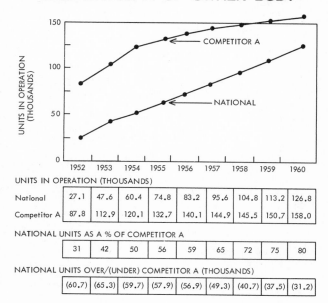

UNITS IN OPERATION (THOUSANDS)

National	27.1	47.6	60.4	74.8	83.2	95.6	104.8	113.2	126.8
Competitor A	87.8	112.9	120.1	132.7	140.1	144.9	145.5	150.7	158.0

NATIONAL UNITS AS A % OF COMPETITOR A

31	42	50	56	59	65	72	75	80

NATIONAL UNITS OVER/(UNDER) COMPETITOR A (THOUSANDS)

(60.7)	(65.3)	(59.7)	(57.9)	(56.9)	(49.3)	(40.7)	(37.5)	(31.2)

This chart shows the estimated number of National and competitor A type X tractors in operation for the years 1952–60.

In 1952, it is estimated that competitor A had approximately 88,000 type X tractors in operation, while National had approximately 27,000 units in use. By 1960, National units in operation had more than quadrupled to a level of approximately 127,000 units. Competitor A units, on the other hand, had increased by almost 100 percent to a level of 158,000 units. During this period, National units as a percent of competitor A increased from 31 percent in 1952 to 82 percent in 1960. At the same time, our variance, in terms of units, decreased from 60,700 in 1952 to 31,200 in 1960.

Because of the importance of owner loyalty, competitor A's advantage in owner body represents an automatic advantage in market penetration as indicated in the succeeding pages.

1960 Type X Replacement Patterns

	Make Purchased			
Make Replaced	*National*	*A*	*Other*	*Total*
National	48%	27%	25%	100%
Competitor A	13	73	14	100
Other	17	20	63	100

SOURCE: Replacement analysis published annually by trade association.

This table indicates the relative loyalty in 1960 of National and competitor A type X tractor owners. In this sample, 48 percent of the National owners who replaced a tractor bought a new National, 27 percent bought an A model, and 25 percent bought some other type X tractor. In contrast, 73 percent of A owners bought a new A, 14 percent bought some type X tractor other than National, and 13 percent of A owners purchased a National tractor when they reentered the market.

EFFECT OF DIFFERENCES IN OWNER BODY ON 1960 TRACTOR PURCHASES

	Make Purchased (thousands of units)			
Make Replaced	*National*	*A*	*Other*	*Total*
National	5.0	2.8	2.6	10.4
Competitor A	3.6	6.4	3.4	13.4
Other	3.7	3.8	12.8	20.3
Total	12.3	13.0	18.8	44.1
Penetration	27.9%	29.5%	42.6%	100.0%
National (under) competitor A:				
Percentage points	(1.6)			
Units	(0.7)			

In this table, we have calculated the effect of owner bodies on type X tractor purchases in 1960. We have used actual figures for the size of National and competitor A owner bodies but have assumed that all other factors, including owner loyalty rates, are equal. In this calculation, we have applied National loyalty to both National and competitor A owner bodies. Based on these premises, one would expect National to have a deficiency in market penetration relative to competitor A of 1.6 percent solely as a result of the differences in the size of the two owner bodies, with National market penetration at 27.9 percent and competitor A penetration at 29.5 percent.

TYPE X TRACTOR WARRANTY EXPENSE[2]

	Model Year						1960 (over)/under 1955	
	1955	*1956*	*1957*	*1958*	*1959*	*1960*	*Per Unit*	*Per-cent*
Engine	$11.30	$ 7.56	$28.05	$28.40	$22.58	$12.76	$(1.46)	(13%)
Transmission	3.70	3.09	3.90	6.60	6.00	7.19	(3.49)	(94)
Hydraulic system	.80	.46	.74	5.21	1.35	.57	.23	29
Electrical	.65	1.14	1.93	3.88	4.40	3.27	(2.62)	(403)
Other	5.03	4.20	5.20	10.97	8.90	7.59	(2.56)	(51)
Total	$21.48	$16.45	$39.82	$55.06	$43.23	$31.38	$(9.90)	(46%)

Some indication of National's type X tractor quality and durability problem is found in the level of our warranty expense as shown in the above table. From 1955 to 1958, our warranty expense on the average type X tractor increased from $21.48 to $55.06, an increase of $33.58 per unit. Since 1958, warranty costs have declined to $31.38, a reduction of $23.68. Expense on all components, with the exception of the hydraulic system, has increased over 1955 levels. It seems clear that warranty costs of over $31 per unit are too high and represent an unsatisfactory level of quality as far as the user is concerned.

The table on page 162 indicates changes in warranty expense and design costs per unit on the N–50 tractor in the 1958, 1959, and 1960 models. In total, during this period, warranty expense has been reduced approximately $33, while design costs have increased $36. Engine warranty expense on this model has declined $40 per unit, while design costs have increased $24. In the case of the transmission, warranty expense has increased $3.30 per unit, despite an increase of $1.77 per unit in design costs.

---

[2] Warranty Expense is the amount spent by National for replacements and repairs to tractors in use for which it had accepted responsibility. The company kept detailed records of such costs, broken down not only in the main classifications indicated above, but also for individual parts within each classification.

NATIONAL N-50 TYPE X TRACTOR— WARRANTY AND DESIGN[3] COST

CHANGES BY YEAR

	1958 (over)/under 1957		*1959 (over)/under 1958*		*1960 (over)/under 1959*		*1960 (over)/under 1957*	
	Warranty	*Design*	*Warranty*	*Design*	*Warranty*	*Design*	*Warranty*	*Design*
Engine	$ 9.80	$(3.74)	$24.00	$(12.99)	$ 6.48	$ (7.62)	$40.28	$(24.35)
Transmission...	(2.69)	(1.31)	.59	—	(1.20)	(.46)	(3.30)	(1.77)
Hydraulic system	(4.48)	(8.90)	3.87	.94	.77	(2.97)	.16	(10.93)
Electrical	(1.93)	—	(.53)	(1.09)	1.13	.32	(1.33)	(.77)
Other	(5.70)	4.17	2.00	(.50)	1.33	(1.73)	(2.37)	1.94
Total	$(5.00)	$(9.78)	$29.93	$(13.64)	$ 8.51	$(12.46)	$33.44	$(35.88)

[3] Design cost refers to the costs of the tractor itself. These costs are a function of the way in which the tractor is designed. For example, the total standard cost of the 1958 model was $9.78 more than the total standard cost of the 1957 model; the designers had devised a more expensive tractor in 1958. In making the comparisons, wage rates and material costs are held constant.

Chapter Five

EXPENSE CENTERS; MANAGED COSTS

The concept of the responsibility center is central to an understanding of management control systems, as explained in the following "Note on Responsibility Centers." The three types of responsibility centers—expense centers, financial performance centers, and investment centers—are the subject of this and the next two chapters.

An expense center is not conceptually the same as a cost center. The cost center is an accounting entity, a device for the accumulation of costs to be charged to products or services; the expense center is an organizational entity. Some expense centers are also cost centers—for example, the departments of a manufacturing plant. This book is not concerned with the cost center concept; that is discussed extensively in books on cost accounting.

The cost elements in an expense center can be classified as engineered costs, managed costs, and committed costs. This chapter focuses on managed costs—those for which standards cannot be determined. The other two types are also important, but an extensive literature concerning them already exists.

Reading 5-1

Note on Responsibility Centers

By Robert N. Anthony*

All organizations, except the tiniest, are made up of smaller organizational units. In a large organization there is a hierarchy of such units, for example, divisions, departments within divisions, sections within departments. If an organizational unit is headed by a supervisor who is responsible for the activities of the unit, then we call the unit a responsibility center.

Every organization has at least one goal, and most organizations have several. The organization exists for the purpose of accomplishing its goal or goals. The work done by each responsibility center presumably contributes, or at least is supposed to contribute, to the attainment of the goal, or goals, of the organization of which it is a part. We take as our central premise that a management control system should be structured in such a way that when heads of responsibility centers are motivated to act in their own perceived best interests they also are acting in the best interests of the whole organization, insofar as this is feasible. We call this premise goal congruence; that is, there should be as much congruence as possible between the goals of the head of each responsibility center and the overall goals of the organization. We recognize that perfect congruence of individual interests and organizational interests is not possible. A more practical statement of the premise, therefore, is that the system should *minimize* the amount of conflict between the goals of heads of responsibility centers and the goals of the whole organization. To the extent that the management control system induces people to act in a way that does not contribute to the goals of the organization, the system is said to be *dysfunctional*.

Note that we make no assumption as to what the goals are. This is an important distinction between our approach and that taken in classical eco-

* Adapted from James S. Hekimian, Introduction to *Management Control in Life Insurance Branch Offices* (Harvard Business School Division of Research), 1965.

nomics. If it is assumed that a company has a single goal and that this goal is the maximization of profit, then certain generalizations about management control systems can be made with confidence. But these generalizations are valid only if the underlying assumption is valid, and there is strong evidence that the assumption of the single goal of profit maximization is not valid for most companies.

OUTPUTS AND INPUTS

Every responsibility center has outputs and inputs. Outputs are the products, services, or other effects created in a responsibility center. Inputs are the resources consumed in this process. The degree to which outputs and inputs can be measured quantitatively varies greatly in different responsibility centers. In a department making a tangible homogeneous product (e.g., cement), the *quantity* of output often can be measured precisely; but when the products are heterogeneous (e.g., different styles and grades of shoes, parts produced by a machine shop), problems arise in summarizing the separate outputs into a meaningful measure of the total. Converting the disparate products to a monetary equivalent is one way of solving this problem. The *quality* of product also involves measurement problems, which often are solved by a go, no-go procedure: either the product is of satisfactory quality, or it is not.

When the outputs are services or other intangibles, the problem of measuring them becomes formidable; it is always difficult and often not feasible to measure, even approximately, the outputs of such staff units as the legal department or the research department of a company, or the outputs of hospitals, schools, government agencies, or churches. Nevertheless, these organizations *have* outputs; the difficulty of measurement does not alter this fact.

In addition to the products and services usually thought of as outputs, responsibility centers produce other intangible effects, some intentional and others unintentional. They may prepare employees for advancement; they may instill attitudes of loyalty and pride of accomplishment (or, alternatively, attitudes of disloyalty and indolence); and they may affect the image of the whole organization that is perceived by the outside world. Some of these outputs, such as better trained employees, are created in order to benefit operations in future periods; that is, they will become inputs at some future time. Such outputs are therefore "investments," since a business investment is a commitment of current resources in the expectation of deriving future benefits.

In the typical responsibility center, inputs are a heterogeneous mixture of resources: labor, materials, and services. Some common denominator must be found if these heterogeneous elements are to be aggregated into a measure of the total resources consumed by the responsibility center. Money is the most frequently used such common denominator. The total resources consumed by a responsibility center, when measured in monetary terms, are the expenses of that responsibility center. Total recorded expenses are at best an approximation of the true inputs. Some inputs are not included as expenses, either because the effort required to translate them into monetary terms is not worthwhile (e.g., minor supplies and services, small amounts of borrowed labor) or because measurement is not possible (e.g., certain types of executive or staff assistance, training).

Output measured in monetary terms often is called revenue, or gross margin. As already mentioned, the monetary measure of input is called expense. In a profit-seeking company, the difference between revenue (or gross margin) and expense is called profit.

TYPES OF RESPONSIBILITY CENTERS

Responsibility centers include expense centers, financial performance centers, and investment centers.

Expense Centers

In an expense center, inputs are measured in monetary terms (i.e., expenses), but no attempt is made to measure output in monetary terms or to relate outputs and inputs in monetary terms. Usually, the departments, sections, or other subunits within a division are treated as expense centers.

Financial Performance Centers

In this type of responsibility center, both inputs and outputs are measured in monetary terms, and the relationship between them is calculated. The financial measurements in a financial performance center are, therefore, inherently broader than those in an expense center.

Our concept of a financial performance center is exactly the same as that of a profit center, as this term is used in profit-seeking companies. We use the broader term, financial performance center, simply because we believe that useful generalizations can be made that are applicable both to profit-seeking and to nonprofit organizations, and we therefore do not want to restrict our investigation to the first type, as use of the term profit center would connote.

The term financial performance center makes it apparent that we tend to emphasize the financial—i.e., monetary—aspects of measurement. This fact should not be taken as an indication that we think these financial aspects are the only, or even the most important, parts of a control system; quite the contrary. We recognize that nonmonetary and even nonquantitative measures are important. We focus on financial devices partly because we believe we can develop generalizations about these that have a broad application across industries and types of organizational units, whereas quantitative but nonmonetary measures (e.g., invoices processed per man-hour, salesmen's calls per day, readership of an advertisement) tend to be specialized to an industry or function.

Investment Centers

The ultimate extension of the responsibility center idea is the investment center, in which the supervisor is responsible not only for profit but also for the assets that he uses. The formal financial measure in a financial performance center is profit; in an investment center it is profit related to assets employed.

EFFECTIVENESS AND EFFICIENCY

The performance of the head of a responsibility center can be measured in terms of his "effectiveness" and his "efficiency." An explanation of these words may help to indicate the inherent limitations of financial measures of performance. By effectiveness, we mean *how well* the manager does his job—that is (to quote the dictionary), "the extent to which he produces the intended or expected result." We use efficiency in its engineering sense—that is, the amount of output per unit of input. An efficient machine generates a given quantity of outputs with a minimum consumption of inputs, or generates the largest possible outputs from a given quantity of inputs.

Effectiveness is always related to the organization's goals. Efficiency, per se, is not related to the goals. An efficient manager is one who does whatever he does with the lowest consumption of resources; but if what he does (i.e., his output) is an inadequate contribution to the accomplishment of the organization's goals, then he is ineffective.

In both expense centers and financial performance centers, a measure of efficiency can be developed that relates actual expenses to some standard—that is, to a number that expresses what expenses should be incurred for the amount of measured output. Such a measure can be a useful indication of efficiency, but it is never a perfect measure for at least two reasons: (1) recorded expenses are not a precisely accurate measure of resources consumed, and (2) standards are, at best, only approximate measures of what resource consumption ideally should have been in the circumstances prevailing.

Effectiveness cannot be measured in financial terms in an expense center. Effectiveness is related to outputs, and in an expense center, by definition, outputs are not measured in financial terms. In some types of financial performance centers, however, an approximate measure of effectiveness is possible. When one goal of the whole organization is to earn profits, then the contribution to this goal by a financial performance center is a mesaure of its effectiveness. This is so because in a financial performance center, by definition, the relationship between outputs and inputs is measured in monetary terms, and profit is a term describing such a relationship; that is, profit is the difference between revenue, which is a measure of output, and expense, which is a measure of input.

Actually, profit is influenced both by how effective a manager is and by how efficient he is; so profit measures both effectiveness and efficiency. However, we see no need here to make a clear-cut distinction between the two types of measures. In other situations, it is feasible and useful to classify performance measures as relating either to effectiveness or to efficiency. In these situations, there is the problem of balancing the two types of measurements. For example, how do we compare the profligate perfectionist with the frugal manager who obtains less than the optimum output?)

Profit is, at best, a crude measure of effectiveness and efficiency for several reasons: (1) monetary measures do not exactly measure either all aspects of outputs or all inputs, for reasons already given; (2) standards are not accurate; and (3) at best, profit is a measure of what has happened in the short run, whereas we are presumably also interested in the long-run consequences of decisions.

MEASUREMENT OF OUTPUTS

If a responsibility center produces a product or performs a service that it sells in the marketplace, then the revenue earned from sales provides a useful monetary measure of its outputs. In situations where this marketplace validation of the value of outputs is absent, serious, and sometimes insuperable, problems of measurement arise.

One such class of situations occurs when the product or service of one responsibility center goes to other responsibility centers within the same organization. Monetary measurement of outputs in these situations requires the use of a transfer price mechanism. Sometimes, this transfer price can be based on an outside market price for the identical product or service, being transferred internally, or for a closely similar one. In these situations, the output measure can be nearly as valid as that obtained from a market transaction. Many services performed internally have useful market analogs. Trucking companies or car rental agencies have selling prices that may be relevant for internal transportation departments; secretarial agencies, for typing pools; engineering and consulting firms, for staff service units; service bureaus, for computers; contractors of various types, for maintenance work; and so on.

When a reliable outside price cannot be found, the difficulty of devising a useful transfer price increases, and in many situations the difficulty is so great that no monetary measurement of outputs is attempted. In such situations, the responsibility center cannot be treated as a financial performance center, by definition, and this is the principal reason why many responsibility centers are not so treated. Many integrated petroleum companies, for example, have explored the possibility of treating their refining operations and their marketing operations as separate financial performance centers, but they generally have concluded that this is not feasible because of the difficulty of valuing the products transferred from the refinery to the marketing division.

MANAGED COSTS

From a control standpoint, the measurable inputs, or the costs incurred, in a responsibility center can usefully be classified into three categories—engineered costs, managed costs, and committed costs.

Engineered costs are elements of cost for which the "right" or "proper" amount that should be incurred can be estimated. Direct labor is an example. Given the specifications for a product, engineers can determine the necessary operations to be performed, and they can estimate, within reasonably close limits, the time that should be spent on each operation. The total amount of direct labor costs that should be incurred can then be estimated by translation of these times into monetary terms by use of a wage rate and multiplication by the number of units produced. Since production engineering is not an exact science, these amounts are not necessarily the exact amounts that should be spent, but the estimates usually can be made closely enough so that there will be relatively little disagreement between informed, unprejudiced men as to what the costs should be. In any case, there can be no reasonable ground for denying that there is a direct relationship between volume and costs; two units require more direct labor than does one unit.

Managed costs (or "discretionary" costs), on the other hand, can be whatever management wants them to be, within wide limits. There is no scientific way of deciding on the right amount or, at least, there is no scientific basis that the management of the particular company is willing to rely on. How much should we spend for research and development? for public relations? for employees' parties and outings? for donations? for the accounting department? No one knows. In most companies, the managed cost category includes costs of all general and administrative functions, all order-getting, and a great many items of factory overhead. In the absence of an engineering standard, the amount to be spent must be a matter of judgment.

Committed costs are those that are the inevitable consequence of commitments previously made. Depreciation is an example; once a company has purchased a building or a piece of equipment, the responsibility center has an inevitable depreciation charge.

In our study of management control systems, we find the problem of managed costs to be the most interesting of the three types of cost. A great deal of work already has been done on techniques for the control of engineered costs, such as the use of standard costs, time studies, and analysis of bills of material. Committed costs pose no particular problem to operating managers. By definition, they are not controllable in the short run, and the only trouble they cause is that, unless these costs are properly identified in control reports, they may give rise to misleading inferences. This problem, however, is easily solved, either by omitting this category of costs from control reports or by structuring the system so that no red flag or variance is permitted to be shown for a difference between the so-called actual and the standard for a committed cost element.

Reading 5-2

Notes on Managed Costs

By Robert N. Anthony

THE PROBLEM

Managed costs are costs for which the optimum relationship between output (i.e., results) and input (i.e., resources consumed) is not known. It follows that there is no scientific way of knowing either (*a*) the optimum of cost for a given or desired output or (*b*) the *direction* of change in cost that represents improvement. For engineered costs there is a presumption that if desired "product" specifications (including quality) are achieved, then the lower the costs, the better the performance. For managed costs, there is no such presumption; it is quite possible that a managed cost should be increased, rather than decreased.

There are limits outside of which costs are clearly too high or clearly too low, but the limits are so broad as not to be helpful in many situations.

Despite the absence of scientific standards, costs must be controlled.

A corollary of Parkinson's first law tends to apply to managed cost situations: Costs tend to increase regardless of what happens to output.

ELEMENTS OF GOOD MANAGEMENT CONTROL

Competent Managers

Competent managers are competent not only in the technical aspects of the function being performed in the responsibility center but also in administration. Even with the best system, it is difficult to obtain good control with mediocre managers, and good managers can overcome the defects of a poor system.

Good Atmosphere

There should be in the organization a climate that fosters the attitude that appropriate attention to efficiency is important. This attitude should permeate the whole organization. Almost invariably, it stems from the attitude of the top management. A good atmosphere and competent managers are more important than all the other points combined.

Question Basic Policies

Reviews of policies and practices of responsibility centers should be made occasionally by persons outside the centers, generally headquarters staff or outside consultants. Often, the main purpose of considering these questions is to establish a burden-of-proof situation, which the responsible manager is expected to rebut if he can. The basic questions asked are these:

1. Should the function be performed at all? (Not every company should do research.)
2. What should the quality level be? (Are we doing too much?)
3. Should it be performed in this way?
4. How much should it cost?

A comparison with similar functions in other companies (e.g., AMA Group Ten[1]; trade association data) is one way of approaching the fourth question. Although there are problems of comparability, although, by definition, there is no way of finding a correct relationship between costs and output, although there is a danger in taking outside averages as a standard, and although many other specific criticisms can be made, nevertheless, these comparisons can be useful. There is a danger of raising quibbling arguments, of failing to see that a technique can be less than perfect and still be better than any alternative. These comparisons often lead to the following useful question: If other companies can get the job done for $X, why can't we?

In some situations (auto dealers, service stations, restaurant chains) there is enough similarity to permit such comparisons to be made regularly among units of the same company; this mechanism then becomes part of the regular performance measurement technique.

Outsiders who ask these basic questions usually are nonexperts in the functions performed, but the experts cannot be expected to analyze their own operations adequately; the manager who says, or even thinks, "We must rely on the judgment of the experts," is at their mercy. Studies by outsiders are likely to have a traumatic effect on managers—second-guessing the experts, challenging the status quo, threatening job security. Because of the possible repercussions, the basic questioning technique is used only at

---

[1] See Peterson Manufacturing Company, page 213.

intervals of several years in a given area; the process may go on continually somewhere in the organization, with a given area being examined perhaps once every five years.

Sometimes, the whole managed cost area is examined at once, especially when (*a*) a new management takes over, or (*b*) there is a major crisis, or (*c*) a new management takes over because of a crisis (e.g., Chrysler), or (*d*) a technological innovation (e.g., computers) occurs. Cost reduction campaigns are another example of company-wide efforts.

Appropriate Policies, Procedures, Guidelines, Rules

These serve to restrict or guide the actions of the manager of a responsibility center. They may range from inviolate ceilings ("There shall be only two secretaries in the personnel office") to general, vague guides. They include wage scales, promotion policies, overtime practices, purchasing practices, allowable travel expense per day, and so on. An important class of such rules is the set of formal limitations on spending, which specify both the limits within which the manager has discretion ("Initiate purchase orders for supplies up to $25") and the approvals required outside these limits.

One function of these rules is to make it easier for the manager to say no to his subordinates; he does not have to judge each request on its merits, which is both unpleasant and time-consuming.

Pieces of Engineered Costs

In managed cost situations, there are elements of engineered costs. These pieces of engineered costs should be searched for and, when located, treated as any other element of engineered cost. The whole controller organization is a managed cost, but certain functions, such as invoicing and payroll, are susceptible to engineering analysis and, hence, to scientific standards. These functions often account for a substantial percentage of total costs.

Engineered standards, at best, show what the cost of performing a specified task should be. They do not answer the question of whether or not the task should be performed at all. In a problem situation, elimination of the task may be a better solution than reducing its cost.

Effective Use of Budgets

For managed costs, by definition, the budget does not show the "correct" amount to spend. At best, it shows an *agreed on* amount, which is an essentially different concept. Budgeted amounts should be arrived at by negotiation between manager and his superior. The current level of spending is a bench mark, or starting point, in the sense that the burden of proof is on the person who proposes to change. Valid reasons for change include price factors (e.g., wage rates), changes in output (e.g., greater work load), and changes in methods. In a tight system, this burden of proof is strong enough to prevent costs from creeping much above the level established by the basic questioning technique, at least for a few years, despite the force of Parkinson's law.

The final budget represents a *bilateral commitment*; the manager commits himself to produce desired results with this level of spending, and the superior commits himself to regard spending as acceptable if it is consistent with the budget.

The budgeted amounts, both as to individual items and as to totals, are of three types: (*a*) a *ceiling* ("You should not spend more than $X for overtime"), (*b*) a *floor* ("You should spend at least $Y for management development"), (*c*) a *guide* ("You should spend roughly $Z for chemicals"). Ordinarily, the items are not explicitly identified as belonging to one of these categories, but it is obviously important that the parties involved have a mutual understanding as to which item belongs in which category.

The budget may permit certain costs to vary with volume, but no one should think that such cost behavior is a necessary or causal relationship, as is the case with engineered costs.

An important part of the process is totaling tentative budgets of the separate responsibility centers to see if the overall result is satisfactory. If costs are judged to be too high in total, cuts often are made. This is an arbitrary process, but by definition there is no rational (i.e., scientific) way of making such cuts.

Satisfactory Measures of Performance

By definition, when actual spending equals the budget, the only valid conclusion is that the manager *conformed to the budget*, which is different from the conclusion that he was efficient.

Appraisal of performance requires judgments both as to effectiveness and as to efficiency. In managed cost situations, effectiveness is likely to be both more important and more difficult to judge than is efficiency. Nevetheless, it is both possible and of some importance to form a judgment as to efficiency.

When actual spending is significantly different from the budget, either higher or lower, an explanation is in order.

GENERAL COMMENTS

We try to convert managed costs into engineered costs. This is an important part of what we mean by progress, when done intelligently. Beware, however, of pseudoconversions ("Our competitors spend 3 percent of sales on research; we must do likewise").

The value derived from any technique should obviously exceed its cost. Beyond a certain point, an elaborate budget or an expensive standard-setting technique or a detailed cost comparison is not worth the effort.

Reading 5–3

Profit Planning

By Marshall K. Evans*

The need for new concepts and techniques of profit planning is felt in many companies today. It is true that we have good financial tools for the planning and control of receivables, inventories, and capital facilities, but these tools alone are not enough.

Without more techniques we are handicapped in dealing with the many trends and cross trends which beset modern industry—increasing sales volume but, on the other hand, falling profit margins, expanding investments in capital facilities, growing cost requirements for product and market development, declining return on investment, and so forth.

The problem is likely to be especially acute in areas such as the electrical industry where expansion has been very rapid. Earnings, the ultimate goal of long-range planning, too easily become the victim of the unbridled growth of different corporate functions.

THE PROFIT PATTERN

Something more than good conventional accounting practice is, therefore, required. Management needs improved ways of dealing with what I shall call the profit pattern of a company or division—its profitability over a period of time, taking into account the particular circumstances and conditions. More specifically:

How can we evaluate the strong and weak points in the profit pattern of a division to establish objectives that are pinpointed to the organization's needs?

How can we compare the financial effects of alternative courses of action designed to improve the basic profit pattern?

---

* Vice-President, Operations Staff of Westinghouse Electric Corporation. From *Harvard Business Review,* July–August, 1959. Reprinted by permission of *Harvard Business Review.*

How can we report the effects of different influences on the profit pattern in order to learn whether objectives are being accomplished and, if not, what changes to make in the plan of action?

In this article I shall show how one company, the Westinghouse Electric Corporation, has answered these questions. Some parts of Westinghouse's solution may be familiar to readers, some parts may not. But the combination of techniques and ideas used is, we believe, an original one, and it is proving helpful to management in its efforts to improve the turnover of assets, profit margins and return on investment.

SEGREGATING COSTS

In the analysis of the profit pattern at Westinghouse, the first step is a vital one. This is to segragate costs and expenses into categories according to the manner in which they respond to short-term changes in the volume of sales. This approach results in three basic cost categories—(1) product costs, (2) committed costs, and (3) managed costs.

Product Costs

The costs which respond directly to changes in the level of production and sales are product costs. These include:

Cost of labor which goes directly into manufacture of the product.

Cost of material which becomes part of the product.

Factory and other overhead costs which are closely allied with production, such as indirect product materials, shop supplies, and some elements of indirect shop labor.

Product costs typically will vary directly with the volume of production and sales, assuming that management has perfect control data, that the mix of production is constant, and that the hourly wage rates and material prices remain unchanged.

Committed Costs

Any costs which remain fixed, over the short term, regardless of the level of production, are committed costs. They are associated primarily with costs of capital facilities such as depreciation charges, insurance, taxes, and rental charges for building and equipment. Over the longer range, these costs will inevitably vary as the result of changes in depreciation policies, the addition and retirement of assets, changes in insurance, and tax rates; but they do *not* respond to fluctuations in volume within the limits of existing facilities.

Managed Costs

All other elements of general overhead expenses are managed costs. The distinguishing characteristic of these costs is that they are subject to management control. For purposes of profit pattern analysis, they may be divided into two sub-classes:

1. *Policy costs*—These are dependent almost entirely on management evaluation and judgment and include such items as expenditures for advertising and for research on new products, new methods, and procedures. Such judgment expenditures may vary widely without any immediate effect or relationship to sales volume.

2. *Operating costs*—Here we include the cost of services and processes over and beyond direct product costs—outlays essential to day-to-day business operation but subject to considerable management judgment as to amount and extent. Examples are expenditures for management and supervisory personnel; factory-related manufacturing services for production planning, purchasing, and quality control; general services such as accounting, industrial relations, and order service.

Managed costs may be considered fixed in relationship to production or sales volume, within limits; they respond primarily to management judgment and decision rather than to volume stimuli.

Although significant changes in the volume of production and sales will ultimately bring pressure to increase or decrease the level of managed costs, a fairly wide range of activity can be satisfied without changing the expenditure level. Since the functions covered by managed costs are generally staffed by salaried personnel, short-term expansion or reduction of work in response to short-term changes in the level of production activity is both impractical and undesirable.

GRAPHIC ANALYSIS

In line with these concepts, the profit pattern may be expressed graphically in a fashion similar to a breakeven chart (see Exhibit 1). Since we have defined committed costs and managed costs as being "fixed" with relation to short-term fluctuations in volume, they may be treated, for the purpose of profit pattern visualization, as constant over the full-volume range. However, product costs by definition vary directly with volume, and are treated as a variable in direct ratio to the number of units produced. The margin between the sales dollar and the product cost per sales dollar contributes to the absorption of managed and committed costs up to the breakeven point, beyond which the margin represents incremental profit.

The important measurements in evaluating the soundness of a particular profit pattern include: ratio of product cost to sales, gross margin over product cost contributed by sales, dollar level of managed and committed costs to be absorbed by gross margin or incremental profit rate, dollar level of the breakeven point, and relationship between actual or projected billings and breakeven point.

Exhibit 1

PROFIT PATTERN

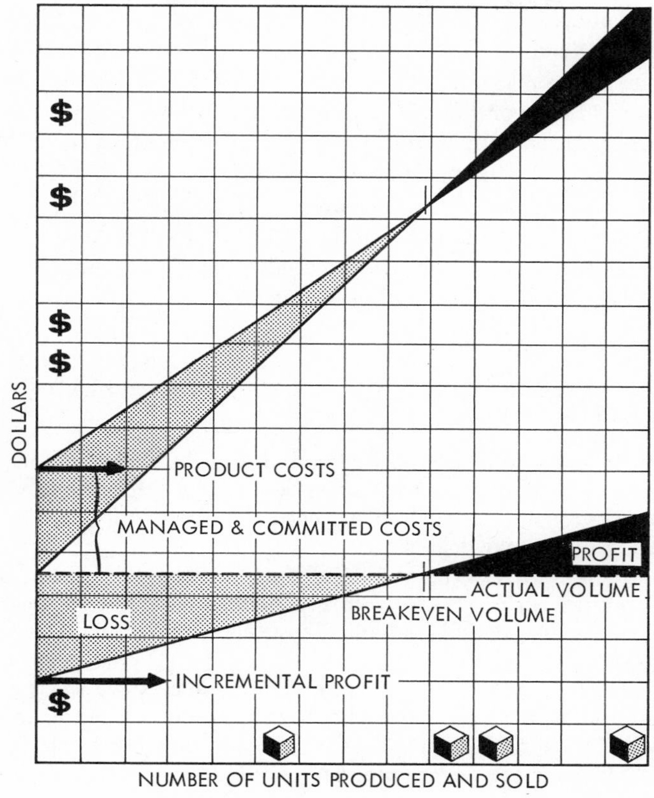

Thus, a given division may be producing inadequate profits because:

(1) Margin between product cost and sales price is too narrow, indicating the need for product cost reduction, a price increase, or both.

(2) Committed and managed costs are too high relative to the level of sales or to the production capacity of the facilities and the organization.

(3) Actual sales volume is too low relative to the breakeven point and the capacity of the plant to break into the profit range.

(4) Not *enough* is being spent upon managed costs—say, advertising or quality control services—to generate profitable volume.

UNDERSTANDING THE CAUSES

Up to this point, the profit pattern analysis principle may appear to be only slightly different from the typical breakeven concept. Except for variations in terminology the *concepts* of profit pattern and breakeven charts are in fact basically the same.

Interpretation

The real difference develops in the concepts which are applied to the *interpretation* of the profit pattern. The pattern itself is seen as a first step only—an indispensable one, but in need of a follow-up. It purports to give only a picture of the condition of a division at a particular point in time.

Furthermore, it is applicable only to a relatively limited range of volume change, beyond which the basic management decisions going into the establishment of a level of managed costs must be re-examined.

Inasmuch as development of a profit pattern does only half the job which needs to be done to develop a meaningful dynamic planning tool, we must move on to the job of understanding the causes.

Changes over Time

Many factors can cause the picture to change between two points in time. For example:

(1) Hourly and salary rates may change as a result of contract negotiations, management policy decisions, merit increases, or changing composition of the work force with relation to length of service.

(2) Selling prices may change.

(3) In a multiproduct division, the mixture of products with different margins over product costs may vary, with resultant change in the total contribution to absorption of managed and committed costs and to the over-all dollar level of income.

(4) Policy decisions by management may result in changed levels of expenditure for policy costs, different approaches to organization structure, and in different concepts of the type of service deemed necessary for design, production, and selling, and for employee and community relations.

(5) New plant investments, purchases of additional capital equipment, retirement of worn-out and obsolete equipment, and changed tax regulations may result in changes in committed cost levels for depreciation, insurance, and taxes.

(6) Prices of purchased materials may change upward or downward, resulting in fluctuations in the product costs per unit.

(7) Changes in the product design may result in higher or lower product cost content per unit.

(8) Improvements in manufacturing methods, automation, and other areas can reduce the product cost content, while at the same time increase committed or managed costs for depreciation, maintenance, and so on.

(9) Changing levels of productivity effort on the part of employees in the shop and office can affect favorably or adversely the levels of both product costs and managed costs.

(10) Improvement of systems and methods in the office operations, including the mechanization of clerical procedures, can bring about reductions in managed costs.

If a clear understanding of the causes for profit variation over past periods is to be developed, it is necessary to isolate and evaluate the effect of the influencing factors. Also, if we want to know what action to take to improve profits in the future, we must have good estimates of the effect of different critical factors in the future. And we must be able to set appropriate objectives for accomplishing improvements which are within the over-all control of management.

In other words, a picture of a company's or a division's operation at a particular point in time is not enough. A sound planning procedure must also take into account the influence of different factors on the organization as it goes from one period to another.

Analysis Form

The development of profit pattern analyses in Westinghouse divisions is expressed in a profit pattern analysis form. Exhibit 2 shows a sample for the "Transmotor Division" (disguised):

Beginning and ending profit patterns are recorded in the first and last columns of the form.

Past trends are analyzed by comparing the profit patterns for two historical years and then developing the influencing factors in the intervening columns.

Future plans are laid by recording in the first column the latest available profit pattern, establishing the objective pattern toward which the division plans to work, and forecasting the effect of influencing factors in between.

Typically the procedure requires entering the expected effects of general wage and material cost changes, and developing by difference the amount of improvement through cost and expense reduction necessary to obtain the desired levels.

Basic Tools

I should emphasize here that certain basic tools must be maintained in order to provide accurately the information that is ultimately carried to the profit pattern analysis. For example:

Continuing indexes of selling prices, labor rates, and purchased material prices should be kept so that management can calculate the relative impact of these changing factors for any given level of production and sales volume.

All Westinghouse divisions maintain formalized cost reduction programs, in which the design and manufacturing, sales, and purchasing engineers study each product, subassembly, and component for the purpose of devising less expensive features, improving manufacturing methods, and utilizing less expensive materials in order to produce a high quality product at a minimum cost.

Organization analysis and planning, as well as office systems and methods analyses, contribute to increased productivity of managed-cost personnel.

The margin over product costs contributed by individual product lines is developed as the basis for review of pricing decisions and policies and for pruning out unprofitable products which cannot, within a relatively short period of time, be placed on a profitable basis through either cost reduction or price revisions.

Exhibit 2

SAMPLE FORM

WESTINGHOUSE
FORM 31 518C

ANALYSIS OF CHANGES IN PROFIT PATTERN — FORM 2

Transmotor DIVISION ______ DEPARTMENT ______ DATE 4-1-59 PERIOD 1958 TO 1960

(Dollars in Thousands)

STMT. 6 LINE NO.	DESCRIPTION	(A) 1958 ACTUAL	(B) INFLUENCING FACTORS – MANAGEMENT CONTROL: MIX CHANGES	(C) GENERAL PAYROLL ADJUST.	(D) DIVISION PAYROLL & MATL. INCR.	(E) POLICY CHANGES	(F)	(G)	(J) REQUIRED COST & EXP. REDUCTIONS	(K) REVISED PATTERN MGMT. CONT.	(L) INFLUENCING FACTORS GENERAL ECONOMIC: PRICE CHANGES	(M) PHYSICAL VOLUME	(N) 1960 PROPOSED	(O) 1959 OBJECTIVE	(P) 1957 ACTUAL	FORM 2 LINE NO.
8	GROSS SALES BILLED	12 500								12 500	+ 500	+1 500	14 500	13 000	12 725	1
9	PRODUCT COSTS - Labor	2 025	- 75	+ 136					- 104	1 982		+ 240	2 222	1 976	2 163	2
10	- Material	4 375	- 150		+ 169				- 132	4 262		+ 510	4 772	4 398	4 454	3
11	- Factory Expense	1 100	- 35	+ 25	+ 18				- 22	1 086		+ 130	1 216	1 110	1 018	4
12	- Other	625		+ 5	+ 26				- 13	643		+ 77	720	638	636	5
13	-															6
14	TOTAL PRODUCT COSTS	8 125	- 260	+ 166	+ 213				- 271	7 973		+ 957	8 930	8 122	8 271	7
17	COMMITTED COSTS	500		+ 14						514		+ 10	524	507	485	8
18	Organization & Other Operating	900		+ 50	+ 30	- 45			- 35	900			900	910	940	9
19	Facilities Program Expense	30			+ 5					35		+ 25	60	35	25	10
20	Manufacturing Development	55			+ 5					60		+ 20	80	60	60	11
21																12
22	DIVISION MANAGED COSTS-MANUFACTURING	985		+ 50	+ 40	- 45			- 35	995		+ 45	1 040	1 005	1 025	13
23	Customer Order Development - Engineering	250	- 50	+ 13	- 6					207			207	215	260	14
24	Standard Development - Engineering	325		+ 17	+ 8				- 15	335		+ 50	385	370	330	15
25	Long Range Major Development	70		+ 5	+ 5	- 50				30			30	40	70	16
26	Standard Development - Tools	95			+ 10					105		+ 25	130	100	100	17
27																18
28	DIVISION MANAGED COSTS-PROD. DEVELOP.	740	- 50	+ 35	+ 17	- 50			- 15	677		+ 75	752	725	760	19
29	Division Advertising	100			+ 5					105		+ 50	155	120	95	20
30	Division & Region Sales - Division Cont.	400		+ 21	+ 10	- 40				391		+ 20	411	385	395	21
31	Division Order Service, Whse. & Shipping	125		+ 5	+ 3					133		+ 5	138	130	120	22
32																23
33	DIVISION MANAGED COSTS - MARKETING	625		+ 26	+ 18	- 40				629		+ 75	704	635	610	24
34	Admin. & General - Division Control	280		+ 15	+ 7	- 25				277			277	264	270	25
35	Foreign Lic.. Royalties & Pat. Can. W Inc.	* 5								* 5			* 5	* 5		26
36	Other Income & Deductions - Net	* 15								* 15			* 15	* 15	* 10	27
38	DIVISION MANAGED - ADMIN. & GENERAL	260		+ 15	+ 7	- 25				257			257	244	260	28
39	TOTAL DIVISION CONTROL MANAGED COSTS	2 610	- 50	+ 126	+ 82	- 160			- 50	2 558		+ 195	2 753	2 609	2 655	29
39b	MARGIN OVER DIVISION CONTROL COSTS	1 265	+ 310	- 306	- 295	+ 160			+ 321	1 455	+ 500	+ 338	2 293	1 762	1 314	30
39c	Margin - % GSB	10.1%								11.6%			15.8%	13.6%	10.3%	31
40	International Sales, Admin. & General	25								25			25	25	25	32
41	Headquarters General Control Expense	300				+ 28				328			328	310	290	33
42	Reg. Sales (App. Div.) Dist. Services	300				+ 40				340			340	305	295	34
43	Headquarters Research & Development	100								100			100	100	90	35
45	TOTAL NON-DIVISION MANAGED COSTS	725				+ 68				793			793	740	700	36
46	TOTAL COMMITTED & MANAGED COSTS	3 835								3 865			4 070	3 856	3 840	37
47	Inventory Change - Effect on IBT	* 50				50						75	75	* 25	20	38
48	INCOME BEFORE TAXES	490	+ 310	- 306	- 295	+ 142			+ 321	662	+ 500	+ 413	1 575	997	634	39
49	IBT AS % GSB	3.9%								5.3%			10.9%	7.7%	5.0%	40
50	BREAKEVEN VOLUME	10 957								10 671			10 596	10 277	10 971	41
51	Breakeven Volume - % GSB	87.7%								85.4%			73.1%	79.1%	86.2%	42
52	Incremental IBT Rate	.3500								.3622			.3841	.3752	.3500	43
2	GROSS ASSETS	7 500								7 500			8 290	7 700	7 650	44
1	% RETURN ON GROSS ASSETS	6.4%								8.7%			19 %	12.9%	8.3%	45

* CONTRA OR LOSS

INFLUENCE FACTORS

The key to useful profit pattern analyses lies in the accurate development of the factors that influence results. These fall broadly into two categories: (1) those which are primarily internal and/or subject to management control, and (2) those which are heavily influenced by external market conditions and competition.

Subject to Control

In the first category, the principal factors are: changes in wage and salary rates, material prices, mix of product lines, decisions to spend or withhold spending in policy areas, and cost and expense reduction accomplishments:

The effect of changes in wage rates is calculated from the provisions of existing labor contracts or from forecasts based on management's objectives in negotiations of new contracts.

To obtain the effect of material prices, it is necessary to keep accurate indexes of past material prices, and to predict the trend of these indexes for the principal types of raw materials and parts purchased. The full dollar impact is developed by applying the forecasted per-unit change to the labor, salary, and material content of the various categories of cost.

The effect of product mix changes can be significant where several product lines are manufactured and sold, and where the margin between product cost and selling price varies from one line to another. A fixed dollar sales volume will be produced at varying product costs depending on the mixture of products involved. This effect is calculated by comparing the product costs for the planned mix with the costs for the actual mix in the base period. The result is increased or decreased cost, depending on whether the mix is unfavorable or favorable.

The cost and expense reduction figures are initially obtained by difference—the difference between the accumulated effect of the other influencing factors and the level of cost and expense required to produce the desired profit result. These figures become the goal for cost and expense reduction during the period involved. They may have to be tempered if the amounts squeezed out by difference are obviously unattainable, resulting also in modification of the profit goal.

External Conditions

Because changes in product selling price and volume are, to a degree, speculative in nature, these are tacked on to the plan after the full effect of the internal influencing factors has been calculated. The objective is to focus maximum attention on profit improvement by internal action, and to avoid too heavy reliance on the external factors in programing for desired profit objectives. This is not to say that programs to improve volume and price realization should not be pushed to the maximum, but rather that expense programing should be done so as to produce a suitable profit at a conservative volume base.

Calculation of the effect of physical volume changes is done by applying the planned product cost ratio to the dollar increase or decrease in sales volume. Required changes in managed cost levels to meet the change in volume are developed by applying the variable elements of budget standards applicable to the various managed cost categories or by management decision as to the level of expenditure needed in marketing areas to produce the planned volume change.

The calculation of the effect of realized price changes can be very simple or extremely difficult, depending on the nature of the product. Where a standard product is involved, application of known or forecasted price changes to the number of units in the volume base will produce the total dollar effect. But in product lines in which units are designed and manufactured to customer specifications, every unit is different and prices are not comparable. In these cases, the calculated effect of price changes is much less precise. The problem may be approached by detailed analysis of cost/price factors for a representative style of product, or an answer may be calculated from a "quoted margin" base, rather than from a total price base.

In any case, even a crude answer is better than no answer at all, and the necessity of at least attempting a calculation has pointed up some basic weaknesses in pricing policies and procedures.

REPORTS TO MANAGEMENT

No planning and control procedure is complete without prompt and accurate feedback of operating results. Management must know how actual profit compares with the objective and with past performances, and to what extent variations from objective and from past performance have been caused by the various influencing factors indicated.

To meet this need, Westinghouse executives have designed a monthly operating report of the type shown on page 185 in Exhibit 3 (filled out, again, for the "Transmotor Division"). The actual results for a month and for the period of the year to date are reported in the profit pattern format. Results are compared with the budget or objectives, and the variances from budget are calculated. In addition, the cause of variance from the objective and from a base period in the past are calculated and reported at the bottom of the form.

Within the various operating divisions, the different categories of expense as reported on the profit pattern are supported by detailed budget statements developing actual budgeted expenditures matched against individual control accounts. Also, product line statements are prepared reporting profits by product line in terms of contrributed margin and of share of general prorated expenses. These subsidiary reports enable top management to evaluate actual performance on an exception basis and direct corrective action to the appropriate area.

Exhibit 3

SAMPLE FORM

FORM 32311

WESTINGHOUSE ELECTRIC CORPORATION
(INCLUDING INTERNATIONAL COMPANY)
STATEMENT OF OPERATIONS & ANALYSIS OF IBT VARIANCE

STATEMENT 6
PAGE ______

MONTH OF March, 1959   19   Transmotor DIV.
__________ DEPT.

(DOLLARS IN THOUSANDS)

CONFIDENTIAL – Information in this statement is not to be released or transmitted outside the Westinghouse Electric Corporation Organization.

LINE NO.	CURRENT MONTH Objective	Actual	Variance	SCH. NO.	DESCRIPTION	YEAR TO DATE Variance	Actual	Objective
1	9.3%	5.4%	* 3.9%		% RETURN ON TOTAL GROSS ASSETS	3.7%	14.0%	10.3%
2	7 625	7 595	30		TOTAL GROSS ASSETS	32	7 588	7 620
3	1.5	1.5	–		ASSET TURNOVER	.1	1.6	1.5
4	1 050	1 075	25		ORDERS ENTERED – CUSTOMER	215	3 220	3 005
5	50	55	5		– INTERUNIT	15	135	120
6	2 575	2 610	35		UNFILLED ORDERS – CUSTOMER	35	2 610	2 575
7	150	125	* 25		– INTERUNIT	* 25	125	150
8	950	920	* 30		GROSS SALES BILLED	110	3 010	2 900
9	142	137	5		PRODUCT COSTS – LABOR	* 20	455	435
10	323	315	8		– MATERIAL	* 59	1 045	986
11	86	82	4		– FACTORY EXPENSE	* 10	242	232
12	57	53	4		– OTHER	20	180	200
13					–			
14	608	587	21		TOTAL PRODUCTS COSTS	* 69	1 922	1 853
15	(342)	(333)	(* 9)		MARGIN OVER PRODUCT COSTS	(41)	(1 088)	(1 047)
16	(.3600)	(.3613)	(.0013)		MARGIN RATIO TO G.S.B.	(.0005)	(.3615)	(.3610)
17	40	41	* 1		COMMITTED COSTS	2	118	120
18	72	70	2		ORGANIZ. & OTHER OPER.	5	215	220
19	5	10	* 5		FACILITIES PROGRAM EXP.	–	10	10
20	–	–	–		MFG. DEVELOPMENT	* 5	10	5
21								
22	77	80	* 3		DIVISION MGD. COSTS – MFG.	–	235	235
23	15	14	1		C.O. DEVELOPMENT – ENGRG.	5	45	50
24	25	22	3		STD. DEVELOP. – ENGRG.	2	70	72
25	3	3	–		LONG RANGE MAJOR DEVELOPMENT	–	9	9
26	5	10	* 5		STD. DEVELOP. – TOOLS	–	10	10
27								
28	48	49	* 1		DIVISION MGD. COSTS – PRODUCT DEVELOP.	7	134	141
29	5	10	* 5		DIVISION ADVERTISING	5	15	20
30	30	32	* 2		DIVISION & REGION SALES – DIV. CONTR.	5	85	90
31	9	8	1		DIVISION ORDER SERV., WHSE. & SHIP.	2	23	25
32								
33	44	50	* 6		DIVISION MGD. COSTS – MARKETING	12	123	135
34	20	19	1		ADM. & GEN'L – DIVISION CONTROL	2	50	52
35	–	–	–		FOR., LIC., ROY. & PAT., CAN. W. INC.	2	* 2	–
36	* 2	* 3	1		OTHER INCOME & DEDUCTIONS – NET	1	* 7	* 6
37								
38	18	16	2		DIVISION MGD. COSTS – ADM. & GEN'L	5	41	46
39	187	195	* 8		TOTAL DIV. MANAGED COSTS	24	533	557
40	2	4	* 2		INT'L SALES, ADM. & GEN'L.	* 1	7	6
41	26	26	–		HDQTRS. GEN'L CONTROL EXPENSE	–	78	78
42	25	25	–		REGIONAL SALES (APPR. DIV.) & DIST. SER.	–	75	75
43	8	8	–		HDQTRS. RESEARCH & DEVELOPMENT	–	24	24
44								
45	61	63	* 2		TOTAL NON-DIV. MANAGED COSTS	* 1	184	183
46	288	299	* 11		TOTAL COMM. & MANAGED COSTS	25	835	860
47	5	–	* 5		INVENTORY CHANGE – EFFECT ON IBT	2	12	10
48	59	34	* 25		INCOME BEFORE TAXES	68	265	197
49	(6.2%)	(3.7%)	(* 2.5%)		INCOME BEFORE TAXES – % G.S.B.	(2.0%)	(8.8%)	(6.8%)
50	800	828	* 28		BREAKEVEN VOLUME	73	2 309	2 382
51	(84.2%)	(90.0%)	(* 5.8%)		BREAKEVEN VOLUME – % G.S.B.	(5.4%)	(76.7%)	(82.1%)

LINE NO.			FROM 1959 OBJ.		ANALYSIS OF IBT VARIANCE — CAUSE OF VARIANCE	FROM 1959 OBJ.	Same Period 1958 Actual	
52								
53								
54			* 20		REALIZED SALES PRICES	10	15	
55			* 4		VOLUME OF G.S.B.	36	197	
56			12		MIX OF SALES	* 7	22	
57			* 2		PRODUCT COSTS – WAGE & NAT'L RATES	* 3	* 52	
58			5		– OTHER	5	35	
59								
60			* 9		MARGIN OVER PRODUCT COSTS	41	217	
61			* 1		COMM., & MGD. COSTS – DIV. – WAGE & MAT'L	* 2	* 20	
62			* 8		– OTHER	28	10	
63			* 5		ADJUSTMENT FOR INVENTORY CHANGE	2	20	
64								
65			* 23		TOTAL VARIANCE – DIVISION CONTROL	69	207	
66			* 2		NON-DIVISION – MANAGED COSTS	* 1	* 3	
67					– OTHER			
68								
69			* 25		TOTAL VARIANCE – IBT	68	210	

* CONTRA IN COST & EXPENSES   * LOSS ON LINE 48   * UNFAVORABLE IN VARIANCE COLUMNS

SPONSORED BY F. E. DALTON

Planning Procedure

What can be done to provide for greater top management participation in setting objectives, for more detailed consideration of basic improvement requirements, and for a closer tie between long-range plans, short-range budgets, and actual results? One helpful step is a new procedure that was developed and put in operation at Westinghouse early in 1957. Experience with it has been extremely favorable, and while small alterations will undoubtedly be made from year to year, it is expected that the basic features of the method will be continued for several years.

The most fundamental change from the procedures formerly used is that planning reviews have been put on a rolling schedule throughout the year. During each month top management reviews the plans and objectives of three to five operating divisions, covering all of the divisions over the 12-month period. This review is attended by the president, executive vice president, other members of corporate top management, the product group general managers, and the vice presidents for sales, engineering, manufacturing, and finance. The division manager is responsible for preparing his plan, reviewing it with his group manager, and then presenting it to the top management committee.

In addition to the profit pattern analysis, the division managers prepare, as part of their presentation to the committee, a five-year projection of market trends for each product line, a forecast of capital facilities requirements, and a projection of working capital requirements for the target year. These projections, together with the profit pattern analysis, are supported by specific plans of action to cope with the particular problems of the division as revealed by the analysis. These action plans may be directed to a reduction of managed costs or product costs, increased sales effort to step up sales volume relative to the breakeven point, shifted emphasis in development to update product designs or increase the speed of developing new products, or modernization or expansion of facilities to meet the requirements of growth or improvement.

Another change in procedure shortens the length of time covered by the planning cycle. Formerly the initial planning called for a fifth-year projection of markets, facilities, and profit margins. But five years, in most of the cases we deal with, is too far in the future for the kind of specific planning called for, and planning so far ahead led to inflation of programs of all kinds tied to long-range market projections. It was decided, therefore, at least for a few years, to focus planning attention on the next full calendar year. To illustrate:

> In January 1958, general company goals for improvement of operations were adopted and communicated to the division managers at a management meeting. In February, top management began to review the objective and plans of each division for the year 1959. Subsequently, detailed plans were reviewed in the light of their contribution to the over-all company objectives as well as to the solution of the specific problems which were facing managers.

Finally, the new procedure provides for a better comparison of objectives and results. Both division and corporate managements receive a periodic playback of long-range plans against short-range budgets and against actual performance to date.

This step permits evaluation of planning deficiences, adjustment of emphasis in planning, and measurement of the planning and operating performance of division managers in terms applicable to each individual situation. It is likely that in future years the length of the planning cycle will be increased, at least for some of those divisions which have long product cycles through booking of orders, design, and manufacture. On the other hand, it is not likely that the longer-range objectives will be disassociated from shorter-range plans and current operating performance.

POINTING UP OPPORTUNITIES

How can profit pattern analysis help management? What kinds of opportunities for improvement can it point up? Westinghouse's experience is a revealing one, and I should like to turn now to some examples of what has been accomplished. It might be argued, of course, that some of these gains might have happened anyway—without profit pattern analysis. It is our conviction, however, that the new approach has revealed problems more clearly and has stimulated prompt and constructive action by management.

Managed-Cost Trends

Confirming pre-existing suspicions, profit pattern analyses revealed that the level and trend of managed costs was unsatisfactory. The analyses not only pointed up the contributing factors, but also provided a means for determining the level to which managed costs should be held if adequate profits were to be earned under various volume conditions. Furthermore, they provided the mechanics for measuring the effect of various alternative management decisions. For example, the cost of a stepped-up program for market penetration could be evaluated in terms of the additional sales volume necessary to overcome the costs of the program and produce a net gain in profitability.

Convincing knowledge of the effect of managed-cost trends and their relative importance in the total cost picture led to an aggressive management drive to contain the growth of these trends. This was done by more careful evaluation of plans to spend money in such judgment areas as product development, sales promotion, advertising, and public relations; by the adoption of formalized industrial engineering techniques for the analysis of paperwork systems and the productivity of nonfactory personnel; also by development of a formalized approach to organization analysis and simplification.

Profit Detractors

A specific program was initiated throughout the corporation for detailed studies of each product line not contributing a normal margin over product costs. Objectives were to determine why the product was not producing adequate margins, what could be done through redesign or improved manufacture to reduce costs, and finally, whenever all alternatives appeared inadequate, to face up to the decision of abandoning that product line. As a result of this approach the loss from these so-called "profit detractors" has been substantially reduced. Several individual product lines have been dropped, and one operating department has been discontinued and its plant disposed of.

In singling out individual product lines for detailed study, courses of action necessary to make them more profitable became obvious very quickly. Before profit pattern analysis these courses of action had been obscured by the fact that the results for individual product lines were lost in general profit and loss figures. Now specific opportunities emerged. Here are some concrete examples:

In come cases it became evident that product cost-selling price relationships were basically good, but sales volume was insufficient to absorb the managed costs associated with the product. This resulted in intensified sales efforts, either through re-alignment of sales responsibility or by the expediture of more advertising and sales promotional funds.

In other cases it was discovered that overhead organizations had been built in anticipation of larger sales volume than could be realized in the foreseeable future. Management decided, therefore, to scale these managed cost structures down to a size suitable for the volume of sales actually being realized.

Situations were also discovered in which a net improvement in over-all profit margins could be obtained by re-alignment of manufacturing or selling responsibilities for "profit detractor" lines. In one case it was discovered that management responsibility for an individual product had been separated from responsibility for the end product in which the "profit detractor" was a component part. Combining the two responsibilities led to more effective direction of development efforts in the component and to expanded use of the component both in the end product division and in the outside market as well.

Cost-Price Squeeze

The profit pattern analysis has dramatically portrayed the seriousness of the squeeze on profits which has been caused by the upward trend of wage and salary rates and raw material costs, and by the historic reluctance of the electrical industry to translate rising costs into higher prices. It has become clear to all levels of management that, unless the rate of increase in wages is brought into line with the rate of increase in productivity of *all* employees, hourly and salary, either prices must rise or profit margins will continue to suffer; and that management policies must be guided accordingly. For example, we see today that:

(1) The attitude with which management approaches the bargaining table to negotiate contract changes needs to be studied with particular reference to the

ability of the company to recover the cost of such wage increases through productivity improvement or price increases.

(2) The whole area of pricing policy and procedures needs to be studied to assure anticipation of contractual increases in costs and to exploit every practical opportunity for assuming price leadership.

Excess Capacity

In a few divisions the profit pattern analyses show that too wide a gap exists between current production levels and the capacity of existing facilities. This gap, for several reasons, makes earning adequate profits virtually impossible despite all efforts to reduce product and managed costs. Accordingly, action has been initiated to step up marketing programs and promotional activities; to increase sales volume relative to the breakeven point; and to reduce excess capacity with its attendant overheads by consolidating production in lower cost location and by closing out or retiring idle or excess plant and equipment.

EXECUTIVE EFFECTIVENESS

To sum up, the profit pattern concept provides for the segregation of income and cost data according to the factors which cause them to change. It provides a means for evaluating the effect on profits of such influencing factors as: price levels, sales volume, mix of product, changing labor and material rates, and cost reductions through redesign and methods improvements.

By segregating the elements of profit performance in these categories, the new concept reveals to management the general lines of approach which must be taken to improve results. Once this is done, specific plans of action and tools for improvement can be utilized, with the profit pattern arrangement facilitating evaluation of various courses of action.

The universal reaction of line managers at Westinghouse, after almost two years of using the profit pattern technique, is that they now have a far better understanding of what is going on in the company and in the various divisions. Consequently, they have been able to plan and carry out programs of action specifically suited to the problems at hand.

Reading 5-4

The Budget Comes of Age

By James L. Peirce*

Any technique of management reaches maturity when, after its earlier mistakes have antagonized human beings sufficiently, it emerges with a new outlook and practice that is in harmony with the basic motivations of people. Budgeting now seems to be undergoing this metamorphosis. Out of the disturbance it has created is appearing a calmer, more orderly, more positive approach.

It is my purpose in this article to add weight to the spreading view that budgeting rests on principles which have more in common with concepts of human relationship than with rules of accounting; and that, if these principles are applied, successful practice is inevitable.

DEFENSIVENESS—THE TROUBLE

There is no doubt that thousands of management people are well grounded in constructive budget practice and derive from it a sense of balance and direction in their business affairs. No businessman who has had extensive experience with an ably managed budget system appears to doubt its value. But there are many more thousands who are so confused on the subject that it might indeed be better for them to discard their budgets entirely than to continue as they are. Surveys have shown that in some quarters budgeting is about as popular among foremen as a layoff, and analyses stress the damage that results from the misuse of budgeting procedures.

Some executives freely admit the shortcomings of their budget practices and acknowledge that they could be remedied by the application of more

---

* Vice-President (finance), secretary and treasurer, A. B. Dick Company. From the *Harvard Business Review*, May–June, 1954. Reprinted by permission of the *Harvard Business Review*.

intelligent human relations. If it is as simple as that, then why cannot budgets be made a welcome and productive feature of all business operation without delay? The answer, I think, is that the problem is not such a simple one—just as human beings are not simple, just as the science of human relationships is not simple, as witness the many failures to apply it effectively.

How shall we go about the task of instilling revitalized ideas in place of negative or shortsighted attitudes?

We can accomplish nothing until we face up to the fact that many of us have acquired a defensive approach to the subject through painful experience. Here we must dig deep into the recesses of thought—not omitting the realm of emotional misconception that colors our word associations. Why do the two words "budgets" and "people" repel each other? Why should they, when taken together, suggest the image of a problem? Why, in fact, should it even be necessary to discuss a positive approach to the matter of budgets and people?

This unhappy reaction comes from the fact that people generally do not like budgets. We must remember that foremen are people first and supervisors second; so are department managers and top executives. Budgets represent restriction. They are in the same category as school bells and Monday mornings. Each of us has entered business life with a primitive aversion to restraint, only thinly veneered by academic training.

Someone should have presented the budget idea to us very constructively in order for us to accept it, much less to enjoy it. If from the very beginning of our careers we had been told, with accompanying evidence, that budgets were a help to us, affording us guidance, stability, and strength, as well as keeping us out of innumerable troubles, our responses would by now be quite different.

But what was our actual experience? Have not many of us been introduced to budgets in business when the budget was blamed, rightly or wrongly, for our failure to get a raise in pay? Have not many of us become acquainted with the budget only as a barrier to spending what we felt were necessary amounts of money for better equipment or performance? Is it surprising, then, that budgets are associated in many people's minds with paucity and niggardliness rather than with planning and direction?

Fortunately, it is not too late to effect a correction in the thinking of the current generation of managers.

ATTITUDES—THE KEY

In probing further, it quickly becomes evident that good attitudes are the key to successful budgeting. When the attitudes of people toward each other are generous, understanding, and based on mutual respect, any technique adopted by management to further effective performance is apt to be successful. When human attitudes are dominated by distrust, criticism, and recrimination, any technique designed to improve performance is likely to fail miserably. In such cases, by a strange twist of human nature, the budgets and those who defend them bear the brunt of the blame for more fundamental errors which are entirely unconnected with budgets.

Budgeting is a trained, disciplined approach to all problems, which recognizes the need for standards of performance in order to achieve a result. Hence it must be built on a base of good organization; otherwise, favorable attitudes have no chance to operate. But at the same time it lives in an atmosphere of perpetual adjustment to the needs and capacities of people. It thrives on such fundamentals as recognition of accomplishment, consideration for the rights of individuals, fair play—in other words, enlightened relationships among people.

Motivation for Budgeting

In exploring budgeting principles as they relate to people, the first consideration should be the motivation for the budget system. Why have one at all? Is the budget a part of a system of over-all planning, in order that all concerned may have a measure of the amounts to be spent, and in order that action may be by design rather than by expediency? Or is the budget a pressure device designed to goad people into greater efforts? It takes a little soul-searching to determine honestly which of these concepts represents the position of a particular management.

Both concepts are prevalent. They may be symbolized by two wooden sticks—one neatly divided into thirty-six one-inch spaces, and the other sharply pointed at one end. The yardstick, symbolizing the planning concept of budgets, may be used, for example, by a foreman to establish standards of performance and cost and to measure actual results in relation thereto; in this sense, it is a tool used by the foreman and his boss in partnership. The pointed stick, a symbol of the pressure type of budget, is always found in the hand of the superior, turned menacingly toward his foremen or workers. The yardstick concept elicits the voluntary effort of men to do their best work. The pointed stick forces a reluctant and minimal performance.

There is plenty of evidence that the choice of the yardstick concept will not diminish the yield from the budget tool in terms of cost reduction. It has been shown again and again that high costs which stubbornly resist all efforts of the pressure type will melt away under the warmth of an approach which is attuned to the basic responses of humanity. The attitude to be adopted here is an enlistment of all concerned in a common effort, with a complete explanation of objectives and methods.

PLANNING—THE FOUNDATION

Next in the line of exploration of principles is the dependence of budgets on general company planning. Although budgeting can be separately applied to any unit of the business, it is far more effective when it rests on a foundation of integrated planning for the entire operation. In the proper sense, it is only one phase of planning. When the planning concept has been adopted, budgets emerge of necessity—budgets with a purpose as deep as the stream of ideas giving direction and drive to the business itself.

The presence or absence of intelligent planning is reflected to a surprising degree in the effectiveness of the people who are asked to operate with a budget system. And this means all the people—from top executives to production-line workers. Individuals are usually more intuitive than we realize. When a budget is built on sound business planning, they respond to that fact without always knowing why.

Meaning of Planning

As used in this discussion, *planning* refers to the predetermination of a course of action in such detail that every responsible unit of the company may be guided thereby. It includes sales forecasting, production scheduling, expense budgeting, and estimating of manufacturing costs and inventory levels. It involves making advance decisions concerning new product development and introduction, merchandising methods, material procurement, and labor rates. In short, planning implies anticipating all the knotty problems to be met by a business during the planning period—usually a year so far as operations are concerned, longer for financial and developmental activities—in other words, facing the problems and making decisions about them *ahead of time* (subject to later revision if necessary).

These decisions are frequently so hard to make in advance that they border on the impossible. Yet they insure a reasonable net profit as no other method can. And on this planned net profit figure—the apex of the planning structure—depends our ability to attract new capital as needed and to compensate management and shareholders.

I need not elaborate the importance of profit planning. I am only concerned here that it be recognized that when budgeting has a hard core of deliberate planning, adhered to by the company's top, middle, and all other management, the budget idea takes on real meaning for all concerned. Without this basis, it can never be completely palatable to those who do not understand how it can benefit them.

Effect on People

Let us examine the effect of the planning process on the people involved in it. In particular, we might first consider the impact on administrative people, for their outlook in the long run determines the attitudes of the larger non-administrative group. What is the planning technique doing to foremen, department managers, division heads? Is it building up or tearing down their confidence in their company's future? Is it affecting favorably or adversely their independence of thought, their self-assurance, their capacity to understand and rely on those around them?

It seems self-evident that planning alone does not afford the entire answer. If a company's administrative personnel are exhibiting what is called "good morale" before the installation of a planning system, the chances are that turning their eyes to the future and asking them to construct together a plan for better achievement can do them no harm, but can do them untold good. With proper explanations, the management can hold forth the legitimate promise of better accomplishment, greater satisfaction, more confident operating, and, ultimately, opportunity for increased compensation.

If, on the other hand, the management is struggling with a discordant staff, perhaps suffering from the blight of fuzzy organization lines or any of the other impediments to good work resulting from a mediocre job of personnel administration, it might be better off to defer trying the planning and control idea until it has put its house in order. Too frequently a well-designed budget system has collapsed after being superimposed on a faulty base of administrative personnel policy. Then the budget is discarded and all concerned return to their familiar bad habits.

CONTROL—THE COMPLEMENT

But there is another phase of budgeting which tests the fiber of men even more than planning. I am referring to control, which is the eternal complement of planning. Neither one is useful without the other, and to budget even the smallest unit of a business implies the presence of control also.

Budget Abuses

It is in the control area that the colossal mistakes of budgeting are made. It is here that the amateurs have censured their subordinates for exceeding budgets, without realizing that they themselves were to blame for inadequate training. It is here that men have become so frustrated under maladministered budgets that they have resorted to all sorts of tricks to conceal the actual results and have padded their budgets to give themselves breathing room. It is here that staff men have usurped authority, merited pay increases have been denied because of budget limitations, and tales have been carried around supervision and up to the top under the guise of budget reporting.

The list of abuses could be prolonged indefinitely. There are many wrong ways to exercise budget control. There is only one right way. Let us then discard the negative approach, since the assertion of an affirmative truth will dissolve all counterfeits.

Control might be quickly and simply defined as a disciplined effort to follow a plan or explain deviations from it. The effort referred to takes the form of self-discipline—voluntary, unified, and cooperative. The deviations from plan are deliberate, foreknown, and authorized. If they are apparently beyond anyone's ability to prevent—as for instance a failure to reach budgeted sales volume—at least they are spotlighted as early as possible, and management has the chance to take whatever action is indicated. Control is simply the modern form of the old formula, "management by exception."

It is, of course, at the point of deviation from the budget that most of the human problems are born. This is, by design, the central point in the entire system—the moment which demands explanation, instruction, decision, argument, or even discipline, as the case warrants—the flash point for management in action.

Common-Sense Departures

It should be evident that the effect of control on people is commensurate with their training and conditioning for it. If they understand thoroughly the meaning and uses of control, they will view it in the light of common sense. They will neither resent it nor be awed by it. They will turn it to the constructive use for which it is intended, and it will become an aid rather than an obstacle.

Perhaps the best way to clarify this common-sense approach is to examine a typical situation in which a manager wishes to make what he believes to be a desirable expenditure not covered in his budget. This problem is encountered daily and solved without friction by management people equipped with knowledge of budget principles and skill in their application—in other words, by the trained minority which shows the same attitudes-in-action of a manager grounded in good budget practice as illustrated in the following case:

The case of a sales promotion manager who is also responsible for advertising —Having been instructed to prepare a budget, he has first carefully completed his sales promotion and advertising plans for the coming period, basing them on discussions with the sales vice president and others responsible for policy and sales objectives. After constructing an acceptable plan, he has converted it into dollars in the form of a budget, which has been approved.

Because he has prepared this budget himself, he is thoroughly familiar with it. It is supported with adequate detail, including schedules of space insertions, estimates of costs of mailings, salary lists, and so on. He has reached an understanding with his "boss" concerning all of these items as a preliminary to approval of the budget. He feels confident that the plan and budget are as nearly right as he can make them.

Furthermore, he knows the implications of accepting this budget as his guide to operations. It is not to be exceeded without approval. It is a commitment that must be honored, and he well understands its importance to the company, his associates, and himself.

Nevertheless, he senses in the attitudes surrounding his budget an element of flexibility. If conditions change, the budget will have to be altered, either upward or downward. The sales promotion manager is not uneasy about this prospect. He is simply alert to recognize such a situation if it should develop.

Now let us suppose that an opportunity is presented to exert extra pressure on a certain market, and it appears that a special direct-mail compaign, supplemented by some local newspaper advertising, will yield good sales result. He knows enough not to throw the whole idea aside simply because it is not provided for in his budget. He has already had a clear understanding with the top sales executive about what to do in such cases. So he goes about preparing a report, including proposed action, cost, and anticipated results; and he presents this report, knowing that it will be given proper consideration, even though it represents an expenditure in excess of budget limits.

The important point here is that this man, as manager of sales promotion, will not be subjected to injustice, censure, or negative treatment of any sort in advancing his ideas. He is fully aware of having a plan and a commitment to abide by it; yet he has assurance that if the interests of the company will be best served by breaking the budget, permission to do so will be forthcoming. All concerned will have an opportunity to evaluate the proposal and to weigh the desirability of deviating from the adopted plan.

How simple this miniature study in budget attitudes! How mature the responses governed by common sense! And yet how often common sense is violated! Is there any reason not to extend this frank approach to the foreman who sees a need for maintenance expenses or a merit increase not embraced in his budget? The frictions, frustrations, and other evils supposed to be inherent in budgets must all be susceptible to eradication in the same sensible manner.

Essential Prerequisites

All this presupposes, of course, that the supervisor in question—regardless of which division of the business he may be in—enjoys a satisfactory working relationship with his immediate superior. It also rests on clear-cut organization lines and the disposition to delegate authority along with responsibility.

Further, the accounting principles used must be well tested, and the accounting administration of high caliber. Strict honesty must govern the determination of the content of budget accounts and of the charges made thereto. Nothing confuses budget operation more quickly than the charging of costs over which the supervisor has no control, unless such items are set out separately and so labeled.

A last important requisite is understanding of the make-up of the budget. Flexible factory budgets especially can be complicated and subject to dispute. The factors used must be clearly explained, with full recognition of their weaknesses. If an item—such as machine repairs, for example—is neither wholly fixed nor wholly variable, but must be treated one way or the other for budget purposes, the shortcomings of the resulting budget figure should be conceded frankly. If scrap and rework costs are subject to dispute between foremen, the situation must be talked out in an air of give-and-take. No plant management should encourage or permit embittered arguments between foremen on such a matter. If all concerned have a clear understanding of the function of the budget and a reasonable attitude toward each other in the framework of modern industrial organization, such disputes will not occur.

COST REDUCTION—THE GOAL

The attitudes we have been discussing should add to, rather than detract from, the effectiveness of budgets in the field of cost control. Most companies operate continuously, in good times and bad, under the pressure of relentless competition, which forces them in turn to devote ceaseless effort to cost reduction. It is perhaps this circumstance more than any other that has given impetus to the spread of budgeting. And it has doubtless given rise to the abuses falling under the general heading of "pressure."

The usual tone of the complaints in this category is to the effect that budgets are used only as a hammer on costs (and at the same time on people), and particularly that the budgets are constantly being tightened and compliance with them enforced indiscriminately. The impression received by a supervisor in this situation is one of constant insistence on better and better performance, continuous blame for failure to meet the budget, and complete absence of credit for his good work. The budget becomes purely a pressure device, against which he must defend himself or lose his job.

The only really effective cure for such a distorted outlook is to substitute, as rapidly as possible, a "let's do it together" attitude for the shortsighted "you do it or else" attitude. The latter may have gained more ground in a plant or office than the management realizes. To correct this attitude may take time and patience, but it is never impossible to blank out negatives and substitute positives in human thinking.

Cost reduction drive is a feature of the American competitive system and is admittedly responsible in large measure for our high living standard. Budgets can be used for such stimulation without enslaving people. They furnish the standard from which to explore cost-savings possibilities. They provide the measure of yield from improved methods. But the attitude surrounding the practice must be right.

Incentives, True and False

This line of thought runs directly into the question of incentive. What incentive does a production supervisor have to reduce costs? Certainly the incentive supplied by threat is negative and, in the long run, ineffective. Direct money incentives, correlated to budget factors, claim some merit but, as we shall see, are fraught with problems. The true incentives, becoming clear after generations of management experiment, are those usually referred to as "intangible," supplemented by wages carefully determined and sympathetically explained.

But as an alternative let us examine for a moment the possibilities of direct money incentives. Some companies use and defend them—and we can have no quarrel with success. The line of reasoning on which they are based runs something like this: "If simple piecework can be an effective incentive for the workman, then the same principle can be applied to the foreman. We will provide a supervisory bonus and include in its computation a factor measuring success in complying with the budget. Savings against the budget will benefit the company and, at the same time, will provide funds for rewarding the foreman."

The fallacies in this reasoning begin to appear early in the process. They arise from two sources: (a) from the almost insurmountable difficulty of setting a completely fair and acceptable budget for this purpose, especially in the light of unforeseeable changes in operating conditions, and (b) from the tendency for the foreman to emphasize budget performance to the detriment of necessary action. It is a distinct temptation to defer maintenance when the need is not urgent and the expenditure would reduce one's own pay check.

As the foreman grows to the stature of a responsible manager, as he becomes more and more able to carry added responsibilities independently (and this is the goal of enlightened management today), the problems of basing incentive pay on budget factors become progressively tougher to handle. The experienced foreman is conscious of the importance of cost reduction, both by training and by virtue of the understanding of the job which his company has given him. He is also conscious of the need to spend money. He is likely to resent being rewarded for unwise penny-pinching as much as being penalized for exceeding his budget when the need for it is evident to everyone.

To a supervisor properly informed and aware of his role as a part of the management team, the real incentive is the satisfaction that comes from knowing that he has given his best effort, evidenced by suitable recognition both financial and in the manner and words of the superior. There is no substitute for the positive kind of understanding that can be developed between a supervisor and the rest of management if all concerned resolve to cultivate it.

By the same token, there is nothing better to assure the success of a cost-reduction program than a foreman with an inspired attitude and a real comprehension of the company's objectives, needs, and policies. To such a man, the budget will be a tool used to measure common achievements, rather than an irritant to the men and women entrusted to his leadership.

MANAGEMENT SUPPORT—THE NEED

One of the rocks on which many systems founder is the lack of top-management support. This is a strange commentary on a management group which, in this country, is generally supposed to have reached the acme of sophistication in the motivation of people. Nevertheless, examine any limping, halfhearted budget system, and note how the "chickens come home to roost" in the president's office.

Even more surprising, it frequently turns out that the top man does not really understand the planning and control concept and the simple interplay of attitudes that make it work. Consequently his allegiance to it is tentative and lukewarm. He constantly questions the methods used and is instinctively distrustful of results. This frame of mind permeates the organization. It bolsters opposition to the budget idea and weakens its proponents.

No budget system can realize its potential value without the unqualified support and understanding of top management. The solution, of course, lies in a process usually known as "education." Actually, it is even deeper than that. The budget idea is an expanding, growing concept—usually pioneered by one man with vision in a company. Little by little, this man—be he president or controller—patiently inculcates the advancing idea on his associates, until it is tested and accepted by all.

Controllers' Mistakes

There is another enemy of successful budget practice which may well be the cause of more of the friction between budgets and people than all the other errors put together. I refer to the misconception on the part of controllers, budget managers, accountants, and other staff people concerning their part in the process.

When a controller takes operating personnel to task for exceeding the budget, he is inviting trouble of the worst kind. His correct course is to report the situation to responsible operating management and, if necessary, to the president, using the same figures and terms in each case. The problem then rests with the president and his operating subordinate, which is exactly where it belongs. It should be discussed and action determined in the direct line organization. No controller should permit himself to be placed in the position of representing the president in such matters—of giving approval to budgets or disapproval to results.

The same principle applies to all staff people concerned with coordinating the budget system, whether they report to a controller, treasurer, or factory accountant. There is impressive evidence that overzealous budget people have caused a great deal of mischief in this field, practically all of it unnecessary. They cannot be blamed individually, of course, for the failure of management to provide the principles needed for good budget practice. The remedy is in the eradication of a vicious set of faulty notions concerning the relationships of staff and line.

One of the first steps is to insist that each manager or foreman establish his own budget. He knows best his potential performance and the extent to which he can commit himself. He may enlist expert help, of course, from the budget man, but under no circumstances should the budget man or controller establish the budget, nor should the foreman be permitted to feel that this is happening. The penalty for violating this rule is the sacrifice of the sense of responsibility that locks a man securely to his budget when he knows it is his own.

Another misconception sometimes indulged by budget men is that they are almost solely responsible for cost reduction; that they alone are expected to seek and find opportunities for cost savings, such as excessive waste, dispensable overtime, carelessness in handling tools, and so on. In some cases, they have apparently been instructed to report such instances to a factory superintendent or even to top management rather than to the responsible first-line supervisor. It is difficult to conceive of a practice that violates more completely the basic principles of good human relations.

Line Organization

This medieval mess will clear itself up once management has established the fact that the line organization is responsible for cost control—fully and absolutely. Using a familiar type of organization, let it be clear that the vice president of manufacturing is charged with the duty of conducting the manufacturing cost reduction campaign; he delegates this work as he sees fit to plant managers, and they in turn to factory superintendents, who then look to the front-line men, the foremen, for control of costs.

The controller and budget men still fit into this picture importantly:

(1) They are equipped to establish and coordinate the budget system, with all of the tools of accounting and cost analysis.

(2) They should be able to teach the operating people how to use it.

(3) They should provide timely and intelligible reporting on performance against budget. (This reporting should of course be tailored to the organization level to which it is addressed. For instance, at the top, the controller is obligated to report that which is pertinent to the president of the company.)

The attitude which should govern the staff people in this field, as in all other staff assignments, is one of maximum helpfulness to the line personnel. Only in this way can the budget man gain the foreman's confidence. If he finds cost-saving ideas, they should be volunteered promptly to the foreman for what use the latter can make of them. Personal credit is not the primary consideration. The budget man's own superior should be adept enough in detecting a skillful job to accord it the recognition it deserves—and one primary evidence of such performance will be a satisfactory relationship with the operating personnel. It is a preposterous notion that a budget man vaults to success on the failures and errors of the line.

CONCLUSION

The specific steps to be taken to improve budgeting practice depend, of course, on the mistakes an organization has been making. A searching self-examination in the light of the known principles of budgeting would seem to be the first move. Having identified the practices in an organization which most clearly abuse these principles, management will find that the corrective steps will present themselves. Courage and patience are needed to follow them.

Summary of Principles

Here, for your convenience, is a summary of points to be considered by any management wishing to establish its budget practice on a sound foundation:

(1) Establish your budget system on the highest possible level of motivation. To be specific, this means using it as a means for setting standards of performance, for measuring actual results, and for guiding management to satisfactory achievement. It means rejecting the use of budgets primarily as a pressure device to goad people into greater efforts. Accept this as a part of the philosophy of your company. Think about it, talk about it, make it a reality. And give more than lip service, even if it is difficult at first to separate the two conflicting motives. A budget program cannot be advanced to the stage of maximum fruition without this step.

(2) Anchor your budgeting firmly in a foundation of company planning. Do not permit it to float unattached—a technique without a clearly thought-out reason for being. The budget is not the plan; it is merely the statement of the plan in the language of figures. First turn the thinking of your organization to basic planning; then ask your people to prepare budgets to effectuate their plans. Plan sales by markets and products, plan development, plan methods of manufacturing, purchasing, and merchandising. Determine the performance required of each department of the business; then budgets become simply the standard of dollars needed to do the job. This is the approach that makes managers out of men.

(3) Establish the meaning of control, and then put it into practice. In particular this requires the manager of each department to establish his own budget, based on his understanding of the job to be done. Top management may not be able to approve as high a figure as he asks for, but it can reach agreement with him as to what he is expected to accomplish and what it will cost. Having done this, he is responsible for planned performance. If he finds it necessary to exceed the budget, he should discuss this action with his superior and ask for advance approval. A budget is neither to be considered sacred nor to be taken lightly. Managers will respond with better attitudes when they understand that the use of the budget is to permit them to control their own operations.

(4) Insist on a clear-cut organization structure. A budget system cannot thrive without it. Each department should have a responsible manager, vested with authority commensurate with his responsibilities. He should have a clear understanding both as to the individual to whom he reports and as to the people who report to him. These are well-known precepts. A searching organization audit may be needed to determine whether they are being followed. The limitations on budget success are precisely marked by the degree of organization soundness.

(5) Arrange for good, common-sense accounting and complete, simple, and prompt explanations of the contents of the items. This requires an accounting staff that is more concerned with the operating facts than with the techniques of balancing the books. Extreme care should be devoted to seeing that no supervisor has in his budget any item over which he does not have control. This area is fraught with debatable items and unending technical complications. If your house is not in order in this respect, almost any amount of effort is justified to put it in

shape. And unless you are the exception to the rule, it will cost more money initially than you expect to pay, in terms of staff salaries and, perhaps, outside consulting services. The cost is usually well justified, however, in the end result.

(6) In the field of cost control, use your budget as a tool to be placed in your foremen's hands—not as a club to be held over their heads. To implement this rule, it may be a good idea to design an educational program. Meetings attended by line and staff supervisors may prove an effective vehicle. Cost reduction must be placed on the basis of mutual effort toward a common aim. The creation of this atmosphere is an essential, definitive step in budget practice.

(7) Insure the active participation of top management. The budget program cannot succeed otherwise. The way of going about this step depends on your organizational status. If you are the president and question how well you measure up to this requirement, examine your thinking critically and ascertain which of the points in this article, if any, arouse resistance in your thought. Discussion with a controller other than your own may afford a fresh view. In any case, set aside the time to explore and understand the subject fully and to practice budgetary control in your daily affairs. If, however, you are a controller, your course in enlisting top-management support is one of patient, untiring teaching, until your case is won and the planning and control idea is in the warp and woof of your company's thinking.

(8) See that the controller and his staff express the correct attitude for the responsibility they undertake with respect to budgets. It is the controller's job to establish, maintain, and coordinate a budgetary system—in fact, a complete system of planning and control. But this work must be accomplished through authorized management. He must not enforce his instructions nor issue orders. He and his staff must be devoted to producing, reporting, and interpreting information—to making the planning and control machinery run. He is wholly a staff executive, and his only honors stem from the confidence of his associates. This he earns by honestly providing the control service and refraining from making operating decisions. Perhaps the cultivation of this attitude is the most productive single step of all, because from it the impetus to take the other steps may flow.

I have refrained from specifying the manner in which these ideas might be made known, or "sold," to the administrative groups. The task is essentially one for controllership. It is the most challenging project the controller is privileged to conduct, and it gains momentum as he enlists the support of top management and of supervision at all levels.

The actual method of carrying on this unremitting campaign varies from company to company, but there is a predominant tendency to rely largely on daily contacts. The controller and his staff—all the budget men and cost accountants—spread the idea in their working conversations. Meanwhile, special attention is continuously given the top echelon by the controller himself. Relatively few companies appear to hold regular educational or discussion meetings for this purpose.

It is interesting that all of the eight steps listed have their roots deep in personnel administration—that each one is, in the final analysis, the reflection of a problem involving people.

Deeper Significance

The present era demands a new appraisal of our daily work. The symptoms of budget irritations may point to deeper meanings in the spiritual emancipation of mankind. We are beginning to learn that no tool can be used effectively unless the hand that guides it is rightly motivated. Like all other techniques of business, the budget should be a door open to more satisfying and profitable work—not an instrument of torture.

Then it will be known that what you can do without a budget you can do better with one. It will be seen that the entire planning and control procedure, under whatever name, is a device for freeing men to do their best work—not a machine of restriction and condemnation. This better view is within our grasp today.

Planning is but another word for the vision that sees a creative achievement before it is manifest. Control is but a name for direction. The genius of management cannot fail to turn the budget idea finally into positive channels, so that people individually, as well as business leadership generally, will reap the harvest that it promises.

Case 5–1

New Jersey Insurance Company

On July 16, 1959, John W. Montgomery, a member of the budget committee of the New Jersey Insurance Company, was reading over the current budget report for the law division in preparation for a conference scheduled for the next day with the head of that division. He held such conferences quarterly with each division head. Mr. Montgomery's practice was to think out in advance the questions he wished to ask and the points he thought he should make about each division's performance.

The law division of the New Jersey Insurance Company was responsible for all legal matters relating to the company's operations. Among other things, it advised company management on current and prospective developments in tax and other legislation and on recent court decisions affecting the company, it represented the company in litigation, counseled the departments concerned on the legal implications of policies such as employee benefit plans, and it examined all major contracts to which the company was a party. It also rendered various legal services in respect of the company's proposed and existing investments.

As shown in Exhibit 1, the head of the law division, William Somersby, reported directly to top management. This relationship insured that Mr. Somersby would be free to comment on the legal implications of management decisions, much the same as would an outside counsel. The law division was divided into five sections. This case is concerned with only two of these sections, the individual loan section and the corporate loan section. It does not attempt to completely describe the work of these two sections or the professional service rendered by the lawyers.

INDIVIDUAL LOAN SECTION

The individual loan section was responsible for the legal processing of loans made to individuals and secured by mortgages on real property. The

Exhibit 1

NEW JERSEY INSURANCE COMPANY
Partial Organization Chart

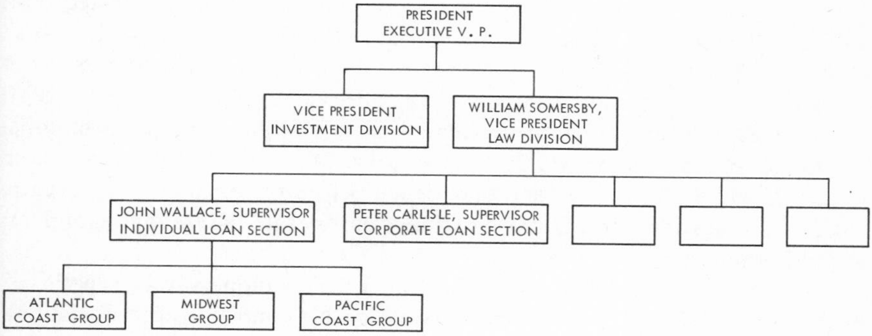

loan instruments were submitted by independent companies situated throughout the country. The company made no loans directly to individual borrowers, although at one time it had made direct loans in the New Jersey area. Most common among the loans submitted by the independent companies were FHA, VA, and conventional loans on homes, ranging in amounts from $10,000 to $20,000. These loans usually were made directly by banks or similar financial institutions organized for the purpose. They would batch together a number of loans and sell them to NJIC in a package. The insurance company purchased many thousands of such loans each year.

The investment division of the company was responsible for establishing the terms of these loans, including their amount, interest rate, and maturity. An independent company would submit to the investment division an offer to sell a mortgage loan. It was the function of this division to determine whether or not the property to be mortgaged and the mortgagor were acceptable to NJIC for a mortgage loan. After the proposed loan was approved and its terms worked out, the investment division would forward to the law division the note, mortgage, and related papers which it received from the seller.

The major function of the individual loan section was to perform the legal work necessary on all new loans purchased and on all existing loans. Among other things, it had to check all the loan instruments to make sure they did, in fact, protect the interests of NJIC as required by law and by the investment division. Organizationally, the section was divided into three groups, each headed by an attorney and each responsible for a geographical section of the country—Atlantic Coast, Midwest, and Pacific Coast. In addition to the three attorneys who headed regional groups, there were two other attorneys—one who helped out in busy spots and took over a group in case of sickness or vacation, and another who was in a training status.

Other than these five attorneys and a supporting secretarial staff, the section was comprised of 26 so-called mortgage examiners. These were persons who had had no formal legal training, but who had been carefully selected and company trained to check over and approve certain of the loan transactions that came into the section. Because of the repetitive nature of the routine loan transactions, management believed that properly selected and trained laymen could, under the supervision of lawyers, perform this task, which at one time had been performed only by lawyers. Problem cases were referred by the mortgage examiners to the attorneys. John Wallace, head of of the individual loan section, estimated that it took about three months initially to train a person to do this type of work. It then took about a year and a half of on-the-job training and experience before the examiner achieved a satisfactory rate of output, and two to three years before the average examiner reached optimum performance.

Since the work performed by the mortgage examiners was repetitive, management felt that it could exercise considerable control over a substantial part of this section. Based on a time study, a work standard of 12 loan transactions per examiner per day had been established some years previously, and this standard later was raised to 15. Records were maintained within the section of the number of loan transactions received each day, the number processed by each examiner, and the backlog.

In evaluating the work of individual examiners, some judgment had to be exercised in applying this standard. For example, in the Atlantic Coast group, an examiner sometimes received a batch of loan transactions in which the mortgaged properties were in a single, large housing subdivision. The legal issues in these transactions tended to be the same. In other parts of the country, however, loans tended to come from scattered localities and thus would be quite different from one another in many respects. A supervisor, therefore, in applying the standard would have to be familiar with the type of work an examiner was doing.

BUDGET PROCESS

Although considerable control could be achieved over the output of individual examiners, control over the entire section was a more difficult problem. Each September, the budget committee of the company issued a memorandum to all division heads, asking them to prepare a budget for the operation of their division during the following year.

The basic intent of the budget process was to get division heads to plan and report in advance the scope of their operations for the following year. Usually, the budgets were prepared by anticipating first the changes in activity levels from the current year and then the cost implications of these changes. Management checked each individual budget for reasonableness, and also checked the total expected cost and revenue to insure that the overall anticipated profit was satisfactory. The budget was viewed as a device for informing management of the plans a division head had for the coming year so that management could appraise these plans in relation to what other divisional heads had planned and in relation to company policy. The budget was also considered to be a measure of a division head's ability to plan his division's operations and then to operate in accordance with that plan.

On receipt of the budget committee's memorandum in September, division heads began forecasting operations within their divisions for the following year. First, each section head made plans for his section. For example, the individual loan section obtained an estimate of the amount of money that the investment division would have available for individual loans in the following year. Based partially on this estimate and partially on its estimated needs for other activities, the individual loan section developed a budget. This estimate, along with the estimated budgets for the other sections of the law division, was reviewed by Mr. Somersby. The law division then sent its budget to the budget committee for review. Usually, the law division's figures were accepted. Each quarter during the year, actual performance to date was compared with budgeted performance. Heads of divisions were required to explain large deviations from projected estimates.

Although management within the law division could, in theory, vary the size of the staff in the individual loan section, in fact, there was great reluctance to increase or decrease the work force unless a definite trend in volume was apparent. One reason for this was company policy. The company felt a great responsibility toward its employees, and as a matter of policy would lay off or discharge employees only for serious offenses. This same policy made management reluctant to hire new employees unless there was assurance that the need for them was permanent. Therefore, the law division tended to maintain a staff sufficient to handle a minimum work load, and it supplemented this with overtime.

Another reason for the tendency to maintain a level work force of mortgage examiners was the cost of selecting and training them. Management went to great pains to select outstanding clerks for these jobs. This was followed by a thorough course of study and on-the-job training. Because of this large investment, management wanted to be sure that anyone trained for this job would be needed permanently in the section.

Management within the individual loan section, in attempting to achieve control over the section as a whole and yet in keeping with company policy, had devised several controls. Occasionally, when the work load lessened, supervisors would call the investment division to see if they could get some work that, although perhaps not quite ready to be sent over as a complete batch, could, nevetherless, be sent in parts. Also, since in periods when loan applications were low foreclosures tended to increase, the mortgage examiners were trained to handle some aspects of foreclosures, and this provided a degree of dovetailing in the work flow. Other than these measures, however, the division preferred to rely on overtime work. The use of outside law firms was out of the question for this type of work because of the far greater cost, even in comparison with overtime wages.

CORPORATE LOAN SECTION

The corporate loan section was a much different kind of operation. A corporate loan, generally for a much larger amount than an individual loan, was one made directly by NJIC to a borrower, such as an industrial or commercial enterprise or a public utility. The loan might be either secured or unsecured. An important advantage to a borrower of this type of loan, as compared with a loan evidenced by a bond issue sold to the general public, was that the borrower was not required to furnish a formal prospectus or file a registration statement with the SEC.

In this type of loan, financial determinations such as the amount of the loan, interest rate, timing of repayments, restrictive covenants, and so forth were made by the investment division, as was the case with individual loans, but by a different section in that division. Because of the size and complexity of corporate loans, the corporate loan section worked closely with the investment division people who made these financial determinations. This involved sitting in on the negotiations and rendering advice on all the terms of the transaction. It was the responsibility of the corporate loan section to insure that the final loan instruments protected the interests of NJIC in the manner intended by the financial people.

On this type of loan, for various reasons, the corporate loan section almost without exception retained well-known outside counsel. One important reason was that an opinion from such an independent law firm contributed to the marketability of the investment in the event of a sale at a later date. Further, in many of these transactions, a number of other investors were involved, and NJIC's law division could not appropriately represent these other investors. If NJIC was the leading investor, it did, however, select the outside counsel to be retained. In addition, it was not possible, without greatly increasing the size of the present staff, for company attorneys to handle all the legal work connected with this type of loan, especially at the time of peak loads. Under this system, any one lawyer had a large number of loan negotiations in process at all times with various outside counsel, and this was beneficial both to the individual and to the company in providing lawyers with a broad base of experience in a variety of situations. The background and experience of company attorneys assured the company of consistency of policy in the negotiation of direct placements.

A substantial part of the work in corporate loans consisted of drafting legal documents. The extent to which company attorneys relied on outside counsel to perform parts of this work depended on the complexity of the transaction (company attorneys tended to do more of the work on more complex transactions) and on how busy company attorneys were. In general, company attorneys handled as a minimum enough of the work to be thoroughly familiar with all aspects of the transaction. In many cases, they prepared the first drafts of all legal papers. But in the event that first drafts were left to outside counsel, company attorneys reviewed the work and redrafted it as necessary.

Borrowers were required to pay all expenses incurred in employing outside counsel. However, NJIC made clear to both prospective borrowers and to outside counsel that the counsel were representing NJIC and that their loyalty belonged to NJIC, much the same as for a company attorney. Even though the borrower paid the fee for outside counsel, the head of the corporate loan section, Peter Carlisle, checked closely on the fees charged by outside counsel. Over the years, a thorough tabulation of fees charged for different types of legal work throughout the country had been built up. Mr. Carlisle, simply by referring to this tabulation, could readily determine whether a particular fee was apparently out of line. If there was any substantial deviation, he looked into the case more closely to determine if there was some reasonable explanation; if not, he discussed the matter with the outside counsel and adjusted the fee. Over the years, NJIC had established excellent working relationships with many law firms throughout the country.

The control procedure in this section was substantially different from that in the individual loan section. At the initiation of each transaction, Mr. Carlisle was consulted by the attorney to whom it was referred. Reassignments to equalize the work load of the various attorneys were made as necessary. A degree of control also was achieved through weekly staff conferences with Mr. Carlisle. At this conference, lawyers raised individual problems they had encountered. In addition to keeping Mr. Carlisle informed in detail on what was going on, the conference provided an opportunity for each staff member to draw on the experience of other lawyers, and it served as a vehicle for developing a consistent policy on various matters. Also, the discussion of current negotiations made it more likely that in case of illness another lawyer would be prepared to take over the work.

Another control device was the current work assignment report which each attorney in the section submitted to Mr. Carlisle. Because corporate loan transactions took varying amounts of time to complete, ranging from several weeks to many months, it was found that daily and, in some cases, weekly reports were not feasible. Accordingly, each attorney submitted a report when his work situation suggested to him that a new one was desirable. Each report covered all the time elapsed since the preceding report.

At the top of this report the lawyer briefly indicated his current work status, such as “fully occupied’ ’or “available.” Although a detailed format was not prescribed, in general the report described briefly how the lawyer’s present jobs were going, what kinds of problems were involved, and what he had completed since his previous report. These reports, in addition to supplementing Mr. Carlisle’s knowledge of what was being done in this section, helped tell who was available for more work.

The amount of time a lawyer had to spend on a particular job was not predictable. Major variables were the number and complexity of restrictive covenants in an unsecured note, for example, and the terms and provisions of the security instruments in a secured transaction. The number and complexity of the various covenants in these security instruments did not necessarily vary with the size of the loan, but depended, rather, on the nature, size, and credit standing of the corporate borrower. Many times, a relatively small loan was more complicated than a larger one.

Also, even though the details of a loan had been worked out initially to the satisfaction of the borrower and NJIC, and even though the loan had been in effect for a considerable period of time, borrowers frequently came back to NJIC to ask for waivers or modifications; that is, they requested changes in the restrictive covenants, the terms, or other conditions or agreements. Such events increased the difficulty of planning in advance how a lawyer was to spend his time.

Unusually heavy work loads in the section were met not only by overtime but also by increasing to the extent feasible the amount of work given to outside counsel. Within limitations, the lawyer responsible for a particular job generally decided how much work would be assigned to outside counsel.

Although the corporate loan section followed the same budget procedure as the individual loan section, one of the variable factors—that is, the extent to which work was delegated to outside counsel—did not affect the budget, since the borrower paid for these services.

BUDGET REPORTS

Mr. Montgomery was thoroughly familiar with the background information given above as he began his review of the law division's budget performance for the first half of 1959. The report he had before him consisted of a summary page for the law division (Exhibit 2) and a page for each of the five sections, two of which are shown in Exhibits 3 and 4. The budget figures on the report were one-half the budget for the year.

QUESTIONS

1. In what ways does Mr. Somersby control the operations of the sections of his division? In what ways does top management control the operation of the law division?

2. What possibilities for improving control, if any, do you think should be explored?

3. As Mr. Montgomery, what comments would you make and what questions would you ask Mr. Somersby about the performance of the two sections of the law division for the first six months of 1959?

Exhibit 2

NEW JERSEY INSURANCE COMPANY
Budget Report, Law Division
First Six Months, 1959

Sections	*Budget*	*Actual*	*Over Budget*	*Under Budget*
Individual loans	$231,676	$253,098	$21,422	
Corporate loans	163,737	151,944		$11,793
[Three other sections omitted]	—	—	—	—
Total	$945,872	$944,260		$ 1,612
Number of full-time employees	166	160		6

Exhibit 3

NEW JERSEY INSURANCE COMPANY
Budget Report, Individual Loan Section
First Six Months, 1959

Costs	*Budget*	*Actual*	*Over Budget*	*Under Budget*
Employee costs:				
Salaries, full time	$141,364	$144,067	$ 2,703	
Salaries, part time	—	—		
Salaries, overtime	1,000	12,644	11,644	
Borrowed labor	—	2,362	2,362	
Employee lunches	6,822	7,672	850	
Insurance, retirement, etc.	18,931	19,642	711	
Social security	3,861	4,227	366	
Total	$171,978	$190,614	$18,636	
Direct service costs:				
Photography	$ 3,682	$ 4,267	$ 585	
Tracing	148	276	128	
Mimeograph	163	235	72	
Reproduction	103	206	103	
Total	$ 4,096	$ 4,984	$ 888	
Other costs:				
Rent	$ 28,092	$ 28,092	$	
Office supplies	907	1,227	320	
Equipment depreciation and maintenance	4,776	4,776		
Printed forms	1,537	2,147	610	
Travel	1,134	1,262	128	
Telephone and telegrams	3,031	3,476	445	
Postage	1,223	1,291	68	
Prorated company services	14,724	14,962	238	
Professional dues	20	40	20	
Miscellaneous	158	227	69	
Total	$ 55,602	$ 57,500	$ 1,898	
Grand Total	$231,676	$253,098	$21,422	
Number of full-time employees	46	46		

Exhibit 4

NEW JERSEY INSURANCE COMPANY
Budget Report, Corporate Loan Section
First Six Months, 1959

Costs	*Budget*	*Actual*	*Over Budget*	*Under Budget*
Employee costs:				
Salaries, full time	$109,680	$101,872		$ 7,808
Salaries, part time				
Salaries, overtime	1,200			1,200
Borrowed labor				
Employee lunches	4,130	3,742		388
Insurance, retirement, etc.	13,891	11,845		2,046
Social security	3,006	2,742		264
Total	$131,907	$120,201		$11,706
Direct service costs:				
Photography	$ 655	$ 541		$ 114
Tracing	292	106		186
Mimeograph		27	$ 27	
Reproduction		14	14	
Total	$ 947	$ 688		$ 259
Other costs:				
Rent	$ 16,781	$ 16,781	$	$
Office supplies	740	1,182	442	
Equipment depreciation and maintenance	3,096	3,096		
Printed forms	178	366	188	
Travel	772	752		20
Telephone and telegrams	910	1,134	224	
Postage	168	156		12
Prorated company services	8,085	7,343		742
Professional dues	80	80		
Miscellaneous	73	165	92	
Total	$ 30,883	$ 31,055	$172	
Grand Total	$163,737	$151,944		$11,793
Number of full-time employees	26	24		2

Case 5-2

Peterson Manufacturing Company

"For controlling direct labor and raw materials costs, we have had standard cost based on scientific measurements; for decisions on fixed asset investments, we have been using rather sophisticated return-on-investment calculations; but we have lagged behind in inventing even a most primitive technique for controlling such overhead items as advertising, research and development, and personnel, although these costs have grown in their relative importance over the recent years." Thus began Mr. Toomey, controller of the Peterson Manufacturing Company, in describing a control technique recently adopted by his company. He proceeded,

What makes the planning and control of these costs difficult, is, fundamentally, the difficulty in defining and measuring output—that is, benefit or result intended from the incurrence of these costs—and establishing predictable relationships between costs (input) and the result (output), if definable at all. For example, what is the benefit of adding another personnel man? How are advertising expenses related to sales volume? These questions cannot be meaningfully and operationally answered. If the research department or personnel department asks for an additional man, we have no way of judging whether the request is justifiable or not. More basically, we have no idea, in the first place, whether or not the current level of services rendered by these departments is adequate. Obviously, we need a reasonably objective standard in order to prevent constant haggling between those who request additional manpower or expenditure in these areas and those who must approve or deny such requests.

Briefly put, the standard on which our new technique is based is industry data—that is, how much other comparable companies are spending on advertising, R&D, personnel, etc. We are aware that what other companies do is not necessarily correct; nevertheless, such information provides a workable starting point of analysis. Suppose your company spends 20 percent of sales dollars on R&D, while a comparable company, company A, spends only 14 percent, the industry average being 16 percent. We would be curious to find out why our R&D effort is out of line in comparison with company A and with the industry. Is the difference a result of considered company policy, or is it something else?

SOURCE OF INDUSTRY DATA

A prerequisite for the effective use of the new technique of controlling these overhead costs at the Peterson company was the availability of reliable industry data. Fortunately, the company was a participant in the American Management Association's "Group Ten" project. Under this program, approximately 200 participating companies (in 1963) supplied Group Ten headquarters with detailed information on how many employees were doing what kind of work, and with supplementary financial information on such items as sales, operating expenses, and income. Group Ten headquarters processed the information on a computer, calculating industry averages and ratios for various functions, and sent each participant these tabulations in what is called the Red Book.

All participants were required to follow a uniform definition of functions so as to increase comparability. Exhibit 1 gives Group Ten's form for reporting information according to the prescribed functional groupings. A few examples of definitions and instructions on classification are given in the appendix. Although only code names were used for companies cited in the Red Book, each participant was supplied with a separate list of codes and actual company names so that it could identify companies with which it believed it could make useful comparisons. Frequently, one company would call another company to exchange more detailed information than that given in the Red Book. From time to time, at the request of participants, Group Ten carried out a special study for more detailed information on a specific function. The Group Ten membership fee was $675 a year.

According to Mr. Toomey, a major benefit of Group Ten participation came from the soul-searching self-appraisal that participants had to make in classifying employees into the uniform functions defined by Group Ten. Other benefits were limited to what the participants chose to do with the Red Book data. Mr. Toomey believed that Peterson was one of the companies that made good use of the data. Following are his descriptions of two examples of how Peterson used the information.

Example 1: Control of Personnel Function

"When we receive a new Red Book, we first compare the number of employees for our company with the industry average in each of the 60 functions defined by Group Ten. Then for further analysis we select a number of functional areas that seem out of line—that is, overstaffed.

Exhibit 1

PETERSON MANUFACTURING COMPANY

Furnished by Group Ten

Manpower Utilization—Unit Report

DIVISION UNIT:

Line	FUNCTIONAL GROUPING	Actual Number of Employees on Payroll as of: A (Exempt)	B (Non-Exempt) Salaried	Hourly	Tot Non Ex	TOTAL A+B	C Outside Services
1	EXTRACTING OR PRODUCING						
2	Production Workers						
3	Maintenance Workers						
4	1st Line Supervisors						
	A. Production						
	B. Maintenance						
	C. 1st Line Supv. Sub-Total (A+B)	( )	( )	( )	( )	( )	( )
5	Management and Staff						
	GROUP TOTAL						
8	MANUFACTURING OR PROCESSING						
9	Production Workers						
10	Maintenance Workers						
11	1st Line Supervisors						
	A. Production						
	B. Maintenance						
	C. 1st Line Supv. Sub-Total (A+ B)	( )	( )	( )	( )	( )	( )
12	AUXILIARY SERVICE						
	A. Utilities and Waste Disposal						
	B. In-Plant Trans. & Material Handlg.						
	C. Inspecting or Testing						
	D. Receiving, Storing, Shipping						
	E. Prod. Planning, Sched. Expediting						
	F. Devising, Prod., Maint., Jigs. Etc.						
	G. Aux. Serv. Sub-Total (A – F)	( )	( )	( )	( )	( )	( )
13	Management and Staff						
14	GROUP TOTAL						
16	TRANSPORTING						
17	Marine						
18	Motor Truck						
19	All Other						
20	Management and Staff						
21	GROUP TOTAL						
23	Design, Creat. Devel., Research						
24	Oriented toward Extracting or Producing						
25	Oriented toward Processes or Mfg.						
26	Oriented toward Products or Marketing						
27	Oriented toward Facilities						
28	Oriented toward New Creations or Disc.						
29	Auxiliary Service						
30	Management and Staff						
31	GROUP TOTAL						
33	MARKETING						
34	Sales Representatives – Consumer						
35	1st Line Supervisors – Consumer						
36	Sales Representatives – Industry						
37	1st Line Supervisors – Industry						
38	Customer Servicing						
	A. Order Hand. Billing, Non-Tech. Serv						
	B. Serv. & Repair after Prod. Is Sold						
	C. Tech. Explan. of Existing Applic.						
	D. Cust. Serv. Sub-Total (A – C)	( )	( )	( )	( )	( )	( )
39	Advertising & Sales Promotion						
40	Market Research & Sales Statistics						
41	Management and Staff						
42	GROUP TOTAL						

Exhibit 1—Continued

Line	FUNCTIONAL GROUPING	Actual Number of Employees on Payroll as of:					C Outside Services
		A (Exempt)	B (Non-Exempt) Salaried	Hourly	Tot Non Ex.	TOTAL A+B	
44	GENERAL ADMINISTERING						
45	Accounting and Auditing						
46	Finance, Insurance, Tax						
47	Economics, Budgeting						
48	Credit and Collections						
49	Personnel						
50	External Relations						
51	Purchasing						
52	Traffic						
53	Office Services						
	A. Mail, Messenger, Repro, Etc.						
	B. Centralized Type & Steno Pools						
	C. Centralized Files & Archives						
	D. Office Serv. Sub-Total (A – C)	( )	( )	( )	( )	( )	( )
54	General Management Aux. Service						
55	Operations Improvement						
	A. Industrial Engineering						
	B. Operations Research						
	C. Systems and Procedures						
	D. Scien. & Tech. Program & Coding						
	F. Op. Imp. Sub-Total (A – D)	( )	( )	( )	( )	( )	( )
56	Tabulating & Electronic Computing						
57	Legal and Secretarial						
58	General Management						
59	GROUP TOTAL						
61	Specific Accessory Functions						
62	TOTAL EMPLOYEES						

"In September, 1959, the personnel function was selected as one of the overstaffed areas that needed special management attention. According to the Red Book, our ratio of personnel staff to the number of employees served was the fourth highest among 35 companies that we think are roughly comparable to Peterson. The number of personnel staff per 1,000 employees was 22.0 for Peterson and 16.6 on the average for the 35 companies.

"Shortly thereafter, we received the result of a special, detailed study of personnel staff made under Group Ten sponsorship. In this study, the personnel function was further broken down into 10 subfunctions, and the interested companies supplied the figures for these subfunctions. After a careful analysis of all relevant information obtained from the special study and from our own investigation, we sent out the following memorandum to each operating division."

INTEROFFICE CORRESPONDENCE

February 10, 1960

TO: *Operating Division General Managers*
FROM: *Sean Toomey, Controller*
SUBJECT: *Manpower Utilization*
Personnel Function

This report provides a further breakdown of the personnel function data distributed on October 5, 1959. The function has been exploded into 10 personnel activities to provide an opportunity for detailed comparisons and analysis.

Table 1 presents the suggested staffing ranges for the operating divisions in terms of the number of personnel staff per 1,000 employees. These ranges were developed by comparative analysis and judgment in conjunction with the personnel division. It is believed that they can be used effectively as guides for staffing divisions.

As used in the table, "personnel people" includes both individuals performing personnel functions in the operating divisions as well as an allocated portion of the individuals on the central personnel staff. (For the basis of allocation, see Table 2 and a paragraph below that explains the table.)

For the total company, it should be noted that the suggested ratio is lower in five of the ten categories, remains the same in four, and is up in one. The total shows a lowering of the ratio by 4.2 per thousand employees. This will drop our rank from fourth to sixth in the 35 companies.

Tables 2–9[1] show for the individual divisions the applications of the suggested staffing ratios.

Distribution of personnel staff of the central service divisions was based on the time spent on each operating division as estimated by the service division staff. Personnel staff by activity was supplied by you in November, 1959.

The ratio of personnel staff to 1,000 employees is shown, and the resulting ranking in the operating divisions.

The last two columns show the application to the division of the suggested staffing ratio. Although the *total* suggested ranges are the only figures of major significance, the detail by activity may give you clues as you apply the range to your division.

Mr. Toomey continued, "Dispatching this memorandum was virtually all we did, but the result was very pleasing. First of all, the availability of an objective standard put the burden of proof on the division. Second, the memorandum made

[1] Only Table 2 for division A is included in this case.

Table 1

PETERSON MANUFACTURING COMPANY

Suggested Staffing Ranges, February, 1960

(Ratio Personnel People per 1,000 Employees)

Personnel Activities	*Empl. & Place.*	*Train & Educ.*	*Labor Rel.*	*Wages & Sal.*	*Ben. & Serv.*	*Health & Safe.*	*Pub. & Comm.*	*Sugg. Syst.*	*Per. Res.*	*Per. Adm.*	*Total*
Present ratio (Sept. 1959)	2.9	.8	1.4	2.1	2.0	8.3	.3	.8	.3	2.6	22.0
Ranking in 35 companies*	6	7	8	4	6	1	8	4	9	6	4
Suggested ratio	2.4	.8	1.4	1.7	2.0	5.4	.8	.6	.4	2.3	17.8
The resulting ranking*	8	7	8	6	6	7	8	5	5	9	6
Present range:†											
Low	1.1	.1	.8	1.2	.9	3.3	.1	.3	0	1.2	13.2
	to	to	to	to	to	to	to	to	to	to	to
High	3.8	1.5	3.6	4.8	2.8	11.1	1.2	2.0	.5	3.1	26.3
Suggested range:†											
Low	1.1	.1	.8	1.2	.9	3.3	.1	.3	0	1.2	13.2
	to	to	to	to	to	to	to	to	to	to	to
High	2.8	1.5	2.3	2.2	2.4	6.3	0.9	1.0	.5	2.8	18.5

* Ranking: Highest Ratio = #1 rank.

† Ranges represent the highest and lowest among all Peterson divisions.

Table 2

PETERSON MANUFACTURING COMPANY
Personnel Function
Summary, September, 1959

Division A

Personnel Activities	Number of Personnel People: In Operating Division	Number of Personnel People: From Central Serv. Div. for Oper. Div.	Number of Personnel People: Total	Personnel People Per 1,000 Employees: Ratio	Personnel People Per 1,000 Employees: Present Operating Division Rank	Personnel People Per 1,000 Employees: Suggested Range
1. Employment and placement	1.2	.3	1.5	1.1	(8)	1.1 to 2.8
2. Training and education	.7	.1	.8	.6	(5)	.1 to 1.5
3. Labor relations	2.4	1.8	4.2	3.0	(3)	.8 to 2.3
4. Wage and salary administration	1.7	—	1.7	1.2	(8)	1.2 to 2.2
5. Benefits and services	2.7	1.1	3.8	2.7	(3)	.9 to 2.4
6. Health and safety	12.0	2.1	14.1	10.1	(2)	3.3 to 6.3
7. Publications and communications	.7	—	.7	.5	(5)	.1 to .9
8. Suggestion system	2.4	.1	2.5	1.8	(2)	.3 to 1.0
9. Personnel research	—	—	—	—	—	0 to .5
10. Personnel administration	1.2	.5	1.7	1.2	(8)	.8 to 2.8
Total	25.0	6.0	31.0	22.2		
Suggested range:						
Low			18			13.0
High			26			18.5
Total employees in division: 1,400						

the division aware of and interested in the problem. Third, the divisions had detailed information if they cared to analyze further.

"To be sure, we heard a lot of complaints from the divisions. Typical were the comments that our company was different from the 'comparable' companies, and therefore the averages were without much meaning; that the divisions should not be charged for personnel staff of the central service divisions; and that one division was different from other divisions. To these, our answer was always that the data in the memorandum were to be taken only as 'guidelines', and it was up to the division managers to change the size of the personnel staff on the basis of the data. At any rate, whatever the feeling may have been, the important fact is that the divisions reduced personnel staff by 10 percent on the average in two years' time. The following is a progress report:"

INTEROFFICE CORRESPONDENCE

January 23, 1962

TO: *Operating Division General Managers*
FROM: *Sean Toomey, Controller*
SUBJECT: *Personnel Function—Progress Report*

This is a progress report aimed at showing how far we have come since the first study of personnel staff made in September, 1959. The result is gratifying to all of us. From September, 1959, to November, 1961, there was a reduction in personnel staff of 31 men, from 363 to 332, despite an increase, though slight, in the total number of employees of the company.

In 1960, we set the goal of a company-wide ratio of 17.8 personnel people for every thousand employees, and a range of 13.0 to 18.5 personnel people per thousand people for the operating divisions; the current figure was 22.0. In November, 1961, the company-wide ratio of personnel people per thousand employees was 20.0.

Table 3 summarizes the progress we have made and shows, in addition, how far we have to go in attaining the goals set up in the 1960 report.

Example 2: Control of Production Planning, Scheduling, and Expediting Function

The controller continued, "In Example 1, comparison with other companies led to a reduction of manpower, but it should not be inferred that the new technique is always aimed at economizing the number of employees. In many cases, seemingly overstaffed functions—compared to other companies—were left intact after a careful analysis; in a few cases, studies actually led to an increase in the number of employees.

"For instance, a few months ago Red Book data indicated that our production planning, scheduling, and expediting function might be overstaffed, since our company's ratio of sales to the number of employees engaged in these functions was low compared to that of other comparable companies. Accordingly, we initiated a special analysis. First of all, we had to determine what this particular staff function was contributing to the company. Of many indicators of the function's contribution, the most important, we decided, was inventory turnover—namely, the ratio of sales to inventories. Here, our company ranked among the top few of the comparable companies. The conclusion was that we were satisfied with the level of number of employees engaged in the function. I do not recall specifically, but our staff even did a fancy calculation of the cost of additional employees compared to the savings—chiefly in capital cost—from quick inventory turnover, and it was a considerable amount."

QUESTIONS

1. Is this approach useful in the Peterson Manufacturing Company?
2. Is it likely to be useful in companies generally?

Table 3

PERSONNEL FUNCTION COMPARISON

1959–61

	Division Population		*Number of Personnel People*						*Difference in Total Personnel Staff, 1959–61*	*Reduction Required to Achieve Top of Range (18.5 per 1,000 employees)*	
			September, 1959			*November, 1961*					
	1959 Sept.	*1961 Nov.*	*On Div. Payroll*	*Allocated*	*Total*	*On Div. Payroll*	*Allocated*	*Total*		*1959 Sept.*	*1961 Nov.*
A	1,400	1,623	25	6.0	31.0	31	5.5	36.5	+5.5	5.0	6.5
B*											
C*											
D	3,117	3,096	64	9.6	73.6	52	7.8	59.8	—13.8	15.9	2.5
E*											
F*											
G*											
H*											
Totals	16,524	16,580	321	42.5	363.5	299	33.3	332.3	—31.2	57.8	25.6

* The figures for these divisions are omitted in order to make it more difficult to identify the divisions.

Appendix

Extracts from Group Ten Definitions

Examples of Definitions and Instructions on Group Ten Functional Groupings Used in Manpower Utilization—Unit Report[2]

. . . Report the manpower utilized for the various basic functions *without regard* to our job titles or traditional names of our "departments," divisions, etc. This is necessary because such varied departmental names are used to describe the same work in other companies. Definitions of functional categories may be thought of as revolving around action-words. What *specific work* does the employee *do* during his work day?

. . . If a person holds a position that falls into more than one functional category, classify the employee according to the function that consumes the greatest amount of time. Do not use additional categories.

NOTE: If the number of such employees has a significant effect on line percentages, then the entire group should be allocated by percent to their appropriate functions.

Occasionally difficulty has been reported with the classification of special groups, task forces, and the like. Most of these difficulties disappear when the group or task force unity is broken up and individuals are considered by what they are doing. Departments, divisions, special groups, task forces, etc., rarely can be classified en masse. It is essential to carry out the functional classification on an individual basis.

Column A generally is to be used to record the number of those employees who are exempt from the U.S. Wage and Hour Law, or not covered by it. . . .

Column B generally is to be used to record the number of those employees who are *nonexempt*—that is, covered by the U.S. Wage and Hour Law. . . .

---

[2] These examples refer to the form given in Exhibit 1.

Trainees are to be included in the functions for which the training is preparing them.

In collecting data this year, provision has been made for recording on *each line* where appropriate, an estimate of the number of people our company avoids having on its regular staff because of its purchase of outside services. For example, in the Personnel function outside medical practitioners are frequently used rather than staff doctors; in the operations improvement function outside industrial engineers may perform work in our company that is handled by its own staff in another company.

Line Definitions

Please read all line definitions and review the entire form before proceeding. . . .

1. *Extracting or Producing*

   A general heading controlling lines 1 thru 6. Employees concerned with prospecting for, extracting and producing materials for subsequent processing, refining and other manufacturing operations. Examples are exploring, mining, drilling, petroleum producing and farming.

2. *Production Workers*—Nonexempt—generally hourly employees in mining, drilling, farming and related occupations, except maintenance.

8. *Manufacturing or Processing*

   A general heading controlling 8 thru 14. Employees concerned with the processing, refining, fermenting, manufacturing, assembling, or packaging of products and the necessarily related occupations of storage, flow of products, materials and utilities.

11. *First Line Supervisiors*—All positions in which the work is accomplished by the direct supervision of production and maintenance workers (lines 9 and 10). Exclude group leader, lead hand or others who spend more than half of their time doing the same work as those they supervise—Show supervisors' secretaries or clerks on line 13B.

12. *Auxiliary Service*—Employees performing service functions related specifically to manufacturing, fabricating, or processing. Include also all first line supervisors of auxiliary personnel in each line.

    A. Utilities and Waste Disposal. . . .

    E. Production planning, production scheduling and dispatching (including preparation of bill of materials and formulation), floor expediting and materials control. Typical titles: Inventory Clerk, Production Planning Manager, Perpetual Inventory Clerk, Expeditor, Scheduler, Job-Time or Machine Utilization Record Clerk. . . .

44. *General Administering*

    A general term controlling lines 44 thru 59. A group of general functions not specifically part of the functions of producing, manufacturing, transporting, creating and designing or marketing covered elsewhere. . . .

49. *Personnel*—Activities related to personnel or industrial relations including recruitment, employment and placement, training (except sales), education and development; labor relations; wage and salary administration; employee benefits and services; health, medical and safety; employee publications and communications; suggestion systems; personnel research; personnel administration and records. Certain apparently related items not specifically listed here belong on Line 61, for example, guards and firemen.

Case 5–3

Global Chemical Company

The Global Chemical Company was a medium-size concern specializing in the development of products and processes both for itself and for other firms in the chemical industry. In some respects, the company was a "job-shop" research laboratory for the chemical trade; it frequently received requests from other members of the industry for the development of a special product or process. The company maintained offices in the major cities throughout the United States. It also operated chemical plants in Amarillo, Texas; San Bernadino, California; Philadelphia, Pennsylvania; and Dubuque, Iowa, in which it produced a standard line of chemical products. Since the company's progress depended to a large extent on its ability to tailor products and processes to meet the specific needs of customers and to develop new products for its own organization, the research division was generally considered to be one of the most important parts of the company, and, as such, occupied a proportionately large share of management's attention.

In the spring of 1964, the Global management was reviewing the company's research activities with a view toward possible improvements in its control over research expenditures and in the appraisal of the profitability of its research program.

RESEARCH DIVISION

The division of research was headed by a director, whose staff consisted of a controller, a purchasing agent, and a number of department heads—one for each of the types of research shown in Exhibit 1. The administration and business department was in the charge of the research division controller.

The facilities of the research division consisted of a group of buildings located on the outskirts of Baltimore, Maryland. The central plant housed most of the executive staff and office personnel. Department heads also had their laboratories in this building, as did the head of the chemical division.

Exhibit 1

ANALYSIS OF RESEARCH APPROPRIATION PROGRAM FOR 1964

Engineering research	$ 300,000
Organic chemical research	250,000
Inorganic chemical research	110,000
Maintenance services for research plant	375,000
Product research	125,000
Physics research	100,000
Pilot plant research	100,000
New product research	115,000
Administrative and business department	95,000
Total Research Appropriation	$1,570,000

A second building housed the remaining scientific laboratories, and a third housed pilot plant operations. Engineering development was carried on in a fourth building, located adjacent to the other three facilities.

Global employed over 200 research personnel in all: 90 were directly connected with the research work, 33 were service personnel, 60 were clerical workers, and the remaining 20 comprised the executive group.

For the three years 1961, 1962, and 1963, research expenditures ranged from $1.5 million to $1.8 million. Although the annual research expenditures had consistently amounted to about 3 percent of sales, no company policy related the amount of such outlays to expected sales revenues.

The general direction of the company's research activities came within the purview of the board of directors, who established broad company research policy and exercised general control over the program. In fact, the board had established a standing committee whose purpose was to maintain close contact with the research program through continued review and appraisal of the conduct and results of research operations. This committee, which consisted of the board chairman, the president, executive vice-president, director of research, and the chairman of the research committee, provided whatever guidance and direction it considered necessary to insure effective research activities. Typical of the kinds of questions on which the standing committee offered guidance to the research division were these:

1. Should emphasis be placed on the development of new products or on the improvement of existing ones?
2. What particular fields of research may prove profitable in the long run?
3. When should the division intensify efforts on a particular product and when drop products for which the prospects appear dim?
4. How should it dispose of new products developed—for example, how appraise the sales potential of new products, how decide when a new item is ready to be turned over to an operating division for production?
5. What are the potentials of by-products arising from new processes or products?

BUDGETING PROCEDURE

The budgeting procedure for the division started at the level of the departments listed in Exhibit 1. Each department head prepared budget estimates, using as a basis the expenditures he expected to be required during the budget period for projects already in progress and for those expected to be started during the year. In making these estimates, the department head was guided by the advice and direction of the director of research who, in addition to his own thoughts, reflected the opinions and expectations of the standing research committee. The assistance of the research controller and his office also was available to department heads in the preparation of their budgets.

Each departmental budget was broken down according to two detailed classifications as well as (1) by project, as illustrated in Exhibit 2, and (2) by type of expense, as shown in Exhibit 3. When the departmental budgets were completed, the research controller combined them into a master budget for research divisions as a whole, which was broken down by two classifications of detail: (1) by department, as shown in Exhibit 1, and (2) by type of expense, as shown in Exhibit 3. The master budget, after review by the company controller, was submitted to the chairman of the research committee for presentation to the research committee and board of directors for approval and fund appropriations.

Exhibit 2

RESEARCH DIVISION—ENGINEERING RESEARCH DEPARTMENT
ESTIMATED EXPENDITURES BY PROJECTS, 1964

		Estimate, 1964				
Title of Project	*Number*	*Total*	*Over-head*	*Total Direct*	*Labor*	*All Other Direct*
Water installation improvement	342	$18,352	$8,300	$10,052	$8,000	$2,052
etc.						

CONTROL OF EXPENDITURES

Close control was exercised in assuring that research expenditures were made in accordance with budget authorizations. Because carrying out a research project consisted primarily of the efficient use of research personnel, especially close watch was maintained over labor costs. No department head was allowed to commence a new project unless he could demonstrate that sufficient time for research was available to assure reasonable progress. Salary increases, and increases or decreases in research personnel, were made only after a careful analysis of the effects of the change on the divisional budget and on departmental budgets.

Exhibit 3

RESEARCH DIVISION EXPENSE—BUDGET, 1964

	Effective Monthly Salary Payroll as of October 1, 1963	Engineering Research Department Control *Budget 1964*	*Budget 1963*	*Actual 8 Months 1963*
Total Expense—Net		$	$	$
Income credits				
Expense transfers				
Total (excluding income credits)				
Executive labor	($)			
Supervision and clerical labor	($)			
Shop direct labor	($)			
Research labor	($)			
Service labor	($)			
Overtime salary pay				
Power, light, and heat				
Maintenance material, and service				
Raw materials				
Operating supplies				
Suggestion awards				
Traveling and expense				
Auto depreciation and insurance				
Auto operating expense				
Auto taxes				
Office operating expense				
Office operating appliances				
Dues, subscriptions, and memberships				
Telephone and telegraph				
Professional services				
Storage and handling expense				
Advertising (publications)				
Payroll taxes and retirement benefits				
Surveys				
Unclassified				
Taxes				
Insurance premiums and service				
Depreciation				
Rents and royalties				

The approval of the director of research was required for any addition of personnel to the research staff. Although department heads could approve requisitions for materials costing up to $250, anything above that figure had to be approved by the research controller, and requisitions amounting to over $500 also had to be approved by the director of research. In addition, all requests for materials in excess of $1,000 and all maintenance and capital expenditures required the approval of the treasurer.

The Global company used a wide variety of reports in its efforts to control the cost of its research operations. Each department head received a monthly report showing expenses, by project, for the month, for the year to date, and for the life of the project. Exhibit 4 illustrates the form of this report. The labor costs on this monthly report were supported by a detailed breakdown showing the time spent by each research worker on each project.

A monthly report of actual versus budgeted expenses also was sent to the research committee, along with a letter of transmittal explaining any significant differences between budgeted and actual costs. A monthly summary of expenses by accounts (as in Exhibit 3) and for each department also was made to the director of research and the research committee. Exhibit 5 illustrates the form of this report; account titles were supplied in the columns. Quarterly reports similar to the monthly reports also were submitted to the research committee, and with the quarterly report there was a written review, prepared by the director of research, describing progress to date and appraising the future prospects of each project. On the basis of this review, the director of research and the research committee decided for each whether the project should be dropped, continued as planned, or modified in any respect.

In addition to these monthly and quarterly reports, the research controller prepared interim reports for department heads when the expenses for a particular project had reached the budgeted limit or when it appeared that a project might run over its budget. On the basis of this report, the department head might request an additional appropriation to continue the study if he believed that further work was warranted by the results already accomplished.

The controller prepared annual reports showing comparisons of budgeted against actual expenses, along with the actual expenses for the previous year and the budget for the ensuing one. These reports included a review of last year's operations, with explanations of variations of actual from budget, both by type of expense and by project.

In an effort to tie in research more closely with the actual production of its products, the Global management was, in 1964, experimenting with a new idea for guidance and control of its research program. Previously, the costs of the research division had not been distributed either to product costs or to the operating divisions of the company. The division's expenses were, instead, shown in the company's income statement as a separate deduction. The company had based this practice partially on the premise that research benefited the company as a whole and partially on the fear that the distribution of research expenses among operating divisions might cause

Exhibit 4

MONTHLY REPORT OF PROJECT

	CUMULATIVE FROM INCEPTION	CUMULATIVE CURRENT YEAR	TOTAL MONTH EXPENSE	OVERHEAD APPLIED	TOTAL DIRECT COSTS	LABOR	MATERIAL AND SUPPLIES	SHOP WORK AND ASSAYS	OTHER	
YEAR					PRIOR YEARS					
Prior to 1958										
1958										
1959										
1960										
1961										
1962										
1963										
MONTH					CURRENT YEAR					
JANUARY										
FEBRUARY										
MARCH										
APRIL										
MAY										
JUNE										
JULY										
AUGUST										
SEPTEMBER										
OCTOBER										
NOVEMBER										
DECEMBER										
TOTALS										

Current Year Estimate __________ Total Estimate __________

Project __________

Current Year __________ Project No. __________

Program __________

Exhibit 5

MONTHLY EXPENSE REPORT TO DEPARTMENT HEADS

CURRENT YEAR ____________________

				MONTHLY	
JANUARY					
FEBRUARY					
MARCH					
APRIL					
MAY					
JUNE					
JULY					
AUGUST					
SEPTEMBER					
OCTOBER					
NOVEMBER					
DECEMBER					
				CUMULATIVE	
MONTH	BUDGET				
OF	CURRENT				
JAN.	LAST YR.				
2 MO.	BUDGET				
THRU	CURRENT				
FEB. 28	LAST YR.				
3 MO.	BUDGET				
THRU	CURRENT				
MAR. 31	LAST YR.				
4 MO.	BUDGET				
THRU	CURRENT				
APR. 30	LAST YR.				
5 MO.	BUDGET				
THRU	CURRENT				
MAY 31	LAST YR.				
6 MO.	BUDGET				
THRU	CURRENT				
JUNE 30	LAST YR.				
7 MO.	BUDGET				
THRU	CURRENT				
JULY 31	LAST YR.				
8 MO.	BUDGET				
THRU	CURRENT				
AUG. 31	LAST YR.				
9 MO.	BUDGET				
THRU	CURRENT				
SEPT. 30	LAST YR.				
10 MO.	BUDGET				
THRU	CURRENT				
OCT. 31	LAST YR.				
11 MO.	BUDGET				
THRU	CURRENT				
NOV. 30	LAST YR.				
12 MO.	BUDGET				
THRU	CURRENT				
DEC. 31	LAST YR.				

the research program to be unduly influenced by the special interests of divisional managements. Since such distribution would result in lower short-run divisional profit figures, there might be a tendency for division heads to oppose research expenditures that, in the longer run, would prove profitable to the company as a whole. The research director was aware of this apparent conflict of interests and, since he very highly valued the cooperation of operating division heads, he was eager to avoid any change that might antagonize them.

The board of directors, however, was concerned about the overall profitability of Global's research program. Although the directors knew that a certain portion of the company's research expenditures were directed to basic research and could not readily be prorated to specific products or divisions, they believed that some types of research could be attributed to products or divisions. Some board members held that if each product was made to bear its share of allocable research costs, the company's whole research program stood a better chance of showing a profit than it then did. For example, product development costs and the cost of pilot plant operations might well be distributed to products or producing divisions. Because of the significance of the research activity to the company's profitability and progress, however, the board was extremely apprehensive lest it take action that would in any respect jeopardize the effectiveness of its research operations.

QUESTIONS

1. Does Global Chemical Company exercise effective control over its research expenditures?
2. Should Global's research expenditures be allocated to products and/or divisions?

Case 5-4

National Motors, Inc.

William Franklin, controller of the Panther automobile division of National Motors, a manufacturer of numerous products including a wide line of automobiles and trucks, was faced with a difficult decision in August, 1960. Four months previously, the manufacturing office had submitted a supplemental budget in which it had requested additional funds for increased administrative costs in its operations control department. The controller's office had written a memorandum in reply, explaining why it thought this request was not justified, and the manufacturing office had now answered this memorandum.

Mr. Franklin now had three possible courses of action: (1) to concur with the manufacturing office's position, in which case the request would undoubtedly receive the necessary approval of the general manager; (2) to continue his opposition, in which case his views and those of the manufacturing office would be placed before the general manager, who would decide the issue; and (3) to reply with a further analysis, in the hope that the manufacturing office would become convinced of the soundness of his position.

During the last quarter of 1959, the Panther automobile division had absorbed the manufacturing activities of the Starling automobile division. Prior to this, the Starling division had a mechanized system of parts control in its operations control department. The Panther division, on the other hand, had been using a manual system in its corresponding department.

In December, 1959, a study was made to determine which system would serve the division best. On the basis of an estimated reduction of 23 salaried people and of $138,000 in salary and other costs in the operations control department because of mechanization, the decision was made to completely mechanize the Panther division system of parts control. The results of this study were concurred in by the manufacturing office of the Panther division. The appendix explains National Motors' method of controlling administrative expenses in general.

MANUFACTURING OFFICE'S PROPOSED SUPPLEMENTAL BUDGET

In April, 1960, the manufacturing office proposed in a supplemental budget that the Panther operations control department, now servicing both Starling and Panther automobiles, be alloted for 1960 a personnel ceiling of 109 people to handle the combined work load. Its proposal and reasoning are summarized in Exhibit 1 and in the following paragraphs.

Exhibit 1

PERSONNEL CEILINGS FOR OPERATIONS CONTROL DEPARTMENT IN 1960
Proposed by Manufacturing Office

Positions	*Starling Commitment 12/31/59*	*Starling Savings*	*Proposed Levels Starling*	*Proposed Levels Panther*	*Totals*
Manager and secretary	2	2	—	2	2
Specifications control	20	12	8	17	25
Design parts control	31	12	19	48	67
Planning and control	7	3	4	11	15
Total	60	29	31	78	109

Exhibit 1 shows the Starling division's personnel ceiling commitment as of December 31, 1959, the expected saving in numbers resulting from the consolidation, and the proposed ceiling for 1960. Since the manufacturing office believed that the new consolidated system of parts control in the operations control department was going to be about the same as the Starling division's mechanized system, the standards that it used to develop the proposed personnel requirements were based on the Starling division's work load and authorized personnel levels for 1959.

Specifications Control Section (25 people)

The work load determinant used in this activity was the number of specifications requests to be processed. In the previous year, 20 employees had been approved in the Starling division's specifications control section: 5 were clerical and supervisory, 10 processed specifications requests, and 5 were involved in specifications follow-up. The specifications control procedure currently used in the Panther division operations was generally the same as that used by Starling. But in the future, the specifications follow-up procedure would no longer be done in this section or, for that matter, in the operations control department.

In 1959, the 10 analysts in the Starling specifications control section had processed 2,964 specifications requests, or an average of 296 specifications each.

In the Panther division, 3,680 specifications requests had been processed during 1959. The manufacturing office believed that a comparison of both Starling and Panther data, as shown in Exhibit 2, indicated that there was a definite relationship between the number of specifications requests processed and the number of unique, new model parts.

Exhibit 2

RELATIONSHIP OF NUMBER OF PARTS TO SPECIFICATION REQUESTS

Division	*Number of Unique Parts*	*Number of Specifications Requests*	*Specifications Requests per Unique Part*
Panther	8,810	3,680	.42
Starling	6,584	2,964	.45
Total	15,394	6,644	.43

On the basis of the above calculations, the manufacturing office estimated the total number of specifications requests for 1960 for both Panther and Starling automobiles, and the personnel required to handle this work load as in Exhibit 3.

Exhibit 3

ESTIMATES OF PERSONNEL REQUIREMENTS FOR SPECIFICATIONS CONTROL SECTION, 1960

A. Specifications Requests and Equivalent Personnel

Division	*Estimated Number of Unique Parts**	×	*Specifications Requests per Unique Part*	÷	*Actual Output per Man*	=	*Equivalent Personnel*
Panther	11,600		.42		296		16.5
Starling	4,800		.45		296		7.3
Total	16,400						23.8

B. Salaried Personnel Requirements

Division	*Equivalent Personnel*	*Less Planned Efficiency (approx. 10%)*†	*Less Planned Overtime (approx. 5%)*	*Salaried Ceiling Required*
Panther	16.5	1.7	.9	14
Starling	7.3	.8	.4	6
Total	23.8	2.5	1.3	20

C. Other Personnel Requirements

Position	*Panther*	*Starling*	*Total*
Section supervisor and secretary	2	–	2
Unit supervisor	1	1	2
Clerk-typist	–	1	1
Total Fixed	3	2	5‡
Total Salaried and Other			25

* The Panther division had added a new car to its line, and the Starling division had dropped one.

† "Planned efficiency" reduces the calculated personnel requirements to a level approximately consistent with the lowest work load level anticipated during the coming year. In order to handle periodic work load increases during a year, the department is forced to improve its efficiency and, if necessary, to utilize overtime or temporary clerical help from outside agencies.

‡ Same as Starling commitment of December 31, 1959.

Design Parts Section (67 people)

The number of unique parts to be processed was used as the general work load determinant in this section. In 1959, for 6,584 parts there were 27 specifications coordinators in the Starling division budget for an average of 242 parts per coordinator. According to Exhibit 4, which was drawn up in the manufacturing office, 58 specifications coordinators would be required to handle the combined work load in 1960, plus nine supervisors and clerical workers.

Exhibit 4

ESTIMATES OF PERSONNEL REQUIREMENTS FOR DESIGN PARTS SECTION, 1960

A. Specifications Coordinators Requested

Division	*1960 Parts Count*	*Estimated Output per Man*	*Equivalent Personnel Required*	*Less Planned Efficiency (approx. 10%)*	*Less Planned Overtime (approx. 5%)*	*Ceiling Required*
Panther	11,600	242	48.0	4.7	2.3	41
Starling	4,800	242	19.8	1.9	.9	17
Total	16,400		67.8	6.6	3.2	58

B. Supervisory and Clerical Workers Requested

Position	*Panther*	*Starling*	*Total*
Section supervisor and secretary	2	–	2
Unit supervisors	2	1	3
Clerk-typists	3	1	4
Total	7	2	9
Unit supervisors to coordinators	1:20	1:17	1:19
Clerk-typists to coordinators	1:13	1:17	1:15
Total for the Section			67

Exhibit 5

ESTIMATE OF PERSONNEL REQUIREMENTS FOR PLANNING AND CONTROL SECTION, 1960

Position	*Starling Personnel*	*Number of Unique Parts for Starling, 1959*	*Parts per Person*
Programming computer	3	6,584	2,195
Programming timing and coordination	2	6,584	3,292

	Number of Unique Parts, 1960		*Estimated Output per Person*	*Equivalent Personnel*		*Personnel Ceiling Requested*		
	Panther	*Starling*		*Panther*	*Starling*	*Panther*	*Starling*	*Total*
Program timing and coordination	11,600	4,800	3,292	3.5	1.5	4	2	6
Programming	11,600	4,800	2,195	5.3	2.2	5	2	7
Total				8.8	3.7	9	4	13
Section supervisor and secretary								2
Total for the Section								15

Planning and Control Section (15 people)

The requirements for this section were determined by the manufacturing office as shown in Exhibit 5, based on an overall work load indicator of number of parts to be handled.

Manager's Office (2 people)

A personnel ceiling of two was requested: the manager and his secretary.

Estimated Dollar Requirements

The manufacturing office estimated that a total of $1,458,000 would be needed to operate the consolidated operations control department for 1960. This figure was broken down as follows:

Personnel	$1,160,000
Material and supplies	45,000
Computer services	245,000
Miscellaneous	8,000
Total	$1,458,000

Personnel Expenses. This estimate was based on the figure for actual salaries plus approved fringe benefits, in accordance with the level of requested salaried personnel ceilings.

Materials and Supplies. This expense was about $10,000 higher than the 1959 Starling actual. According to the manufacturing office, the job to be accomplished now was about two-and-one-half times the job accomplished by the Starling division in 1959, but the expense was only 30 percent greater. This was a result of efficiencies in programming and reporting, which, in turn, would result in savings in materials and supplies.

Computer Services. Starling had spent $190,000 in 1959 to accomplish a job that was about 40 percent as great as the combined Starling–Panther job. Included in the proposed amount was $34,000 for start-up cost associated with the conversion of the manual Panther system to a mechanized system. Therefore, the real cost was $211,000, or only about 10 percent more than the 1959 Starling actual. The manufacturing office was proposing to do a job 150 percent greater than that done at Starling for only 10 percent more money. This was said to be the result of efficiencies in programming and reporting.

ANALYSIS BY THE CONTROLLER'S OFFICE

The controller's office did not concur with the manufacturing office's proposal. It summarized both the 1960 Panther division's budget and the Starling division's budget as approved prior to the consolidation, and compared these figures with those proposed by the manufacturing office. This summary is shown in Exhibit 6 and is explained in the following paragraphs.

Exhibit 6

BUDGET COMPARISON FOR SALARIED PERSONNEL PREPARED BY CONTROLLER

	Panther Division		*Starling Division*		*Total*	
Budget Status	*Number*	*Dollars (000)*	*Number*	*Dollars (000)*	*Number*	*Dollars (000)*
Approved	76	$722	55*	$668	131	$1,390
Proposed	78	974	31	484	109	1,458
Net change	(2)	($252)	24	$184	22	($ 68)
Explanation of Changes						
Savings from mechanization of Panther system	23†	$138†	—	$—	23	$ 138
Savings from consolidation	—	—	24	184	24	184
Proposed increase to Panther budget	(25)	(390)	—	—	(25)	($ 390)
Net change	(2)	($252)	24	$184	22	($ 68)

( ) = Adverse effect on profit.
* Reflects the transfer of five specifications follow-up personnel out of the specifications control system.
† Based on study of December, 1959, concurred in by manufacturing office.

Although the proposed combined Panther and Starling budgets for 1960 showed a decrease of 22 salaried personnel, there was an increase in cost of $68,000.

The manufacturing office had referred to a saving of 24 people and $184,000 in the Starling division. This reduction, according to the controller, was the result of (*a*) a reduction in the 1960 parts count and (*b*) a reduction of supervisory and clerical personnel. This saving of 24 people, therefore, had nothing to do with mechanization and would have occurred under either a mechanized or a manual system.

Although the main reason for mechanizing the Panther division's system of parts control had been financial savings, the controller calculated what the combined budget would have been if, in fact, the Starling division's system had been changed to a manual one comparable to the one in use by the Panther division prior to the consolidation. The budget requirement for the Panther division, of course, would not change. However, 35 people and $406,000 would be required for the Starling division, on the basis of Panther division's standards as developed in the manufacturing office's analysis. Thus, a comparison between the manual system and the mechanized system was as shown in Exhibit 7.

According to Exhibit 7, the effect of the mechanization and the consolidation on the 1960 Panther budget, which was based on a manual system, was to increase the 1960 salaried personnel level by two people and to increase costs by $252,000. The controller was at a loss to know why these increases should result from mechanization. Moreover, the manufacturing office had committed itself to a saving of 23 people and $138,000 in the

Exhibit 7

CONTROLLER'S REVISED BUDGET COMPARISON FOR SALARIED PERSONNEL, 1960

System	*Panther Division* *Number*	*Dollars (000)*	*Starling Division* *Number*	*Dollars (000)*	*Total* *Number*	*Dollars (000)*
Combined manual systems	76	$722	35	$406	111	$1,128
Proposed mechanized systems	78	974	31	484	109	1,458
Difference between cost of mechanized system and manual system	(2)	($252)	4	($ 78)	2	($ 330)

Panther division, whereas the current proposal was 25 people and $390,000 *over* the levels committed.

The controller believed that budget figures under a *combined mechanized system,* instead, should be as shown in Exhibit 8.

Exhibit 8

CONTROLLER'S PROPOSED BUDGET, 1960

Salaried Personnel	*Panther*	*Starling*	*Total*
Number	53	31	84
Budget dollars (000)	$584	$484	$1,068

In this calculation, the Panther division's number of salaried personnel was based on the premechanization figure (76) minus the saving agreed to by the manufacturing office as a result of mechanization (23). The Panther division's budget dollars were based on the same sort of analysis—$722,000 minus $138,000. Starling division's figures were those used in the preceding table, based on a reduced parts count, supervisory savings, and the functional transfer of personnel. The budget figures for the new division have been 84 people and $1,068,000.

On the basis of its analysis, the controller's office recommended that the manufacturing office at least not increase its 1960 costs for the operations control department over the level that would have occurred under a combined manual system. This meant a dollar budget of $1,128,000. Personnel reductions would be required to contain costs within recommended levels; these were set forth in Exhibit 9.

PROTEST FROM THE MANUFACTURING OFFICE

The manufacturing office did not accept the controller's recommendation of a reduction of 25 salaried people and $330,000, though it agreed that, generally speaking, a mechanized operations control system should not be any more costly than the previously used manual system.

Exhibit 9

DETAIL OF CONTROLLER'S RECOMMENDED BUDGET, 1960

Proposals	Panther *Number*	Panther *Dollars (000)*	Starling *Number*	Starling *Dollars (000)*	Total *Number*	Total *Dollars (000)*
Manufacturing office's request	78	$974	31	$484	109	$1,458
Controller's recommended reductions:						
Salary mix	—	85	—	—	—	85
Overtime	—	27	—	21	—	48
Required personnel (to meet financial objective)	25	197	—	—	25	197
Total Recommended Reductions	25	$309	—	$ 21	25	$ 330
Total Recommended Level	53	$665	31	$463	84	$1,128

Work Load Content and Volume Adjustments

One of the arguments of the manufacturing office was that its proposed Starling–Panther budget included additional people to handle actual work load volume increases over the estimated levels used in developing the 1960 Panther budget for a manual system. The parts counts estimates used in developing the 1960 manual budget and the proposed consolidated mechanized budget were as shown in Exhibit 10.

Exhibit 10

REVISED ESTIMATES OF NUMBER OF UNIQUE PARTS

Division	*1960 Original Budget Estimates*	*Current Known Conditions*
Panther	10,200	11,600
Starling	—	4,800
Total	10,200	16,400

According to the manufacturing office, in addition to increased work as a result of the added work load of the Starling division there had been an increase of 1,400 parts in the Panther division as a result of understated original estimates. This increased parts count would have resulted in a requirement for at least 10 more people under the manual system, at a cost of about $90,000, plus an estimated $4,000 for operating expenses.

Unavoidable Increases in Salary Mix

As a result of Starling–Panther consolidation and the consequent personnel changes, the average salary per employee retained in the operations control department had increased significantly. This resulted from the retention of employees on the basis of seniority. The approved budget provided for an average annual salary of $7,044. The Starling–Panther budget proposed by the manufacturing office for 1960, based on actual salaries, provided for an average annual salary in excess of $7,800. Therefore, if average salaries had remained unchanged after the consolidation, the manufacturing office's budget proposal would have been $91,560 less, as shown in Exhibit 11.

Exhibit 11

BUDGET INCREASE DUE TO SALARY MIX

Salary Base	*Proposed Ceiling*	×	*Average Annual Salary*	=	*Total Annual Salaries*
At approved budget rates	109		$7,044		$767,796
At proposed budget rates	109		7,884		859,356
Difference					($ 91,560)

Association with Integrated Data Processing Plan

By implementing the mechanized operations control system, the manufacturing office contended that it had taken an inevitable step included in the company's integrated data-processing plan, which provided for eventual establishment of a completely mechanized master parts control system. This step would make it possible to significantly reduce the original expense estimates associated with setting up this master system.

The original proposal, submitted prior to the consolidation of the two divisions, contained cost estimates of $94,887 during 1960, and $104,672 each year thereafter for providing a master parts control system to preproduction control. According to the manufacturing office, these cost estimates would have been increased to $111,872 and $159,241, respectively, as a result of the consolidation if a manual system were used. As a direct benefit of implementing a mechanized operations control system, however, the manufacturing office believed that it could show a saving of $103,000 during 1960 and $98,000 for each year thereafter. See Exhibit 12.

Exhibit 12

EFFECTIVE COST DECREASE DUE TO MECHANIZATION

Revised Cost Factors	*1960*	*1961 Going Level*
Original cost estimates	$ 94,887	$104,672
Cost of consolidation and revised assumptions based on manual system	16,985	54,569
Total cost estimates to include effect of consolidation based on a manual system	$111,872	$159,241
Reduction in cost estimates to give effect to consolidation based on mechanized system	8,700	61,010
Savings directly associated with a mechanized versus manual system	$103,172	$ 98,231

Nonrecurring Cost Penalties

The manufacturing office's proposed budget included a nonrecurring cost penalty of $112,305, resulting from the change in organization and procedure. This was compromised of $72,305 in salaries and wages, and $40,000 in computer expense. If work volume remained at the same levels in future years, the manufacturing office felt that its budget could be revised as follows:

Exhibit 13

FUTURE SAVING OF NONRECURRING COSTS

Budget Items	*1960*	*Future Years*	*Reductions*
Average personnel ceiling	117	109	9
Personnel costs	$1,158,876	$1,086,571	$ 72,305
Computer expense	245,000	205,000	40,000
Other operating costs	54,136	54,136	—
Total	$1,458,012	$1,345,707	$112,305

Functional Improvements and Advantages

The manufacturing office contended, furthermore, that a mechanized operations control system offered certain other advantages over a manual system.

1. It provided a single and better integrated program progress report that reflected the status of engineering, manufacturing, and purchasing actions against schedules on a more timely basis than did a manual system.
2. It provided a master file that, once stored in the computer, could be used to produce other useful information.
3. It was compatible with the objective to mechanize the issuance of specifications and would result in a more efficient method of handling this activity. The manufacturing office said that it could not put a dollar value on these advantages, but that it was reasonable to expect them to yield cost savings.

Summary

A cost comparison for a manual versus a mechanized operations control system, based on the above adjustments, was as shown in Exhibit 14.

The manufacturing office concluded its arguments by pointing out that the mechanized system cost only $41,000 a year more than a manual system, as shown in the preceding table, rather than $330,000 more, as stated by the controller.

QUESTION

Take a position on the problem stated in the second paragraph of the case. In order to make a judgment on this problem, you should make a careful analysis of the arguments advanced by the controller's office and by the manufacturing office.

Exhibit 14

MANUFACTURING OFFICE'S SUMMARY OF ADJUSTED COST ESTIMATES

Costs	*1960 Cost Comparison (000)* *Manual System*	*Mechanized System*
Unadjusted costs:		
Panther division	$ 722	$ 974
Starling division	406	484
	$1,128*	$1,458**
Increases:		
Parts count	(94)	—
Average salaries	(92)	—
Implementation of mechanized operations control system in accordance with company's integrated data processing plan	(112)	(9)
Total Adjusted Costs	$1,426	$1,467

* Estimated by controller's office.
** Proposed by manufacturing office.

Appendix

Summary of Controller's Description of the Control of Administrative Expenses

Administrative expenses included such expense items as salaries and wages, operating expense, program expense, and assessments for certain divisional activities. Controlling administrative expenses in many ways is similar to the control of manufacturing costs. It is one of the most unpopular and sensitive jobs in the divisional controller's office, because it involves the exercise of control over the addition and elimination of people.

Annual Budgets

Annual budgets are submitted by all divisions and serve as the basis for the control system, performance evaluation, and forecasting of expenses. These budgets are commitments by the individual divisions that they will contain their spending within the committed levels unless they receive approval from the general manager for a supplemental budget.

Personnel Ceilings

A second means of controlling expense is that of setting personnel ceilings, which are limits on the number of people employed. This system of control is useful in reducing to a meaningful size the problem of establishing, analyzing, and controlling budget levels.

Supplemental Budgets

Using supplemental budgets is a technique of continuing budget adjustments. They must be justified on the basis of changed conditions from those existing when the original budget was approved. Through this system, the division reaps the advantage of a detailed review and management approval of all programs prior to the spending of funds. Many companies permit the expenditure of funds, and then ask the spending departments to justify, on an after-the-fact basis, any unfavorable variances. Our system provides more opportunity for coordinated and informed management decision-making.

Management Reports

To make any control system effective, there must be a meaningful system of management reports. Only through usable management reports can management be kept informed and be provided with the basis for performance evaluation, forecasts of costs, and the pinpointing of troubled areas.

DETAILS OF THE ADMINISTRATIVE EXPENSE CONTROL SYSTEM

Annual Budgets

Assumptions. Probably one of the most important things in an annual budget review is the establishment of a realistic timetable and the *development of budget assumptions* by the budget section of the controller's office. Divisions will tend to base their budget proposals on different assumptions unless instructed otherwise.

Objectives. With these assumptions, the next step is to *establish budget objectives.* Objectives are realistic forecasts of next year's administrative expenditures based on known assumptions. To develop objectives, the budget section of the controller's office must normally begin with the current budget, including all supplemental budgets of a continuing nature, and then adjust for any known changes, such as projected cost reductions, increases based on new programs, and so forth. The objectives are then reviewed and approved by the general manager who, in turn, informs the divisions that this is to be the basis for their budget planning. These objectives become the primary bench mark against which the division's proposals are reviewed. If a division's proposal is within the objective, the proposal is usually approved as submitted. However, if a proposal is over the objective, the division must explain in detail the reasons for variance.

Instructions. With the assumptions and the objectives established, the *issue of budget instructions* to the divisions is a routine job. It is very important, however, that a complete and clear set of instructions be issued. It is important that a budget analyst go through them personally with each division and make certain they are understood. The budget section does not save money. It is primarily a "back pressure" on the divisions that are, in fact, the money savers. Therefore, a close working relationship with the divisions and a good selling job by the personnel of the budget section are essential.

Standards. As opposed to the majority of the manufacturing budgets, administrative expense budgets are primarily fixed budgets. Through years of reviewing these budgets, however, it has been found that work load standards, quite similar to those employed in variable budgets, can be established for most fixed positions. For instance, in the general manufacturing office, work load in the plant management staff can be partially measured by the number of automobile lines and the number of assembly plants; or in the production scheduling department, work load can be measured by the number of unique parts weighted by the number of plants to which they are released.

Budget Analysis and Review. With the receipt of the budget submission from the divisions, a detailed analysis is performed by the budget section. One of the significant determinations is the appropriate bench mark from which to measure overall changes in work load. Objectives, of course, are of primary importance. However, actual spending performance in the current year is also used as a bench mark. Probably the single most important tool used in reviewing the detail of budgets is a complete organization chart and statement of functions. This tool is the basis of personnel evaluations and serves to isolate duplication and overstaffing. The organization and systems departments assist the achievement of this goal by giving the controller's office a list of recommended system changes with resulting personnel reductions.

Presentation of Final Budgets for Management Approval. When the controller's analysis of the budgets is completed, his comments and recommendations are made available to the divisions. If appropriate levels can be agreed on through conferences with the divisions, the budget proposals are submitted to the general manager. If the controller's offices and a division cannot reach agreement, the budget proposal is submitted to the general manager together with a clear, concise statement of the area of disagreement. Recommendations of the divisional controller's office carry a great deal of weight with the general manager, and in a substantial majority of cases our position, when different from that of a division, is upheld. Budgets are not considered just as bench marks, but as actual commitments by divisions.

Personnel Ceiling

Numbers. One of the primary advantages of utilizing a salaried personnel ceiling control is that dealing with numbers of people, as opposed to dollars, brings the problem to a more manageable size. Understanding the need for, and justification of, 8,000 people is clearly much easier than that for the vague figure of $136 million. Moreover, once the justification for the number has been established, the budget dollars follow with very little added analysis.

Time Element. Another significant feature of the personnel ceiling control system is the time advantage it provides. Departments cannot hire or transfer people in excess of the authorized ceiling, and this rule provides a firm before-the-fact control on these administrative expenses. In the case of budget dollars, on the other hand, inappropriate spending cannot be determined until a budget performance report is issued, approximately a month after the expenditure has been made. This feature of the personnel ceiling control puts teeth into the principle of management approval on a before-the-fact basis.

Disicipline. Under our budget system, if salary in a division is under budget in total the division is generally not required to explain an overrun in an individual account. On the other hand, by having a personnel ceiling control as well as a budget control a division cannot use up underruns in other accounts by *adding* people over authorization. This adds much more discipline in administrative expenditures, and prevents unauthorized increases in personnel, which in the long run are the source in one way or another of most administrative costs.

Supplemental Budgets

Purposes. Another important feature of the control system is the concept of supplemental budgets. The annual budgets established each fall are outdated almost before they are submitted. The continual changes in plans and programs caused by the volatile nature of the automobile industry do not permit fixed commitments. Moreover, the process of justifying budget supplements by the operating divisions requires them to take time to plan in detail how they propose to spend money. In addition, the system of supplemental budgets provides the general manager with a continuing source of information as to what changes are taking place and what new programs are being planned. It also provides him with a means of altering direction or giving directions to a division before expenditures have been committed.

Variable Adjustments. These are automatic adjustments to a division's budget, and include such changes as functional transfers between departments, division-wide changes in fringe benefits or wage rates (such as a change in the cost-of-living allowance), and volume and work loads in areas that operate under an approved variable budget. Divisions are not required to anticipate these items.

Approval by Management. The supplemental budget system provides for controller's office concurrence and general manager's approval for all proposals on a before-the-fact basis.

Planning and Justification by Activities. The supplemental budget system requires operating management to plan and justify expenditures in terms of benefits to the division.

Commitments. Through the supplemental budget procedure, divisions are asked to demonstrate the financial desirability of new programs. Then it becomes our job to identify and establish these proposed benefits as commitments. For instance, the establishment of the Auburn sales district was proposed by the sales office. Obviously, in the administrative area there are only increased costs associated with a new district. However, we specifically obtained a commitment for additional volume from the sales office. This commitment, if met, will result in substantial added sales to the division, and these incremental sales will more than offset the added administrative costs.

Management Reports

As with any control system, the key to its success is the information it provides to management. Without meaningful and concise reports to management, good analytical work can be wasted.

Performance Reporting. On a monthly basis, each activity's performance against budget is reported to the general manager. Also, on a semimonthly basis, the performance of each activity with respect to its salaried ceiling commitment is reported. Each of these reports is accompanied by a brief letter, pointing out any problem areas that need management attention.

Forecast Reporting. All forecasts are developed by the individual divisions and then reviewed by the budget section. These forecasts are then consolidated and included in the division's profit reporting system.

Product Line Reporting. As the division's profit reporting is segregated by product line, the administrative area is required to allocate its cost by product line. Although the majority of our costs are not specific to individual product lines, we do determine specific costs in the case of new product programs.

Forward Model Program Reporting. With the many new forward model programs in existence or being planned, reporting in this area has become a particularly important part of our reporting job. Administrative expense, particularly in the manufacturing and purchasing areas, can be substantial during the preactivation period of a new program and requires adequate visibility to insure its proper control.

Financial Review. This is another tool to direct management attention to a problem area. It can deal with either a specific problem or a general problem. For example, financial reviews have been prepared that analyze a particular truck line and all the problems peculiar to it. Also, financial reviews have been made which study a sudden increase in administrative costs. The only requirement for preparing a financial review is that the problem be significant for management attention and action.

Chapter Six

FINANCIAL PERFORMANCE CENTERS; TRANSFER PRICING

In financial performance centers, or profit centers, both revenues and costs are measured in financial terms. The problems, therefore, include those discussed in the preceding chapter on expense centers, plus the new problems associated with revenue. Of these, we have elected to focus here on the problem of transfer pricing.

When products or services are sold outside the company, the measurement of revenue is relatively easy. For products or services furnished to another unit within the company, however, the problem is difficult, for the company must construct its own substitute for the market mechanism that establishes external values.

Reading 6–1

Profit Performance Measurement of Division Managers

By Joel Dean*

I. INTRODUCTION

In introduction we shall touch on (A) the importance, (B) the difficulty and (C) the role of profit centers in measuring executive performance.

A. Importance

Measuring executive performance is important in five ways:

1. It directs top management's supervision and assistance to where it is most needed and where it will be most productive.
2. It shapes the future executive team by indicating whom to promote, whom to retain and whom to remove.
3. It directs the activity of executives toward high scores on the aspects of performance on which they are measured and judged.
4. It gives job satisfaction directly by letting the executive know how he is doing.
5. It provides the objective, factual foundation for sound incentive compensation.

B. Difficulty

Measuring executive performance in a big company is difficult. The performance you want to measure is achievement of the company's goals. Measuring the executive's contribution to this achievement is made complex by the

---

* President of Joel Dean Associates and professor of business economics, Columbia University. From *The Controller*, September, 1957. Reproduced by permission of Financial Executives Institute.

fact that the corporation usually has several objectives which overlap and in some degree conflict: profits, growth, market share, and eternal life.

Profits should be the corporation's dominant goal in view of its obligation to stockholders and to a free enterprise society, but other objectives contribute in diffuse ways to long-run profits and thus cannot be ignored in measuring executive performance. Hence, the main executive performance you want to measure is contribution to the corporation's profits today and tomorrow.

The problem is made more difficult by the fact that facets of executive activity are numerous and contribute to profits in complex ways. There are few profit-determining activities that are absolutely good or bad in themselves. To make the most money often requires foregoing a high score in one activity in order to push another (e.g., high quality product vs. low cost of making it).

To combine performance measures of separate activities requires proper weights which are hard to determine and change continuously. For example, a textile mill manager is scored on (1) quality control, (2) cost compared with standards, (3) safety, (4) equipment modernity, (5) production volume, (6) meeting delivery deadlines. How should these facets of performance be weighted?

Thus, responsibility for profits in a big company is in danger of being diffused. This makes measurement hard and cuts economic efficiency of the firm. Decentralization, i.e., setting up profit centers, is a promising way to overcome this diffusion of profit responsibility.

C. Role of Profit Center Decentralization

For measuring performance, executives can be put in two groups: (1) Staff specialists, (2) businessmen, i.e., profit center (i.e., division) managers.

Complex problems of measuring and weighting executives' contributions to profits are best solved by dividing the corporation into semiautonomous profit centers whose management is measured by the contributions his center makes to corporation's overhead and profits.

A big, integrated multiple-product company functions best if made into a miniature of the competitive free enterprise economy. You can do this by dividing firms into independent operating units which act like economic entities free to trade outside as well as inside the company.

Powered with the right incentives, each profit center in maximizing its own contribution profits will do what will also maximize the profits of the entire company. It works the same way that selfish profit-seeking by individual firms in a private enterprise society generates the high productivity and automatic economic adjustments of a competitive economy.

II. REQUIREMENTS FOR PROFIT CENTER PERFORMANCE MEASUREMENT

To make a profit center system achieve these desired results of stimulating and measuring executive performance, it is necessary to:

A. Mark off profit centers correctly
B. Establish economically sound intracompany transfer prices and business arrangements
C. Measure the contribution profits of the profit center correctly
D. Determine realistic standards of contribution profit performance
E. Establish incentives in the form of executive compensation and nonmonetary rewards that will induce profit center managers to do what will be best for the corporation as a whole.

A. Profit Center Boundaries

The problem of marking off profit center boundaries has two aspects: (1) Segregating service functions from profit centers, (2) defining the scope of each profit center.

Service centers comprise staff activities which cannot be satisfactorily measured in terms of profit performance. Profit centers and service centers shade into one another so that each company's solution needs to be different. The contribution of a service center to company profitability may be great but is hard to isolate and measure definitively.

The problem of gearing staff service to profit performance is partly solved by pulverizing staff services and distributing among profit centers, where the activity must be justified economically.

Some services could be sold on a profit center basis but institutional arrangements would be too complicated and burdensome, e.g., engineering. Some services might not be used enough or in the right way if made a profit center, e.g., legal department or economics department.

The second problem is to define the scope of each profit center. A profit center is defined as a semiautonomous group of facilities and functions chosen so that profit performance can be the main guide to evaluation of divisional performance and the main guide by which the division manager makes his critical decisions.

Decisions involve economic choices among mutually exclusive courses of action. Each decision requires balancing of various kinds of costs and revenues. The company's interest lies not in maximizing a particular kind of revenue or minimizing a particular kind of cost in isolation but in maximizing the difference between all revenues and all costs. Hence the scope for profit performance measurement should be a major guide in marking off profit center boundaries.

The details of divisional boundaries and institutional arrangements are important. Failures and frustrations of decentralization are often traceable to bad boundaries and rules. Boundary lines determine how well a particular profit center functions in the corporation's interests, i.e., minimize conflicts of interest. Good boundaries make the profit performance of the division manager more meaningful, produce better incentives, supervision and development guides.

Four economic tests can be applied in marking off profit centers: (1)

Operational independence, (2) access to sources and markets, (3) separable costs and revenues, and (4) managerial intent.

1. Operational Independence. Unless a division has a large measure of independence it will have inadequate scope to reach decisions on a profit-oriented basis and hence delegation will be defeated. The division manager needs discretion over buying, production, scheduling, inventories, product-mix and pricing. This discretion should be exercised under broad rules of the game established centrally.

2. Access to Sources and Markets. Independent access to sources and markets is essential if make-or-buy decisions are to be made correctly. It is also essential for make-or-sell decisions, i.e., choice between selling a product at an early stage of the process or later (e.g., cured vs. uncured hams).

Access to outside sources and markets is most useful if outside markets are highly flexible in the long run, i.e., capable of either supplying or absorbing the company's needs without extreme price disturbances. Markets which appear too imperfect in the short run frequently are not over a period of months or years, e.g., major components of an automobile.

3. Separable Costs and Revenues. Profit centers should be marked off so as to minimize the necessity for cost and revenue allocations, since these are necessarily arbitrary and contentious.

Contribution profits of the division can be defined so as to exclude central and other costs outside the profit center manager's control. But when these controllable profits are too small a part of the total, a profit center does no good.

4. Managerial Intent. No division's contribution can be measured solely by its profits but this must be a good measure of performance if the division is to be a profit center.

Top management must be resolved to abide by the behavior and performance and the impersonal guidance of the price system which this measure of divisional performance implies.

B. Economic Transfer Prices

A second underlying requisite of effective profit center controls is competitive intracompany transfer prices negotiated in arm's length bargaining by profit center managers.

Transfer pricing must preserve profit-making autonomy of the division manager so that his divisional profit performance will coincide with the interests of the company. Small differences in unit price of transfer products make big differences in division profits and executive bonuses.

Conflicts of interests can be held at a minimum by transfers at marginal cost, but this prevents meaningful division profit performance and undercuts the main gains of profit center control.

Competitive negotiated transfer prices can be obtained by applying these simple principles:

a. Buyers and sellers completely free to deal outside or inside the company.
b. Prices determined by negotiation between buyers and sellers with a minimum of arbitration.
c. Negotiators have access to data on alternative sources and markets and have facilities for using the markets.

C. Measurement of Profit Contribution

A third requirement is good measurement of the profit contribution of the division. Performance measurement of profit center management must be geared to the multiple and overlapping goals of the corporation.

Performance Areas. Key performance areas can be grouped and labeled in various ways. One pattern is:

1. *Current Profitability,* the dominant measurement, will be discussed later.
2. *Growth* is usually conceived as sales growth, either absolutely or relatively to the industry. Frequently it is best measured in terms of market share. In whatever way it is measured, growth usually requires the development of a market franchise. This is generally achieved at the expense of some short-run profits. But presumably, it contributes to more distant profits and hence it is a part of the picture of the management's profit performance.
3. *Progress* has many dimensions. Three important ones are
   a. Investment in ideas. Research is at the expense of short-run profits, designed for long-run survival.
   b. Modernity and acceptability of the product. Sometimes this, too, causes short-run profit sacrifice.
   c. Productivity. This can be indicated by output per man hour and rate-of-return on facilities investments.
4. *Executive Development:* investment in people for future profits.

The last three factors, growth, progress and people, though measurable in their components, are hard to weight and reconcile with current profitability. The key question is whether the right amount of near profits were sacrificed in attaining these various determinants of distant profits. The answer requires high-level judgment and technical familiarity with the kinds of investment in market franchise, in ideas, in facilities, and in people that are entailed.

Measurement of the current profitability of a division entails three kinds of considerations:

1. The concept of profits
2. The form in which that profit concept will be used
3. The measurement of profits.

Profit Concepts. As to the concept of profit there are three choices:

a. Book net profits
b. Real net profits
c. Contribution profits

Book net profits tie into the stockholder reports, have a surface acceptability and are not very fudgible. But they embroil executives in fruitless debates about allocation of corporate overheads over which they have no control and raise moot questions about capital consumption costs of plant acquisitions at widely differing price levels.

Real net profits may settle the latter questions (inflation and depreciation) but do not settle problems of allocation of overhead beyond the division manager's control.

Contribution profits have fewer of these drawbacks being confined to costs and revenues over which the profit center manager has control.

Form of Profits. As to the form in which any of these three profit concepts may be expressed, there are three choices:

1. As dollar amounts
2. As percentage of sales
3. As a rate-of-return on investment

All three forms are useful in measuring different aspects of executive performance. For best results each needs to be compared with a suitable bogey.

1. Contribution profit dollars aid economic decision-making by focussing division management energies on dollars of added profit.

2. Contribution profits as a per cent of sales facilitate comparison with past performance and with comparable outside companies. Standing alone and without a bogey this performance measure is misleading.

3. Contribution profits at a return on investment provides the most important guide to top management in evaluation of profit center performance.

Measurement of Profits. Technical problems of profit-performance measurement are in practice less formidable than they appear to many newcomers.

A moderately good approximation to contribution profits can be drawn from most accounting systems with few adjustments given correct profit center demarcation and transfer prices. Isolating the book value of investment used by the division is always possible with some rough approximations.

Determination of the economic value of the book investment can be done quite cheaply with a tolerable degree of accuracy, once the concept is accepted. Current assets have book values and real values generally close enough together. Other assets can be adjusted to replacement value or disposal value by sampling and index numbers with adequate accuracy. If the concept of economic investment rather than book investment is unacceptable the defect is not fatal, particularly when the company has grown fast so that most of its assets are at recent price levels.

D. Standards of Profit Performance

Standards of profit performance, our fourth requirement, is a big, complex subject. In this analysis we can only mention four thoughts.

1. Measurement of profit performance of division managers achieves in itself many of the benefits of decentralization. Indeed a good case can be made for not attempting to formalize the standards of profit performance. Instead, leave this to the informal judgment of top management, which must in any event tailor the standard to the individual division and take many dimensions of longer-term profit performance into account, e.g., growth, progress and executive development.

2. Lack of standards should not hold up decentralization: rough standards can be used first and refined later.

3. Historical perspective is essential in developing performance standards: back-casting of comparable performance measurements will be needed.

4. Par for the profit center course should also take account of economic climate and competitive conditions in the industry. Sometimes this can be done roughly by comparison with the earnings of independent firms of approximately the same product line.

E. Incentive Compensation

The final requirement for effective profit center operation is incentives which will power the profit center manager to maximize his division's contribution-profits now and in the future. The following basic considerations should underlie the development of a balanced plan for incentive compensation of the managers of profits center divisions:

1. Objective measurements of profit performance are in themselves incentives to the kind of man who makes a good division manager. But profit center control will be most effective if powered with incentive compensation which is geared dominantly to the contribution profits of the division.

2. Incentive compensation should fit the organizational environment and personality of the profit center management: (a) independence, (b) economic sophistication and (c) minimal concern about bureaucratic politics. This means it should be geared to his division's performance.

3. Since incentives are a reward for extraordinary performance the base salary should approximate a competitive level and the ceiling or target bonus should be 40 to 50 per cent of this salary though it is hard to find a principle to justify any ceiling.

4. The company's total incentive compensation fund should be based on a maximum percentage of corporate net income which may each year be put into the fund after deducting compensation for capital—a symbol of good faith to the stockholders. (Example, General Motors, 12% of net income after deducting 5% of net capital.)

5. The amount of incentive compensation for any profit center manager should be determined by group judgment preferably at the board level based on multiple measurements of profit performance, compared when feasible with objectively determined standards.

6. Whether the payment should be in cash, in deferred compensation or in stock options ought to be tailored to the financial personality of the manager rather than determined by uniform formula.

Reading 6–2

Notes on Transfer Prices

By Robert N. Anthony

GENERAL COMMENTS

Unless a transfer price can be constructed, a responsibility center cannot be a financial performance center, even if it furnishes a significant amount of output to other units inside the company. In appraisal of a transfer price, the basic criterion is the extent to which it promotes goal congruence.

There are two broad classes of transfer prices: (1) market-based prices and (2) cost-based prices. A transfer price may be used either for products (including parts or components) or for services (including various types of staff services).

THE IDEAL SITUATION

A transfer price will induce goal congruence if *all* the conditions listed below exist. Rarely, if ever, will all these conditions exist in practice. The list, therefore, does not set forth criteria that must be met in order to have a transfer price. Rather, it suggests a way of looking at a situation (*a*) to see what changes should be made in order to improve the operation of the transfer price mechanism, or (*b*) to decide that a transfer price mechanism is inappropriate because conditions sufficient to provide an adequate degree of goal congruence do not exist.

Competent People

Ideally, the manager should be interested in the long-run as well as the short-run performance of his responsibility center, but many division managers do not have an adequate interest in long-run performance. Staff people involved in negotiation and arbitration of transfer prices also must be competent.

Good Atmosphere

Managers must regard profitability as measured in their income statement as an important goal, and as a significant consideration in the judgment of their performance. They should perceive the transfer prices as being just.

A Market Price

The ideal transfer price is based on a well-established, normal market price for the identical product or service being transferred, a market price that reflects the same conditions (quantity, delivery time, etc.) as the product or service to which the transfer price applies. (Although less than ideal, a market price for a *similar* product is better than no market price at all.)

Freedom to Act

Alternatives should exist, and managers should choose the alternative that is in their own best interests. In particular, the buying manager must be free to buy outside. This ideal clearly cannot be met completely in an organization, for if top management placed no limitations on the actions of subordinates, it would be abrogating an important reason for the organization's existence. Also, top management intervenes to forestall or correct mistakes in division managers' judgment.

Full Flow of Information

Managers must know about the available alternatives and the relevant costs and revenues of each.

Negotiation

There must be a smoothly working mechanism for negotiating "contracts" between divisions.

MARKET-BASED PRICES

If a market price exists, use it. A transfer price based on a market price is preferable to a transfer price based on cost. An important ground rule is this: If an inside division is willing to meet an outside market price and wants the business, it can have the business.

A distress or buy-in market price ordinarily should not be used as a basis for reducing an existing transfer price, or for setting a new transfer price. (But sometimes it is desirable to go outside to take advantage of a distress price.) When the market price can be ascertained only by requests for a bid, such requests must be made with restraint, because outside vendors will not knowingly prepare bids for business they are, in fact, not going to get. Usually, it is good practice to accept a significant proportion of outside low bids.

Once a transfer price is established, there may be a mechanism for adjusting it automatically for changes in cost factors (e.g., wage rates), design characteristics, etc., so as to avoid the need for finding a new market bench mark every time these changes occur. The company's own selling price for similar items may be used as a market price. The price to the most-favored customer should govern.

COST-BASED PRICES

In the absence of a market price, the transfer price must be built up from cost. The rules for constructing such a price must be prescribed by top management, rather than being negotiated by the divisions. In the absence of a detailed price formula, negotiation on a "fair" price is not feasible because the buying division does not have the power associated with a threat to go outside. There should be a negotiation mechanism for attempting to settle disputes about interpretation of the rules. Negotiation must focus on whether the ground rules are, in fact, being followed. (See below, the references to negotiation and arbitration.)

If feasible, the cost should be a *standard cost*. If it is an actual cost, then the selling division can bury its inefficiencies in the transfer price. If at standard cost, inefficiencies show up in the income statement of the selling division. If feasible, the concept of using the direct costs of the "most efficient producer," plus depreciation on actual assets, plus other overheads at standard amounts and standard volume is a good one for normal transfers. A price based on incremental costs is appropriate for capacity-filling or other special types of transactions.

If practicable, there should be a mechanism to insure that the selling division benefits from savings arising from new methods; otherwise, it will not be motivated to introduce new methods. One possibility is to leave the standard cost unchanged for a period of time after a new method is introduced. The profit margin should be a *standard* profit margin. If feasible, it should be a standard return on assets employed. If this is not feasible, it should be a standard percentage of standard costs.

NEGOTIATION AND ARBITRATION

Unless managers have full freedom to act, negotiation will not always produce an equitable result, because the parties will have unequal bargaining power; that is, one party does not have the power of threatening to take his business elsewhere, and the other party does not have the power to refuse to do the work. Since managers rarely, if ever, have full freedom to act, there must be an arbitration mechanism to insure an equitable result.

The ground rules should provide that disputes go to arbitration fairly quickly. Prolonged bickering over transfer prices is dysfunctional. The controller, or someone in the controller organization, conceptually has a neutral point of view and therefore should make a good arbitrator.

There should be a way to appeal from the arbitrated decision to top management. Top management should act on these appeals in such a way as to signal (*a*) that the appeal procedure is not a fiction, but (*b*) that appeals not well supported are unwelcome.

WHEN A TRANSFER PRICE SHOULD NOT BE USED

When top management *requires* divisions to use a service in the corporate best interests (e.g., internal auditing), the service should probably be furnished at no charge to the division. When top management *desires* divisions to use corporate staff services (e.g., public relations), it may be desirable to furnish these services without charge. However, the desired result may be accomplished with a transfer price that is less than cost; the price is in the nature of a "corporate subsidy."

A transfer price may be used even though a manager has much less than complete control over his output, as, for example, when product designs and/or production schedules are established elsewhere. If, however, the head of a responsibility center is not expected to make decisions that effect the quantity, the quality, or the mix of output, then a transfer price often should not be used. (Even in these circumstances, a transfer price may be used because of its value in controlling the *buying* division.)

If output is fairly homogeneous (e.g., cement), a quantitative, nonmonetary measure of output may be adequate. There may be no need for a "common denominator" monetary measure. If the best available *monetary* measure of output is a misleading indication of *real* output, then a transfer price should not be used. If a transfer price would induce too much competition and not enough cooperation, it should not be used.

Reading 6–3

Interdivisional Pricing

By John Dearden*

An interdivisional pricing system is required whenever a company having internal financial transactions decentralizes profit responsibility. Under a system of decentralized profit responsibility, the interests of the company must coincide with the interests of the division; that is, the action a divisional manager takes to maximize divisional profits should also maximize company profits. In developing an internal pricing system, the most important consideration is that it support the financial control system by maintaining consistency between company and divisional interests.

In this article I shall (1) consider some aspects of interdivisional pricing that are particularly important in the proper functioning of a financial control system; and (2) describe methods which have been used to establish and administer successful systems of interdivisional prices. I shall be concerned only with companies that have a significant amount of internal financial transactions; the discussion, generally, does not apply to companies with little or no internal sales and purchases.

FINANCIAL CONTROL

The problems of establishing and administering an interdivisional pricing system so that it is consistent with the financial control system are neither theoretical nor academic. Profits have been lost (and, for that matter, are probably still being lost) because this consistency was not observed, and the effectiveness of financial control systems has been impaired because internal

* From *Harvard Business Review,* January–February, 1960. Reproduced by permission of the *Harvard Business Review.*

pricing systems were inadequate. To demonstrate the importance of this point, let us look at four actual cases:

The first two illustrate how profits were lost because pricing rules created a conflict between divisional and company interests.

The third demonstrates how profits were lost when prices were not maintained in accordance with the rules, even though the rules were correct.

The fourth case describes the effect that arbitrary pricing methods have on the acceptance of the financial control system by divisional personnel.

Case 1: Design Changes

So that the manufacturing divisions of one large company would have an incentive to initiate design changes that would result in reduced manufacturing costs, the following rule was established:

"Once it has been established that a supplying division's price for a part or component is at competitive levels, any savings made by a supplying division by means of an officially approved design change, initiated by the supplying division, is to accrue to that division until the end of the model year."

Instead of creating the desired results, this rule encouraged the supplying divisions to hold off initiating design changes until the beginning of a model year. For example:

If the model year started in October, a change initiated in August would benefit the division for only two months. There would be every incentive to hold off the change until October, at which point the savings would accrue for a full twelve months (assuming, of course, that the part did not go out of production).

The situation was corrected by allowing the manufacturing divisions to keep the savings for exactly twelve months.

Case 2: Negotiation

A division was purchasing an identical part from both an outside source and a company division. The rules provided that, in cases of this type, the internal price would be exactly the same as the outside price. The buying division would be able to negotiate prices with the outside source more effectively if it knew the manufacturing costs of the part. But the selling division was reluctant to give any information to the buying division that would reduce the outside price because the inside price would also be reduced. Although a lower price was clearly to the benefit of the company, it was to the disadvantage of the division.

The conflict of interests was resolved by making a price reduction by an outside vendor effective internally one year later, *if* the selling division assisted the buying division by providing the necessary cost information.

Case 3: Cost Reduction

For three years a manufacturing division had been supplying a part to another division of the company for a price of $10.00. The rules provided that this part should be priced at competitive levels. When the buying division discovered that it could have been buying the part from an outside company for $8.50, a price reduction was immediately requested. The manager of the manufacturing division stated that the outside price figure could not be correct because his costs were $9.25.

The dispute was submitted to a central staff group for arbitration. After reviewing all the circumstances, the central staff group concluded that the $8.50 price was valid. The divisional manager then promptly took steps to reduce the cost of the part by making some design changes, effecting savings in direct labor costs, and improving material utilization. His costs were reduced to $8.00 a unit and the division was again in a profit position. It was evident that the failure of the buying division to maintain prices at lower levels had resulted in a loss of profits to it of as much as $1.25 a unit for three years.

Of course, it may be argued here that the poor cost situation should have been corrected by the manufacturing division without the pressure of a price reduction. This may be true, but the fact is that, rightly or wrongly, there is a tendency to assume that costs are satisfactory when profits are satisfactory. Without pressures of some kind, manufacturing processes tend to stabilize because the easiest, least risky course of action is to maintain the status quo.

If possible, divisions should be subjected to the same competitive pressures on costs that are experienced by independent companies. If prices are allowed to remain at levels higher than competition, this benefit is lost. Worse, management may be led by the artifically high profits of the selling division to believe that all is satisfactory in it, while improvements that may not be feasible are looked for in the division that is paying these prices. This kind of trouble can be avoided, as I shall show later, by a decentralized profit control system.

Case 4: Arbitrary Arbitration

An interdivisional price dispute was submitted to the central staff for arbitration. The difference between the buying division's proposal and the current price was $0.40 a unit; the volume was about 100,000 units a month. The staff decided to "split the difference" and the price was reduced by $0.20 a unit.

The plant manager of the selling organization was very disturbed when he heard of this decision. It reduced his profits $20,000 a month, and he had worked all year to reduce his costs $10,000 a month. A "split-the-difference" reason was not too convincing in such circumstances. As he might have pointed out, arbitrary pricing methods tend to defeat one of the most important purposes of decentralizing profit responsibility—to make divisional personnel profit-conscious.

OVER-ALL APPROACH

How can management develop an internal pricing system that is consistent with the objectives of sound financial control? I should like now to outline the main features of a complete internal pricing system. Although, to my knowledge, no single company has a pricing system exactly like the one I propose, all the methods and techniques which I recommend are being successfully used in some company at the present time.

Parts & Service Groups

One of the most important day-to-day activities that is affected by the internal price level is the analysis of make-or-buy problems. Because it is important for interdivisional prices to be at the level that will provide a proper basis for these decisions, there is a definite advantage to classifying all parts and services sold within a company according to the possibility of buying them from an outside source. As I shall explain later, this will also simplify the administration of the pricing system.

Parts and services may be classified in three categories:

A. *Items that will probably never be produced by an outside supplier*—Parts in this category include: (a) those for which no outside source is available; (b) those made within the company because of the necessity for maintaining secrecy; and (c) those which it is company policy to manufacture because control over the production process is essential (to maintain quality standards or meet some other goal). To illustrate, in the case of one of the large automobile manufacturers this category of parts would include engines (for which there is no outside supplier) and body stampings (which may be manufactured inside for reasons of secrecy).

B. *Items for which a change from manufacturing to buying or vice versa must be made on a more or less long-term basis*—Items in this category include parts requiring a substantial investment in specialized equipment or trained personnel. If a company is to start producing a part of this kind, it must generally be committed for a considerable future period because of the investment required. Conversely, if the company stops producing the part, it could involve idling (and possibly disposing of) equipment and also separating trained personnel. This would imply a more or less permanent withdrawal. To use the example of the automobile industry again, automatic transmissions would fall into this classification.

C. *Items for which the source may be changed on a short-term basis*—This category includes parts produced on general-purpose equipment or equipment involving a relatively small investment.

Pricing Rules

The first step in the recommended pricing system is to classify all parts into one of the three categories just described. The general pricing rules applicable to each of these categories follow:

Class A. I propose that, whenever possible, parts that require no make-or-buy decision be priced at long-run competitive levels. Since no direct competitive information is available for many of these items, it is generally not practicable to compare productive efficiency. For this reason, as well as the fact that decisions on choice of supplier do not depend on the prices of the items, it is not quite so compelling that exact competitive levels be maintained. However, it is desirable, although not imperative, to maintain prices at competitive levels so that the profits of a division making Class A products will be comparable to the profits of the other divisions.

Class B. I recommend that items requiring a long-term make-or-buy decision be priced at the long-term competitive price level. If the prices are allowed to reflect temporary fluctuations resulting from short-run supply and demand conditions, management might acquire a mistaken idea about their profit contribution to the company. To illustrate:

> Assume that a company has its own forging plant manufacturing gear blanks exclusively for other divisions of the firm, and that these particular parts necessitate a substantial investment in specialized equipment. Assume further that during the past year several large companies have integrated into the manufacture of forgings by building their own forge plants. Excess capacity has thus been created in this segment of the industry. As a result, gear blank forging prices have fallen to the point where this business is not yielding a satisfactory profit to the efficient producers. At what level should interdivisional profits be set?
>
> They should not be based on the low prices *if* these prices are temporarily depressed and *if* it is expected that they will rise as soon as some of the companies either go out of business or enter some other field of endeavor. Short-term low prices such as these are not valid as a basis for establishing interdivisional prices because management might be misled into deciding the company should stop producing these forgings (which might be just what competitors are hoping for, for it would relieve some of the industry's excess capacity and help prices return to the previous level).

Regardless of other considerations, a price that is expected to increase if a company stops manufacturing the item would be incorrect for internal pricing under the proposed system. It is not the lowness of prices that makes them invalid. Temporarily high prices are an equally poor base for pricing Class B items. What matters is the fact that the levels are temporary while the choice of source must be relatively permanent.

The answer to the question. "How long is temporary?" will differ in each case. Generally, it should be related to the effective life of the equipment involved. If, for instance, equipment is subject to obsolescence and has to be replaced every three years, a price that is likely to hold for three years would be considered long term and valid for interdivisional pricing. In the absence of any specific termination period, I have found that three to five years is a good general measure of what is "long term."

Class C. Items that require relatively little capital investment or that are manufactured on general-purpose equipment, and that therefore require only a short-term make-or-buy decision, may be priced on the basis of current competitive price levels (whether temporary or not). A temporary price is a perfectly good basis for a temporary make-or-buy decision. If, for example, the price of a part is temporarily depressed, it may be purchased until such time as the price increases to the point where it becomes profitable to manufacture it again.

SOURCE DETERMINATION

Many discussions of interdivisional pricing include the generalization that the buying and selling divisions should deal with each other as though they were independent companies. The procedure usually requires the manufacturing division to submit a bid (along with a number of outside firms) to the buying division; the buying division, on the basis of these bids, decides which source will supply the part.

This procedure has the advantage of simplifying the administration of the internal pricing system because the divisions treat each other as if they were independent companies. It is my opinion, however, that giving the buying division the right to decide whether or not to buy a part from within the company can prove to be a very costly method of administration. In effect, make-or-buy decisions are being delegated to a divisional purchasing agent (or even a buyer). The buying division, whose profits may be relatively unaffected, is responsible for deciding whether a part is to be made within the company or purchased from an outside source. But the selling division, whose interests coincide closely with those of the company, must compete on the same terms as any outside company.

In general, would it not be more logical to let the *selling* division decide whether it will produce a part or not? Any change in company profits from the decision either to make or buy will be reflected in the financial statements of the selling division. It is, therefore, in a position to evaluate the desirability from a company-wide point of view of manufacturing a part. (This may not be strictly true if the selling division buys component parts from some other division. But, secondary company sources are usually minor. If there are significant purchases from a second company location, the two manufacturing divisions should prepare a joint study.)

On the other hand, the buying division is not in a position to evaluate a make-or-buy decision from a company viewpoint. On the contrary, its interests are frequently to buy from outside sources, even at the same price. I have known of instances where a division has placed business outside the company because it was able to put more pressure on the outside supplier for service. The value of this extra service was small but the cost of idle facilities was considerable.

Recommended Policy

I believe that it is neither practicable nor desirable for divisions to deal completely with each other as though they were independent companies. I suggest the following alternative:

(1) The original source of Class B parts should be determined by a central staff group (either purchasing, finance, or manufacturing—or a committee of all three), and subsequent changes in source of supply should be made by mutual agreement between the divisions or, in case of dispute, arbitrated by the central group.

(2) In the case of Class C parts, the selling division should have the right to appeal to the central group in any case where it believes that what the buying division wants to do is contrary to company interests. In most transactions, however, no quarrel is likely to occur. From an administrative viewpoint, therefore, it is more practical to let the buyer make the preliminary decision whether to purchase outside or inside. If the seller does not object, the decision stands; on the other hand, if the seller does object, an appeal can be made on behalf of the selling division's and the company's interest.

The proposed method of source determination retains much of the administrative advantage of allowing the divisions to deal with each other as independent companies because Class C parts normally constitute a large portion of the total number of parts, although a small portion of the total dollar sales. Most transactions, therefore, will be negotiated at the local level, and the central staff will not be bothered. At the same time, the company is protected against uneconomic actions in choosing suppliers.

ESTABLISHING PRICES

What specific techniques are helpful in establishing and maintaining interdivisional prices? Let us turn to this question now, keeping in mind that pricing a part depends partially on its classification. I shall assume, therefore, that parts classification as well as decisions involving sources of supply have been made in accordance with my previous recommendations.

Class C Parts

In general, the pricing of Class C parts will be the easiest of the three groups. These parts may be priced with a minimum of administrative effort because the negotiating divisions can deal with each other at arm's length (or close to it). If satisfactory prices cannot be agreed on, the buying division may be given the right to have the part made by an outside supplier, subject to appeal by the selling division.

As have indicated, the prices of Class C parts should be established and maintained on the basis of current competitive levels. The division should meet competitive prices no matter how low, or give up the business.

Prices may be changed any time that competitive price levels change, subject only to agreement between divisions. For example, the buying division may request a price reduction from the selling division whenever the part can be purchased more cheaply from another vendor, provided there is no time limit on the agreement. If a time limit exists, the manufacturing division must meet the lower price on expiration of the agreement or give up the business.

Class B Parts

As earlier suggested, Class B parts should be priced at current competitive levels, adjusted for any short-term abnormalities. But may it not be difficult to determine the level of competitive prices exactly? Fortunately, where the competitive price level is difficult to estimate, there is frequently little opportunity for changing the sourcing pattern of a part and, therefore, little danger of choosing the wrong source of supply if the internal price varies somewhat from the competitive level. Conversely, where there is the real and continuing alternative of buying a part from an outside source, competitive price levels are usually available.

Here are some of the methods that have been used successfully in obtaining or approximating competitive prices:

1. *Published price lists*—Wherever possible, it is desirable to use a published price list for establishing interdivisional prices because this is usually the cheapest and most exact source of competitive price data. Price lists exist for many raw materials such as steel or glass and for standard parts such as nuts, bolts, tubes, and so forth. In certain specialized areas (e.g., meat packing), market prices are available at several points of production.
2. *Price quotations*—Published price lists and market quotations are often unavailable. To obtain data on differentiated products, management must turn to other means. Quotations from outside suppliers are one of the best sources of competitive price data for these products. The quotations must, of course, be obtained in good faith and not merely to help set internal prices. Not only is it unfair to request a quotation from a company when there is no intent to award it the business, but the supplier soon discovers what is happening and prepares his quotations accordingly.
3. *Current prices*—If a buying division purchases identical parts from both inside and outside sources, the price paid to the outside source—adjusted, of course, for differences in the conditions of the sale—may be used for internal pricing. Similarly, if a manufacturing division is selling an identical part to an outside source as well as to the inside source, the outside price provides a simple and accurate basis for setting the internal price.
4. *Prices formerly paid to an outside supplier*—When the source of a part is changed from an outside vendor to an inside division, the last valid price paid for this part will generally be a satisfactory basis for the internal price. (This price

will, of course, have to be adjusted periodically for the effect of design changes as well as for changes in the general cost level of raw material and labor.)

But caution should be exercised in deciding what the last valid price is. For instance, a vendor may adjust his price either upwards or downwards when he knows that he is to lose the business. Such price changes, frequently the direct result of the change in source, should be reviewed carefully to be sure that the new price is at a reasonable, long-term competitive level.

5. *Prices paid for similar parts*—Some internal prices may be based on the price of a similar part that is either purchased from an outside supplier or sold to an outside purchaser. The price of the outside part can be adjusted to reflect differences from the item produced inside the firm. Note that in the case of design differences which require different processing systems and therefore different costs, management wants to know what the cost differential would be if the part under consideration were produced as efficiently inside the firm as the outside item.

6. *Historical price data*—Most companies have a wealth of historical data that may be used as a basis for establishing competitive price levels for internal parts. The extent that this information may be used and the methods for using it depend, of course, on the problem to be solved.

For example, one company needed to establish prices on a group of castings sold entirely within the organization. No outside quotations existed for these parts. The purchasing department obtained the price that was currently being paid for all castings purchased from outside vendors. It also took the data on parts purchased within the past three years and brought these prices up to date by making adjustments for changes that had occurred in the general level of casting prices.

Each of these castings was then brought into a conference room, weighed, and classified into one of several groups, depending on its size and complexity. A price per pound was established for each group based on the outside purchase prices. The prices per pound were, of course, established on a judgmental basis, rather than according to the arithmetic average of all the castings in a particular group. Some prices had to be discarded completely because the part was produced in very low volume or had design peculiarities.

The final step was to classify all of the internal parts into groups corresponding to the classification of the outside parts. Prices were calculated by multiplying the appropriate price per pound by the weight of the part.

This method proved to be an effective and reasonably simple means for setting the prices of a number of complex castings. Incidentally, the study more than paid for itself since it pointed out several inconsistencies among the prices of outside parts, and the company was able through negotiation and changing sources to effect an over-all reduction in the cost of purchased castings.

Adjusting for Changes

Periodically, prices should also be adjusted for changes in competitive conditions. Once a year, perhaps, the buying division should request reductions if prices have gone down for any of the outside-purchased Class B parts that formed the basis for establishing the interdivisional prices. In the case of increases, the supplying division should initiate the necessary price action. More frequent adjustment tends to create an unnecessary work load, and less frequent adjustment leads to the danger that interdivisional price levels may get too far out of date and create a distortion in the divisional profit statements.

Price adjustments should not, of course, be made for changes in the efficiency of the manufacturing division. Such changes rarely, if ever, affect the competitive price level. Furthermore, if prices move up and down as efficiency is reduced or improved, the supplier would have little incentive to work on his costs.

Class A Parts

There are two pricing categories into which Class A parts may be divided: (1) those parts for which competitive prices may be approximated, and (2) those parts for which competitive prices cannot be reliably estimated. The first group may be priced in the same manner as Class B parts; the second group requires some other techniques.

The main need is for prices that will provide an incentive to maximize the rate of return on the investment under the control of the divisional manager. Rules for calculating these prices must be established with sufficient precision to allow the divisions to negotiate and establish their own rates. Although each case should be treated individually, the following methods have proved useful in establishing prices on manufactured parts for which no competitive standards exist:

1. *Calculate the cost of producing the part to be priced*—This should be the expected cost of a modern, efficient producer using the best methods and equipment.
2. *Calculate a profit allowance*—This profit, expressed as a percentage of the necessary investment, should be equal to the return that an efficient producer would be expected to earn. The investment should include an allowance for working capital and be based on the current replacement value of the equipment used in making the cost estimate. When costs are based on equipment actually in use, the book value of that equipment may be used instead of the replacement value.
3. *Calculate the price by adding the cost and the profit*—This is the final step.

It will be necessary, of course, to provide the divisions with specific, detailed instructions so that they will have a basis for negotiations. And if the part is very complicated, it may be necessary for the central staff to establish the initial price for it.

Once a price is established, it should be adjusted periodically for changes in design and changes in costs that are not controllable by the manufacturing division. It should *not* be adjusted for changes in efficiency or for facilities added to gain efficiency.

In the case of complicated assemblies does this approach result in an excessive amount of work? Such might appear to be the case, particularly when current facilities and methods are out of date and the price must be calculated on hypothetical costs and facilities.

However, the analysis necessary to establish a price is precisely the same type of analysis that should be undertaken to plan the action needed to correct the out-of-date condition. Further, when the interdivisional price is based on an efficient level of cost and the difference between the actual and the efficient cost level is reflected as a variance from profit objective, management is constantly made aware of the profit effect of the outdated facilities and inadequate methods.

A simpler version of this technique is to use actual costs as a basis for the price in combination with a profit markup that is less than the divisional profit objective; the purpose is to give the divisional management an incentive to improve efficiency. For instance:

> It was decided in one case that the current manufacturing costs of a part were not at an efficient level. The price could be calculated by adding a 10% return on the investment to the actual costs of production. If the profit objective was then set at 20%, the division would be under pressure to correct the inefficiencies.

Although this method has the advantage of ease of calculation (because it does not require the costs of some hypothetical producer), it has disadvantages: (1) a plan to improve efficiency should be made whether or not interdivisional pricing is involved, and (2) it is an arbitrary method and may tend to undermine the acceptance of the financial control system.

SPECIAL PROBLEMS

In almost every decentralized financial control system, special pricing problems arise that are not covered by any of the preceding methods. Four problems in particular deserve attention here.

Separate Marketing Division

In some instances it may be desirable to have a separate division whose principal function is to market a line of products. Assume that Division A is responsible for marketing a line of electrical appliances that are manufactured by Divisions B, C, and D of the same company. How should the prices that Division A is to pay be calculated?

Some companies establish the purchase price to Division A on the basis of a percentage of the outside selling price. For example, the percentage might be 80 percent, leaving a margin of 20 percent to cover the division's sales promotion and administrative costs as well as profits. But this method is undesirable because it gives the merchandising division only a small part of the benefits of judicious pricing—usually one of its principal responsibilities. And, worse, it could create an incentive to keep prices low at the expense of profits because the merchandising division would be relatively unaffected by price reductions. To illustrate:

If an appliance sells for $100, Division A pays 80% of the selling price ($80), leaving $20 to cover profits and costs. A reduction in price of 10% means a new selling price of $90, a new purchase price of $72, and a new cost and profit allowance of $18. Although company profits have been reduced $10, Division A has absorbed only $2 of the loss. It can make up this loss with a relatively slight increase in volume.

A more realistic price to the merchandising division would be one based on the cost of manufacture, preferably, the efficient-producer cost of the Class A parts. In this way, the full impact of price changes falls on the merchandising division, where it belongs in such a case.

What about having the division pay a price per unit? This may tend to keep the selling price too high because the benefits of higher volume resulting from greater utilization of fixed plant and equipment do not accure to the merchandising division. To correct this situation, the price paid by Division A could be divided into two parts: (1) a unit price based on the variable costs plus a profit on the variable assets; and (2) a fixed amount, charged each month, based on the fixed costs associated with producing the assemblies plus a profit on the fixed assets used.

If this approach is used, the merchandising division's effort to maximize divisional profit will also maximize company profit.

Interdivisional Disputes

An interdivisional pricing system must provide in some way for the possibility that two divisions may not be able to settle a price. There are several methods in common use for settling such disputes:

(1) Both of the divisional managers involved in the dispute meet with a top executive (e.g., the president, executive vice president, or vice president of finance). The meeting is generally conducted informally with no written presentation; the price is usually settled during the course of this meeting without a detailed review of each of the division's proposals. The decision is quick but arbitrary.

(2) The dispute is submitted formally to a committee established for the purpose of arbitrating price disputes. Each party generally submits its position to the committee in writing. The committee, with the help of a staff, analyzes the proposals of both parties and publishes a decision.

(3) Disputes are submitted to a central staff (probably finance or purchasing). The staff analyzes the proposals of each party and publishes a decision.

Probably no single one of these methods is completely satisfactory. In any case, however, the individual or group with final authority must be high enough in management to assure acceptance of the decisions, and to make it extremely difficult for divisional managers to apply undue pressure.

It helps to assign to a staff office (usually finance or purchasing), the task of recommending a settlement, but giving divisional management the right to appeal. If the staff recommends an appropriate settlement and either party disagrees with its recommendation, the matter is then referred to management for final arbitration—to a top executive or committee if the problem is a major one, to lower-level managers if it is not.

Always, however, it is important to keep alive the possibility that *any* recommendation may be appealed to top management. This assures the divisions that a careful and unbiased study will be made by the staff group responsible for reviewing price disputes.

Chronic Quarreling

One of the most annoying problems associated with many interdivisional pricing systems is the acrimonious debate and the resulting ill feelings which so frequently accompany price negotiations.

Inasmuch as the selling division is not concerned about selling its product and the buying division is not concerned about its source of supply, divisional personnel can be much more cavalier in the treatment of each other than if they represented independent companies. Sometimes this animosity between divisions can reach ridiculous extremes. I know of one instance in which the engineers of a buying division were refused admittance to a company plant that was freely accessible to engineers from a competing concern.

I know of no completely satisfactory answer to this problem. One of the most important considerations is the choice of people to conduct the negotiations. Many difficulties can be attributed to those who are doing the negotiating, rather than to the technical problems associated with establishing the price, as the following example clearly illustrates:

> For a period of three years, in one instance, a division had to have nearly every price settled by arbitration. After the person responsible for settling price disputes was replaced, the division successfully settled all such problems thereafter without arbitration.

Although disputes are the result of many causes, it may be well to review the personnel involved in areas where the number of price disputes is inordinately large.

Accepting the Costs

In making a decision to decentralize, the cost of establishing interdivisional prices should be included as an added expense of the move. If the decision for decentralization is made because the change seems profitable, the cost of regulating interdivisional prices should *not* be considered a waste any more than the cost of preparing divisional financial statements. The direct savings from price negotiations—frequently significant—should not be expected to equal the direct cost of administering the internal pricing system.

Of course, I do not imply that every effort should not be made to keep the system as simple and inexpensive as possible, consistent with the objectives of the financial control system. My point is simply that there is no royal road to interdivisional pricing, that a naive internal pricing system will not support a sophisticated and complex financial control system. Shortcutting the pricing process will often weaken financial control in the same way that reducing the analysis of a proposed budget can weaken budgetary control.

CONCLUSION

Interdivisional pricing is a means to an end, not an end in itself. It is an essential part of a decentralized profit control system in any company where divisions buy from and sell to each other. The financial control system is only as good as the interdivisional prices on which the financial statements are based.

The most important requirement of interdivisional pricing is that it be consistent with the financial control system. The division and the company as a whole have vital mutual interests. The interdivisional pricing system can lend valuable support to these interests—or work against them. It is all up to top management.

Case 6–1

Birch Paper Company

"If I were to price these boxes any lower than $480 a thousand," said James Brunner, manager of Birch Paper Company's Thompson division, "I'd be countermanding my order of last month for our salesmen to stop shaving their bids and to bid full-cost quotations. I've been trying for weeks to improve the quality of our business, and if I turn around now and accept this job at $430 or $450 or something less than $480, I'll be tearing down this program I've been working so hard to build up. The division can't very well show a profit by putting in bids that don't even cover a fair share of overhead costs, let alone give us a profit."

Birch Paper Company was a medium-size, partly integrated paper company, producing white and kraft papers and paperboard. A portion of its paperboard output was converted into corrugated boxes by the Thompson division, which also printed and colored the outside surface of the boxes. Including Thompson, the company had four producing divisions and a timberland division, which supplied part of the company's pulp requirements.

For several years, each division had been judged independently on the basis of its profit and return on investment. Top management had been working to gain effective results from a policy of decentralizing responsibility and authority for all decisions except those relating to overall company policy. The company's top officials believed that in the past few years the concept of decentralization had been successfully applied and that the company's profits and competitive position had definitely improved.

Early in 1957, the Northern division designed a special display box for one of its papers in conjunction with the Thompson division, which was equipped to make the box. Thompson's staff for package design and development spent several months perfecting the design, production methods, and materials to be used. Because of the unusual color and shape, these were far from standard. According to an agreement between the two divisions, the Thompson division was reimbursed by the Northern division for the cost of its design and development work.

When all the specifications were prepared, the Northern division asked for bids on the box from the Thompson division and from two outside companies. Each division manager was normally free to buy from whatever supplier he wished; and even on sales within the company, divisions were expected to meet the going market price if they wanted the business.

In 1957, the profit margins of converters such as the Thompson division were being squeezed. Thompson, as did many other similar converters, bought its paperboard, and its function was to print, cut, and shape it into boxes. Though it bought most of its materials from other Birch divisions, most of Thompson's sales were made to outside customers. If Thompson got the order from Northern, it probably would buy its linerboard and corrugating medium from the Southern division of Birch. The walls of a corrugated box consist of outside and inside sheets of linerboard sandwiching the fluted corrugating medium. About 70 percent of Thompson's out-of-pocket cost of $400 for the order represented the cost of linerboard and corrugating medium. Though Southern had been running below capacity and had excess inventory, it quoted the market price, which had not noticeably weakened as a result of the oversupply. Its out-of-pocket costs on both liner and corrugating medium were about 60 percent of the selling price.

The Northern division received bids on the boxes of $480 a thousand from the Thompson division, $430 a thousand from West Paper Company, and $432 a thousand from Eire Papers, Ltd. Eire Papers offered to buy from Birch the outside linerboard with the special printing already on it, but would supply its own inside liner and corrugating medium. The outside liner would be supplied by the Southern division at a price equivalent of $90 a thousand boxes, and it would be printed for $30 a thousand by the Thompson division. Of the $30, about $25 would be out-of-pocket costs.

Since this situation appeared to be a little unusual, William Kenton, manager of the Northern division, discussed the wide discrepancy of bids with Birch's commercial vice-president. He told the vice-president: "We sell in a very competitive market, where higher costs cannot be passed on. How can we be expected to show a decent profit and return on investment if we have to buy our supplies at more than 10 percent over the going market?"

Knowing that Mr. Brunner had on occasion in the past few months been unable to operate the Thompson division at capacity, it seemed odd to the vice-president that Mr. Brunner would add the full 20 percent overhead and profit charge to his out-of-pocket costs. When asked about this, Mr. Brunner's answer was the statement that appears at the beginning of the case. He went on to say that having done the developmental work on the box, and having received no profit on that, he felt entitled to a good markup on the production of the box itself.

The vice-president explored further the cost structures of the various divisions. He remembered a comment that the controller had made at a meeting the week before to the effect that costs which were variable for one division could be largely fixed for the company as a whole. He knew that in the absence of specific orders from top management Mr. Kenton would accept the lowest bid, which was that of the West Paper Company for $430. However, it would be possible for top management to order the acceptance of another bid if the situation warranted such action. And though the volume represented by the transactions in question was less than 5 percent of the volume of any of the divisions involved, other transactions could conceivably raise similar problems later.

QUESTIONS

1. In the controversy described, how, if at all, is the transfer price system dysfunctional?
2. Describe other types of decisions in the Birch Paper Company in which the transfer price system would be dysfunctional.

Case 6–2

Automobile Dealership Accounting

The management accounting systems recommended to dealers by the major automobile manufacturers—General Motors, Ford, Chrysler, and American—were basically similar. These systems were recommended primarily on the grounds that they would be useful, first, in the management of the dealership, and only secondarily as a means of providing the manufacturer with comparable information from all its dealers. Indeed, figures from the "departmental" aspect of the system, which is described in this note, often were not even reported to the manufacturer.

The dealer was urged to develop monthly income figures for each of the following departments: (1) new car sales, (2) used car sales, (3) service, and (4) parts and accessories. If relevant, there also were departments for truck sales, leasing, and other identifiable activities.

The service department, in addition to doing service work for customers, also did internal work for the new car department, for which customers were not charged (preparation of new cars and making repairs in response to customer complaints), and for the used car department (reconditioning). Methods of charging for this internal work varied. In some dealerships, there was a standard price for each type of job; others charged an hourly rate that included direct labor cost plus an allowance for overhead and profit. In some dealerships, the price for internal work was the same as that charged outside customers; in others, there was a discount for internal work, so that the transfer price, although in excess of cost, was less than the retail price. For example, the hourly rate for internal work might be 90 percent of the rate charged customers.

Service departments qualified as profit centers for several reasons. They generated revenue from internal work. Interdepartmental charges ordinarily were *not* made at cost. There was a market price for service work done for customers, but this price sometimes was changed after negotiation with the customer, and prices to customers did not cover all types of service work. For example, they did not cover new care preparation, which amounted to about $40 or more per car. Similarly, the parts and accessories department was a profit center. Parts used in reconditioning used cars were charged to the used car department at a price that ordinarily included an element of profit.

Automobile dealerships usually are not large businesses. For the 21,000 member dealers of the National Automobile Dealers Association, the average dealer in 1959 had a net worth of $119,000 and employed 17 people.

QUESTION

Are the dealers well advised to use a profit center system?

Case 6-3

Strider Chemical Company

On December 9, 1960, the president of the Strider Chemical Company, which had sales of around $75 million, announced that on January 1, 1961, the company would be reorganized into separate divisions. Until that time, the company had been organized on a functional basis, with the manufacturing, sales, finance, and research departments each under one man's responsibility. Six divisions were to be set up—four by product group and two by geographical area. Each division was to have its own production, sales, and accounting staff, and a general manager who would be responsible for its operation. The division's operating performance was to be judged by the profit it produced in relation to the investment assigned to it. It was anticipated that the procedure for computing the investment base and the return thereon would have to be carefully worked out if the resultant ratio was to be acceptable to the new division managers as a reasonable measure of their performance.

One of the biggest obstacles to the establishment of the desired monthly profit and loss statement for each division was the pricing of products for transfer from one to another of the various divisions. At the time the divisions were established, the company's president issued a policy statement upon which a pricing procedure was to be based. The president's statement follows.

STATEMENT OF POLICY

The *maximum*, and usual, price for transfers between profit units is that price which enables the producing unit to earn a return on the investment required, consistent with what it can earn doing business with the *average* of its customers for the product group concerned.

Established prices will be reviewed each six months or when a general change in market prices occurs.

DISCUSSION

Pricing policy between operating units is particularly important, because to the extent that the price is wrong, the return on one segment of the business is understated, and the return on another is overstated. This not only gives a false measure of how well individuals are performing, but also may make for bad decisions on the business as a whole, which will affect everyone.

Certain elements of expense that may not be found in intracompany relations are:

1. Deductions for cash discounts,, freight, royalties, sales taxes, customer allowances, etc.
2. Usual selling expenses and, in many cases, order and billing services.
3. Certain customer services by the research laboratories, such as sales services where this applies.

The producing division that acts as a supplier will establish a price by discounting its *regular price* structure for the elements listed above which apply.

In case the buying division disagrees with the price as computed above, it will explain the basis of its disagreement to the president, who will decide what is to be done.

We are hopeful that this policy will work out equitably, giving each division a fair basis for the business they do. If, in practice, it is found that the policy is not working properly, is complicated in its application or calculation, or is working a hardship, the policy will have to be changed.

The largest of the newly formed divisions, the Williams division, was strongly affected by the problem of transfer prices, since about 23 percent of its sales would be to other divisions.

With only three weeks before the separation into divisions, it was important that a schedule of prices be quickly established for the transfer of products between divisions. The Williams division's task was complicated by its large number of products. There were several hundred different compounds and materials for which a price had to be fixed. It was, therefore, partly for the sake of expediency that the Williams division chose to set the prices on the basis of direct manufacturing cost. The figures used in this method were more readily available than those used in setting a price based on the current market price.

A week after the president's policy statement on transfer pricing had been distributed, the Williams division issued an interpretation of the policy which stated its proposed method for setting prices for the sale of products by the Williams division to other divisions. The key paragraphs from this statement were as follows:

The Williams Division will charge the same price to another division as it charges to the average of its existing customers, less an allowance for those expenses incurred with average customers but not with interdivisional customers.

These non-comparable expenses to be deducted include Sales Deductions and a part of Selling Expenses. The prices will be calculated in terms of a markup or multiplier factor on Direct Manufacturing Cost. A markup will be recalculated each six months, based on the prior twelve months' experience with regular customers.

The markup for the first six months of 1961 will be 1.41 times Direct Manufacturing Cost as shown by the following computation which uses actual data for the 12 month period ended October 31, 1960:

		$	%
Gross sales to outside customers		$5,126,328	
Less: Amounts not applicable to internal sales:			
a) Freight, royalties, sales taxes	$ 58,625		
b) Selling expenses	260,123		
Total Deductions		318,748	
Adjusted sales		$4,807,580	100
Direct manufacturing cost		3,404,923	71
Margin		$1,402,657	29
Computation: 100 ÷ 71 = 1.41 times			

By the end of March, 1961, the president had received a number of letters from division managers, raising questions about transfer prices. Three of these are summarized below.

1. The Williams division questioned the price which the Johnson division had established for compound A, a raw material for the Williams division. The Johnson division had initially calculated a markup of 1.33, computed in the same way the Williams division computed its markup of 1.41. At a markup of 1.33, however, the Johnson division would show a net loss, since the division had not operated at a profit in the preceding 12 months. It therefore raised its markup to 1.41, the same as that used by the Williams division. At this markup, it would show about the same profit as that of the Williams division. The Williams division argued that this markup violated company policy.

2. The International division questioned the transfer price of several products it purchased from the Williams division for sale abroad. It said that at these prices the International division could not meet competitive prices in European markets and still make a profit.

3. The Western division purchased chemical B from the Williams division for resale to its own customers. It submitted data to show that at the computed transfer price the Western division would be better off to manufacture chemical B in one of its own plants. Rather than do this, it proposed that the transfer price be cut by 15 percent, which would still leave a margin over direct manufacturing cost for the Williams division.

As of the end of March, the president had not acted on any of these letters, other than to reply that existing relationships between divisions should be continued until further notice, and that after the questions had been decided, adjustments in transfer prices would be made retroactive to January 1.

In view of the numerous questions that had already arisen about the markup, the president was considering the possibility of transferring all products at cost, without any markup.

QUESTION

What changes, if any, should be made in the transfer price practices of Strider Chemical Company?

Case 6–4

General Appliance Corporation

ORGANIZATION

The General Appliance Corporation was an integrated manufacturer of all types of home appliances. As shown in Exhibit 1, the company had a decentralized, divisional organization consisting of four product divisions, four manufacturing divisions, and six staff offices. Each division and staff office was headed by a vice-president. The staff offices had functional authority over their counterparts in the divisions, but they had no direct line authority over the divisional general managers. The company's organization manual stated: "All divisional personnel are responsible to the division manager. Except in functional areas specifically delegated, staff personnel have no line authority in a division."

The product divisions designed, engineered, assembled, and sold various home appliances. They manufactured very few component parts; rather, they assembled the appliances from parts purchased either from the manufacturing divisions or from outside vendors. The manufacturing divisions made approximately 75 percent of their sales to the product divisions. Parts made by the manufacturing divisions were generally designed by the product divisions; the manufacturing divisions merely produced the parts to specifications provided to them. Although all the manufacturing divisions had engineering departments, these departments did only about 20 percent of the total company engineering.

TRANSFER PRICES

The divisions were expected to deal with one another as though they were independent companies. Parts were to be transferred at prices arrived at by negotiation between the divisions. These prices were generally based on the actual prices paid to outside suppliers for the same or comparable parts.

Exhibit 1

GENERAL APPLIANCE CORPORATION

Organization Chart

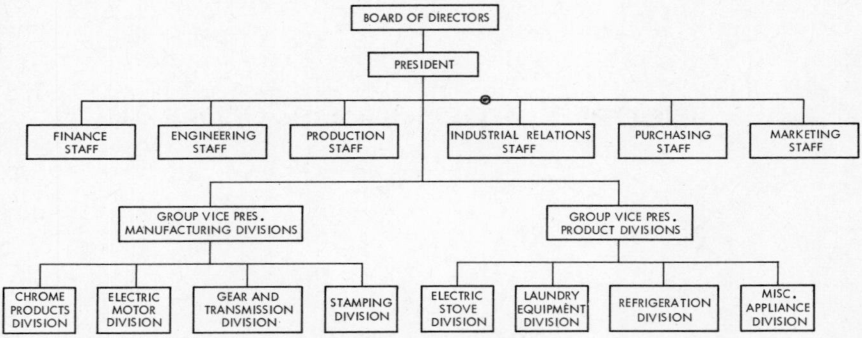

These outside prices were adjusted to reflect differences in design of the outside part from that of the inside part. Also, if the outside price was based on purchases made at an earlier date, it was adjusted for changes in the general price level since that date. In general, the divisions established prices by negotiation among themselves, but if the divisions could not agree on a price they could submit the dispute to the finance staff for arbitration.

SOURCE DETERMINATION

Although the divisions were instructed to deal with one another as independent companies, in practice this was not always feasible, because a product division did not have the power to decide whether to buy from within the company or from outside. Once a manufacturing division began to produce a part, the only way the product division buying this part could change to an outside supplier was to obtain permission of the manufacturing division or, in case of disagreement, appeal to the purchasing staff. The purchasing staff had the authority to settle disputes between the product and manufacturing divisions with respect to whether a manufacturing division should continue to produce a part or whether the product division could buy outside. In nearly every case of dispute, the purchasing staff had decided that the part would continue to be manufactured within the company. When the manufacturing divisions were instructed to continue producing a part, they had to hold the price of the part at the level at which the product division could purchase it from the outside vendor.

In the case of new parts, a product division had the authority to decide on the source of supply. Even for new parts, however, a manufacturing division could appeal to the purchasing staff to reverse the decision if a product division planned to purchase a part from an outside vendor.

STOVETOP PROBLEM

The chrome products division sold to the electric stove division a chrome-plated unit that fitted on the top of the stove; the unit had to be resistant to corrosion and stain from spilled food. It was also essential that the unit remain bright and new-looking. The chrome products division had been producing this unit since January 1, 1958; prior to that time, it had been produced by an outside vendor.

The unit in question was produced from a steel stamping. Until June, 1959, the stamping was processed as follows:

Operations	*Processes*
1	Machine buffing
2	Nickel plating
3	Machine buffing
4	Chrome plating
5	Machine buffing

About the middle of 1958, the president of General Appliance Corporation became concerned over complaints from customers and dealers about the quality of the company's products. A customer survey appeared to indicate quite definitely that in the previous year the company's reputation as a producer of quality products had deteriorated. Although this deterioration was believed to have been caused principally by the poor performance of a new electric motor, which was soon corrected, the president had come to the conclusion that the overall quality of the company's products had been decreasing for the past several years. Furthermore, he believed that it was essential for the company to reestablish itself as a leader in the production of quality products. Accordingly, early in 1959 he called in the production vice-president (i.e., head of the production staff office) and told him that for the next six months his most important job was to bring the quality of all products up to a satisfactory level.

In the course of carrying out this assignment, the production vice-president decided that the appearance of the chrome-plated stovetop was unsatisfactory. Until now, the bases for rejection or acceptance of this part by the quality control section of the chrome products division were a corrosion test and an appearance test; appearance was largely subjective and, in the final analysis, dependent on the judgment of the quality control man. In order to make the test more objective, three tops were selected and set up as standards for the minimum acceptable quality. Because better than average units were selected, rejects increased to over 80 percent. Personnel from the chrome products division and the production staff jointly studied the manufacturing process to find a way of making the stovetops conform to the new quality standards. They added copper plating and buffing operations at the beginning of the process, and a hand-buffing operation at the end of the manufacturing cycle. The total cost of these added operations was 40 cents a unit. As soon as the new operations were put into effect in June, 1959, the rejection rate for poor quality declined to less than 1 percent.

In July, 1959, the chrome products division proposed to increase the price of the stovetop by 45 cents; 40 cents represented the cost of the added operations, and 5 cents was the profit markup on the added costs. The current price, before the proposed increase, was $5.00 a unit. This price had been developed as follows:

Price charged by an outside producer (12/31/58)	$4.50
Design changes since 12/31/58	.25
Changes in raw materials and labor prices since 12/31/58	.25
Price as of June 30, 1959	$5.00

The electric stove division objected to the proposed price increase, and after three weeks of fruitless negotiations it was decided that the dispute should be submitted to the finance staff for arbitration. The positions of the parties to the dispute are summarized below.

Chrome Products Division

In a letter to the vice-president for finance, the general manager of the chrome products division stated that he believed he was entitled to the increased price because:

1. He had been required by the production staff to add operations at a cost of 40 cents a unit.
2. These operations resulted in improved quality that could benefit only the electric stove division.
3. The present price of $5.00 was based on old quality standards. Had the outside supplier been required to meet these new standards, the price would have been 45 cents higher.

Electric Stove Division

The general manager of the electric stove division, in appealing the price increase, based his position on the following arguments.

1. There had been no change in engineering specifications. The only change that had taken place was in what was purported to be "acceptable appearance." This was a subjective matter that could not be measured with any degree of precision. Further, both the particular case and the possible effects of establishing a precedent were objectionable. "If we were to pay for any change in quality standards, not accompanied by a change in engineering specification, we would be opening up a Pandora's box. Every division would request higher prices based on giving us better quality based on some subjective standard. Every request by this division to a manufacturing division to improve quality would be accom-

panied by a price increase, even though we were requesting only that the quality be brought up to competitive levels."

2. The electric stove division had not requested that quality be improved. In fact, the division had not even been consulted on the change. Thus, the division should not be responsible for paying for a so-called improvement that it neither requested nor approved.

3. Whether there was any improvement in quality from the customer's viewpoint was doubtful, although to the highly trained eye of the quality control personnel there may have been an improvement. The customer would not notice a significant difference between the appearance of the part before and after the change in quality standards.

4. Even if there were an improvement in quality perceptible to the consumer, it was not worth 45 cents. By adding 45 cents to the cost of the stove, he could add features that would be far more marketable than the quality improvement.

5. Any improvement in quality only brought the part up to the quality level that the former outside producer had provided. The cost of the improved quality, therefore, was included in the $5.00 price.

Finance Staff Review

The finance staff reviewed the dispute. In the course of this review, the engineering department of the production staff was asked to review the added operations and comment on the acceptability of the proposed cost increases. The quality control department of the manufacturing staff was asked to verify whether quality was actually better as the result of the added operations and whether the new units were of higher quality than the units purchased from the outside vendor 18 months ago. The engineering department stated that the proposed costs were reasonable and represented efficient processing. The quality control department stated that the quality was improved and that the new parts were of superior quality to the parts previously purchased from outside sources.

THERMOSTATIC CONTROL PROBLEM

One of the plants of the electric motor division produced thermostatic control units. The laundry equipment division bought all its requirements for thermostatic control units (about 100,000 a year) from the electric motor division. The refrigeration division used a similar unit, and until 1956 it had purchased all its requirements (20,000 a year) from an outside supplier, the Monson Controls Corporation. In 1956, at the request of the electric motor division, the refrigeration division purchased 25 percent of its requirements from the electric motor division. In 1957, this percentage was increased to 50 per cent, and in 1958 to 75 percent. In July, 1958, the refrigeration division informed the Monson Controls Corporation that beginning January 1, 1959, it would buy all its thermostatic control units from the electric motor division. The refrigeration division made these source changes as a result of electric motor division requests which were, it said, "in the best interests of the company." The units made outside and inside were comparable in quality, and the price paid to the electric motor division was the same as the price paid to the Monson Controls Corporation. The laundry equipment division also paid this same price to the electric motor division.

In 1955, the demand for this kind of thermostatic control unit was high in relation to the industry's production capacity. Between 1956 and 1959, several appliance companies, including the General Appliance Corporation, built or expanded their own facilities to produce this unit, so that by the middle of 1958 the production capacity of the independent companies considerably exceeded the demand. One of the results of this situation was a declining price level. Prices of the Monson Controls Corporation had been as follows:

1955	$3.00
1956	2.70
1957	2.50
1958 (January–June)	2.40

As a result of these price reductions, which the electric motor division had met, the profits of the electric motor division on this product had dropped from a before-tax profit of 15 percent on its investment in 1955 to nearly zero in 1958.

In August, 1958, after being told it could no longer supply the refrigeration division, the Monson Controls Corporation reduced its price to the refrigeration division by 25 cents, retroactive to July 1. The price reduction was not reflected immediately in the intracompany price, because the three divisions involved had agreed to use $2.40 for the entire year.

In October, 1958, the electric motor division and the refrigeration division were negotiating 1959 prices. The refrigeration division proposed a price of $2.15, the price paid to the Monson Controls Corporation. The electric motor division, however, refused to reduce its prices below $2.40 to either the refrigeration division or the laundry equipment division. After several weeks of negotiations, the disagreement was submitted to the finance staff for settlement.

Electric Motor Division

The electric motor division based its refusal to accept the last price reduction of the Monson Controls Corporation on the premise that it was made as a last, desperate effort to continue supplying General Appliance Corporation with this part. (Monson Controls Corporation continued to supply General Appliance Corporation with other products, although this control unit had been the major item.) As support for this premise, the electric motor division indicated that at the lower price it would lose money. Since it was as efficient as the Monson Controls Corporation, it concluded that Monson must also be losing money. The price was, therefore, a distress price and not a valid basis for determining an internal price. To support its case further, the electric motor division pointed out the downward trend in the price of this part as evidence of distressed pricing practices growing out of the excess capacity in the industry.

The general manager of electric motor division stated that it was going to take all his ability and ingenuity to make a profit even at the $2.40 price. At $2.15, he could never be in a profit position; and if forced to accept a price of $2.15, he would immediately make plans to close the plant and let outside suppliers furnish all the thermostatic control units.

Laundry Equipment Division

The laundry equipment division based its case for a $2.15 price on the intracompany pricing rules that required products to be transferred between divisions at competitive prices. The general manager pointed out that his annual volume was 100,000 units a year, compared to a total of only 20,000 for the refrigeration division. He believed that with his higher volume he could probably obtain an even more favorable price if he were to procure his requirements from outside the corporation.

Refrigeration Division

The refrigeration division based its case on the fact that the division not only could, but did, buy the thermostatic control unit from a reliable outside supplier for $2.15. The division was sure that the Monson Controls Corporation had capacity to produce all its requirements and would be happy to do so for $2.15 a unit. Since patronage had been transferred to the electric motor division only as a favor and to benefit the company as a whole, the refrigeration division believed it was unjust to make it pay a higher price than it would have paid if the division had never allowed the business to be taken inside the company.

As further evidence to support its case, the refrigeration division pointed to an agreement made with the electric motor division at the time it had agreed to purchase all its requirements of the thermostatic control unit from that division. This agreement read, in part: "In the event of a major pricing disparity, it is agreed that further model requirements will be competitively sourced [i.e., sourced to the lowest bidder]."

The refrigeration division stated that in the light of the major pricing disparity it should be allowed to request quotations from outside suppliers and place the business outside should such a supplier bid lower than the electric motor division.

Finance Staff Review

In the course of arbitrating this transfer price dispute, the finance staff asked the purchasing staff to review the outside market situation for the thermostatic control unit. The purchasing staff replied that there was excess capacity and that, as a result of this, prices were very soft. Eventually, the prices would rise either when the demand for comparable units increased or when some of the suppliers went out of business. The purchasing staff had no doubt that the refrigeration division could purchase all its requirements for the next year or two for $2.15 a unit, or even less. The purchasing staff believed, however, that if all the corporation's requirements for this unit were placed with outside suppliers, the price would rise to at least $2.40 because this action would dry up the excess capacity.

TRANSMISSION PROBLEM

The laundry equipment division began production of automatic washers shortly after the end of World War II. Initially, it had purchased its transmissions from two sources—the gear and transmission division and the Thorndike Machining Corporation. The transmission had been developed and engineered by the Thorndike Machining Corporation. In consideration of an agreement to buy one half of its transmissions from the Thorndike Machining Corporation, the General Appliance Corporation had been licensed to produce the transmission. The agreement ran from 1949 to 1959; at the expiration of the 10 years, General Appliance would have the right to use the design without restrictions.

In early 1957, nearly two years before the end of the agreement, the management of the General Appliance Corporation decided that it would not extend the agreement when it expired, but that it would expand the facilities of the gear and transmission division enough to produce all the company's requirements. Accordingly, in March, 1957, the Thorndike Machining Corporation was notified that beginning January 1, 1959, the General Appliance Corporation would manufacture all its own transmissions and, consequently, would not renew the current agreement.

This notification came as a surprise to the Thorndike Machining Corporation; furthermore, its implications were very unpleasant, because the General Appliance Corporation took its major share of the output of an entire plant, and there was little likelihood that the lost business could be replaced. The Thorndike Machining Corporation consequently faced the prospect of an idle plant and a permanent reduction in the level of profits.

In April, 1957, the president of the Thorndike Machining Corporation wrote to the president of the General Appliance Corporation, asking that the decision not to extend the current agreement be reconsidered. He submitted a proposed schedule of price reductions that would be made if the current agreement was extended. He stated that these reductions would be possible because (*a*) Thorndike would be better off to obtain a lower price than to abandon the special-purpose machinery used for transmissions and (*b*) it expected increases in productivity. These proposed reductions were as follows:

Present price	$14.00
Price effective 7/1/57	13.50
Price effective 1/1/58	13.00
Price effective 7/1/58	12.50
Price effective 1/1/59	12.00

The letter further stated that the corporation had developed a low-cost transmission suitable for economy washers; this transmission was designed to cost $2.00 less than the present models, and could be made available by January 1, 1959.

On receiving a copy of the letter, the general manager of the laundry equipment division reopened the issue of continuing to buy from the Thorndike Machining Corporation. He had been interested in adding to the line a low-cost automatic washer, and the possibility of a $10 transmission appealed to him. The general manager of the gear and transmission division, however, was interested in expanding his production of transmissions, and to satisfy the laundry equipment division he offered to develop a unit that would be comparable in price and performance to the proposed Thorndike Machining Corporation's economy unit. The offer was set forth in a letter signed by the general manager of the gear and transmission division, dated April 22, 1957. The general manager of the laundry equipment division accepted this offer, and no further question was raised about continuing to buy from the Thorndike Machining Corporation.

During the next two months, the engineering departments of the gear and transmission and the laundry equipment divisions jointly determined the exact performance features needed for the economy transmission; some of these features were different from those of the proposed Thorndike transmission. In June, 1957, the general manager of the gear and transmission division wrote a letter to the general manager of the laundry equipment division, outlining the agreed-on engineering features and including the following price proposal:

Proposed selling price of Thorndike model		$10.00
Probable cost (assuming 10% profit)		9.00
Add:		
Cost of added design features	$ .85	
Increased cost of material and labor since date of quotation	.75	1.60
Total Cost		$10.60
Profit		1.06
Adjusted Price of G & T Unit		$11.66

The letter went on to say: "Because a price of $11.66 will not give us our objective profit, we propose to sell you this unit for $12. We believe that this is a fair and equitable price, and decidedly to your benefit."

This letter was never acknowledged by the laundry and equipment division.

In October, 1957, the gear and transmission division submitted a project proposal to the top management of the corporation, requesting money to build facilities to produce the new economy transmission. The project proposal included a profit projection based on a $12 price. The laundry equipment division was quoted in the project proposal as agreeing to the price. There was no objection to this statement from the laundry equipment division personnel who were asked to comment on the proposed project. The project was approved, and the gear and transmission division proceeded to buy and install the equipment to produce the new transmission.

In the latter part of 1958, the gear and transmission division opened negotiations with the laundry equipment division on the price of the new transmission, proposing $12 plus some minor adjustments for changes in cost levels since the previous year. The laundry equipment division refused to accept the proposed price and countered with an offer of $11.21, developed as follows:

Proposed selling price of Thorndike model		$10.00
Adjustments:		
Cost of added design features	$ .85	
Cost of eliminated design features	(.50)	
Increased cost of material and labor since date of quotation	.75	
Net cost change	$1.10	
Profit on added cost	.11	
Total Price Increase		1.21
Proposed Price		$11.21

The gear and transmission division refused even to consider this proposal, and after several days of acrimonious debate both divisions decided to submit the dispute to the finance staff for arbitration.

Laundry Equipment Division

The laundry equipment division based its case on the following argument:

1. The division could have purchased a transmission, comparable in performance characteristics to the gear and transmission division's unit, from the Thorndike Machining Corporation for $11.21.
2. The gear and transmission division had agreed to this price in consideration of being allowed to produce all the transmissions.
3. The intracompany pricing policy was that the supplying divisions should sell at competitive prices.

The general manager of the laundry equipment division stated that it would be unfair to penalize him for keeping the transmission business inside the corporation as a benefit to the gear and transmission division, particularly in the light of the promise made by the general manager of the gear and transmission division.

The general manager also stated that he had not protested the price proposal included in the May, 1957, letter because he believed that it was then too early to open negotiations. His cost analysts had not evaluated the proposal, but he assumed that the gear and transmission division was approximately correct in its evaluation of the cost differences from the Thorndike unit. His position was that the difference of 34 cents between the adjusted Thorndike price and the quoted gear and transmission price was not worth negotiating until nearer the production date. The laundry equipment division had naturally assumed that the gear and transmission division would live up to its agreement, and therefore regarded the request for $12 as just a negotiating gimmick.

Gear and Transmission Division

The gear and transmission division based its case on two arguments.

1. The $10 quotation of the Thorndike Machining Corporation was invalid because it represented a final desperate effort to keep a share of the transmission business. A price of this nature should not form a long-term intracompany pricing base. If the Thorndike Machining Corporation had received the business, it would have eventually raised its price.
2. The laundry equipment division did not object to the gear and transmission division's price proposal until after the facilities to build the transmission were already in place. The $12 price was used in the calculations that showed the profitability of the project, and on which the project approval was based. If the laundry equipment division wished to object, it should have done so when the project was presented to top management. Because facilities were purchased on the assumption of a $12 price, the laundry equipment division should not be allowed to object after the money has been spent.

Finance Staff Review

A review by the finance staff disclosed the following.

1. If the Thorndike Machining quotation of $10 were adjusted for the cost effect of changes in performance characteristics and the increase in general cost levels since the original quotation, the price would be $11.25, or approximately the same as that proposed by the laundry equipment division. The price of $11.66 developed by the gear and transmission division was in error because it failed to allow for a design elimination that would reduce the cost of the Thorndike unit by 50 cents.
2. At $12, the gear and transmission division could expect to earn an after-tax profit of 15 percent on its investment; this was equal to its profit objective. At the $11.25 price, the division would earn about 6 percent after taxes.
3. The purchasing staff stated that in its opinion the transmission could be obtained from the Thorndike Machining Corporation at the quoted price level for the foreseeable future.

QUESTIONS

1. As a member of the finance staff, how would you settle these intracompany disputes? How would you explain your decision to the general managers involved?
2. Should the company's intracompany price policy and its procedure for negotiating differences be changed?

Case 6–5

Hartford Locomotive Company

Hartford Locomotive Company's Canadian division was a wholly owned subsidiary. It manufactured and sold industrial and railroad locomotives only in Canada. Most of the major components of these locomotives were shipped from Hartford's plants in the United States. Those parts and materials that could not be easily supplied by the parent corporation were procured either in Canada or from Europe.

Among the items transferred to the Canadian division by the parent corporation were large gears. Each year, the Canadian division ordered between $150,000 and $600,000 worth of gears from Hartford's locomotive department for use in original equipment and as replacement parts. These gears were precision parts, which met high performance standards and whose manufacture required considerable know-how and technical skill. The quality of Hartford gearing was a critical element in the satisfactory operation and long life of Hartford locomotives. This gearing not only was used in Hartford equipment, but also had a ready market as replacement parts in competing locomotives.

Late in 1959, the Canadian division notified the locomotive department that in 1960 it would use an estimated $425,000 in gears for original equipment alone. It proposed, however, that it procure these parts from a large British firm rather than from the parent organization. By so doing, Canadian division expected to save over $100,000 as a result of a lower price and lower import duty. This estimate was based on a quotation the Canadian department already had received from the British manufacturer.

Personnel in the locomotive department calculated that, whereas Canadian division might realize a substantial saving, Hartford, as a whole, would lose if the gearing in question was purchased outside. They opposed the change for this reason. Furthermore, they objected to the Canadian division's proposal because it would involve giving Hartford's blueprints and process sheets for gears to the British firm. This company could then manufacture and sell replacement gears for use on Hartford equipment in the United States and especially abroad.

INTERDIVISIONAL TRANSFER PROCEDURES

This situation raised for review the history of intracompany transfer procedures. Until 1946, Hartford had purchased all its gearing from outside vendors. In that year, John Gray, head of the locomotive department, attempted to interest James Stigler, head of the components department, in adding a wing to a components department plant to make gears for its own use and for sale outside. Mr. Gray argued that there would be a large market for diesel electric locomotives and, hence, a sharply rising demand for gears. He believed that the components department had the know-how to manufacture gears of a higher quality than those then made outside. Such quality would become increasingly important, he thought, as higher-powered locomotives were built.

Mr. Stigler did not agree with Mr. Gray's prognostications. Furthermore, he was unwilling to invest money in a plant for making gears, because he believed that with such an expenditure he would lower his average return on investment—at that time, 10 percent after taxes.

In an informal meeting with Mr. Stigler, Mr. Gray then proposed that the components department build and operate a plant to make gears solely for the locomotive department and that the locomotive department guarantee an annual 10 percent after-tax return on investment. In addition, Mr. Gray's department would absorb each year any unliquidated shop overhead and engineering costs. Under this arrangement, gears would be transferred to the locomotive department at prices calculated to cover full cost and yield a 10 percent return on investment. These prices would be set at the beginning of each year on the basis of estimates of requirements prepared by the locomotive department. At the end of the year, a book adjustment would be made between divisions to account for over- or underliquidations of both fixed cost and return on investment. The components department head agreed to this proposal, and the arrangement then was formalized in an exchange of letters. This agreement had no time limit and was still in effect in 1959.

To implement the arrangement, a gear committee had been established, with representatives from both departments. This committee audited the costs of the gear plant and approved accounting statements for this operation. In addition, locomotive department engineering personnel worked with engineers at the gear plant on design problems and on quality control. Manufacturing volume fluctuated greatly from one year to the next. In some years, the fixed costs and return on investment were substantially overliquidated, and the locomotive department received a sizable year-end credit. In other years, the accounting transaction went in the other direction.

Almost from the start of this operation, the Canadian division purchased gears through the locomotive department. The Canadian division was charged one price for gears to be used in original equipment and a somewhat higher price for gears it sold to customers as replacement parts. The second figure was based on list price to users less a distributor's discount of 12 percent. This was the price at which the locomotive department sold to independent locomotive repair shops in the United States. An import duty of 22.5 percent was added to these prices charged the Canadian division.

Recently, Canadian division managers had expressed some dissatisfaction concerning the purchasing arrangements between that division and the parent company. They believed they should enjoy more independence in reaching decisions on such matters as source of supply. One member of the gear committee believed that he had seen this sentiment growing in the Canadian division, and he suspected that this feeling might be related to reports he had read concerning growing objections in Canada to the degree of foreign influence over Canadian manufacturing companies.

ANALYSIS OF THE CANADIAN DIVISION'S PROPOSAL

One member of the gear committee calculated that Hartford would be out of pocket by about $50,000 annually if the Canadian division bought gears from the British manufacturer. His estimates were as given in Exhibit 1.

This calculation was presented at a gear committee meeting in November, 1959. At this same meeting, a representative of the components department stated that the management of his department thought the time had come to revise the arrangement Mr. Gray and Mr. Stigler had worked out many years earlier. This representative said that the components department should now assume responsibility for the gear plant investment, and should sell gears directly to the locomotive department and to the Canadian division at market prices. These prices could be easily determined because several gear manufacturers sold to Hartford competitors at fairly standard prices. The components department representative stated that at a recent meeting of department heads Hartford's executive vice-president had said that loading a product with multiple profits was not a good practice, and that the profit on the product belonged with the investment. Finally, it was noted that Mr. Gray and Mr. Stigler, who had worked out the original deal, had both retired several years earlier.

QUESTIONS

1. Should the Canadian division be permitted to purchase gears from Britain in 1960?

Exhibit 1

COST ANALYSIS

Cost to Hartford Locomotive Company in 1960 if Canadian Division's Gear Requirements Were Procured from an Outside Vendor

	Full Cost	*Out of Pocket*	*Difference*
Material	$134,507	$134,507	$ —
Labor	14,424	14,424	—
Shop overhead*	104,437	25,459	78,978
Shop cost	$253,368	$174,390	$ 78,978
Direct engineering*	$ 20,272	$ —	$ 20,272
Packing costs	13,895	13,895	—
Return on investment*	26,260	—	26,260
Cost to large locomotive	$313,795	$188,285	$125,510
L.D. Margin (10%)	31,379		
Price to Canadian division	$345,174		
Duty paid by C.D. (22.5%)	77,664		
Total paid by C.D.	$422,838		

	Cost of Gears Internally Supplied	*Cost of Gears Purchased in Britain*
Out-of-pocket costs	$188,285	$288,044†
Duty (22.5%)	77,664	—
Duty (10%)	—	28,804
Total out-of-pocket cost	$265,949	$316,848
Out-of-pocket cost		265,949
Net cost of external purchase		$ 50,899

* Underliquidations on this item charged to the locomotive department.
† Price quotation obtained by Canadian division from British manufacturer on basis of preliminary negotiations.

2. Assuming that the gears are to be manufactured internally, what should the transfer price be?

3. Assuming that the gears are to be purchased from Hartford, how should the revenues to be recorded for the locomotive department and the components department be arrived at?

Case 6-6

Zemblan Electronics Corporation (A)

In April, 1963, S. C. Halloway, corporate controller of the Zemblan Electronics Corporation, received the following memorandum from J. D. Walcott, controller of the tube division:

INTEROFFICE MEMORANDUM

April 5, 1963

To: *S. C. Halloway*
From: *J. D. Walcott*
Subject: *Recommendation on the method of determining the divisional share of cost-based government contract fees*

When one of our equipment or systems divisions that has a cost-reimbursable government contract engages a sister components division to produce necessary components for the contract, it is only fair that the components division be given a fair share of the total fee receivable from the government.

At present, fees are shared among the divisions through after-production negotiations without regard to the initial estimate of the fee. I propose, with our division managers' approval, that regardless of whether the actual production cost is over or under the estimated cost the components divisions should be given the fee credit as originally estimated. The following two examples illustrate the present and suggested methods.

Example 1. A year ago, the Santa Ana systems division asked from us a "bid" for 7,000 units of a certain type of ceramic part. We estimated the total production cost of $294,000 and added a 10 percent profit of $29,400 for the part, and on this basis obtained the order from the systems division. When the job was completed and the parts delivered, we billed the systems division for the amount of $256,900, as calculated below:

Actual total production cost	$227,500
Originally estimated profit	29,400
Total Price	$256,900

But the systems division has written back to us that we would be allowed a credit of only $245,700, as calculated below:

Actual total production cost		$227,500
Allowable profit		18,200
Total cost	$227,500	
Actual profit % earned on the contract	8%	
	$ 18,200	
Total Price Allowable		$245,700

The systems division and we are still negotiating as to what fee we are entitled to. The systems division argues that it cannot allow any more profit than 8 percent, instead of 10 percent as originally agreed on, because actual costs on the overall contract exceeded the initial cost estimate on which the overall fee on the contract was based. We feel, however, that we are entitled to 10 percent profit, because decrease in total profit on the contract was caused by the systems division itself or other subcontracted divisions, not by our division. If anything, we should be rewarded for being efficient enough to show a cost underrun. If my proposal is adopted, we shall automatically receive the originally estimated profit of $29,400 without going through meaningless after-production negotiations.

Example 2. We have recently finished producing 1,000 units of KTN 21 tube for the La Jolla equipment division. Our original bid was based on the following estimate:

Estimated total production cost	$1,250,000
Estimated profit ($1,250,000 × 7%)	87,500
Estimated Total Price	$1,337,500

Unfortunately, however, our actual cost has turned out to be $350,000 above our estimate, that is, $1,600,000. We have billed the Equipment Division as follows:

Actual production cost	$1,600,000
Originally estimated profit (see above)	87,500
Total Price	$1,687,500

Despite a cost overrun of $350,000, we have asked as our share of the fee only $87,500 as originally estimated by us and accepted by the equipment division.

The proposed method of fee determination would eliminate uncertainty and unnecessary after-production negotiations.

It had been Mr. Halloway's practice to answer as soon as possible all inquiries, recommendations, and memoranda from any individuals in the company, and he wanted in this instance, too, to express his opinion promptly on Mr. Walcott's memorandum. Before a final ruling on the specific recommendation, however, he wanted to be sure that his decision would be consistent with Zemblan's management philosophy of decentralization, policies governing interdivisional relationships, and other aspects of interdivisional pricing.

Zemblan, a fast growing, large electronics company with sales of $400 million in 1962, consisted of six highly decentralized divisions—three equipment divisions and three components divisions. The equipment divisions were the Santa Ana systems division, the La Jolla equipment division (mostly for government contracts), and the commercial (nongovernmental) apparatus and equipment division. The tube division, of which Mr. Walcott was the controller, was one of the three components divisions. Approximately 70 percent of the total outside sales of the company were made by the equipment divisions, and 30 percent from the components divisions. Although policy with respect to operating components divisions was nowhere written or otherwise made explicit, at least one executive thought the divisions were indispensable for the long-run survival and continued growth of the company, because technological advances in the equipment divisions—the basis of the company's success—were made possible largely through inventions and breakthroughs originating in the components divisions.

The divisions were allowed or encouraged to lead their own lives, with minimum interference from the top management. A major criterion in the evaluation of the divisional performance was the return on investment. The elements in the return-on-investment calculation were materially controllable by the division management.

A list of products made by each division was drawn up and approved by top management; a division could not make the products listed by other divisions. Otherwise, the divisions could manufacture and sell almost any products within their capabilities. The equipment divisions were free to purchase their component needs either internally or externally, that is, either from their sister components divisions or from outside suppliers. The components divisions were also free, in general, to sell their products internally or externally, except for a few classified items. The volumes of internal and external purchases were significant for all equipment divisions; the volumes of internal and external sales were significant for all components divisions.

Prices for the interdivisional transactions not covered by government contracts were determined through arm's-length negotiations between the divisions concerned. Therefore, all transfers from the components divisions to the commercial apparatus and equipment division were so priced. For the transactions covered by government contracts—that is, transactions between the government equipment divisions and the components divisions—the determination of transfer prices was more complex. If the contract held by the buying division was noncost-recoverable—that is, of the fixed-price type—the procedure was the same as that involving nongovernment contracts.

If the contract was of cost-recoverable type—e.g., cost plus a fixed fee (CPFF)[1]—the process was as follows: First, the buying division would ask

[1] In a CPFF contract, the company is reimbursed for its actual cost (in accordance with a detailed definition of cost) plus a fixed dollar amount of fee. The dollar amount of the fee is determined when the contract is signed, and is based on a percentage (from 3 percent to 12 percent, depending on the risks involved) of the *estimated* cost. The CPFF contract is used only when the uncertainties involved in contract performance are of such magnitude that it is not possible to establish a firm price or an incentive arrangement at any time during the life of the contract.

the selling division to submit a bid. Second, the selling division would estimate its recoverable production cost (the cost elements included in the government's definition of cost), and the profit or fee percentage anticipated by the buying division on the overall contract, and submit the price thus determined to the buying division. Sometimes, the buying division adjusted downward the fee percentage allowable to the selling division according to the additional risk it was taking as the "prime contractor." Third, if this bid was acceptable, the buying division would award an order to the selling division. Fourth, the selling division would produce and deliver the parts and invoice the buying division. Fifth, the buying division would either accept the amount in the invoice, or would protest and begin negotiations with the buying division.

If a dispute arose, it might be over the fee or profit element alone, as in Example 1 of the above memorandum. In other cases, it might be over the cost element also, if the actual cost substantially exceeded the estimated cost of the original bid. If the actual cost was below the estimate, Mr. Halloway said, "the buying division had to be charged at the actual cost (plus profit element), because the government agency would not allow any more than the actual cost." Thus a dispute over the cost element arose only when the actual was above the estimate. The divisions, according to Mr. Halloway, were encouraged to resolve disputes between themselves; the corporate management intervened rarely and only with reluctance.

"Of course, if the buying division could recover the actual cost from the government," Mr. Halloway said, "it was for the good of the company that the buying division should be charged at the actual cost and try to recover it." But when a cost overrun could not be wholly recovered because a maximum price ceiling was specified in the contract, "the dispute was real"; according to Mr. Halloway, "neither the selling nor the buying division likes to absorb the loss." The cause of cost overrun could be inefficiency, carelessness, wrong forecast, unforeseen technical difficulties, error in the buying divisions' specifications, or any combination of these.

Mr. Halloway felt that he had been greatly restricted by government procurement regulations in choosing the best method of transfer pricing. He preferred, he said, negotiated prices based on market as transfer prices, but the government tended to prefer the cost-based transfer prices.

The Armed Services Procurement Regulation on intracompany transfer pricing was as follows:[2]

Charges for materials, services, and supplies sold or transferred between plants, divisions or organizations, under a common control, ordinarily shall be allowable to the extent of the lower of cost to the transferor or current market price. However, a departure from this basis is permissible where (i) the item is regularly manufactured and sold to the contractor through commercial chan-

[2] Department of Defense, *Armed Services Procurement Regulation,* 15–202.22 (e) (Washington, D.C.: U.S. Government Printing Office, 1960).

nels, and (ii) it is the contractor's long-established practice to price interorganization transfers at other than cost for commercial work; provided, that the charge to the contract is not in excess of the transferor's sales price to his most favored customer for the same item in like quantity, or the current market price, whichever is lower.

If an equipment division first asked for bids both from its sister division and from an outside supplier, but finally decided to award the subcontract to the sister division, government auditors would require "costs" as transfer prices, although an objective outside market price was available in the bid made by the outside supplier. Likewise, if a components division was asked to make a bid by its sister equipment division and by an outside equipment manufacturer (the last two competing for the same government contract), and if the sister equipment division was awarded the contract and gave the components division the job, the transfer price had to be based on cost. On the other hand, if the outside equipment division obtained the contract and subcontracted with the Zemblan components division, the price would be a negotiated market price. Mr. Halloway had been asking government auditors to broaden their interpretation of the clause and to allow transfer pricing based on the negotiated market price.

Mr. Walcott made the following comments in relation to his memorandum.

My proposal is fair to everyone concerned. Under the recommended method, we are not always the winner: We will be rewarded if we are efficient; we will be penalized if we are inefficient.

We are willing to go further than the proposal. We would be happy if we were held responsible for the estimates of both cost and profit—not just the estimate of profit, as suggested in the present proposal. Penalize us if we couldn't meet the bid price, including both cost and profit element; reward us if we economize on our costs.

In connection with Example 2 in my memorandum, I don't know exactly how the La Jolla equipment division made the decision to give us the KTN 21 job, but it is possible that it had asked a couple of outside suppliers to make a bid, and the suppliers' bid price might have been higher than ours. If the suppliers' bid had been lower than $1,600,000 it would have been unfair for the La Jolla division to be charged $1,600,000 by us. The best way would be to make the initial bid price final, no matter what the actual cost is.

QUESTION

What should the transfer price policy be?

Case 6–7

Zemblan Electronics Corporation (B)

On September 1, 1964, Zemblan Electronics Corporation issued a new written policy pertaining to interdivisional pricing for the following types of government contracts and subcontracts: (1) cost-reimbursable, (2) redeterminable, and (3) incentive. (See Zemblan Electronics Corporation A for a description of the company and of the former policy.) Under this new policy, the transfer price was to be determined, whenever possible, on the basis of a fixed price established before actual production and not subject to any change based on differences between the selling division's estimated and actual costs.

The new policy set up five kinds of items and a rule for establishing the transfer price for each, as follows:

Nature of Item	*Transfer Price Rule*
1. Adequate competition exists[1]	A firm fixed price not in excess of lowest competing price
2. Standard commercial items regularly manufactured and sold by Zemblan in substantial quantities to the general public, provided they are specifically identified in the procurement manual	Zemblan's most-favored-customer price
3. When a buying division specifically agrees to a fixed price transfer for some reason (e.g., the item is of such value as not to justify the administrative expense of individual costing)	Fixed price established by selling division and agreeable to the government

[1] Adequate price competition was defined in detail. The key point of this definition stipulated that there must exist at least two qualified outside offers.

4. No competition exists, but a sound cost estimate can be obtained in accordance with ASPR 3–807, 2 (c)[2] and the government contracting officer agrees to a fixed price transfer	Firm fixed transfer price based on cost without a profit allowance to be adjusted up or down after production of item
5. None of above cases applies	Actual cost or estimated cost subject to some upward or downward adjustment after costs are finalized (such as items in Zemblan A)

The policy statement provided that the buying division, whenever possible, establish a market price for the item through solicitation of bids from outside suppliers before awarding any subcontract to an internal division.

The company's policy pertaining to interdivisional pricing in cases when there was a fixed price contract or when the transaction was not covered by a government contract remained the same as it had been for these situations; that is, the price was determined through arm's-length negotiations between the divisions concerned.

For the first and third of the above categories of items, the new policy represented a change from the former practice of basing the transfer price on cost plus a fee negotiated by the buying and selling divisions after completion of production. The fourth category was new.

As of March, 1965, the company was not certain whether the government would accept this change in all situations. It had reason to believe, however, that it would obtain general acceptance since it had tested this new policy in contract negotiations. The company's initial basis for this belief was the ASPR regulation quoted in Zemblan A, citing two situations in which a departure was permissible from the cost-to-the-transferor or current-market-price basis of determining a transfer price. Furthermore, in recent months the government had proposed to industry a revision to ASPR that reflected a coming change in government policy that seemed to move in the same general direction as the change in Zemblan's transfer pricing policy.

Management of the Zemblan company knew that the Department of Defense was making every effort to reduce the number of cost-plus-fixed-fee contracts (CPFF) and increase the number of incentive-type contracts. In 1964, two basic types of incentive contracts were in use, other than firm fixed price.

1. Cost Plus Incentive Fee (CPIF). In this type of contract, the cost is estimated at the beginning and then a profit percentage and an incentive fee schedule is negotiated, thus arriving at a target price. If the contractor meets the cost, he receives the profit agreed on. If he goes over the cost, his profit is greatly reduced. Essentially, he pays out of his pocket for a percentage of the cost overrun. If the contractor goes under the cost estimate, he receives an additional profit. Fundamentally, he keeps a portion of the cost underrun.

[2] Armed Services Procurement Regulations (Revision 5, dated May 11, 1965).

2. Fixed Price Incentive (FPI). This type is similar to CPIF, but with a ceiling price.

The Department of Defense was especially interested in expanding the use of CPIF contracts. It believed that use of such contracts would lead to reducing defense expenditures by making contractors more competitive and, thus, more cost conscious.

Zemblan management believed that its new transfer pricing policy, though inspired by the government's growing interest in incentive-type contracts, would lead to significant benefits to the Zemblan company as well as to the government. Management also believed that in cases of items in the first category described in the policy statement, the selling division would, indeed, be encouraged under the new policy to be more competitive and thus would attempt to reduce its costs. This result would increase the possibility of selling to commercial customers some of the items now being sold only to the government. Most transfers fell into this first category.

The company's manager of government accounting, Donald F. Alton, who reported to the corporate controller for government activities, cited an example of a transformer line Zemblan had manufactured for many years under cost-plus-fixed-fee contracts. The government continued to purchase this transformer, although it had a capability of lasting beyond its required use or beyond the lifetime of the system of which it was a part. This high quality was reflected in a correspondingly high cost. On the commercial front, the company had been unsuccessful in marketing its transformer lines. Alton thought that if the transformer division had been given some incentive for cutting costs on government contracts it could and would have designed some products that might have achieved success in outside competitive markets, while still meeting the government's minimum needs.

Another expected advantage of Zemblan's new interdivisional policy was that it would reduce administrative paper work. Now, once a transfer price was set, it could not be changed, and there was no room for renegotiation between the buying and selling divisions. This policy, if accepted by DOD might have the further effect of reducing the need for government auditors and company accounting personnel to spend time analyzing costs of each item in a contract manufactured within the company.

Long before the company formally adopted the new policy, one of the component division managers had been operating as though such a policy were in effect. He had once said to Mr. Alton:

> We can't determine our costs. Our items are of a joint process, and it is impossible to separate the joint costs and allocate them to each type of item in the process. My approach is to quote a fixed selling price to a sister division. In no circumstances will I accept a cost-plus contract. If I can't beat an outside competitor's price, then I think the systems division should go to the outside. If I feel I can afford to sell him the item at a competitive price, then I will submit my bid and hope I'm low bidder and receive the job.

All problems concerning interdivisional transfers normally were referred to James R. Heiler, director of interdivisional business policy. Mr. Heiler reported to the corporate director of manufacturing and purchasing services. According to Heiler, most problem situations fell into one of two categories:

1. Those arising from the failure of the two parties involved in a prospective transfer to reach agreement.
2. Those arising from the failure of one party to perform to the satisfaction of the other.

Whereas Heiler used to spend a great deal of his time resolving disputes such as those described in Zemblan Electronics A, the new policy virtually eliminated those kinds of cost overrun and cost underrun disputes. Heiler believed that his most important job was to "sell Zemblan to Zemblan." He developed his views further, as follows.

My chief job in these purchase orders is to try to keep purchases from being made outside the company in cases where we have an internal division that can produce a similar item at an equal price. It's easy for a division manager to agree with this policy. It is also easy for a laboratory director to agree. It's the lower-level people who can cause problems in this regard. An engineer might from past experience be familiar with a specific GE component, or maybe just happen to employ it in a prototype system he designs because he had one handy. We can't (nor should we) require a man to specify Zemblan, while at the same time we impose on his division decentralized profit responsibility. When the system goes into production, he specifies the GE component in the engineering drawings. The system subsequently is designed around the particular properties of that GE component. Perhaps Zemblan has the same component or, at least, could manufacture it at a competitive price. Or perhaps the system could have just as easily been designed around a Zemblan component's characteristics.

We are trying to corrrect this kind of situation. One remedy is to set up what we call a candy-store operation. By this, I mean that we allow a local distributor to set up a little sales outlet inside the plant of a systems division, thus making it possible for the systems division to purchase a quantity of one or two of a given part. Formerly, the systems division engineering staff might not have bothered to place an order for just one or two Zemblan parts when they could walk down the street and with no red tape pick up a part from a local retail supplier. If necessary, we supply our parts on consignment to these "candy stores." Furthermore, we now make sure that there is a local supplier carrying a wide line of Zemblan products.

Other steps we have taken to encourage internal purchasing are these:

1. We have simplified the paper work required for our interdivisional transfer.
2. We have encouraged the introduction of savings in the quality control operation (e.g., arrangements where the selling division performs the necessary quality control checks, obviating or at least lessening the need for the buying division's duplicating this effort).

But you can see that our components divisions have to compete just like any outside supplier to obtain orders from our systems divisions. Although their salespeople may have no trouble presenting their stories to sister divisions, the components divisions cannot ignore the job of marketing their products. Of course, if an internal division cannot meet the price of an outside supplier, then he does not get the order.

Even that is not so clear cut. On any substantial order, I check into the costs very carefully to find out why our inside division is unable to meet an outside price. We go through a formal make-or-buy procedure in these cases. A make/buy committee might be called in to analyze the problem.

We don't always accept the bid of an outside company as being valid either. We must only accept a bid of an outside supplier who is qualified to produce a given part. To become qualified, a supplier must submit his product to a series of environmental tests which may take from three to six months and may cost from $5,000–$10,000. Furthermore, a supplier must be considered to be financially capable of fulfilling his contract.

Against this background, Heiler thought about what kinds of issues he might have to resolve as the new transfer pricing policy was being implemented. What would he do if a systems division refused to acknowledge that a components division was qualified and, as a result, placed with an outside manufacturer an order that might otherwise have been placed internally. He knew that there was much judgment involved in determining whether or not a supplier was "qualified." Heiler also wondered what he would do if an outside company submitted to a Zemblan systems division a bid that was less than the Zemblan components division's bid for the same item, but greater than the components division's out-of-pocket cost of producing that item.

One of the first transfer pricing problems referred to Heiler after the new policy became effective concerned a make-or-buy decision by the Santa Ana systems division for an electronic module containing two basic parts. The quantity required was 2,000 of each part. Because of technical considerations, the two parts had to be purchased from the same supplier. Santa Ana had received the following quotation:

Bidder	*Item*	*Unit Price*	*Extension*
Outside Company A	Part #1	$54.10	$108,200
	Part #2	72.50	145,000
Total Bid			$253,200
Outside Company B	Part #1	$64.40	$128,800
	Part #2	81.60	163,200
Total Bid			$292,000
Zemblan Components Division	Part #1	$48.90	$ 97,800
	Part #2	88.10	176,200
Total Bid			$274,000

The Zemblan division's cost breakdown was as follows:

Materials	$129,000
Direct labor	19,420
Overhead	73,500
General and administrative	43,800
Profit	8,280
	$274,000

A further analysis by Heiler showed that the components division's out-of-pocket costs of producing this module were about as follows:

Materials	$129,000
Direct labor	19,420
Incremental overhead costs	37,580
	$186,000

He further noted that the components division had some idle capacity. Heiler believed that it would be in the company's interest to develop some production competence for this module.

QUESTIONS

1. Who should get the contract for the two parts described at the end of the case? If *not* the Zemblan components division, how would you justify this decision?

2. If you decide the business should go to the Zemblan components division, what should be the transfer price? Why?

Case 6–8

Kosal Company

Division A of the Kosal Company processed a variety of consumer and industrial products from a single basic raw material.[1] Approximately 65 percent of its output, measured by weight, consisted of a line of consumer products distributed through retail stores. Division B was responsible for marketing this line. Approximately 25 percent of its output was sold by division A directly to large industrial users. The remaining 10 percent was marketed by division B, also to industrial users, but these customers were in industries different from those contacted by division A's sales organization. The margin on all industrial sales was considerably less than that on consumer products. This division of marketing responsibility existed for sound business reasons and was not open to question.

Divisions A and B were two of ten profit centers in the Kosal Company. Each was measured by its performance with respect to return on investment. Products were transferred from division A to division B at a unit price that corresponded to actual cost, including the following elements:

	Approximate Proportion
Raw materials	80%
Labor and variable overhead	8
Nonvariable overhead	12
	100%

Also, 75 percent of the investment in division A was assigned to division B for the purpose of computing return on investment. This investment consisted of property, plant, equipment, and inventory, all of which was "owned and operated" by division A.

[1] This case is necessarily heavily disguised. Think of the raw material as either a basic mineral (such as coal, sulphur, or borax) or a basic agricultural product (such as grain or sugar beets).

This transfer price resulted in friction between divisions A and B, primarily for three reasons:

1. As in many process industries, unit costs were significantly lower when the plant operated at capacity. Indeed, the principal reason for accepting the low-margin industrial business was to permit capacity operations. There was general agreement that acceptance of such business at a low margin, or even at something less than full cost, was preferable to operating at less than capacity. In recent years, the company had always operated at at least 98 percent of capacity.

Division A alleged that division B was not aggressive enough in seeking this capacity-filling volume. Division A believed that division B could increase the volume of consumer sales by increasing its marketing efforts and by offering more attractive special deals, and that it could do more to obtain industrial business at a price which, although not profitable, nevertheless would result in a smaller loss than that which division A incurred from sales made to the industry it served. This additional volume would benefit the company, even though it reduced the profit margin of division B. Division B admitted that there was some validity in this argument, but pointed out that it had little incentive to seek such business when it was charged full cost for every unit it sold. Division A's profit on its sales to its industrial customers averaged 2 percent of revenue, and it often booked such business at a loss.

2. Division B complained that it was charged for 75 percent of the investment in division A, but that it did not participate in any of the decisions regarding the acquisition of new equipment, inventory levels, etc. It was generally agreed that the people in division A were technically more competent to make these decisions.

3. Division B complained that since products were charged to it at actual cost, it must automatically pay for production inefficiencies that were the responsibility of division A.

A careful study had been made of the possibility of relating the transfer price either to a market price or to the price charged by division A to its industrial customers. Because of differences in product composition, however, this possibility had been definitely ruled out.

Division B currently earned about 20 percent pretax return on investment, and division A earned about 6 percent. Division A's return, although less than division B's, was regarded as satisfactory, since it compared favorably with the earnings of those competitors who were primarily processors.

One proposal for solving the problem was that the transfer price should consist of two elements: (*a*) a standard monthly charge representing division B's fair share of the nonvariable overhead, plus (*b*) a per-unit charge equivalent to the standard material, labor, and variable overhead costs applied to each unit billed. Investment would no longer be allocated to division B. Instead, a standard profit would be included either in the fixed monthly charge, in the per-unit charge, or both.

Among the questions raised about this proposal were the following: (1) Should the amount of nonvariable overhead charged to division B be on the basis of its current actual share of the volume, on an historical average of volume, or on budgeted volume? (2) If on budgeted volume, what would prevent division A from preparing a budget that gave it too low a share of the overhead? (3) Should the variable costs be charged at actual or at standard? (The company had standard costs, but not everyone agreed that they were correct.) (4) How should the standard profit be determined?

Top management of the Kosal Company was convinced that, some way or other, the profit performance of divisions A and B should be measured separately; that is, it ruled out the simple solution of combining the two divisions for profit-reporting purposes. It was agreed, however, that the basis of measurement need not necessarily be return on investment .

QUESTION

How should the Kosal Company set transfer prices?

Chapter Seven

INVESTMENT CENTERS

The ultimate extension of the responsibility center idea is the investment center, in which the manager is responsible not only for profit but also for the assets that he uses. In an investment center, in addition to the problems of revenues and cost discussed in the two preceding chapters, there are two new problems:

1. What assets (and, in some cases, liabilities) should be included in the "investment base" of the investment center, and how should each of them be measured? The answer to this question is derived not from the rules of accounting but, rather, from a consideration of the best way of motivating managers to make wise decisions on the acquisition, use, and disposition of assets.
2. How should profits be related to assets employed? There are two general approaches to this problem: (*a*) the simple ratio of profits to assets employed, called return on investment; and (*b*) the residual income approach (described, e.g., in the General Electric Company Case), in which a capital charge (which is a percentage of assets employed), is deducted from profit.

Reading 7-1

Problem in Decentralized Financial Control

By John Dearden*

What techniques are most commonly employed for calculating the current investment assigned to the division of a decentralized company?

Why are these techniques ineffective in accomplishing management objectives? Why do they fail to motivate divisional managers properly, and thus lead to unnecessary fluctuations in a division's rate of return?

How *can* current investment be calculated so that current profits will be stated correctly and the financial control system strengthened?

Correct techniques of calculating a division's current investment should be no more difficult to work out and no less simple to administer than faulty techniques. Yet the methods used by division managers in large, decentralized corporations today are, to the best of my knowledge, *universally* incorrect. The errors may affect current profits adversely and weaken the financial control system of the corporation. Accordingly, they deserve careful top-management attention, even though their long-run effects on profits are not as serious as the results of incorrect methods of calculating fixed investment.

PURPOSES DEFEATED

To begin with, what conditions need to be satisfied before the top management of a corporation can safely decentralize the responsibility for operating decisions to divisional managers? Two conditions, it seems to me, are particularly important here:

* From *Harvard Business Review,* May–June, 1961. Reproduced by permission of the *Harvard Business Review.*

(1) Top management must be assured that the divisional manager will make the same decisions, within the limits of his ability, that would be made by top management itself if it were doing his job. In other words, headquarters must be assured that divisional management will act in the best interests of the company.

(2) Top management must have a way of evaluating the effectiveness of the divisional manager in pursuing the profit goals of the company.

The method customarily used to accomplish both of these conditions is to evaluate the divisional manager on the rate of return that he earns on the investment under his control. The theory is that if each divisional manager earns a satisfactory return on the divisional investment, the company will earn a satisfactory return. The divisional manager who is evaluated on the basis of this return will be motivated to do everything within his power to maintain it at a satisfactory level and, wherever possible, improve it.

It is vital to the effective operation of a decentralized profit-control system, therefore, that action taken by a local manager to improve the division's rate of return also improve the company's rate of return to a corresponding degree. Otherwise, the system will be motivating the divisional manager to take action that, from a corporation-wide viewpoint, is unprofitable.

As for the evaluation problem, under any system of financial control the divisional manager should clearly be appraised by more than a single criterion, and this seems to be widely recognized. The general business situation during the evaluation period and the state of the division when the manager was first appointed are examples of one kind of circumstance that affects results. Again, ability to develop subordinates is an important factor. Nevertheless, in most decentralized profit-center systems the rate of return earned by a division is the most *influential* factor in evaluating performance. It is doubly important, therefore, that the rate represent the effectiveness of management action as accurately as possible.

It is my opinion that present methods of calculating the current investment for which the divisional manager is held responsible encourage decisions that may affect divisional profits adversely. The techniques thus fail to provide the proper motivation to executives. Moreover, they actually cause fluctuations in the division's rate of return over which the manager has little, if any, control. As a consequence, the rate of return as a top-management evaluation tool is weakened.

PRESENT TECHNIQUES

Although specific techniques for calculating divisional current investment differ somewhat from company to company, they are all essentially similar:

Cash is usually determined by formula.

Other current assets and current liabilities are included at their actual end-of-month balances.

Intracompany receivables and payables are included either at their actual end-of-month balances or are calculated by a formula that is intended to approximate what the actual levels would have been if the divisions had been independent companies.

Let me describe each of these techniques precisely so that we can be specific about their weaknesses when we go on to discuss them.

Estimating Cash

In most decentralized profit-center systems, cash is controlled centrally because this is a more efficient way of utilizing it than allowing each division to control its own. The usual method is to provide each accounting location daily with enough cash to cover the day's expenditures. At the same time, the accounting location deposits all of each day's receipts to an account which automatically transfers it to a central bank. Because of this system of cash control, the actual cash amount on the *books* of a division is nominal, and is not the amount that would be required if the division were an independent company.

But most companies wish to hold the divisional manager responsible for the amount of cash he would require if he were operating an independent business. The purpose of assigning the division a "normal" amount of cash is to make the organization's rate of return correspond to its contribution to the corporate rate of return. If the divisional investment included only a nominal amount of cash, a 15 percent return by the division might represent only a 12 percent return to the corporation. Another reason for assigning "normal" levels of cash is to facilitate comparisons between the divisional rate of return and the returns of outside companies.

One common method of assigning cash to a division is as a percent of annual sales. For example:

> In developing an investment figure for calculating the rate of return, the division would use 5 percent (or some other percentage) of annual sales as the amount of cash. The specific percentage is obtained by dividing the estimated average cash requirements of the company for some future period by the estimated average annual sales. Once the percentage is established, it is changed only when it becomes significantly incorrect. For instance, General Motors has been using 4½ percent of annual sales for divisional cash balances since the 1930's.

Another common method for estimating the cash balance is to use actual expenses incurred by the division during some particular period of time (e.g., the previous month). There are several variations of this method, such as using out-of-pocket expenditures rather than total expenses.

Although specific techniques do differ, all of these methods of cash determination have one thing in common: *they are related directly to the volume of sales or production.*

Other Accounts

Receivables from outside customers are usually reflected in the investment base at their actual balances, while intracompany receivables are shown either at actual balances (if the accounting for inside receivables is the same as that for outside receivables) or at some approximation of what the actual balances would be if the divisions were independent companies. For example, intracompany receivables could be established at the previous month's sales, if the usual credit terms in the industry were 30 days net. Notes receivable and prepaid expenses, when they are carried on the divisional books, are generally reflected at the actual end-of-month balance.

To the best of my knowledge, *inventories* are always included in the investment base at book value.

As for *payables*, in many systems the divisional rate of return is calculated on the basis of "assets employed," which include only the accounts on the left-hand side of the balance sheet. Other systems employ the concept of "working capital" and calculate divisional rate of return on an investment base that consists of fixed investment plus working capital. When the latter concept is used, working capital is calculated by subtracting the payables from the current assets.

Payables are usually handled in the same manner as receivables: outside payables are included at the actual end-of-month balance; intracompany payables are included either at their actual balance or on the basis of a formula reflecting industry credit terms.

Typical Calculation

A division in a typical decentralized profit control system might calculate its current assets at the end of each month as follows:

Cash—5 percent of the current month's sales annualized.
Outside receivables—the actual end-of-month balance.
Intracompany receivables—current month's intracompany sales.
Inventories—end-of-month book value.

The current assets calculated from the above rules would be added to the fixed investment for which the divisional manager is responsible to obtain the assets employed by the division. This amount would then be divided into the monthly profit (and multiplied by 12) to obtain the rate of return earned by the division.

A common variation is to subtract payables. In this event, instead of calculating rate of return on "assets employed," the computation is made on the basis of "net investment." The net investment includes the "working capital" plus the fixed investment which has been assigned to the division.

INCORRECT INVENTORY DECISIONS

Now let us see why the methods just described (a) motivate division managers to do the wrong things, and (b) lead to fluctuations in the divisional investment base that weaken the rate-of-return system as a top-management evaluation tool.

Inventory management is a good place to start. It is the area where the most serious problems are created by the traditional techniques of calculating current investment. Here trouble arises because of:

The need to earn the same return on inventories as on fixed assets.
The inadequacy of divisional profit objectives as a yardstick in making order and reorder decisions.
The fluctuations caused in inventory levels.

I shall examine each of these topics in turn.

Conflict with Profit Goals

Since inventories are reflected in divisional assets employed at book value, the manager of a division is expected to earn a return on these inventories. If the profit objective is to earn 30 percent on the assets employed, the division will be expected to earn \$0.30 each year for every \$1.00 of inventory on the books. This means that a divisional manager would sacrifice \$0.30 in profits to decrease his inventory \$1.00. To illustrate:

Assume that a divisional manager could increase his sales by increasing the number of items maintained in inventory. If the annual profit from the added sales would be \$25,000 and the average increase in inventories would be \$100,000, his rate of return would be 25 percent. If the divisional profit objective were 30 percent, the manager would not take this action to increase his sales.

Confusion over Stock Levels

Another problem occurs in calculating the quantity of an inventory item to order. These principles are involved:

(1) The most economic order quantity is the one that minimizes the combined cost of *ordering* (preparation of purchase order and setup cost) and the cost of *carrying* the inventory (cost of the capital tied up in inventory plus the cost of warehousing).

(2) The higher the cost of carrying inventory, relative to the ordering cost, the lower will be the economic order quantity.

(3) The use of a high carrying charge (such as 30 percent) in the calculation of economic order quantity will reduce the level of inventories but will increase the costs resulting from carrying low inventories; it could lead, for instance, to high setup costs, frequent stock-outs, and premium freight (wihch are all actual, out-of-pocket expenses).

The use of a 30 percent carrying charge in making inventory decisions would be correct, according to the accepted order and reorder rules, if the cost of financing marginal inventories were 30 percent. In most companies, however, the cost of financing additional inventories is much lower than the divisional profit objective. As a matter of fact, the financing cost is frequently only the loss of income from investing in short-term treasury notes, whereas the divisional profit objective tends to approximate the rate of return that is used to decide whether or not to make a proposed capital investment.

There can be a wide difference between the proper rate of return required for an investment in fixed equipment and the proper rate of return for an investment in additional inventories. The rate of return required for carrying additional inventories would, in fact, be normally *much less* than the profit objective of the average division in the typical decentralized company. Consider the following points:

While an investment in fixed assets may commit the company to a program for several years in the future, an investment in more inventory may be reversed within a month or even within a week. When cash is available, often it may be invested in inventories more profitably than in government securities.

If the cost of capital used to calculate inventory levels is reduced, inventories will rise and cash will fall a corresponding amount. If cash is needed subsequently, the reverse procedure may take place.

Since the change in inventory levels is affected principally by the fast-moving parts (which may turn over as frequently as once a week), it is possible to liquidate marginal inventories very quickly.

Even if a company's cost of carrying additional inventories did approximate the average divisional profit objective, the latter would still not be a satisfactory rate as a base for inventory decisions. This is because the cost of capital to be used in making inventory decisions will change from period to period, depending (among other things) on the cash position of the company. Also, the cost of capital will be the same for all divisions while the profit objective tends to be different for each division. Yet every decentralized control system with which I am familiar makes it to the division manager's best interests to use the profit-goal figure in deciding on inventory levels.

Financial Control Problem

One method that has been employed to avoid the mistakes just described is to establish a company-wide cost-of-capital percentage to be used by all divisions in making inventory decisions. In cases with which I am familiar, this percentage ranges from 4 percent to 10 percent. Although such a step will ensure correct action with respect to inventory levels, it will tend to undermine the effectiveness of the financial control system. To illustrate:

Assume that a division manager, by much effort, reduces his administration costs by $30,000. Assume also that, at the same time, his inventory is increased by $100,000 because the company has excess cash and therefore reduces the cost-of-capital percentage to be used in making inventory decisions. This means that he must net $30,000 more in profits (still assuming a 30 percent profit goal) because of the larger base for computing rate of return, so that his savings in administrative costs are wiped out and he is back where he started. His efforts are not reflected in his profit showing because of a chance event in the corporation's cash situation.

In the light of cases like this, it is difficult to explain to a divisional manager that he must earn 30 percent on his investment and yet use only 5 percent, let us say, as the cost of capital when determining how much the inventory part of this investment should amount to. From his point of view, it would be far preferable to use a high cost of capital, whether realistic or not, because that would mean lower inventory levels and a better profit showing.

Undesirable Fluctuations

A final difficulty is caused by inventory fluctuations. It should be understood, of course, that the principal reason that inventories are necessary is the unpredictability of demand. The amount of stock on hand at any particular time is a function of the difference between forecasted demand and actual demand. If demand is higher than expected, inventories will be temporarily low as stock is used to fill the unanticipated demand. Conversely, when demand is less than expected, inventories will be temporarily high until purchases are adjusted to take account of the lower demand and the higher stock.

When inventories increase, the rate of return of the division decreases. It is therefore to the division manager's benefit to take action to ensure that inventories are not high, particularly at the end of the month. Again let me illustrate:

> Assume, as in our previous example, that a division is expected to earn a profit of 30 percent before taxes on its investment. It will then be economic for the manager to spend up to 30 cents for every dollar by which he can reduce inventories. It will also be to his benefit always to forecast demand with a low bias and meet commitments on an emergency basis, as long as the additional cost of the emergency orders is less than 30 percent of the reduction in inventories resulting from the forecast bias. Yet this action is clearly uneconomic if the cash released by the reduction in inventories is worth only about 5 percent (as it is likely to be).

Even if the division manager does not keep his inventories uneconomically low, the normal fluctuations will tend to distort his profit performance. The effect of controllable profit action (e.g., reductions in unnecessary overhead or increases in sales) may be offset or exaggerated by noncontrollable fluctuations in the level of inventories, which alter the rate of return shown on the books. Thus, the evaluation of profit performance by top management is made more difficult.

Cumulative Impact

In summary, the inclusion of inventories in the divisional investment base may encourage uneconomic action on the part of the operating head and may also reduce the effectiveness of rate of return on investment as a measure of performance. If management is required to use one rate of return for making its inventory decisions, yet expected to earn a higher rate of return on its investment, the financial control system will be weakened; the divisional executives will surely tend to think of the system as unfair, or at least as inaccurate. Top management at headquarters will also find it more difficult to put pressure on the local manager to increase his rate of return when, at the same time, he is expected to take action that will reduce this return (e.g., increase inventories when the cost of capital goes down).

OTHER FAILURES

What about the effect of prevailing methods of computing current investment on the management of other accounts?

Receivables & Payables

Because they are less subject to divisional control, receivables and payables do not present as serious a problem as inventories. Nevertheless, the inclusion of receivables and payables in the investment base at the actual end-of-month balances can result in uneconomic action on the part of the divisional manager. Furthermore, as with inventories, fluctuations in these accounts can create a distortion in the profit performance of the organization. In the following cases of action actually taken by divisional managers to reduce their investment bases, note the conflicts with broad corporate interests:

A divisional manager refused to ease credit terms in order to increase volume when the marginal business was expected to earn only 20 percent on the increased assets. Most of the increased assets were in receivables. The increased profit on assets, exclusive of receivables, was forecast to be 45 percent. At this time, the company had substantial amounts of money in short-term government notes, paying less than 3 percent.

A divisional manager insisted that an all-out effort be made to collect as much as possible of the accounts receivable (many of them only a day or two delinquent) at the end of each month. This created ill will on the part of the customers and also caused additional collection expenses. The cash from collecting the receivables was placed in a demand deposit.

A divisional manager held up paying as much of his accounts payable as he could during the last week of the month. The delay increased his accounts payable on the books at the end of the month and reduced his working capital. The action accomplished nothing for the company but created considerable ill will among the suppliers.

These are examples of extreme action. Most divisional managers have very little to say about credit terms or payment schedules and, consequently, tend to ignore receivables and payables (as they should). Fluctuations in the balances of these accounts, however, will be reflected in the rate of return, creating an unnecessary and undesirable distortion in profit performance.

The inclusion of receivables and payables at actual end-of-month balances not only causes fluctuations in the rate of return which have nothing to do with profit performance; but it fails to provide any positive motivation to divisional management.

My conclusion, therefore, is that traditional techniques which require the divisional manager to earn a return on actual receivables (or working capital with actual payables subtracted) are incorrect because they may result in unprofitble actions and, under the best of conditions, accomplish no positive good.

Cash & Other Accounts

Because they are usually calculated by formula, the cash, intracompany receivables, and intracompany payables are treated together. As previously indicated, the formula for determining cash is usually based on sales or expenditures; the formula for receivables is based on sales; and the formula for payables is based on purchases.

The divisional manager can do nothing about the level of these three items because, being calculated by formula, they result automatically from doing business. The purpose of including them in the investment base is to make the divisional investment approximate the level which would exist in an independent business.

Of all items of current investment, the cash, receivables, and payables—when calculated by formula—are likely to cause the least trouble. When sales are low, these assets are low; thus, the effects of reduced profits are mitigated. Conversely, when sales are high, the assets are also high. Fluctuations in the level of current assets, therefore, tend to be acceptable to the divisional manager. Investment is high when he can afford it; and it is low when he cannot.

Still, the formula method for calculating cash and receivables can result in overstating divisional investment when a division is expanding. To illustrate:

Division A is interested in producing a product now being purchased from an outside concern by division B of the same company. A study shows the expected profitability of this venture to be as follows:

Annual sales	$100,000
Annual profit	5,000
Investment:	
Equipment	40,000
Additional inventories	10,000
Cash—10% of sales	10,000
Receivables—8% of sales	8,000
Total Investment	$ 68,000

From the divisional point of view, the increase in investment is $68,000 and the expected rate of return from going into the business is 7.4 percent ($5,000 profit divided by $68,000 investment). It is quite possible, however, for the actual increase in the *company's* working capital to be only nominal. For example, the increase in inventories in division A might be offset by lower inventories in division B because, with the part now produced inside the company, it may no longer be necessary to maintain a reserve supply. Also, company receivables would not increase at all, and the rise in other working-capital requirements might be small.

Consequently, the company's actual investment might be only, say, $45,000—perhaps $40,000 for equipment plus $5,000 for additional working capital. The rate of return for the company as a whole would, therefore, be 11 percent. Yet if the required rate of return that the division heads were trying to meet were 10 percent, they would want to reject the investment.

RECOMMENDED METHOD

What *would* be a satisfactory method for calculating the current investment to be assigned to a division? The approach I shall recommend is, to the best of my knowledge, untried in any large corporation. However, it is based on a good deal of practical experience with and observation of the problems that managers face.

Basic Principles

First, it is important that working capital, rather than current assets, be used. Cash, receivables, part of inventories, and payables represent a revolving fund that cannot logically be separated (as they are with present techniques). Also, it is working capital that represents the company's investment in the business. High payables may (and frequently do) accompany high current assets, but if the payables were low and current assets also low, the investment would be no greater.

Secondly, in assigning working capital to a division, the amount should approximate *the level that would be required if the division were an independent company*. Consequently, before considering the recommended method of calculating divisional investment in working capital, it will be useful to review the functions of working capital:

Working capital is the excess of current assets over current liabilities. In the typical company it is made up of two things:

1. An amount to protect the company against insolvency in case of a temporary shutdown.
2. A base amount of inventory that would not be liquidated during the shutdown period.

You will note that I have considered working capital as being maintained largely to protect the company against a temporary shutdown (from a fire or strike, for example). I believe that this is the essential use of working capital. It is true that some companies, being on a hand-to-mouth basis, need working capital merely to meet current bills. I believe, however, that this is not typical of the average decentralized company; and, in any event, the condition is not generally desirable and should be corrected as soon as funds are available. It is too dangerous to run the risk of becoming insolvent the moment that production is stopped.

Note also that under my concept of working capital, credit terms do not affect the amount that is required. However, the amount of *cash* needed will vary, because it serves as the buffer against a shutdown. For example, if receivables average 2 days and payables 30, more cash is required as protection because receivables will stop 2 days after the last sale has been made while payables will continue for a month after the last item has been produced. If, however, the receivables average 30 days and the payables only 2, the amount of the receivables would act as protection against a shutdown for 28 days; consequently, a correspondingly smaller amount of cash would be required.

The amount of working capital that a company must carry is also affected by the *base* amount of inventory. Because this represents inventory that cannot be liquidated during the shutdown period, it cannot be used to protect the company against possible insolvency during this period. Inventory which can be liquidated will, of course, provide protection in the same way as cash and receivables.

If we accept these concepts, a company will need current assets in excess of current liabilities equal to the base amount of inventory *plus* the amount of the cash outlay which would be required during the shutdown period. The longer the shutdown period that management wants to protect against, the greater must be the working capital.

Assigning Working Capital

To make proper assignments of working capital to the divisions, three main steps are important:

Step 1: Calculate the total working-capital requirements of the company as follows:

(a) Decide how many days' protection against shutdown is needed. (If no policy is available on this point, estimate the average days' protection that has been available over the past two or three years.)

(b) Estimate the amount of inventories that would not be sold during the protection period. (This is the base inventory.)

(c) Calculate the total amount of net cash outlay that would be required on a shutdown basis during the protection period.

(d) The sum of these base inventory and cash requirements is the company's working-capital requirement.

Step 2: Calculate the working-capital requirements of the divisions as follows:

(a) Determine the inventory in Step 1(b) that applies to each division.

(b) Determine the cash outlays in Step 1(c) that apply to each division. (As for the central staff outlays that will have to be allocated, the amount can usually be decided on the basis of the division's sales dollars or amount of fixed investment relative to other divisions.)

(c) The sum of the two preceding amounts for each division is the working capital that should be assigned to it. This is the amount of current investment on which the divisional manager should be required to earn a return.

Step 3: Once a division has been assigned its working capital, the amount would be changed only for the following reasons:

(a) *Expansion of operations*—When a division submits a capital-expenditure proposal involving the expansion of its operations, the proposal should include an estimate of the increased working capital that will be required.

If the project is approved, the divisional working capital should be increased by the amount included in the proposal.

(b) *Contraction of operations*—If a division's operations are contracting, it can request a reduction in its assigned working capital equal to the reduction in the company's working capital that has resulted from the contraction.

(c) *Changes in the company working capital*—Every few years, a review of the working-capital allocation to the corporation should be made. Where significant changes have taken place, a reallocation of working capital to the divisions should be made.

Advantages

The recommended method for calculating divisional investment has these advantages:

Division managers will not spend time and money trying to reduce current assets or increase current liabilities. Once specific rules are established for the collection of receivables, the payment of payables, and decisions for inventory levels, there will be no motivation to do other than follow these rules. If top management believes that a divisional manager should be given a financial incentive to control inventories, he can be charged a percentage for all inventories in excess of the base amount. This percentage might represent the company's cost of carrying the marginal inventories.

Fluctuations in working capital will not affect a division's rate of return because the amount of capital assigned to it will change only with a change in the scope of its operations. By eliminating these noncontrollable fluctuations, the rate of return becomes a more effective tool for evaluating profit performance.

The increase in divisional working capital associated with an expansion project will be the same as an increase in the company's. The division will, therefore, have the same basis for evaluating a proposed investment as the company has.

The recommended method is easier to calculate and administer than traditional techniques. Adjustments to the working-capital base are made automatically when a capital-investment proposal is approved. Also, the working-capital requirements need to be calculated only once, and then reviewed only every few years or so, in contrast to many traditional techniques requiring monthly calculation.

Alternative Techniques

If a company believes that the amount of work required to make the calculations just described is unwarranted, there are alternative methods for obtaining adequate approximations with less effort. These approximations, although not as satisfactory as the amounts obtained using the recommended method, are much better than the investment obtained by using traditional techniques.

One way to make such an approximation would be to determine the company working-capital requirements by averaging the monthly or quarterly actual working capital over the past two years. (This step assumes that the company's working capital is adequate.) Then allocations of this capital could be based on the *gross fixed assets* of each division. Working-capital requirements are to a considerable degree determined by the size of the business, and gross fixed assets are a reasonable indication of size. Though there are other indications of size (e.g., sales dollars or number of employees), gross fixed assets are more stable and can be used to increase or contract the working-capital base assigned to a division. Here is an example of how this method would operate:

If a company has working-capital requirements of $1,000,000 and gross fixed assets of $4,000,000, divisional working capital would be established as equal to 25 percent of its gross fixed assets. If, subsequently, the division expanded its operations, its working capital would be increased by 25 percent of the additional investment in facilities.

Where the foregoing method is used, management would, of course, have to make more frequent revisions of its working-capital figures than it would with the approach earlier recommended.

Another method which has been employed to overcome the objections to traditional techniques is to leave current investment out of the divisional base entirely. Although this is better than continuing with traditional techniques, I do not recommend it because of the following drawbacks:

The rate of return earned by the division will be considerably higher than that earned by the company.

Divisional rates of return cannot be compared directly with the rates of competitors.

Divisional performance will be measured on a base different from that included in the capital-investment proposals. (Capital-investment proposals *must* include an estimate of the change in working capital that is expected to result.)

These objections are not nearly so serious as the ones raised with respect to traditional methods. Moreover, there are ways of overcoming some of them. For example, in comparing divisional performance with that of an outside competitor, the competitor's working capital can be estimated and eliminated from the calculation of its rate of return.

CONCLUSION

The techniques presently employed in decentralized profit-center systems for calculating the current investment of a division are not effective in promoting the best interests of the company. These techniques tend to motivate divisional management to take action that is detrimental to the over-all interests of the company. They result in fluctuations in the divisional investment base over which the divisional manager has little or no control. Moreover, some of the techniques result in increasing divisional investment more than the actual increase in company investment when an expansion program is undertaken. As a consequence, attractive programs from a corporate point of view may be unattractive to the division.

The surprising thing about traditional techniques is that *they are all ineffective*! Yet correct techniques are easy to calculate, install, and administer. The new approach described in this article will, in my opinion, overcome all of the disadvantages of the older methods. It will give managers both in the divisional organization and at headquarters a better appreciation of what they are trying to do and how well they are doing it.

Reading 7–2

Problem in Decentralized Profit Responsibility

By John Dearden*

Why do most systems of decentralized profit responsibility fail to create a community of interests between company and division?

How do conventional methods of calculating a division's investment in facilities actually encourage divisional managers to make decisions that are *inconsistent* with over-all company interests?

What methods will ensure a community of interests between company and division? Would it be advantageous, for purposes of profit evaluation, to assign a value to divisional facilities that is not reflected in the books of account?

One of the principal advantages of decentralizing profit responsibility is that top management may delegate the day-to-day operating decisions to divisional management and concentrate its efforts on long-range planning and overall corporate problems. Before operating responsibility may be safely delegated, however, top management must be assured that divisional executives will act in the best interests of the company as a whole. This means that company interests and divisional interests should coincide.

COMMUNITY OF INTERESTS

Supposedly, what is accomplished by making the divisional manager responsible for earning a satisfactory rate of return on the investment at his disposal is a community of interests. The theory is that if all divisions earn a satisfactory return on investment, the company's return will be satisfactory. If each divisional manager is evaluated in terms of the rate of return earned

* From *Harvard Business Review*, May–June 1960. Reproduced by permission of the *Harvard Business Review*.

on the investment assigned to his division, he will be motivated to earn a satisfactory return and will, therefore, be acting in the best interests of the company. Top management then is able to delegate operating responsibility with the assurance that, within his ability, the divisional manager will make the same decisions that would have been made by top management.

On the surface, the problem of assuring a consistency of interests between company and division may not appear very difficult. After all, is not the objective simply to develop divisional statements that so reflect the financial effects of decisions made in the organization that its return on investment will be increased when a manager's decision increases the company's return, or decreased when a decision reduces the company's return? Yet, although the objective may be stated with ease, most systems of decentralized profit responsibility fail to accomplish it. Many systems actually encourage *incorrect* decisions by divisional management.

This situation is particularly common in investment decisions, and in this article I shall examine an especially important area of a decentralized financial control system—viz., the investment amount assigned to a division for the facilities under its control; assess the present, conventional approaches; and set forth a new system for meeting the still unanswered needs.

WORST COMBINATION

The objective of any decentralized financial control system as it applies to the investment in facilities is to provide an incentive for divisional management to purchase, retain or retire facilities in accordance with the best interests of the company. The divisional financial statements should be prepared so that the organization's rate of return will be satisfactory when correct action is taken. The extent to which the divisional financial statements will reflect a community of interests between the company and the division in the area of facility investment depends on two major factors:

The method of valuing the facilities.
The method of depreciation.

These two factors are so vital in evaluating the effectiveness of a decentralized profit control system that it will be necessary to treat them in some detail.

A common combination of these two factors is to show facilities on the divisional books at their gross book value and depreciate them at a composite rate. Gross book value in most instances is the original cost of the facilities; accumulated depreciation is not subtracted. The composite method of depreciation is one in which depreciation is calculated by groups of assets, and the rate is based on the estimated average life. When an asset is retired, it is assumed to be fully depreciated, regardless of its age.

The assumption is that, on the average, assets will last for the estimated life. If one asset is retired earlier than the estimated average life, another will last longer than the average. The important point for financial control is that, with this method of depreciation, *no gain or loss* is reflected on the financial statements when an asset is retired because it is assumed to be fully depreciated.

Diametric Interests

The combination of assigning fixed assets to a division at their gross book value and accounting for depreciation on a composite basis is, from the viewpoint of financial control, perhaps the worst method commonly used today. That company and divisional interests often may be diametric can be demonstrated by two actual cases:

1. *Idle equipment*—The manager of a division on a plant visit noticed that some testing equipment was idle. This testing equipment had cost $100,000 and occupied approximately 150,000 square feet. There was no immediate use for the floor space.

The divisional general manager questioned the plant manager about the equipment and was told that it had not been used for about a year. Moreover, the plant manager stated that he would have no use for it unless some changes were made in one of the products that he was manufacturing. If changes were made, he would use this equipment for testing because the regular production equipment could not be used for this purpose.

The divisional manager knew of no immediate plans for product change and suggested that the equipment be scrapped to reduce the investment on which he was expected to earn a return. The plant manager scrapped the equipment, and a year later, when the product was changed, new testing equipment was purchased for $130,000.

The division's investment was reduced $100,000 for the year following the scrapping of the testing equipment because, on retirement, the gross book value of the facilities was reduced by $100,000. The depreciation expense of the division was reduced by $10,000. (The depreciation rate for this equipment was 10 percent.) The division benefited in the following manner for the year after the equipment was scrapped:

	Profit	*Investment*	*Rate of return*
If equipment had not been scrapped	$500,000	$2,000,000	25.0%
With equipment scrapped	510,000	1,900,000	26.8
Benefit from scrapping equipment	10,000 (increase)	100,000 (decrease)	1.8 percentage points

But while the divisional manager improved his rate of return on investment some 1.8 percentage points by having the test equipment scrapped, this decision resulted in the company losing $130,000 (less the value of any improved features that the new equipment had).

2. *More efficient machine*—The general manager of a division requested a

study of whether or not a machine should be replaced. The new machine would cost $100,000 and last ten years; the before-tax savings in operating costs were estimated to be $20,000 per year. The machine to be replaced had a gross book value of $75,000 and no scrap value.

An analysis showed the following effect on the profits of the division from purchasing the new machine:

Investment in new machine	$100,000	
Less retirement of old machine	75,000	
Net increase in investment		$25,000
Savings in operating costs	$ 20,000	
Less increase in depreciation costs*	2,500	
Net savings		$17,500
Rate of return of savings on additional investment		70%

* $10,000 on new machine less a $7,500 reduction from retiring the old machine.

The divisional manager purchased the new machine because it yielded such a high return. Yet if we calculate the *company's* return using, for the sake of simplicity, the so-called accounting method (comparable results would be obtained with more sophisticated techniques), the picture changes:

Investment		$100,000
Operating savings	$20,000	
Less depreciation	10,000	
Profit before taxes		$ 10,000
Rate of return		10%

Realities of Conflict

The foregoing cases demonstrate the problems associated with using the gross book value of facilities as the investment base for evaluating divisional performance. The general manager of the division is encouraged to scrap assets that are not being used or that are not earning a satisfactory return on their book value. He is encouraged to replace assets any time the cost savings from a new investment are attractive enough to show a good return on the difference between the cost of the new asset and that of the old. To make the point, let us set up an extreme case:

Suppose a manager buys a machine for $100,000 today. A year later a similar machine costing $100,000 is developed that will reduce operating costs by a small sum such as $1,000 a year. It would improve the divisional rate of return to purchase this machine. It is easy to see that the division's interests and the company's interests are radically different under such a system.

It may be argued that divisional management has the company's interest at heart and therefore would not purposefully act in a manner that would be detrimental to the company in any way. This may be generally true, but differences of interest between company and division are still undesirable. The danger I have suggested is not a figment of the imagination. The cases given, although disguised, are not hypothetical. *They happened.* As a matter of fact, it was the occurrence of one of these events that first made me aware of the problem.

Inherent Defects

The failure of the gross book value approach to cement divisional and corporate interests is due to reasons that are built into the system:

(1) In many instances, divisional management does not *realize* that it is not acting in the best interests of the company when it retires assets as soon as they become idle. The concept that the book value of the assets represents "sunk costs" and that there must be a more positive reason for retiring assets than reducing the book value is often difficult for the production-oriented manager to grasp. I have known financial analysts who also had trouble grasping this concept.

(2) Frequently, a strong factor in the promotion of a divisional manager is his aggressiveness in pursuing his goals. It should not be surprising, therefore, to find that he has a tendency to take the most direct route to increasing the division's return. If this requires certain action (such as getting rid of idle assets), the manager will not look at the pros and cons too long. He will take the action necessary to improve his return. This is particularly true when he is having difficulty meeting his profit objective.

(3) It is true that all companies have procedures for approving proposed capital expenditures so that divisional managers generally are not able to take action that is clearly uneconomic (such as retiring the one-year-old $100,000 machine in my hypothetical illustration because a new model saves $1,000 annually). There will be, however, a bias toward replacing equipment too soon. As a result, any questionable decision will tend to be resolved in favor of retirement or replacement.

(4) A situation in which a divisional general manager is expected to act in a way not to his best interests tends to destroy some of the value of a decentralized profit responsibility system. The manager may be inclined to take the system a little less seriously and to believe that perhaps he is playing a bookkeeping game. Worse still, top management must also take a division's profit performance less seriously in evaluating its management. Top executives cannot put pressure on the divisional manager to increase his rate of return on investment and, at the same time, expect him to ignore several obvious means of accomplishing this end. In such a situation, there cannot help but be a general weakening of the effectiveness of the financial control system.

For the foregoing reasons, I believe that valuing divisional investment at gross book value and depreciating this investment on a composite basis is an approach that should not be used in a financial control system. To the extent that this combination is used and has not created the problems described here, I can only say that divisional managers evidently are not yet aware of some of the possible methods of improving their rates of return. My advice is to watch out for the consequences when they wake up.

OTHER FAULTY METHODS

Other methods of calculating a division's investment also have serious disadvantages. Let us take three of the most common ones and examine their shortcomings.

Unit Depreciation

If, instead of composite depreciation, unit depreciation is used, the situation is only somewhat better. Unit depreciation is a method that accumulates depreciation for each piece of equipment separately. Under this method, a loss or profit is taken when an asset is retired. Divisional managers would not be tempted, therefore, to retire a relatively new machine for a slight cost advantage because of the adverse effect this action would have on divisional profits.

But even though control is improved where unit depreciation is used, there are still the following inconsistencies between company and divisional interests:

As soon as equipment becomes fully depreciated, all of the problems described in the previous section again exist. If the asset is retired, the individual investment is reduced. If the asset is not earning the objective profit, there is every incentive to retire it because the investment can be reduced with no adverse effect on profits. There could still exist, therefore, the tendency to replace assets too soon if they are fully, or nearly fully, depreciated.

The fact that a loss must be taken may affect the decision to replace an asset. The book loss, of course, should have no effect on a replacement decision. For example, assume these conditions:

Present machine:	
Cost	$250,000
Accumulated depreciation	100,000
Scrap value	0
Proposed new machine:	
Cost	$300,000
Annual operating savings	100,000
Estimated life	10 yrs.

From a company viewpoint, the return on the investment in the new machine would be calculated as follows:

New investment		$300,000
Operating savings	$100,000	
Less depreciation	30,000	
Net profit		$ 70,000
Rate of return		23%

But from a divisional viewpoint, the return from the investment in the new machine would be:

	First Year	Subsequent Years
Added investment	$ 50,000	$ 50,000
Operating savings	100,000	100,000
Less		
Depreciation	5,000	5,000
Loss on the retirement of fixed assets	150,000	—
Net profit (loss)	$ (55,000)	$ 95,000
Rate of return	—	190%

Who can say that the divisional manager would not take into account the $55,000 loss in the first year? If he needed the profit then, he might defer the replacement until some more favorable year. And because a replacement decision is principally a timing decision, this delay might well be to the disadvantage of the company.

The real objection to the results just described is, however, a more fundamental one: When divisional rates of return can differ from company rates by the margin demonstrated in the example, there is little community of interests between the division and the company with respect to the replacement of facilities.

My conclusion is that the use of unit depreciation is better than using composite depreciation only because extreme mistakes are unlikely, but it still leaves much to be desired.

Net Book Value

The difference between the gross book value and accumulated depreciation, i.e., net book value, generally provides a much better base for a decentralized profit control system than gross book value. As I have already demonstrated, the method of depreciation plays an important role in the effectiveness of the method of assigning divisional responsibility for facilities. I shall consider, therefore, both the unit and composite depreciation methods in evaluating the use of net book value as a basis for valuing divisional facilities.

Along with Unit Depreciation. The use of net book value together with unit depreciation overcomes the problem that the divisional manager will be motivated to scrap fully or nearly fully depreciated assets that are not currently earning a satisfactory return. Because fully depreciated assets have no net book value, no reduction in investment results from retiring them. The divisional manager will keep them until other relevant factors (such as need for space) indicate that it is economical to scrap or replace them. In this respect the interests of the division and the interests of the company coincide.

To some extent, however, there exists the second problem that was discussed in the preceding section. If the assets are replaced or scrapped before they are fully depreciated, the division may have to show a loss in the period that this action is taken. Although the accounting loss on a piece of equipment is not a valid consideration in making a replacement decision (except as it affects the timing of income tax payments), it does affect the division's profit and could influence the division manager's decision.

Along with Composite Depreciation. What if composite depreciation is used with net book value instead of unit depreciation? This combination overcomes nearly all the disadvantages raised in previous sections. An asset is considered to be fully depreciated when it is retired. Since scrapping it will not reduce the investment, there is no bookkeeping incentive to retire assets not earning a satisfactory return. Furthermore, no profit or loss is reflected when an asset is retired; therefore, this factor cannot influence the divisional manager when he makes a replacement decision. When facilities are purchased, the divisional investment is increased by the total cost of these facilities; therefore, the investment on which the division's return is measured is the same as the investment on which the company's return is measured.

The only difference between divisional interests and company interests is that the division can reduce depreciation expense by retiring an asset. For example, assume that a division has a $10,000 machine that is not being used. If the composite depreciation rate for this equipment is 10 percent, the machine is generating $1,000 a year in depreciation expense. By scrapping the machine, the divisional general manager can reduce his costs $1,000 a year, although this clearly is not a real saving to the company. As a practical matter, however, this possibility is usually not very serious because it is to the division manager's benefit to keep equipment if he has any chance of using it again. If he were to scrap a machine and subsequently have to buy another to take its place, his investment would be increased by the cost of the new machine. This tends to make him cautious about premature retirements.

Even the disadvantage of artificial depreciation savings from scrapping equipment is overcome if declining-balance, composite depreciation rates are used. Under the declining-balance method (in which the depreciation percentage is applied to the net book value) retiring an asset does not reduce depreciation costs because the net book value is unaffected by retirement.

Disadvantages in Use. But while we may conclude that a combination of net book value and composite depreciation will assure consistency of interests between division and company with respect to the replacement or retirement of facilities, there are two disadvantages of the approach, both concerning the valuation method:

> *A significant problem arises where assets, although quite serviceable, are old in terms of years.* Not only will the net book value be low because of the relatively large amount of accumulated depreciation, but the original cost is also likely to be low (i.e., considerably less than the replacement value). This situation is particularly evident with facilities that were purchased prior to World War II.
>
> As a result of the low valuation, the rate of return may be particularly high. This may have these undesirable effects:
>
> —Management (both corporate and divisional) may be led by the high return on investment into believing that the division's profits are satisfactory. This may or may not be the case. A substantial amount of inefficiency can be offset by low depreciation charges and small investment responsibility. The fact that a division's rate of return is high is no guarantee of satisfactory performance on the part of its personnel. When assets carry abnormally low values, top management is handicapped in comparing profit performance between divisions.
>
> —The divisional management is sometimes reluctant to dilute the artificially high rate of return by adding facilities that will yield a lower return than is cur-

rently being enjoyed. If this situation were carried to a ridiculous extreme, a divisional manager with fully depreciated assets (i.e., value zero) would never add a single piece of new equipment if he could help it. Since any profit at all gives him an infinite return on his zero investment, any additional investment will reduce this rate of return.

The fact that the value of divisional assets is tied to the accounting records makes an inflexible arrangement that is sometimes undesirable. For example, take this case:

> A division found it necessary to close one of two plants because the demand for its products had declined to the point where two-plant operation was uneconomical. One of the plants was built prior to World War I and had a very low book value. The other was built after World War II and had a relatively high book value. Even though the newer plant was considerably more efficient, a higher rate of return could be earned by consolidating operations in the old plant. The divisional manager did, of course, favor closing the new plant even though it was clearly to the company's advantage to close the old one instead. (The potential sales value rather than the book value was the important figure from the company's viewpoint.)

The two problems just described are, it seems, to me, the main ones for management consideration. There are, of course, others. For instance, it is sometimes argued that use of net book value results in a decreasing investment base so that the divisional rate of return improves automatically with the passage of time. This could be true in the case of a division with mostly new assets, but it is not true in most cases; divisional assets usually are of different ages, and the new replacements tend to offset the reduction from added depreciation amounts.

PROPOSED SYSTEM

I believe that there is considerable merit in assigning a value to divisional facilities for profit evaluation purposes that is not reflected in the books of account. I shall outline one such system and indicate its advantages over the methods which are generally being used in business today.

Principal Features

The proposed system has five main features. Let me describe them briefly.

1. *The facilities assigned to a division are valued at their current economic value.* This is normally replacement cost minus accumulated depreciation. In establishing these values, we should consider the following points:

> The accumulated depreciation will not be the same amount that is reflected in the accounting records. It will be the estimated replacement value of the facility multiplied by the fraction of life that has already been used. For example, assume that a machine was purchased six years ago for $100,000 and has an accounting life of ten years. The replacement cost today of that machine is $150,000 and its estimated life as of today is nine years. The investment for which the di-

vision manager is responsible is $150,000 minus accumulated depreciation of $60,000 which is calculated as follows:

> Replacement value of equipment = $150,000
> Estimated life = 15 years (equipment is 6 years old now and is expected
> to last 9 more years)
> Estimated life that has expired = 6/15
> Accumulated depreciation = $150,000 × 6/15 = $60,000

The book value of $100,000 minus accumulated depreciation of $60,000 does not enter into the calculation.

Any obsolete or idle equipment will be valued, not at its replacement cost, but at its worth to the company. I recognize, of course, that the worth of a certain machine or plant could become quite a controversial issue, but even a rough approximation of economic values is better in this case than using book or replacement value.

An adjustment will be made where there is a significant difference between the equipment in use and the type of equipment that would be purchased if the equipment were to be replaced. This situation could occur where surplus equipment has been adapted to an alternative use instead of being scrapped.

2. *Once established, the divisional investment is reduced annually by an addition to the accumulated depreciation amount.* This depreciation is not the amount booked in the accounting records but is based on the values included in the investment record. I recommend the use of a depreciation method where the amount of depreciation is calculated by applying the rate to the depreciated value of the equipment. Also, for reasons already stated, I believe that the composite depreciation method should be used.

A declining-balance, composite depreciation method offers two advantages: (a) since the rate is applied to the net value of the investment, the retirement of an asset will not reduce the depreciation expense; and (b) this method will reduce considerably the clerical cost of maintaining the investment on an up-to-date basis, as I shall explain later.

3. *There is no reduction in either investment or depreciation expense when an asset is retired.* The depreciation is calculated on a composite basis, and when an asset is retired, the gross investment is decreased but the accumulated depreciation is also decreased an equal amount. This would leave the net investment the same after retirement as before. Depreciation, being calculated on the net investment, would also be unchanged by the retirement.

4. *All additional investments in facilities, after the initial evaluation has been made, are added to the investment base at cost.*

5. *Asset values may be changed in unusual circumstances.* Three examples of such circumstances are:

> When a new manager assumes control of a division, he may be justified in requesting relief for poor investments made by his predecessor.
>
> When an unusual change takes place in a division, such as closing an entire plant, it may be desirable to adjust the investment values to reflect this change.
>
> Although under current conditions I believe that it will be unnecessary con-

tinually to readjust facility values for changes in price levels, some provision should be made to bring asset values in line with price levels where deviations are significant (e.g., a foreign plant in a country experiencing significant inflation).

Record Duplication

One may object to the proposed method on the grounds that it is expensive to operate because it requires duplicating much of the fixed asset accounting records. I believe that this is not true. The initial estimate of the replacement cost of all assets may require careful analysis, depending on the degree of precision that is desired. An adequate approximation may be obtained without an undue amount of work, and almost any approximation of replacement value is better than using original cost.

The assets could be classified into several broad categories (e.g., heavy and light machinery, buildings, land, vehicles, furniture, and fixtures) and by broad age classifications (e.g., pre-World War II, World War II, 1946–1949, and so on). Approximations of changes in price levels are available from several sources and could be used to estimate the replacement costs of the present complement of fixed assets. Accumulated depreciation could be estimated by category on the basis of the average age of each particular group.

After the replacement value of the assets has been estimated, they may be classified into several broad groups for depreciation purposes. A depreciation rate to be applied to the net book value of each of the groups is then established. Because this rate will be applied to the depreciated value of the asset, the only work required to keep the investment up to date is to add the value of new investments to the appropriate group. This is why the proposed method of depreciation *simplifies* the clerical task and cost of keeping the investment values up to date, rather than complicating the job. As assets are retired, they are assumed to be fully depreciated and the net value of the investment is unaffected.

It is not necessary to keep a record of the investment value of the retired asset because no adjustment is required when the asset is retired. The entire operation can be kept very simple without significant loss in accuracy by adjusting the investment base once a year only. At the end of each year, new investments made during that year are added to the investment base. At the same time, the depreciation for the year is calculated and subtracted. For monthly income statements, one twelfth of this amount is used as a charge against divisional income each month. Thus, the entire process of keeping the investment base current can be organized to take very little additional time and expense.

Varied Advantages

I believe that the proposed method has the following advantages over methods currently used for valuing divisional assets in decentralized profit center systems:

The investment base of the division is such that each manager is motivated to act in the best interests of the company in replacing or retiring facilities.

Divisional profits more nearly reflect the value to the company of the investment in the divisional assets. In particular, rates of return will not be abnormally high because the asset values are abnormally low.

The division has a more realistic base for pricing and costing its products (except when it is the company philosophy to seek to recover from its present customers only the historical cost of the facilities used).

Top management has a more useful tool for evaluating divisional management. In the first place, comparisons of the rates of return of the various divisions will be more meaningful. Secondly, the financial control system is more flexible than if the divisional investment were tied to the company's books of account. For example, if a divisional manager makes a series of poor investments in equipment and is replaced, the assets can easily be adjusted to reflect realistic values in the investment base. In this way, the profit performance of the new manager will be unaffected by his predecessor's mistakes.

CONCLUSION

An effective decentralized financial control system must establish a community of interests between the company and the division. The divisional manager must be motivated to take action that is consistent with company profit objectives. This motivation is created by establishing a system which maximizes divisional profit performance when correct action is taken and by measuring divisional effectiveness on the basis of this profit performance.

Many of the financial control systems currently in operation today fail to create this community of interests, particularly in the area of the replacement and retirement of facilities. The disparity between company and divisional interests varies with the particular method used for assigning values to divisional facilities. No method using the book value of facilities is completely satisfactory, and some methods actually encourage incorrect decisions.

It is my belief that the only completely satisfactory method for assigning values to divisional facilities is one that uses replacement values and is not tied directly into the books of account. Not only can such a method help to improve performance and appraisal, but it is also economical and sometimes actually simplifies the task of keeping satisfactory records and accounts.

Reading 7–3

Accounting for Capital Costs

By Robert N. Anthony

This note is concerned with a deficiency in current financial accounting statements—namely, "return on investment" as developed from these statements does not match the conceptually correct concept of return on investment as used in making investment decisions. It shows how this deficiency can be overcome, lists some of the advantages of a system that would overcome it, and points out practical difficulties of applying the proposed change in accounting.

THE NEED

The usual accounting measurement of return on investment does not match the concept used when an analyst estimates the return on investment of a proposed capital acquisition. The meaning of return on investment used by the analyst is illustrated by the figures in Exhibit 1. This exhibit demonstrates that a proposed investment of $1,000, estimated to earn $250 cash per year for five years, is expected to earn 8 percent on the amount at risk each year.

Exhibit 1

ANALYSIS OF INVESTMENT

Year	Total Earnings (a)	Return at 8% of Investment Outstanding (b)	Balance Capital Recovery (c) = (a−b)	Investment Outstanding End of Year (d)
0	$—	$—	$—	$1,000
1	250	80	170	830
2	250	66	184	646
3	250	52	198	448
4	250	36	214	234
5	250	19	231	3*

* Due to rounding.

The analyst does not actually make the year-by-year calculation shown in Exhibit 1. He has a technique that tells him directly that the return on such an investment is 8 percent. The exhibit merely demonstrates the precise meaning of return on investment to the analyst—namely, the $250 annual earnings will, over the five-year period, both recoup the investment of $1,000 and also yield a return of 8 percent on the amount of the investment that has not yet been recouped at the end of any year. For example, in the first year the whole $1,000 is outstanding; 8 percent of this, or $80, is "set aside" as return, and the remainder of the $250 earnings, or $170, goes to reduce the investment, making it $830. In the second year, the return is 8 percent of $830, or $66, and so on.

In the situation illustrated above, the return *is* 8 percent in the sense that the investor (if things work out as expected) recoups the amount of capital he has risked and receives 8 percent each year on the funds still at risk that year. This meaning of return on investment is universally accepted in capital budgeting analysis.

However, if the investment is made and if the earnings are, in fact, $250 per year, the usual accounting records will not show a return of 8 percent, either in any single year or in an "average" year. For example, under the straight-line method of depreciation the accounting records would show the following results:

Year	Gross Assets	Average* Net Assets	Net Income†	Computed Return On Gross	Computed Return On Net
1	$1,000	$900	$50	5%	5.5%
2	1,000	700	50	5	7.1
3	1,000	500	50	5	10.0
4	1,000	300	50	5	16.7
5	1,000	100	50	5	50.0

* Average of beginning and ending book values.
† Cash earnings, $250, minus depreciation, $200. Income taxes are included in the calculation of net earnings.

The computed return on gross assets makes no allowance for the fact that part of the initial investment is being recovered each year, and this return is therefore understated. The computed return on net assets does, through the depreciation mechanism, allow for the recovery of the initial investment, but the pattern of recovery implied by the straight-line method of depreciation is by no means the same as the pattern of recovery implicit in the concept of return on investment, which is that shown in Column (*c*) of Exhibit 1. Use of an accelerated depreciation method (such as double declining balance or sum-of-the-years' digits) makes the discrepancy even greater, because the pattern of the accelerated methods is the opposite of that in Column (*c*); Column (*c*) shows *increasing* amounts of recovery each year.

A SOLUTION

The solution proposed for this problem consists of two related rules:

1. Use a method of depreciation that matches the implicit recovery of the investment.
2. Make a charge for the use of capital as an element of cost.

In the situation illustrated above, the annuity method of depreciation matches the investment recovery; that is, the annual amounts credited to accumulated depreciation and debited to depreciation expense in the annuity method are the same as those in Column (*c*) in Exhibit 1. Thus, the reported net income of each year would be 8 percent of the net asset value at the beginning of that year. This change, taken by itself, would therefore make the financial statements reconcilable with the financial concept of return on investment. The annuity method of depreciation was more common 50 years ago than now. It is still used by some utilities. It is in accordance with generally accepted accounting principles, which state that *any* "systematic and rational" method of distributing net asset cost over useful life is acceptable.

With respect to the second rule, the capital charge would be taken as a percentage of the book value of the assets employed. What percentage to use is discussed in more detail below, but roughly it corresponds to the company's required-earnings rate.

In the situation described above, if the capital cost is figured at 8 percent and if earnings actually were $250 each year, the reported net income would be zero. For example, in Year 3, the income statement (disregarding all items other than those relevant to this investment) would be as follows:

Revenue		$250
Depreciation	$198	
Capital charge	52	250
Net income		0

An income statement constructed in accordance with these rules, and for an investment estimated to earn exactly the expected earnings rate, would show zero "income" in each year that the actual situation came out exactly as estimated, and would show positive or negative "income" in years in which the estimates were exceeded or not realized, respectively. Presumably, the accounting principle would be that capital is charged as a cost at a rate that expresses a "normal" earnings rate for the company, and projects accepted because they showed a higher-than-normal rate would result in an increase in "income" on the income statement to the extent that these expectations were realized.

The capital cost would be substantially higher than actual interest charges. The excess is an imputed cost, and imputed costs cannot be recorded under current accounting principles (although such a practice was advocated by some accountants many years ago and is in accordance with the economists' concept of cost). A change in accounting principles, therefore, would be necessary.

ADVANTAGES

Performance Measurement

The problem arose initially because of the impossibility of measuring divisional performance in a way that matched the reasoning process that led to decisions on acquiring assets. Conceptually, the proposal would solve this problem, although there are a number of practical difficulties, as described below. To the extent that a division reports net income, it is presumably more than paying its way—it is earning more than a normal return on the capital that it uses. This is perhaps the best single measure of divisional performance. It also keeps management attention focused on the necessity of earning a satisfactory return.

Pricing

The system would result in a different method of pricing, and this might well be an improvement over the system which calculates normal prices on the basis of a percentage markup over cost. Price under the proposed system would include an allowance for return on investment of the assets used to make the product. Furthermore, prices would tend to be even from year to year, thus avoiding the error of reducing prices when, for example, a labor-saving machine is introduced.

Leasing

Under the present system, divisions can often improve their computed return on investment by leasing assets rather than purchasing them, even though purchase would be in the best interests of the company as a whole. This is because the implicit interest in a long-term, noncancelable lease contract, although higher than the cost of borrowing funds, is less than the return of a division of average profitability. In these circumstances, leasing an asset of average profitability would add something to the division's income without affecting its investment and, therefore, would increase its ratio of income to investment, which is return on investment. Purchase of such an asset would increase the investment base. Use of capital charge would lessen this discrepancy (although it would not remove it entirely unless the capital charge corresponded to the implicit interest cost in the lease, which might not be desirable on other grounds).

Income Taxes

A company need not, and ordinarily does not, keep its internal accounting records in a way that conforms to income tax regulations; thus, the proposal can be considered quite apart from any effect on the computation of taxable income. Nevertheless, it is interesting to consider the implications of an income tax based on the principles suggested above. For one thing, making the capital cost a deductible item would at least partly remove the distinction between borrowed capital and equity capital that exists in the present tax structure and which has undesirable social consequences. It also would reduce the double taxation of dividends. The rate at which the capital charge is calculated for tax purposes would probably have to be set by the government.

As a practical matter, this change in the definition of taxable income would be unacceptable to the Congress unless balanced by another proposal that makes up for the income that otherwise would be lost. Taxing capital gains as ordinary income is one possible quid pro quo.

Follow-up on Decisions

With the present system, it is difficult to check up, after the fact, on the soundness of investment decisions, since accounting figures do not conform to the figures used in making the decision. Under the proposed system, such a check could easily be made. Management could determine how well the proposal worked out in practice, and thus have a basis for appraising the competence of the analyst and the soundness of the analytical process.

DIFFICULTIES

The balance sheet under the proposed system would show too high a net book value figure, since the market value of assets (disregarding price level changes) tend to follow the declining-balance curve. It is doubtful whether anyone can make a practical use of the balance sheet figures for net book value in any event, however, and balance sheet implications will not be discussed further.

The concept works out perfectly in the situation illustrated in Exhibit 1, because the annual earnings are level. The annuity method of depreciation would not give the right results for any earnings pattern other than a level one. Many, but by no means all, investments do have a projected earnings pattern that is reasonably level from year to year. Some companies that have investigated this proposal have found that most investments fit into one of a very few categories of earnings patterns. The most common alternative to the level pattern is the new-product pattern, characterized by a curve that increases slowly at first, then increases more rapidly, reaches a ceiling, and tapers off. It seems likely that these alternative earnings patterns can be identified, and that depreciation schedules can be calculated that will fit reasonably well the investment recovery implicit in them.

The determination of the normal-earnings rate used to figure the capital charge is a difficult problem. Many studies indicate that an attempt to find it via the cost-of-capital route is unsatisfactory because of the difficulty of finding the cost of equity capital. Nevertheless, companies do decide on a rate for decision-making purposes, and even though it is determined subjectively, this same rate can be used in the proposed accounting system. The possibility exists for using different rates for different divisions, and within divisions for different categories of assets, in order to reflect differences in risk.

CONCLUSION

A system can be useful even though it is less than perfect. Undoubtedly, it is not practicable to devise depreciation methods that fit all conceivable earnings patterns. Nevertheless, if in a given company two or three earnings patterns fit most of the investments reasonably well, then a system developed from these patterns would reflect the facts reasonably well and certainly would be superior to the systems currently used.

The mechanics of such a system would be:

1. Book assets initially at cost.
2. Write off this cost over the useful life of the asset, using a depreciation method that reflects the anticipated capital recovery pattern. For assets with projected level earnings, this is the annuity method.
3. Make a capital charge to income, determined by multiplying the net book value of assets by a normal-earning rate.

Case 7–1

Diversified Products Corporation*

The Diversified Products Corporation manufactured consumer and industrial products in more than a dozen divisions. Plants were located throughout the country, one or more to a division, and company headquarters was in a large eastern city. Each division was run by a division manager and had its own balance sheet and income statement. The company made extensive use of long- and short-run planning programs, which included budgets for sales, costs, expenditures, and rate of return on investment. Monthly reports on operating results were sent in by each division and were reviewed by headquarters executives.

The Able division of the Diversified Products Corporation manufactured and assembled large industrial pumps, most of which sold for more than $1,000. A great variety of models were made to order from the standard parts that the division either bought or manufactured for stock. In addition, components were individually designed and fabricated when pumps were made for special applications. A variety of metalworking machines were used, some large and heavy, and a few designed especially for the division's kind of business.

The division operated three plants, two of which were much smaller than the third and were located in distant parts of the country. Headquarters offices were located in the main plant, where more than 1,000 people were employed. They performed design and manufacturing operations as well as the usual staff and clerical work. Marketing activities were carried out by sales engineers in the field, who worked closely with customers on design and installation. Reporting to Mr. Allen, the division manager, were men in charge of design, sales, manufacturing, purchasing, and budgets.

---

* Although not previously copyrighted, this case was written by Professor William Rotch, University of Virginia, published by Intercollegiate Case Clearing House (ICH4C53R), Soldiers Field, Boston, and reproduced here with the permission of the author.

The division's product line had been broken down into five product groups, so that the profitability of each could be studied separately. Evaluation was based on the margin above factory cost as a percentage of sales. No attempt had been made to allocate investment to the product lines. The budget director said this not only would be difficult in view of the common facilities, but also such a mathematical computation would not provide any new information, since the products had approximately the same turnover of assets. Furthermore, he said it was difficult enough to allocate common factory costs between products, and even margin on sales was a disputable figure. "If we were larger," he said, "and had separate facilities for each product line, we might be able to do it. But it wouldn't mean much in this division right now."

Only half a dozen men ever looked at the division's rate of return, for other measures were used in the division's internal control system. The division manager used shipments per week and certain cost areas such as overtime payments to check on divisional operations.

THE DIVISION MANAGER'S CONTROL OF ASSETS

During 1957, the total assets of the Able division were turned over approximately 1.7 times, and late that year they were made up as follows:

Cash	12%
Accounts receivable	21
Inventory:	
Raw material	7
About 3% metal stock	
About 4% purchased parts	
Work in process	11
About 7% manufactured parts	
About 4% floor stocks	
Finished goods	2
Machinery (original cost)	29
Land and buildings (original cost)	18
	100%

Cash (12 Percent of Total Assets)

The Able division, like all divisions in the Diversified Products Corporation, maintained a petty cash account in a local bank to which company headquarters transferred funds as they were needed. This local working account was used primarily for making up the plant payroll and for payment of other local bills. Payment of suppliers' invoices as well as collection of accounts receivable was handled by headquarters for Able as well as for most of the other divisions.

The division's cash account at headquarters was shown on the division's balance sheet as cash and marketable securities. The amount shown as cash had been established by agreement between top management and the division manager, and was considered by both to be about the minimum amount necessary to operate the division. The excess above this amount was shown on the division's balance sheet as marketable securities, and earned interest from headquarters at the rate of 3 percent a year. It was this account which varied with receipts and disbursements, leaving the cash account fixed as long as there was a balance in the securities account. It was possible for the securities account to be wiped out and for cash to decline below the minimum agreed on, but if this continued for more than a month or two, corrective action was taken. For Able division, the minimum level was equal to about one month's sales, and in recent years cash had seldom gone below this amount.

Whether or not the company as a whole actually owned cash and marketable securities equal to the sum of all the respective divisions' cash and security accounts was strictly a headquarters matter. It probably was not necessary to hold this amount of cash and securities, since the division accounts had to cover division peak needs and, from headquarters' point of view, not all the peak needs necessarily occurred at the same time.

The size of a division's combined cash and marketable securities accounts was directly affected by all phases of the division's operations that used or produced cash. It also was affected in three other ways. One was the automatic deduction of 52 percent of income for tax purposes. Another was the payment of "dividends" by the division to headquarters. All earnings that the division manager did not wish to keep for future use were transferred to the corporation's cash account by payment of a dividend. Since a division was expected to retain a sufficient balance to provide for capital expenditures, dividends were paid generally only by the profitable divisions that were not expanding rapidly.

The third action affecting the cash account occurred if cash declined below the minimum, or if extensive capital expenditures had been approved. A division might then "borrow" from headquarters, paying interest as if it were a separate company. At the end of 1957, the Able division had no loan and had been able to operate since about 1950 without borrowing from headquarters. Borrowing was not, in fact, currently being considered by the Able division.

Except for its part in the establishment of a minimum cash level, top management was not involved in the determination of the division's investment in cash and marketable securities. Mr. Allen could control the level of this investment by deciding how much was to be paid in dividends. Since only a 3 percent return was received on the marketable securities and since the division earned more than that on its total investment, it was to his advantage to pay out as much as possible in dividends. When asked how he determined the size of the dividends, Mr. Allen said that he simply kept what he thought he would need to cover peak demands, capital expenditures, and contingencies. Improving the division's rate of return may have been part of the decision, but he did not mention it.

Accounts Receivable (21 Percent of Total Assets)

All accounts receivable for the Able division were collected at company headquarters. Around the twentieth of each month, the accounts were run off and the report was forwarded to the division. Though, in theory, Mr. Allen was allowed to set his own terms for divisional sales, in practice it would have been difficult to change the company's usual terms. Since Able division sold to important customers of other divisions, any change from the net-30-days terms would disturb a large segment of the corporation's business. Furthermore, industry practice was well established, and the division would hardly try to change it.

The possibility of cash sales in situations in which credit was poor was virtually nonexistent. Credit was investigated for all customers by the headquarters credit department, and no sales were made without a prior credit check. For the Able division, this policy presented no problem, for it sold primarily to well-established customers.

In late 1957, accounts receivable corresponded to 45 average days of sales. This exceeded the 30-day credit period as a result of a slight increase in shipments the month before, coupled with the normal delay caused by the billing and collection process. Mr. Allen could do almost nothing directly to control the level of accounts receivable. This asset account varied with sales, lagged behind shipments by a little more than a month, and departed from this relationship only if customers happened to pay early or late.

Inventory, Raw Material Metal Stock (about 3 Percent of Total Investment)

In late 1957, inventory as a whole made up 20 percent of Able division's total assets. A subdivision of the various kinds of inventory showed that raw material accounted for 7 percent; work in process, 11 percent; and finished goods and miscellaneous supplies, 2 percent. Since the Able division produced to order, finished goods inventory was normally small, leaving raw material and work in process as the most significant classes of inventory.

The raw material inventory could be further subdivided to separate the raw material inventory from a variety of purchased parts. The strictly raw material inventory was composed primarily of metals and metal shapes, such as steel sheets or copper tubes. Most of the steel was bought according to a schedule arranged with the steel companies several months ahead of the delivery date. About a month before the steel company was to ship the order, Able division would send the rolling instructions by shapes and weights. If the weight on any particular shape was below a minimum set by the steel company, Able division would pay an extra charge for processing. Although this method of purchasing accounted for the bulk of steel purchases, smaller amounts were also bought as needed from warehouse stocks and specialty producers.

Copper was bought by headquarters and processed by the company's own mill. The divisions could buy the quantities they needed, but the price paid depended on corporate buying practices and processing costs. The price paid by Able division had generally been competitive with outside sources, though it often lagged behind the market both in increases and in reductions in price.

The amounts of copper and steel bought were usually determined by the purchasing agent without recourse to any formal calculations of an economic ordering quantity. The reason for this was that since such a large number of uncertain factors continually had to be estimated, a formal computation would not improve the process of determining how much to buy. Purchases depended on the amounts on hand, expected consumption, and current delivery time and price expectations. If delivery was fast, smaller amounts were usually bought. If a price increase was anticipated, somewhat larger orders often were placed at the current price. Larger amounts of steel were bought, for example, just before the 1956 steel strike, when steel negotiations were expected to result in a price increase, and perhaps also in a delay in deliveries.

The level of investment in raw material varied with the rates of purchase and use. Mr. Allen could control this class of asset within a fairly wide range, and there were no top management directives governing the size of his raw material inventory.

Inventory, Purchased Parts and Manufactured Parts (about 11 Percent of Total Assets—4 Percent from Raw Material, 7 Percent from Work in Process)

The Able division purchased and manufactured parts for stock to be used later in the assembly of pumps. The method used to determine the purchase quantity was the same as that used to determine the length of production run on parts made for work-in-process stocks.

The number of parts bought or manufactured was based on a series of calculations of an economical ordering quantity (EOQ). Since several thousand different items were bought and manufactured, these calculations had been made routine so that most of the work was done by clerks with the aid of an inventory control work sheet, Exhibit 1. This sheet had been prepared by headquarters staff personnel, and was used throughout the company in conjunction with two tables drawn up by each division. To show how this procedure worked, an actual computation is shown in Exhibit 1 for a hypothetical part called a gremlet.

Section I of the worksheet shows two methods of calculating the value of future quarterly requirements. In the first method, the clerk considered two quarters of past activity and, with the aid of the first of the two tables, filled in the estimated requirements for the next quarter. This table is simply an automatic method of weighting the average of the two quarters, applying a weight of three to the most recent quarter and a weight of one to the quarter before. In the example furnished, 83 dozen gremlets were used last quarter

Exhibit 1

INVENTORY CONTROL WORK SHEET
Order Quantity and Review Point
(Long Form)

Item / Style No. / Size	P D S	Ledger Codes	PROBABILITY ACCOUNTS SINGLE DELIVERY	PROTECTION
Description: Blue Gremlets	End Use: fasten box top	Unit Measure: dozen	☑ Purch. ☐ I.W.R. ☐ Self Mfd.	1 Stock out in 2 yrs

REQUIREMENTS

I. A. PAST ACTIVITY

Past six month activity (from ledger)

1st	53	(most recent past)	4th	28
2nd	12		5th	6
3rd	18		6th	20

3 Mo. Total 83 ——→ 83

X $ 1.77 Std. Cost — 6 Mo. Total 137

- $ 147 Val. (L) — X $ 1.77 Std. Cost

- $ 242 Val. (M)

From Requirements Table where (L) & (M) intersect read indicated future quarterly requirements [$ 133] (N)

OR

B. PAST ACTIVITY AND FUTURE TREND

Past three months activity (from ledger)

1st ____ (most recent past)
2nd ____
3rd ____
3 Mo. Total ____

% Rate should not exceed (+) (-) 25%. When quarter to quarter changes are erratic, consider the Planned Approach.

X ____ % Rate of future trend

- ____

X $ ____ Standard Cost

- [$ ____] (P) Value of future quarterly requirements

ORDER QUANTITY

II. 1. Quarterly requirements (I. (N) or (P) $ 80
2. Set up value (if self mfd.) $ -
3. EOQ (from OQ Table) $ 149
4. No. times/yr. stock is ordered 2.1
5. EOQ Units $\frac{\text{Line 3 \$ 149}}{\text{Std. Cost \$ 1.77}}$ = [84] 75 EOQ Units

REVIEW POINT

III. 1. No. demands during expected delivery time

No. demands past 3 mos. (from ledger) 8 / Calendar Days 90 = No./Day .09 (S)

x E.D.T. (from Delivery Time Schedule) 30 (F)

= No. Demands during E.D.T. 2.7 (T)

2. From O.R.P. table where No. demands (line 1 (T). above) intersect with No. times/yr. stock is ordered (II. line 4) read O.R.P. — O.R.P. Dem. [3.8]

3. O.R.P. in Units

a. Average size of demands: Past 3 mos. activity (I. A or B) - Units 83 / No. demands past 3 mos. (Line 1, before division) 8 = 10.4 (U)

x O.R.P. demands (line 2) = 3.8

b. O.R.P. - Units = [40]

NOTE: Post O.R.P. in units on ledger record and reset signal devices.

CONCLUSION

IV. 1. Present Stock Balance 0
2. On Order 0
3. Total Stock 0 (24 issued 3/19)
4. O.R.P. (III. line 3b) 40
5. Difference
a. Total under ORP (line 4-3) - ____
b. Total over ORP (line 3-4) + ____
6. If the difference under or over, (5a or b above) is within 10% (‡) of the O.R.P. (4 above) follow this general rule: (Ø) place a requistion for the E.O.Q.(*) (II. line 5) and schedule delivery for the E.D.T. (III. line (F)) in this case.

____ days from today's date ____

Equals order schedule date [3/28/58] Short date

7. If a positive difference and the difference (5b above) is greater than 10% (‡) do not place a requisition now. Wait until new O.R.P. is reached and recalculate.
8. If a negative difference and the difference (5a above) is greater than 10% (‡) place the requisition for the E.O.Q. (II. line 5) and calculate the length of time total stock (3 above) will last.

(Size Dem. (III. 3 (U)) ____

X (Dem./Day (III. 1 (S)) ____ Days Total Stock Will Last

(Units/Day) ____ Total Stock (Line 3)

Refer to EDT (III. line 1 (F) and schedule requisition for the shortest time. In this case.

____ days from today's date ____

‡ Equals Order Schedule Date [ ]

Subject to change based upon local policy.

Ø See operating procedure (Part IV. Sec. 7A) for exception.

* If the new order quantity plus the total (3 above) does not exceed the O.R.P. (4 above) place an additional requisition(s) for the economical order quantity and schedule as required.

Subject to Quantity Discount ☐ YES ☐ NO	If special information is considered, check here and record on other side. ☐
Ordering & Storage Limitations, etc. ☐ YES ☐ NO	Minimum Quantities ☐ YES ☐ NO
Work Sheet By & Date	Reviewed By & Date

and 54 dozen the quarter before. The clerk located the dollar value (standard cost) of the most recent quarter on the left side of the table ($147), moved across that line to the column corresponding to the value of gremlets used in the last half year ($242), and read off the estimated future quarterly requirements ($133). The alternative method for estimating future activity was used when only three months' activity was known, or when a definite trend was anticipated. In such cases, instead of using the table to weight past activity, the clerk applied a percentage rate of change, not to exceed ±25 percent.

In transferring the indicated quarterly requirements from section I to section II, a clerk in the Able division made the first of the two special adjustments by the application of a factor of .6 to the indicated requirements ($133), thereby reducing them to the $80 shown on line 1 of section II. The factor had been established at .75 by the division manager sometime before 1957 and was changed to .6 late that year. By changing this factor, the division manager could reduce or increase across-the-board inventories of both purchased and manufactured parts.

In section II of the work sheet, the quarterly requirements are converted into an economical ordering quantity with the aid of the order-quantity table. In this table, two constants were combined with the estimated requirements—the incremental cost of handling an additional order and the inventory carrying charge. The order cost used by the Able division was a constant of $3.14 for outside orders, but for manufactured parts it varied with the cost of machine setup. The carrying charge was 9 percent of the average value of the inventory; this covered the cost of capital tied up—considered to be about 4.5 percent—and the cost of insurance, inventory taxes, and obsolescence. When quarterly requirements were $80 worth of gremlets, the table said that $149 worth should be ordered, or 84 dozen. This, then, was the economical order quantity for gremlets if the future requirements were expected to be only 60 percent of past requirements.

In determining what the actual order would be, the inventory control supervisor applied the second special adjustment, ranging from 0 to 75 percent or more. He based this on his judgment of what would be needed and the speed of delivery. In special situations, he asked the advice of his superior, the superintendent of production, and on rare occasions the decision actually was made by the division manager. In this particular case, the economical order quantity of 84 dozen gremlets was revised downward to 75 dozen because the division manager had made a general request that inventory be reduced. The remainder of the work sheet concerned the order review point and scheduling of the order.

A second work sheet was used for making an analysis of quantity discounts when they were available. Exhibit 2 shows a copy of a work sheet filled out for widgets, of which the division used 21,000 each year. The economical order quantity for widgets as calculated on the order quantity work sheet was 1,500 at 19 cents each. One half-cent per unit could be saved if orders

Exhibit 2

INVENTORY CONTROL WORK SHEET
Quantity Discount Analysis

DWG. & ITEM PART OR STYLE NO.	PDS	UNIT MEAS.	DESCRIPTION
Widgets			

(A) ANNUAL REQUIREMENTS	21,000	UNITS	SUPPLIER Staple Co.

		(B) ORDER QUANTITY	(C) UNIT PRICE	(D) ORDERS PER YEAR (A ÷ B)	(E) MATERIAL COST PER YR. (A X C)	(F) DECREASED MATERIAL COST (IE - IIE)	(G) ADDITIONAL ORDERING & CARRYING COSTS (FROM TABLE)	(H) DECREASE OR INCREASE IN COST (G - F)
I	E.O.Q. DATA	1,500	.19	14	3990.00	XXXXX	XXXXXXX	XXXXXX
II DISCOUNT SCHEDULE	1.	5,000	.185	4	3885.00	105.00	50.20	54.80
	2.							
	3.							
	4.							
	5.							
III COST REDUCTION AND RETURN ON ADDITIONAL INVESTMENT	6. COST REDUCTION -	LARGEST NEGATIVE VALUE IN COLUMN (H)						-$ 54.80
	7. ADDITIONAL INVESTMENT -	(DISCOUNT QTY. 5,000 X DISCOUNT PRICE .185) ÷ 2					- (E.O.Q. 1500 X STANDARD PRICE .19) ÷ 2	-$ 320.00
	8. RETURN ON ADDITIONAL INVESTMENT -	(COST RED. ÷ ADD. INVEST.) X 100						- 17%
APPROVALS	PURCHASING			DATE		INVENTORY CONTROL		DATE

of 5,000 were placed, making a total annual saving of $105. From this saving was subtracted the net increase in ordering and carrying costs, which was taken from a table, leaving a net increase or decrease in cost as a result of the larger orders. In the example, $54.80 is the net cost reduction, which is a 17 percent return on the $320 average increase in investment.

Whether 17 percent was a sufficient return to prompt the ordering of larger quantities depended in the Able division on other related factors. The inventory control supervisor who made the decision considered general business conditions, the time required to use up the larger order, the specialization of the particular part, and any general directives made by the division manager concerning inventory levels. A return below 15 percent was probably never acceptable, more than 20 percent was required in most instances, and any quantity discount yielding 25–30 percent or more usually was taken, though each case was judged individually. In the example shown, 17 percent was considered not sufficient, both because it was on the borderline of acceptability and because the division manager had requested a general reduction in inventories.

The level of purchased and manufactured parts inventory in the Able division varied with changes in rate of consumption and purchase. If the rules for calculating economical order quantity were adhered to, inventory levels increased with usage; and for all items whose annual requirements were above \$4.36,[1] the rate of inventory change was less than the rate of usage change. Thus, an increase in sales yielding the same percentage profit on sales would, under strict application of the rules, provide a higher return on investment. However, application of the two adjustments in determining economical quantities destroyed this relationship. In times of anticipated downturn, the adjustments tended to accelerate inventory reduction; in times of expanding sales, relaxing the adjustments tended to accelerate the buying and production of parts. Thus, the division manager, by setting the first adjustment factor and the general tone of the second adjustment, controlled the level of his parts inventory with considerable flexibility.

Inventory, Floor Stocks (about 4 Percent of Total Investment)

Floor stock inventory consisted of parts and components being worked on and assembled. Items became part of the floor stock inventory when they were requisitioned from the storage areas, or when delivered directly to the production floor. Pumps were worked on individually, so that lot size was not a factor to be considered. Mr. Allen could do little to control the level of floor stock inventory, except to see that there was no excess of parts piled around the production area.

Inventory, Finished Goods (2 Percent of Total Investment)

As a rule, pumps were made to order and for immediate shipment. Finished goods inventory consisted of those few pumps on which shipment was delayed. Control of this investment was a matter of keeping it low by shipping the pumps as fast as possible.

Land, Buildings, and Machinery (47 Percent of Total Investment)

Since the Able division's fixed assets, stated at gross cost, comprised 47 percent of total assets at the end of 1957, the control of this particular group of assets was extremely important. Changes in the level of these investments depended on retirements and additions, the additions being entirely covered by the capital budgeting program.

Diversified Products Corporation's capital budgeting procedures were described in a planning manual. The planning sequence was as follows:

1. Headquarters forecasts economic conditions. (March)
2. The divisions plan long-term objectives. (June)
3. Supporting programs are submitted. (September) These are plans for specific actions, such as sales plans, advertising programs, and cost-reduction pro-

---

[1] If ordering costs were \$3.14 per order, and carrying costs were 9 percent of average inventory, and the average inventory was considered to be one-half of the ordering quantity, then average inventory when economical-size orders were made equaled $4.175\sqrt{A}$, where A is the annual requirements in dollars. By differentiating this equation, it can be found that average inventory increased faster than A until A was equal to \$4.36; thereafter, average inventory increased more slowly.

grams, and include the facilities program which is the capital expenditure request. The planning manual states under the heading, "General Approach in the Development of a Coordinated Supporting Program," this advice:

> Formulation and evaluation of a supporting program for each product line can generally be improved if projects are classified by purpose. The key objective of all planning is return on assets, a function of margin and turnover. These ratios are, in turn, determined by the three factors in the business equation—volume, costs, and assets. All projects, therefore, should be directed primarily at one of the following:
>
> To increase volume.
> To reduce costs and expenses.
> To minimize assets.

4. Annual objective is submitted. (November 11, by 8:00 A.M.) The annual objective states projected sales, costs, expenses, profits, and cash expenditures and receipts, and shows pro forma balance sheets and income statements.

Mr. Allen was "responsible for the division's assets and for provision for the growth and expansion of the division." Growth referred to the internal refinements of product design and production methods as well as to the cost-reduction programs. Expansion involved a 5- or 10-year program, including about two years for construction.

In the actual capital expenditure request there were four kinds of facilities proposals:

1. Cost-reduction projects, which were self-liquidating investments. Reduction in labor costs was usually the largest source of the savings, which were stated in terms of the liquidation period and the rate of return.
2. Necessity projects. These included replacement of worn-out machinery, technical changes to meet competition, and facilities for the safety and comfort of the workers.
3. Product-improvement projects.
4. Expansion projects.

Justification of the cost-reduction proposals was based on a comparison of the estimated rate of return (estimated return before taxes divided by gross investment) with the 20 percent standard, as specified by headquarters. If the project was considered desirable and yet showed a return of less than 20 percent, it had to be justified on other grounds and was included in the necessities category. Cost-reduction proposals made up about 60 percent of the 1958 capital expenditure budget, and in earlier years these proposals had accounted for at least 50 percent. Very little of Able division's 1958 capital budget had been allocated specifically for product improvement and none for expansion, so that most of the remaining 40 percent was to be used for necessity projects. Thus, a little over half of Able division's capital expenditure was justified primarily on the estimated rate of return on the investment. The remainder, having advantages that could not be stated in terms of the rate of return, was justified on other grounds.

Mr. Allen was free to include what he wanted in his capital budget request, and for the three years that he had been division manager his requests had always been granted. However, no large expansion projects had been included in the capital budget requests of the last three years. Most of the capital expenditures had been for cost-reduction projects, and the remainder were for necessities. Annual additions had approximately equaled annual retirements.

Since Mr. Allen could authorize expenditures of up to $100,000 per project for purposes approved by the board, there was, in fact, some flexibility in his choice of projects after the budget had been approved by higher management. Not only could he schedule the order of expenditure, but in some circumstances he could substitute unforeseen projects of a similar nature. If top management approved $50,000 for miscellaneous cost-reduction projects, Mr. Allen could spend this on the projects he considered most important, whether or not they were specifically described in his original budget request.

For the corporation as a whole, about one quarter of the capital expenditure was for projects of under $100,000, which could be authorized for expenditure by the division managers. This proportion was considered by top management to be about right; if, however, it rose much above this fraction, the $100,000 dividing line would probably be lowered.

QUESTIONS

1. For each asset category, discuss whether the basis of measurement used by the company is the best for the purpose of measuring divisional return on investment. If, in your opinion, it is not the best, suggest an improvement.

2. Comment on the general usefulness of the return-on-investment measure. Could it be made a more effective device?

Case 7–2

Long Manufacturing Company

The Long Manufacturing Company, with 1956 sales of just over $100 million, operated six plants which produced different but related products for sale to other companies or consumers. Each plant was operated independently by a plant manager whose performance was judged by several factors, one of the most important being the return the plant made on the investment that had been allocated to it.

The investment figure used in the calculation had, since the system was started, included all the investment over which each plant manager had control. Until the spring of 1957, two classes of investment were not included in the division's investment base—headquarters investment and research investment. The first was small (.2 percent of the company's total net investment), since most of the headquarters facilities were rented. Until recently, research investment had also been small, but by the spring of 1957 had grown to just over 1 percent of the company's total net investment, and it was expected that more money would be invested in research facilities in the near future.

In late 1956, the president of Long Manufacturing Company asked that all the company's investment be distributed in some way to all the operating divisions. This would, he stated, make the reported return on investment by the plants more realistic as indicators of how well the company as a whole was doing.

The recommended method of distribution of investment was to be based initially on the allocation of expenses. Distributed investment would bear the same relationship to total investment as allocated expenses bore to total expenses. If a division had 20 percent of total research expenses allocated to it, it would carry 20 percent of total research investment. The allocation of expenses for both research and headquarters activities was, in turn, according to a simple average of three weighting factors: net realization or sales less freight and discounts; net book value of the property assigned to the plant;

and payroll or total salaries and wages. Thus, if a division had 10 percent of the company's total net realization, 9 percent of total net book value of property, and 14 percent of the directly assignable payroll, the division would be allocated 11 percent of the headquarters and research expenses. It would also now be allocated 11 percent of the research and headquarters investment. One exception to the allocation of research expenses by formula occurred in the case of expenses in the nature of technical service costs. These were charged directly to the plant for which the work was done. In theory, this exception had seemed reasonable; in practice, however, the line separating technical service from research was difficult to define.

A memorandum was issued to all plants early in 1957, explaining the forthcoming allocation of headquarters and research investment. The memorandum made the following statements about the allocation of research investment.

Allocation of Total Gross Investment to Plants

Currently, the plants do not include in their operating investment base any of the facilities that serve the entire company, e.g., research. Inclusion of these facilities will mean that the operating return on investment should now measure the performance of the total assets in the company.

Recommended Method of Allocation of Research Investment to Plants

Distribution on the Basis of Research Expenses. This makes use of readily available figures and adds a measure of flexibility, for distribution depends on the annual budgeted research expenses. This incorporates a measure of their value received from research during the year. Over a period of time, allocation of the research gross investment will be improved as more precise expense figures are developed.

Soon after this memorandum was issued, the financial analysis manager received from one of the division managers a letter which said, in part:

. . . I question the advisability of allocating research investment to the divisions. As you know, we exercise no direct control over research expenditures; consequently, we are unable to control the effect of increased research investment on our return. It seems to me the return on investment concept will be a more meaningful tool to the divisions if our investment base includes only those items over which we have some degree of control. . . .

The financial manager knew that though it was the company's research director who actually planned what was to be worked on by his research staff, the plant managers did have some influence on the research director's decisions through periodic discussions with him. Furthermore, two of the plant managers were on the board of directors, and in directors meetings they could exercise some influence over the choice of research projects.

With these facts in mind, the financial analysis manager wrote an answer to the plant manager's letter. This read, in part, as follows:

Letter to a Division Manager from Financial Analysis Manager

. . . The major item that had not formerly been carried by the plants in their investment base is the investment in research. This is now included so that returns will be based upon the *total* investment in the company. Wo do not believe that the company could long exist without research. And we believe that the plants and products they produce benefit from the research and should, therefore, carry their share of such investment.

Your point on exercising direct control over research investment is well taken. However, I do not feel that this is an issue, and I do question the implication that a plant manager has no degree of control over research.

Return on investment is an anlytical tool that we have tried to make uniformly applicable to as many general and specific problems as possible. We have attempted to make it equally applicable in measuring past performance and providing a guide for current problems, as well as in giving a basis for decisions affecting the future. It is not a perfect yardstick, but it does come close.

There is no reason why this tool cannot be designed by plant management to serve its particular purposes at any level within the plant. I am thinking here of plant managerial control and would be glad to work with you on this. . . .

QUESTION

Assume that you are administrative assistant to the president, and that he has asked you to comment on the question(s) raised in the case. What would you say to him?

Case 7–3

Antol Company

The Antol Company consisted of a central corporate office and 20 operating divisions scattered throughout the United States. Each operating division produced and marketed a line of products unrelated to those of the other divisions. There was little interaction among the divisions. Personnel were moved from one division to another only in exceptional circumstances. Interdivisional transfers of products were insignificant.

Although primary responsibility for managing a division rested with the division president, the central corporate management made basic policy decisions, provided permanent capital for the divisions, and approved capital expenditures, long-term financing, and salaries of division presidents and vice-presidents. Major tools of top management control of the activities of the divisions were the balance sheet and income statement prepared monthly by each division. The corporate controller regularly summarized and analyzed these financial statements in a report prepared for the executive committee. In this report, he described the causes of significant deviations from the budgets, and showed the percentage return on net worth for each division.

This percentage was viewed as a key indication of divisional performance. It was found by dividing divisional earnings by divisional net worth. Divisional earnings was defined as the net earnings of the division after all charges properly allocable or attributable to the division, including depreciation, an administrative service charge equal to 1 percent of net sales of the division (which for all divisions was about equal to the cost of the central corporate organization), plus a net worth capital charge equal to .5 percent per month of divisional net worth. Divisional net worth was defined as net total assets less total liabilities as shown on the divisional balance sheet, Exhibit 1. For the purpose of determining the net total assets, cash was fixed at an amount agreed on between the division and the corporate management as necessary for day-to-day operation; inventories were valued at the lower of fifo cost or market; and property, plant, and equipment were included at

Exhibit 1

FORM OF DIVISIONAL BALANCE SHEET

ASSETS

	End of this Month	*Beginning of Year*
Current Assets:		
Cash		
Accounts and notes receivable, less: Reserves		
Inventories		
Raw material and supplies		
Work in process and finished goods		
Other		
Inventory reserves		
Total Inventories		
Prepaid and deferred expenses		
Other current assets		
Total Current Assets		
Notes receivable, noncurrent		
Property, Plant, and Equipment:		
Land and buildings		
Machinery and equipment		
Other property		
Less: Reserves for depreciation and amortization		
Property, plant, and equipment, Net		
Other assets		
Total Assets		

LIABILITIES AND NET WORTH

Current Liabilities:		
Notes payable, banks		
Current portion of long-term debt		
Accounts payable		
Accrued liabilities		
Accrued federal taxes on income		
Other current liabilities		
Total Current Liabilities		
Long-term debt		
Other liabilities and deferred income		
Total Liabilities		
Net worth		
Total Liabilities and Net Worth		

net book value after allowance for depreciation. All divisions used the unit, double-declining-balance method of depreciation.

QUESTIONS

1. Assuming that Antol top management wished to calculate one overall ratio that related earnings to investment, as a measure of a division manager's performance, do you think the formula described above is probably as good as any? If not, in what respects should it be changed?

2. If you need more information before definitely recommending a change, what information would you seek? Why?

3. Do you think top management was basically correct in regarding percentage return on net worth (as possibly modified by your answer to Question 1) as an important figure? Is some other single indicator of performance even more important?

4. Antol Company paid a substantial bonus to division managements. The bonus was based in part on a calculated measure of performance, but the bonus so calculated was subject to change in accordance with the judgment of corporate top management. To the extent that a calculated figure is used, would you recommend the percentage return on net worth as the best figure to use? Presumably, the bonus would be calculated on the basis of the excess of the actual return over some agreed-on budgeted return. If you think some other figure would be preferable, please describe it.

Case 7–4

Lemfert Company

Lemfert Company was a large manufacturing company organized into divisions, each with responsibility for earning a satisfactory return on its investment. Division managers had considerable autonomy in carrying out this responsibility. Some divisions fabricated parts; others—here called end-item divisions—assembled these parts, together with purchased parts, into finished products and marketed the finished products. Transfer prices were used in connection with the transfer of parts among the various fabricating divisions and from the fabricating divisions to the end-item divisions. Wherever possible, these transfer prices were the lowest prices charged by outside manufacturers for the same or comparable items, with appropriate adjustments for inbound freight, volume, and similar factors.

Parts that were not similar to those manufactured by outside companies were called type K items. In most fabricating divisions, these items constituted only 5 to 10 percent of total volume. In division F, however, approximately 75 percent of total volume was accounted for by Type K items. Division F manufactured 10 such items for various end-item divisions; they were less than 5 percent of the total cost of any one of these end-item divisions. The procedure for arriving at the transfer price for type K items is described below.

First, a tentative transfer price was calculated by the value analysis staff of the corporate purchasing department and was submitted to the two divisions involved for their consideration. This price was supposed to be based on the estimated costs of an efficient producer plus a profit margin. An "efficient producer" was considered to be one conducting its purchasing and using modern equipment in a manner that could reasonably be expected of the company's principal competitors.

The material cost portion of the total cost was based on current competitive price levels. Direct labor cost was supposed to reflect efficient processing on modern equipment. Overhead cost represented an amount that could be expected of an efficient producer using modern equipment. Depreciation expense, expenditures on special tooling, and a standard allowance for administrative expense were included in the overhead figure.

The profit margin was equal to the divisional profit objective applied to the cost of the assets employed to produce the product in question. Assets employed was the sum of the following items:

Cash and receivables—18 per cent of the total manufacturing cost.

Inventories—the value of the optimum inventory size required at standard volume.

Fixed assets—the depreciated book value (but not less than one-half original cost) of assets used to fabricate the part, including a fair share of buildings and other general assets, but excluding standby and obsolete facilities.

The percentage used for cash and receivables was based on studies of the cash and receivable balances of the principal outside manufacturers of parts similar to those manufactured in the fabricating divisions. The standard volume was an estimate of the volume that the plants should *normally* be expected to produce, which was not necessarily the same as current volume or projected volume for the next year.

For an average division, the budgeted profit objective was 20 percent of assets employed, but there were variations among divisions. The divisional budgeted profit objective multiplied by the assets employed, as calculated above, gave the profit margin for the item. This profit was added to the cost to arrive at the suggested transfer price, which then was submitted to the two divisions. If either the buying or the selling division believed that the price thus determined was unfair, it first attempted to negotiate a mutually satisfactory price. If the parties were unable to agree, they submitted the dispute to the controller for arbitration. Either party might appeal the results of this arbitration to the executive vice-president.

QUESTIONS

1. Are these the best transfer price practices for the Lemfert Company? If not, how should they be revised?

2. For what types of companies would the revised policy not be best? Why?

3. Do you think the attempt to measure profitability in division F is worthwhile? If not, how would you measure performance in this division?

Chapter Eight

OVERALL SYSTEMS

The cases in this chapter are intended to facilitate a pulling together of the concepts discussed in the preceding chapters, especially the preceding three chapters. Each case describes a system, or a proposed system; the essential task is to examine the extent to which it facilitates the management control process, and to suggest how observed weaknesses can be corrected.

Case 8–1

Acton Life Insurance Company

It was the third week in July, 1962. The Quarterly Operating Review Report for the southern region of the Acton Life Insurance Company (see Exhibit 1) had recently been distributed. William Bailey, sales manager of the southern region, was visiting the home office in Boston for the purpose of discussing this and related reports with John McFarland, vice-president of sales. Much of the discussion related to the performance of the six branch agencies in the southern region. Mr. Bailey had been sales manager of that region for five months; formerly he had been a branch manager in the eastern region. This was his first visit to the home office since he had assumed his new duties.

Exhibit 1

QUARTERLY OPERATING REVIEW REPORT
Southern Region—Second Quarter, 1962

Branch	*First-Year Premiums*	*First-Year Expenses**	*First-Year Expense Ratio*
Atlanta	$34,608	$14,298	41.3%
Birmingham	30,002	9,817	32.7
Charlotte	22,807	6,610	29.0
Nashville	45,846	11,146	24.3
New Orleans	47,723	10,400	21.8
Tampa	38,185	7,215	18.9
Averages: Region	$36,529	$ 9,914	27.2%
Averages: Company	$38,117	$ 9,449	24.8%

* The expenses associated with the acquisition of new business, including salaries of salesmen. In the full report, 12 additional columns were included, showing a breakdown of the total expenses of the branches and certain adjustments.

MR. BAILEY: Our Atlanta branch had the best performance this past quarter. Just look at the volume of business it put on the books over the last three months—over two and three-fourths million. This works out to about $550,000 per salesman, which is way ahead of the other branches.

MR. MCFARLAND: Bill, don't you remember our discussion on performance yardsticks during my visit to your office earlier this year? I made a particular effort to explain why we feel that sales volume is not enough, that we have to relate the value of these sales to the cost of making them. For some time now, we have been using the ratio of first-year expenses to the total of first-year premiums. This is what the Operating Review Report is all about. Looking at this report, we can see that the Tampa branch was your best branch last quarter. Your Atlanta branch was actually your poorest performer.

MR. BAILEY: That's not the way I understood it when I was a branch manager under Eddie Petanski. I had the impression that the volume of business we booked was the really important yardstick: Don't we pay branch managers commissions on the basis of volume? Aren't all the awards we hand out based primarily on volume—the million-dollar round table, the president's club, and so on? All the branch managers I ever knew felt this way. In fact, we went even further; when we got together to compare performance, we usually ended up by looking at the total amount of commissions we had earned. After all, the real test is how much the company pays us for our efforts.

MR. MCFARLAND: Well, we're supposed to be using this expense ratio. It was put in before I became VP, and I thought by now we were all using it. We're not even satisfied with this measure, however, and have been turning out another report to be used in conjunction with the Quarterly Operating Review Report to help interpret the expense ratio. This is the Quarterly Profit Report (see Exhibit 2) which you've also received. . . . There it is, at the bottom of that pile of papers. This shows that even your Tampa branch didn't do as well as it appeared to on the basis of its expense ratio.

MR. BAILEY: Hold on, Jack, now you've really got me confused. I looked over the Quarterly Profit Report when I got it, and compared these profit factors with previous periods to spot trends, as you suggested. But I didn't use it as you did just now. In fact, I don't see how I can relate these five measures to the expense ratio and to sales volume accomplishments and come up with anything meaningful on performance. I'd just be shooting in the dark. And I'd bet this is true with the other sales managers.

MR. MCFARLAND: You're probably right. It's pretty difficult to relate so many factors together and come up with a meaningful appraisal of performance. What we've been trying to do is to get a better indication of profitability of the business booked by each branch than the expense ratio tells us. The best we've come up with so far is the set of five factors.

MR. BAILEY: Well, I can see what you're driving at, but I just don't think you can do it. What we have now doesn't seem to get us much closer and is much too complicated. Besides, as an ex-branch manager, I'd bet most of our branches believe that volume of business is the primary yardstick.

MR. MCFARLAND: Bill, I don't think there is much to be gained by push-

Exhibit 2

QUARTERLY PROFIT REPORT
Southern Region—Second Quarter, 1962

Branch	*Face Value of Insurance Sold (000)*	*First-Year Premiums*	*Average-Size Policy*	*Average-Size First-Year Premium*		*Premium Collection Frequency**	*Two-Year Lapse Ratio†*
				Amount	*Per $1,000 Ins.*		
Atlanta	$2,763	$34,608	$ 8,735	$109.88	$12.53	6.2	8.4
Birmingham	1,588	30,002	6,606	125.60	18.90	7.0	5.2
Charlotte	1,700	22,807	14,388	193.75	13.42	4.6	13.6
Nashville	2,364	45,846	11,927	230.00	19.39	2.8	12.9
New Orleans	1,916	47,723	13,211	328.53	24.91	3.7	18.3
Tampa	2,507	38,185	9,406	140.07	15.23	4.7	6.8
Averages: Region	$2,140	$36,529	$10,928	$215.19	$19.69	4.2	10.9
Averages: Company	$2,310	$38,117	$12,520	$287.51	$22.96	4.9	5.3

* The average number of times per year that premiums were collected per policy.

† The fraction of the number of policies sold in a given 12-month period that lapsed during the following 2-year period, computed as a running average.

ing our review of performance any further at this time. Some of these same problems have been bothering me for some time now. I think what I'll do is discuss this performance appraisal problem with Mr. Runyan [president of the company] during our regular meeting on Friday. Your points will be very helpful in this discussion. Thanks for bringing them up.

BACKGROUND

Acton Life Insurance Company was a stock company, formed in 1909. It was licensed to do business in all the 50 states, the District of Columbia, and most of Canada. At the beginning of 1962, 56 branches served these areas. It had a total of about $4.5 billion of insurance in force, and its total sales volume in 1961 was about $650 million.

The lines of insurance offered by Acton Life consisted primarily of ordinary life, accident and health, group life, and various annuities. As of 1962, the company sold its entire line of insurance through independent brokers, approximately 20,000 in number. As independent brokers, they were not required to sell Acton policies exclusively. Many also sold policies of the same general types written by other insurance companies.

The basic organization of Acton Life followed the general pattern in the industry. This was a functional type, consisting of six departments: actuarial, legal, sales, investment, underwriting, and administrative services. At the head of each of these departments was a vice-president who reported to the president. The organization chart as of 1962 is shown in Exhibit 3.

The sales department was responsible for directing the operations of the various branches, through which relationships with the independent brokers

Exhibit 3

SIMPLIFIED ORGANIZATION CHART

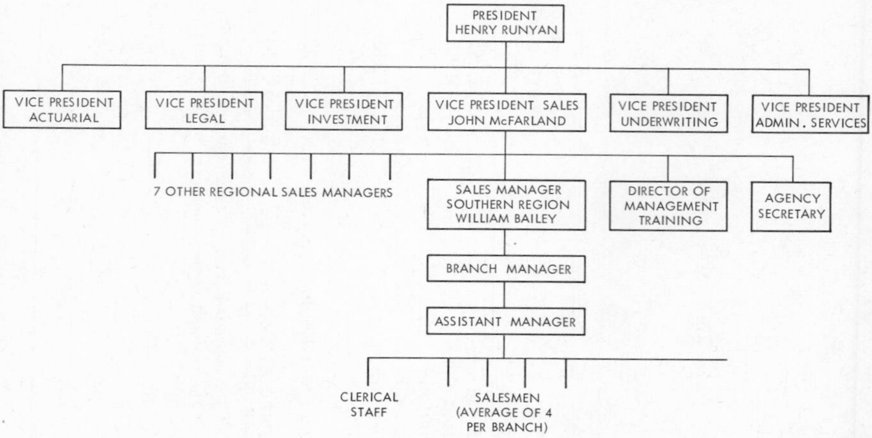

were established and maintained. The company planned to expand the number of branches as rapidly as it could over the following few years in order to serve a larger number of brokers. The branches were grouped into eight geographical regions, each region having from four to eleven branches. For each region, there was a sales manager, who reported to the vice-president of sales. The heads of two staff activities (agency secretary and management training) also reported to the sales vice-president.

A manager was in charge of each of the branches. His primary responsibilities were the direction of the selling effort of his branch, selecting and developing salesmen, participating in negotiating contracts with brokers, and supervising the office personnel required to service the policies sold by these brokers. In general, a branch manager was paid entirely in commissions on the business booked through his branch. However, new branch managers were paid a fixed salary for a period of five years, or until the commissions they would otherwise receive consistently exceeded the salary.

The average number of salesmen working for a branch was four. The major activities of the salesmen were calling on and developing contracts with brokers, helping them to start making sales, and following up from time to time to make sure their sales efforts were satisfactory. Branch salesmen were paid salaries only; commissions for selling the insurance were earned by the independent brokers.

In all branches except a few of the smaller ones, there was an assistant branch manager. Each branch also had a small clerical staff.

MEETING WITH THE PRESIDENT

At his regular Friday morning meeting with Mr. Runyan, Mr. McFarland brought up the problem of measuring the performance of branch managers. He summarized the discussion he had had earlier in the week with Mr. Bailey. To help highlight the problem, Mr. McFarland had prepared a summary, showing the type of statistics currently being employed, either formally or informally, in the appraisal of a branch manager's performance (Exhibit 4). Data for this table, except that on commissions, were taken from the Quarterly Operating Review Report (Exhibit 1) and the Quarterly Profit Report (Exhibit 2). The southern region was chosen for illustrative purposes because of the deficiencies in current practice there that had been brought out in Mr. McFarland's recent discussion with Mr. Bailey.

Mr. Runyan said that of late he had become concerned with a closely related problem—the need for a more rational approach to the planning and control of branch operations. Recently, he had read a doctoral dissertation in which the author proposed a solution to this problem. Mr. Runyan suggested that Mr. McFarland study this proposal and, if it looked sufficiently promising, discuss it with his sales managers. In any event, the president wanted Mr. McFarland's considered opinion regarding the utility of the

Exhibit 4

SELECTED MEASURES OF PERFORMANCE
Southern Region—Second Quarter, 1962*

Branch	First-Year Expense Ratio	Average-Size Policy	Average-Size First-Year Premium		Premium Collection Frequency	Two-Year Lapse Ratio	Face Value of Insurance Sold (000)	Total Commissions Received†
			Amount	Per $1,000 Ins.				
Atlanta	41.3%	$ 8,735	$109.88	$12.53	6.2	8.4	$2,763	$2,940
Birmingham	32.7	6,606	125.60	18.90	7.0	5.2	1,588	2,350
Charlotte	29.0	14,388	193.75	13.42	4.6	13.6	1,700	2,130
Nashville	24.3	11,927	230.00	19.39	2.8	12.9	2,364	4,660
New Orleans	21.8	13,211	328.53	24.91	3.7	18.3	1,916	4,960
Tampa	18.9	9,406	140.07	15.23	4.7	6.8	2,507	3,290
Averages	27.2%	$10,928	$215.19	$19.69	4.2	10.9	$2,140	$3,390

* Prepared by John McFarland for purposes of analysis and discussion.

† Prepared by branch managers.

proposal for Acton Life and his recommendations for a course of action. Mr. McFarland agreed to submit a report of his conclusions and recommendations by October 1.

EVALUATION OF THE PROPOSAL

Over the weekend, Mr. McFarland considered how best to reach a meaningful appraisal of the proposal. He finally decided to send an abstract of it to each of his eight sales managers and to ask for their reactions to the idea of its adoption by Acton Life, either completely or in a modified form. Accordingly, on Monday, July 30, he asked his assistant to prepare such an abstract and to have it ready by the end of the week. A copy of the abstract, including four attachments, is shown in Appendix A.

After reviewing and approving the abstract, Mr. McFarland dictated a covering memorandum to his sales managers. In this memorandum, he asked them to read the entire abstract carefully and focus attention on the feasibility of its adoption by Acton Life. He also asked for written comments, both favorable and critical. In order to have the branch managers' point of view represented, he suggested that each sales manager discuss the proposal with one or two of the better managers in his region and incorporate their comments, appropriately identified, as part of the memorandum each would submit.

To ensure that the proposal would not be dismissed quickly as impractical, Mr. McFarland stated that in his opinion the concept of ECTP (expected contribution to profit), around which the proposal was constructed, appeared to have considerable merit. Although use of the concept in a system for planning and controlling branch operations would constitute a novel and somewhat radical step for a life insurance company, the concept had sufficient possibilities, he thought, to be considered seriously and with an open mind. In order to give everyone sufficient time for study and discussion, Mr. McFarland set September 15 as the deadline for submission of comments.

As of September 16, Mr. McFarland had received memoranda from all eight sales managers. He immediately began to analyze the comments in terms of the principal arguments for and against the proposal. In the process, he prepared a summary, included here as Appendix B. Five reaction patterns are highlighted in the summary:

1. Cost of implementing and administering the proposed planning and control system.
2. Method of calculating the expected contribution to profit (ECTP).
3. Concept of a profit measure at the branch level.
4. Applicability of the proposal in practice.
5. Defense of the industry.

In reviewing this summary, Mr. McFarland noted that comments by 10 branch managers had been submitted in addition to those from the 8 sales managers. The summary represented the opinions of 18 of his best managers.

With his summary before him, Mr. McFarland pondered what recommendations he should make to the president. He wanted to be sure that they resulted from an objective weighing of the advantages and disadvantages of the proposal, including a realistic appraisal of the benefits to be derived by Acton Life and the problems likely to be encountered. He also wanted to accompany his recommendations with a summary of supporting arguments, together with an action plan for implementing his recommendations.

QUESTIONS

1. Disregarding the practical problem of obtaining acceptance, do you believe the expected contribution to profit approach is conceptually sound?
2. Assuming that the approach is sound, what steps should be taken next?

Appendix A

Summary of Proposed Planning and Control System for Branches*

SCOPE OF THE PROPOSAL

This proposal applies primarily to the administrative needs of the branch manager and higher levels of management in planning and controlling the operations of branch agencies within a life insurance company. It is anticipated that parts of the proposal will also have utility for various classes of decision problems, such as the establishment of insurance premiums, the setting of commission scales, and the design of incentive systems.

* Abstracted from a Doctoral Thesis.

This proposal does not apply directly to the planning and control of central staff activities, such as the legal department or the actuarial department. However, the proposal is fully compatible with the more traditional practices for planning and controlling such staff activities.

OBJECTIVES SOUGHT BY PROPOSAL

The objectives this proposal seeks to achieve are as follows:

1. To provide a satisfactory basis for branch managers to use to relate the financial worth of results achieved to the costs incurred in order to realize these results.
2. To provide both top management and branch managers with an improved system for planning and controlling the operation of individual branches.
3. To motivate branch managers to do what is in the best interest of the company.

COMPONENTS OF THE PROPOSAL

The proposal consists essentially of two parts:

1. *Expected contribution to profit*—a measure of the worth to the company accruing from the sale of an individual policy calculated at the time of sale. Use of this measure makes possible the calculation of the contribution to the company's profit arising from the operation of any branch.
2. *Improved planning and control system*—an overall planning and control system for the management of branch agencies of life insurance companies that incorporates the above profit calculations.

EXPECTED CONTRIBUTION TO PROFIT

Nature of the Problem

A major obstacle in the way of improving systems for planning and controlling the operations of branches is the lack of an adequate measure of the worth of accomplishments or results generated by branches. Most of the measures used currently are related to the volume of policies sold, either expressed directly as the aggregate of the face value of these policies, or indirectly as premiums collected or as commissions paid. Usually, expenses of operating a branch are related to these sales figures in some way, often in the form of a ratio; the implication of this practice is that there exists a certain standard ratio (based on past performance, or a current average, or both) that indicates profitable or, at least, desirable performance. Some management personnel believe that sales volume accomplishments should not be the end-all, and that some better measure of the worth of accomplishments should be developed against which to weigh the cost of achieving these accomplishments. A few believe that the problem is one of trying to operate a profitable branch without any idea of what profits are.

Everyone interviewed agreed that the various types of insurance policies differed considerably as to their worth to the insurance company. For example, it was generally acknowledged that a company gained less from selling a $1,000 term policy than from selling a $1,000 endowment policy. However, no practical way had been found as yet to measure the difference in gain and to incorporate it into a system for planning and controlling sales efforts.

Analysis

In many industries the worth of the accomplishments of a branch was measured in terms of the gross profit on the sales volume it generates; against this were charged the expenses of acquiring this gross profit in order to arrive at the amount contributed to net profit. For the life insurance industry, this approach had never seemed possible because of accounting practices pertaining to the time the profit from a policy was realized. However, this obstacle resulted from an accounting convention, and accounting *need not* stand in the way of developing an improved measure of worth to guide the internal management of an insurance company.

As a result of discussions with management personnel, it was decided that in order to be truly useful any measure of worth should meet the following criteria:

1. Reflect the worth to the company of the sale of a particular policy.
2. Do this in monetary terms.
3. Do this as of the time a policy is sold.

If such a measure could be developed, it would make possible the calculation of a form of "profit" accruing to the company from the operation of any branch. An examination of the practice of the industry in computing premiums and of the expectations of the industry regarding actual performance in the three areas making up this premium calculation suggested that such a measure could be developed.

Basically, every life insurance premium was developed from three separate factors: a projected mortality rate, a projected interest rate, and a projected loading charge. Realistically, also, companies considered competition in setting a final premium; in practice, this consideration usually resulted in an adjustment in the loading factor. Given the three factors, insurance actuaries calculated an approximate premium for any kind of policy the company cared to sell.

All three of these factors in practice were deliberately set conservatively. Because the projected mortality rate was based on the actual mortality rate during some *past* period, companies were, in effect, assuming that the mortality rate was higher than it actually would be. But the mortality rate actually had been decreasing steadily over the years, and this trend was expected to continue. Thus, with the collection of every premium, the company expected a gain from overestimating mortality.

In projecting interest rates, companies tended to be very conservative in their estimates of the rate of return they would earn on their investments. The actual return on investments usually was higher than the assumed return; thus, the premium resulted in a gain from the interest assumption.

Finally, companies tended to overestimate the total loading charge required, thereby creating a third expected gain. In a stock company, a profit allowance usually was included as an explicit element of the loading charge, whereas in a mutual company an equivalent result was produced by the deliberate overstatement of costs.

In sum, then, because of the current practices of computing life insurance premiums, companies expected a gain from savings from the allowance for mortality, excess interest earned, and the loading charge.

Proposed Solution

Therefore, it was argued, there was built into every life insurance premium an expected contribution to profit (hereafter referred to as ECTP). This ECTP occurred *at the time of sale* of a policy. It was further argued that this ECTP could be calculated and that this figure could serve the purpose of a "profit" figure for a branch. These conclusions were valid because *at the time of sale*, for each policy sold, one could calculate:

1. *The expected gain included in the mortality charge.* This was the difference between the premium actually charged—based on the assumption that projected mortality experience would parallel past mortality experience—and the premium that would be needed to cover *expected* mortality. That is, the mortality rate actually experienced would not be so high as assumed, death benefits would not be paid out so soon as assumed, and, therefore, companies would have more of the insurance premiums left for contribution to profits. In computing annuity premiums, insurance companies actually employed mortality rates lower than those they employed in computing life insurance premiums. A company's expectations regarding future mortality experience would fall somewhere between these two sets of rates.
2. *The expected gain from the interest charge.* This was the difference between the premium actually charged—based on a conservative assumption as to interest earned on investments—and the premium that would be charged if it were based on *expected* interest earnings. For most companies, estimates of future earning rates on their investments were regularly made by their investment departments.
3. *The expected gain from the loading charge.* This was the difference between the total amount of loading in a particular premium and the actual amount of variable expense of selling that policy (commissions, medical fees, taxes on premiums, and so forth). Although the separation of variable expenses might be difficult to make, it was generally considered to be feasible. Even if this separation

could not be made with a high degree of accuracy, the resulting error would be constant for all policies, and thus its effect on the proposed planning and control system would be minor.

Thus, for each year a particular policy was expected to be in force, an expected gain could be calculated *at the time of sale*. The present value of this stream of expected year-by-year gains from each policy sold is the *expected contribution to profit*. This represents the additional *worth* to the company *now* of selling a particular policy.

Given this calculation of ECTP, a branch manager could exercise intelligent control over his responsibility for the acquisition of business. This would be accomplished by relating the total ECTP of a branch to its cost of acquiring business.

Example Showing Calculation of ECTP

To illustrate the foregoing description, a sample calculation of ECTP is presented for a $1,000 term insurance policy with a life of 20 years sold to a man, age 35, with premium payments to be made over the first 10 years. Although this is not one of the common types of policies offered by life insurance companies, it does involve most of the calculation techniques that need to be employed for the more common types—straight life insurance, limited payment life, endowment.

Mortality. Let us assume that the company uses a standard mortality table, such as the 1941 Commissioners Standard Ordinary Mortality Table, for setting premiums on its policies. This, then, is the company's *projected* mortality table. However, the company really *expects* mortality to be lower than that assumed in this table; an *expected* mortality table can readily be developed for this purpose.

Interest. Let us assume that this company uses a 2.5 percent interest rate in calculating its premiums, and that its investment department *expects* it to earn 3 percent on its investments.

Calculation of Net Premium.[1] Given the foregoing assumptions and the facts regarding the type of policy, we can proceed to calculate the net premium on both a *projected* and an *expected* basis. These calculations are shown in Attachments A and B.

In each year of the life of the policy (20 years), the company assumes that it will pay out the face amount of a fraction of all such policies, equal to the projected mortality rate for the particular age of the insured in that year. By applying appropriate discount factors for the projected rate of earnings on the company's investments (2.5 percent), the present value of the stream of such projected payments over the life of the policy can be computed. This series of calculations is summarized on the left-hand side of Attachment A. The present value of this stream of projected payments is $124.78.

[1] Net premium takes account of mortality and interest only. Loading must be added to arrive at the gross premium which the insured is charged.

The policy in the example calls for the payment of premiums by the insured over the first 10 years that the policy is in force or until his death, if he dies in that period. Thus, the company anticipates that it will receive a premium payment during each of these 10 years from the insured, who survive until the next year when another premium is due. By applying the same series of discount factors and structuring the calculation on the basis of each dollar of net premiums received, the company can compute the present value of such premium payments. This series of calculations is summarized on the right-hand side of Attachment A. The present value of this stream of receipts is 8.77 per dollar of net premium.

The net premium for this policy is that amount which equates the present value of these two streams. It is computed by dividing the first present value figure by the second figure: $124.78 ÷ 8.77 = $14.24. The resulting figure is the *projected* net premium for this sample policy. This is the type of calculation actually made by the actuarial department of an insurance company in arriving at net premiums.

The *expected* net premium is calculated in exactly the same way. The only differences in the calculations result from the substitution of *expected* values in place of *projected* values for death rates, survival rates, and interest rates (Attachment B).

On the basis of the calculations shown in Attachment A, the projected net premium is $14.24; this is the net premium to be included as a part of the gross premium charged the insured. By charging this premium, the company expects a composite gain from mortality and from interest equal to $4.09 ($14.24 less $10.15, the net premium calculated on an expected basis—from Attachment B). The expected gain from mortality alone is $3.61, and that from interest alone is 40 cents; the remainder of the total gain—8 cents—results partially from mortality and partially from interest. This total gain of $4.09 is expected for each year the policy remains in force.

Calculation of Gross Premium. To calculate the gross premium, a loading charge is added to the net premium (projected basis). This loading charge is determined on the basis of a loading formula, which is usually stated in terms of a percentage of net or gross premium and a fixed amount per $1,000 of insurance. For this example, we shall assume that this loading comes to $6.65. Thus, the gross premium is calculated to be $20.89 ($14.24 plus $6.65). For each such $1,000 policy sold now, the company would expect to collect $20.89 each year for the next 10 years, assuming that the policy remained in force.

Expected Contribution to Profit. Of the gross premium of $20.89, the company *expects* that $10.15 will be added to the reserve for death claims, on which a 3 percent return will be earned. In selling this policy, the company also *expects* to incur incremental expenses equal to the variable portion of the costs built into the loading formula. By subtracting both the $10.15 and the variable costs in the loading from the gross premium, a figure is obtained

Attachment A

CALCULATION OF PROJECTED NET PREMIUM FOR 10-PAYMENT, 20-YEAR TERM POLICY, BASED ON PROJECTED MORTALITY AT 2.5 PERCENT

Calculation of Present Value of Projected Death Claim Payments over Life of Policy

Age of Insured	Projected Death Rate per 1,000	×	Face Value of Policy	×	Discount Factor	=	Present Value
35	4.590		$1,000		.9756		$ 4.48
36	4.838		1,000		.9518		4.60
37	5.102		1,000		.9286		4.74
38	5.381		1,000		.9060		4.88
39	5.694		1,000		.8839		5.03
40	6.022		1,000		.8623		5.19
41	6.381		1,000		.8413		5.37
42	6.763		1,000		.8207		5.55
43	7.173		1,000		.8007		5.74
44	7.622		1,000		.7812		5.95
45	8.097		1,000		.7621		6.17
46	8.605		1,000		.7436		6.40
47	9.154		1,000		.7254		6.64
48	9.731		1,000		.7077		6.89
49	10.360		1,000		.6905		7.15
50	11.020		1,000		.6736		7.42
51	11.724		1,000		.6572		7.71
52	12.466		1,000		.6412		7.99
53	13.259		1,000		.6255		8.29
54	14.086		1,000		.6103		8.60
Total Present Value (X)							$124.78

*Calculation of Present Value of Projected Premium Payments per Dollar of Net Premium**

Age of Insured	Projected Survival Rate	×	Dollar of Net Premium	×	Discount Factor	=	Present Value
35	1.0000*		$1.00		1.0000		$1.00
36	0.9954		1.00		.9756		0.97
37	0.9906		1.00		.9518		0.94
38	0.9855		1.00		.9286		0.92
39	0.9801		1.00		.9060		0.89
40	0.9744		1.00		.8839		0.86
41	0.9684		1.00		.8623		0.84
42	0.9620		1.00		.8413		0.81
43	0.9552		1.00		.8207		0.78
44	0.9481		1.00		.8007		0.76
Total Present Value (Y)							$8.77

$$\text{Net Premium} = \frac{(X)}{(Y)} = \frac{\$124.78}{\$8.77} = \$14.24$$

* First premium payment due immediately.

Attachment B

CALCULATION OF EXPECTED NET PREMIUM FOR 10-PAYMENT, 20-YEAR TERM POLICY, BASED ON EXPECTED MORTALITY AT 3 PERCENT

Calculation of Present Value of Expected Death Claim Payments over Life of Policy

Age of Insured	*Expected Death Rate per 1,000*	×	*Face Value of Policy*	×	*Discount Factor*	=	*Present Value*
35	2.981		$1,000		.9709		$ 2.89
36	3.206		1,000		.9426		3.02
37	3.448		1,000		.9151		3.16
38	3.706		1,000		.8885		3.29
39	3.984		1,000		.8626		3.44
40	4.280		1,000		.8375		3.58
41	4.598		1,000		.8131		3.74
42	4.935		1,000		.7894		3.90
43	5.297		1,000		.7664		4.06
44	5.683		1,000		.7441		4.23
45	6.094		1,000		.7224		4.40
46	6.532		1,000		.7014		4.58
47	6.998		1,000		.6810		4.77
48	7.490		1,000		.6611		4.95
49	8.016		1,000		.6419		5.15
50	8.571		1,000		.6232		5.34
51	9.158		1,000		.6050		5.54
52	9.779		1,000		.5874		5.74
53	10.432		1,000		.5703		5.95
54	11.119		1,000		.5537		6.16
Total Present Value (X)							$87.89

*Calculation of Present Value of Expected Premium Payments per Dollar of Net Premium**

Age of Insured	*Expected Survival Rate*	×	*Dollar of Net Premium*	×	*Discount Factor*	=	*Present Value*
35	1.0000*		$1.00		1.0000		$1.00
36	0.9970		1.00		.9709		.97
37	0.9938		1.00		.9426		.94
38	0.9904		1.00		.9151		.91
39	0.9867		1.00		.8885		.88
40	0.9827		1.00		.8626		.85
41	0.9784		1.00		.8375		.82
42	0.9738		1.00		.8131		.79
43	0.9689		1.00		.7894		.76
44	0.9636		1.00		.7664		.74
Total Present Value (Y)							$8.66

$$\text{Net Premium} = \frac{(X)}{(Y)} = \frac{\$87.89}{\$8.66} = \$10.15$$

* First premium payment due immediately.

which is the yearly expected contribution resulting from the sale of this policy. These computations are summarized in Attachment C.

All that remains is to compute the present value of these expected annual contributions in order to determine the ECTP from selling this policy.

In order to make this computation, it is necessary to select a discount rate—that is, a rate by which we may calculate the present value of the annual contributions to profit. For this particular application, the rate selected should provide for the likelihood that a portion of the total number of policies of this particular type of insurance will lapse during each year because of death or surrender as well as for the time value of money. For this example, a lapse ratio of 5 percent and an opportunity cost of money of 3 percent[2] are employed for these two purposes, respectively; the mathematical combination of the two factors yields a single discount rate of approximately 8 percent.[3] Applying the discount factors for this rate to the annual contributions calculated in Attachment C gives a present value of $42.72; this amount is the ECTP that can be said to result from selling this policy.

Use of ECTP

The suggested method of making an ECTP calculation provides a valid profit figure at the branch level. It measures the additional current worth to the company of the sales made by a branch. And it is available at the time decisions regarding selling efforts are being made.

Admittedly, this figure is not a precise measure of realized profits in an accounting sense. Since we must necessarily be looking to the future in any such calculation, and since the future is filled with uncertainties, the results of such a calculation must necessarily have a high likelihood of being different from the profit actually realized.

This fact is of no practical concern, however. The principal objective of the concept of ECTP is to make available as good a figure as possible for planning and control purposes. Certainly, the best profit figure available at the time a relevant decision is to be made (realizing that this may be something less than perfectly accurate) will be more useful than a perfectly accurate figure (if there is such a thing) that is not available until sometime after the decision has been made.

The concept of ECTP also provides a new tool for use in analysis of different types of policies. Most companies now rely on first-year premiums or face value of policies sold as a measure of accomplishment, and both branch managers and salesmen generally are motivated to achieve as high a volume of either one (or both) as possible. Yet, it is obvious that neither first-year

---

[2] For an insurance company, the opportunity cost of money is the rate of return it expects to earn on the incremental investments in its portfolio.

[3] These two discount factors are combined mathematically as follows:

$$1/(1.05)^n \times 1/(1.03)^n = 1/(1.0815)^n.$$

Attachment C

CALCULATION OF EXPECTED CONTRIBUTION TO PROFIT

Year	(1) Gross Premium Collected	(2) Expected Net Premium	(3) Variable Loading Expenses as a Percentage of Gross Premium						(4) Expected Survival Rate	(5) Annual Contribution to Profit [(1) − (2) − (3)] × (4)	(6) Discount at 8%	(7) ECTP (5) × (6)
			55%	33%	27%	5%	2%	2%				
0	$20.89	$10.15	$11.49	$6.89	$5.64	—	—	$0.42	1.000	$(13.70)	1.000	$(13.70)
1	20.89	10.15	—	—	—	$1.04	$0.42	0.42	.997	8.83	.959	8.47
2	20.89	10.15	—	—	—	1.04	0.42	0.42	.994	8.81	.888	7.82
3	20.89	10.15	—	—	—	1.04	0.42	0.42	.990	8.77	.823	7.22
4	20.89	10.15	—	—	—	1.04	0.42	0.42	.987	8.74	.762	6.66
5	20.89	10.15	—	—	—	1.04	0.42	0.42	.983	8.71	.705	6.14
6	20.89	10.15	—	—	—	1.04	0.42	0.42	.978	8.67	.653	5.66
7	20.89	10.15	—	—	—	1.04	0.42	0.42	.974	8.63	.605	5.22
8	20.89	10.15	—	—	—	1.04	0.42	0.42	.969	8.59	.560	4.81
9	20.89	10.15	—	—	—	1.04	0.42	0.42	.964	8.54	.518	4.42
												$42.72

NOTES: Present Value of Annual Contributions to Profit at 8% is $42.72.
Expected Contribution to Profit as a result of selling this policy is $42.72.

premiums nor face value of policies sold necessarily indicates any relation to profitability or worth to the company. To the extent that a reasonable profit measure for individual policies is made available, branch managers will be far better able to direct their sales forces to work in the interests of the company. Through the use of this concept, salesmen may be induced to concentrate on the more profitable policies and to relate their selling efforts to the ECTP of a policy rather than to the first-year premium or face value.

IMPROVED PLANNING AND CONTROL SYSTEM

Essentials of a Planning and Control System

In devising a planning and control system, one must take into consideration the purposes for which the system will be used. For planning purposes, the system should provide the best information available in order that management may be able to make intelligent decisions. These decisions may be nonrecurring (whether to open a new branch) or recurring (how to operate a branch). For control purposes, the system should provide information needed by management to measure conformance to plans and to identify causes of deviations from plans.

A sound *planning* effort embraces the following factors:

1. *A profit orientation.* For a stock company, the reason is obvious. The company is in business to make a profit for its stockholders; therefore, it must relate all its plans to the profit motive.

2. *An operational tool.* Since plans must be carried out by operating people (sales managers, not budget committees), they must be expressed in terms that will be meaningful to the decision-makers at the operating level.

3. *A plan of action.* Often, a plan is confused with a forecast. A forecast is simply an extrapolation of the past into the future, based on certain expectations of the future. A plan, on the other hand, should be a projected statement of results and the cost of attaining those results, based on specific actions that management intends to take in order to achieve the stated results.

The main requirement for effective *control* by management is that the control portion of the planning and control system it uses is tied to the planning portion so that managers are motivated to use it to achieve the results set out in the operating plan. The essentials of a control system are these:

1. *A measure of performance.* Actual performance must be measured and related to planned performance. Deviations from the plan and reasons for the deviations must be determined.

2. *A responsibility center.* Performance measures must be associated with the people who are responsible for, or who can affect, performance. (For this proposal, these are the branch managers.) The intent of this requirement is not necessarily to fix blame but to make a responsible supervisor aware of the effect of his daily decisions. As he becomes aware of his responsibility, he can be expected to make his decisions in light of plans and goals previously set forth.

In brief, then, an effective planning and control system enables a company to set goals in meaningful terms and to measure the attainment of those goals. The system should be so designed as to create an environment such that each responsible supervisor, acting in his own interests, will be motivated to make decisions that are in the best interests of the company as a whole.

Key Features of Proposed System

The core of the proposed planning and control system is the establishment of each branch as a profit center, with the branch manager as the responsible supervisor. The appropriate profit figure for a particular branch is the ECTP earned by the branch minus the expenses incurred by that branch in generating this ECTP. Operating plans are expressed in terms of ECTP and the expenses needed to achieve that ECTP. Actual expenses are deducted from the ECTP actually generated by the branch to determine the profit contributed by the branch; this total profit then is compared to the planned profit. Deviations from planned performance are shown for each element of ECTP and expense. The analysis of these deviations and the taking of appropriate corrective action are vital elements in the proposed planning and control system.

In designing this system, a company must take two vital precautions: (1) to match with ECTP only those expenses incurred to generate ECTP and (2) to limit the expenses chargeable to a branch to only those controllable at the branch level.

Looking at the second requirement first, we see that various kinds of expenses incurred in the operation of a branch are controllable to a significant extent by the branch manager. Some are controllable only over a fairly long period of time, whereas others are controllable to a considerable extent on a day-to-day basis. In recognition of this variation in controllability as a function of time, all branch expenses are segregated, under the proposal, into three classifications—long-range controllable expenses, annual controllable expenses, and day-to-day expenses. The expenses segregated in each of these categories are as follows:

Long-Range Controllable Expenses	*Annual Controllable Expenses*
Rent	Management salaries
Depreciation: furniture	Advertising
equipment	Training
	Net advances to salesmen

Day-to-Day Expenses

Clerical salaries	Travel
Postage	Entertainment
Stationery and supplies	Loss on advances to salesmen
Telephone and telegraph	Miscellaneous
Repairs and maintenance	

Attachment D

HYPOTHETICAL LIFE INSURANCE COMPANY PROFIT SCHEDULE, 1963

Branch A
Profit Schedule, 1963

	Total		*Service*		*Acquisition*			
	Budget (a)	*Actual* (b)	*Budget* (c)	*Standard Allowance** (d)	*Budget* (e)	*Actual* (f)	*Variance* (g)	(h)
Expected Contribution to Profit								
Baker	$ 30,000	$ 36,000	—	—	$ 30,000	$ 36,000	$ 6,000	20%
Donovan	30,000	33,000	—	—	30,000	33,000	3,000	10
George	15,000	12,000	—	—	15,000	12,000	(3,000)	(20)
Henderson	5,000	4,000	—	—	5,000	4,000	(1,000)	(20)
Levin	35,000	31,000	—	—	35,000	31,000	(4,000)	(11)
Lannigan	60,000	65,000	—	—	60,000	65,000	5,000	8
Ramos	40,000	39,000	—	—	40,000	39,000	(1,000)	(2)
New hires—three	5,000	7,000	—	—	5,000	7,000	2,000	40
Total ECTP	$220,000	$227,000			$220,000	$227,000	$ 7,000	
Controllable Branch Expenses								
Long range:								
Rent	$ 6,600	$ 6,600	—	—	$ 6,600	$ 6,600	$ 0	0
Depreciation on furniture and equipment	400	400	—	—	400	400	0	0
Annual:								
Management salaries	17,000	17,000	—	—	17,000	17,000	0	0
Advertising	5,000	4,800	—	—	5,000	4,800	(200)	(4)
Training	1,000	750	—	—	1,000	750	(250)	(25)
Net advances to salesmen	2,500	3,600	—	—	2,500	3,600	1,100	44

Clerical salaries	29,000	30,000	$7,000	$7,575	22,000	22,425	425	2
Postage	1,100	1,200	200	196	900	1,004	104	12
Stationery and supplies	1,500	1,600	360	400	1,140	1,200	60	5
Telephone and telegraph	3,400	3,600	—	—	3,400	3,600	200	6
Repairs and maintenance	500	100	—	—	500	100	(400)	(80)
Entertainment	1,500	1,400	—	—	1,500	1,400	(100)	(7)
Travel	2,800	3,000	—	—	2,800	3,000	200	7
Loss on advances	500	1,500	—	—	500	1,500	1,000	200
Miscellaneous	600	560	—	—	600	560	(40)	(7)
Total Expenses	$ 73,400	$ 76,110	$7,560	$8,171	$ 65,840	$ 67,939	$ 2,099	
Branch profit					$154,160	$159,061	$ 4,901	
Home office support						$150,000		
Net profit						$ 9,061		
Lapse ratio					5.0%	4.7%		

* *Service Allowance:*

	Number of Units	Standard Time	Average Clerical Salary	Standard Clerical Cost	Total Clerical Cost
1. Clerical Salaries					
PNBB	650	4 hrs.	$1.50/hr.	$6.00	$3900
Collecting Premiums	1300	1½ "	"	2.25	2925
Paying Claims	500	1 "	"	1.50	750
Total	2450				$7575

2. Postage: $0.08 × 2450 units = $196.
3. Stationery and supplies: 25.1% of $1,600 = $400.

Total—Budget and Actual: the total amount of ECTP generated by each component (i.e., salesman), and the total of each class of expense.

Service—Budget and Standard Allowance: the allowances credited to the branch for the performance of its service functions. Calculation of these allowances is shown at the bottom of the report.

Acquisition—Budget: for each line item, the amount in the Total, Budget column less the *budgeted* amount for each service allowance.

Acquisition—Actual: for each line item, the amount in the Total, Actual column less the allowance (if any) in the Service, Standard column.

Variance, $: for each line item, the dollar difference resulting from the subtraction of the amount in the Acquisition, Budget column from the amount in the Acquisition, Actual column. Negative amounts are shown in parentheses. For components of ECTP, positive values are favorable variances and negative values are unfavorable variances. For elements of expense, negative values represent overspending and positive values underspending; whether these variances are favorable or unfavorable can be judged only in the light of the particular circumstances giving rise to the variance.

Variance, %: the magnitude of the dollar variance shown in the preceding column expressed as a percentage of the amount in the Acquisition, Budget column.

The first requirement can be understood best by regarding the mission of a branch agency as consisting of two functions: (1) the acquisition function, or the job of selling insurance policies; (2) the service function, or the job of maintaining insurance in force. The expenses incurred for the service function do not create, or result in, ECTP. Therefore, these service expenses should be excluded from the matching of branch expenses against ECTP.

These service expenses can be classified in the following three categories:

1. *Putting new business on the books:* checking over the application and other forms to see that everything is in order, setting up the appropriate accounting records, and mailing out the policy.
2. *Collecting premiums:* sending out bills, changing beneficiaries, arranging for loans, and performing other routine service.
3. *Paying claims:* final disbursement of cash, closing the records, and carrying out other details involved in terminating a policy.

The procedure for excluding these service expenses from the determination of the profit contributed by a branch consists of the following basic steps. Clerical time standards are established for each of these service activities; this may be done on the basis of time and motion studies, although an average of actual past performance could serve the purpose. The number of units of work (e.g., number of premiums processed or number of new applications processed) actually handled by a branch are multiplied by the time standard for the particular unit, and the resulting number of standard hours is multiplied by the average clerical wage at a particular branch. The resulting dollar figure is an allowance or credit for the service work performed during a reporting period by the branch. This expense credit is deducted from the appropriate expense classification, with the balance of these expenses charged to the acquisition function. Nonclerical service expenses (e.g., supplies) are credited in the same proportion that the clerical cost allowance bears to the total of clerical expense.

Example of Proposed Control Report

A hypothetical control report to be employed in the proposed planning and control system is shown as Attachment D. The report relates to the operations of a particular branch and covers the calendar year 1963. The first portion of the report presents the components of ECTP, identified by the individual salesmen who have generated the ECTP by their sales activities. The middle portion presents the various expenses of operating a branch, grouped by controllability classification. Below the line for total expenses are three lines involving profits: branch profit, the difference between actual ECTP and the total actual expenses; home office support, an allocation of the fixed expenses of running the home office; and net profit, the amount remaining after the allocated home office expense has been deducted from the branch profit. The reason for this deduction is simply that the branch profit figure otherwise will always seem high, both because it gives credit (through ECTP) for profit not yet realized and because it is, in fact, only a contribution to profit. The purpose of this deduction is to make the manager aware of the amount of support he is receiving from the home office and to which the branch must contribute. For other purposes, the branch profit or ECTP is the appropriate figure.

Eight columns of figures are presented in the Profit Schedule (Attachment D).

Appendix B

Summary of Managers' Comments on Proposal

Cost of Implementing and Administering the Proposed Planning and Control System

Six comments related to the cost consequences of adopting the proposal. Four men felt that the proposed system would be much more costly than the present system; there would have to be an ECTP figure for each policy, and new calculations would have to be made each year on the basis of expected figures; present measures were really good enough. One man also felt the proposal might be more costly than the present system, but it would be worthwhile to devote some effort to finding out. One man felt that cost of proposal seemed high, "but people often don't realize how costly the present system really is." If the proposal were adopted, it would substitute in many instances for work already being done and would eliminate the need for doing some other work. He felt, however, that a straight cost comparison was not valid; the important consideration was whether or not the proposed system would supply better information and thus make possible better decisions; in particular, the motivation of branch managers would be better directed.

Method of Calculation of ECTP

Eight comments related to the method of calculating ECTP. All eight men felt that the calculation was headed in the right direction, assuming that some sort of profit figure at the branch level was wanted; the idea of a gain from mortality, a gain from interest, and taking the present value of the expected cash flow was believed to be sound if one wanted to do this kind of thing. The idea of earning a contribution to overhead was not very well understood.

Three men wondered why there was not expected gain from loading. Two men said the calculation made a lot of sense to them; for the first time, they had an idea of what actuaries did. Three stated that if the calculation could be made they would have little trouble applying it pretty much as suggested in the proposal.

Concept of a Profit Measure at the Branch Level

Sixteen comments pertained to the idea of employing a profit measure for the planning and control of branch operations.

Three men felt that the concept of profit was not appropriate in the life insurance business; life insurance companies, through their salesmen, should sell insurance on the basis of people's needs; salesmen generally were trained first to recognize a client's insurance needs and then to try to satisfy those needs with the client's available funds; if profits became a matter of concern, salesmen and branch managers would be induced to try to sell the more profitable policies rather than to satisfy clients' needs.

Thirteen men believed the concept was useful, the extent of usefulness ranging from limited to broad.

> At one extreme—limited usefulness: A regional manager stated that he had asked the actuarial department to make this kind of calculation from time to time just to see how various branches were making out, but he doubted that the information would be useful to managers in general.
>
> At other extreme: A branch manager commented that it was just the tool he needed to do his best job; if he could somehow relate his decisions to the effect they would have on company profits, he would make better decisions in the long run and also would have an easier time making them.

Several men commented that they always had thought something like this should be done, but either had not pursued it or had not been able to convince others of the merit of the idea.

Applicability of the Proposal in Practice

Of the 13 men who had positive, favorable reactions, in varying degrees, to the concept of a profit measure at the branch level, 10 made comments on how well they expected the proposal would work in actual practice.

Five men felt it would work, with the following qualifications:

One suggested that it be tried out on a few branches to see how it worked.
One was uncertain whether the calculation actually could be made.
Three suggested that the proposal be reviewed by a committee.

Five men believed that the proposal could work, but would not work in actual practice because of lack of acceptance; reasons for this opinion were categorized as follows:

Tradition: Sales volume had always been the accepted measure of accomplishment in the insurance industry; almost everyone had become accustomed to this orientation; trying to effect such a radical change as substituting a profit measure for a sales measure would take a long, long time.

Status: Certain people, both within the company and within the industry in general, who had achieved positions of prominence on the basis of the traditional volume measures would not have been promoted to such positions if their performance had been measured by their profit contribution (best example was those who sold mostly group insurance); a number of such people were in key positions in top management; these people were not likely to act favorably on a proposal that as much as told them they were not so important as they had imagined, and probably should not be in the positions of prominence they currently occupied.

Profit Image: A lot of people in the industry would not like others' talking about the insurance business as being profit oriented; the image of a life insurance company as a benevolent institution catering to the public good should not be risked.

Defense of the Industry

Three comments were categorized as a defense of current practices of the life insurance industry; they focused on the importance of being conservative in one's expectations about the future (e.g., mortality tables, interest assumptions, and loading expenses), especially in light of the public interest being served and the indefinite nature of the business.

Case 8–2

Metropolitan Bank (A)

Metropolitan Bank, with deposits averaging well over a billion dollars, was one of the largest banks in the United States. Its banking operations were conducted in a main office and several dozen branch offices located throughout the metropolitan area it served. A partial organization chart is shown in Exhibit 1.

Exhibit 1

METROPOLITAN BANK
Partial Organization Chart

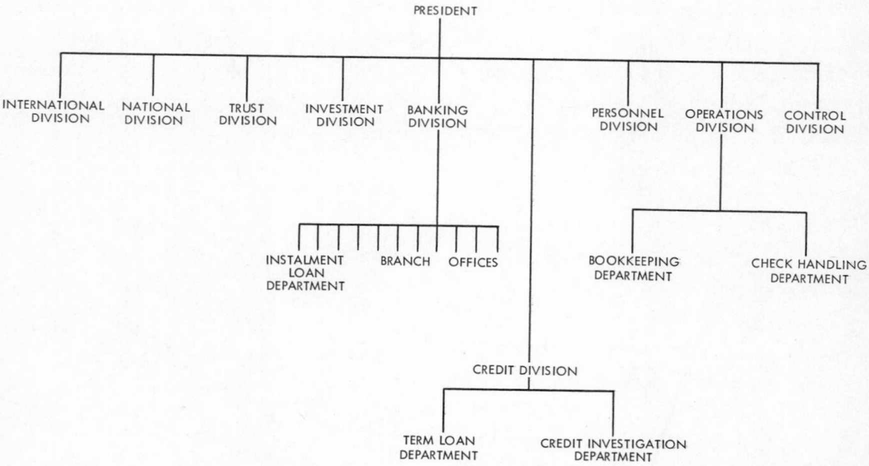

Branch offices operated as if they were independent banks. They served individual, commercial, and industrial customers by accepting demand, savings, and time deposits, by extending various types of loans, and by performing other services normally expected of a bank. The sizes and operating characteristics of the branches varied over a wide range. Average deposits outstanding ranged from $1 million to over $100 million; average loans outstanding, from no loans to over $100 million. Moreover, the ratio of deposits to loans varied considerably from one branch to another; most branches had more deposits than loans, but a few had more loans than deposits. In brief, both the magnitude and composition of assets and liabilities were significantly different among the different branches. Inasmuch as these differences were related to the geographical location of the branches, the difficulty of evaluating and comparing the performances of branches for the purpose of overall planning and control was inherent in the situation. The design and operation of a planning and control system for this purpose was the responsibility of the control division.

Among various reports reaching top management, the quarterly comparative earnings statement (see Exhibits 2 and 3) played a central role in the evaluation of branch performance. The report was designed to show the extent to which branches attained three important goals: (1) branches should operate within their budgets; (2) branches should grow in deposits and loans; and (3) branches should earn satisfactory profits. Accordingly, the statement showed for each branch the budgeted and actual amounts of deposits and loans outstanding, and income, expenses, and earnings for the current quarter, the year to date, and the year to date for the preceding year.

BUDGET

In early November, each branch prepared a budget for the following year for submission to headquarters of the banking division and to top management. The branches were furnished a booklet containing sample forms, 24 pages of detailed instructions, and a brief set of policy guides from top management to facilitate the preparation of their budgets. The policy guide for 1961 is given in its entirety in Exhibit 4. The instructions gave the procedures to be followed in arriving at the budget amounts for specific items. It was, for instance, specified that the starting point for forecasting was to be the prior year's figures on the quarterly basis, that the income item interest on loans was to be derived from the projected volume of loans and loan rates, that painting cost should not be included in the item for building maintenance expense, and so on.

Since Salaries was the biggest single expense item, and the hiring and releasing of employees involved considerable cost, utmost care was required in budgeting this item. Branches were instructed to arrive at staffing requirements for the next year after a thorough examination of anticipated increases in productivity arising from mechanization or otherwise improved operating procedures, of anticipated changes in the volume of activity, and of advantages and disadvantages of using overtime or temporary or part-time help. If the number of the required staff of a branch thus determined exceeded the

Exhibit 2

COMPARATIVE STATEMENT OF EARNINGS, 1960

Branch A

(Dollars)

3rd Quarter 1960 *Actual*	1960 *Budget*		*January 1 thru September 30* 1960 *Actual*	1960 *Budget*	1959 *Actual*
		Income:			
13,177	12,600	Interest on loans	33,748	35,200	
6,373	4,800	Service chgs.—regular A/C's.	14,572	14,100	
3,816	3,600	Service chgs.—special ck.	11,114	10,700	
1,168	1,300	Safe deposit rentals	4,317	4,500	
2,237	2,154	Installment loans (net)	5,126	5,406	
—	—	Special loans (net)	—	—	
1,010	1,200	Fees, comm., other income	3,321	3,300	
27,781	25,654	Total Direct Income	72,198	73,206	
104,260	102,148	Interest on excess (borr.) funds	324,434	306,166	
132,041	127,802	Gross Income	396,632	379,372	
		Expenses:			
32,363	32,617	Salaries	96,151	97,164	
2,955	2,955	Deferred compensation	8,865	8,865	
5,232	4,689	Employee benefits	14,925	14,067	
11,485	11,489	Rent and occupancy	34,398	33,947	
6,824	7,560	Interest on deposits	20,455	21,780	
9,458	8,090	Other direct	25,688	23,930	
3,128	3,097	Office administration	9,676	9,725	
19,183	17,642	Service departments	57,059	52,399	
6,415	5,061	Indirect and overhead	14,964	14,273	
97,043	93,200	Gross Expenses	282,181	276,150	
34,998	34,602	Net Earnings before Taxes	114,451	103,222	
18,955	18,741	Income tax prov. (credit)	61,987	55,906	
16,043	15,861	Net Earnings after Taxes	52,464	47,316	
12,655,000	12,550,000	Average deposits—Demand	13,134,000	12,650,000	
979,000	1,100,000	Savings	986,000	1,057,000	
55,000	55,000	Time	40,000	43,000	
233,000	190,000	U.S.	213,000	183,000	
13,922,000	13,895,000	Total	14,373,000	13,933,000	
900,000	870,000	Average loans	775,000	827,000	
5.82	5.76	Average loan rate	5.82	5.69	
		Earning rate on:			
4.08	3.95	Excess (borr.) funds	4.05	3.95	
6.50	6.40	Savings deposits	6.46	6.40	
26.5%	27.1%	Net earnings ratio (before taxes)	28.9%	27.2%	
		Memo:			
—	—	Losses—before taxes	—	—	
—	—	Recoveries—before taxes	—	—	

Exhibit 3

COMPARATIVE STATEMENT OF EARNINGS, 1960

Branch B

(Dollars)

3rd Quarter 1960 Actual	3rd Quarter 1960 Budget		January 1 thru September 30 1960 Actual	January 1 thru September 30 1960 Budget	1959 Actual
		Income:			
951,617	833,300	Interest on loans	2,646,813	2,202,750	
7,015	7,400	Service chgs.—regular A/C's.	24,020	21,900	
8,211	7,600	Service chgs.—special ck.	23,384	22,600	
2,049	2,100	Safe deposit rentals	6,712	7,100	
9,202	9,478	Installment loans (net)	21,402	23,790	
—	212	Special loans (net)	85	556	
8,081	3,100	Fees, comm., other income	22,517	12,800	
986,175	863,190	Total Direct Income	2,744,933	2,291,496	
(191,650)	(121,960)	Interest on excess (borr.) funds	(430,444)	(121,493)	
794,525	741,230	Gross Income	2,314,489	2,170,003	
		Expenses:			
69,308	62,633	Salaries	197,572	185,634	
5,646	5,646	Deferred compensation	16,938	16,938	
9,180	7,989	Employee benefits	25,833	23,967	
27,674	27,775	Rent and occupancy	82,726	83,375	
15,878	18,230	Interest on deposits	47,589	52,650	
25,637	23,660	Other direct	86,112	71,400	
17,232	17,072	Office administration	53,321	53,606	
89,724	95,719	Service departments	290,082	283,531	
22,406	18,001	Indirect and overhead	53,643	51,166	
282,685	276,725	Gross Expenses	853,816	822,267	
511,840	464,505	Net Earnings before Taxes	1,460,673	1,347,736	
277,212	251,576	Income tax prov. (credit)	791,100	729,934	
234,628	212,929	Net Earnings after Taxes	669,573	617,802	
67,901,000	70,000,000	Average deposits—Demand	69,425,000	72,667,000	
2,354,000	2,700,000	Savings	2,328,000	2,600,000	
74,000	90,000	Time	52,000	66,000	
5,194,000	1,900,000	U.S.	4,086,000	1,733,000	
75,523,000	74,690,000	Total	75,891,000	77,066,000	
72,129,000	65,000,000	Average loans	67,446,000	57,666,000	
5.25	5.10	Average loan rate	5.24	5.10	
		Earning rate on:			
4.08	3.95	Excess (borr.) funds	4.05	3.95	
6.50	6.40	Savings deposits	6.46	6.40	
64.4%	62.7%	Net earnings ratio (before taxes)	63.1%	62.1%	
		Memo:			
—	—	Losses—before taxes	5,559	—	
66	—	Recoveries—before taxes	798	—	

Exhibit 4

COVERING MEMORANDUM FOR 1961 BUDGET INSTRUCTIONS

It is customary for the committee to summarize for your general guidance current thinking regarding deposits, loans, and loan rates. The expectations outlined below are for the overall bank. Therefore, it is important that the head of each earning unit analyze the impact of expected general economic trends on the conditions peculiar to his own area of activity in order to project specific goals which he may reasonably expect to attain.

Deposits

There is every indication that money market conditions will be such that demand deposit levels in our area will expand. In our judgment, we anticipate at least a 5 percent growth in demand deposits for all banks. Our overall goal, however, should be set somewhat higher to reflect an improvement in our relative position. Savings deposits will continue to climb moderately. Current rates for time and savings deposits should be used to project interest costs.

Loans and Loan Rates

In all probability loan demand will slacken seasonally in the early months of 1961; in fact, many economists believe that the decline may continue through the second quarter of the year. We firmly believe that sometime between the March tax date and early in the third quarter, loan demand should strengthen.

For the most part, the recent decline in the prime rate is reflected in the loan rate structure at this time. Accordingly, except where necessary rate adjustments are still anticipated, the existing rate structure should prevail.

Expenses

Before preparing the budget, it is imperative that each supervisor closely evaluate every controllable expense in his area and consider all means of economizing and reducing costs, particularly in such areas as personnel staffing, overtime, entertainment, stationery, etc. The salary administration policies explained on pages 19 and 20 in the Budget Instructions* should be strictly followed.

In order to complete the budget for the entire bank by year-end, your full cooperation is necessary in meeting the deadlines which appear in the attached General Instructions.

BUDGET COMMITTEE

October 7, 1960

---

* The policies referred to are as follows:

Your current appraisal of each employee's performance as E (excellent), AA (above average), A (average), or P (poor) is to be shown immediately following the individual's name on schedule 4A, as a guide for your own budgeting and for the subsequent review by the budget committee.

Exhibit 4—Continued

> Salary administration policies, as expressed in Bulletin III of the Personnel Policies Manual, are not expected to change during 1961. Our salary rates are competitive, and as in recent years, any projected increases should be based solely on merit or, where plans are sufficiently advanced, on anticipated bona fide promotions.
>
> In general, the budget committee anticipates that we will be able to maintain our competitive position with total bankwide increases to deserving employees, averaging no more than 5 percent of their salaries. In order to achieve this purpose, all departments must cooperate in observing the following guides:
>
> *a*) In all cases, *merit* and not length of service is to be the basis for the forecasting of increases.
>
> *b*) Individual merit increases should be roughly 5 to 5½ percent of the range midpoint, with no increase less than $156 nor more than 10 percent of the range midpoint, ($500 maximum), and in multiples of $1.00 weekly.
>
> *c*) Individual increases exceeding the guidelines in (*b*) above should be thoroughly documented both in budget submittal and in subsequent actual review for salary purposes.
>
> *d*) An employee rated average should not receive appreciably more than the midpoint of his salary range. The top half of the range is reserved for those employees who demonstrate above-average performance.
>
> *e*) In case of promotion, the increase or increases to be scheduled should normally bring the salary within a reasonable period to the minimum for the new job.

number previously authorized by top management, the reason for the difference had to be thoroughly documented and substantiated to banking division headquarters and the budget committee. Top management was extremely critical of subsequent requests by the branches for staff increases which had not been reflected in the budgets.

In general, there were two types of income and expense items—those directly identifiable with a particular branch, and those not directly identifiable with a particular branch. Branches were instructed to budget only those direct expenses under their control. Indirect expenses were allocated to branches by the control division. In addition, the budgeting of certain direct expenses, such as depreciation of fixtures, employee benefits, and deferred compensation, was done by the control division because the branches had only secondary control over these expenses.

DEPOSITS AND LOANS

In the lower part of the comparative statement were shown the budgeted and actual loans and deposits outstanding. Both top management and branch managers exercised a close watch over these primary indicators of the level of the branch's operation. The controller, however, believed that the ultimate test of the office performance should not rest with these items but, rather, with earnings. He maintained that the effect of changes in deposits and loans should and would be reflected in the earnings statement.

EARNINGS STATEMENT

The control division had encountered a number of serious problems in trying to produce an earnings statement that would be most useful for the branches and for the management of the banking division. Some problems were basic to all types of business; some were peculiar to banking. The fundamental cause of the problems, however, lay in the fact that not all income and expense items could be measured precisely or directly identified with particular offices. Specifically, some of the questions asked were these: What should be the basis for determining the credit for a branch that generated deposits in excess of its own requirements for funds? What share of general administrative expenses, including the salaries of top management, should be charged to each branch? How should the expenses of the personnel division, the bookkeeping department, the check clearance department, the credit department, etc., be allocated to branches? The control division resolved some of these problems in the following ways.

Installment Loans

Record-keeping, issurance of coupon books, and part of collection work for installment loans generated by all branches were handled centrally by the installment loan department, and income earned from installment loans was, therefore, credited initially to this department. This income was, in large part, attributable to the branches that generated the loans and was, therefore, redistributed to them. The current procedure was to distribute gross operating income less the cost of "borrowed" funds and operating expenses of the department on the basis of the total direct installment loans generated by the branch during a revolving annual cycle.

An alternative basis that had been considered was to apportion the net income of the installment department according to the number of payments received by branches, since this measure of activity reflected the clerical time spent for coupon handling. This alternative was not adopted, on the grounds that it did not give branches enough motivation to seek more new installment loans, particularly since customers could make their installment payments at any branch they chose. An alternative basis considered was the amount of average loans outstanding. The controller thought this might be more equitable than the currently used basis, but he was of the opinion that the gain to be obtained from the adoption of the new basis was not large enough to offset the additional necessary record-keeping.

Interest on Excess (or Borrowed) Funds

Branches and other operating units with funds available for investment in excess of their own requirements for loans, cash, and other assets shared in the net earnings of the investment division; branches and other operating units whose asset requirements exceeded their available funds were charged for funds "borrowed." There was a wide variation in the ratio of deposits to loans among branches, and some branches were credited with the interest on excess funds in an amount higher than their direct income. An example of the calculation of this important income or charge item is shown in Exhibit 5.

As shown in the top section of Exhibit 5, the first step was to compute the amount of excess (or borrowed) funds for the branch. Funds were divided into two pools: (1) special pool—earnings from special long-term, high-yield, municipal securities, which were considered as an investment of part of the savings and time deposits; and (2) regular pool—earnings from other portfolio securities investments, interest on certain loans, and sundry earnings. As a rule, the special-pool investments yielded a higher rate of return than the regular-pool investments.

Third, branches with savings deposits were credited at the interest rate of the special pool on the basis of their pro rata share of savings deposits. Net savings deposits in excess of the principal of investment in the special pool, together with excess funds other than savings deposits, received pro rata credit from the earnings of the regular investment pool. Branches that borrowed funds were charged at the regular pool rate. In summary, the two rates from the two pools were as follows:

Special pool rate:	Net earnings of special pool/special pool securities principal (part of total savings deposits)
Regular pool rate:	Net earnings from regular pool/excess funds less borrowed funds less special securities principal

For the first three quarters of 1960, the budgeted regular pool rate and special pool rate were 3.95 percent and 7.81 percent; the actual rates, 4.05 percent and 7.88 percent, respectively. Thus, for branch A the interest on excess funds for the first three quarters was calculated as shown in the lower section of Exhibit 5.

Rent and Occupancy Cost

Some branches operated in leased space whereas others operated in bank-owned buildings. The first group was charged with the actual rent paid, but the second was charged with the "fair rental value," which was determined by outside real estate appraisers. The practice was thought to put the two groups on the same footing. The fair rental value charges were internal bookkeeping entries offset by credits to real-estate accounts, which were maintained for each bank-owned building. These accounts, therefore, indicated the profitability of each building. The determination of the fair rental value was not difficult, and there had been no significant controversies involving its calculation.

Exhibit 5

CALCULATION OF INTEREST INCOME ON EXCESS FUNDS, BRANCH A
First Three Quarters of 1960

Calculation of Excess Funds

		(In thousands)
Total demand deposits	$13,134	
Less: Reciprocal bank balances; float	(727)	
Plus: Treasury tax and loan a/c	221	
Adjusted demand deposits	$12,628	
Less: Reserve at 18%	(2,273)	
Net demand deposits		$10,355
Savings deposits	$ 1,026	
Less: Reserve at 5%	(51)	
Net savings deposits		975
Net deposits available for investment		$11,330
Less: Loans, cash, other assets		(1,229)
Net Excess Funds		$10,101

Calculation of Interest Income on Excess Funds

	Principal		*Annual Rate*		*Three Quarters*		*Interest*
In special investment pool (63%)	$ 614,000	×	7.88%	×	¾	=	$ 36,270
In regular investment pool (37%)	361,000	×	4.05%	×	¾	=	10,962
Savings deposits (100%)	$ 975,000	×	6.46%	×	¾	=	$ 47,232
In regular investment pool—demand deposits	9,126,000	×	4.05%	×	¾	=	277,202
Net excess funds	$10,101,000						
Interest on excess funds							$324,434

Advertising

General or institutional advertising was charged to other indirect expenses. (See below for the allocation of other indirect expenses.) Advertising related to a specific branch was charged directly to that branch, except that when advertising was placed in mass media, such as radio, television, and newspapers with general circulation, 33 percent of the expense was allocated to other indirect expenses and 67 percent was allocated to the specific branches involved. The theory of the exception was that when mass media were used, the whole bank benefited to a certain extent.

Banking Division Headquarters and General Administration

All expenses of the banking division headquarters, including the salaries of officers in the division headquarters, were allocated to branches on the basis of their prior year's average gross deposits. The figure for average gross deposits was considered as the best single measure of branch activity.

The salaries of general administrative officers of the bank were first allocated among divisions on the basis of the time spent on problems of each division as estimated by each officer. The amount of general administrative salaries thus allocated to the banking division was, in turn, allocated among branches on the basis of gross deposits in the prior year. All other general administration expenses were charged on the same basis.

Bookkeeping Department

Much of the bookkeeping work was centralized for the whole bank. However, since the central department had been established only in 1959, several offices continued to do their own bookkeeping in 1960. The expenses of the central bookkeeping department were, therefore, allocated only to the branches it serviced. There were eight functional cost centers in the bookkeeping department, and each cost center had its own basis of allocation. The bases of four of the cost centers are given below.

1. *Regular Bookkeeping Cost Center.* In the bookkeeping department, a permanent clerical staff was assigned to process the accounts of each branch. Allocations to branches were based on the salaries of this assigned staff, plus fringe benefits and related overhead costs.
2. *Bank Ledgers Cost Center.* Allocation was on the basis of debit and credit activity as determined by an analysis made from time to time. Inasmuch as the main activity of this cost center was the posting of transactions to ledger sheets, the number of debit and credit entries was preferred to any other basis, e.g., number of accounts. A new survey of debit and credit statistics was made by the analysis department whenever it was believed that there had been a material change from the prior survey period and, in any event, at least once a year.
3. *Special Checking Cost Center.* Same as 2.
4. *Special Statement Section.* Allocation was on the basis of number of accounts handled. The activity of the section was to send out special statements on customers' special requests.

Before adoption of the current method based on the cost center concept, weight of statements mailed out had been the basis of allocation for the expenses of the entire department. The current practice was regarded as more accurate, because there were very few temporary movements of staff and machine services from one cost center to another and because there was a significant variation in the activity measures of the cost centers.

According to the controller, the main controversy involving the expenses of the bookkeeping department was not with respect to the basis of allocation but, rather, with respect to the absolute level of expenses of the department. Complaints were heard from those branches serviced by the department to the effect that they were handicapped relative to branches that did their own bookkeeping, because the cost charged by the central bookkeeping department was considerably higher than the cost that would be incurred if the branch did its own bookkeeping. The controller thought branches that had this opinion failed to recognize that the bookkeeping expenses shown in the earnings statements of the branches with their own bookkeeping were only part of the true bookkeeping cost, because an appropriate portion of supervisory salaries, occupancy costs, supplies, etc., was not included in the item. When the bookkeeping was centralized for a branch, the benefit gained from relieving the supervisors of supervising bookkeeping activity usually appeared as increased loans and deposits, and better management generally.

Check Clearance Department

The total cost of this department was divided among 12 functional cost centers, based on the number of employees assigned to each and the volume of its work. The cost of each cost center was, in turn, charged to branches. Examples of the basis of allocation are given below.

1. *IBM proof machine operation—exchanges:* allocated on the basis of number of checks handled.
2. *IBM proof machine operation—deposits:* allocated on the basis of the number of deposit items.
3. *Check desk:* allocated on the basis of number of checks handled.
4. *Transit clerical:* allocated on the basis of number of deposit items.
5. *Supervision:* allocated to the various check clearance department cost centers in ratio to labor costs.

As was the case with the bookkeeping cost centers, the measures of activity (checks handled and number of deposit items) were based on periodic surveys and remained unchanged until significant changes in the relative activity of branches indicated the need for a new survey. Every cost center's activity was reviewed at least once a year for this purpose.

There were two important sources of trouble in allocation of the expenses of the check clearance department. One was that branches cashed checks issued by other branches; the other was that branches received deposits for customers whose accounts were in other branches. In the periodic activity analyses made to determine the basis of allocating cost, the "number of checks cashed" was the number of checks actually cashed in the branch, whether or not the account was located in the branch. Similarly, the "number of deposit items" was the number of deposits made in the branch. Although it had been believed that the effect of these interbranch services largely offset one another, a recent study by the control division indicated that they, in fact, resulted in distortions with respect to certain branches. The control division was currently working on a method of allocation by which the charge would be made to the branch that benefited most; that is, the branch in which the account was located.

Credit Investigation Department

Although most branches had their own credit analysis staffs, they often asked the central credit department to make investigations. The expenses of the central credit investigation department, therefore, were allocated to the branches that requested its service. The basis of allocation was the number of requests for credit investigation weighted by the typical time required for the analysis performed. The weight for the various types of investigation was determined by the analysis department on the basis of an actual time study.

Term Loan Department

Income from term loans was credited to the branches that generated the loans. Officers of the term loan department actively counseled the branches in negotiating terms with customers, in drawing up loan contracts, and in reviewing existing loans. It was therefore necessary that the expenses of the term loan department be allocated to the branches that used its service. The basis of allocation was the number of loans considered, the number of loans outstanding, and the number of amendments to existing loans, weighted by the unit handling time of each of three classes. In order to determine the weight, the analysis department asked the staff of the term loan department to estimate the time spent on each class.

Personnel Division

The expenses of this division were allocated to all operating units in the ratio of the number of employees in each operating unit to the total.

Other Indirect Expenses

Items of a general overhead nature, such as expenses of the accounting division (except the direct cost of examining a branch, which was charged directly), cost of the senior training program, general institutional advertising, contributions, etc., were included under this heading. The basis of allocation of these expenses among branches was the ratio of annual operating expenses (excluding other indirect and interest on deposits) of each branch to the total operating expenses of all branches.

CONTROLLER'S VIEWS ON ALLOCATIONS

The controller believed that some arbitrariness was inevitable in the allocation of the income and expense items described above. With dozens of branches, each with its own operating characteristics, it was impossible to have a "perfect" or "right" system for all of them. What was more important, according to the controller, was agreement on the part of the branch managers that the system was generally equitable. If managers agreed on the fairness of the system, he believed, it was likely to be a success. They therefore, let it be known to branch managers that the system was always open for revision, and he encouraged them to make known any criticisms they had. After the control division had done its best to find a workable system, the initiative for suggesting changes was with the branch managers. The controller said that several changes had been made as a result of branch managers' suggestions.

He warned them, however, against a blind and apathetic acceptance; the acceptance should be positive and constructive. On acceptance of the system, branch managers should be concerned with the reported result and make necessary efforts to improve it. Thus, he said, branch managers were told clearly that the earnings statement was used to evaluate their performance. This, he thought, attached sufficient importance to the matter to prevent any possible indifference.

ATTITUDES OF BRANCH MANAGERS ON ALLOCATIONS

The managers of two offices, A and B, held different opinions about the system. The operating characteristics of these branches were different, as indicated by their comparative statements of earnings for the third quarter of 1960, reproduced in Exhibits 2 and 3. Branch A was relatively small and deposit-heavy, did its own bookkeeping and operated in a leased space, whereas branch B was larger, loan-heavy, used the centralized bookkeeping department, and operated in a bank-owned building. Their annual earnings statements of recent years are shown in Exhibits 6 and 7.

Comment by Manager of Branch A

The statement is useful because I like to see, at least quickly, whether I am within the budget and what caused the deviations from it, if any.

The earnings of our branch are relatively low, because the volume of business is limited by the location. We have more deposits than our loan requirements; consequently, we get credit for the excess funds. In fact, as you see, for the first three quarters of 1960, interest on excess funds was more than four times the total direct income. The 4.05 percent rate on the excess funds seems fair enough, but we try always to increase our own loans in order to increase our earnings. However, the location of our office is a limiting factor.

Since rent and occupancy is the actual rent paid to the owner of the building, we can't have any quarrel about that, but the service department charges are certainly too high. We don't have any control over these costs; yet we are charged for them. I am not complaining that this is unfair; on the contrary, I believe branches should share the burden. My only misgiving is whether those service departments are doing enough to cut down their costs.

About one half of the service department expenses charged to our branch is for check clearing service. Although I don't know the basis of allocation, I don't doubt that it is fair. Besides, even if I should have some questions about the basis, probably it wouldn't reach up there; the communication channel from here to the top is long and tedious.

At present, we do our own bookkeeping, but soon this will be centralized. I have heard some managers complain that the cost charged to them for the centralized bookkeeping is higher than the cost when they did their own bookkeeping. However, such intangible gains as prestige and customer relations may justify

Exhibit 6

CONDENSED ANNUAL EARNINGS STATEMENTS, BRANCH A

(In thousands)

	1960 Budget	1959 Budget	1959 Actual	1958 Budget	1958 Actual	1957 Budget	1957 Actual	1956 Actual	1955 Actual
Total direct income	$ 98	$ 93	$ 90	$ 87	$ 89	$ 99	$ 90	$ 99	$ 82
Interest on excess funds	409	364	381	327	316	299	287	263	355
Gross income	$ 507	$ 457	$ 471	$ 414	$ 405	$ 398	$ 377	$ 362	$ 437
Expenses:									
Salaries	$ 130	$ 129	$ 125	$ 125	$ 125				
Deferred compensation	12	10	10	8	9	$ 140	$ 147	$ 132	$ 114
Employee benefits	19	19	18	17	17				
Rent and occupancy	45	46	45	45	47	47	49	43	43
Interest on deposits	30	30	27	19	19	9	11	6	4
Other direct	32	29	31	30	30	*	*	*	*
Office administration	13	15	13	17	16	*	*	*	*
Service departments	70	58	61	57	57	67	69	62	44
Indirect overhead	18	18	21	19	16	*	*	*	*
Gross expenses	$ 369	$ 354	$ 351	$ 337	$ 336	$ 315	$ 329	$ 296	$ 256
Net earnings before taxes	$ 138	$ 103	$ 120	$ 77	$ 69	$ 83	$ 48	$ 66	$ 181
Average gross deposits	$13,975	$13,550	$13,707	$13,573	$12,948	$14,540	$13,442	$15,057	$21,504
Average loans	$ 820	$ 820	$ 810	$ 746	$ 737	$ 990	$ 927	$ 1,139	$ 1,093

* Changes in accounting procedure make these items noncomparable with later years.

Exhibit 7

CONDENSED ANNUAL EARNINGS STATEMENTS, BRANCH B

(In thousands)

	1960 Budget	1959 Budget	1959 Actual	1958 Budget	1958 Actual	1957 Budget	1957 Actual	1956 Actual	1955 Actual
Total direct income	$ 3,077	$ 2,725	$ 2,532	$ 2,214	$ 2,201	$ 2,338	$ 2,395	$ 1,959	$ 1,172
Interest on excess (borrowed) funds	(177)	157	222	154	263	73	(32)	209	556
Gross income	$ 2,900	$ 2,882	$ 2,754	$ 2,368	$ 2,464	$ 2,411	$ 2,363	$ 2,168	$ 1,728
Expenses:									
Salaries	$ 249	$ 255	$ 256	$ 245	$ 247				
Deferred compensation	22	19	21	17	18	$ 250	$ 264	$ 236	$ 232
Employee benefits	32	34	33	30	31				
Rent and occupancy	111	105	104	104	105	106	108	65	85
Interest on deposits	71	75	66	51	52	19	25	12	10
Other direct	95	93	108	84	86	*	*	*	*
Office administration	71	85	76	86	83	*	*	*	*
Service departments	379	383	360	356	345	361	380	315	224
Indirect and overhead	65	64	72	60	51	*	*	*	*
Gross expenses	$ 1,095	$ 1,113	$ 1,096	$ 1,033	$ 1,018	$ 878	$ 928	$ 829	$ 814
Net earnings before taxes	$ 1,805	$ 1,769	$ 1,658	$ 1,335	$ 1,446	$ 1,533	$ 1,435	$ 1,339	$ 914
Average gross deposits	$77,410	$79,885	$75,853	$72,063	$73,899	$73,415	$69,683	$70,740	$73,433
Average loans	$58,000	$56,000	$49,702	$48,971	$47,095	$50,000	$49,945	$44,460	$28,378

* Changes in accounting procedure make these items noncomparable with later years.

a little higher cost. At any rate, we wouldn't have any choice if top management decides to centralize our bookkeeping. It may be better in the long run.

Although I don't know exactly what items are included in other direct and indirect and overhead expenses, I don't think they are excessive. The control division is trying to be fair.

In summary, I think the statement is useful, but there are many factors you should consider in interpreting it.

Comment by Manager of Branch B

The statement is a fair measure of how branches are doing. It is true that the location of a branch has a lot to do with its operation; in evaluating a particular branch, the location is an important element to be taken into account. To take the extreme case, you don't need a branch in a desert. If a branch can't show earnings after being charged with its fair share of all costs, perhaps the purpose of its existence is lost.

High volume and efficient operation have contributed to our high level of earnings. Our branch has more loans than can be sustained by our own deposits; thus, we are charged with interest on borrowed funds on the theory that we would have to pay the interest if we borrowed from outside. Of course, by increasing deposits we could meet the loan requirements and add to our earnings a good part of the interest on borrowed funds; indeed, we have been trying to lure more deposits to our branch. Quite apart from this special effort, however, we do not neglect to seek more loan opportunities, for loans increase earnings even after the interest charge.

Our office is in a bank-owned building, but instead of controversial depreciation and maintenance charges we are charged with the fair rental value. We are satisfied with this practice.

The bookkeeping of our branch is centralized. I believe we could do it for less money if we did our own bookkeeping; but competing banks have centralized bookkeeping departments, and we have to go along. I suspect there are some intangible benefits being gained, too.

If I really sat down and thoroughly examined all the allocation bases, I might find some things that could be improved. But the fact of life is that we must draw a line somewhere; some arbitrariness will always be there. Furthermore, why should our branch raise questions? We are content with the way things are.

Comments by Banking Division Headquarters

We call this report [Exhibits 2 and 3] our Bible, and like the actual Bible, it must be interpreted carefully. Many factors affect the performance of a branch that do not show up on the report. For example, in an area that is going downhill the manager of a branch has to work terribly hard just to keep his deposits from declining, whereas in a growing area, the manager can read the *New York Times* all day and still show an impressive increase in deposits. The location of the branch in the neighborhood, its outward appearance, its decor, the layout of its facilities—all can affect its volume of business. Changes in the level of interest rates, which are noncontrollable, also have a significant effect on income. At headquarters, we are aware of these factors and take them into account when we

Exhibit 8

BRANCH OFFICE REPORT

1960

Location and Office No. A

	All Dollar Amounts in Thousands Unless Otherwise Stated	JAN.	FEB.	MAR.	APRIL	MAY	JUNE	JULY	AUG.	SEPT.	OCT.	NOV.	DEC.	YEAR AVERAGE	
	DEPOSITS - AVERAGE														
1	Demand - (Ind., Part., Corp.) $	14 038	13 473	12 330	12 919	13 108	12 911	12 596	11 907	12 746	12 202				1
2	Demand - Banks $	50	50	-	-	-	-	-	-	-	-				2
3	Special Checking $	221	218	220	251	235	216	237	244	236	219				3
4	Treas. Tax & Loan Account $	118	149	238	124	270	321	232	202	265	196				4
5	Savings $	987	974	1 001	990	976	1 012	972	978	986	1 013				5
6	Christmas Club $	15	23	30	35	41	46	51	55	60	63				6
7	Time $	-	-	-	-	-	-	-	-	-	-				7
8	Total $	15 429	14 887	13 819	14 319	14 630	14 506	14 088	13 386	14 293	13 693				8
	NUMBER OF ACCOUNTS														
9	Demand (Ind., Part., Corp.)	1 515	1 513	1 507	1 503	1 516	1 511	1 514	1 497	1 478	1 473				
10	Demand - Banks	1	-	-	-	-	-	-	-	-	-				
11	Special Checking	868	865	884	892	894	900	903	911	939	948				
12	Savings	585	587	593	589	587	591	593	587	621	645				
13	Christmas Club	540	536	534	538	533	530	526	519	516	511				
14	Time	-	-	-	-	-	-	-	-	-	-				
15	Total	3 509	3 501	3 518	3 522	3 530	3 532	3 536	3 514	3 554	3 577				
	LOANS													YEAR AVERAGE	
16	Total Loans - Average $	723	755	720	627	672	773	841	889	971	961				16
17	Instalment Loan - Volume $	20	24	36	31	35	22	25	34	27	39				17
18	Spec. Loan Dept. - Month End $	-	-	-	-	-	-	-	-	-	-				18
	NUMBER OF BORROWERS														
19	Total Loans	48	58	50	49	51	54	55	60	62	63				
20	Instalment Loans - Made	24	37	46	50	32	30	28	45	44	39				
21	Special Loan Dept.	-	-	-	-	-	-	-	-	-	-				
22	Staff - Number of Officers	4	4	4	4	4	4	4	4	3	3				
23	No. of Employees - Auth. Budget	25	25	25	25	25	25	25	25	25	25				
24	Total	29	29	29	29	29	29	29	29	28	28			YEAR - TOTALS	
25	Overtime & Supper Money Payments (To nearest dollar) $	276	135	273	93	496	123	536	370	350	220				25
	SERVICE CHARGES (To nearest dollar)														
26	Regular Checking Accounts $	1 543	1 578	1 445	225	2 550	858	2 378	1 998	1 997	1 833				26
27	Special Checking Accounts $	1 017	1 119	1 220	1 397	1 223	1 322	1 313	1 237	1 266	1 340				27
28	Total $	2 560	2 697	2 665	1 622	3 773	2 180	3 691	3 235	3 263	3 173				28

Income and Expense By Quarters And Cumulative

To Nearest Dollar	1st Quarter	2nd Quarter	Jan. thru June	3rd Quarter	Jan. thru Sept.	4th Quarter	Jan. thru Dec.
Gross Income $	133 060	131 531	264 591	132 041	396 632		
Gross Expenses $	92 050	93 088	185 138	97 043	282 181		
Net Before Taxes $	41 010	38 443	79 453	34 998	114 451		
Net After Taxes $	18 799	17 622	36 421	16 043	52 464		

	1st Quarter	2nd Quarter	Jan. thru June	3rd Quarter	Jan. thru Sept.	4th Quarter	Jan. thru Dec.
Average Loan Rate	5.80	5.83	5.81	5.82	5.82		
Earn. Rate-Excess Funds	4.02	4.06	4.04	4.08	4.05		
Earn. Rate-Savings Deposits	6.52	6.55	6.54	6.59	6.55		

Exhibit 8—Continued

BRANCH OFFICE REPORT—SUPPLEMENT

1960 Location and Office No. A

	All Dollar Amounts in Thousands	JAN.	FEB.	MAR.	APRIL.	MAY	JUNE	JULY	AUG.	SEPT.	OCT.	NOV.	DEC.	YEAR TOTALS	
	Regular Checking Accounts - Number														
1	Opened - New	26	17	7	15	16	17	10	9	14	11				1
2	Opened - A/C Trans. within Office	-	1	1	1	4	-	1	-	-	-				2
3.	Opened - A/C Trans. from other Off.	-	1	1	-	3	-	2	-	1	-				3
4	Total Number Opened	26	19	9	16	23	17	13	9	15	11				4
5	Closed	24	17	12	17	6	19	9	17	24	14				5
6	Closed - A/C Trans. within Office	-	2	1	2	2	-	-	8	6	1				6
7	Closed - A/C Trans. to other Offices	4	3	2	1	2	3	1	1	4	1				7
8	Total Number Closed	28	22	15	20	10	22	10	26	34	16				8
9	Net Opened or Closed	-2	-3	-6	-4	+13	-5	+3	-17	-19	-5				9
	Regular Checking Accounts Average Deposits Closed - Monthly														
10	Closed $	16	7	3	15	7	14	4	11	18	7				
11	Closed - Trans. within Office $	-	19	2	4	2	-	-	6	4	1				
12	Closed - Trans. to other Offices $	5	6	2	-	1	3	1	1	2	2				
13	Total Average-Closed Accts. $	21	32	7	19	10	17	5	18	24	10				
	Accounts Since Jan. 1st- Cumulated*														
14	*No. Opened (Line 1)	26	43	50	65	81	98	108	117	131	142				
15	No. Closed (Line 5)	24	41	53	70	76	95	104	121	145	159				
16	*Opened-Current Mo. Avg. (Line 14) $	83	191	162	143	120	102	120	109	114	127				
17	Closed-Total Avg. Bal. (Line 10) $	16	23	26	41	48	62	66	77	95	102				
	Business Development													YEAR TOTALS	
18	No. of calls - Customers	3	8	7	4	10	8	6	9	5	5				18
19	No. of calls - Prospects	3	4	4	4	1	4	2	6	5	5				19
20	Total	6	12	11	8	11	12	8	15	10	10				20
21	Spec. Checking Accts - Opened	26	21	31	21	19	22	15	33	37	29				21
22	Spec. Checking Accts - Closed	13	24	12	13	17	16	12	25	9	20				22
23	Spec. Checking Accts - Net	+ 13	- 3	+ 19	+ 8	+ 2	+ 6	+ 3	+ 8	+ 28	+ 9				23
24	Savings Accounts - Opened	17	9	22	9	15	24	15	9	52	39				24
25	Savings Accounts - Closed	21	7	16	13	17	20	13	15	18	15				25
26	Savings Accounts - Net	- 4	+ 2	+ 6	- 4	- 2	+ 4	+ 2	- 6	+ 34	+ 24				26
27	S.D. Boxes - New Rentals	9	6	3	9	3	6	5	6	4	-				27
28	S.D. Boxes - Surrendered	9	4	9	11	12	10	6	7	7	3				28
29	S.D. Boxes - Net	-	+ 2	- 6	- 2	- 9	- 4	- 1	- 1	- 3	- 3				29
30	No. of Personal Money Orders Sold	523	543	583	643	421	467	447	419	452	367				30

Exhibit 9

BRANCH OFFICE REPORT

1960

Location and Office No. B

No.	All Dollar Amounts in Thousands Unless Otherwise Stated		JAN.	FEB.	MAR.	APRIL	MAY	JUNE	JULY	AUG.	SEPT.	OCT.	NOV.	DEC.	YEAR AVERAGE	
	DEPOSITS - AVERAGE															
1	Demand - (Ind., Part., Corp.)	$	76 738	68 526	68 509	68 654	65 716	67 602	66 723	64 335	70 017	70 912				1
2	Demand - Banks	$	475	475	350	150	275	520	524	350	258	125				2
3	Special Checking	$	506	506	509	562	534	516	512	508	475	465				3
4	Treas. Tax & Loan Account	$	1 689	3 065	4 776	1 824	5 078	4 761	4 757	4 786	6 038	6 026				4
5	Savings	$	2 359	2 301	2 340	2 320	2 359	2 210	2 349	2 328	2 385	2 493				5
6	Christmas Club	$	19	28	35	45	54	61	67	75	81	89				6
7	Time	$	-	-	-	-	-	-	-	-	-	-				7
8	Total	$	81 786	74 901	76 519	73 555	74 016	75 670	74 932	72 382	79 254	80 110				8
	NUMBER OF ACCOUNTS															
9	Demand (Ind., Part., Corp.)		3 561	3 585	3 631	3 622	3 565	3 556	3 569	3 617	3 619	3 591				
10	Demand - Banks		1	1	1	1	1	1	1	1	1	1				
11	Special Checking		1 840	1 862	1 853	1 850	1 893	1 891	1 871	1 894	1 885	1 909				
12	Savings		1 509	1 510	1 511	1 518	1 507	1 531	1 523	1 526	1 642	1 707				
13	Christmas Club		600	602	734	731	728	723	721	720	715	708				
14	Time		-	-	-	-	-	-	-	-	-	-				
15	Total		7 511	7 560	7 730	7 722	7 694	7 702	7 685	7 758	7 862	7 916				
	LOANS														YEAR AVERAGE	
16	Total Loans - Average	$	64 277	67 796	66 835	62 033	61 763	67 926	72 386	71 644	72 356	65 851				16
17	Instalment Loan - Volume	$	80	86	134	124	103	110	98	115	90	123				17
18	Spec. Loan Dept.-Month End	$	3	-	-	-	-	-	-	-	-	-				18
	NUMBER OF BORROWERS															
19	Total Loans		378	381	372	390	398	403	408	430	434	409				
20	Instalment Loans - Made		86	83	118	121	97	107	106	120	112	110				
21	Special Loan Dept.		1	-	-	-	-	-	-	-	-	-				
22	Staff - Number of Officers		8	9	9	9	9	9	9	9	9	9				
23	No. of Employees - Auth. Budget		42	42	43	43	43	43	43	43	43	43				
24	Total		50	51	52	52	52	52	52	52	52	52			YEAR - TOTALS	
25	Overtime and Supper Money Payments (To nearest dollar)	$	756	238	139	127	139	21	195	78	16	80				25
	SERVICE CHARGES (To nearest dollar)															
26	Regular Checking Accounts	$	3 081	2 786	2 263	3 048	2 430	3 399	2 620	2 067	2 328	2 876				26
27	Special Checking Accounts	$	1 963	2 251	2 504	2 834	2 755	2 867	2 865	2 645	2 701	2 674				27
28	Total	$	5 044	5 037	4 767	5 882	5 185	6 266	5 485	4 712	5 029	5 550				28

Income and Expense By Quarters And Cumulative

To Nearest Dollar		1st Quarter	2nd Quarter	Jan. thru June	3rd Quarter	Jan. thru Sept.	4th Quarter	Jan. thru Dec.
Gross Income	$	766 538	753 426	1 519 964	794 525	2 314 489		
Gross Expenses	$	290 733	280 398	571 131	282 685	853 816		
Net Before Taxes	$	475 805	473 028	948 833	511 840	1 460 673		
Net After Taxes	$	218 109	216 836	434 945	234 628	669 573		

	1st Quarter	2nd Quarter	Jan. thru June	3rd Quarter	Jan. thru Sept.	4th Quarter	Jan. thru Dec.
Average Loan Rate	3.18	5.29	5.24	5.25	5.24		
Earn. Rate-Excess Funds	4.02	4.06	4.04	4.08	4.05		
Earn. Rate-Savings Deposits	6.52	6.55	6.54	6.59	6.55		

Exhibit [illegible]—Continued

BRANCH OFFICE REPORT—SUPPLEMENT

1960

Location and Office No. A

	All Dollar Amounts in Thousands	JAN.	FEB.	MAR.	APRIL	MAY	JUNE	JULY	AUG.	SEPT.	OCT.	NOV.	DEC.	YEAR TOTALS	
	Regular Checking Accounts-Number														
1	Opened - New	54	54	38	32	21	32	33	49	43	46				1
2	Opened - A/C Trans. within Office	10	9	50	5	6	10	5	46	8	4				2
3	Opened - A/C Trans. from other Off.	4	4	7	5	1	5	11	9	3	6				3
4	Total Number Opened	68	67	95	42	28	47	49	104	54	56				4
5	Closed	32	17	40	31	47	30	21	39	32	28				5
6	Closed - A/C Trans. within Office	14	19	2	16	35	20	12	7	10	53				6
7	Closed - A/C Trans. to other Offices	5	7	7	4	3	6	3	10	10	3				7
8	Total Number Closed	51	43	49	51	85	56	36	56	52	84				8
9	Net Opened or Closed	+ 17	+ 24	+ 46	- 9	- 57	- 9	+ 13	+ 48	+ 2	- 28				9
	Regular Checking Accounts Average Deposits Closed - Monthly														
10	Closed $	129	37	181	158	160	32	72	42	40	91				
11	Closed - Trans. within Office $	226	48	31	42	34	694	39	107	346	157				
12	Closed - Trans. to other Offices $	294	107	15	20	5	247	36	44	70	67				
13	Total Average - Closed Accts. $	649	192	227	220	199	973	147	193	456	315				
	Accounts Since Jan. 1st-Cumulated*														
14	*No. Opened (Line 1)	54	108	146	178	199	231	264	313	356	402				
15	No. Closed (Line 5)	32	49	89	120	167	197	218	257	289	317				
16	*Opened-Current Mo. Avg. (Line 14)$	603	907	1 378	1 584	1 544	1 709	2 419	2 634	2 484	3 066				
17	Closed-Total Avg. Bal. (Line 10) $	129	166	347	505	665	697	769	811	851	942				
	Business Development														
18	No. of calls - Customers	129	148	153	115	140	215	117	103	160	136				18
19	No. of calls - Prospects	89	46	39	48	51	44	29	50	33	34				19
20	Total	218	194	192	163	191	259	146	153	193	170				20
21	Spec. Checking Accts - Opened	70	62	28	66	64	55	67	60	91	87				21
22	Spec. Checking Accts - Closed	33	40	37	69	21	57	87	37	100	63				22
23	Spec. Checking Accts - Net	+ 37	+ 22	- 9	- 3	+ 43	- 2	- 20	+ 23	- 9	+ 24				23
24	Savings Accounts - Opened	63	54	54	63	47	65	56	53	173	122				24
25	Savings Accounts - Closed	93	53	53	56	58	41	64	50	57	57				25
26	Savings Accounts - Net	- 30	+ 1	+ 1	+ 7	- 11	+ 24	- 8	+ 3	+116	+ 65				26
27	S.D. Boxes - New Rentals	8	11	7	14	15	10	14	6	15	7				27
28	S.D. Boxes - Surrendered	8	9	8	8	9	13	14	6	14	13				28
29	S.D. Boxes - Net	-	+ 2	- 1	+ 6	+ 6	- 3	-	-	+ 1	- 6				29
30	No. of Personal Money Orders Sold	1 410	1 636	1 578	1 648	1 165	1 140	1 244	1 157	1 134	1 084				30

read the reports. The unfortunate fact is that some managers—for example, those in declining areas—may not believe that we take them into account. Such a manager may worry about his apparently poor performance as shown on the report, and this has a bad psychological effect on him.

One other difficulty with the report is that it may encourage the manager to be interested too much in his own branch at the expense of the bank as a whole. When a customer moves to another part of town, the manager may try to persuade him to leave his account in the same branch, even though the customer can be served better by a branch near his new location. We even hear of two branches competing for the same customer, which certainly doesn't add to the reputation of the bank. Or, to take another kind of problem, a manager may be reluctant to add another teller because of the increased expense, even though he actually needs one to give proper service to his customers.

Of course, the earnings report is just one factor in judging the performance of a branch manager. Among the others are the growth of deposits compared with the potential for the area; the number of calls he makes soliciting new business (we get a monthly report on this); the loans that get into difficulty; complaint letters from customers; the annual audit of his operations made by the control division; and, most important, personnel turnover, or any other indications of how well he is developing his personnel. Some of these factors are indicated in these statistics [see Exhibits 8 and 9], which are prepared at banking division headquarters.

QUESTIONS

The general question is: What are the strong and weak points of the budget-reporting-performance evaluation system of the bank in reference to its branch operations? What improvements would you suggest?

Examples of specific topics you should consider are:

1. What characteristics of banking make its management control system different from that of a manufacturing operation?
2. What is the relationship between the earnings statement and the branch office reports?
3. Would you recommend calculating a return on investment for each branch? If so, how would you determine the investment base?
4. Should noncontrollable costs be omitted from the earnings statement? If so, what items would be affected?
5. In comparing actual with budgeted interest on loans, should a noncontrollable variance be developed which represents the effect of changes in the general level of interest rates?

Case 8-3

Metropolitan Bank (B)

The controller of the Metropolitan Bank considered, from time to time, various proposals for improving the bank's management control system. He originated some of these ideas himself; some came from other men in the bank. Three of these proposals are described in this case.

BONUS FOR BRANCH MANAGERS

It was proposed that branch managers be paid a bonus based on a comparison of actual and budgeted net earnings for the branch. In order to make such a comparison equitable, certain changes in the branch income statement would be required. For example, actual net income would probably be adjusted to eliminate the effect of changes in the general level of interest rates. The vice-president who made this proposal said that he realized that net earnings only partially measured performance, but he believed that other factors could not be readily quantified or, if quantifiable, that a bonus plan incorporating other factors would be too complicated.

CENTRAL BOOKKEEPING DEPARTMENT MADE A PROFIT CENTER

It was proposed that the bookkeeping department be made into a profit center; that is, its services be billed to the branches and to other users at a price that would include cost plus an element of profit, instead of the present practice of billing branches at cost.

The bookkeeping department was starting to perform certain record-keeping services for bank customers. For example, it did the record-keeping for payments on their accounts receivable. A company would ask its credit customers to mail their payments to a certain post office box, which the Metropolitan Bank then emptied. As the bank added electronic data processing equipment, such services for customers were expected to increase and to include payroll accounting and accounts payable accounting for customers who did not have electronic equipment. For customers with personal checking accounts, the bookkeeping department also made monthly payments of bills, such as insurance premiums, mortgage payments, installment loan repayments, and utility bills. One authority estimated that 75 percent of the checks then written in the United States might eventually be eliminated by the growth of these practices. Customers would be charged a fee for such services.

Branch revenue currently included a service charge for each deposit made and each check drawn to cover both the costs of the bookkeeping department and the costs of tellers and related activities at the branches, plus a profit. Revenue from the new services would presumably be credited to the branch where the account was located.

Advocates of the proposal also saw advantages in the relationship between the bookkeeping department and the branches if the fee charged the branches for bookkeeping services included an element of profit.

CREDIT FOR CUSTOMERS' ACCOUNTS SHIFTED TO ANOTHER BRANCH

It was proposed that when a customer shifted his account from one branch to another, the income from the account (reflected principally in the service charge and interest on excess funds items) should be divided equally between the branches for one year. There was a feeling that branch managers tended to hold an account, even when the customer moved, whereas they should refer the customer to the branch nearest to him. The proposed rule was designed to overcome this tendency. The accounting problems involved in dividing the income were believed to be minor.

QUESTION

What is your opinion on each of the three proposals? You need not necessarily consider the proposals exactly as stated; that is, if you think a proposal has the germ of a good idea but is wrong in some of its details, you should suggest how it might be improved.

Case 8–4

Empire Glass Company

ORGANIZATION

Empire Glass Company was a diversified company organized into several major product divisions, one of which was the glass products division. This division was responsible for manufacturing and selling glass food and beverage bottles. Each division was headed by a divisional vice-president who reported directly to the company's executive vice-president, Landon McGregor.

Mr. McGregor's corporate staff included three men in the financial area—the controller, the chief accountant and the treasurer. The controller's department consisted of only two men—Mr. Walker and the assistant controller, Allen Newell. The market research and labor relations departments also reported in a staff capacity to Mr. McGregor.

All the product divisions were organized along similar lines. Reporting to each product division vice-president were several staff members in the customer service and product research areas. Reporting in a line capacity to each individual vice-president were also a general manager of manufacturing and a general manager of marketing. The general manager of manufacturing was responsible for all the division's manufacturing activities. Similarly, the general manager of marketing was responsible for all the division's marketing activities. Both of these executives were assisted by a small staff of specialists. Exhibit 1 presents an organization chart of the glass product division's top management group. All the corporate and divisional management group were located in British City, Canada. Exhibit 2 shows the typical organization structure of a plant within the glass products division.

PRODUCTS AND TECHNOLOGY

The glass products division operated a number of plants in Canada producing glass food and beverage bottles. Of these products, food jars consti-

Exhibit 1

EMPIRE GLASS COMPANY
Glass Products Division Top Management and Staff

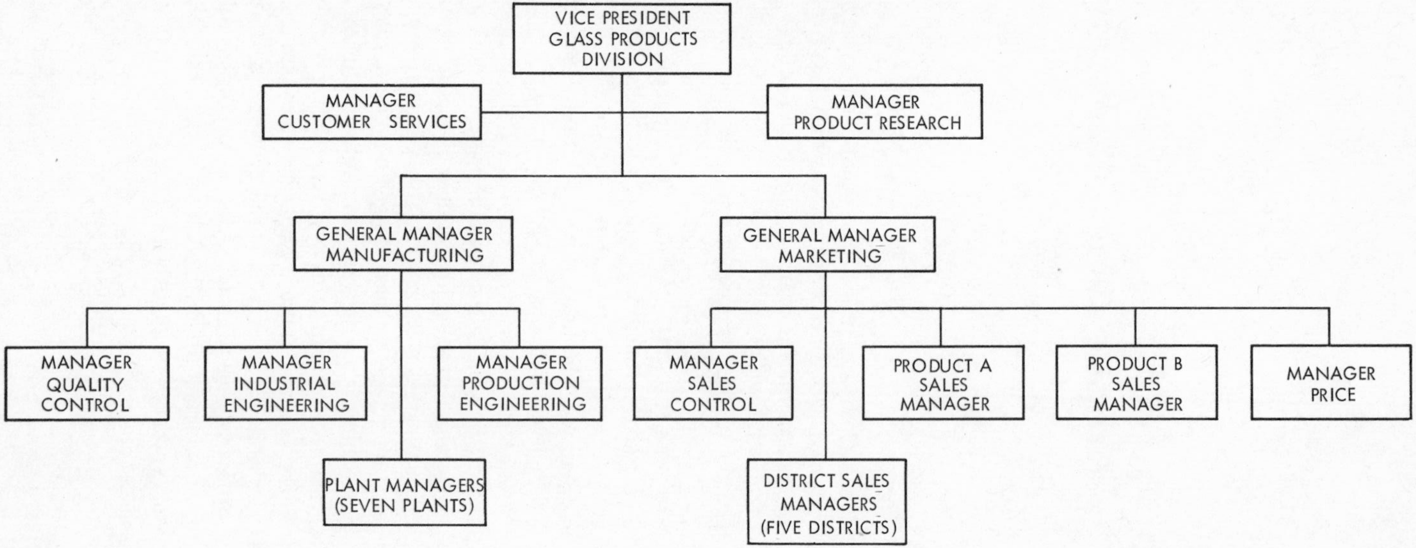

Exhibit 2

EMPIRE GLASS COMPANY
Typical Plant Organization—Glass Products Division

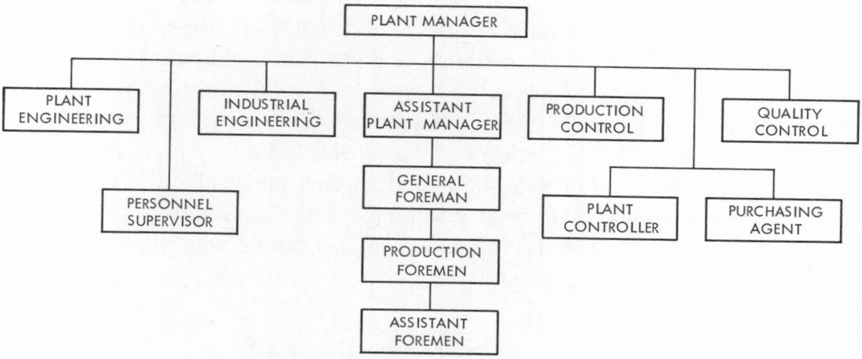

tuted the largest group, including jars for products like tomato catsup, mayonnaise, jams and jellies, honey, and soluble coffee. Milk bottles and beer and soft drink bottles were also produced in large quantities. A great variety of shapes and sizes of containers for wines, liquors, drugs, cosmetics, and chemicals were produced in smaller quantities.

Most of the thousands of different products, varying in size, shape, color, and decoration were produced to order. According to British City executives, during 1963 the typical lead time between the customer's order and shipment from the plant was between two and three weeks.

The principal raw materials for container glass were sand, soda ash, and lime. The first step in the manufacturing process was to melt batches of these materials in furnaces or "tanks." The molten mass was then passed into automatic or semiautomatic machines, which filled molds with the molten glass and blew the glass into the desired shape. The ware then went through an automatic annealing oven or lehr, where it was cooled slowly under carefully controlled conditions. If the glass was to be coated on the exterior to increase its resistance to abrasion and scratches, this coating—often a silicone film—was applied at the lehr. Any decorating (such as a trademark or other design) was then added, the product inspected again, and the finished goods packed in corrugated containers (or wooden cases for some bottles).

Quality inspection was critical in the manufacturing process. If the melt in the furnace was not completely free from bubbles and stones (unmelted ingredients or pieces of refinery material), or if the fabricating machinery was slightly out of adjustment, or molds were worn, the rejection rate was very high. Although a number of machines were used in the inspection process, including electric eyes, much of the inspection was still visual.

Although glassmaking was one of the oldest arts, and bottles and jars had been machine molded at relatively high speed for over half a century, the glass products division had spent substantial sums each year to modernize its equipment. These improvements had greatly increased the speed of operations and had substantially reduced the visual inspection and manual handling of glassware.

Most of the jobs were relatively unskilled, highly repetitive, and gave the worker little control over work methods or pace. The moldmakers who made and repaired the molds, the machine repairmen, and those who made the equipment setup changes between different products were considered to be the highest classes of skilled workers. Wages were relatively high in the glass industry. Production employees belonged to two national unions, and for many years bargaining had been conducted on a national basis. Output standards were established for all jobs, but no bonus was paid to hourly plant workers for exceeding standard.

MARKETING

Over the years, the sales of the glass products divisions had grown at a slightly faster rate than had the total market for glass containers. Until the late 1950's, the division had charged a premium for most of its products, primarily because they were of better quality than competitive products. In recent years, however, the quality of the competitive products had improved to the point where they now matched the division's quality level. In the meantime, the division's competitors had retained their former price structure. Consequently, the glass products division had been forced to lower its prices to meet its competitor's lower market prices. According to one division executive:

> Currently, price competition is not severe, particularly among the two or three larger companies that dominate the glass bottle industry. Most of our competition is with respect to product quality and customer service. . . . In fact, our biggest competitive threat is from containers other than glass. . . .

Each of the division's various plants shipped their products throughout Canada to some extent, although transportation costs limited each plant's market primarily to its immediate vicinity. While some of the customers were large and bought in huge quantities, many were relatively small.

BUDGETARY CONTROL SYSTEM

In the fall of 1963, James Walker, Empire Glass Company controller, described the company's budgetary control system to a casewriter. Mr. Walker had been controller for some fifteen years. Excerpts from that interview are reproduced below.

To understand the role of the budgetary control system, you must first understand our management philosophy. Fundamentally, we have a divisional organization based on broad product categories. These divisional activities are coordinated by the company's executive vice-president, while the head office group provides a policy and review function for him. Within the broad policy limits, we operate on a decentralized basis; each of the decentralized divisions performs the full management job that normally would be inherent in any independent company. The only exceptions to this philosophy are the head office group's sole responsibilities for sources of funds and labor relations with those bargaining units that cross division lines.

Given this form of organization, the budget is the principal management tool used by head office to direct the efforts of the various segments of the company toward a common goal. Certainly, in our case, the budget is much more than a narrow statistical accounting device.

Sales Budget

As early as May 15 of the year preceding the budget year, top management of the company asks the various product division vice-presidents to submit preliminary reports stating what they think their division's capital requirements and outlook in terms of sales and income will be during the next budget year. In addition, corporate top management also wants an expression of the division vice-president's general feelings toward the trends in these particular items over the two years following the upcoming budget year. At this stage, head office is not interested in too much detail. Since all divisions plan their capital requirements five years in advance and had made predictions of the forthcoming budget year's market when the budget estimates were prepared last year, these rough estimates of next year's conditions and requirements are far from wild guesses.

After the opinions of the divisional vice-presidents are in, the market research staff goes to work. They develop a formal statement of the marketing climate in detail for the forthcoming budget year and in general terms for the subsequent two years. Once these general factors have been assessed, a sales forecast is constructed for the company and for each division. Consideration is given to the relationship of the general economic climate to our customers' needs and Empire's share of each market. Explicitly stated are basic assumptions as to price, weather conditions, introduction of new products, gains or losses in particular accounts, forward buying, new manufacturing plants, industry growth trends, packaging trends, inventory carry-overs, and the development of alternative packages to or from glass. This review of all the relevant factors is followed for each of our product lines, regardless of its size and importance. The completed forecasts of the market research group are then forwarded to the appropriate divisions for review, criticism, and adjustments.

The primary goal of the head office group in developing these sales forecasts is to assure uniformity among the divisions with respect to the basic assumptions on business conditions, pricing, and the treatment of possible emergencies. Also, we provide a yardstick so as to assure us that the company's overall sales forecast will be reasonable and obtainable.

The product division top management then asks each district manager what he expects to do in the way of sales during the budget year. Head office and the divisional staffs will give the district sales managers as much guidance as they request, but it is the sole responsibility of each district sales manager to come up with his particular forecast.

After the district sales managers' forecasts are received by the divisional top management, the forecasts are consolidated and reviewed by the division's general manager of marketing. Let me emphasize, however, that nothing is changed in the district sales manager's budget unless the district manager agrees. Then, once the budget is approved, nobody is relieved of his responsibility without top management approval. Also, no arbitrary changes are made in the approved budgets without the concurrence of all the people responsible for the budget.

Next, we go through the same process at the division and headquarters levels. We continue to repeat the process until everyone agrees that the sales budgets are sound. Then, each level of management takes responsibility for its particular portion of the budget. These sales budgets then become fixed objectives.

Manufacturing Budgets

Once the vice-presidents, executive vice-president, and company president have given final approval to the sales budgets, we make a sales budget for each plant by breaking down the division sales budgets according to the plants from which the finished goods will be shipped. These plant sales budgets are then further broken down on a monthly basis by price, volume, and end use. With this information available, the plants then budget their gross profit, fixed expenses, and income before taxes.

The plant manager's primary responsibility extends to profits. The budgeted plant profit is the difference between the fixed sales dollar budget and the sum of the budgeted variable costs at standard and the fixed overhead budget. It is the plant manager's responsibility to meet this budget profit figure, even if actual dollar sales drop below the budgeted level.

Given his sales budget, it is up to the plant manager to determine the fixed overhead and variable costs—at standard—that he will need to incur so as to meet the demands of the sales budget. In my opinion, requiring the plant managers to make their own plans is one of the most valuable things associated with the budget system. Each plant manager divides the preparation of the overall plant budget among his plant's various departments. First, the departments spell out the programs in terms of the physical requirements, such as tons of raw material, and then the plans are priced at standard cost.

The plant industrial engineering department is assigned responsibility for developing engineered cost standards and reduced costs. Consequently, the phase of budget preparation covered by the industrial engineers includes budget standards of performance for each operation, cost center, and department within the plant. This phase of the budget also includes budgeted cost reductions, budgeted unfavorable variances from standards, and certain budgeted programmed fixed costs in the manufacturing area, such as service labor. The industrial engineer prepares this phase of the budget in conjunction with departmental line supervision.

Before each plant sends its budget into British City, a group of us from head office goes out to visit each plant. For example, in the case of the glass products division, Allen Newell, assistant controller, and I, along with representatives of the glass products division manufacturing staffs visit each of the division's plants. Let me stress this point: We do not go on these trips to pass judgment on the plant's proposed budget. Rather, we go with two purposes in mind. First, we wish to acquaint ourselves with the thinking behind the figures that each plant manager will send in to British City. This is helpful, because when we come to review these budgets with the top management—that is, management above our level—we will have to answer questions about the budgets, and we will know the answers. Second, the review is a way of giving guidance to the plant managers in determining whether or not they are in line with what the company needs to make in the way of profits.

Of course, when we make our field reviews we do not know about what each of the other plants is doing. Therefore, we explain to the plant managers that while their budget may look good now, when we put all the plants together in a consolidated budget the plant managers may have to make some changes because the projected profit is not high enough. When this happens, we must tell the plant managers that it is not their programs that are unsound. The problem is that the company cannot afford the programs. I think it is very important that each plant manager has a chance to tell his story. Also, it gives them the feeling that we at headquarters are not living in an ivory tower.

These plant visits are spread over a three-week period, and we spend an average of half a day at each plant. The plant manager is free to bring to these meetings any of his supervisors he wishes. We ask him not to bring in anybody below the supervisory level. Then, of course, you get into organized labor. During the half day we spend at each plant we discuss the budget primarily. However, if I have time I like to wander through the plant and see how things are going. Also, I go over in great detail the property replacement and maintenance budget with the plant manager.

About September 1, the plant budgets come into British City, and the accounting department consolidates them. Then, the product division vice-presidents review their respective divisional budgets to see if the division budget is reasonable in terms of what the vice-president thinks the corporate management wants. If he is not satisfied with the consolidated plant budgets, he will ask the various plants within the division to trim their budget figures.

When the division vice-presidents and the executive vice-president are happy, they will send their budgets to the company president. He may accept the division budgets at this point. If he doesn't, he will specify the areas to be reexamined by division and, if necessary, by plant management. The final budget is approved at our December board of directors meeting.

Comparison of Actual and Standard Performance

At the end of the sixth business day after the close of the month, each plant wires to the head office certain operating variances, which we put together on what we call the variance analysis sheet. Within a half-hour after the last plant report comes through, variance analysis sheets for the divisions and plants are compiled. On the morning of the seventh business day after the end of the month, these reports are usually on the desks of the interested top management. The variance analysis sheet highlights the variances in what we consider to be critical areas. Receiving this report as soon as we do helps us at head office to take timely action. Let me emphasize, however, we do not accept the excuse that the plant manager has to go to the end of the month to know what happened during the month. He has to be on top of these particular items daily.

When the actual results come into the head office, we go over them on the basis of exception; that is, we only look at those figures that are in excess of the budgeted amounts. We believe this had a good effect on morale. The plant managers don't have to explain everything they do. They have to explain only where they go off base. In particular, we pay close attention to the net sales, gross margin, and the plant's ability to meet its standard manufacturing cost. Incidentally, when analyzing the gross sales we look closely at the price and mix changes.

All this information is summarized on a form known as the Profit Planning and Control Report No. 1 (see Exhibit 3). This document is backed up by a number of supporting documents (see Exhibit 4). The plant PPCR No. 1 and the month-end trial balance showing both actual and budget figures are received in British City at the close of the eighth business day after the end of the month. These two very important reports, along with the supporting reports (PPCR No. 2, PPCR No. 11) are then consolidated by the accounting department on PPCR-type forms to show the results of operations by division and company. The consolidated reports are distributed the next day.

In connection with the fixed cost items, we want to know whether or not the plants carried out the programs they said they would carry out. If they have not, we want to know why they have not. Here, we are looking for sound reasons. Also, we want to know if they have carried out their projected programs at the cost they said they would.

In addition to these reports, at the beginning of each month the plant managers prepare current estimates for the upcoming month and quarter on

Exhibit 3

EMPIRE GLASS COMPANY

Profit Planning and Control Report No. 1

MONTH: Income Gain (+) or Loss (-) From Prev. Year	MONTH: Income Gain (+) or Loss (-) From Budget	MONTH: Actual	Ref.		YEAR TO DATE: Actual	YEAR TO DATE: Income Gain (+) or Loss (–) From Budget	YEAR TO DATE: Income Gain (+) or Loss (–) From Prev. Year
			1	Gross Sales to Customers			
			2	Discounts & Allowances			
			3	Net Sales to Customers			
%	%		4	% Gain (+)/Loss (-)		%	%
				DOLLAR VOLUME GAIN (+)/ LOSS (-) DUE TO:			
			5	Sales Price			
			6	Sales Volume			
			6(a)	Trade Mix			
			7	Variable Cost of Sales			
			8	Profit Margin			
				PROFIT MARGIN GAIN (+)/ LOSS (-) DUE TO:			
			9	Profit Volume Ratio (P/V)			
			10	Dollar Volume			
%	%	%	11	Profit Volume Ratio (P/V)	%	%	%
Income Addition (+)					Income Addition (+)		
			12	Total Fixed Manufacturing Cost			
			13	Fixed Manufacturing Cost-Transfers			
			14	Plant Income (Standard)			
%	%	%	15	% of Net Sales	%	%	%
Income Addition (+) Income Reduction (–)					Income Addition (+) Income Reduction (–)		
%	%	%	16	% Performance	%	%	%
			17	Manufacturing Efficiency			
Income Addition (+)					Income Addition (+)		
			18	Methods Improvements			
			19	Other Revisions of Standards			
			20	Material Price Changes			
			21	Division Special Projects			
			22	Company Special Projects			
			23	New Plant Expense			
			24	Other Plant Expenses			
			25	Income on Seconds			
			26				
			27				
			28	Plant Income (Actual)			
%	%		29	% Gain (+)/Loss (–)		%	%
%	%	%	30	% of Net Sales	%	%	%
			36A				
Increase (+) or Decrease (-)				EMPLOYED CAPITAL	Increase (+) or Decrease (-)		
			37	Total Employed Capital			
%	%	%	38	% Return	%	%	%
			39	Turnover Rate			

______ Plant ______ Division ______ Month 19____

Exhibit 4. EMPIRE GLASS COMPANY

Brief Description of PPCR No. 2—PPCR No. 11

	Individual Plant Reports
Report	*Description*
PPCR No. 2	Manufacturing expense: Plant materials, labor, and variable overhead consumed. Detail of actual figures compared with budget and previous year's figures for year to date and current month.
PPCR No. 3	Plant expense: Plant fixed expenses incurred. Details of actual figures compared with budget and previous year's figures for year to date and current month.
PPCR No. 4	Analysis of sales and income: Plant operating gains and losses due to changes in sales revenue, profit margins and other sources of income. Details of actual figures compared with budget and previous year's figures for year to date and current month.
PPCR No. 5	Plant control statement: Analysis of plant raw material gains and losses, spoilage costs, and cost reductions programs. Actual figures compared with budget figures for current month and year to date.
PPCR No. 6	Comparison of sales by principal and product groups: Plant sales dollars, profit margin and P/V ratios broken down by end product use (i.e., soft drinks, beer). Compares actual figures with budgeted figures for year to date and current month.
	Division Summary Reports
Report	*Description*
PPCR No. 7	Comparative plant performance, sales and income: Gross sales and income figures by plants. Actual figures compared with budget figures for year to date and current month.
PPCR No. 8	Comparative plant performance, total plant expenses: Profit margin, total fixed costs, manufacturing efficiency, other plant expenses and P/V ratios by plants. Actual figures compared with budgeted and previous year's figures for current month and year to date.
PPCR No. 9	Manufacturing efficiency: Analysis of gains and losses by plant in areas of materials, spoilage, supplies and labor. Current month and year to date actuals reported in total dollars and as a percentage of budget.
PPCR No. 10	Inventory: Comparison of actual and budget inventory figures by major inventory accounts and plants.
PPCR No. 11	Status of capital expenditures: Analysis of the status of capital expenditures by plants, months and relative to budget.

forms similar to the variance analysis sheets. Since our budget is based on known programs, the value of this current estimate is that it gets the plant people to look at their programs. Hopefully, they will realize that they cannot run their plants on a day-to-day basis.

If we see a sore spot coming up, or if the plant manager draws our attention to a potential trouble area, we may ask that daily reports concerning this item be sent to the particular division top management involved. In addition, the division top management may send a division staff specialist—say, a quality control expert if it is a quality problem—to the plant concerned. The division staff members can make recommendations, but it is up to the plant manager to accept or reject these recommendations. Of course, it is well known throughout the company that we expect the plant managers to accept gracefully the help of the head office and division staffs.

Sales-Manufacturing Relations

If a sales decline occurs during the early part of the year, and if the plant managers can convince us that the change is permanent, we may revise the plant budgets to reflect these new circumstances. However, if toward the end of the year the actual sales volume suddenly drops below the predicted sales volume, we don't have much time to change the budget plans. What we do is ask the plant managers to go back over their budgets with their staffs and see where reduction of expense programs will do the least harm. Specifically, we ask them to consider what they may be able to eliminate this year or delay until next year.

I believe it was Confucius who said: "We make plans so we have plans to discard." Nevertheless, I think it is wise to make plans, even if you have to discard them. Having plans makes it a lot easier to figure out what to do when sales fall off from the budgeted level. The understanding of operations that comes from preparing the budget removes a lot of the potential chaos and confusion that might arise if we were under pressure to meet a stated profit goal and sales declined quickly and unexpectedly at year-end, just as they did last year. In these circumstances, we don't try to ram anything down the plant managers' throats. We ask them to tell us where they can reasonably expect to cut costs below the budgeted level.

Whenever a problem arises at a plant between sales and production, the local people are supposed to solve the problem themselves. For example, a customer's purchasing agent may insist he wants an immediate delivery, and this delivery will disrupt the production department's plans. The production group can make recommendations as to alternative ways to take care of the problem, but it's the sales manager's responsibility to get the product to the customer. The salesmen are supposed to know their customers well enough to judge whether or not the customer really needs the product. If the sales manager says the customer needs the product, that ends the matter. As far as we are concerned, the customer's wants are primary; our company is a case where sales wags the rest of the dog.

Of course, if the change in the sales program involves a major plant expense which is out of line with the budget, then the matter is passed up to division for decision.

As I said earlier, the sales department has the sole responsibility for the product price, sales mix, and delivery schedules. They do not have direct responsibility for plant operations or profit. That's the plant management's responsibility. However, it is understood that sales group will cooperate with the plant people wherever possible.

Motivation

There are various ways in which we motivate the plant managers to meet their profit goals. First of all, we only promote capable people. Also, a monetary incentive program has been established that stimulates their efforts to achieve their profit goals. In addition, each month we put together a bar chart which shows, by division and plant, the ranking of the various manufacturing units with respect to manufacturing efficiency.[1] We feel the plant managers are one hundred percent responsible for variable manufacturing costs. I believe this is true, since all manufacturing standards have to be approved by plant managers. Most of the plant managers give wide publicity to these bar charts. The efficiency bar chart and efficiency measure itself is perhaps a little unfair in some respects when you are comparing one plant with another. Different kinds of products are run through different plants. These require different setups, etc., which have an important impact on a position of the plant. However, in general, the efficiency rating is a good indication of the quality of the plant manager and his supervisory staff.

Also, a number of plants run competitions within the plants which reward department heads, or foremen, based on their relative standing with respect to a certain cost item. The plant managers, their staffs, and employees have great pride in their plants.

The number one item now stressed at the plant level is *quality*. The market situation is such that in order to make sales you have to meet the market price and exceed the market quality. By quality I mean not only the physical characteristics of the product but also such things as delivery schedules. As I read the company employee publications, their message is that if the company is to be profitable it must produce high-quality items at a reasonable cost. This is necessary so that the plants can meet their obligation to produce the maximum profits for the company in the prevailing circumstances.

---

[1] Manufacturing efficiency $= \dfrac{\text{total actual variable manufacturing costs}}{\text{total standard variable manufacturing costs}} \times 100\%$

The Future

An essential part of the budgetary control system is planning. We have developed a philosophy that we must begin our plans where the work is done —in the line organization and out in the field. Perhaps, in the future, we can avoid or cut back some of the budget preparation steps and start putting together our sales budget later than May 15. However, I doubt if we will change the basic philosophy.

Frankly, I doubt if the line operators would want any major change in the system; they are very jealous of the management prerogatives the system gives to them.

It is very important that we manage the budget. We have to be continually on guard against its managing us. Sometimes, the plants lose sight of this fact. We have to be made conscious daily of the necessity of having the sales volume to make a profit. And when sales fall off and their plant programs are reduced, they do not always appear to see the justification for budget cuts. Although I do suspect that they see more of the justification for these cuts than they will admit. It is this human side of the budget to which we have to pay more attention in the future.

QUESTION

Comment on the strong points and the weak points in the management control system of Empire Glass Company. What changes, if any, would you suggest?

Chapter Nine

LONG-RANGE PLANNING

Formal long-range planning as used here refers to a systematic way of preparing estimates for a whole enterprise, including balance sheets and income statements, for a number of years in the future; the usual number is five.

Such long-range planning for industrial enterprises, although relatively new, is attracting considerable attention, particularly in large corporations and in companies in fields with a rapid pace of technological progress.

The need for long-range planning by the managements of such companies is clear: new products, new markets, and new production processes are increasingly available for those with the imagination to see them and the determination to act. It is by no means clear, however, that a formal long-range planning mechanism is a worthwhile part of the planning process in all these companies. A central question, therefore, is: What types of companies should engage in formal long-range planning? In other words, although no one can disagree with the desirability of thinking about the future, it is by no means certain that the value derived from five-year projections of balance sheets and income statements is worth the considerable amount of effort required to compile them.

A second question, assuming that formal long-range planning is worthwhile in certain circumstances, is: What is the best way to do long-range planning? The Northwest Aggregates case is certainly not given as a model, but analysis of what happened in that company may suggest useful ways of answering this question.

Reading 9–1

Basic Approach to Long-Range Planning

By George A. Steiner*

This paper centers on two basic points. First, there is no generally accepted definition of long-range planning. Second, partly—but not wholly—because of this, there are different approaches to long-range planning, many of which are equally acceptable and successful.

The focus of this paper is on long-range planning in large business organizations. Much that is said, however, is applicable to smaller business firms and to non-business organizations.

WHAT IS LONG-RANGE PLANNING?

Justice Holmes once observed that "A word is not crystal, transparent and unchanged. It is the skin of a living thought and may vary greatly in color and content according to the circumstances and the time in which it is used."[1] This is certainly true of long-range planning. The words mean different things to different people, at different times in the same company, and among companies.

While I do not aspire to resolve the semantic problem associated with these words in this article, it is important to discuss different definitions. In dealing with approaches to long-range planning we should at least organize our confusion by talking about definitions. Perhaps of more importance is

---

* Director, division of research, and professor of business administration, Graduate School of Business Administration, U.C.L.A. Presented at the annual meeting of the Academy of Management, Pittsburgh, Pa., December 27, 1962. Portions of this material appear in Chapter 20 of *Managerial Long-Range Planning*, by G. A. Steiner, copyright 1963, published by McGraw-Hill Book Company.

[1] *Towne* v. *Eisner,* 215 U.S. 418 (1917).

the fact that in the business world, at least, actions follow concepts. What is done in the name of long-range planning follows definitions of the term, and vice versa.

Among the current crop of jocular definitions might be mentioned these: Long-range planning is missing the forest *and* the trees. Long-range planning is asking "what's for dinner?" instead of "what's for lunch?" Long-range planning is putting off until tomorrow what should be done today. But, there are more substantive definitions.

Long-range planning deals with the futurity of present decisions. Decisions are made only in the present. Actions taken today will have long-range consequences and long-range planning examines these evolving chains of cause and effect.

Long-range planning is the examination of future alternatives open to a business to provide a framework, perspective, or umbrella, within which current decisions can be made. Long-range planning, in this view, is the setting of future goals and the basic strategies to achieve them. These serve as guides to current operating decisions.

Long-range planning is choosing from among alternative courses of action. Planning is the conscious determination of courses of action to achieve objectives. In the development of objectives and the means to achieve them, choices have to be made. Long-range planning does this over an extended period of time.

Long-range planning deals with a stream of commitments of resources over time. Long-range planning examines consequences of commitments over time plus choices open when committed resources become liquid or uncommitted. Since commitments vary greatly in time and become uncommitted continuously, long-range planning is a continuous process extending well beyond the ending of a "sunk" commitment.

Long-range planning makes forecasts about matters of importance to business and helps the firm adjust to them or surmount them if they are not acceptable. For example, it treats such questions as: "Evolving technology will make our product obsolete in the next few years. What shall we do about it?" Making the discovery and examining ways to overcome the problem constitute long-range planning in this definition.

Long-range planning is the development of an image of what the company should be like in some future time.

Long-range planning is the development of a comprehensive and uniform program of plans for the entire company reaching out over a long period of time. Here is the idea that long-range planning results in specific actions to be taken over a long period of time in a fashion comparable to details of a community's master physical development plan.

This definition also accommodates the idea that long-range planning is an integrating framework for all company plans and decisions. It provides a comprehensive basis within which each of the functional area plans can be integrated one with another and all with an over-all plan for the entire enterprise. To do this does not imply the building block precision inherent in the above definition.

Long-range planning, in my view, encompasses all these ideas and a few others. Long-range planning is the conscious determination of courses of action to achieve prescribed goals. Planning is deciding in advance what is to be done, when it is to be done, how it is to be done, and who is to do it. Long-range planning attempts to do this for extended periods of time. The further ahead, however, the less is the detail. Long-range planning is a process which begins with long-range objectives and develops from them concrete targets or goals for achievement. It establishes policies and strategies for achieving these goals. The process examines the future consequences of present decisions and also provides a perspective, an overall frame of reference, for making present decisions. It develops detailed sub-goals and sub-plans and means to achieve them. The closer to the present the more detailed they are. It assures that sub-plans are implemented. Long-range planning also should include review of performance toward goals and insure that an appropriate feedback of progress is applied in the planning cycle.

Viewed this way, the distinction between long- and short-range planning becomes blurred. Each influences the other. In addition, the definition accommodates a great many different approaches, sequential steps, and planning structures.

Because of the semantic confusion associated with long-range planning I suggest the phrase should be abolished. It creates more problems than solutions. Rather, for the present, it might be better to speak of corporate planning as having a variety of parts. One might be long-range strategic planning. This would encompass objective and goal setting, as well as the development of broad policies and strategies to achieve them. Another facet might be detailed programming of activities to fit within these strategies. These programs could encompass both current one-year (or shorter) operational plans and intermediate-range plans extending over a period of years. Corporate planning, of course, could also include different plans covering functional areas. Clearly, the parts of corporate planning could also be categorized in other ways.

For our purposes the important point is that in the absence of a uniform acceptable definition of long-range planning, and in light of the variety of currently used definitions of the term, there inevitably must be, by the very definition of terms, a variety of approaches to long-range planning.

WHAT MAJOR FACTORS INFLUENCE BASIC APPROACHES TO LONG-RANGE PLANNING?

Fundamentally, all planning must be predicated upon the basic analytical problem-solving steps which are generally familiar. In the simplest model, the steps are these: determine and define the problem, collect all pertinent facts, consider all possible alternatives to solve the problem, choose a solution or solutions, and take action to solve the problem. In a more sophisticated form for a business enterprise the following steps may be differentiated: lay out a plan for the plan; establish objectives and goals; prepare planning premises; search for alternative courses of action; evaluate alternative courses of action; select a course or courses of action to follow; formulate necessary derivative plans in functional areas; assure the proper implementation of plans; and provide adequate review of performance. The last two steps might be considered control rather than planning. I have included them here simply to cover a complete planning program.

These steps are generally recognized and accepted. How companies go about building planning programs from them, however, varies tremendously. As the old Japanese couplet observed:

> Though there may be many paths about the foot of the mountain
> Yet, when the top is reached, the same moon is seen.

A thumb-nail sketch of a few major considerations influencing basic approaches to long-range planning is as follows. First, as noted above, the definition of long-range planning is of major consideration. A company that thinks of long-range planning as a process of framing the corporate image will go about the job in a different fashion from one which takes action on the basis of the last definition given.

Second, characteristics of the top management will be important. One approach will be followed if this philosophy is accepted:

> Don't worry about the future
> The present is all thou hast
> The future will soon be present
> And the present will soon be past.

Quite another approach will be followed if the top management believes, as Ernest Breech did, that it is their business to make trends rather than to follow them.

Third, organization of the company will be important in the approach to planning. A company having strong product divisions considered to be profit-making centers will have an approach different from a centrally controlled company divided into functional departments.

Fourth, is the way plans are structured. A company that wishes to develop a coordinated and comprehensive planning program which includes all important elements of the company, and ties tightly together short-range, intermediate-range, and long-range strategic plans will follow an approach considerably different from a company that does not seek such comprehensive coordination.

A final factor is the stage of evolution of the long-range planning program. I have concluded on the basis of empirical study that companies with multiple divisions have gone through about five observable stages in the development of long-range planning programs. These steps were generally confirmed by the participants in, and papers prepared for, the UCLA research seminar on long-range planning, noted above, and by a study of the Stanford Research Institute.[2] This evolution deserves more than passing mention in this paper.

Business firms generally get involved in formal long-range planning as a result of a major problem or the general feeling that since other companies are doing it perhaps they also should. In either event an evolutionary process frequently sets in which typically goes through the following stages.

Stage one is entered when an individual or a committee is assigned to look into the matter. If an individual is assigned he frequently is the controller, but may be an assistant to the president, a vice president, or a person interested in the job. If a group is assigned the task it is composed of the senior staff of the president. Staff specialists may be invited to advise the group on some problems. A good bit of information is collected and focused on special problems. Solutions are recommended and actions taken. Corporate objectives are developed and a more permanent and integrated planning program is discussed and recommended.

At the end of about one year a planning director is appointed and the next stage begins. He is given a small staff which includes economic, financial, engineering, and perhaps scientific talent. The mix depends, of course, much upon the company and industry. The work of this group does not follow a typical pattern but generally includes the development of corporate goals, examination in detail of the strengths and weaknesses of the company, analysis of the evolving environment in which the company will operate, surveys of where the company is heading, identification of new fields for corporate growth, and creation of a basis for the development of a comprehensive corporate planning effort. Division personnel participate in individual studies.

Around the beginning of the third year plans are laid for the first comprehensive plan and the next stage begins. The central corporate planning group gives general guidance to the divisions for their development of a plan. Frequently the plan covers the next five-year period. But parts of it may extend beyond five years. Once these plans are completed they are submitted to the central planning group for integration, aggregation and assessment. The divisional plans are examined in light of corporate goals and often a gap appears between divisional projected developments and corporate goals. The problem then becomes one of how to fill this gap. Or, as often happens, divisional capital requirements are well beyond the financial capability of the corporation. This calls for drastic revisions of plans, tapping new sources of capital, or re-examining proposed courses of action. While the resulting plans are by no means considered by anybody as being perfect, they result in important decisions for action.

On the basis of the value to the corporation of this stage, the planning director is made a vice president and planning becomes formalized in the

[2] R. Hal Mason, "Organizing for Corporate Planning," *Proceedings of the Long Range Planning Service Client Conference,* Stanford Research Institute, Menlo Park, California, 1962.

divisions. The central staff continues to give guidance to the divisions in the planning program but turns more to over-all corporate development problems. Presentation of division plans are made directly to top management. At the divisional levels, planning coordinators are appointed and report in a staff capacity to general managers.

Planning becomes firmly established in the company in the final stage and the central planning staff begins to exercise a more critical evaluative review of divisional activities in relationship to company objectives. The work of the central planning staff expands in other directions to be noted shortly. At the divisional level the planning coordinators are given responsibility both for long-range and short-range planning, thereby assuring a close relationship between the two. In addition, they begin to take on control activities in conjunction with their current operating planning responsibilities. On behalf of the general manager these control activities concern evaluation of performance in relation to plans.

These stages seem to me to have been followed by so many companies and a number of government agencies that they appear to be somewhat typical. Since we know so much more about planning today than we did ten years ago, the sequence of stages of a company now entering the ranks of formalized long-range planners may be a little different and the evolutionary process considerably telescoped in time. For any individual company, of course, the sequence of stages and methods of operation may vary much from this presumably typical pattern.

On the basis of these major factors affecting approaches to planning it is obvious that a variety of approaches not only is possible but predictable. They range from one extreme in which an individual company chief executive has his goals and strategies in his own mind and communicates them to others only as required. Ernest Tener Weir may illustrate this end of the spectrum. At the other extreme is the very large corporation with a series of planning staffs in central headquarters and in the divisions and with a set of formalized planning programs, the results of which are made generally available as guides to decision-making throughout the enterprise. In between, of course, are many other approaches.

Rather than attempt a panoramic survey of the many possible different approaches it seems more fruitful to present a composite, or typical, structure of planning arrangements in large enterprises. For this purpose I present the case of the large, decentralized corporation having had much and sophisticated long-range planning experience. The following composite picture is based upon examination of a number of structures of large organizations.

PLANNING PATTERNS IN A LARGE MULTI-DIVISIONAL CORPORATION

In size the company may have from 25,000 to 50,000 or more employees, sales in the hundreds of millions, and powerful product divisions operating as semi-autonomous profit-making centers. The company may also have small product divisions. Products of the company are not homogeneous and are subject to rapid obsolescence. The setting is one in which top management has given unflinching support to forward and comprehensive planning for many years. This is enough background description for our purposes here.

The corporation has a strong board of directors, vitally interested in looking ahead and preparing for the future. The chairman of the board is a past president of the company and takes seriously his duties to assure continuing survival, growth, and prosperity of the company through the uncertainties of the future. This responsibility is discharged by giving guidance to and checking appropriately on results of activities of the president, who has authority over corporate staff.

The president in turn takes seriously his obligation to minimize current "fire-fighting" and spends an appropriate amount of time on the future of the enterprise. He has a policy-making committee to help in decision-making, composed of his top vice presidents. Reporting to one of these vice presidents, or to the president himself is the central planning staff.

The central planning staff has six major functions. First is development planning. Included in this function are diversification planning, the development of new areas for company growth, planning new product developments, and undertaking special studies of major interest to the company and its divisions, such as important potential future environmental changes. These studies sometimes have a very long time dimension. (The Ford Motor Company, for example, is undertaking a study of transportation needs and patterns in the year 2000.) They point out new directions for the company, lay strategies for the company, and provide a basis for current decision.

Second is the development of comprehensive strategic plans covering rather long periods of time. These plans may be reviewed and revised periodically, such as once each year. Or they may be developed only when considered necessary, with supplementary examination of changes affecting the plans which are made annually. The strategic plans cover the objectives which the company should seek over a long period of time. Specific goals may be set for sales, profits, assets, capital structure, share of market, employment, staffing patterns, and organization. Plans cover problems of the company in achieving the goals and specific strategies to overcome the problems and hit the targets. Strategies cover all relevant major activities of the company: products, manpower, financial, management personnel, industrial relations organization, marketing, public relations, and research and development.

The inclusion of all relevant considerations in the development of strategies does not mean, of course, that the central planning department is the sole custodian of long-range planning in the company. Other parallel staff groups have functions which necessitate their looking ahead and laying plans. For instance, there are long-range plans of the organization planning department. The vice president of sales may be developing long-range marketing plans, the vice president of research and development may be preparing long-range research plans, the vice president of manufacturing may be developing long-range capital facility expenditure plans, the vice president of finance may be preparing long-range financial plans, and the vice president of personnel may be developing long-range management training, selection and staffing plans. There are, of course, other possibilities depending upon corporate headquarters organization.

But the central planning staff operations serve to integrate, to bring together all these planning efforts into one consolidated framework. Staff from these other areas participate in the strategic planning operation. A committee may exist to aid this coordination. But it is the responsibility of the central planning staff to get the planning document together for presentation to top management for review, approval, and action. Even though the document may comprehensively cover all corporate activities, the central planning staff does not assume the authority for making parts of the corporate planning job lodged in other corporate staff departments.

Third is guidance to the divisions in their planning beyond immediate operations. This may take the form of procedural and substantive guidance. In the case of the former, the staff serves to assure some uniformity in the procedures followed by the divisions in developing their plans. This may take the form of establishing uniform time schedules, forms for presenting data, rules for preparing data, and procedures for presentation of plans to top management. Substantive guidance may take a variety of forms. Of basic importance is the establishment of assumptions to guide the planning effort, such as product allocation among the divisions. The staff may make forecasts of environmental factors of importance to the divisions for their guidance. Included would be forecasts of demand by major customers, price trends for material purchases, economic trends (e.g., Gross National Product), technological trends, and general industry competitive conditions. The strategic plans also provide general guidance. The central staff also stands ready to help the divisions upon request with substantive problems. Throughout this process there is continuous discussion among the central planning staff and corporate management and staff, and between corporate staff and division staff.

Fourth, the central staff reviews plans prepared by the divisions. While the divisions make plans based upon the guidance of the central planning staff, the plans are presented by the divisions directly to the executive vice president or to a top management committee. These plans are both one-year operational and long-range plans. The central planning staff reviews these plans after presentation to top management for any major problems which they may create. In addition, the central planning staff reviews division plans to evaluate the extent to which the aggregated plans for the corporation as a whole move toward corporate objectives.

Fifth, the central planning staff may make long-range plans for weak divisions, or at least set forth strategies to resolve current or anticipated difficulties. The staff may also examine long-range problems of a particular division as a basis for management action with respect to that division.

Finally, of course, top management from time to time makes specific requests for staff assistance covering a variety of problems having both short- and long-range time dimensions.

In large divisions the planning activities are lodged in the office of a vice president of long-range planning. This individual coordinates the work of the major departments in the division. A major device to help him is a division committee of which he is chairman and on which are represented the persons responsible for major staffs in the divisional central offices and persons responsible for planning in the departments of the division. This committee is a forum for discussing goals and objectives of the division and their relations to those of the corporation as a whole, the annual planning activities with their array of procedures and problems, developments of importance in the annual preparations of plans, and a review of the completed plans.

The vice president of long-range planning is responsible for the following major functions: maintaining liaison with both the headquarters planning offices, the divisional general manager, and other divisional personnel; giving broad procedural guidance to the departments in the development of their plans; giving substantive guidance in the form of economic, technical and other forecasts of environment, some of which are made with other divisional staff and personnel; coordinating the planning operation; aggregating the plans for top management review and approval; analyzing problems brought to light in the plans; and presenting the plans, with the help of department representatives, to management in the central headquarters office. Throughout the process there is continuous discussion between the central planning group and the general manager, central staff offices, and departmental personnel who make the plans. There is, of course, at the departmental levels a comparable relationship with department heads and other managers.

Three sets of plans are made: a corporate strategic long-range plan, a divisional five-year intermediate-range plan, and the divisional one-year operational plan. Special long-range studies, which eventually move into formal plans, are made at all levels in the company. All are tied together because the planner in the departments is responsible for both long-range and short-range planning, and at the divisional headquarters level the vice president of long-range planning is also responsible for aggregating the divisional short-range plan and relating it to the medium- and long-range plans.

VARIATIONS FROM THE COMPOSITE PICTURE

While the above illustration may be considered a composite or typical arrangement in a large sophisticated corporation, it does not *exactly* describe any planning patterns in any corporation with which I am familiar. In practice there are variations from the description. Some of the important variations are as follows.

First is the role played by the board of directors. In some companies the board takes a direct hand in guiding and evaluating divisional long-range planning. This is true at E. I. duPont de Nemours, Inc. In other companies the board does not assume its proper responsibilities in long-range planning.

Second, top management in many companies strongly supports formalized long-range planning throughout the enterprise. In other companies planning staffs struggle to make their efforts felt.

Third, the power of central planning staff directors varies considerably. In some companies top management relies too heavily on recommendations of staff. This gives staff considerable power. In other companies central planning staff exercises little influence in decision-making. On the whole, however, where central planning staffs exist they exert important influence over decisions.

Fourth, not all companies that have sophisticated long-range planning have planning departments. In some companies, Ford Motor Company, for instance, traditional central corporate staffs are under the direction of a vice president who coordinates the long-range planning programs of the company. At Continental Oil the members of the Management Executive Committee, except for the President, comprise the Long-Range Planning Committee. The Coordinator of Long-Range Planning is the Administrative Secretary of the Committee. In some companies, division general managers coordinate their long-range planning in meetings with the executive vice president.

Fifth, in some companies the planning director reports directly to the president. In very large companies reporting is usually through a vice president. Standard Oil Company of Indiana has an interesting arrangement where Dr. Lawrence A. Kimpton, who heads the long-range planning program, reports directly to the President and is also a member of the Board of Directors.

Sixth, the degree to which division plans tie into central corporate staff strategic planning varies widely. At Ford, for example, central finance staff develops suggested goals of return on assets and earnings per share of stock. These are bases for discussions between the President and division managers, out of which goals are set for the divisions' operations. At Lockheed Aircraft Corporation, the President asks the divisions to look at the strategic plans as guides for their action. There is not a direct compulsion for the divisions to act in response to these general plans. In some areas, however, the President will take direct action on the basis of the plans.

Seventh, the scope of planning varies. In some companies, formalized integrated long-range planning encompasses all major activities of the enterprise. In others, each functional area engages in long-range planning and only the loosest sort of coordination takes place at top management councils. These variations exist not only among companies but in individual companies over time.

Eighth, the planning period varies among companies. The general pattern seems to be strategic planning moving into the future as far as seems practicable. Usually this is five to ten years for most parts of the strategic planning, but beyond that for other parts, as appropriate. Then, rather detailed intermediate-range plans covering four or five years seem to be the vogue in large corporations. These plans cover sales, profits, facilities, manpower, research and development, and comparable functions. The first year of the four- or five-year plans constitutes the current operating plan. The long-range strategic plan provides a framework for the intermediate-range plan, but the connection is loose. The relationship between the short-range one-year and the intermediate-range plan, however, is very close. This pattern suggests that long-range planning might well be divided into major parts. One is strategic planning and the other programming. The first lays out broad preferred guidelines for the company and divisions. The second translates these into specific proposed and operational plans. In large companies this distinction has merit.

Ninth, planning in companies centrally controlled, with homogeneous products, or with functional divisions, is frequently conducted on a somewhat different basis. At Continental Oil and American Airlines, for instance, the corporate long-range planning department does not have a counterpart in the divisions. It operates in much the same fashion as the central planning department in the case illustration. But instead of integrating the plans of the divisions it integrates the plans of the corporate headquarters staff who are in charge of the different functional areas. The more heterogeneous the product lines, as at Bendix Aviation, for example, and the more sophisticated and changing the technology, as in the aerospace industry, the greater is the need for decentralization of long-range planning groups. In such instances, the divisional long-range planning staff may act in much the same fashion as the central planning staff in a company controlled centrally.

Finally, the actual operational steps taken to accomplish the planning programs vary much. This is not the occasion, however, to discuss them. To do so would involve more detail than should be accommodated in this article.

SOME REQUIREMENTS FOR SUCCESSFUL LONG-RANGE PLANNING

It is fitting to close this analysis with requirements for successful long-range planning because they will determine the preferred approach. Since the subject has been dealt with in the literature I shall be very brief.

First, top management support and interest in long-range planning is indispensable to its success.

Second, top management must make use of at least some of the recommendations of long-range planning staffs. Failure to take action or continuous vacillation will bring results which will weaken the planning staff efforts.

Third, planning staffs must be continuously reminded that line managers, not they, make operating decisions.

Fourth, plans should be put into writing for everyone to see who has a need to know.

Fifth, adequate implementation machinery should be available to carry out decisions.

Sixth, planning should not be separated from operating. In large enterprises this principle generally results in central headquarters providing guidance for the development of plans by the operating sections whose plans are then presented to top management for its review and approval. Central planning groups must, of course, have knowledge in depth of operating conditions, and operating people should be familiar with central corporate planning activities. A healthy mixture of knowledge and liaison is important in improving planning.

Seventh, a careful balance should be struck between the use of committees and reliance on one or two men working alone. Either extreme is dangerous.

Eighth, it should be recognized that life is so complicated that it is impossible to tie together all plans into a complete coordinated set of relationships. The further out in time the less detail is appropriate and the looser are the relationships among parts of the planning program. In developing current operational plans, tighter relationships are possible and desirable.

SUMMARY AND CONCLUSIONS

This article points out that there are many definitions of long-range planning. The semantic confusion surrounding the words long-range planning suggests they should be abandoned and, in the absence of more inspired definitions than now exist, corporate planning should be spoken of as having different parts. This article does not set out to resolve the definitional problem. Rather, different definitions are noted because in practice approaches to longe-range planning depend much upon definitions.

Approaches to long-range planning also depend upon such considerations as the characteristics, interests, and methods of operation of top management; the organizational and authority structure of the company; the way in which different plans are prepared and integrated; and the evolution of long-range planning. Many companies have gone through a series of discernible steps in the development of long-range planning. The stage of development also determines in important measure the approach to planning.

Because it is impossible in a short article to exhaust the different approaches to planning, a case illustration of typical planning patterns in a large, multi-divisional, and sophisticated planning company is given as a basic frame of reference. General variations found in practice to this composite picture are presented. These are followed by a brief list of requirements for successful long-range planning.

Case 9–1

Northwest Aggregates Corporation (A)

In November, 1960, Leroy Cunningham, president of Northwest Aggregates Corporation, met with William H. Milford, the company's marketing vice-president and John Van Sickle, the company's financial vice-president and controller, to inform them of his decision to hold a conference of the company's entire executive group in April, 1961. Mr. Cunningham told Mr. Milford and Mr. Van Sickle that he had been very well pleased with the results of a three-day conference on budgeting that Mr. Van Sickle had organized earlier in the year, and that he believed programs of this kind could be an exceptionally useful device for obtaining closer coordination among the diverse segments of Northwest's business. He stated his conviction that the previous session, which concerned corporate budgeting procedures, had significantly increased both the interest in and understanding of the ways in which the division managements could utilize this tool. He also said that the meetings had provided a very useful medium for allowing division officers to become better acquainted with one another and for emphasizing to the management of each division that it was a part of a very large corporation being guided by the central management group.

The name Northwest Aggregates Corporation had been adopted by the long-established Seattle Stone Company in 1956, when it started a program of expansion, largely through the acquisition of existing independent companies. The corporation became one of the first nationwide producers of commercial aggregates (i.e., sand, gravel, and crushed stone) in the United States. Most of the 6,000 other companies in the industry conducted local operations.

The Seattle Stone Company was a family-owned firm, and members were still active in the management of Northwest Aggregates. Robert P. Stearns, son of one of the founders, was president from 1957 to 1959, and then became chairman of the board and general manager of the materials division. Leroy

Cunningham had been a partner in the law firm that had handled the Stearns family's business for many years. He was involved in the original acquisition plans and negotiations, and had joined the company in 1957 as executive vice-president. He became president in 1959.

As of 1960, Northwest Aggregates consisted of nine divisions, each still managed by the officials incumbent at the time of acquisition, which had been effected through an exchange of stock. Typically, these men had founded or grown up with their companies.

Summary descriptions of these nine divisions are as follows.

Seattle Stone division. The original company. Quarried, processed, and sold commercial aggregates in the states of Washington and Oregon. Also processed and sold slag, a steelmaking by-product used in highway and railway bed construction.

Wilson Stone division. Acquired in December, 1956. Produced and sold commercial aggregates in Idaho. John R. Stearns, president, was a cousin of Robert P. Stearns.

Titan Detinning division. Acquired in December, 1956. Purchased tinplate scrap, separated the steel (95 percent) from the tin (4 percent), and sold these products. Plants located near tinplate users in San Francisco, Chicago, and Houston.

Western Concrete pipe division. Acquired in December, 1956. Produced and sold concrete pipe. Nine plants located in five Northwest states.

Empire Chemical division. Acquired December, 1957. Produced brine from wells; manufactured this raw material into chlorine, muriatic acid, caustic soda, and related chemicals; and sold these to industrial users.

Materials division. Acquired December, 1957. Produced and sold commercial aggregates, primarily in Chicago.

Farrell Brothers division. Acquired December, 1957. Produced and sold commercial aggregates in Oregon.

Klamath Falls Rock Products division. Acquired in fall of 1958. Engaged in the construction of highways, bridges, dams, tunnels, and airports in 15 western states.

J. F. L'Esperance and Sons division. Acquired in fall of 1958. Produced and sold commercial aggregates and engaged in the general construction business, principally in Idaho.

By 1960, sales of the expanded company had increased over fourfold, to about $120 million. Sales revenue was derived in approximately the following proportions:

Commercial aggregates, concrete, and similar material	60%
Concrete pipe products	12
Chemicals	14
Products recovered from tin scrap	14
Total	100%

The corporate officers of Northwest Aggregates consisted of a small group, including several officers of the Seattle Stone Company and Farrell Brothers.

As of 1958, none of these men had staff reporting to him, except Mr. Van Sickle, who supervised 23 people, and Mr. Strange, who, as vice-president for administration, had a small staff. By 1960, staff activities included market research, personnel policy, sales to major customers, budgetary control, and purchasing; the total annual expense of the headquarters office was approximately $2 million.

The divisions operated with considerable autonomy. In 1958, the principal report to headquarters was a monthly profit statement, prepared in whatever format the division wished. In 1959, a budget system was introduced, and headquarters approval was required for the annual operating budget, projected balance sheet, and capital expenditures. Initially, each division used the same format for its budget it had used for the monthly profit statement. A more uniform procedure and format applicable to all divisions was devised for the 1960 budget and was continued for 1961. Few divisions had used a budget of any kind prior to 1959.

Mr. Cunningham had proposed the conference for April, 1961, believing that it would be highly advantageous to discuss some question of major importance to the company. Since the subject of the past meeting had been in the financial area, he asked Mr. Milford, in marketing, to take on the responsibility for proposing an agenda for the next meeting. He suggested that Mr. Van Sickle could undoubtedly make some real contributions to this decision and asked that he assist Mr. Milford. Before terminating this session with the two men, Mr. Cunningham added that he felt the only weakness of the last meeting was that it had taken place at a very large resort hotel and the temptation for officers to miss meetings in favor of golf or tennis had been strong. He though it desirable, therefore, to plan that the April meeting be held at some much less glamorous location, where those attending would give complete attention to business problems for the duration of the conference.

Two days after the November meeting, Mr. Milford and Richard Aronson, director of market research, met with Mr. Van Sickle and Edward Carrol, the corporate treasurer, to discuss specific problems around which the session could be organized. Almost immediately, Mr. Milford and Mr. Aronson suggested that the subject should be long-range planning, which they said was the most topical subject of interest to management. To back up their position, Mr. Milford stated a number of reasons for their selection.

Mr. Milford recalled that early in the previous month Mr. Cunningham had set up a top management committee composed of Messrs. Milford, Van Sickle, Minter, Strange, and others, with the assignment of developing a definition of short-term, intermediate-term, and long-term corporate objectives. Mr. Milford reminded those present that the committee had met twice and had voted, at its second meeting, to defer further action until committee members could find out just what plans Mr. Cunningham had in mind for the company. Mr. Milford suggested that the April meeting could provide a good opportunity for an exchange of ideas about corporate objectives. Corporate management would be in a better position to select among competing objectives after a full discussion of the positions and potential of the operating divisions.

Also, a number of business reasons substantiated an interest in long-range planning. First, the company could always expect a sizable cash flow to result from its aggregates operations because of the nature of that business. Because of the heavy initial investments required, depreciation was a significant element of cost, and, hence, unless substantial capital investments were planned in advance, considerable amounts of uncommitted cash were likely to accumulate. Mr. Milford contended that the company was in no way prepared to allocate these funds intelligently without a continuing program of attention to operating programs more than one year in the future.

Second, market research studies indicate that in the next five years requirements for commercial aggregates in the United States were likely to grow by about 60 percent. For Northwest Aggregates, this rate would mean an increase in total sales of close to $50 million by the end of that period. Mr. Milford argued that since roughly $1.00 in capital had to be invested in property and equipment to support $1.00 in yearly sales of aggregates, definite plans had to be made for obtaining this amount of capital.

Third, it was recognized that many personnel and organizational changes were likely to occur in the next five years. One lively topic of debate was whether or not replacements existed within the company or could be found outside on retirement of the founders, who currently managed several of the aggregates divisions. It also was recognized that the divisional form of organization that Mr. Cunningham had adopted was appropriate for controlling the corporation as it was constituted at present, but it was not at all clear that this form would continue to be desirable if major changes in the character of the company's managerial personnel were to occur. Mr. Milford believed that attention should be given immediately to this problem, and that the preparation of long-range operating plans for each division would give the headquarters group more information on which to make these key decisions.

Fourth, there was considerable uncertainty as to where the future strength of the company lay. Many individuals tended to look to the future of Northwest Aggregates in terms of growth by mergers and acquisitions of other producers of aggregates. Others, however, believed that the future for Northwest Aggregates was brightest in the chemicals and detinning divisions, and that funds would eventually be channeled from the aggregate operations into these other businesses. Whichever of these one believed in, Mr. Milford contended, there was certainly no question about the fact that Northwest aggregates was engaged in a number of different businesses and that some formal long-range planning would definitely help to give better answers to these questions.

Finally, Mr. Aronson presented a short report on technological developments likely to occur in the aggregates industry. He pointed out that significant progress had been made in the area of developing lightweight aggregates, and that a number of completely new, and highly superior, products could be expected within the next decade. He reminded the group that steelmaking processes and iron ore compositions were changing considerably, and that sources of slag, the major product of the company's Seattle Stone division, were likely to disappear shortly. He stated that, all in all, he believed it was imperative for the Northwest company to begin to consider problems of this kind and to extend its planning time horizon beyond the one year provided in the budgeting program.

After these arguments had been presented, Mr. Van Sickle voiced his complete agreement with the need to consider all these questions. He recognized that each of them was of vital importance to the company's future and that they comprised the most important decisions currently facing the company. He stated, however, that he was "appalled at the thought of having another budgeting meeting in April." He believed that the central management had been emphasizing budgeting as strongly as it possibly could over the past few years, and that the divisions were not yet prepared to accept the concept of a formal long-range budgeting meeting. He said:

> Frankly, Bill, I was thrilled when Leroy threw the ball to you to come up with a marketing theme for this coming conference. I've pushed these characters about as far as I can at the moment, and progress has been fine. I'd hate to lose it by adding a five-year plan to their tasks at a premature stage. I'll tell you that I'd be scared to death of a long-range planning meeting where I'd have to get up and tell them how to plan their businesses for the next five years, when they don't really know how to plan for the current year yet. I believe that the best way to handle this meeting is to come up with a marketing issue—one that will be interesting and informative. Maybe new products or something—but for Pete's sake, let's keep away from the budgeting angle for a while.
>
> I'll tell you something else. We don't want these boys to get engaged in a lot of theoretical poppycock. Unless divisions are adequately prepared, they can't possibly do a good job of coming up with figures that will mean anything. And until the budget is refined, they just won't have the basic data on which to base good, sound long-range plans. These questions that you are proposing are wonderful, but the divisions aren't yet capable of doing much about them.

Mr. Milford and Mr. Van Sickle finally agreed that they would consult with Mr. Cunningham on the proposal. Mr. Van Sickle conceded that if Mr. Cunningham approved, and gave the topic his strong, personal endorsement, the chances for obtaining some worthwhile results would be improved.

QUESTION

1. Should the executives of Northwest Aggregates attempt long-range planning in 1961?

2. Assuming that the operating divisions are to be asked to present long-range (five-year) plans at the April, 1961, meeting, what instructions, advice, and assistance should the corporate headquarters give them in preparation for the meeting?

Case 9–2

Northwest Aggregates Corporation (B)

On January 17, 1961, Leroy Cunningham, president of Northwest Aggregates Corporation, wrote identical letters to the presidents of the company's nine divisions to announce a meeting of all corporate and division top management personnel to be held in Los Angeles, April 10 through April 12. Extracts from his letter follow:

> For this meeting, we will turn our attention to longer-range planning. With this in mind, the theme of the meeting will be: Northwest Aggregates Corporation—1966.
>
> In this connection we will ask each division to present its plan of operations for the year 1966, contrasting it with 1960 operations in terms of market potential, product interest, sales facilities and plant capacity, organization structure and manpower, and profits. We wish such presentation to reveal the steps that the division will pursue during 1961 to 1965—including the major problems that will be solved—in attaining the 1966 concept of operations. Furthermore, we would wish to have a discussion of the techniques used in developing the program.
>
> We hope that this effort will be developed as carefully and as wisely as present circumstances permit, but we realize that this first approach will be subject to modification and improvement. Indeed, the April program is intended to be a first step toward attainment of the advance planning and workable techniques we all need. . . . Within the limitations of time available to you prior to this meeting, however, we desire that this long-rang planning effort be a fully conscientious one. The purpose of the meeting is twofold. First, we are desirous of laying a strong foundation for a more formal long-term planning effort to be completed at some date not too far in the future. Second, we wish to educate ourselves as to the best methods available to us of developing sound long-range plans.

In the months that followed, all the divisions received from corporate headquarters, particularly from the market research department, a considerable amount of material containing data for possible use in preparation of the divisions' 1966 plans, and specific instructions as to certain techniques to be used. For example, market research provided its estimates of market potential indices based on 1960 markets for various types of construction activity. A communication from John Van Sickle, the vice-president for finance, indicated that the divisions should not attempt to allow for any assumed inflation of the dollar, except insofar as it would affect their relative competitive position. They were to prepare their forecasts in 1960 dollars and assume that inflation, if any, would affect them and their competitors equally with regard to costs as well as prices.

THE APRIL MEETING

On April 10, 1961, over 100 senior corporate and division officials gathered in the conference room of the Pacific Cabana Motel in Los Angeles for the Division Presidents 1961 Meeting. Also among those present were four guests, who had agreed to serve as a panel to listen to the presentations at the meeting and offer their criticisms at the end. The guests included Frederick LaSalle, controller of Mammoth Motors, Inc., one of the nation's largest automobile manufacturers, who had promised to give a short talk on the benefits that his company saw in long-range planning; Professors Gordon N. Thompson and H. John Mack of Pacific University business school, consultants to the company; and Dr. John Herbert, of Western Economics Corporation, an economic consultant permanently retained by the company.

The program lasted for three days. On the first two, a spokesman for each division presented its plans for five years hence. Each speaker was alloted an hour for his talk plus a group discussion. On the third day, the consultants talked on the presentations and the planning process in general, and there was further group discussion. The meetings opened with remarks by the president on the purpose of the gathering, and closed with comments by the board chairman.

It was the consensus of those who attended the meeting that the different divisions had used their one-hour allotments in surprisingly different ways. It was obvious that the planning activity had been taken fairly seriously by some, but had not been given much attention by others. For example, the Seattle Stone division's presentation consisted of little more than an appraisal of the current marketing problems that the division faced. In essence, the presentation summarized the facts that had been uncovered in the course of the division's budgeting for 1960, when executives had realized that it had become necessary to raise slag prices because of the rapidly changing characteristics of the market.

On the other hand, some divisions went to the extent of preparing a formal presentation, having it printed, and distributing it to the assembled group at the end of their hour. Two examples of this are the presentation of the Farrell Brothers division, summarized below, and that of the Empire Chemical division, summarized as the appendix. (The actual presentation of Empire Chemical was much more detailed than the summary in the appendix; it ran to 20 pages.) These plans illustrate two different approaches to the long-range planning assignment.

Farrell Brothers Division Presentation

Sales—Looking Ahead to 1966

In attempting to forecast our position in our market area in 1966, we have used the following procedure. First, we have analyzed our actual sales and profits for the years 1958, 1959, and 1960, and our budgeted sales for 1961. These sales figures we have divided into three categories—commercial, portable, and joint ventures. Next, we predicted sales at each of our existing commercial plants yearly through 1966, leaving out any existing plant that might cease operation during this period. The same procedure was followed with regard to our portable plants. Then, we made provisions for our tentative new commercial operations, effective the year in which we plan to put them into operation. Therefore, we arrived at a combined total unit sales and revenue for each year 1962 through 1966. To arrive at our sales figures for existing commercial plants, we took into consideration the following factors:

1. Estimated rate of population growth in each market area.
2. Estimated construction expenditures.
3. Programmed highway department expenditures.
4. Competitive climate.

To arrive at probable sales from portable operations, we gave main consideration to possible base and paving projects to be let in isolated areas and our chances of supplying a given percentage of this material. By using the five portable plants we now have, on an average we can produce a maximum of 1½ million tons per year. During the next five years, we are likely to get and produce a minimum of 1 million tons per year; therefore, we took an average of 1¼ million tons per year at an average price of $1.20 per ton for the year 1962, and $1.25 per ton for the years 1963, 1964, 1965, and 1966.

Finally, we pinned down the estimated start of operations at each new proposed plant, and attempted to predict the sales and average price at these locations from the start of operations up through 1966. Exhibit 1 is a summary of our anticipated sales activity 1962 through 1966. The trend of sales from our plant is on the decline, due to competition from various sources that provide in several cases a competitive truck haul into Eugene. We hope to offset some of this loss in sales by negotiating a lower freight rate into Halsey and the establishing of a materials yard to be stocked with materials from Coos Bay. You can see by the population trends shown in the exhibit [omitted here] that Douglas County had a 30 percent increase in population from 1950 to 1960. This indicates the tremendous construction materials potential in this county.

In Cascade County, we sell stone and sand on a commission basis at Toketee Falls. Our anticipated sales for these two operations in tons, average prices, dollar amount, and commission income received were estimated. We also estimated our

Exhibit 1

FARRELL BROTHERS DIVISION

Anticipated Sales Activity, 1962–66

(Thousands of dollars or tons, except price figures)

	1962	*1963*	*1964*	*1965*	*1966*
Existing commercial plants:					
Tons	5,313	5,434	5,693	5,731	5,809
Average price	$1.30	$1.29	$1.31	$1.31	$1.31
$—sales	$6,907	$7,010	$7,458	$7,508	$7,610
Tentative new operations:					
Tons	165	860	610	570	610
Average price	$1.22	$1.28	$1.33	$1.32	$1.34
$—sales	$201	$1,101	$811	$752	$817
Portable operations:					
Tons	1,250	1,250	1,250	1,250	1,250
Average price	$1.20	$1.25	$1.25	$1.25	$1.25
$—sales	$1,500	$1,563	$1,563	$1,563	$1,563
Totals (three items above):					
Tons	6,728	7,544	7,553	7,551	7,669
Average price	$1.28	$1.28	$1.30	$1.30	$1.30
$—sales	8,608	$9,674	$9,832	$9,823	$9,980
Joint venture operations:					
Tons	1,175	1,255	1,205	1,245	1,275
Average price	$1.22	$1.22	$1.23	$1.23	$1.23
$—sales	$1,434	$1,531	$1,482	$1,531	$1,568

Exhibit 2

FARRELL BROTHERS DIVISION
Projected Operating Statement, 1962–66

	1962	*1963*	*1964*	*1965*	*1966*
Total sales	$9,470,774	$10,617,543	$10,757,520	$10,747,080	$10,910,270
Cost of sales	6,264,080	6,766,722	6,479,313	6,420,853	6,441,877
Gross profit	$3,206,694	$ 3,850,821	$ 4,278,207	$ 4,326,227	$ 4,468,393
S.G. & A. expense	928,293	926,927	945,464	965,412	984,891
	$2,278,401	$ 2,923,894	$ 3,332,743	$ 3,360,815	$ 3,483,502
Joint venture income	328,646	339,244	347,686	353,620	354,848
Pretax net income	$2,607,047	$ 3,263,138	$ 3,680,429	$ 3,714,435	$ 3,838,350

sales for ready-mix concrete in cubic yards, average price per cubic yard, dollar amount of sales, and gross profit for the years 1962, 1963, 1964, 1965, and 1966 (see Exhibit 2).

This presentation was supported by additional exhibits giving (1) population changes in totals and percentages from 1950 to 1960, by counties, for the districts served, and (2) income from commission sales and sales of ready-mix concrete, in dollars and tons, for 1961 to 1966.

In addition, there was some explanation of the adjustments made to current figures in order to project the figures used in the operating statement, Exhibit 2. The categories mentioned were variable labor, fixed labor, fuel, repairs and maintenance, supplies and other costs, depreciation, taxes, insurance, leases of equipment, rent on land, capital expenditures, sales expense, and general and administrative expense. Variable labor, as an example of an item given relatively full treatment, but still brief, was expected to remain unchanged from 1961, when a 5 percent increase was added, through 1964, when an unexplained 1.5 cents per ton was added. Increased efficiency of plant was credited with keeping down this cost. Fuel cost, at the other extreme, was assumed to stay unchanged. General and administrative expense was increased overall by 1.5 percent. The supporting reasoning mentioned the addition of a general superintendent and 1.7 percent increase for merit raises. Other components of this expense item were listed; these were expected to increase by an unnamed amount. The comment on this item closed with this statement: "However, we do not believe that the amount of individual increase warrants further elaboration thereon."

Comments on Presentations

At the panel discussion on Wednesday morning, April 12, Professor Thompson, speaking on behalf of the whole panel, complimented the divisions on the generally high standard of their presentations. He said he had been amazed that the job had been done so seriously, since this was the first attempt at long-range planning within the company. He said that it had been obvious that all members of the division management groups had participated in the preparation of their plans, which was as it should have been. He was glad that members had avoided the temptation of having only the division controllers prepare plans. He said, however, that one consequence of setting few ground rules was that many different approaches had been followed. He recommended that the company proceed to set up a pattern for the preparation of future plans so as to achieve some uniformity in presentation and method of analysis. As an example of what he had in mind, he suggested that all divisions incorporate in their plans a form that he proceeded to illustrate on the chalkboard, using a set of hypothetical figures he had prepared on a recent consulting assignment (see Exhibit 3). The firm required each division to specify its profit expectations for its current "base" of operations, and then to specify, year by year, how these profit expectations would be affected by any and all changes in operations from the current base. The changes contemplated could be grouped into categories, such as abandonments, expansion, new ventures, and others, as appropriate. He suggested that the form provide columns for several years in advance, so that, in effect, the list below the base operations line would provide a ready reference list of all planned changes in operations.

Exhibit 3

SUMMARY OF LONG-RANGE PROFIT PLAN
Form Proposed by Gordon N. Thompson
($000)

DIVISION EXAMPLE AGGREGATE	1962			1963			1964			1965			1966		
	Pre-Tax Earnings	Average Invest-ment	Depre-ciation	Pre-Tax Earnings	Average Invest-ment	Depre-ciation	Pre-Tax Earnings	Average Invest-ment	Depre-ciation	Pre-Tax Earnings	Average Invest-ment	Depre-ciation	Pre-Tax Earnings	Average Invest-ment	Depre-ciation
BASE OPERATIONS	2,500	20,600	2,060	2,500	20,600	2,060	2,500	20,600	2,060	2,500	20,600	2,060	2,500	20,600	2,060
Normal Replacements				(26)	300	30	(80)	875	88	(130)	1,450	145	(190)	2,075	208
Retirements and Dispositions				28	(275)	(28)	80	(800)	(80)	105	(1,050)	(105)	165	(1,650)	(165)
Fully Depreciated Items				6		(6)	22		(22)	30		(30)	40		(40)
Loss of AG-Lime Markets				(35)	(55)		(85)	(95)		(130)	(115)		(160)	(125)	
Reduced Production Volume - Quarry One							(65)	(50)		(140)	(80)		(275)	(150)	
Abandonment of Quarry Two - Worked Out										(350)	(700)	(60)	(335)	(900)	(75)
Sub-Totals	2,500	20,600	2,060	2,473	20,570	2,056	2,372	20,530	2,046	1,885	20,105	2,010	1,745	19,850	1,988
Return on Investment (%)		12.136			12.022			11.554			9.376			8.791	
Acquisition - 5 Yard Shovel - Pit One	7	155	10	15	350	20	20	400	20	75	400	20	75	400	20
Acquisition - 10 RM Concrete Trucks	15	200	10	35	400	20	40	450	20	65	475	20	80	500	20
Stripping Overburden - Quarry Three	(500)														
Increased Capacity - Quarry Four	20	350	15	55	600	30	65	650	30	100	700	30	150	700	30
Joint Venture - Project A				(25)	350		60	750		175	750		225	350	
Addition - Quarry Five							(45)	800	50	115	1,500	100	215	1,500	100
Addition - Quarry Six										135	750	40	260	1,200	80
Increase in Sales Volume - Pits										50	65		75	225	
Sub-Totals	2,042	21,305	2,095	2,553	22,270	2,126	2,517	23,580	2,166	2,600	24,475	2,220	2,825	24,725	2,238
Return on Investment (%)		9.585			11.464			10.674			10.507			11.426	
Stripping Overburden - Quarry Three	250			(250)											
Acquisition 5 RM Concrete Trucks Cancelled	(6)	(75)	(5)	(10)	(175)	(10)	(15)	(225)	(10)	(20)	(225)	(10)	(20)	(275)	(10)
Sub-Totals	2,286	21,230	2,090	2,293	22,095	2,116	2,502	23,355	2,156	2,580	24,520	2,210	2,805	24,450	2,228
Return on Investment (%)		10.768			10.378			10.713			10.522			11.472	
Sale of Idle Real Property	50	(100)			(100)			(100)			(100)			(100)	
Loss from Strike/Wage Settlement Quarries	(340)	(275)		(45)	25			50			50			50	
Additional Profit-Joint Venture, Project BB	210														
Unrecoverable Loss in Sales Volume - RM	(250)	(150)													
Sub-Totals	1,956	20,705	2,090	2,248	22,020	2,116	2,502	23,305	2,156	2,580	24,470	2,210	2,805	24,400	2,228
Return on Investment (%)		9.447			10.209			10.736			10.544			11.496	

Reactions to the Meeting

A few days after the conclusion of the meeting, Mr. Cunningham circulated a confidential memorandum to senior head office executives, including Mr. Milford and Mr. Van Sickle. The memorandum set out some of Mr. Cunningham's conclusions about the division presidents' meeting. Major excerpts follow.

If we are to be realistic, we have to recognize that few tangible results were achieved at the meeting. The diversity in approach that we saw indicates only too clearly how much further we still have to go to get our long-range planning properly organized. However, I do feel that the exercise in thinking ahead was valuable for all our divisional executives, and I am in favor of continuing this requirement. We should not underestimate the significance of the pressure that we imposed on our operating men (all successful businessmen in their own right) by requiring them to stand up in front of a group of fellow executives and present their divisions' long-range plans.

The factor that concerns me most in regard to our planning is that the plans presented by the division presidents could be said to be no more than an academic exercise, for at least two reasons:

1. "Acceptance" of the plans at the April meeting did not imply any commitment on the part of corporate management to support or approve the divisions' proposals, in effect, included in the plans. There has been no change in our policy of corporate management's approving capital budgets on an annual basis.
2. There has been no suggestion that the plans as presented represent long-range standards against which divisional performance will be evaluated.

On the one hand, therefore, I find myself in favor of the continuation of this activity on an annual basis, with some emphasis given to Gordy Thompson's proposal that we standardize procedures and require greater detail in the presentations. On the other hand, I have a lurking suspicion that we may be getting ourselves involved in an activity that is useless in practice, and for this reason potentially dangerous.

Please let me have your comments. I ask that you regard the contents of this memorandum as highly confidential.

When Mr. Van Sickle received this memorandum he laughed involuntarily. "Looks like Leroy is having second thoughts about long-range planning now. Well, I warned him, didn't I?"

QUESTIONS

1. On balance, was the effort to make long-range plans worthwhile?
2. Should Northwest Aggregates try it again? If so, how can the process be improved?

Appendix

Empire Chemical Company Division—1966

Presented by: CHARLES SOMERS, *Division President*

April 11, 1961

All of us who have participated in preparing this report on Empire Chemical Company division—1966, feel, I believe, that in the circumstances prevailing this year this has been a most strenuous, although beneficial exercise. We have felt, at times, that the current extreme pressures of market competition have made it particularly difficult for us to devote the concentration of effort that such a study requires and to reliably predict future marketable quantities and prices of chemicals, which comprise our logical fields of interest, but this is probably a usual reaction to an unusual problem of this kind. We have, we believe, projected a program that we think can be achieved.

In making these projections, we have considered, but have not included, possible acquisitions of existing domestic chemical operations that would complement and add to our present operations. We have also considered possible foreign operations, particularly those of a character that would permit an equity ownership participation by Northwest through use of our engineering and know-how rather than cash as a basis for acquiring the equity. The attitude of our government in respect to possibly limiting domestic business opportunities, or even harassing domestic industry, while subsidizing investments abroad is an important factor with which we must reckon.

Much of the accomplishment projected is dependent on successful completion of certain process studies now underway in our research and development department. Success also depends on obtaining top-notch performance from our present personnel as well as securing high-caliber additional personnel for various key positions that will need to be filled as this program is carried into effect.

In laying out this future program, we have compared ourselves with the chemical process industry in general and, more particularly, with selected companies within this industry that most nearly resemble our own. This chemical industry has, over the past 10 years, shown a sales growth rate of approximately 5.6 percent. A 6 percent per annum growth rate is projected by economists to apply over the next five years. In this connection, although we think highly of economists we are not too confident about predicating *all* our plans on the predictions of economists, since these predictions are very frequently found to be at variance with the actual results achieved. I have heard it said that if all economists were carefully placed end to end they would still wind up pointing in all directions.

If we compare Empire's net sales growth with selected companies within the chemical process industry, whose growth rate is shown at the predicted industry average of 6 percent per year, it may be seen that Empire's sales are favorably related to sales of these companies. Our projection indicates that Empire's net sales are expected to rise from a 1961 budget level of $15.9 million to a 1966 level of $34.9 million, an increase of 119 percent. It is expected that our gross assets value will rise from $29.1 million in 1961 to $60.1 million in 1966; pretax profits go from a 1961 budget level of $3.2 million to a 1966 level of $8.6 million, an increase of about 170 percent. Return on gross assets for the 1961 budget is 11 percent, while the 1966 return on gross assets is projected to be 14.4 percent. These earnings, I believe, compare well with better-operated companies in this industry. Appropriate adjustments have been made for interest charges, other income, marketable securities, etc., in order to improve the validity of this comparison. However, research charges without commensurate benefit of research results also burden Empire's results.

In projecting our future growth, we have used as bench marks our 1960 performance, our budgeted 1961 performance, and a projected performance that we call program A. This depicts our present facilities plus those capital expenditures essential to bring present assets to the maximum production level by the expenditure of a relatively nominal amount of capital funds, already in the 1961 budget, for a so-called "de-bottlenecking" program. We have then projected an expected sales increase of our present product line that we feel can be achieved over the next several years, based on a detailed study by areas and by product line. We find that there is an expected stabilized level of earnings for these facilities some time during the period of 1963–64, and that this performance would envision net sales of $15.3 million, pretax earnings of $3.6 million, and a return on gross assets of 12.5 percent.

It might be well to state here that in making these projections we have employed present-day market prices and present wage and salary costs. While it is not likely that either of these factors will actually prevail in 1966, we feel that there is no other sufficiently reliable basis on which we can predicate our predictions. In arriving at this approach, as well as in our overall planning of this presentation, we have used outside counsel, particularly Arthur D. Little, Inc. They are in complete concurrence in utilizing this approach. While this base program of operations shows improvement in earnings over our 1961 budget position, it does not provide for a growth rate commensurate with the growth of the industry over the five-year period, nor for a desirable level of earnings-to-gross-assets ratio.

Our plans to improve this base program have been divided for convenience into two programs—a B program, which we call the "Salina Expansion Program," and a C program, which we call our "Non-Salina Expansion Program."

In regard to the B program, we think that the first element to be considered is that of a significant expansion to our chloromethanes plant. This could be accomplished at a total estimated cost of about $1.2 million (facilities plus working capital), and if chlorine from the Salina plants were available at cost for this expansion the profitability on the added investment would be very high expressed as a return on gross assets. [Mr. Somers then went into the details of these proposals.]

Empire is currently enjoying about 0.05 percent of the chemical process industry business. It is known that chemical process industry sales are expected to grow at the rate of 6 percent per year for the next 10 years, and gross national product is expected to grow at a rate of 3.9 percent per year. This means that if our net sales grow at the rate of 6.0 percent we grow slightly faster than the GNP, but we amount to no more in the chemical process industry five years from now than we have during the past few years. We, as a young company, will have ceased to grow out of adolescence and attain the maturity of stature in the industry accorded to a healthy, growing company. It is probably an oversimplification to say that when a business loses momentum it loses position as a going concern, and when it loses position as a going concern, property values may be lost. If we are limited to plan A, we are a smaller portion of the industry in 1966; if we adopt plan C (see below), we move from a position of 0.05 percent (to the chemical process industry) to 0.09 percent (an improvement of about 80 percent).

The expansions at Salina also serve the purpose of broadening our product line by at least one chemical—namely, phenol—as well as keeping us abreast of expected realizable growth in our sales of carbon tet, chloroform, and methylene chloride.

We have also planned the possibility of production of chemicals new to our line at an eastern seaboard location (plan C). These products will be produced in a chloroethanes plant by a technique currently being perfected on a pilot plant basis in our research and development department. The products are chemically closely related to our present line of chlorinated hydrocarbons. Market investigation indicates that we have a reasonable expectation of accomplishing the sales of these products in the quantities and at the prices used in our projections.

The capital costs for such a program would amount to \$6.5 million and would produce added sales of about \$8.5 million, with pretax profits of \$2 million for a return on gross assets of about 30 percent. Hydrocarbons and chlorine for such an operation are projected to be purchased and, according to recent information, we have reason to believe that these purchases can be effected at prices approximating those used in our projection.

[Mr. Somers also explained this proposal at some length, and concluded as follows.]

I should like to have several of our group take a few minutes to give you some of the details which underlie this projection. I think it is appropriate to have such further details supplied in respect to fiscal planning, sales, and plant operations. These will be covered respectively by our controller, D. M. Drake; our sales manager—chemicals, J. C. Sheahan; and our vice-president in charge of manufacturing and research and development, Bruce D. Barclay.

Summary of the Financial Commentary of D. M. Drake

The financial commentary of the controller backed up Mr. Somers' remarks. It contained a detailed exhibit, including an earnings statement and figures for asset values and return on assets with 1961 budget figures, 1960 actual, and projections for each of the three alternative plans, A, B, and C, and their components.

His remarks explained and supported the assumptions on which the figures were based. Among other things, the division had had professional market studies made. His concluding statements dealt with capital requirements and the expected timing of a returning cash flow:

> If we assume for the moment that the most advantageous schedule was adopted in keeping with the sales forecast, we can count on a significant increase in cash flow during the five-year period in question. In fact, as much as one half of the required new money can be generated from increased earnings and depreciation during this period. The net new money would therefore be close to \$16 million.

Summary of Sales Organization, 1961–1966, Commentary of J. C. Sheahan

The sale, manager for chemicals described his sales program with special attention to each of three so-called "problem areas"—caustic soda, muriatic acid, and pentachlorophenol. Plans related to projected sales, the necessary sales force, changes in the existing sales force, and the possible changes in sales territories, all in specific reference to plans A, B, and C. He concluded on this optimistic note:

> We in sales enthusiastically endorse these plans which have been submitted and accept them as a realistic challenge. We look on them as an opportunity to contribute to our own department, the growth of Empire Chemicals, and the growth of Northwest Aggregates Corporation.

Summary of the Manufacturing and Technical Organization, 1961 through 1966, Commentary of B. D. Barclay

In his supporting document, the vice-president in charge of manufacturing, engineering, and research and development presented further material on plans and policy contemplated as corollary to the five-year plans. His horizon extended even beyond the five years, and his remarks covered quantitative and nonquantitative factors.

Recognizing the place of research and development in the chronology of product development, and their particular importance in the chemical field in general, he outlined specific plant and personnel expansion plans for the department for the near and more distant future, although plans A, B, and C did not depend on new product development. Specific projects were under way, however.

For the engineering department, also, he had specific plans, and announced a change in policy—namely, to assign a greater proportion of engineering work to outside professionals. He projected a modest increase in size, however.

As for manufacturing, he supported specific increases in plant and personnel in direct response to the overall plans, and announced policies for staffing, including consideration of assigning several functions to one individual in small plants, identifying positions to be filled, and planning transfers and upgrading. He foresaw problems in recruiting:

> We shall need to hire during the five-year period at least 60 additional engineers and chemists. This in itself will require an intensification of our recruitment activities in a market which is scarce of capable people and is predicted to become more competitive during this period of the golden sixties.

Chapter Ten

CAPITAL BUDGETING

Capital budgeting has two main facets—an analytical technique for examining individual proposals, and a system.

It is assumed that the student already has some familiarity with the analytical facet, specifically, that he understands the general concept of present value and that he knows how to use one or more of the techniques that help managers decide which proposed investments should be undertaken and which should be rejected. A satisfactory, practical analytical apparatus is by no means completely worked out, however. The analytical cases in this chapter are restricted to just one of the major problems on which there is a disagreement among the experts, namely: How, if at all, should differences in risk and uncertainty be brought into the formal analysis?

A second problem for which no good solution currently exists involves the choice of a discount rate or rates. The article by John F. Childs deals with one aspect of this problem.

Although the cases in this chapter treat with some advanced techniques, the student is cautioned not to lose sight of the fact that the most serious source of difficulty in real-life situations is that of obtaining good estimates for the numbers cranked into the analytical apparatus. If the estimates are not good to start with, arguments about the fine points of technique are pointless.

The other facet of capital budgeting is the system used to insure that individual proposals get considered by the proper management people, that the aggregate of individual projects makes a sensible total of a capital budgeting program, and that approved projects are, in fact, implemented. The International Harvester case is the vehicle for discussing such a system.

Reading 10–1

Note on Deferred Investments

By Robert N. Anthony

The general approach to problems involving the proposed acquisition of capital assets is well worked out: the amount of investment required is estimated; the earnings resulting from the investment are estimated, year by year; the present value of these earnings[1] is found by use of an appropriate discount rate; and if this present value is high enough, as compared with the investment, the proposal is accepted.[2] This approach works well if the investment involves a single outlay made when the project starts, that is, at time zero.

Difficulties arise, however, if the investment outlays are spread over a considerable period of time. This happens either when the investment is physically acquired in several time periods (for example, a plant requiring two or three years of construction), or when the investment outlays are represented by lease payments, payments under a conditional sales agreement, or other financial arrangements that are spread through time. Such investments are called deferred investments. The approach to analyzing proposals involving deferred investments is discussed in this note.

Before discussing this approach, let us briefly review some basic concepts. First, what precisely is meant by the term return on investment? Any investment involves the commitment of funds. Ordinarily, a businessman makes an investment with the expectation of earning a satisfactory return on the funds he thus risks. The rate of return on the investment is the annual return divided by the amount of funds at risk.

To take the simplest situation, if a business buys land for $1,000, if it receives earnings of $80 a year for five years (or any number of years) from

---

[1] The term earnings refers to the cash inflow resulting from the investment. In accounting terms, it is the increase in after-tax net income plus depreciation.

[2] For a more complete description, see Robert N. Anthony, *Management Accounting: Text and Cases* (Homewood, Ill.: Richard D. Irwin, Inc., 1964), chap. 19.

the rental of this land, and if it sells the land for $1,000 at the end of this period, its annual return on this investment is $80/$1,000 = 8 percent. If, on the other hand, a business buys a machine for $1,000, if it receives earnings from it of $250 a year for five years, and if the machine has zero value at the end of five years, the problem of finding the return on investment is more complicated. This is because part of the $250 annual earnings must go to recoup the $1,000 investment, and only the remainder can be counted as return. The usual discounting technique shows that this investment also has an annual return of 8 percent, in the same sense as the investment in land, namely: the $250 annual earnings for five years recoups the $1,000 investment and provides for a return of 8 percent on the amount of investment not yet recouped.

Many practical problems arise in applying this basic concept to real-life situations. In part, these problems have to do with making realistic estimates of the key figures—earnings, investment, and the length of life. In part, they arise because the return-on-investment calculation applies only to those aspects of the problem that are reduced to monetary terms. Nonmeasured factors (e.g., quality, management's ability to assimilate the investment) and objectives other than earning a satisfactory return (e.g., increased share of the market, prestige, employees' welfare) are always important, and often are dominant in practical situations. Without in any way minimizing the importance of these practical difficulties, we shall restrict this discussion to the measured factors in the problem.

DEFERRED INVESTMENTS

The usual procedures work well when the investment is made in one lump sum at the inception of the project—for example, when a machine is purchased for cash or its equivalent. If, however, the payments for the machine are spread over time, these techniques can yield peculiar results. If a company has a minimum required earnings rate on new investments of 10 percent, then a proposed project involving an investment of $1,000 with estimated annual earnings of $250 for five years would not be acceptable since, as we have already seen, the indicated return on such a project is only 8 percent.

But suppose the company had an opportunity to buy the identical machine under a conditional sales agreement, with a down payment of $100 and five annual payments of $200 each. The calculated rate of return exceeds 40 percent, shown as follows: The "investment" made at time zero becomes $100, and the net cash inflow becomes $250 earnings minus $200 payments, or $50 a year. The discount rate that equates the present value of the inflows to the $100 "investment" turns out to be in excess of 40 percent (the present value of $1,000 a year for five years at 40 percent is $2.035; for $50, the present value is 50 x $2.035, or $102, which exceeds the$100 "investment").

Can it be that this hitherto undesirable investment has become, by the simple act of spreading the payments over time, an extremely attractive proposition? Common sense indicates that if the original proposition, as a business proposition, was unattractive, then it has not suddenly become extremely attractive just because the method of paying for it has been changed.

To carry this line of reasoning to the extreme, it can be seen at once that if the down payment were eliminated entirely, the indicated rate of return would be infinite if the installment payments were any amount less than $250 a year. Does the elimination of a down payment make such a proposition infinitely desirable—a proposition that we should certainly accept? Clearly, not.

What happened was that the calculation did not take into account that the proposal to purchase a machine under a conditional sales agreement was one that involved both an investment and the means of financing it. The net cash flow of $50 a year was the difference between two essentially unlike figures—earnings of $250 and the finance payment of $200. In problems of this type, the financing aspect must be treated separately from the investment aspect rather than merged with it in a single set of cash-flow figures.

In order to explain why this is so, we go back to the basic considerations involved in the company's choice of its financial structure. For simplicity, we shall disregard the differences among the various types of secured and unsecured debt and preferred and common stock, and shall state that the basic financial question a company must resolve is the proper proportion of debt and equity. We shall further simplify by assuming that this "proper" ratio is determined by arriving at what is believed to be the proper balance between (*a*) cost and (*b*) risk; that is, we shall disregard such considerations as possible loss of voting control. Debt typically has a low cost (i.e., a low interest rate) and imposes a high risk (i.e., periodic payments must be made, regardless of the level of income; otherwise serious financial consequences will ensue). Equity typically has a high cost (i.e., investors will typically accept an equity position only when they foresee a high return) and a low risk to the company (i.e., dividends can be lowered or passed without serious consequences). Thus, the greater the proportion of debt, the lower is the total cost, but the higher is the risk to the company.

Judgments as to the "right" proportion of debt are made both by management and by investors; the actual proportion of debt in the capital structure will be the lower of these two judgments, since investors are unwilling to furnish debt capital in excess of the proportion they consider safe (i.e., that has a tolerable amount of risk), and management is unwilling to commit the company to a higher proportion of debt than *it* feels is safe. We need not consider further how the "right" proportion is decided on. The fact is that in a given company at a given time a proper proportion has been decided on, and the same proportion will continue as a basic financial guide until either management or investors change their judgments as to the correct balance of cost and risk. It is important to note that these financial judgments relate to the capital structure of the whole company; they are not usually related to specific investment proposals.

The *actual* debt–equity ratio will, of course, be in constant change, since new borrowings, new investments, dividend payments, and the like are made from time to time rather than continuously. Nevertheless, there will always be a tendency for the actual ratio to converge on the "proper" ratio. As already pointed out, neither management nor investors will willingly permit the proportion of debt to become too high, because this would go counter to their judgment as to the appropriate amount of risk. Management will not permit the proportion of debt to become too low, because too large a proportion of funds would then consist of the high-cost equity.

Let us now fit the proposed purchase of a machine into this financial framework. Assume that, for reasons of no concern to us, management and investors have decided that the "right" proportion in our company is 40 percent debt and 60 percent equity. A very simple balance sheet might then appear as follows:

Various assets	$10,000	Debt	$ 4,000
		Equity	6,000
Total Assets	$10,000	Total Equities	$10,000

If the company's income, after taxes but before interest, was $1,000 a year, its return on investment would be 10 percent, and if it paid out this $1,000 as interest and dividends to its investors the company's balance sheet would continue indefinitely as above; that is, the company would be in a "steady state."

If the company "expands" by buying a $1,000 machine for cash, it would tend to finance this purchase by incurring $400 additional debt and $600 additional equity; otherwise its "right" debt–equity ratio would be upset. (Recall that we are here discussing only tendencies. Actually, in order to avoid the trouble of obtaining additional debt and equity for each equipment acquisition the average company would obtain relatively large chunks of debt at one time, and would build up equity gradually through retained earnings; but this does not change the basic tendency.) If the machine has a life of five years, there will be an additional depreciation expense of $200 a year, and if earnings from the machine amount to $250 a year, there will be $50 additional profit a year.[3] Note that total annual income will now be $1,050, total investment will be $11,000, and the return on investment will shrink

[3] The foregoing is described in terms of the income statement. If the reader wishes to visualize this situation in terms of a steady-state company, he should assume five machines, each costing $200, with one being replaced each year. This gives a more exact, but also more complicated, statement of the new steady-state situation.

to 9.5 percent. This fact jibes with our earlier analysis, which indicated that the machine had a return of only 8 percent; its relatively low return pulls down the average return on investment in the company as a whole.

But suppose that the same machine is acquired on a conditional sales agreement. The installment payments are definite, fixed obligations; that is, they are debt. If we assume, for simplicity, that the amount to be recorded as a liability is exactly $1,000 (which might or might not be the case), then the balance sheet prepared after acquisition of the machine would be:

Various assets	$11,000	Debt	$ 5,000
		Equity	6,000
Total Assets	$11,000	Total Equities	$11,000

At first blush, this proposition may appear attractive, because if the after-tax cost of debt is, say, 2 percent, then $50 a year will be added to earnings but only $20 to interest requirements, so the stockholders will gain the difference of $30. This is true as far as it goes. The trouble is that the balance sheet given above cannot be tolerated, for the debt ratio has now risen above the permitted 40 percent. Unless the company wishes to shrink the scale of its operations, it must now obtain $1,500 of additional equity to restore the "proper" ratio. Moreover, it must invest this $1,500 in income-producing assets if the 10 percent rate of return on all assets is to be maintained; in fact, this $1,500 increment must be invested so as to earn at least 13 percent if the overall return is to remain at 10 percent. (Return from the $11,000 of assets is assumed to be $1,050; return required to earn 10 percent on $12,500 = $1,250; $1,250 − $1,050 = $200 additional required; $200 is 13 percent of $1,500.) Thus, instead of having a very high, or even an infinite return, as the cash-flow type of analysis indicates, the installment purchase turns out to be unsatisfactory, as demonstrated by the fact that it must be offset by another investment of greater than average earning capacity if the overall average rate of 10 percent is to be maintained.

PROCEDURE

The error in the cash-flow analysis arose because the annual installment payments were netted against the earnings for the year. This should not have been done. Instead, the installment payments should have been replaced by a figure representing the present value of the liability that was created; this is the true amount of investment involved in the proposition. This present value is found by discounting the installment payments at a rate equivalent to the cost of debt. This rate, which would normally be in the vicinity of 4 percent to 7 percent before taxes (2 percent to 3.5 percent after taxes) is much lower than the company's required earnings rate. Often, this present value turns out to be approximately the same as the cash purchase price, because the installment payments may have been derived from the cash price by the application of the same discount rate.

For example, in the installment-payment situation described above, assuming a debt cost of 4 percent, the equivalent investment turns out to be almost the same as the $1,000 cash purchase price, as shown in this computation:

Item	*Year*	*Amount*	*Discount Factor at 4%*	*Total*
Down payment	0	$100	1.000	$100
Installments	1–5	200	4.452	890
Equivalent investment				$990

The return on an investment of $990, with earnings of $250 a year for 5 years, is less than 10 percent (present value at 10 percent is $250 × 3.791 = $948).

The discount rate may be either a pretax or an after-tax rate, depending on how income taxes are handled in the particular analytical procedure. The choice can be decided by testing each possibility against a simple set of figures and seeing which gives the more sensible answer.

In summary, when the outflows represent a definite commitment that is in the nature of debt, these outflows should not be netted against inflows in the return-on-investment analysis. Instead, the present value of the stream of payments should be found by discounting them at a rate equivalent to the cost of debt. This present value amount is the investment. The equivalent investment thus computed can then be compared with earnings in the usual manner.

LEASES

The approach described above is applicable whenever the series of future payments represents a definite obligation on the company—that is, when the payments are in the nature of debt. A lease agreement may or may not represent such an obligation. If the lease is for a short term or is easily cancelable (as are leases for telephone equipment and certain types of office equipment, for example), the company's borrowing power is unaffected; payments made under such leases properly may be netted against earnings. If, on the other hand, the lease is almost equivalent to a conditional sales agreement (as is the case with so-called "financial leases," i.e., leases that require a series of noncancelable fixed payments), then the investment is equal to the present value of the series of lease payments, discounting them at a low rate. The discount rate used may be the same as the rate used for a stream of debt payments, or it may be slightly (say, 0.5 percent) higher if the analyst believes that the lease does not affect the company's borrowing capacity quite so stringently as would an out-and-out debt arrangement. The important point is that in an investment analysis these contractual lease payments are properly capitalized, even though accountants do not capitalize these payments and show them as liabilities on the balance sheet.

IMPLICATIONS FOR OTHER FLOWS

The problem we have been discussing is a problem only because the proposed project involved a certain type of financial arrangement as one of its essential aspects. If the proposed project had involved only an investment made for cash, the problem would not have arisen. Some analysts would go one step further and argue that there are other types of cash flows which, even though they do not, strictly speaking, involve financial arrangements, are essentially similar to debt payments, and that these flows should be treated in the same manner.

Those who advocate this approach point out that "risk" as used above is practically synonymous with "uncertainty." Investors are willing to supply debt capital at a low rate because of the low degree of uncertainty (or high degree of certainty) that they will receive the stated payments. They require a high return on equity capital in view of the much greater uncertainty of receiving dividends. As a general rule, the lower the uncertainty of payment, the lower the cost of the funds.

The estimated cash flows in an investment project also differ as to the certainty that they will be made. A cash investment made at the inception of the project has complete certainty. The tax shield provided by a depreciable investment is fairly certain, subject only to changes in the tax rate or in the method of calculating allowable depreciation, and to the earning of some taxable income by the company as a whole (not merely from the project in question). The incurrence of some types of overhead costs is also relatively certain once the decision to go ahead with the project has been made. At the other extreme, the generation of revenue from an untried new product has a high degree of uncertainty.

It can be argued that by analogy with the treatment of installment payments discussed above all cash flows should be discounted at rates reflecting the relative certainty of their occurrence, ranging from zero for immediate cash outlays, through a low rate for flows that are as certain as debt payments, to a rate comparable to the cost of equity capital for quite uncertain flows such as the revenue from new products. A few companies do, in fact, use this reasoning with respect to the depreciation tax shield, but the practice is, at present, not widespread.

CONCLUSION

Although the analysis made above depends in part on tendencies, which may not be correct for certain specific situations, and although part of it reasons from analogy, which is dangerous, the following conclusions seem warranted:

1. The procedure of netting cash inflows against cash ouflows gives results that are clearly unreasonable when the outflows are contractual obligations but the inflows are uncertain estimates. Such flows should not, therefore, be netted.

2. When the outflows are financial payments on debt obligations, or on obligations similar to debt, a procedure that discounts these flows at a low rate to give an "equivalent investment" produces results that are clearly reasonable. This equivalent investment can then be used as the investment amount in any of the usual analytical techniques.

3. Since the low rate was associated with a low uncertainty of payment, an argument can be made that, in general, flows should be discounted at rates corresponding to their uncertainty; but few companies actually follow such a practice.

Reading 10-2

Profit Goals for Management

By John F. Childs*

The success of a company today depends to a great extent on correct decisions on major capital expenditures. The principal question and a difficult one: What should be the goal in deciding on whether to give a project the green light? Profits are the catalyst in our free enterprise system and management's guide in expansion. Therefore, management needs answers to the question: What profit goals should be used for expansion purposes?

This article will deal primarily with the application of profit goals to plant expansion, and with that type of plant expansion which is relatively independent of the rest of the company's operations. However, the ideas discussed are the foundation for thinking in the many other areas: acquisitions, plant abandonment, parts of financial policy such as capital structure determination, etc.

THE IMPACT OF EXPANSION

If a company makes a mistake in this area, how serious is it? When a company expands, management directs the flow of the savings of our nation into means of production. Uncalled-for expansion has serious consequences:

Investors are hurt because of the effect on profits!

All companies in an industry suffer because overexpansion by one company will depress prices in the entire industry and restrict profits!

Our entire economy is blighted because capital directed where it is not needed means production of the wrong goods and a reduction in usable goods and consequently our standard of living. Furthermore, if excessive expansion

---

* Vice-president, Irving Trust Company. From *Financial Executive,* February, 1964. Used by permission of Financial Executives Institute.

occurs in a prosperous period, it will accentuate the business cycle and the unemployment problem!

Thus, a smooth flow of capital into production, where it is needed, is essential to our economy. And yet, this is one of management's most difficult areas. It requires the best possible judgment with regard to the profit element.

THREE PARTS TO PROFIT DETERMINATION IN EXPANSION

The analysis of an expansion program includes three parts:

1. A *forecast* of sales, expenses and capital outlays.
2. A *profitability calculation based on the forecast*. In other words, what rate of return will the forecast produce? Allowance must be made for the time value of money. This can only be done by such methods as "discounted cash flow" or "present value." Such methods as payback, return on original investment, and return on average investment are inadequate.
3. *Establishing a profit goal*. Before the final decision can be made, it is necessary to establish a profit goal as a cutoff rate of return on capital. This is the rate with which the project's profitability can be compared, in order to determine whether there is sufficient profit to justify the project.

Part 3, profit goal, is our present subject. In order to simplify the explanation, some ABC types of examples will be used. Since all top management should understand the subject, the article is written so that those only casually acquainted with finance can grasp it. However, the subject is truly a part of finance and the greater a person's financial knowledge the more readily the subject can be understood.

What we are seeking is a rate of return on capital which can be used as a goal to determine whether the forecast profit rate on capital to be invested in an expansion project is sufficient to justify a project.

UNSOUND GOALS

If you ask managements what goal they use for expansion decisions, you will find that each has some goal, but you may be surprised at their rationale. In order to start our thinking on the subject we will review some of the goals that managements feel have value. Some of them are obviously wrong. Others may seem reasonable and their errors only become apparent after the complete discussion of the subject.

Profit as a Percent of Sales. It leaves out the amount of capital required to produce the sales. The rate must always be related to the investment required to produce the profit.

Interest Rate on Long-Term Debt. What about the common stockholders if the company just earned its interest or slightly over its interest? Interest is a part of the cost-of-capital, but only a part because it overlooks the rate that should be earned on the money the common stockholders provide.

Interest on Long-Term Debt and Dividends on Common. If two identical companies had different dividend policies, their goals would be different. And suppose a company had no debt and paid no dividends—what then, a zero goal? Of course, the real reason that dividends alone are no measure is the fact that it ignores the importance of earnings per share to the stockholders.

Company's Experienced Return-on-Capital. Experienced return-on-capital can be expressed by dividing total income (interest plus net earnings after taxes before dividend) by total long-term capital (long-term debt, preferred stock and common equity). If this were used as a goal, a company with poor earnings would tend to perpetuate its failure; a company with high earnings might think it should forego profitable investments unless the past rate were achieved. Neither is the rate that other companies in the industry have earned any good as a goal. All these rates leave unsolved what is correct as a minimum goal.

Improving Common Stock Earnings Per Share. This is one goal which some executives and financial analysts consider sound. I do not dispute the fact that managements should attempt to increase earnings per share, but it is not just that simple as far as new investment is concerned. Suppose an industrial company is earning an inadequate return of 6 percent on its total capital which results in earnings per share on its common stock of $1.00 and the company is considering an expansion program which will increase earnings per share to $1.25. The question immediately arises whether this is sufficient to justify the project. There must be adequate earnings per share, but what is adequate? The ultimate test must be based on a proper profit goal as a percent return on new investment. I will explain more fully why I object to earnings per share as a goal at the end of the article after I have developed the tools to work with.

WHERE CAN MANAGEMENT LOOK FOR AN ANSWER?

There is a competitive market for capital in our system of private capital just as there is a competitive market for other types of goods and services. Furthermore, capital has a cost, and to be successful a company must earn enough to cover all costs, including capital costs. Very briefly, a company should earn at least something above the bare minimum rate which investors require to induce them to provide all the capital, that is the cost-of-capital. We are really interested in three rates:

Cost-of-Capital, that is the cost to attract capital.

Return-on-Capital Target—the rate a company should earn on its capital, which should be at least somewhat above the cost-of-capital.

Expansion Profit Goal—well above the cost-of-capital to take care of risk elements in expansion.

Broadly speaking, cost-of-capital includes two elements. One element is the amount necessary to induce people to invest and save their money rather than hold it idle or spend it. The other element is the amount necessary to compensate investors for the risk they take. Therefore, it is the nature of the company and its risk which determines the cost-of-capital. We will define cost-of-capital at this point and hope that the explanation which follows will make its meaning clear.

Cost-of-capital is the over-all composite percent net cost rate, after allowing for underwriters' compensation and expenses of financing, which investors require to induce them to provide all forms of long-term capital, in a competitive market, on an average over a period of years.

FRAMEWORK FOR REASONING

In order to have a base for our thinking, we will start with a look at how capital flows into a corporation and how it is put to use. This may seem elementary, but it is often lost sight of. A look at a balance sheet will give us the best picture. Assume that you start a new industrial company with the simplified balance sheet shown in Exhibit 1; practically any balance sheet can be summarized in a similar manner.

Exhibit 1

BALANCE SHEET

Assets		*Liabilities*		
Current assets	$100	Current liabilities		$ 50
Plant	50	Long-term capital		
		Debt	$20	
		Common equity	80	100
Total	$150	Total		$150

When determining cost-of-capital, we will be looking to the right-hand side of the balance sheet and dealing with the total capital of $100. It comes from investors through the sale of long-term securities—debt $20 and common equity $80. All common equity, whether it be the stated or par value, capital surplus or earned surplus, should be treated alike for cost-of-capital purposes. There is no distinction so far as the common stockholders are concerned. It all represents part of their ownership. Surplus arising from retained earnings is equivalent to raising new common equity. In fact, as earnings are plowed back, a company regularly raises new common equity. If management made a distinction as regards the rate to be earned on earned surplus, stockholders would be well advised to have the company pay out all its earnings in dividends and then raise new equity money by sale of stock to stockholders. If you question this statement, consider a private company with one stockholder. Would he accept a lower return on money he leaves in versus money he put in? Stockholders of a publicly owned company should not be treated differently by management.

When applying a profit goal we will be working with assets on the left-hand side. It is necessary to visualize the relationship between the two sides of the balance sheet so that the rate obtained on the right-hand side will be correctly associated with the assets on the left. Therefore, we must note that the $100 of long-term securities provide the money for $50 of plant and $50 of working capital. (Current assets $100 less current liabilities $50.) The working capital is required to earn the same rate as the plant.

In order to cover the entire subject of cost-of-capital we should discuss capital structure and the cost of debt, but to save space we will skip them. A further point we will omit is the question of costs associated with current liabilities. Generally, such costs are so small as not to be important; in any event, they can be handled fairly readily.

Cost-of-capital would actually be easy to understand and calculate if all capital consisted of debt since its cost is the interest rate. The problem becomes difficult because of the common equity part of our capital structure. Does it have a cost and how can it be calculated? We will concentrate on trying to answer this question.

AN ALL-DEBT CAPITAL STRUCTURE TO ASSIST IN EXPLANATION

Before we try to answer the question of the common cost rate, let's take another view of the capital structure in the simplified balance sheet shown, that is, the $20 of debt and $80 of common equity. For the moment, let's reason in terms of debt securities since we can probably agree that debt has a cost.

If we assign an interest rate of five percent to the $20 of debt, the picture would be as shown below. Forget about the tax savings that interest produces; we are now only talking about the rates that investors require, and they do not pay the corporate tax. We will cover the effect of interest on taxes later on.

	Amount	*Rate*	*Cost*
Debt	$20	5%	$1.00
Common	80		

Now let's change the composition of our capital structure and first substitute a layer of $30 of junior debt for $30 of the common equity. Since the added debt would be junior and in a more risky position, it would require a higher rate. For illustrative purposes let's use six percent. For an industrial company, we have already added much more debt than would be wise from the point of view of sound financial policy but, purely for the purpose of illustrating the idea of cost-of-capital, let's go one step further and substitute a third layer of $49 more junior, junior debt for $49 of common. Certainly, no ordinary investor would purchase such debt, and any rate we assign to it would be a pure guess. But, if we did try to sell it to anyone, the type of person who might be interested would be a so-called "money-lender." If you have ever heard about the rates they charge, you are aware of their magnitudes. At least, it is not inconceivable that with 99 percent total debt that the rate on the third layer might be between 10 percent and 20 percent; let's use 15 percent. The picture would be as follows:

	Amount	*Rate*	*Cost*
Debt	$ 20	5%	$ 1.00
Junior debt	30	6	1.80
Junior, junior debt	49	15	7.35
Common	1		
	$100		$10.15

Thus, leaving out the cost for the remaining $1.00 of common and just using the debt costs as above, the over-all cost for 99 percent of our capital is about 10 percent.

We used this approach as a first step in explaining cost-of-capital to show that:

1. All capital has a cost, whether it be debt or equity. Merely substituting debt for equity or vice versa does not change the fact that there is a cost to all capital.
2. Capital is not cheap. As the debt becomes more junior the interest rate must rise because of the added risk. The common stock has all the risk with no junior security protecting it, and, in fact, it must provide protection for the senior securities. Therefore, the common should justifiably receive a substantially higher rate.
3. The rate we are trying to seek for a cost-of-capital is the over-all composite cost of all the capital. It is the composite rate which must be used as a basis for the goal in deciding how much should be earned on assets when an expansion program is being weighed.

Sometimes managements are attracted to the idea of applying the increment cost rate to a particular project. This mistake is most often made in connection with lease financing,[1] which is a form of debt financing. This is wrong. If a company sold debt securities and used the proceeds to build a a factory, the goal should still be based on a composite rate of all the company's capital. It could not sell the debt unless it had some common equity.

[1] These remarks are not to be confused with the necessity of comparing the cost for one type of security with the cost rate for the other similar types of securities, when deciding on how to finance. For example, the rate on one type of debt obligation such as a lease should be compared with the rate on the other types of debt and not with equity or with a composité figure

Visualize the situation which would arise if a company did use the rate on the type of security sold to raise money for a particular project. The goal would shift depending on whether it used debt or equity even for the same type of project.

With this background, we can attack the difficult task—the cost of the common equity. As stated above, common stock does not have a cost in the sense that debt has a cost, but common stock has an economic cost. Some people prefer such a term as "required earnings rate."

In essence, when a person buys a stock he looks forward to receiving two benefits: dividends as they are paid in the future, and capital appreciation. It is future prospects of these two elements that induce stockholders to pay a price for common stock. But both dividends and market appreciation come from future earnings per share. Many things affect the price of a stock, but the principal factor which includes all the returns that accrue to the common stock are the earnings per share. The price is affected by both the amount and quality of earnings.

The measurement of the common cost rate on the basis of this concept is not easy to explain. First, let's look at an old guidepost for pricing a common stock. The old rule of thumb for the price-earnings ratio of a stock, without prospects of growth, was ten times. This meant that a stock earning $10 per share would sell for $100 as long as it had prospects of earning the $10. Since a company would have to earn the $10 in order for it to maintain the common stock at a price of $100, then the percentage earnings rate would be 10 percent. This, in essence, is what is meant by a cost rate for the common, but unfortunately, it is not that simple.

The important point is that the cost rate for common is the relationship of price to *future* prospects of earnings rather than to current earnings per share. Current earnings are over the dam once a stock is purchased; all gains to the stockholders come from future earnings. Past earnings may well be a guide to future earnings, but they are not what benefit the common stockholders. This is particularly important to keep in mind for growth stocks which sell at high price-earnings ratios.

There is another more subtle point with regard to the common cost which we have alluded to, but not explained. There are actually three earnings per share which we have to choose from. This can be illustrated by the simple figures below:

a. Price of stock	$100
b. Current earnings per share	5
c. Estimated potential earning per share by company	8
d. Expected potential earning per share by investors	10

These simple examples of estimated and expected earnings per share and those that follow are supposed to reflect the full future potential earnings power including all growth prospects.

Now then, what is it that makes investors pay $100 per share for the stock—$5, $8 or $10? It is the *investors' expectations* of $10! Thus, the cost rate for common, or in other words, the rate that induces investors to buy the stock, has to be based on the price investors pay for a stock related to the prospects of earnings that *they expect* to receive. The rate is:

Common Cost Rate—

$$\frac{d}{a} = \frac{\$\ 10}{\$100} = 10\%$$

Eventually, if the company's estimate of $8 proved to be correct rather than the $10 the investors expected, and this became known to investors, the price of the stock would fall to $80 per share. Then, the common cost rate would still be 10 percent that is, the same expectancy rate by investors. Actually, as noted above, no future single earnings per share figure can represent investors' full expectations if there are prospects for continuous growth.

We have to add one further point with regard to common cost. To simplify the picture, we have left out financing costs. If a company's common stock sells for $100 per share in the market, and it sold some new stock, the net amount it would receive per share would be less than the $100 because of financing costs. A company should be able to sell stock through rights if it is required to do so for its stockholders' benefit. As a rough rule of thumb, a figure of 10 percent is a reasonable allowance for financing costs and rights value, for cost-of-capital purposes, for a large, relatively stable company like an electric utility. For a large, well-situated industrial company a slightly higher figure of 15 percent may be used. There may be variations from these percentages depending on the circumstances surrounding a particular common offering, but they are sufficiently within the range of reasonableness for our purposes. Therefore, our illustration for the common cost rate would have to be modified by allowing 15 percent for financing costs.[2] The common cost rate would be $10 ÷ $85, giving a rate of 11.8 percent. The figures, which we have used to describe the common cost rate, are shown in the diagram in Exhibit 2. For illustrative purposes, the bond cost rate is also included.

Our explanation has admittedly compounded the problem of actually figuring the common cost rate. Investors' expectations at times may be above, below, or the same as is actually realized by the company in the future. In the long run, as their errors become apparent, the market should eventually correct itself to conform to reality. However, either excessive optimism or

[2] There is one possible small difference between funds raised through the sale of stock and retained earnings. A stock sale involves financing costs, but none is associated with retained earnings. Therefore, it may be contended that a slightly lower rate can be applied to earned surplus to the extent of financing costs. There is a good argument against any difference: a company should earn enough on its equity in order to be able to pay out all its earnings in dividends if it chose to do so and still cover its cost-of-capital. This article treats all equity the same.

Exhibit 2

COST RATE ILLUSTRATION

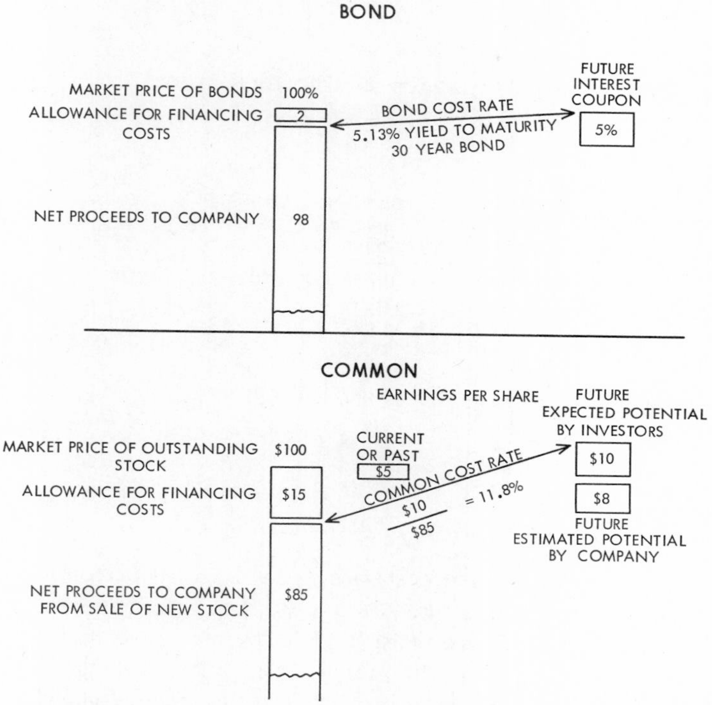

pessimism may persist for a long time and failure to take it into account can lead to meaningless results in the common cost rate. We will see how to try to handle the idea of expected earnings when we get to actual common cost rate calculations. At this point we can, at least, define the common cost rate. The common cost rate is obtained by dividing the net amount a company would receive from the sale of common stock, after all financing costs, on an average over a period of years, including both favorable and unfavorable market conditions, into all future benefits the stockholders expected to receive when they bought the stock.

COMMON COST: SOME ACTUAL FIGURES

To turn to some actual figures, let's look at a company which, aside from some ups and downs, has exhibited a relatively stable earnings picture in recent years. With such a situation, on an average over a period of years, the relationship of current earnings to price should give some indication of the common cost rate. A discussion with some qualified security analysts confirmed the fact that investors generally viewed the stock as lacking any marked growth prospects during the period. Without revealing the company's name, figures for the common stock for the past ten years are shown in Exhibit 3.

Exhibit 3

HISTORICAL DATA ON A COMMON STOCK

Years	*Earnings Per Share*	*Dividends Per Share*	*Book Value Per Share*	*Average Market Price*	*Average Market Price Discounted 15%*	*Earnings Divided by Market Price Discounted 15%*
1962	$10.83	$6.00	$120.33	$123.93	$105.33	10.3%
1961	7.71	6.00	115.50	126.18	107.25	7.2
1960	9.03	6.00	113.97	120.18	102.24	8.8
1959	13.08	6.00	111.33	129.39	109.98	11.9
1958	7.02	6.00	104.46	97.14	82.56	8.5
1957	11.43	7.20	103.47	107.82	91.65	12.5
1956	12.03	6.90	97.53	134.07	113.97	10.6
1955	15.51	5.79	90.15	124.50	105.81	14.7
1954	9.81	5.01	81.09	112.14	95.31	10.3
1953	9.78	5.01	76.77	75.36	64.07	15.3
Average						11.0%

On this basis, the common cost rate would be 11.0 percent. There are reasons to suggest that this figure is too low: First, the figures indicate that common stockholders might at least have had some expectation of growth. Secondly, the stock market was at a relatively high level during recent years. Thus it would seem to be justified to increase this figure somewhat on the basis of judgment. As an approximation we might use 12 percent as a cost for common. The capital structure, during this ten-year period included six percent of senior securities and 94 percent common equity. Therefore, the overall cost-of-capital would be only slightly less than the common rate, or about 11.5 percent. The nature of this company's business in terms of risk was such during the ten-year period that one would expect the cost-of-capital to be above that for the average for industrial companies.

A word of caution should be noted here: Merely because a company's earnings have been level does not necessarily mean that investors expected them to be level. If investors had hopes of increased earnings and were willing to pay high prices for the stock on such hopes, then the technique used of relating earnings per share to adjusted market price would give too low a common cost rate. Figures for cost-of-capital purposes can only be used properly after a review has been made of the investors' attitude towards the company. As an example, one of the large companies in the chemical industry showed a ratio of earnings per share to price, adjusted for financing costs, on an average over the past ten years of 5.1 percent. There was some increase in earnings, but certainly not enough to justify such a low rate. The low earnings-price ratio was accounted for by the fact that the company was in a business which was considered to have great prospects. Furthermore, this particular company had large expenditures for research, which made investors feel that the future earnings prospects would be very favorable. If they are not realized, a price adjustment is inevitable.

Now turning to the question of the significance of price-earnings ratios for growth stocks, it is interesting to note the following remark (*New York Times,* June 17, 1962) made by Secretary of the Treasury Douglas Dillon about stock prices before a Senate Finance Committee: ". . . many investment advisors believe that a stock selling at a price 15 times earnings was probably on a pretty sound basis. . . ." It has been suggested that some managements may have taken the reciprocal, or price-earnings ratio of 6.7 percent, as a clue to the common cost rate. If investors did not expect growth in earnings, would they be willing to buy stocks on such a price-earnings basis? Obviously not! Cost-of-capital measurement must take into consideration expectations of investors. This can be illustrated by taking a look at a typical picture of increasing earnings. We will use as an example, Moody's Common Stock Average for 125 industrials. As a matter of fact it showed average price-earnings for the past ten years of 15.5 times. The figures are shown in Exhibit 4.

Exhibit 4

MOODY'S COMMON STOCK AVERAGE
125 Industrials

Years	*Earnings Per Share*	*Market Price*	*Price-Earnings Ratios*	*Market Price Discounted 15%*	*Earnings Divided by Market Price Discounted 15%*
1962	$11.10	$189.95	17.1	$161.46	6.9%
1961	9.61	199.90	20.8	169.91	5.7
1960	9.62	173.18	18.0	147.20	6.5
1959	9.85	186.26	18.9	158.32	6.2
1958	8.31	149.81	18.0	127.34	6.5
1957	10.27	143.65	14.0	122.10	8.4
1956	10.35	149.41	14.4	127.00	8.1
1955	10.51	130.66	12.4	111.06	9.5
1954	8.38	95.81	11.4	81.44	10.3
1953	7.71	76.05	9.9	64.64	11.9
Average			15.5		8.0%

The earnings to adjusted price shows an average figure of eight percent. Obviously, this is too low, because investors must have expected some growth in earnings. Assuming that their expectations were the same as were actually realized by these companies, how do we allow for it in obtaining a common cost rate? There is no easy answer.

The following approach gives some interesting figures: Assume that investors looked one year ahead when they purchased stock and that on the average their forecasting was correct. This would call for dividing each adjusted price into the next year's earnings. This would give us an 8.5 percent. If we did it for two years ahead, it would be 9.3 percent, and for three years ahead 9.5 percent. These figures are too low because in each case they give no effect to still further growth which investors would be entitled to expect. If investors felt that all growth in earnings would disappear after three years, they would certainly lower their market appraisal drastically.

Since we are trying to interpret how investors viewed the picture, we cannot come up with any exact figure, but at least it would not seem unreasonable to take 11 percent as a rough figure. The companies included in the index had a debt ratio of about 15 percent. Assuming a five percent interest rate for the debt and applying 11 percent to the equity would give an approximate composite cost-of-capital of about 10 percent. This is a reasonable figure for the cost-of-capital for an industrial company.

No pat rule can be given to determine the common cost rate for a particular company. Space does not permit a discussion of other approaches. All the circumstances surrounding a company must be considered, having in mind the way the investors view it. In some situations it may be impossible to use a company's own securities to determine the rate. Then a company must arrive at a figure based on judgment, having in mind the nature of its risk as compared with the risk for other types of companies for which there are known figures. This problem always exists for a privately owned company since there are no market prices for its securities. True, the owner of a privately owned company can disregard cost-of-capital and even run his company at a loss if he chooses to do so, since it is his property. However, presumably he will wish to run it so as to make the same profit as though his capital were invested in a similar type of publicly owned company. Thus, a privately owned company should wish to apply the same principles.

The above qualifications on the approximate nature of the common cost rate may make it appear as though the over-all cost-of-capital cannot be determined sufficiently accurately to be of real value. However, it is not really necessary to refine a cost-of-capital closely for an industrial company —in an expansion program, forecasts of sales expenses and expenditures are bound to contain substantial errors and the calculated profitability of a project is only an approximate figure. This approach is based on sound principles and an understanding of the idea will assist management in arriving at sound conclusions.

SOME COMPOSITE RATES

To give you an idea of the magnitude of the figures for certain types of business, we will now present a few approximate figures in summary form without proof. We include figures on regulated industries because much work has been done in this field. Furthermore, they give us a good reference point for comparison. Because of the relatively stable nature of their business, they are the lowest rates we can expect to find. The rate for any industrial company should be substantially higher.

The rates shown in Exhibit 5 apply to total capital after taxes for investors. We will discuss the treatment of taxes subsequently.

Exhibit 5

APPROXIMATE RATES

	Cost-of-Capital	*Return-on-Capital Target*	*Expansion Profit Goal*
Electric utility		6½ to 7%	
Telephone		8%	
Department stores	8%	At least above bare cost	up to 20%
Industrial company, average	10%		
Textile	13%		

The spread between the three rates depends on many factors. In regulated industries the spread is small. On the other hand, managements of industrial companies may set the expansion goal well in excess of cost-of-capital for many reasons. How much the spread should be above cost-of-capital in order to arrive at the expansion profit goal is a matter of judgment. It must take into account the fact that when a company goes into a new venture there is added risk because of the lack of familiarity with the business. Basically, allowance must be made for the fact that if in each new venture, a company used the cost-of-capital as its goal, and it failed in some of its ventures, the average return would be below cost-of-capital. It has been reported[3] that some major companies have used 20 percent after taxes as an expansion goal.

It is interesting to note that the managements of companies which have shown good profits recognize the importance of setting high profit goals. On the other hand, companies which have shown poor results argue that they cannot find projects which will provide high profits so they struggle with themselves and in the end usually lower their goals. This can only lead to perpetuation of poor performance with all the unfortunate consequences of misdirecting capital.

If there is a significant variation in risk between products, a company will wish to set different goals. This may have to be handled on the basis of judgment, because it may be impossible to find any evidence in the securities markets. This may appear difficult at first, but once a person has become familiar with the subject, satisfactory figures can be established.

---

[3] Variability of Private Investment in Plant and Equipment. Materials submitted to the Joint Economic Committee Congress of the United States (87th Congress, 2nd Session). Part II, Some Elements Shaping Investment Decisions—Page 14.

In recent years, more and more companies are turning to investing in foreign countries. The risk will obviously depend on the country. However, on the basis of logic, there must be at least some increase in risk in any foreign investment over a similar type of investment in this country. There are the added risks of foreign exchange problems and political attitudes towards foreign investment. It seems that some companies today, in their eagerness to enter the foreign market, are underestimating the risk element.

The question sometimes arises whether a company can take on some independent projects below the cost-of-capital if other projects are sufficiently high so that the average of all projects is satisfactory. No! This is misdirecting capital. This is entirely different from the question of how to handle certain types of investment which contribute no direct income such as recreational facilities for employees, etc. To provide a satisfactory return on all capital, the deficit on such investment must be made up on the income-producing projects.

TAX TREATMENT

We have defined cost-of-capital as the rate required to induce investors to provide long-term capital and we refer to it as the "to investor rate." Thus far, we have not been concerned with the effect of corporate income taxes. How to handle it depends on the purpose to which the rate is to be applied. There are various ways to treat taxes; we will discuss three of them:

1. *To Investor Rate.* As already stated, the rate to investors provides the starting point for calculation of cost-of-capital. It disregards corporate taxes. Investors are not directly concerned with the taxes the corporation pays. This rate which is the target for return-on-capital can be used to compare with the company's past experienced return to determine whether it has been sufficient.[4]

The company's experienced return is derived by adding the net income after taxes, before any dividends to the interest charges on long-term debt, and dividing the total by the total capital structure. This is referred to above under the title "Company's Experienced Return-on-Capital." It is comparable with the "to investor rate."

When using cost-of-capital for this purpose, the spread above the cost-of-capital and goal can be much smaller than the spread for an expansion profit goal. To be successful, a company should earn at least something above cost-of-capital.

2. *To Company, Pre-Tax Rate.* The nature of this rate is obvious; it gives the cost to the company before income taxes.

3. *To Company, After-Tax Equivalent Rate.* A project's profitability is gen-

---

[4] Actually, a company, to be successful, should earn such a return on its capital giving effect to a present value of its assets. Also, in analyzing policies with regard to plant abandonment and making additional capital expenditures in order to save existing investment, current values of existing plant must be used. The cost-of-capital approach should be applied within the framework of these values. These situations sometimes present some nice complications.

erally figured after the taxes which apply to the income of the particular project. This does not take into account the tax savings that will accrue to the company if it has some interest charges on long-term debt.

Therefore, to make the goal comparable with the profit rate calculated for the project, adjustment is made in the goal for the tax savings if the company has some debt in its capital and thus some interest charges. It is an after-tax rate, adjusted for the tax savings resulting from the interest charges. This is the expansion profit goal rate generally used to compare with the profitability of a project figured on a discounted cash flow basis.

Assuming a 50 percent income tax rate, these three rates can be compared as shown in Exhibit 6. Of course, there should be substantial allowance for the amount above the cost-of-capital when a company sets a profit goal.

Exhibit 6

EFFECT OF TAXES

	Capital Structure	Rate	*I* To Investors	*II* To Company, Pre-Tax	*III* To Company, After-Tax Equivalent
Debt	$ 15	5 %	0.75	0.75	0.375
Common	85	10.5%	8.925	17.85	8.925
Cost-of-Capital	$100		9.675	18.60	9.300

EFFECT OF CAPITAL STRUCTURE ON COST-OF-CAPITAL

One of the controversies about cost-of-capital revolves around the question of the effect of varying debt ratios on cost-of-capital. Pure economic theory tells us that cost-of-capital is dependent on the risk of the enterprise and not the way the capital structure pie is divided between debt and equity. Here we are talking about the "to investor rate" and not considering the effect of interest on tax savings. This idea is based on the principle that as debt is increased, the common stock becomes more risky and the rate on the common must rise so that the two combined equal the same overall cost. For example, suppose one person owned all the company: could he change the cost-of-capital by exchanging half of his stock for debt so that his investment would consist of 50 percent debt/50 percent equity? Obviously, it makes no difference to him how the pie is divided; the over-all risk is the same. Now, suppose the two different securities are owned by different investors, would they take lower rates on each or on either one so that over-all cost would be lower? Not on the basis of pure theory.

However, as a practical matter, the markets for debt and equity are not entirely overlapping and debt may be used up to a certain point without substantially increasing the common cost rate so that there will be a decrease in the over-all cost. Then within an added range of debt there will be some increase in the cost of debt and equity but not in the over-all cost. At some point, as debt is further increased, risk is added to the capital structure so that the rate of debt and equity rise to such an extent as to cause an increase in the over-all cost-of-capital. The amount of debt which each company should carry will depend on all the surrounding circumstances.

There are those who erroneously believe that the cost-of-capital can be reduced by piling on all the debt the traffic will bear. They contend that debt, with interest deductible for tax purposes, is cheap and common is expensive, therefore, using all the debt possible will result in a decrease in the over-all cost-of-capital. The proponents of this idea fail to consider the greater risk to the common and the fact that the rate on both debt and common will increase so as to cause an increase in the over-all cost. This may be labeled the short-range view. In the short run, during a bull market, when investors are not worrying about the possibility of adverse developments, they may tend to disregard the danger of too much debt. Of course, they have in the back of their minds that they will sell their stock before the company encounters adversity.

From the long-range point of view of the stockholders, the short-range approach must be assiduously avoided. The company does not have the mobility of a security holder who can sell out if he expects trouble. A company will have to consider the effect on cost-of-capital when adversity is encountered. During such periods an overly heavy debt burden may jeopardize the stockholders, it may hurt dividend payments, and it may put a company in a difficult position in raising new capital on a reasonable basis. Thus, there are many reasons why it is best for a company in the long run to keep its debt within the highgrade category.

These ideas are shown in the diagram in Exhibit 7 as they might apply to an industrial company. The figures, bond ratings, etc. are for illustrative purposes only and not supposed to represent their relationship for any specific company.

If you are familiar with the many factors which affect security prices, you will realize that adequate statistical proof is not readily available. It is impossible to isolate the effect of debt ratio from all the other factors which affect security prices so as to determine its effect alone. Those efforts at statistical proof which have been based on an earnings-price ratio are wrong because they do not measure the common cost rate properly.

EARNINGS PER SHARE AS A GOAL—WHY A FALLACY

Management should attempt to increase earnings on existing investment. However, as was mentioned under "Unsound Goals" some managements erroneously hold to the belief that increasing current earnings per share is a

Exhibit 7

DEBT RATIO EFFECT ON COST OF CAPITAL—ILLUSTRATION

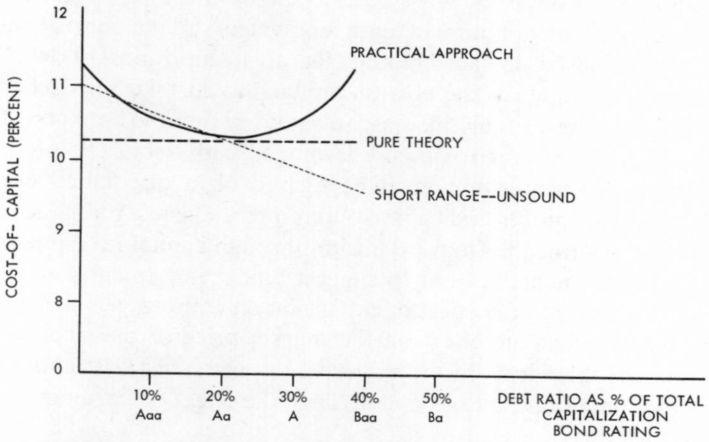

sound goal for new expansion or acquisitions. Now we have the tools to show why this is a fallacy. There are numerous ways in which earnings per share can be increased. In all instances if the new investment earns at least something more than the cost-of-capital, the common stockholders will benefit. However, if it earns less than the cost-of-capital, the stockholders will ultimately experience a loss even though current earnings may show some improvement. We will illustrate this point with an example.

Suppose that a company with great prospects has one share of stock outstanding, earning $4.00 per share, which sells for $100 or a four percent earnings-price ratio. It has a chance to acquire a privately owned company which has one share of stock outstanding, earnings $6.00 per share currently and with potential earnings per share of $8.00 per share. The risk in the business to be acquired, we will assume on the basis of cost-of-capital, is 10 percent. It acquires the second company by issuing another share and swapping it on a share-for-share basis. Thus, in effect, it pays $100 per share for the new company. After the acquisition, the total current earnings will be $10 and earnings per share will be $5.00. Thus, the earnings per share of the acquiring company will be increased from $4.00 to $5.00. However, since the stock to be acquired is only worth $80 on the assumption that the risk is 10 percent, the acquiring company will be hurt by a capital loss of 20 percent in the new investment when it fails to live up to investors' expectations and earn the 10 percent. Since this loss will be spread over two shares after the acquisition, the average capital loss will be 10 percent.

It is not hard to find examples of companies which have acquired many companies through exchanges of stock and the results have ultimately been disappointing even though current earnings may show some increase. This is bound to occur if managements follow the theory of basing acquisitions on increasing current earnings per share and pay exorbitant prices in relation to potential profits.

An acquisition with stock must be calculated on the basis that the company has invested an amount of cash equivalent to the market value of common stock. Based on that amount, the acquisition must show a return above the cost-of-capital. The cost-of-capital should take into account the risk of the enterprise and any increase in rate if in fact the common stock of the company to be acquired is highly leveraged with debt. The profitability calculation for an acquisition must be figured on a discounted cash flow analysis of forecast profits and capital outlays, etc. The test for an acquisition is no different in principle from expansion through capital investment.

The above comments are not to suggest that management should fail to pay careful attention to the effect of expansion on earnings per share because of the possible immediate effect on the market price of the stock and thus the common stockholders. In other words, projects must first and foremost meet the goal based on cost-of-capital. Then the effect on earnings per share should be examined.

Actually, correctly interpreted earnings per share can even be used as a test, but it must conform to the idea of cost-of-capital as previously explained. It is the earnings per share expected by investors which must be achieved. The test thus conforms to the cost-of-capital approach. All the qualifications observed in that approach must be kept in mind.

A quick comment about some other examples which require a knowledge of the principles we have discussed. Suppose a company is earning 30 percent on its capital, can it expand at a lower rate on new capital without hurting the common stockholders? The answer is yes, as long as the company achieves at least something above the cost-of-capital on the new investment. What about the case of a company having excess funds invested in government bonds earning four percent? In order to increase earnings per share, it wants to go into a project which will earn eight percent but has a risk equivalent to a 10 percent cost-of-capital. This would be a mistake on the basis of the principles we have discussed.

In conclusion, an understanding of cost-of-capital will assist managements in making many types of decisions on a sound basis. Profits are the key to our free enterprise system. Our economy, including the consumers, employees and savers, is directly dependent for its continued progress on management decisions based on a correct understanding of this vital key.

Case 10–1

International Harvester Company

In 1960, International Harvester Company invested more than $60 million in about 5,000 individual projects involving capital assets. This case describes the policies and procedures relating to these capital expenditures.

International Harvester was the world's leading manufacturer of farm equipment, among the top six or seven automotive businesses in the world, producers of a wide range of construction equipment (earthmovers, crawler tractors, etc.), and makers of steel and various other items of which fiber and twine was the largest single group. In 1960, the company's total sales were $1.7 billion.

CAPITAL BUDGETS AND APPROPRIATIONS

The capital investment and expenditure process at Harvester included two distinct preliminary stages: compilation of the capital budget and the actual appropriation of funds. The capital budget was the vehicle for financial planning in that it established a limit on the total amount to be used for capital expenditures during a specific fiscal period. The appropriation process, on the other hand, provided an opportunity to appraise in detail the various individual expenditure proposals.

The Capital Budget

At the heart of the preparation of the company-wide capital budget was the formulation of individual budgets by the respective operating divisions and affiliated companies. Examples of these statements are given in Exhibit 1. (The supplementary sheets referred to in that exhibit contained one line for each project, giving a brief description and the estimated expenditures for the project in the budget year and each of the three succeeding years.) The

Exhibit 1

19X2 CAPITAL BUDGET, AS COMPILED IN OCTOBER 19X1 FOR X DIVISION

	Amount Reappropriated or Appropriated	*Estimated 19X2 Expenditures*
Reappropriations from prior year, estimated:		
Works A	$ 100,000	$ 100,000
Works B	200,000	150,000
Works C	300,000	275,000
Engineering	50,000	50,000
Sales department	45,000	45,000
Total	$ 695,000	$ 620,000
To be appropriated in 19X2:		
(*a*) Items over $200,000, per supplementary sheet #1	$ 9,550,000	$ 7,750,000
(*b*) Items over $100,000, not over $200,000 per supplementary sheet # 2	740,000	640,000
(*c*) All other, per supplementary sheet #3:		
Blanket appropriations	300,000	300,000
Other	950,000	800,000
Total to be Appropriated	$11,540,000	$ 9,490,000
Total Reappropriations and Appropriations	$12,235,000	
Estimated expenditures on works manager's authority		$ 140,000
Total Estimated Expenditures		$10,250,000
Estimated amount not to be capitalized in 19X2		750,000
Balance to be added to property account		$ 9,500,000
Estimated property disposals and special credits to property account		400,000
Net addition to property in 19X2		$ 9,100,000
Provision for depreciation:		
On beginning property balance	$ 5,000,000	
On current year's additions	500,000	
Total		$ 5,500,000
Less: Accumulated depreciation on property disposed of		300,000
Net addition to depreciation reserve in 19X2		$ 5,200,000
Estimated addition to net property in 19X2		$ 3,900,000

company-wide budget, with a few minor exceptions, consisted simply of a consolidation of the divisional and subsidiary budgets. Budgets designed for use by the board of directors were compiled twice annually, just prior to the beginning and to the midpoint of the fiscal year (October 31 and April 30, respectively). The first was designated the original budget for the firm, and the second was a revised version. When "approved in principle" by the board, they became the official budgets on the basis of which various segments of the company proceeded to carry out expenditure plans.

Budgets were also prepared quarterly for the finance group, consisting of the board chairman, the president, and certain members of top management. Those of October 31 and April 30 were identical to the ones compiled for the board of directors, except that they included, in addition, estimates of major expenditures (generally involving investments of $200,000 or more) to be made during the ensuing three years. The revisions for January 31 and July 31 also set forth long-term as well as short-term planning, but were not formal budgets and included only the major projects contemplated. They were designed primarily to point up changes that had occurred and progress made since previous budget submissions.

Six members of the finance group were directors of the corporation as well as company officers. As such, they were familiar both with the plans of the operating divisions and with the thinking of the board of directors, and were, therefore, in a position to indicate to the operating units whether proposed projects might or might not be viewed favorably when they were formally submitted to the board. The early exposure of the finance group to proposed future investments provided the operating divisions with the opportunity to pretest the acceptability of their programs and to select for greater concentration those items which appeared to have the most support.

Preparation of this budget was described in the company's 65-page "Capital Expenditure Policies and Procedures" manual. The manual did not prescribe a set method for the development of subsidiary and divisional budgets, although it did assign responsibility for so doing (as well as responsibility for most other phases of the capital expenditure process) to the controllers of the units involved. In practice, expenditure proposals typically originated at all levels of an operating unit. In most cases, expenditure proposals required approval by an authority higher than the level of the proposal's originator.

Ordinarily, staff personnel in the operating units screened expenditure proposals by rough payback estimates, where applicable, as they were brought forth and initiated the investment justification process. At the time a major project was included in the division's capital budget, it was expected to have been formulated to the point where, as a minimum, the following details were known: (1) the acreage and cost of any land to be acquired in connection with the project; (2) for any proposed plant expansion, the number of square feet involved, and the estimated cost; (3) the approximate cost of any proposed plant rearrangement; (4) the approximate number of machine tools to be acquired, their general nature, and the estimated aggregate cost (if the project was very large, a reasonable breakdown of this requirement as among major product units was desirable—that is, so much for crankshafts, so much for pistons, so much for cams, etc.); and (5) approximate cost of tooling, split between that provided for I.H. plants and that to be furnished to vendors (also to be identified by broad totals with major product units). Smaller projects were subject to less detailed requirements, although in such instances the originators and the review groups always were aware that prior to actual appropriation of funds a well-defined justification would have to be prepared.

The sum of an operating unit's depreciation expense plus its earnings (less an allowance for dividends) was regarded as a rough guide to what the individual division could normally expect to spend in total as capital investment in a given year. Additionally, the various management groups involved were continually in touch with one or another of the responsible parties in parent-company management (the executive vice-president overseeing their particular operations, for example), and thereby had an indication of what expenditure allowance they could expect. These overall guides were not restrictive; that is, they were not considered so important as a carefully developed set of individual projects.

The most formal opportunity to discuss individual operating unit prospects with top management was afforded at annual, fiscal year-end meetings between division or subsidiary executives and the parent company's operations review committee. The committee, composed of board members who were also company executives, reviewed results of the units' activities over the preceding year, including capital expenditures made during the period. During its meeting, operating unit executives also had an opportunity to discuss future plans, projects in process, and other projects which they had previously approved but which at the end of the year had not been expended. In the process, individual management groups could sound out top management thinking on future plans. Since the majority of operations review committee members were also members of the finance group, they were, as a rule, already familiar with the divisions' major plans for the future.

In addition to formal meetings with the operations review committee, division management also held periodic consultations with the assistant comptroller for capital budgets, J. W. D. Wright.[1] The week preceding the submission of one of the required capital budgets was officially designated capital budget review week, and during this period Mr. Wright met with officials of each operating unit to discuss with them the items they had tentatively set down in their budgets. Since Mr. Wright was a member of the finance group and also was closely familiar with indicators of Harvester's financial position (such as the firm's cash projections), he was able to make useful comments on the preliminary budgets.

Mr. Wright's position regarding the development of operating units' capital budgets was not restricted to the capital budget review week conferences. Since the origination and investigation of projects was a continuous process and the formal development of capital budgets merely the method of summing up the process as of a particular point in time, Mr. Wright was constantly in touch with the operating units, discussing prospective projects as they became evident. Although projects included on the budgets did not require figure support as to likely savings, profitability, or other justification, most proposed projects were investigated with this end in mind long before

[1] In 1961, Mr. Wright became comptroller of the company.

they were included as prospective expenditures. Often, either before embarking on the investigation or when rough results were available, individual managers checked with Mr. Wright about pursuing the matter further. Or, more commonly, Mr. Wright was asked to discuss the relative merits of cost-saving opportunities versus expansion plans, new methods of ascertaining the return on investment, or the progress of previously budgeted projects.

As the final stage in compilation of the formal capital budget, Mr. Wright consolidated the individual budgets into a single document (which retained the breakdowns shown in Exhibit 1) and added such items as did not appear on the operating units' budgets. He then made copies of the consolidated budget available to the executive vice-presidents and the president. These men made any additional changes they deemed advisable and informed the respective operating divisions accordingly. After final approval by the board of directors, the capital budget was "considered to be accepted as a basis of operation." Each part constituted the accepted budget for the operating unit concerned.

Appropriation of Funds

The approved capital budgets were vehicles of financial planning; they included the amounts proposed to be expended, but neither contained an analysis of the merits of expenditure plans nor constituted a spending authorization. The authorization function was performed at the time a specific appropriation of funds was requested. The way in which it was performed depended on the nature of the project to be approved, the amount of money involved, and the reason for the expenditure.

According to Harvester's capital expenditures manual, the term appropriation was used to designate "a sum of money formally approved to be spent on a clearly defined project for additions or improvements to the capital facilities of the company or its subsidiaries, or for unusual repairs to, or maintenance of, those facilities." The manual also stated, "appropriations approval is not so much the authority to spend a given sum of money as it is the authority to accomplish, through spending not in excess of a certain maximum amount, certain specific purposes as outlined in the appropriation request and accompanying papers."

Harvester's appropriation request form, WF–88 (see Exhibit 2), listed six categories that could be used, individually or in combination, as the "basis of request." The manual expanded on the subject, stating that

> . . . among the reasons for requesting appropriations were the following:
>
> 1. Addition of new production, distribution, or service facility.
> 2. Equipping for the addition of a new product, or product line .
> 3. Equipping for an increase in production schedules.
> 4. Equipping to bring out a new model or make design changes.
> 5. Replacement of worn out equipment, or equipment with high maintenance costs, for cost reduction.

Exhibit 2. APPROPRIATION REQUEST

Date ______ Proposition No. ______ From ______ Division / Department

Project ______

______ Works or Location ______

	Capital	Noncapital	Government Account	Total
WF-365 Building Engineering Service Department				
WF-365 ______ Works				
WF-365 ______ Works				
WF-365 ______ Works				
WF-365 ______ Works				
WF-365 ______ Works				
WF-365 ______ Works				
WF-365 ______				
Totals				

Further explanation of project, desired completion date, etc.:

APPROVALS Name and Title	Date

This request was given Appropriation No. ______

on ______

BASIS OF REQUEST (Show amount for each purpose)	Amount
Expansion of activities	
Replacements to maintain schedules	
Unusual maintenance	
Improved working conditions or safety	
New models or design changes *	
Cost reduction or savings **	
Total, as above	

*Product Committee Report No. ______ approved on ______19___

by ______

**Estimated annual cost reduction or operating savings $______

APPROVED ______ Works Auditor

WF-88-Y-Plain
Printed in United States of America

6. Replacement of machinery or equipment with that of a more efficient kind for cost reduction.
7. Plant rearrangement programs and/or mechanization of production or processes for cost reduction.
8. Equipping to manufacture components presently purchased for cost reduction.
9. Overhauling or rebuilding machine tools.
10. Unusual or extraordinary maintenance.
11. Equipment to improve working conditions or to reduce safety hazards.

In addition to this functional classification of reasons for requesting expenditures, appropriations also were classified on the basis of the type of asset to be acquired. The work sheet from which a WF–88 form was compiled provided nine categories for detailed descriptions of proposed expenditures. Under land improvements, for example, subheadings of landscaping, water, gas, sewer systems, railroad tracks, and miscellaneous were included.

In cases where appropriations were to be made for *cost reduction* purposes, the amount of anticipated savings was shown on the WF–88 form. If the amount of funds to be committed was expected to exceed $25,000, a covering letter also was required, in which a detailed explanation of savings was to be shown. Similarly, in cases where funds were to be appropriated for *purposes other than cost reduction*, covering letters setting forth the merits of the project involved were to be prepared. Harvester's manual suggested in detail the facts that should be included in such letters. Approval authority was limited by the amount of money expected to be involved, as follows:

Management Level	*Maximum Approval Authority*
President	$200,000
Executive vice-presidents (3)	100,000
Vice-presidents (10)	25,000
General managers	15,000
Directors of engineering, manufacturing, etc.	10,000
General superintendents, regional sales managers, etc.	5,000
Manager, consumer relations	2,000
Parts department managers, etc.	1,000
District managers	500

Approval authority was also limited by the purpose for which the expenditure was intended. Below the level of executive vice-president, authority to approve was restricted to projects over which the approving source had direct line authority or clearly specified responsibility. In the case of subsidiary companies, the president of the individual firm was given authority over expenditures of between $5,000 and $20,000, depending on the size of the organization. Above whatever maximum amounts applied in their particular subsidiary, these individuals were expected to solicit an "opinion" from appropriate parent-company sources. The authority to render opinions was identical with respect to dollar amounts to the authority to approve expenditures within the parent company itself.

With the exception of appropriations for less than $1,000, a set of accounting records was maintained in the parent-company offices for each appropriation request. Monthly summaries of appropriations approved under delegated authority were submitted to the board of directors by the president. The figures were shown on a monthly and on a cumulative basis, and were compared with the most recent capital budgets. Unspent balances at the end of a fiscal year (budgeted and appropriated amounts which had not actually been spent) required "reappropriation" during the following period before the spending was considered authorized. The balance of reporting requirements consisted of periodic reports to the general management as to the extent to which anticipated profit investments had actually been realized; these reports are brought up in a subsequent section of the case.

The capital budgeting manual stated that "appropriated funds may not be used for other than the stated purpose of the appropriation." Changes could be made, however, in the method whereby the purpose was achieved, so long as the total amount of funds expended did not exceed the original estimate. For example, if an original appropriation provided for the purchase of 10 lift trucks and sufficient money was available to purchase 11, that could be done, provided proper approval was obtained. Up to 5 percent in excess of the amount originally allocated could be spent on a given project without requesting a new appropriation, provided the total amount thereby committed did not exceed the upper limit of approval authority of the person originally passing on the project.

In the event that approved amounts of money turned out to be greater than actually necessary for the performance of a project, and if the unneeded funds equaled more than $10,000, a formal notice of cancellation was required to be submitted to the board of directors. Smaller amounts of unneeded funds were expected "to cancel themselves" at the end of the year, when all outstanding appropriations were automatically canceled. In no case, however, were unexpended funds for one project to be applied to other projects without a new formal appropriation.

Certain expenditures were covered by so-called blanket appropriations made to the operating units. Specifically, these expenditures were for office or service station purposes that could be forecast on an annual basis with a high degree of accuracy, such as delivery trucks, furniture, or signs. An administrator was appointed for each blanket appropriation approved at the beginning of the year by the board, and he was required to pass on all proposed expenditures made out of the appropriation. The manual emphasized that blanket appropriations were not to be used for purposes other than those for which they were granted, and specifically not to absorb overruns on individual appropriations.

CRITERIA FOR PROJECT EVALUATION

More than one-third of the capital budgeting manual was devoted to defining and illustrating methods for the evaluation of expenditure proposals. The criteria by which various projects were judged differed according to the purpose for which individual expenditures were intended. Cost reduction and new-income producing proposals were ordinarily judged by one of several formulas based on payback plus a return on investment. For example, the following rules were given with respect to investments in equipment.

> A standard of acceptability should provide for an objective rate of return on investment and also an allowance for a normal degree of risk in the project. This risk measures the possibility of obsolescence of either the product or the equipment before the equipment wears out.
>
> For special purpose equipment full recovery of investment, along with an 8 percent return after taxes, should be provided for within a period not longer than ⅔rds of the equipment life, or 8 years, whichever is the shorter period. The limitation of 8 years applies almost wholly to machine tools which are depreciated over 15 years in Harvester automotive plants and over 18 years in implement plants.
>
> For general purpose equipment full recovery of investment, along with an 8 percent return after taxes, should be provided for within a period not longer than 80 percent of the equipment life or 10 years, whichever is the shorter period. General purpose equipment life has, of course, a lesser degree of risk because it is largely unaffected by possible obsolescence of the *product* (the equipment being capable of being switched over to other work) and subject only to the risks of *equipment* obsolescence.

Exhibit 3 shows a sample calculation as given in the manual. The manual also included a short-cut table, which eliminated almost all the calculations for proposals that had these characteristics: (1) the investment consisted entirely of equipment—no working capital; (2) the equipment was to be depreciated for tax purposes by the sum-of-years'-digits method; and (3) the pretax savings were estimated to be the same each year. For example, the table showed that for a project where the ratio of investment to pretax savings is 2.5 to 1, and the estimated life is five years (as in Exhibit 3), the investment would be recouped and 8 percent earned in a period of 44.8 months.

The 8 percent return-on-investment rate mentioned in the manual represented a rough "weighted-average-cost-of-capital," based on the company's outstanding funded debt, preferred stock, and common stock plus retained earnings. Actual costs were used for the first two categories. The cost of equity capital was estimated by attempting to arrive at the amount of dividends that should be paid in order to maintain the common stock at a market price considered appropriate, along with the amount of earnings that would

Exhibit 3

EXAMPLE OF EQUIPMENT ANALYSIS

Consider the case of a proposed investment of $10,000 in equipment with five-year life, estimated to return pretax income on a specific basis of $4,000 annually before depreciation on the new equipment, with no added working capital required, and no salvage value obtainable from the equipment to be replaced. Assume depreciation for tax purposes by the sum-of-the-years'-digits basis, a tax rate of 52%, and an objective earnings rate of 8% after taxes. The cash net income contributed by the project is the total of the savings after deduction of the 52% tax liability thereon, and the tax benefit arising from the fact that the depreciation provisions are deductible items on the tax return. In this method of depreciation the deductions are 5/15, 4/15, 3/15, 2/15, and 1/15, respectively, over the first five years, 15 being the sum of the digits representing the five years. Note the following:

Year	*Pretax Income*	*Same After 52% Income Taxes*	*Provision for Depreciation*		*Depreciation Tax Credit @ 52%*	*Total Cash Net Income*
1	$ 4,000	$1,920	5/15	$ 3,333.33	$1,733.33	$ 3,653.33
2	4,000	1,920	4/15	2,666.67	1,386.67	3,306.67
3	4,000	1,920	3/15	2,000.00	1,040.00	2,960.00
4	4,000	1,920	2/15	1,333.33	693.33	2,613.33
5	4,000	1,920	1/15	666.67	346.67	2,266.67
Total	$20,000	$9,600		$10,000.00	$5,200.00	$14,800.00

The computation of the required 8% return and the progressive payback of the investment (i.e., the excess of the cash net income over the amount required for an 8% return on beginning-of-year investment) are as follows:

Year	*Investment Beginning of Year*	*8% Return*	*Cash Net Income*	*Payback on Investment*	*Unrecovered Investment End of Year*
1	$10,000.00	$800.00	$3,653.33	$2,853.33	$7,146.67
2	7,146.67	571.73	3,306.67	2,734.94	4,411.73
3	4,411.73	352.94	2,960.00	2,607.06	1,804.67
4	1,804.67	144.37	2,613.33	2,468.96	(664.29)

This calculation shows that the investment is recovered, together with an 8% return, in about 3¾ years.

be needed to be able to pay such a dividend. The cost of International Harvester's capital calculated on this basis, after taxes, was 8.2 percent.

The manual was considerably less specific on the subject of "strategic" investments, or those designed to provide for replacement of existing and profitable products subject to future style changes, than on savings or new-income projects. In general, the manual recommended that as many of the relevant figures as possible be supplied with expenditure proposals that could not be justified with full and specific quantitative data, together with such other information as was deemed appropriate by the proposing source.

In practice, unusually sizable or difficult projects encountered were subjected to far more detailed and sophisticated analysis than was apparent from the manual. Normally, such analysis took place under Mr. Wright's general supervision, and reports containing economic forecasts, cash flows, present value analysis, and technical data were submitted to top executive groups or to the board of directors. In the same fashion, proposals for the expenditure of amounts of money requiring direct approval by the board—relatively few in number—were given intensive analysis on an individualized basis.

APPROPRIATIONS REVIEW COMMITTEE

As indicated earlier, Harvester's capital expenditure administrative network included a three-man group known as the appropriations review committee. The committee consisted of two production engineers and an accountant, and was responsible for reviewing the overall plans of proposed projects involving expenditure of $10,000 or more—roughly 400 projects per year. "Overall plans" were further defined to include such items as "the relationship of proposed production methods (including primarily, machinery) to other divisions regarding the utilization of dormant or developable facilities; surveys of methods of tooling proposed; . . . spot checks of prices and delivery dates; and assurance that all capital expenditures stand on their own two feet under specific recommendations and appropriations, and elimination of borderline items from overall or blanket appropriations." The group was viewed as a sufficiently important checkpoint for new proposals so that many division personnel consulted with the committee's members about the feasibility of prospective projects before they went to the trouble of working up detailed analyses.

DIVISION AND PLANT ADMINISTRATION

Whereas top management tended to look at the system in terms of underlying philosophy and effectiveness, those involved with capital expenditures at the division and plant level were primarily concerned with the functional aspects of the procedures. One division comptroller expressed his main responsibility as being "to see that the individual plants follow the procedures and exercise care in charging the expenditures to the right account." Another had delved more deeply into the theory of the expenditure process and, consequently, worked closely with the so-called "advance cost group" to assist in the preparation, evaluation, and presentation of various major proposals. This group, present in each division, was quite similar in function to the parent company's appropriations review committee, and had as one of its major responsibilities the task of working with individual planning groups within the division. Each division also maintained a number of staff groups, such as the new products committee, the materials committee, or the engineering research committee, with either specific or concomitant responsibility to screen and/or work up expenditure proposals.

At the plant level, considerable emphasis was placed on development of projects. The means by which such development took place varied widely, depending in part on the particular capital equipment needs of a given plant, and in part on the size and importance of its operations. At some of the larger plants, several staff groups, which might include, for example, a products planning committee, a cost reduction committee, or a procedure analysis group, spent a large proportion of their time investigating and developing new expenditure possibilities. In smaller plants, individual superintendents and foremen generated ideas for such projects as equipment replacement, modification of processes involving new equipment, and adding capacity. At both the plant and division levels, the process of assembling a workable set of project proposals in time for a particular budget deadline was generally one of screening out all but the most attractive suggestions from an abundance of ideas.

POST-COMPLETION AUDIT

Harvester had tried various systems for post-completion audits of projects in order to ascertain verified forecasts. It was extremely difficult, however, to develop a system for gathering the type of required information usable at the parent company level. For one thing, analysis of an individual project's performance required that detailed records be kept on virtually all phases of the project. For another, the savings analyses almost inevitably had to be made by much the same group that had worked out the project in the first place. Finally, even more difficult problems were connected with the definition of savings itself. Was it not necessary, for example, to determine whether an employee replaced by a machine was occupied productively elsewhere or had been let go, in order to verify that his replacement had really led to a cost reduction?

To cope with this problem, Harvester had developed a standard form to be submitted once a year to the responsible divisional office by the appropriate cost centers for certain individual projects. This form showed the estimated and actual investment, the estimated and actual savings, and the reasons for significant differences between estimated and actual.

Mr. Wright was not entirely satisfied that this post-completion review procedure was the best that might ultimately be devised. He noted that reports to date had shown remarkable accuracy of original savings estimates, with almost 99 percent average fulfillment of goals.

PROBLEM AREAS

In Mr. Wright's view, a wide number of problem areas continued to exist in the administration of the capital budgeting and expenditure program. Among the more important of these were the following.

1. *Volume of Projects.* Harvester processed approximately 5,000 projects per year. Of these, the majority were for outlays of between $5,000 and $10,000, and did not require detailed investigation by representatives of the parent company. The remaining projects, however, were still sufficiently great in number so that a disproportionate amount of time for their review was required of top executives. The board of directors, for example, which was required to look only at projects above $200,000, averaged four or five of these per monthly meeting.

2. *Differences in Ability to Propose Projects.* Some staff members at the division level were more skillful at writing up and justifying proposed expenditures than were their counterparts in other divisions. Although standard form letters had been suggested by the new manual, there still were many instances in which local personnel believed the apparent merits of individual proposals were affected by the quality of the supporting paper work.

3. *Biased Forecasts.* In earlier manuals no overspending allowances had been permitted in project investment estimates (additional funds required separate appropriations), with the result that investments in many cases were overstated initially. The present and preceding manuals *did* authorize overspending to the extent of 5 percent, but, in fact, this provision was resorted to in less than 5 percent of the projects.

4. *Inadequate Information.* In many cases, commitments had to be made before a good part of the pertinent information was available. In several product lines (those involving style changes, particularly), decisions would have to be made a year or more ahead of actual production time—long before reliable estimates of sales volume were worked up—in order to assure that all phases of the production process would be under way when required. Under these conditions, as one man put it, the amount of funds necessary to satisfy the projected requirement was really just an "educated guess."

5. *Timing and Timeliness.* There were three fairly distinct aspects to this problem. First, the question of preparation was involved. To what extent and at what level should individual projects be formalized, and by what method should they be directed to the person empowered to approve them? Second, there were the time dimensions of action. How much time should be permitted or expected to elapse between development of a project possibility, acceptance in principle (as part of the budget), appropriation, and expenditure? This time span could obviously be very costly in terms of foregone benefits, especially in the case of high-yield projects. For most large projects requiring recognition in one of the budgets, however, there was a lag of at least several weeks in the approval chain alone. Furthermore, should more immediately important projects, or more profitable ones, be differentiated from those which, while acceptable, were relatively less imminently necessary or attractive? If so, how should this be done? Finally, when was a given project developed enough to be reviewed fairly? How much

time should be devoted to the review? What use could be made of the data that resulted from the review, which obviously was after the fact?

QUESTIONS

1. What are the key issues involved in the overall capital budgeting program?

2. How does each aspect of the program fit the company's objectives of maximizing the long-term interests of stockholders?

Case 10–2

Problem on Deferred Payment Investments

SITUATION

A company with a required earnings rate of 10 percent has decided to install a certain type of automatic machine. It is considering four makes. It estimates that any of the four will result in a savings of labor and other cash costs of $800 annually for five years as compared with not acquiring a machine. Lease and interest payments were disregarded in arriving at this $800 figure. Income taxes are to be disregarded. No machine will have a residual value. The four machines are offered on the following terms:

Machine A: Outright purchase, $3,000 cash.
Machine B: Purchase in five annual installments of $712 (seller receives $3,000, plus 6 percent interest on the unpaid balance).
Machine C: Noncancelable, five-year lease, $750 a year.
Machine D: Conditional sales agreement calling for a payment of 90 percent of audited savings annually for five years, with the maximum payment to be $750 in any one year. The buyer has no other obligations.

PROBLEM

The problem is to devise a method of calculation that will rank these proposals in the order of their attractiveness. The following points should be noted:

1. According to one method of calculation, the choice between C and D is indifferent. At a required earnings rate of 10 percent, the present value of the investment in each is $2,843 ($750 × 3.791), and since each has the same earn-

ings they have the same profitability or return on investment. Actually, D is clearly more attractive than C.

2. Some methods say C is preferable to A. The equivalent investment, $2,843 in C, is less than the $3,000 in A, and estimated earnings are the same. Others say C is equally attractive as A, but not better. A similar contrast can be made between B and A.

3. According to one method of calculation, B, C, and D are all infinitely desirable, and therefore equally desirable. It can be argued that since they all have cash inflows exceeding cash outflows each year, the rate of return in each case is infinite.

Case 10-3

Bevis Petroleum Company

H. C. Caldwell, manager of the production department of the Bevis Petroleum Company, was considering a proposal for Bevis to buy producing oil property owned by R. M. Bentley. Mr. Bentley offered to sell the property for $2.34 million, but for tax reasons he wished this amount to be paid to him annually over a 10-year period.

Exhibit 1 shows a schedule of expenditures and estimated receipts for this property. Explanation of the columns is as follows:

Column 1 is the schedule of payments to Mr. Bentley. On the assumption that the deal is closed at the end of 1955, the first payment, $390,000, would be made at the end of 1955, and other payments would be made at the end of the years specified. When the deal is closed, Bevis would give Mr. Bentley a non-interest bearing note for $2.34 million.

Column 2 is the estimated capital expenditures that good engineers say should

Exhibit 1

SCHEDULE OF EXPENDITURES AND RECEIPTS FOR OIL PROPERTY PURCHASE

(000 omitted)

Year	*Col. 1 Payments to Seller*	*Col. 2 Additional Expenditures*	*Col. 3 After-Tax Cash Income*	*Col. 4 (Col. 3 less Col. 2)*	*Col. 5 Net Cash Flow*
1955	$390	$350	$	$ (350)	$ (740)
1956	130	50	387	337	207
1957	130		377	377	247
1958	130		351	351	221
1959	130		351	351	221
1960	130		338	338	208
1961	130		338	338	208
1962	130		338	338	208
1963	130		325	325	195
1964	130		234	234	104
1965	780		143	143	(637)
1966			143	143	143
1967			143	143	143

be made within the next five years to improve the property. The amount is fairly definite (subject to price changes), but the timing depends on circumstances. The timing of the expenditures shown in Exhibit 1 is at the end of the year indicated, and is conservative.

Column 3 is the estimated cash inflow, consisting of sales revenue from crude oil sold, less cash lifting, moving, and selling costs, and less income taxes. Columns 1 and 2 have been used in the income tax calculations, but do not otherwise influence Column 3 figures. The property was producing crude oil in 1955. The quantity of crude oil remaining in the property was based on good geological estimates. The selling price estimate, of course, depends on future market conditions. Cost estimates are based on good experience. In short, the figures in Column 3 are as good as, but no better than, competent, experienced people can make them.

Columns 4 and 5 are self-evident.

The Bevis Company recently had borrowed $150 million on 30-year sinking fund debentures, at 4 percent (2 percent after taxes). The company planned to earn at least 15 percent after taxes on funds invested in producing oil properties.

Mr. Caldwell explained that he had considered the following possible ways of evaluating the proposal:

1. Our first thought was to find the time-adjusted discount rate that would bring the present value of Column 5 to zero. This turns out to be around 22 percent.

2. At the time the deal is closed, however, Bevis would have to give the seller a note for $2.34 million, payable without interest on the schedule indicated in Column 1. This would be a fixed obligation, irrespective of the performance of the producing properties, and would have to be carried as a memorandum note on our balance sheet.

In effect, therefore, we are borrowing $2.34 million from the seller, just as we would from a bank or other lending institution, and are investing the proceeds of the loan in the purchase of these properties. The situation (except for the zero interest rate) is, thus, no different from some other project that might make use of the funds secured from our $150 million 30-year sinking fund debentures. Following this line of thought, the $2.34 million is spent at the time the deal is made, and we should find the discount rate that makes the present value of Column 4 equal to $2.34 million. This turns out to be around 5 percent.

3. The "loan" of $2.34 million is peculiar in that it carries no interest charge. It might be said, however, that it relieves us of the need for borrowing an equivalent amount at a cost of 4 percent, or 2 percent after taxes. By discounting Column 1 at 2 percent, we can get the present value of our future obligation to the seller. This turns out to be $2.08 million. We may then find the discount rate that makes the present value of Column 4 equal to this, which is about 7 percent.

QUESTIONS

1. What is the expected return on this investment? (NOTE: If you conclude that none of the methods described in the case gives the expected

return, indicate how you would make the calculation and what the approximate result would be. You are not asked to make the actual calculations. Assume that the arithmetic leading to all figures given in the case is correct.)

2. Should Bevis Petroleum Company purchase the property?

3. What procedure should the company follow in the future in analyzing investment proposals of the type described in the case?

Case 10–4

Lakeside Oil Company*

In January, 1958, Mr. Karsten, treasurer of the Lakeside Oil Company, received a memorandum from Mr. Bocatelli, manager of the service station division. A few days earlier, Mr. Bocatelli had opposed a plan to lease and operate a chain of service stations and restaurants. The capital investment committee, of which Mr. Karsten was chairman, had tentatively approved this proposal on the ground that it showed an adequate return on the investment. In his memorandum, Mr. Bocatelli set out to explain and support his belief that the plan did not, in fact, show an adequate return.

The proposal referred to was operation of a chain of ten service stations and four restaurants to be built on a new automobile turnpike. When the offer first came to Lakeside's attention, it had been suggested that Lakeside lease the properties from the Turnpike Authority for 25 years, agreeing to pay a flat minimum annual rental of $782,300, plus an additional annual rental based on sales of gasoline and food. In the course of negotiations, the flat minimum rental was increased by a supplemental annual amount of $474,800 to be paid during the first five years only. The supplemental amount was occasioned by an unexpected increase in the estimated costs of building the properties. These minimum rental figures were equal to the level repayment schedule needed to amortize loans of $10 million and $2 million over 25 and 5 years, respectively, both including interest at 6 percent. The Turnpike Authority—the corporation set up by the state to borrow funds, and to construct and operate the toll highway—intended to borrow these amounts.

The calculations originally made by the capital investment committee to evaluate this proposal are summarized in Exhibit 1. The committee considered that from Lakeside's standpoint the lease was a form of investment, since it committed the company to a fixed financial burden over a number of years in the future, and they calculated the amount of the investment by taking the present value of all the flat annual payments guaranteed by Lake-

---

Exhibit 1

CAPITAL INVESTMENT COMMITTEE'S APPRAISAL

Capital Investment

Annual flat rental $782,300	
(Amortizes $10 million 6% bank loan over 25 years)	
Capitalized at 16% (782,300 × 6.10*)	$4,772,000
Annual supplemental rental $474,800	
(Amortizes $2 million 6% bank loan over 5 years)	
Capitalized at 16% (474,800 × 3.27*)	1,553,000
Equipment and fittings	150,000
Total Capital Investment	$6,475,000

* Present value of $1.00 per year for n years at 16 percent.

Calculation of Annual Cash Income

	¢ Per Gallon of Motor Fuel	*$ Per Year at 40 Million Gallons Motor Fuel*
Gross margins:		
Motor fuel	11.1	4,440,000
Motor oil	1.5	600,000
Service and labor	.6	240,000
Miscellaneous sales	1.1	440,000
Restaurant sales	3.7	1,480,000
Total Gross Margin	18.0	7,200,000
Less: Variable expense	5.2	2,080,000
Pretax profit before fixed expense	12.8	5,120,000
Less: Fixed expense		444,000
Pretax profit before gallonage sales rental		4,676,000
Gallonage sales rental	*Rental Base*	*$ Per Year*
Motor fuel, 40,000,000 gal.	4.4¢ gal.	1,760,000
Motor oil, (sales of $2,000,000)	4%	80,000
Service and labor (sales of $400,000)	4%	16,000
Miscellaneous sales (sales of $1,800,000)	4%	72,000
Restaurant sales (sales of $8,960,000)	10%	896,000
Total		2,824,000
Pretax profit before annual rental expense		1,852,000

	Years 1–5	*Years 6–25*
Pretax profit before annual rental expense	$1,852,000	$1,852,000
Annual rental expense	1,257,100	782,300
Pretax profit after rental expense	$ 594,900	$1,069,700
Income taxes at 50%	297,450	534,850
Annual cash income	$1,554,550	$1,317,150

Calculation of Rate of Return

Present value of $1 per year for years 1–5 at 22%	$2.86	
Present value of $1,554,550 cash income for years 1–5		$4,450,000
Present value of $1 per year for years 6–25 at 22%	$1.65	
Present value of $1,317,150 cash income for years 6–25		$2,170,000
Present value of total cash income at 22%		$6,620,000

Since this is slightly more than the present value of the capital investment, the rate of return is a little better than 22%.

side. For this calculation, they used a discount rate of 16 percent, which was the weighted before-tax cost of capital to Lakeside.

The revenue from the investment, from Lakeside's viewpoint, was the profit expected to be derived from sales of gasoline and food, less the additional rental based on sales volume. Past experience with similar projects had shown the profit ratios and operating costs that might be expected. The committee applied these estimates to traffic forecasts supplied by the Turnpike Authority. These forecasts indicated that Lakeside could conservatively expect to sell an average of 40 million gallons of motor fuel per year. This would result in annual cash income of $1,554,550 in the first five years, and $1,317,150 thereafter. The discount factor that made this stream of cash income over 25 years equal the original investment was approximately 22 percent, and therefore the committee concluded that the project had a rate of return of 22 percent.

On the basis of some informal discussion, Mr. Bocatelli gathered that at least one or two members of the capital investment committee, along with himself, did not agree with the majority opinion. Mr. Bocatelli's calculations are summarized in Exhibit 2. He reasoned that this lease represented a fixed financial burden over a number of years, somewhat the same as long-term debt. Since Lakeside had recently sold $215 million of its 25-year bonds at 4.5 percent, he thought that a discount rate of 2.25 percent would be appropriate in that this was equivalent to the current after-tax cost of borrowing to Lakeside. Since Mr. Bocatelli had taken account of the after-tax cash flow resulting from the lease payments in calculating the capital investment, the appropriate income figure for appraisal purposes in his calculation would be $926,000. The discount factor that made this stream of earnings over 25 years equal the original investment was a little below 10 percent. "This is a far cry from a 22 percent return," said Mr. Bocatelli, "and I'm sure we can find far more profitable projects than this one."

However, before any formal action could be taken on the matter, an unexpected problem arose. In the original plan, the Turnpike Authority intended to borrow the funds needed for construction of the property from the Trowton National Bank, using the long-term lease from Lakeside as security. In December, however, the authority's legal counsel ruled that such a loan would be illegal. By state legislation, the authority had been set up as a special corporation, wholly owned by the state. The legislation clearly defined limits on the type and amount of funds the authority could borrow. In December, 1957, the top limit on bank loans had been reached, and a further extension of credit was, therefore, not possible.

Another member of the committee, Mr. Lewis, thereupon conceived the idea of creating a special corporation that would act as an arm's-length intermediary, thereby overcoming the legal restrictions on financing. This corporation, temporarily called X Company, would lease the properties directly from the Turnpike Authority, and immediately sublease them to Lakeside. Using the sublease as security, X Company would borrow the funds needed,

Exhibit 2

SUMMARY OF MR. BOCATELLI'S FIRST APPRAISAL

Capital Investment

Annual flat rental $782,300	
Capitalized at a discount rate of 2.25% over 25 years after taxes of 50% on the rental (782,300 × 50% × 19.03*)	$7,444,000
Annual supplemental rental $474,800	
Capitalized at a discount rate of 2.25% over 5 years and after taxes at 50% on the rental (474,800 × 50% × 4.68)	1,111,000
Equipment and fittings	150,000
Total Capital Investment	$8,705,000

Calculation of Rate of Return

Pretax profit before annual rental expense (from Exhibit 1)	$1,852,000
Income taxes at 50%	926,000
After-tax income for *appraisal* purposes (does not include lease expense)	$ 926,000
Present value of $1 per year for 25 years at 10% $9.077	
Present value of $926,000 annual income for 25 years ($926,000 × 9.077)	$8,405,000

Since $8,405,000 is slightly less than the investment of $8,705,000, the rate of return is slightly below 10%.

* Present value of $1.00 per year for n years at 2.25 percent.

which it would then advance to the Turnpike Authority. The money would be borrowed by X Company from the Trowton National Bank under exactly the same conditions as had been previously arranged for the Turnpike Authority. Two separate loans were to be made—for $10 million and for $2 million, each at 6 percent. The $10 million would be repaid over each of the next 25 years, including interest, by equal annual payments of $782,300; the $2 million would similarly be repaid over each of the next 5 years by equal annual payments of $474,800. Lakeside would pay exactly the same annual rent as previously arranged, but in this case payments would be made to X Corporation instead of to the Turnpike Authority.

Since the proposed investment was now tied more closely to this particular scheme of financing, Mr. Bocatelli was prompted to make a new study, which is summarized in Exhibit 3, and to use a different discount rate in calculating the present value of the lease. In his opinion, all other costs were identical with those in his original study. He used a rate of 3 percent, because this was the after-tax cost of this particular piece of credit. The use of this new rate changed the total investment cost to $8,111,000, and consequently resulted in a rate of return of less than 11 percent. "This new development, along with a fictitious corporation and a fancy scheme for financing, makes very little difference in my appraisal," said Mr. Bocatelli. "I'm still very much opposed to this proposal."

At this point, Mr. Jones, another member of the investment committee, offered a completely different argument in favor of the plan. Mr. Jones said he could not for the life of him see why there was so much argument over

Exhibit 3

SUMMARY OF MR. BOCATELLI'S SECOND APPRAISAL

Capital Investment

Annual flat rental $782,300	
Capitalized at a discount rate of 3% over 25 years and after taxes of 50% on the rental (782,300 × 50% × 17.572*)	$6,873,000
Annual supplemental rental $474,800	
Capitalized at a discount rate of 3% over 5 years and after taxes at 50% on the rental (474,800 × 50% × 4.582)	1,088,000
Equipment and fittings	150,000
Total Capital Investment	$8,111,000

Calculation of Rate of Return

After-tax income for appraisal purposes (from Exhibit 2) (does not include lease expense)	$ 926,000
Present value of $1 per year for 25 years at 10% $9.077	
Present value of $926,000 annual income for 25 years ($926,000 × 9.077)	$8,405,000

Since $8,405,000 is slightly more than the investment of $8,111,000, the rate of return is slightly higher than 10%.

* Present value of $1.00 per year for n years at 3 percent.

the proposal. "After all," he said, "we pay out $1,257,100 ($782,300 + $474,800) in rentals before taxes, or $628,550 after taxes. We take in $926,000 after taxes. We therefore have a profit of almost $300,000 after taxes for the first five years, and considerably more thereafter. What is all the argument about?"

As there seemed to be some confusion among members of the capital investment committee, Mr. Karsten adjourned the meeting until the next morning, when a final decision would have to be made. He asked each member to carefully reconsider his position on the matter. It was important that there should not be such a wide difference of opinion among the senior executives of the company on such a basic matter. Mr. Karsten wondered what position he should take at the following day's meeting of the capital investment committee.

QUESTION

What position should Mr. Karsten take at the meeting of the capital investment committee? Be prepared to back up your recommendation with appropriate figure work and justification for any assumptions you have made.

Chapter Eleven

INFORMATION HANDLING

In the framework described in Chapter 1, information handling was shown as a process separate from management control. Nevertheless, there is obviously a close relationship between these two processes, and for this reason some material on information handling is included in the book. Emphasis is on the management rather than the technical aspects of the subject. No prior knowledge of computers is assumed.

Reading 11-1

Management Information Systems and the Computers

By John Dearden

In many companies, management is concerned with the extent to which computers should be used to automate their information systems. A more important concern, however, is the *adequacy* of the management information system, particularly in the strategic planning and management control areas. Consequently, it appears to us that it is vital to examine the quality of the management information system *first* and to consider automating it *second*. Not all management information can be improved by the use of a computer. Nor does all information generated by a computer qualify as management information.

The most important consideration for the business manager is to have an effective management information system. To the extent that computers help in this, he should use them. He should not make the mistake, however, of thinking that extensive computer use guarantees a good management information system. For example, take the case of a very large, multidivisional company with which we are familiar. This company has extensive computer applications in the areas of production control and accounting. In production control, this company successfully uses computer information systems to schedule and control an extremely intricate, multiplant production process. In the accounting field, it has a well-integrated computer system for payroll, general accounting, billing, payment of payables, and cost accounting. In short, it has made good use of computers and, in fact, has been cited by at least one authority as a model for others to follow in adopting computer systems. Yet this company has *no* formal (and practically no informal) system for long-range planning; it has no budgets of any kind; its cost accounting system is archaic and, consequently, seriously inaccurate. In other words, this company is being run by the seat of the pants in spite of extensive computer installations. It has a totally inadequate management information system. And, incidentally, its profit performance reflects this situation.

This company is exceptional only because of its size. Most companies of even a quarter of the size of this one have much better management information systems. In many medium-sized companies, however, it has been our experience that management is not using one-tenth of the information that could be made available *without a computer*. At the same time, the management of these companies seems to be deeply concerned that unless they acquire additional computer capacity they will be left behind competitively.

On the other hand, poor utilization of a computer does not mean that the company has an ineffective management information system. In one large company with which we are familiar, the computer is used only for routine data processing. The production control and inventory control systems are handled by a combination of tabulating equipment and manual processing; budgets and costs are prepared on tabulating equipment. In spite of this, management has an adequate control system.

The important consideration for management, therefore, is the effectiveness of the information system and not whether to acquire computer capability. For these companies with computers, it is important that the computers be used effectively, but using them effectively is not so important as having an effective management information system. It is important to understand that these two factors (the effectiveness of the computer installation and the effectiveness of the management information system) are not necessarily the same. The optimum situation is, of course, to have both good computer systems and good management information systems, and this is the idea toward which a company should work.

WHEN SHOULD MANAGEMENT CONSIDER AUTOMATION?

In order to generalize about the appropriateness of acquiring a computer, it is necessary to distinguish between routine data processing systems and management information. Also, management information must be divided further into operational control, management control, and strategic planning.[1]

Routine Data Processing

Although hard and fast rules cannot be laid down as to the kind of company that should automate its routine data processing systems, two characteristics can be used as a general guide in specific situations—size of company and proportion of data processing cost to total cost.

Size of Company. Much has been written in the past year or two concern-

[1] See Reading 11–2, "Can Management Information Be Automated?" for a definition of these three management functions.

ing the entrance of the small business into the computer field. The increase in availability of service centers and the development of small computers, such as the IBM 1440 series and the Remington-Rand 1000 series, have brought computer capability to the small company. One should not be misled by this trend into thinking that size is no longer important in determination of potential computer use. We believe that it still is an important factor. Although the size of a data processing application is a major factor in determination of the cost of the hardware, the size may have little to do with the cost of the systems and programming work. For example, it might cost nearly as much to develop a billing system for a company with $1 million in sales as for a company with $50 million in sales. To management, this fact means that when the level of activity is high computer applications may pay off handsomely, even though the initial cost of systems development and programming is high. If the activity is low, however, the computer must be restricted to those systems having relatively low development and programming costs. Size, therefore, continues to be an important consideration. The larger the company, the more likely it will be that it can use a computer economically for the routine processing of data.

Proportion of Data Processing Cost to Total Cost. Somewhat related to size is the proportion of total company costs devoted to routine processing of data. This is important for two reasons: (1) the larger the proportion of total cost spent in data processing, the larger will be the absolute cost and, hence, probably, the number of profitable computer applications; (2) the greater the proportion of data processing cost, the more vulnerable the company is to competitive action.

The first of these points, we believe, is clear. The second, however, deserves a little further explanation. If a significant portion of a company's costs is incurred in routine data processing, failure to take advantage of new developments in this area could be very serious if competitors were to take advantage of these developments. This could be true of a small company as well as a large one, although new developments are most likely to apply to the large company. Consequently, managements of companies that incur a substantial proportion of their costs in data processing must spend more time and money keeping up to date on new developments than do managements of other companies. For example, it is more important for managers of banks and insurance companies to be aware of the latest developments in data processing equipment and systems than it is for managers of typical manufacturing enterprises.

Operational Control

Although the potential use of a computer in routine data processing is significantly influenced by the size of a company, this conclusion is not necessarily true of operational control systems. The key indication of potential computer use in the operational control area is the existence of a complex operational control problem—for example, a warehouse operation with a large number of different parts, or a production operation with a complex scheduling problem. Since the payoff in this type of computer application results from improved performance, the amount of data handling is not the key factor. From a management point of view, therefore, the existence of a complex operational control system makes it reasonable to seriously consider the possibility of automation.

Management Control

We believe that a computer will not significantly improve the quality of a good management control system, although it may reduce the cost of operating the system. For example, we believe that the managements of companies like Du Pont, General Motors, Ford, or General Electric, to name a few, will not be able to make better decisions in the management control areas as a result of having their management control systems on a computer. This statement does not mean, however, that we think the development of the computer will not have an effect on management control. We believe that the opposite will be true, for two reasons:

1. New developments in high-speed data processing are having the effect of making management examine its information system. It would be the height of folly simply to automate an old and inadequate information system. As a consequence, many management control systems are being greatly improved. (Note, however, that usually the same objectives could be accomplished with a manual system.)
2. As a result of the lowered cost of handling data, some companies have adopted more sophisticated management control systems than they believed were economically justified before automation. This is particularly true where the information systems have been properly integrated. It has been discovered that the marginal cost of an improved management control system is relatively small.

This development has particular significance for the manager of the medium-size company. (The small company does not generally need an extensive, formal management control system, whereas large companies already have adequate management control systems.) The implication to the manager of the medium-size business is this: increased automation of information systems has indirectly resulted in upgrading the management control systems of many medium-size businesses. The development could have significant competitive consequences for those companies that do not improve management control systems.

Strategic Planning

The computer technique best adapted to assist strategic planning is the general business simulation.[2] We believe that two conclusions bear on the

[2] See Jay Forrester, *Industrial Dynamics* (Cambridge, Mass.: The M.I.T. Press and John Wiley & Sons, Inc., 1961).

relation of company characteristics to the use of simulation models for strategic planning.

1. With the present state of the arts, the general business simulation will be confined principally to the large company. The cost of developing and operating a general business simulation makes it uneconomic for the small- to medium-size business.

2. The better a company can predict the revenue variables—volume, price, and product mix—the more valuable a simulation will be as an aid to testing long-range policy decisions. Public utilities, for example, should find a simulation model more reliable than will automobile manufacturers. In the automobile industry, the results of any simulation run will be determined by the assumptions as to volume and mix of sales.

We believe that management in large, relatively stable businesses should think seriously about experimenting with the development of general business models.

Reading 11-2

Can Management Information Be Automated?*

By John Dearden

During the past year or two, systems specialists have been developing an approach to management information systems which, if left unchecked, could cause serious problems to the companies that adopt it. This approach has been described in several articles appearing in a number of periodicals in recent months. A typical article describes an intricate, multiplant scheduling system, controlled centrally by a large-scale computer. Each plant has a smaller computer with lines feeding directly to the central computer. The computer automatically schedules production, and it maintains current information on inventory levels at hundreds of points throughout the system. When stoppages occur, the computer reschedules, on an optimum or near optimum basis, all parts of the system affected by the stoppage.

Although different in detail, each article describes an elaborate, computer-controlled information system and, invariably, concludes with a statement somewhat like this:

> This is just the beginning. In the near future, the information system will be extended to provide top management with nearly instantaneous information on what is happening throughout the company.

Mention is usually made of large-scale memories, point-of-action recorders, nonimpact printing, and visual display of information. The impression given is that in the near future every board room will have its computer which top executives will be able to interrogate directly and have answers instantaneously flashed on a screen. These new information systems presum-

* From *Harvard Business Review,* March–April, 1964. Used by permission of the *Harvard Business Review.*

ably will make it possible for the top executives of a company to control, at all times, extensive and complicated industrial empires.

The purpose of this article is to demonstrate that this approach to management information systems is sheer nonsense and, worse, that it can lead to severe management problems in the companies attempting to use it. Specifically, I will try to show that:

Complex computer-controlled systems solve a limited type of management problems.

For the most part, only the lower levels of management are directly affected by automatic information systems.

The techniques that make present computer systems successful do not apply at all to more general management problems.

Attempts to apply these techniques to more general management information systems can have serious consequences for the companies that try.

My reason for writing this article is not to reassure top managers that they are in no immediate danger of becoming obsolete. Rather it is to point out the possible consequences of unrestricted automation of management information systems.

MORE MEANINGFUL APPROACH

It appears to me that one of the principal reasons for the existing confusion about the use of computers by management results from failing to segregate management's function in a meaningful manner.

Typically, management is divided into the two categories of middle management and top management. And usually neither of these terms is defined—just because no meaningful definition is possible. The term middle management, although used a great deal in articles on automated information systems, is completely useless. It can include everyone from an assistant foreman to an executive vice-president. How can any logical generalizations be made about such an all-embracing function?

A more meaningful approach to analyzing the potential use of computers in management information systems is to:

—Break down management functions in terms of the type of information required to carry them out.

—Review the characteristics of information systems which make them most adaptable to automation.

Based on this information, it then becomes possible to evaluate how computers can *improve* the information available to management and, consequently, how they can improve management's ability to carry out its functions.

Management's Functions

I propose to classify management's functions in this order:

1. *Strategic planning*, which consists of (a) determining corporate policies

and objectives; (b) deciding on any changes in these policies and objectives; and (c) deciding on the resources to be devoted to attaining these objectives.

2. *Management control,* which consists of (a) dividing the strategic plans into logical subdivisions; (b) providing the funds to carry out the subdivisions of the plan; (c) assigning the responsibility for carrying out each of the subdivisions of the plan to some individual; and (d) following up to see that the assignment is being satisfactorily carried out.

3. *Operational control,* which consists of (a) determining the specific men, equipment, material, and information necessary to accomplish the subdivision of the plan; (b) assigning these resources so that the plan can be carried out in the most efficient manner; and (c) comparing actual results with plans and taking corrective action where appropriate.

The following generalizations may help to clarify these definitions:

For practical purposes strategic planning may be thought of as deciding on long-range plans and objectives; management control, as supervising and evaluating operational personnel; and operational control, as carrying out the day-to-day operations of the business.

In a large company there can be several levels of each of these management functions. For example, strategic planning and management control can take place at the corporate, group, and division levels. Each level, however, is subject to the restrictions placed on it by the group above. Operational control can also occur at the corporate, division, and plant levels. For example, the corporate level can decide which division will manufacture each product in the monthly production schedule. The division can schedule the production by plants. Within the plant, the plant manager schedules production by department and machine. It is even possible for the foreman to schedule the production within his department. (This, however, is unusual today except in the small, job-shop type of operations.)

In a small enterprise the same person may perform the strategic planning, the management control, and the operational control.

The distinction between strategic planning, management control, and operational control is not completely determined by the hierarchy within a company. Even in large companies, top management frequently performs functions that, strictly speaking, are operational. (For example, it is not unusual for a top-management committee to decide *how* the advertising budget is to be spent.) Conversely, people who are normally responsible for operational control may execute management control. (For example, a plant manager may assign to his general foremen more or less complete responsibility for planning and controlling the production of the items that are to be manufactured.)

Determining Suitability

Next we must recognize that a computer can be used to best advantage in processing information which has these general characteristics:

Interacting Variables. One of the computer's most important features is its ability to perform arithmetic and logic operations at tremendous speed. This feature is required for solving problems which have a number of interacting variables. In fact, until the development of the computer, mathematical models with a relatively small number of variables could not be solved by hand calculation in time to provide any help to management. Linear programming was one of the earliest uses of the computer in solving problems of this nature.

Reasonably Accurate Values. It must be possible to place fairly accurate values on the coefficients of the equations. Also, the equations themselves should express accurately the relationships among the variables. This requirement is important because the results of any calculation are no more accurate than the assumptions on which the calculation is based. If it is not possible to develop a mathematical model with a high degree of reliability, there is considerable question as to whether it is worthwhile to develop a model at all. General approximations, taking into account only the principal variable, may be just as satisfactory and much cheaper to calculate.

Speed. The value of a computer in an information system will tend to vary directly with the necessity for speed. Before the development of the computer, much information could not be used to help management make a decision because it could not be provided in time.

Repetitive Operations. The computer can most profitably be applied to repetitive operations. There are three reasons for this:

(1) In order to use a computer for decision making, it is necessary to anticipate all decisions that must be made and to program the computer accordingly. This is usually practicable only where the same operations are repeatedly undertaken.

(2) A repetitive operation is generally required to develop a reliable mathematical model. (This is particularly true if the mathematical model contains probabilistic elements.)

(3) The cost of developing an information system or mathematical model can be substantial. If it is used only occasionally, it may be of questionable economic value.

Need for Accuracy. In general, the greater the degree of accuracy that is required in the output, the more likely it will be that a computer will be helpful. A digital computer can be programmed to obtain results with almost any degree of accuracy (assuming, of course, that the information to be provided to the computer has the same degree of accuracy). If great accuracy is not required, it might be cheaper to use general approximations than to develop and use a more exact computer system.

Large Amounts of Information. As previously stated, computers are able to handle large amounts of data quickly; it is logical, therefore, that the larger amounts of information that must be processed, the more likely it will be that a computer can be profitably employed.

MEETING FUNCTIONAL NEEDS

Now that we have defined management's functions and noted the characteristics of information systems which make them suitable for the computer, we can analyze the potential of computers to improve the information required to discharge each of the three types of management functions—operational control, management control, and strategic planning.

Operational Control

It is evident that many operational control systems will be generally adaptable to automation, with production scheduling being probably the best suited. A typical production scheduling and control system will have all of the characteristics that make effective automation likely. There are many interacting variables; yet, because of the physical nature of the system, reasonable values can usually be placed on these variables. Speed of information is also very important. In fact, instantaneous information is frequently desirable, because an unanticipated change in one part of the system can affect other parts and it is vital to make adjustments quickly. For example, the breakdown of a machine producing a given part affects the entire scheduling system. The schedule must be adjusted to take into account the change in the availability of the part; otherwise, a line may be shut down at some point.

Production scheduling and control, furthermore, is a repetitive operation. Not only does it go on each day, but schedules are constantly being revised for changes in sales plans or production capability. Because of the repetitive, routine nature of production scheduling, accurate decision rules can be built into the computer program. Moreover, these systems require accuracy; rough approximations are rarely satisfactory. Finally, they usually involve handling large amounts of data. In summary, therefore, the typical production scheduling and control system has all the characteristics of an information system that make it adaptable to automation. For this reason the most advanced computer applications have been in this area.

Although production scheduling offers the *best* use of a computer, other operational control systems are also adaptable to automation. For example, inventory control systems have been successfully automated for many years. In the field of research and development, PERT and CPM systems are proving effective devices in planning and controlling these operations. It is clear that in the next few years automation will be extended to other operational control systems. The problem is, however, whether management information systems other than those devoted to operational control are also adaptable. If they are not, it is incorrect to assume that the automation of production scheduling systems is the *first* step in automating higher management information systems.

Management Control

I believe that management control systems are so different from operational control systems that the techniques which have proved successful in automating inventory and production control systems are not at all applicable to the typical management control system and, if used, will result in weakening the entire structure of the management information system. To demonstrate this, let us look at a typical management control system—a manufacturing expense budget and reporting system.

Annually, a budget covering direct labor and manufacturing overhead costs is prepared by the plant controller, tentatively approved by the plant manager, and submitted to top management for final approval. Expenses have been divided between fixed and variable so that they may be adjusted monthly to reflect the actual volume of production. The budget has been developed department by department so that each department manager (or general foreman) can be held responsible for his portion of it.

After approval, the budget becomes the basis for a monthly report. Each month the budgeted costs are adjusted to the actual level of production. The budget figures are then compared by expense series (e.g., indirect labor, supplies, utilities) to the actual costs, and the resulting variances are analyzed.

The budget becomes the basis by which management exercises control over factory cost:

Management can tell whether costs are in line with plan. If they become significantly out of line, management can take action.

Management can evaluate the factory manager on the basis of his performance. If his performance is not satisfactory, management may replace him or strengthen his staff.

Management can tell whether corrective action has been taken effectively. For example, assume that the cost of scrapped parts in January is out of line with the budget. If the plant manager assures management that this condition has been corrected, it is possible to determine from the February report whether, in fact, it has.

In addition to these uses, the budget is a communication device to tell the factory manager exactly what is expected of him. It is also a device to motivate him to stay within the budget. He knows that there is the possibility of some undesirable action if he does not do so.

It is quite possible to put the budget reporting system on a computer with some savings in data-handling cost. It is unlikely, however, that the automation of the budgetary control system will improve significantly the quality of the information available to management. Here is the reason:

First, there are not many complex, interacting variables. The principal concern is actual cost and budgeted cost. The use of a computer will not, in itself, provide any improvement over the manual handling of this information. To be sure, it would be possible to use more complex formulas for adjusting the budgeted expense to the actual level of production. But my personal experience indicates that this has limited usefulness because the relationship of a cost factor to a volume factor is frequently not constant. As a consequence, a linear approximation provides as good an estimate as does a more complex, exponential curve.

Next, it is not possible in most cases to determine exactly what the level of expense should be. There is little advantage in running approximate levels of expense through complex mathematical equations; the results will still be approximate.

Finally, in budgetary control systems speed is not so critical a factor as it is in operational control systems. The budget shows the summation of what has happened throughout the month. It is not, therefore, an instrument for taking direct action. (For example, no one waits for the budget report before fixing a broken steam pipe.) Even if the budget report came out the first day after the end of the month, something could have happened thirty days ago about which management would not have been informed. Consequently, whether a budget report is issued five days after the end of the month or eight days after is of little consequence. If top management wants to know immediately when certain things happen in a plant, it must rely on another communication system than the budget. (Instructions requiring the plant manager to telephone top management when certain conditions arise may be all that is required to cover the unusual contingencies.)

These same qualifications apply to other management control information systems such as profit budgets, standard cost variances, and income statements. Each is similar to expense budgets in its unlikely adaptability to automation.

Perhaps the most important difference between the management control and the operational control systems, however, lies in the automation of the decision-making rules. Decision rules *can* be programmed into the operational control system because of its repetitive and routine nature. But I do not see how this can be done to any degree in the management control system.

The computer is designed to make a great many routine decisions in a short period of time. This is the quality that gives it an advantage over human decision making. Management control decisions, however, are not usually routine at all, and it becomes infinitely more difficult to program a computer to make these decisions correctly. Furthermore, there are not a great number of them to be made. Consequently, speed of decision making is not a vital factor. Many management control decisions are made only after a long period of deliberation (e.g., the replacement of a plant manager), and the effect of these decisions may be felt for a considerable period in the future. These decisions are entirely different from operational decisions, and, given the present state of the arts, they are not adaptable to automation.

Strategic Planning

As might be expected, the techniques used in the automation of production scheduling and control systems cannot be applied to strategic planning.

Speed of information—in terms of hours or days—is practically never vital. Furthermore, it is not usually possible to determine values precisely, because strategic planning always involves predicting future events, many of which have no close precedent. Finally, complete accuracy of results is neither possible nor necessary. There is rarely any significant repetition, and there are usually no requirements for handling large amounts of data. (An exception to this is where a computer is used for data reduction and analysis when statistical studies are made as part of the strategic planning for a particular course of action.) With these facts in mind how, then, could one conclude that it is practicable to program the computer to make strategic decisions automatically?

About the only characteristic of strategic planning that fits into the computer capabilities is that strategic decisions sometimes involve many interacting variables. Because of this, the general business simulation may prove to be of considerable value in strategic planning. The general business simulation, however, is entirely different from the typical automated operational control system and is aimed at solving a different set of problems.[1] The general business simulation is designed to allow management to test the long-range effects of different courses of action before making a decision as to which course to embark on.

BETTER INFORMATION

So far I have tried to show, first, that the computer can be used to automate only certain types of operational control systems and, second, that it is unwarranted to assume that these same techniques can be used to improve the information systems of higher levels of management activity. Assuming this is true, there still remains the question: What harm can it do if systems efforts are directed to trying to apply these techniques to improve the quality of top-management information? I believe that there are two undesirable consequences:

Time and money are spent on developing systems that will decrease the quality of management information if installed.

Attention is directed away both from better means of improving management information and from more useful computer applications.

Let us examine each of these consequences more closely.

Impaired Information

Since most people agree that top-management decisions themselves cannot be automated, the general approach to improving these decisions appears to be to use the computer to increase the amount of information available to management, as well as to increase the speed with which this information is

[1] See Jay W. Forrester, "Industrial Dynamics: A Major Breakthrough for Decision Makers," *Harvard Business Review,* July–August, 1958, p. 57.

available: the more information available, the better the decision. This end is to be accomplished by having vast amounts of data stored in a computer memory, by having this information constantly updated by point-of-action recorders, by having direct interrogation of the data stored in the computer's memory available to the executive, and by having immediate visual display of the answer.

But nowhere is the all-important question asked: "*What* is management going to ask the computer?" Certainly budget performance information (or, for that matter, any financial data) would not be available on an instantaneous basis. Most companies find a month too short a period of time for an accurate budget on financial reports. Would management want hourly or daily profit information? Ridiculous! Even if it were available, it would be meaningless. In fact, none of the information used in either strategic planning or management control can be practically provided on an instantaneous basis. This information requires periodic accumulation and analysis. In fact, the shorter the period covered, the less reliable it is.

What, then, could be the value of having this type of information available in a computer's memory for management to interrogate at will?

If management control or strategic planning information is not available on the computer, what information *would* be available to top management? It would be the only information that it makes any sense to collect and update continuously—operational control data. Conclusion: *the information available to management in these advanced computer control systems would be almost exclusively operational control information.* All the computer could supply, when interrogated, would be such things as inventory levels (by any part desired) or production records!

And what is management to do with this information when it is flashed on the board room screen? There is only one thing that it can do—harass operational personnel. Since the information can be neither meaningful nor useful to top management—because top management is too far removed from the scene of operations—all top managers can do is ask why certain things are happening. How else could they use instantaneous inventory level or production rate information?

One of the most common mistakes in management information systems has been that of providing one level of management with information designed for use by another level. Not only is this information frequently meaningless to those at the one level, but it obscures the fact that certain decisions must be made there and the necessary information for making these decisions is absent.[2] At the time when some headway at correcting this problem is being made, is the computer to take us several steps backward by making available to top management *all* of the information required by operational management?

---

[2] See John Dearden, "Accounting and Budgeting for Research and Development Costs," *The Financial Executive,* November, 1963, p. 20.

It appears to me, therefore, that if a company is successful in installing a management information system such as just described, it will cause serious problems when management attempts to use it. First, top management will be deluged with information that it can only use to check up on operating management. And if top management uses this information to try to control operations, it will be performing the function of the operational manager. A company will end up in the ludicrous position of having two groups performing the operating function and no one handling strategic planning or management control.

Even if top management does not try to interfere with operating management, the hourly or daily information generated by the computer will just waste top managament's time and direct its efforts away from more important things. Even if management is provided only with "exception" information, the system will not be improved, other than that less management time will be devoted to reading useless information. (Notice also that you do not need an elaborate computer installation to communicate when something is seriously wrong in the operating area, which is the only time when top management should be concerned.)

There are some data that top management may want on a 24-hour basis. For example, in many companies sales data are provided daily to management. The amount of this type of data must be small for anyone who does not perform an operating function. I cannot imagine any circumstance where a complete computer system would be warranted to provide this information. The usual procedure is to accumulate the information that is collected for the operational managers and to submit it to top management. (Remember, if top management needs the data, the person directly responsible must also need it, and, therefore, it has to be collected for his use in any event.)

Misdirected Attention

It is natural for systems personnel to aspire to improving the information available to the higher echelons of management. Anyone familiar with management information systems knows that almost all systems can be improved in some respects and that many can be improved drastically. Many managers today are making decisions using less than one-tenth of the information that would be made available to them *without a computer.*

The faults of most inadequate management information systems, however, cannot be corrected by a computer. The problem lies in faulty methods of collecting costs, inadequate standards, and poor budget procedures (if any exist at all), just to name a few. Adequate cost accounting, expense budgeting, profit planning, and capital budgeting systems are not dependent on a computer (although, admittedly, a computer can frequently reduce the cost of operating them). Attempting to automate top-management information systems is the wrong way to tackle the problem. As a result, correct methods for improving management control systems are obscured and ignored.

Not only does this excessive concern with automating management information systems direct attention away from more appropriate action for improving management information, but also it directs attention away from more useful computer applications. It appears to me that the systems efforts should be directed to automating information systems that have characteristics similar to production scheduling systems and to developing techniques to make it possible to automate ever more complex operational control systems.

CONCLUSION

A computer is able to store vast amounts of data, to retrieve the data quickly, to perform arithmetic and logic operations at a speed measured in millionths of a second. And it can perform these operations practically without machine error. These characteristics make the computer ideally adapted to solving many operational control problems. As a result, some complex and ingenious automatic information systems have been developed in the past few years, particularly in the areas of production scheduling and inventory control. It is incorrect, however, to assume that this is the *first* step in automating management information. The higher levels of management activity have entirely different information requirements, and it is a mistake to assume that these functions are merely a more complex operational function. Consequently, the same techniques that are used to solve operational control problems cannot be applied to management control problems.

The effort in automatic systems development should be directed toward improving and refining the present production scheduling and inventory control systems and to extending these techniques to include other operational control areas, such as marketing and R&D. Efforts should not be directed toward applying these techniques to management control and strategic planning systems.

On the other hand, most companies can improve their management information systems considerably. In nearly every case, these improvements are in no way dependent on the use of a computer. It is important to realize that an automated management information system is not necessarily a good one nor is a manual system a poor one. Many companies have installed the most advanced data-processing equipment and yet employ accounting and budgeting techniques that were out of date 20 years ago.

At some future time it may be possible to automate effectively the higher level management functions. This, however, will require considerable improvements in both equipment and techniques. Consequently, this field is still very much in the domain of the researcher. Management should be aware of this fact when approving the extended use of computers to information systems for the higher management echelon.

Reading 11-3

Seven Deadly Dangers in EDP

By L. R. Fiock, Jr.*

If we consider for a moment that business information system methods prior to electronic data processing (EDP) were analogous to 3,000 coolies moving a hillside with baskets, while the computer does the same job with one atomic blast, then we can imagine the immensity of the conversion and the dangers of the process getting out of control. Consider:

With the coolies, things happen in very small bits; not much control is needed. Within several thousand bucketfuls, work can successfully terminate at any point. No more control is needed than that given by visual estimates.

With the blasting, on the other hand, everything must be done just right the first time or, instead of having a mountain to move, there may be a Grand Canyon to fill. But if everything goes right, tremendous time and money can be saved. In short, the new computer way requires skill, better planning, more precise control; the potential gain is great, but the price of failure is dramatic.

In setting up EDP, some managers have tried the middle road and said, "Let's develop the whole plan, a piece at a time." This is rather like giving motorized wheelbarrows to the 3,000 coolies. True, it is a little more modern, and there is not such an imminent risk of failure. But at the same time it is still quite close to the oldest method, and there is small gain. And, worse, by such half-hearted methods one learns little about how to handle the big EDP jobs.

---

* Supervisor of the management analysis section of the industrial engineering department, General Dynamics Corporation. From *Harvard Business Review,* May–June, 1962. Used by permission of the *Harvard Business Review.*

Today EDP is still many different things to different people, according to their varying experiences.

Why is there so little real management knowledge about EDP? Well, let's look at the history of ordinary computer installations.

First, there came tab machines; these have been a boon to the accountant for years because his purpose is to set down each bit of activity with its like kind, and then to sum them up. Eventually, multipliers were invented that could be of some use in areas outside of accounting; so other people came to accounting to have work done. Then the computer came along, and the company simply set up a manager of data processing—still under accounting.

This seemed perfectly logical. Is the computer not complementary to tab equipment? For instance, some will contend that, as a matter of very practical fact, a payroll can be done for a facility hundreds of miles away. But, within a facility, computers and tab equipment must be nuzzled up within inches of each other or life just cannot go on.

Strange? Not at all. Nobody bothered to explain the application of computers to the operating man; thus, he was presumed by default to be unaffected. The machine salesmen naturally courted the people with whom they had always dealt; and few at this time knew computers actually might offer the greatest advances in areas outside of accounting.

Besides, there were strong reasons for thinking the computers still belonged in accounting. One proposition which got wide play held that the computer, crammed full of operating data, is the device which will allow the controller to do what he should do—*control*. Another idea was that a large part of the effort of accounting people is taken up in adding operating statistics. Might not machines eventually be programmed to such an all-encompassing extent that they could take raw data from the field and, untouched by human hands, summarize it in all necessary forms? If the accountant did not possess the machine, he was therefore going to suffer deeply himself.

In most companies things went along quietly while the accounting jobs were converted over to a computer. But then someone was impressed by the sophisticated controls being developed at another company. Inquiry began; a committee was set up.

Here we begin to observe an utter and astonishing inconsistency in company behavior patterns all across our large industrial complexes. Research people were probing in a disciplined, scientific manner at the very edge of man's knowledge, in such a way as to calibrate the meaning of each little element observed. Meanwhile, back on the operating side, companies behaved in an appallingly unsophisticated fashion. Committees of managers were formed, none of whom was really educated to the effect computers might have on operating controls. Naturally, the programs they voted into existence had little chance of achieving the results top management wanted.

In desperation, the committees often loaded the machines up with anything carrying an impressive title.

What is the moral? Simply this: if businessmen were more knowledgeable about some of the dangers involved in setting up and evaluating an EDP installation, maybe they would be able to protect their companies better from the waste of time and money. At least a beginning toward this goal could be made if executives were aware of the most common EDP pitfalls that yawn before them. Such a beginning is what I hope to accomplish in this article.

1. POOR PROCUREMENT

Just how you go about acquiring EDP equipment clearly plays a major role in the success you can expect to achieve. When managers thoughtlessly procure equipment as a natural progress item, they can easily preclude any possibility of success simply by buying the wrong equipment. This is fairly easy to do. Salesmen have a natural affinity for bypassing the technician and selling directly to top management. After all, in the final analysis, the top executives are the ones who must be sold, so why not start with them? And when salesmen deal with top managers, they rely on tricky little gimmicks which they would not dare to use with technicians.

One of the most prevalent practices has been a demonstration of the great advantages of some device that just sits and waits for a challenge, whereupon it throws out answers in a fraction of a second. The implication is that obviously this genie-like response alone is of tremendous value. What the salesman may fail to mention is that the preparation of the question and the handling of the answer constitute the stickiest part of the problem. He also fails to mention that the logic of this little beast, waiting breathlessly to perform, is so narrow that it reacts only to a very limited set of stimuli, and to build any type of control system might require a multitude of these devices. Once the device is placed in the hands of the operating men, disenchantment soon sets in, for he finds the machine relatively useless. He then faces the dubious choice of running the thing just for window dressing or tackling the unthinkable task of telling the boss he was wrong.

So, too, EDP acquisition as the result of the urging of one or two operating functions usually results in paying for more capability than is used. A good application initiated under conditions like these sometimes falls by the wayside simply because other jobs do not develop in time to raise the equipment utilization to a satisfactory level. Once caught in this low-level utilization situation, a company faces the choice of sustaining the high cost until other jobs can be developed or of regressing and relinquishing the effort to date. At its very best, though, this approach is most likely to culminate in a jumbled load of unrelated tasks.

It is often just as dangerous to base the acquisition on the command of a data-processing manager to whom a new installation can mean a glamorous but expensive prestige symbol. The principal benefit of such installations is frequently the fact that the data-processing people can then attend technical conferences as full members of the fraternity rather than as country cousins. At these conferences, the talk is sprinkled with tape density, drive speed, really big numbers, very small numbers, and random numbers. Payroll, labor distribution, and account closings may be talked about as highly important technical achievements.

Or, worse yet, the computer people sometimes end up attempting to assume the role of high priests to the brain which is going to radiate the "new way" to all when it "goes on the air." They ignore all people who have operating experience, and concern themselves with looking for a place to apply some new trick techniques. They may subtly try to create the aura that their mystic methodologies are practically "molded" into the hardware. Is it any wonder that some consultants and even some manufacturers are also pretty smooth at this approach?

Certainly it is fair to conclude that digital computers, properly handled, are clearly the greatest managemnt tool to appear in many decades. But a well-planned management improvement program should be the only incentive to spark an acquisition. Such a program recognizes the need for solid preparation and includes consideration of the needs of all affected organization elements far in advance of delivery. It recognizes, too, that while a single program can mechanize only a few clerical procedures, a properly connected chain of programs offers the possibility of reshaping internal operating policies.

2. IGNORANCE OF PROCEDURES

Perhaps the most universal way in which managers shortchange themselves in their use of computers is by failing to realize the shortcomings in their present methods. Most executives do not know how much their intended policies are prostituted at the lower levels of execution to fit expedients or available methods. Full computer potential will never be reached until blissful misimpressions of present policy execution are shattered.

There have been reams written about the need for executives to do some soul-searching before they embark on a computer romance. But when these dissertations are boiled down, most simply state that the current conflict is about procedure: (1) as it is laid down in the book, (2) as the line functions think they are doing it, and (3) as it is actually happening. Add to this mosaic of conflicts the techniques which could not have existed previously that computers have made possible; the situation fairly cries out for thorough diagnosis before anyone can feel safe in pushing the button on the machine that is going to outperform the people it is replacing.

However, if you are going to take the step, you should accept the fact that over 8% of the getting ready is self-analysis and planning. Writing instructions for the machine actually will amount to less than 20% of your effort. Without a study phase, your efforts with the computer will be analogous to those of the man who buys a fine high-fidelity phonograph, but never sets the instrument to match the recording curves of the records in his library. High performance will be at your finger tips, but you can fail to attain it simply because you failed to do the analysis warranted by the instrument.

The computer is the first mechanical device which can execute long, complicated policy and procedure. The ability to execute choices—i.e., make decisions—is built into the equipment. A properly designed group of computer programs can attain the control level which is normally considered the policy level. It is up to each user whether he achieves or bypasses the full potential of an EDP installation.

3. "SERVICE" OVER "CONTROL"

The use of business computers in manufacturing organizations has taken two different paths. Some companies use computers on a "service" basis, others to establish a "control network" which tightens the coordination of all functions within the enterprise or within a single facility. And the taking of the "service" path is increasingly recognized as a danger.

Under the "service" approach, top management's direct interest is usually limited to selecting equipment and, possibly, to reviewing rental costs. The manager of each functional area uses the computer at his own discretion in specific phases of his activity. In most cases, under the service approach, each function has programmers assigned on its budget. If programmers are not budgeted to specific areas, then management of the functional area assigns people to work with programmers who are supplied from a pool. In some cases, to avoid employing a large-scale computer, several medium-size computers are allocated to the various areas.

The "control network" approach, on the other hand, requires that there be no more than a single programming staff and operating group at any one facility. The basic principle of a control network is that all of the various functional controls are fabricated into a single operations control system for the entire facility. The intent of the network is to exert a more disciplined enforcement of policy and procedure. Control is tightened—especially over those functions which trigger expenditures of direct labor and material.

The policies which are incorporated into computer programs to control "action documents" (shop orders, purchase orders, stock requisitions, and so on) are also used in simulation programs for predictions. The ability to make secondary use of control policies in simulation programs yields tremendous improvements in all forecasting and prediction activities. Actually, it is possible today to simulate on the computer the exact events which will occur on future days. Examples of simulations used for prediction purposes are load forecasting, departmental budget forecasting, material forecasting, and cash requirement forecasting. Simulation also offers a new policy guidance technique. Just as an established policy can be simulated for prediction purposes, various policy alternatives can be simulated to show probable future conditions under various choices. This principle has been made practical only through the high-speed, mass-data handling capabilities of large-scale computers.

Here is another point wherein the service approach breaks down, for the scattered, independent jobs do not contain enough policy data to support a valid simulation. Thus, there is deepening conviction among industrial companies, universities, and consulting organizations that the control network is far more beneficial than the service approach. In fact, it is becoming so generally popular that many concerns which actually work on a service basis make loud avowals that they have achieved a control network.

If it sets its sights on a control network, upper management should skim by all the interesting specifications of computers. Internal circuitry can be fully exploited by technicians, but only management policy direction can set the goals to be attained within a particular organization. This fundamental often eludes management long after installation.

4. MIDDLE-MANAGEMENT RESISTANCE

Every aspect of an effective EDP installation appears as an unwarranted—indeed ominous—intrusion to middle management. Here is why. Computer programming for a control network demands precise, written definition of all instructions—from basic policy to clerical instructions—many of which were previously verbal. The intense staff activity necessary to force policy definition exceeds any previous attempts at such documentation. No motivation has previously existed for the formalization of policy and procedure that is now required. In a manual system, by contrast, policy develops on a day-to-day basis, some even at the lower management levels. People who are designing highly integrated control systems are only now beginning to discover the amount of subtle decision making which takes place at the clerical level.

The mere presence of so much staff activity is disturbing to the functional manager. He will not voluntarily seek the specialized services of outside staff people. Their activity subjects the department manager to possible unsympathetic outside criticism. Their analyses may scrutinize his detailed procedures, which sometimes are defensively designed because of "weaknesses" in other functional areas. The manager is asked to state a firm policy position for inclusion in a computer program at the time that he is most aware that the conflicts and variances among functions—which otherwise might have remained dormant—cannot remain in this condition. Thus, the entire company may be shaken as a result of old wounds being opened and some areas of uneasy compromise becoming outright challenges. In some cases, this may appear intolerable to various functional areas, and several may join forces in a united front to resist the methods and programming staff.

Hence, the real positions of the various functional managers can become buried under their fears about losing control. These apprehensions can occur even though the functional managers have complete control over all significant decisions affecting their areas. They fear that the increased intensity of coordination between functions may indirectly reduce their managerial prerogatives.

Even in the fortunate circumstance where complete open-mindedness prevails when the analysis is started, some differences of opinion soon appear between line and staff personnel—because intensive operating analyses always disclose possible improvement, and computers inherently permit new types of controls. So, while changes in operating controls are the goal of a well-conceived computer installation, these changes are impeded by the personal fears and ingrained habits of some personnel whose irrational resistance to change stems from the fear that if they admit that improvements in their function are possible, then they are indicting themselves for having lived so long with inefficiency.

But even if an installation is lucky enough to get through these troubled waters, it still has far from calm seas ahead. As the analysis progresses from the study to the development phase, more startling events may occur.

For middle management, moving to a computer operation is like moving into a glass house. Here is why. One reel of computer tape can contain information equivalent to a normal file cabinet. On a fully integrated network, a few reels of tape may contain all of the operating information pertinent to an entire department or division. The tapes are maintained and stored in an area geographically removed from the department. It is conceivable that the tapes could be read on orders from upper management without the knowledge of the departmental manager. In fact, a few reels of tape portraying the status of an entire functional area could fit easily into a briefcase and could be read on other machines at other locations.

The resultant feeling of exposure which confronts the operating manager contemplating these facts is appalling. Given some time to worry, he may well come to this conclusion: "My data could be picked up, read, misunderstood, and I could be fired without ever knowing why!"

At the very least, there is a concern that the shortening of the data link between the "field" and top management will tempt top management to jump to "false" conclusions and not turn to middle and lower management for explanations. Sometimes fears like these can lead middle managers to believe that it is their duty to *shield* from upper management any knowledge of situations which they could, in time, get straightened out themselves.

But suppose all these troubles are overcome by some superb groundwork on the part of upper management and by complete open-minded logic on the part of middle management? What impediments still exist? Simply this: that reliance on staff "outsiders" appears (and indeed *can* be) dangerous from a support standpoint. What assurance do middle managers have that the staff organization will provide adequate facilities for them once they have relinquished their old ways of getting the job done? The answer, it seems clear to them, is none!

5. INADEQUATE STAFF

Computers are not simply faster tabulating equipment, but they have been initially regarded as such in most organizations. Actually, treating a large-scale computer as if it were tabulating equipment can almost assure failure, measured by fiscal standards. One of the most painless ways to squander money on EDP is to allow the placid situation to exist where a machine-operating group graciously services all comers and makes glowing achievement-saving reports to a grateful management. The most overt manifestation of this "just-another machine" attitude is the staff which continues its previous mode of operation—quickly handling little deals rather than analyzing the purpose of the entire business system.

One phenomenon of the current state of the art is the EDP manager who enjoys sudden prestige merely because, compared to the days of "tab," he has a larger staff, a more expensive machine, does business with more people, and his rent bill assures more attention from management. During the next few years, however, some basic standards of excellence should develop and, when this occurs, many installations now counted as successful will be switched to the other side of the ledger.

The mistake is in blindly assuming that the existing staff and its methods are worthy of confidence. The very newness of the control network precludes the existence of check points familiar to management which could serve as bench marks for evaluation of the system. The same unfamiliarity exists about personnel involved. Take, for example, the manager of data processing. Computer work is still so new that the manager of data processing who is merely a flash-in-the-pan can look just as good to his management as can the competent pioneer. The ultimate irony is that the truly valuable manager is likely to be much more controversial than will be the rudderless interloper who is merely trying to be popular while he "fakes" his way along.

Management will have to give some extra attention to EDP until a generation of competent data-processing managers mature—men who can select and develop potential future replacements. But being less than a decade old, business data processing has certainly not reached this stage of normal propagation. Seldom has anything come along which has had throughout all industry such a universal appeal as an attention-getting device for the business politician, even though there have been enough setbacks to make glory grabbers cautious.

Some machine manufacturers are now openly recognizing this problem and are attempting to say what they can about properly and improperly qualified personnel without stepping on customer prerogatives. What they warn about is that many persons who possess sufficient analytical ability, objectivity, and ethics to be safely relied on for systems guidance actually do not have the persuasiveness and sales guile of the pseudoexpert. Furthermore, the person who understands the subtle rules of systems work can seldom be distinguished from the salesman, since the latter can pick up the lingo from trade journals and glibly discourse on basic principles, using all the right catch phrases and terminology.

Setting up a business-methods staff requires a type of person that never existed before in business. Those who guide the invention of new operating controls must have operating experience, knowledge of conceptual organization objectives, and relative freedom of thought. Among these, the requirement of actual operating experience is generally not weighed heavily enough. Because of the importance of operating experience, it is often wise to select from line functions qualified individuals who possess adequate operating experience and stability. Ideally added to these characteristics would be the qualities of leadership, education, creativity, initiative, skepticism, mechanical aptitude, ability to synthesize, and stamina.

A strong business-methods staff, once created, does not necessarily induce any shifting of functional responsibility. Nor is there any dilution of functional authority associated with the computer or methods group. Delegation of responsibility and authority lies, as completely as ever, in the hands of management. The control network will, however, restrict departmental autonomy and, unless care is exercised, can be misconstrued as a juggling of responsibility or authority.

There is another danger to having an inadequate methods staff. Only in the detailed nuances of systems work do realistic demands vary from unrealistic demands. And the generalized arguments which reach top management sound much the same whether they come from a good or a bad staff. Usually, such arguments center on a specific computer program or a particular policy in a computer program. Arguments may arise as to whether *any* computer program could possibly offer improvement in certain areas, and loud disputes over cost and savings are no guarantee that a good application will result. Yet, since achieving the control network depends on fair and accurate evaluation of the subtle systems aspects, management is usually forced to rely upon an effective business-methods staff to build thousands of minute details into a program that will achieve the policy goals of the company.

The capabilities of the staff function might be given a test on some initial applications and the results evaluated. If the staff is given direction to help make the installations successful, and the jobs then fail owing to fallacies in methods and programming by the staff, obviously some changes will be in order. If, on the other hand, the results of the first jobs prove the capabilities of the staff, strong management backing on future assignments is probably wise.

Nevertheless, evaluation of the staff should be conducted continuously. While failure to back a competent staff can mean years of delay in operating improvements and cost reductions, backing of an inadequate staff can turn out to be a horrendous error. There have been numerous debacles where a staff of machine technicians had a burst of authority far in excess of their operating knowledge. Failure of this kind can be far more damaging than even the inefficiencies of the service approach. Even in an established installation, constant precautions are necessary to avoid the machine technician's tendency to act beyond his limited knowledge and authority with the result that information is destroyed or altered.

6. POOR STAFF LOCATION

The forthright solution to staff location is to place the staff in the organization element which most uses the computer. If, however, more than one element in the organization uses the computer, some of the troubles described previously prevail. It is also a mistake to have a staff function such as business methods report to a *particular* line function. In a valid installation, all elements of the organization will be involved, and staff placement cannot satisfy everybody.

Normally it will be proper to place the staff function where the most responsible over-all staff work has previously been assigned. If there is not some specific organization designated to handle staff work, a little deliberation will reveal the organization element which is used to perform major staff chores. Placement of the EDP directly under the manager of the facility seems to be evolving as a pattern. But all too seldom is this the first attempt; it usually happens after one or more riotous misplacements.

Proper organization placement of the staff and machine operation can do much to alleviate the concerns of functional managers about adequate response to their needs. But where is "proper"? Conflicts arise because operating philosophies vary from one area to another throughout an organization. In some companies the industrial engineering department or a similar department acts as fiscal watchdog; in others, it is the controller's department. The advantages and dangers of placing the staff function and computer under the fiscal watchdog should be carefully evaluated. Production managers and procurement managers are skilled at treading the middle road between the conservatism of the fiscal watch dog and the needs of the operating man for schedule performance protection. Should EDP be placed under one of these?

In a manufacturing company, the difference between operating and accounting missions may indicate placement outside the accounting atmosphere. Operating people talk about control, and so do the controller's personnel. Yet there is a vast difference in what each means:

> To an operating man, control is the analytical processes which lead to (1) decisions as to future courses of action, and (2) routine decisions which control the function within the plan.
>
> In the parlance of the controller's personnel, control is surveillance of after-the-fact summations, usually compared to historical norms.

According to the first interpretation, history is made by men who make decisions, who select one course out of infinite choices, over and over again. According to the second, history is recorded in the staid, reserved manner of the scribe who may reconstruct some of the major turns of the battle but who can never know the myriad of choices that had to be made during the battle.

Placing computers in the latter environment could well dampen the responsiveness, flexibility, quality, and proficiency of the line organization. All of us seem to have 20/20 hindsight, and anyone so inclined can be a good Monday-morning quarterback. We think we know, but we are oblivious to the many factors complicating the decision of those who have to choose. Those observing the decision, but not making it, often fail to appreciate the importance of little things. Living in this environment over a long period can cause people unknowingly to insulate themselves from knowledge of operating needs.

Even though there is no staff placement which will satisfy everybody, there is one hedge that may be made to enhance acceptance and reduce risk of failure. This hedge involves splitting the methods and programming staff into two groups. First, this will do much to allay the fears of functional managers that some mogul in command of all programming and in possession of important records could try to become a hero through an information coup with top management. With programming personnel reporting to one major organization element, and the business-methods staff reporting to another element, it would be difficult for either to do any questionable data evaluation without knowledge of the affected functional management.

Another advantage this split provides for top management in the early phases is that any deficiency in either programming or methods capabilities should come to light very early. Business-systems analysts will object quickly and vigorously to an incompetent programming staff—and vice versa. In other words, with both types in a single group reporting to a single head, it will take longer for deficiencies in either or both skills to be revealed. This is certainly the maximum splitting of the staff function which can be considered if the control network is to be achieved. Any further splitting places some of the methods work or programming directly in the functional area; then the benefits offered by the network approach are immediately lost. In either a physiological or social sense, there are almost no people who can pick up the scalpel and operate on themselves.

Splitting of the staff should be considered light of its disadvantages as well as the expedients, for it is purely a temporary hedge. In the long run, the analysts and the programmers need a common head for continued development. It is extremely difficult to keep the two separate skills from developing some undesirable internal strife when separated organizationally. Whether the split should be allowed for a year or two, or for several years, will depend on individual situations. The main factors involved in an answer are the rapidity with which both specialties develop, and the rate of their acceptance by line people.

7. EVALUATIONS ON THE BIAS

Attempts at generalized appraisals have been stymied by the multiplicity of the goals for which various installations have aimed and the diversity of policy which frames the computer environment. No real general practices are yet recognized, and evaluation is further clouded because even the best installations have got off to bumpy starts. True, soon after installation, management begins to request evaluations. But since the people primarily responsible for the machine make the evaluation, the report looks about as glowing for a bad installation as for a good one. Here are some special traps:

(1) The temptation to measure performance through cost-savings analysis alone needs to be avoided. Reductions claimed in cost-savings balance sheets cannot be factually proved or disproved and, indeed, many times are merely the largest figure the traffic will bear without objection in some quarter. The value of management improvements in an effective control network far outweighs any amount of dollar savings which can be claimed. The real benefit to a manufacturing concern lies in disciplined coordination between functions. In manufacturing, the diversity of applications makes development slow and early financial assessment somewhat vague and difficult. During the first few years, a worthwhile valuation of EDP is therefore more a matter of judging guesses as to the future than of measuring firm performance history.

(2) Do not fall for easy-to-figure measures of EDP proficiency. Machine load, for example, means little as a measure. A fully loaded machine can still prove to be a more expensive way of doing the same thing that was being done previously, and people who make self-appraisals are never going to show that. Nor can the effectiveness of the staff be judged by its size, for empire-building is an ever-present danger.

(3) A look at base rental or purchase price alone does not tell much either. Often, the higher cost unit will save many times the difference in rent when the two are considered in the environment of an operation.

How then *can* you measure success? Perhaps the answer boils down to measuring changes in operating ratios. Good indicators are reduced inventories, reduced shortages, personnel reductions, increased flexibility in handling orders, and product changes. In fact, any operating index which would directly register the effects of computer endeavors should be watched.

Then, too, tighter operating policies and procedures offer, perhaps, the most tangible evidence of improvement. Management participates in revising both; so these important measures can be calibrated immediately and and directly without reliance upon elaborate self-appraisals prepared by a biased staff.

But when making changes, do not try to paddle upstream; benefits are achieved best when functional controls are revamped first. Operating procedures can be tightened to obtain better operation and reduced cost. At the same time, revised accounting provisions should be included. Then, when the accounting functions are programmed, new measuring techniques are available for budget and fiscal controls.

If you start downstream, at the recording end of the business, all that can be done in the beginning is to publish the same information a little faster and perhaps in a slightly different form. This seems so clear it makes one wonder why so many people have started at the recording end, rather than at procedure execution.

CONCLUSION

Having examined the seven deadly dangers of EDP, let us see what positive steps companies can take to make their EDP installation a success.

First of all, they must establish some definite goal for their EDP and set up a competent organization to direct all the facilities toward the achievement of this goal. Furthermore, the entire organization should be aware of the goal set, the responsibilities borne by the EDP staff, and those borne by other areas, for the success of the project.

In short, the same direct resolve accorded *any* major endeavor is needed, if a company is to be successful with EDP operating improvements. There is a lot of precedent to be overcome. Some strong policies must be established to guard against improper staff scrutiny of machine-stored operating data. Accomplishing this without inadvertently protecting middle management's vested interests is tricky. But staffs, like anyone else, are capable of either knowingly or incompetently pulling together sets of slanted figures and causing a big stir before things get back into perspective.

With a control network in operation a tremendous amount of data, which never existed before, is available in a form directly accessible only through the staff. This resource should be developed on a fully coordinated basis, as should the policy and procedure controls.

If EDP is left under accounting and a decision is made to move the computer into the field of operating decisions, the difference between the accountant's concept of control and the operating man's concept must be faced squarely and resolved. Though jurisdictional disputes do not always occur, they are not uncommon. Sometimes the aftermath of these is simply that the operating man withdraws to try again another day, figuring that if there is really something there, it is not urgent; he can grapple with it in the future. Most differences seem to concern the way in which each would like to proceed, once the decisions have been made.

The operating man tends to move in with the gusto and optimism of the true entrepreneur. The accountant, on the other hand, is inclined to test the water before taking any plunges. The operating man feels he has made his deductions about water temperature and other factors before deciding to go and sees no reasons to go on an inch at a time. Placed in close association for a prolonged period without a catalyst, these two divergent approaches tend to drift even farther apart.

The best catalyst is a new organization element charged with planning and coordinating all types of control improvements. However, if the staff must be placed in a functional organization (such as accounting, operations, sales, or shipping), there *is* a feasible means for establishing an effective arbitrator.

Set up a czar, judge, umpire—or what have you—reporting to the top man of the facility. His function is to plan, to make the day-to-day rulings, and to keep the top man advised on progress. This is what is commonly called a "project director" or "project coordinator." No line function is responsible to him. He seldom has a staff of more than two or three people. But in regard to this one endeavor, his authority crosses all organization lines. His qualifications and experience must be outstanding so that there is no difficulty in granting him the impunity analogous to that granted to a czar.

The use of operating indexes will continue to prove helpful as prime measuring instruments for corporate survival in a competitive society. Performance targets are the only restraint on the workings of Parkinson's Law. The challenge to invent more sensitive, more precise responders and indicators is mandatory, as industrial efforts become more heterogeneous and products become more complex. However, many of the traditional ratios are becoming either ineffective or reduced in value as foundations for fiscal planning. The advent of the computer in procedure execution should not occur without simultaneous development of performance measures and fiscal planning data.

It is axiomatic that operating controls and surveillance controls have to be developed together. The fiscal planning concepts must specifically operate as constraints on the design of operating controls. If all the facts pertinent to procedure execution are internally stored, a wealth of new data is available for surveillance controls. New performance measuring techniques (being developed in conjunction with revised operating controls) are proving equally effective in elevating organizational proficiency.

The computer is well suited to continual analysis of the same operating data which are used for procedure control. Now performance measures can have exactly known relationships to operating procedures. Unity of purpose and tightening of confidence limits can reach the proportions of a major breakthrough. Inevitably, this trend will serve to bring operating people and control people closer together, especially if both groups are conscious of the serious pitfalls that must be side-stepped if EDP installations are to prove successful.

Case 11-1

United Tool Company

On October 15, 1958, John Flynn, vice-president in charge of United Tool Company's Springfield plant, was reviewing initial steps taken at Springfield to determine its data processing requirements. He had recently received from the data processing committee a computer feasibility study (reproduced in the appendix) and was uncertain as to what action it warranted.

United Tool Company was founded in 1891 for the purpose of making small hand tools. Over the years, its activities expanded enormously through both profitable operations and mergers, and it diversified its activities into such areas as high-precision machine-shop work and the manufacture of electronic components. It had plants in 31 states and employed over 100,000 persons.

Its Springfield plant was used extensively for basic research and experimental production runs. Roughly one-third of the facility was devoted to research, engineering, and administrative uses. Basic research in metallurgy, heat transfer, elasticity, etc., was carried on here. New techniques of assembly and prototype construction were developed in the engineering department. If one of the projects was successful, it was then turned over to another plant, which developed it for commercial application. The rest of the plant's area consisted of foundries, machine shops, and assembly areas. The plant had available certain unique equipment that rendered it the logical supplier of many large, closely machined components. As a result, approximately one-half of its activity was in the form of job shop machining. The plant's work force was in excess of 3,000.

United Tool Company was organizationally decentralized; the head of each plant had broad responsibilities for the plant's overall operation. (See Exhibit 1.) Control was achieved through the submission of a number of cost, production, and other reports, which were sent regularly to headquarters in New York for analysis. In addition, New York had responsibility for approving major capital investments. Acquisition of a computer was

Exhibit 1

ORGANIZATION CHART—SPRINGFIELD PLANT

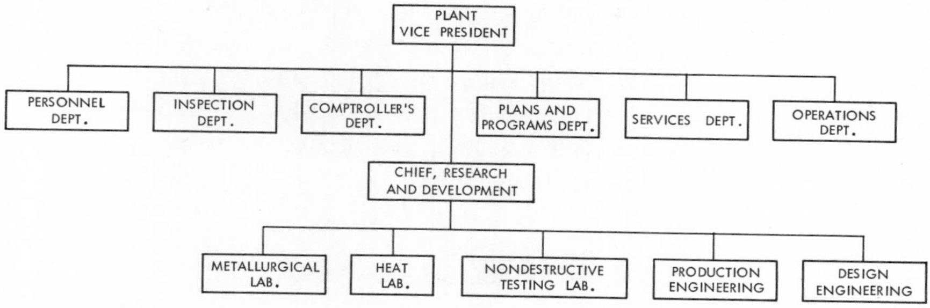

defined as a major capital investment, and New York already had rejected one proposed installation at another plant on the grounds that the initial research had been "superficially carried out."

COST AND GENERAL ACCOUNTING

The accounting information generated at Springfield was dictated by requirements from New York and was covered by appropriate operating regulations. For job orders, performance was measured against established standards, and significant deviations were highlighted for management attention. Direct costing was used internally. The system culminated in a cost of performance budget, which was submitted to New York. In the laboratories and engineering departments, efforts were made to control expenditures by maintaining detailed records on the status of each project. Detailed records were kept on the status of work-in-process inventories, and the administration of purchases and accounts receivable collections was handled here.

PRODUCTION PLANNING AND CONTROL

The production planning and control system provided a detailed record of the progress of a part through Springfield's production centers, and accounted for it as it was completed. This was accomplished by breaking down the system into two separate portions—the planning phase and the operations phase.

In the planning phase, customers' orders were broken down into a list of materials necessary to produce the orders. The various lists of materials were then sorted to get a series of reports showing common materials in different subassemblies of one order as well as materials common to different orders. A master production delivery schedule was then developed.

In the operations phase, work was scheduled to be produced during the following week, and two- and four-week predictions of the future work load were made. In addition, work load forecasts were provided for the machines in each department as well as for all machines of a particular type. Completed production was recorded in a daily production report, and for the foundry in a weekly production report. Since Springfield's production was basically that of a job shop which produced small orders of complex parts, little finished goods or in process inventory was maintained. Advance planning was essential to such a system in order to keep setup time at a minimum and to produce orders on time.

SCIENTIFIC RESEARCH

The data processing requirements of the research, development, and engineering divisions resulted from the need to calculate design specifications from data obtained through experiment and research. An example of the type of computation required is as follows:

> Investigation in the field of applied mechanics involved the elastic stress analysis of notched specimens, cracks, and multiholed plates. The approach to these problems involves determining the coefficients of a complex mapping function and then solving a system of linear equations. The generation of the coefficients of the linear system is accomplished through use of a recursive technique based on the geometry and loading of the experiment. Manual computation of coefficients requires two to three weeks. The resulting system of simultaneous linear equations usually exceeds 25 equations in 25 unknowns and is solved by an iterative technique which requires in excess of three to five days if done manually.

ORIGIN OF FEASIBILITY STUDY

For a number of years, Springfield had had several punched-card machines that had assisted in development of the payroll and some cost accounting information. In 1956, some interest had been shown in the possibility of acquiring a Univac file computer. At that time, however, the New York office believed the field was so new that the officers were unwilling to invest much in it.

During late 1957 and early 1958, members of Springfield's top management held a series of meetings that reopened the possibility of Springfield's attaining benefits from EDP. In April, 1958, a presentation made to Mr. Flynn by several members of the comptroller's office recommended a computer feasibility study. Impressed by their arguments, he authorized in May, 1958, the feasibility study for the installation of automatic data processing equipment. Despite opposition from certain of the research personnel, it was decided at the outset that only a computer capable of meeting both the scientific and commercial interests of the Springfield plant should be considered.

A data processing committee, composed of the comptroller, an assistant to the comptroller, and the assistant manager of systems design (the systems design manager reported directly to the comptroller), was appointed to handle the responsibility of completing the feasibility study. Each department designated one or two men to work with the committee. A scientific subcommittee, made up of a solid-state physicist, a mathematician, and an operations research man, was formed to advise the committee on scientific requirements.

The data processing committee developed a plan consisting of five major phases:

Training for the committee and other personnel.

A survey of areas to which electronic data processing might apply and the gains that would accrue from computer application.

An application study, preparing specifications for manufacturers, reviewing manufacturers' proposals, and the selecting equipment.

Preparation training, developing systems, programming, and debugging.

Conversion to the electronic system.

TRAINING

The initial training consisted of a two-week course called "Automatic Data Processing Systems for the Systems Analyst," conducted by the New York headquarters. This course covered computer characteristics, programming techniques, and practical problems in systems analysis. Two other courses given by consultants were taken. The first covered the feasibility study, programming, and the systems approach pertaining to substitution of equipment or integration of systems. The second included consideration of the organizational placement of EDPS, selection and training of personnel, and problems involved in computer installation. All committee members attended these courses, as well as other courses given by consultants. The personnel assigned to work with the committee attended the two-week course in New York.

THE FEASIBILITY STUDY

The feasibility study covered a preliminary evaluation of the computer requirements in selected areas, notably those areas then served by the punched-card system. The data processing committee report on the feasibility study outlined the activity of the committee and its conclusions. It is presented in full as the appendix.

QUESTIONS

1. What are the principal facts brought out by the study?
2. Do you agree that these facts are supported by adequate evidence?
3. As manager, what action would you take as the result of this study?

Appendix

Feasibility Study for ADPS Equipment at Springfield

SECTION I

BUSINESS DATA PROCESSING

A. Present Methods of Processing Data.

Data are processed either manually or by use of a punch-card Remington Rand system utilizing a 120 Univac Computer.

B. Utilization of Present Data Processing Equipment.

1. The following systems are at present being processed either partially or in whole through our punch-card system.
   a) Payroll.
   b) Personnel files.
   c) Stock accounting, both standard and nonstandard material.
   d) Inventory control, both standard and nonstandard material.
   e) Material cost and distribution.
   f) Cost accounting.
   g) Consolidated project cost.
   h) Production control.
   i) Customer order accounts.
   j) Maintenance and manufacturing control.
   k) New York reporting system.
   l) Miscellaneous reporting for production control, accounting, and maintenance.

2. Springfield's policy is to reduce clerical cost of data processing as much as possible through adapting manual systems to electric accounting machine processes. This practice has resulted in savings of approximately $100,000 a year in the comptroller's area alone. However, use of the 'machine room," now operating on a three-shift basis, has extended beyond its capacity to the point where it is necessary to use the Remington Rand Service Bureau once a quarter in order to meet reporting requirements of New York. The release of many reports is delayed, and the consideration of issuing a new one involves the choice of dropping some present report or not issuing the newly requested data. Thus, the saturation point of a data processing system, which requires the handling of great volumes of cards through sorters, collaters, computer, and printer before reports are released, has been reached. The situation is further aggravated by a high personnel turnover rate in the data processing branch, along with the difficulties involved in finding suitable replacement personnel.

C. Data Requirements of Springfield.

1. In order to carry out daily operations more effectively and to meet New York's reporting requirements, there exists a requirement for Springfield to process and record data. Types of systems which must be provided are:
   a) Production planning, engineering, and control.
   b) Accounting reports.
   c) Budgets.
   d) Program progress reports.
   e) Inventory accounting and control.
   f) Payroll.
   g) Personnel data.
   h) Standard costs and material control.
   i) Customer order accounting.
2. Future data processing equipment will involve an extension of the principle of standard costing and standard labor and material control to other than those in the operations division. This will include support organizations such as plant facilities office and materials office. The integrated approach to systems work available with automatic data processing will enable the utilization of a system of comprehensive accounting in which the accounting records will be maintained so as to more closely tie in work load, manpower, and cost data, and to evaluate the effectiveness of each against a standard or a budget. The implementation of the concept of comprehensive accounting would build flexibility into the system and make fluctuating data requirements of higher headquarters more easy to obtain.

D. Sample Cost of Processing Data at Springfield.

1. In order to determine what Springfield is paying for the processing of

data, a few selected areas were investigated. These areas were production planning and control, accounting, and supply. This information was gathered from the 1959 budget, revised August 1, 1958.

LABOR BUDGET, 1959
(adjusted for leave and retirement)

Production planning and control and production engineering	$ 854,747
Finance and accounting office	459,854
Program analysis branch	81,286
Data processing branch	143,000
Supply branch	161,662
Rental and maintenance budget	33,832
Total	$1,734,381

2. The above figures are presented only to show the magnitude of our present data processing costs, and are not intended to reflect total savings. However, the types of functions performed by these areas are compatible with ADPS processing, and these costs should be reduced considerably on converting to ADPS techniques.

E. Timeliness of Data Transmission and Reporting under Our Present EAM System.

Because of the high volume of integrated data processing systems now employed by the use of our punch-card equipment, the following general conditions exist as to the timelessness of the reports being furnished. In spite of the best effort in its efficient utilization, the present equipment is inadequate to meet the requirements of Springfield. A few selected areas were studied and the following specific examples are given.

1. Financial statements. Scheduled date for receiving this information from data processing branch permits the preparation of statements and closing of books so that financial statements can be issued at the close of the month following the last month being reported—that is, statements as of July 31 are issued August 31. This schedule is the earliest possible one with the present equipment and system. Any speedup of the processing time required for preparation of these statements would have significant results in the timely analysis of the data and the ability to take prompt corrective action.
2. Billing. Monthly billing tapes are scheduled for the fifteenth workday after the close of the month. It takes about one week after receipt of the billing tape to prepare the bills, and about two or three weeks more to receive payment. This means that approximately $4 to $4.5 million is tied up. Each day saved on this cycle frees approximately $100,000.
3. Line item cost data for manufactured items. Because of the limitations of our present equipment, line item costs for manufactured parts are being furnished 30 to 60 days after the item is completed and, in

some cases, as long as 90 days. This means that on short-run production orders the cost of the part is not received until the complete product on order is made and delivered. This does not permit us in all cases to take positive corrective action in order to control costs at the line item until it is too late.

4. Production control reports. The data processing for production control operations is at the present time one of the major applications for EAM. "Daily Production Reports," a weekly two-week schedule, an "Unfinished Work Report," and a "Master Production and Delivery Schedule" are examples of some of the reports prepared. With the exception of the "Unfinished Work Report," there are considerable delays in submitting reports in production control. This difficulty is particularly evident in the handling of crash work route sheets, which are released at the same time the items get into the shop. These actually never get into the two-week schedule because of the length of time it takes to process these items.

SECTION II

Scientific Applications

A. Present Method of Processing Scientific Data at Springfield.

1. The Univac 120 is used to a very limited extent for the processing of scientific data. Springfield laboratories use it occasionally as an aid in performing certain numerical phases in arriving at a solution to selected mathematical problems. However, the restrictions due to the computer's capacity have allowed only infrequent use of it as an assistance in computation work in the research area.
2. Computers located outside the installation are utilized to solve a number of scientific problems that develop in the research area. The materials lab uses the IBM 704 located at Hartford to solve certain problems. The heat lab uses an IBM 650 located in the Boston area to work problems involving the foundry. These problems involve a method of linear programming and a method of furnace chargings.

B. Need for a Computer.

1. The phenomenal benefits that have resulted from the application of high-speed electronic analogue and digital computers to the research area are well known. These benefits have been realized in areas of research in which Springfield is engaged. In certain fields of applied mechanics, for example, in studies in elasticity, particularly as applied to the "thin shell theory," the use of an electronic computer has had enormous effect.
2. The lack of computer facilities at Springfield has deterred those functioning in this area from working on certain problems related to their

field and has forced the finality of certain solutions to problems to be left in general form. Lack of computer facilities make it difficult for those in applied mechanics to keep up with advances made in certain fields.

3. At the present time in the metallurgical laboratory, there is under way a long-range program that involves the study of atomic displacement and characteristic temperatures of certain alloys. Future plans call for the expansion of the above program and the start of the analysis of structural factors of material in the study of single crystals. The present program is slowed down by the lengthy computations necessary to reduce data to desired parameters. Other problems have not been considered because of the computation involved in their study. The computer is much needed in this branch to free personnel from present laborious computations and to speed up and extend present programs outlined above. Not only this, but it will also permit expansion into allied fields in which research outside the installations has advantageously used data processing equipment.
4. Again, in nondestructive testing laboratory attempts are being made to discover and develop nondestructive testing methods for material and equipment. Development of these methods depends on the evaluation of data. The data consist of many parameters, and their combinations under various conditions are of such magnitude and kind as to necessitate the use of an electronic computer. Future plans will create an even greater demand for such equipment.

SECTION III

Conclusions and Recommendations

A. Conclusions.

1. Data processing. As a result of the study thus far devoted to electronic digital computers, it is apparent that a medium-scale computer would be extremely beneficial. As these computers process data at extremely high speeds and have the ability to update and prepare a number of reports with one pass of the basic data, it is believed that a computer would enable Springfield to receive appreciable managerial benefits through improvement in the timeliness and quality of data.
2. Scientific application. As a result of this preliminary examination into the need for a computer in the research area, it is apparent that our research efforts are being hindered because of the lack of modern computational facilities.

B. Recommendations.

1. That this committee proceed with a detailed application study of a production planning and control system, and a comprehensive account-

ing system for the entire plant, excluding research, which will include both quantitative and monetary data. The express purpose will be to design these systems for computer application and for submission to manufacturers for estimates in terms of time and costs for processing on their equipment. From this, the economics and benefits can be measured and a computer selection made.

2. That further study into the specific requirements of our research area be made and incorporated as a separate section in the application study, and be evaluated as the overall computer requirements of Springfield.

SECTION IV

Potential Areas of Computer Application on Installation

Production planning and control (scheduling, forecasting, work load, manpower, machine loading, efficiency reporting, unloading schedule).
General accounting.
Cost accounting.
Headquarters reporting.
Maintenance scheduling and reporting.
Budgeting.
Payroll.
Materials inventory.
Personnel files and reports.
Application of material and time and motion standards.
Literature searching.
Delivery status report processing.

SECTION V

Estimated Costs and Benefits

The estimated costs and direct benefits for a complete study and installation of automatic data processing equipment are detailed in Exhibit 1 by expense classification and by quarters in which the expense is incurred. The quarter starts with June, 1958, when the feasibility study began, and ends with March, 1961.

The process of studying and acquiring a computer falls naturally into six phases as follows:

1. Feasibility study ....June '58 through October '58
2. Application study ....November '58 through June '59
3. Preparation ....July '59 through April '60
4. Installation ....May '60
5. Conversion ....June '60 through July '61
6. Operation ....August '61

Exhibit 1

ESTIMATED COST AND DIRECT BENEFITS FOR A STUDY AND INSTALLATION OF ADP EQUIPMENT

Expenses:	First Year 1 Qtr P*	Jun 58 $†	2 Qtr P	Sep 58 $	3 Qtr P	Dec 58 $	4 Qtr P	Mar 59 $	Second Year 1 Qtr P	June 59 $	2 Qtr P	Sep 59 $	3 Qtr P	Dec 59 $	4 Qtr P	Mar 60 $	Third Year 1 Qtr P	Jun 60 $	2 Qtr P	Sep 60 $	3 Qtr P	Dec 60 $	4 Qtr P	Mar 61 $
A Training		1,270		970																				
B Travel (other than evaluation)		2,126		1,744		1,600		1,600																
C Evaluation of equipment				561		1,329		1,366																
Salaries:																								
D Committee	3	7,400	3	7,400	3	7,400	3	7,400	3	2,476														
E Associated	2	380																						
F Administration									6	8,116	6	12,174	9	16,194	9	16,194	9	16,194	9	16,194	9	16,194	9	16,194
G Analyst			1	1,250	2	1,689	3	5,067	4	7,269	4	7,269	4	7,269	4	7,269	4	7,269	4	7,269	4	7,269	4	7,269
H Programmers					2	1,689	3	5,067	4	7,269	4	7,269	4	7,269	4	7,269	4	7,269	4	7,269	4	7,269	4	7,269
I Operators											1	1,878	3	8,256	3	10,416	7	12,576	7	12,576	10	14,730	10	15,852
J Personnel selection				1,000		1,000																		
K Installation cost																20,000								
L Computer rental																		45,000		45,000		45,000		45,000
M Material																1,500		300		300		300		300
Total Expense		11,176		12,925		14,707		20,500		25,130		28,590		38,988		62,648		88,608		88,608		90,762		91,884
Savings:																								
N Personnel												2,936		2,936		2,936		2,936		38,823		53,787		91,555
O Equipment rental																				2,190		4,380		6,570
Total Savings												2,936		2,936		2,936		2,936		41,013		58,167		98,125
Net expense		11,176		12,925		14,707		20,500		25,130		25,654		36,052		59,712		85,672		47,595		32,595		(6,241)
Cumulative Net Expense				24,101		38,808		59,308		84,438		110,092		146,144		205,856		291,528		339,123		371,718		365,477

* P = People.
† $ = Expense.

The training expense consists of costs incurred for tuition or fees for courses offered by consultants. The cost of evaluation of equipment consists of expenses incurred in travel and per diem in attending approximately a week's seminar in programming, given by the manufacturers of equipment under consideration.

The committee is dissolved after submission of the application study and establishment of the formal ADPS organization in July, 1959. However, a firm basis for the organization is attained through having programmers and analysts work under the guidance of the committee during the application phases of the study.

Personnel costs are those that would be involved in any special testing that may be necessary to guide in the selection of the most highly qualified personnel.

Installation cost is based on the best estimate that can be made without knowing definitely what computer will be installed and the exact location of the installation. A possible location was used in making the estimate and a vacuum tube-type computer was selected in order to be on the high side of such cost.

The computer rental cost includes necessary input and output equipment based upon the situation as it looks at the time of preparing this study. Of course, the application study will refine these estimates.

Direct savings are determined on the basis of the best estimates in the areas listed in Section I, paragraph D, and are phased in at the time they may occur. The anticipated direct savings resulting from a decrease in the needs of personnel in affected areas and the release of equipment at present on hand amount to quarterly net savings of $49,000. The break-even point, where the savings have amortized the computer expense, will occur during December, 1962 or January, 1963. It is believed that these estimates are on a conservative basis, and through an integrated approach to computer utilization and application additional savings may accrue.

Only the direct benefits with respect to cost savings are detailed in Exhibit 1. However, while such direct savings should accrue and are the most readily measured savings, others also are of the utmost importance and are the real motivating factors in determining the need for a computer. As a result of a well-integrated system, the computer should result in a definite improvement in management control by supplying management with meaningful information that is more accurate and more timely as well as impossible to obtain without a computer.

The computer system is also flexible, in that it can be expanded and contracted to meet rather permanent or long-range adjustments in work load.

Case 11-2

The William Carter Company

In late December, 1960, Edward Marzo, manager of the methods department at the William Carter Company, was considering a proposal made by the International Business Machines Corporation that the company acquire an IBM 1410 computer. A large manufacturer of knitwear clothing, the Carter company was not a newcomer to the field of automatic data processing. Prior to December, 1958, the company had had over thirty years of satisfactory experience with punched-card equipment. In 1956, the company had become interested in the acquisition of a computer, and after extensive investigation had ordered a Univac file computer. It was installed on December 10, 1958.

When the computer had been ordered, the following applications had been planned:

1. The entire processing system for customers' orders.
2. Production scheduling for the company's seven plants.
3. Sales statistical analyses currently available for the sales forecasting department, together with several other statistical reports.

Despite some unanticipated delays, by December, 1960, the entire order processing function was being done on the computer. The extra work involved in correcting the delays, however, had caused work on the production scheduling system to fall behind. At that time, some 70 to 80 percent of the systems analysis for the production scheduling application had been completed, and the detailed flow charting had been started; no work had yet been done on writing the programs. Some progress had been made toward achieving the system's third objective, both in terms of systems work and actual programs (25–50 percent of potential realized).

In a recent report to top management, Mr. Marzo had described himself as being basically satisfied with the performance of the computer and the features of the operating systems. The relatively slow operating speed of the machine, however, had had two consequences:

1. The costs of operating the system were higher than had been anticipated.

2. The computer was currently operating two shifts a day to handle the work volume generated by the order processing system. Management believed that the computer should not be scheduled for more than two-shift operations, so as to retain flexibility in case of machine breakdown and also to retain a safety margin for the peak loads of the summer season. This policy meant that with the current setup there was no time to install and operate the production scheduling system or the work on the sales forecasts.

Recalling that the original reason the Carter company had gone into data processing was to achieve benefits in the production area, Mr. Marzo still felt that considerable benefit might accrue to the company from mechanizing this area. He believed that mechanization would result in a better utilization of space and equipment and in a reduction of production lead times, with consequent inventory savings and less obsolescence of fabric. Also, he felt that recent developments in forecasting techniques indicated that a study should be made of the possibility of using the computer for sales analysis and forecasts.

Recognizing this capacity problem as one that was likely to assume serious proportions in mid-1959, Mr. Marzo asked Remington Rand to see if it could develop a core memory to replace the machine's drum memory. He believed that this would sufficiently speed up the machine so that installation of the other systems could be feasible. Although there were repeated indications that Remington Rand would undertake this project, final approval of it and prices were not received until December 16, 1960. Exhibit 1 presents a comparison of the physical features of the machine before and after the installation of the magnetic core memory. Remington Rand said that the unit would be ready for delivery late in December, 1961, and could be hooked up to the machine over a weekend. No revision of the company's present programs would be required.

In the meantime, during 1960 several other computer manufacturers had approached the Carter company in an attempt to convince it that it should adopt their equipment instead. As a result of several months' study by company officials and a large consulting firm, it was decided that the most feasible of these proposed systems was the IBM 1410, a medium-size solid-state computer produced by the International Business Machines Corporation. Exhibit 1 presents a listing of its key physical features compared to those of the Univac file computer, both before and after the addition of the core memory.

In his November presentation to the Carter management, the IBM salesman, in addition to remarking on some of the contrasts indicated in Exhibit 1, made the following remarks concerning the IBM 1410.

Every position of memory can be operated on arithmetically. This means that data do not have to be moved to a separate location, called an accumulator, saving

Exhibit 1

COMPARISON OF OPERATING CHARACTERISTICS OF IBM 1410, UNIVAC FILE WITH DRUM MEMORY, AND UNIVAC FILE WITH CORE MEMORY

Characteristics	*Univac File with Drum Memory*	*IBM 1410*	*Univac File with Core Memory*
1. Solid state	No	Yes	No
2. Power requirements	75 KVA	27.3 KVA	75 KVA
3. Floor space	1,400 sq. ft.	500 sq. ft.	1,400 sq. ft.
4. Air conditioning equipment needed	60 tons	5 tons	60 tons
5. Fixed or variable word length	Fixed (12 digits per word)	Variable	Fixed (12 digits per word)
6. Size of machine memory	1,020 words	10–40K digits	2,000 words
7. Access time (internal storage)*	3.100M	4.5U	4U
8. Add time (6 digit factors)	8.6M	.24M	2.3M
9. Multiply time	33.9M	1.6M	8.9M
10. Divide time	40.0M	6.0M	10.5M
11. Number of instruction	23	190	23
12. External wiring board	Yes	No	Yes
13. Addresses/inst.	3	1–2	3
14. Random access capacity	1,800,000 char.	10,000,000 char.	1,800,000 char.
15. Maximum access time to random access memory	34M	160M	34M
16. Punched cards,† input/output	150R 150P	800R 250P	150R 150P
17. Printer	600 lines/min.	600 lines/min.	600 lines/min.
18. Magnetic characters per second read	10,000	20,000	10,000
19. Length of reel	2,400 ft.	2,400 ft.	2,400 ft.
20. Number of blockettes or records per reel	20,000 fixed length	Variable length	20,000 fixed length

NOTES: The Univac system records of magnetic tape always are of the same size. The IBM 1410 records are variable, depending on the material. For example, on Univac tape, a sales report record for an invoice with two styles would take as much space as a record for an invoice with four styles. On IBM tape, the two-style invoice would only take one-half as much room as the four-style invoice.

* M = one thousandth of a second (millesecond);
U = one millionth of a second (microsecond).

† P = Punch; R = Read.

program steps and simplifying programming. . . . The machine has 15 index registers. Index registers assist in program modification, thus reducing the number of instructions, conserving space, and simplifying programming. . . . There are no control panels. Because of the fast internal speeds, and powerful operations codes, such as the editing commands, all arrangement of input and output data is performed in core memory. This reduces setup time between operations. . . . There is no fixed record length on tape. The features of variable-length tape records, combined with the high recording density of 556 characters per inch, offer several systems advantages. In handling, there will be fewer tape reels. Many reels will be considerably smaller. Fewer tapes mean fewer changes in setups. This saves the time of the operators and the system. It also minimizes operator errors in filing, selecting, and handling. There should also be a really significant savings in tape cost. . . . Earlier this year, we installed four large-scale computers near your office. They were delivered and installed on or prior to their target dates. . . . Included in the programs currently being developed for 1410 customers are the following:

1. Autocodes. By using 1410 Autocodes, a programmer will use a symbolic language that is simpler to learn and easier to use than machine language. Meaningful names for data and instruction locations are used. In addition, programming is simplified through the use of macroinstructions, which generate an entire sequence of appropriate machine instructions from a single statement. Typical macroinstructions pertain to arithmetic operations, logical decisions, and data movement in storage.

2. Input/Output Control System. A high percentage of instructions in any program is related to input-output operations and provides a set of routines that efficiently schedules all input-output operations.

3. Fortran. The Fortran language, which is applicable to the IBM 650, 704, 705, 709, 1620, 7070, 7080, and 7090, as well as the 1410, provides facilities for expressing problems in a symbolic source-language similar to the language of math.

4. Sort and Merge Program. Generalized sort and merge programs for various configuration of 1410 units, including one for a 1410 RAMAC with a single tape unit will be available.

5. Utility System. This set provides frequently needed routines to assist in the testing and operation of your programs. Included are the following:

a) Disk-to-tape and tape-to-disk.
b) Clear disk storage.
c) Clear core storage.
d) Storage print.
e) Trace program.

. . . The 1410 system machine time will be provided to you before the actual installation. Forty hours of test time are provided, and test time for 90 days following installation is not considered use. . . . Special representatives of IBM applied science department are highly trained and experienced in mathematics and the physical sciences, and have a thorough knowledge of our equipment. They are available to consult with your people at any time in the areas of linear programming and operations research. Their contribution will be especially helpful in planning for the production scheduling application.

The original IBM price estimate (see Exhibit 2) indicated that the total rental for the machine would be $12,740 a month. For two reasons, Mr. Marzo believed that this was conservative.

First, the IBM proposal included provision for only four tape drive units. In nearly all cases, four units would be sufficient for handling the actual programming. Experience with the Univac file computer, however, had indicated that tape units were the part of the machine most likely to encounter mechanical failure. At present, with the five Remington Rand units, 15–20 percent of the time one or more was inoperative. In the past, the record had been even more unsatisfactory. Therefore, Mr. Marzo believed that a fifth tape unit was essential.

Exhibit 2

IBM 1410 COST PROPOSAL

Machine	*Description*	*Monthly Rental Cost Component*	*Unit*
1402–2	Card read punch	$ 615	$ 615
	Read 800 CPM		
	Punch 250 CPM		
1403–2	Printer—600 lines per minute, 132 print positions	775	775
1405–1	Disk storage (10 million characters)	965	
	Additional access arm	400	
	Disk storage control	400	1,765
1411–2	Process unit (20,000 positions core memory)	4,550	
	Card read punch adapter	35	
	Disk storage adapter	30	
	Processing overlap	200	
	Tape input-output adapter (2 required)	110	
	Dual synchronizer adapter	325	5,250
1414–2	Input/output synchronizer for 7330 tape units (2 required)	1,000	1,000
1414–3	Input/output synchronizer for card read punch and printer	675	
	Synchronizer storage printer	550	
	Additional	60	1,285
1415–1	Console	250	250
7330–1	Magnetic tape units (4)	1,800	1,800
	Total Monthly Rental		$12,740

Secondly, he felt that an off-line printer would be useful to achieve additional flexibility and speed of operation.

To get some feel for the speed differential between the IBM 1410 and the installed Univac file, Mr. Marzo, in conjunction with an IBM salesman, recorded part of the present order processing system so that it could be run on the IBM 1410 computer. The theoretical processing time for each step was then calculated and added up. This figure was then compared with the known processing times for this operation on the Univac file, and the figures were extrapolated to cover the rest of the operations. On the basis of this study, it was estimated that the IBM 1410 was three to four times faster than the Univac file, and that it would take 70 hours of running time a month to handle the order processing work. A large consulting firm that had worked closely with the Carter company on this effort concurred with these estimates.

Mr. Marzo believed that converting the present set of Univac programs to the IBM 1410 would cost around $75,000. He anticipated that it would take two man-years each by two programmers, which would cost around $40,000. The remainder would be attributed to the supervisor's time and actual clerical conversion costs (e.g., key punching new programs). Because of the reprogramming problems and also because of the long lead time required for an IBM 1410. Mr. Marzo concluded that December, 1962 would be the earliest feasible date for installation. He anticipated that once the machine was installed it would be in use for at least six years before it would need replacement. He anticipated also that if a decision was made to acquire the 1410 the central processing unit with its extra features would be purchased over a five-year period and the rest of the equipment would be rented. (The central processing unit would be depreciated over a five-year period.) He also estimated that because the 1410 was entirely internally programmed it would be up to 30 percent faster to program new projects than was the Univac file with its wired control panel. He also thought that the 1410 would not require so high a caliber of programmer as did the Univac file.

In the face of this competition, Remington Rand made three proposals, each of which provided a price cut to meet the stiffening competition.

1. *Rental Plan.* If the Carter company agreed to rent the computer for three years (1961–64), Remington Rand would install the cores at no additional cost. The basic rent would be $16,740 a month (this included maintenance service and insurance). Second-shift rental would be computed at 50 percent of the first-shift rental on an hourly basis. Thus, if Carter spent an average of one hour a day during the month operating on the second shift, its bill will be increased only by one-sixteenth.

2. *Four-Year Deferred Payment Purchase Plan.* Carter would purchase the file computer on a monthly payment basis, with the magnetic core memory being installed in December, 1961. Monthly payments would be $12,224 in 1961 and $15,187 in 1962–64. In addition, down payments of $19,254 and $5,126 would be made on January 1, 1961, and January 1, 1962. This is based on the following cost figures.

For equipment now installed:	
Current net purchase price (gross price less credit for one-half of rentals already paid)	$385,092
Total carrying charge, 4 years at 6% of remaining balance after each monthly payment	$ 46,564
Maintenance contract	$ 3,633/month
Overtime maintenance	$10/hour
Insurance	$300/year
For 2000-word magnetic core memory to replace 1000-word high-speed drum memory in December, 1961:	
Total purchase price	$102,529
Total carrying charge, 3 years at 6% of remaining balance after each monthly payment	$ 9,271
Additional maintenance	None

3. *Five-Year Deferred Payment Purchase Plan.* The details of this plan were similar to those of the four-year plan, except that the payments for the computer (less the magnetic core memory) would be spread out over five years, and the payments for the magnetic core memory would be spread out over four years. This would result in monthly payments of $10,506 in 1961 and $12,779/month in 1962–65.

Exhibit 3

ANNUAL COSTS ACCRUING TO THE WILLIAM CARTER COMPANY UNDER VARIOUS PROPOSALS

Univac 4-Year Deferred Payment Purchase	*1961*	*1962*	*1963*	*1964*	*1965*
A. Capital investment:					
1. Down payment for computer	$ 19,254				
2. Down payment for cores		$ 5,126			
3. Annual installments for purchase of machine	83,419	88,565	$ 94,027	$ 99,827	
4. Annual core purchase installments..		30,545	32,428	34,429	
Total Capital Investment	$102,673	$124,236	$126,455	$134,256	
B. Cash expenses:					
1. Computer carrying charge	$ 19,680	$ 14,536	$ 9,082	$ 3,275	
2. Magnetic core carrying charge		5,018	3,129	1,130	
3. Regular maintenance contract......	43,596	43,596	43,596	43,596	$ 43,596
4. Overtime maintenance (3 hrs./day 1962, 7 hrs./day other years) rate of $10/hr.	17,500	7,500	17,500	17,500	17,500
5. Insurance	300	300	300	300	300
Total Cash Expenses	$ 81,076	$ 70,950	$ 73,607	$ 65,801	$ 61,396
C. Depreciation:					
1. Chargeable depreciation on machine (straight line)	$ 88,715	$ 88,715	$ 88,715	$ 88,715	
2. Chargeable depreciation on cores (straight line)		34,176	34,176	34,176	
Total Noncash Expenses	$ 88,715	$122,891	$122,891	$122,891	
D. Calculation of tax credit:					
1. Cash expenses plus	$ 81,076	$ 70,950	$ 73,607	$ 65,801	$ 61,396
2. Depreciation equals	88,715	122,891	122,891	122,891	
3. Total expenses	$169,791	$193,841	$196,498	$188,692	$ 61,396
4. Tax credit (50% expenses)	84,895	96,920	98,249	94,346	30,698
E. Calculation cash flow:					
1. Capital investment plus	$102,673	$124,236	$126,455	$134,256	
2. Cash expenses equals	81,076	70,950	73,607	65,801	$ 61,396
3. Total cash outflow	$183,749	$195,186	$200,062	$200,057	$ 61,396
4. Tax credit equals	84,895	96,920	98,249	94,346	30,698
5. Cash drain	$ 98,854	$ 98,266	$101,813	$105,711	$ 30,69

5-Year Deferred Payment Purchase	*1961*	*1962*	*1963*	*1964*	*1965*
A. Capital investment:					
1. Down payment for computer	$ 19,524				
2. Down payment for magnetic core...		$ 5,126			
3. Annual core purchase installments..		22,112	$ 23,588	$ 25,064	$ 26,540
4. Annual machine purchase installments	63,883	68,443	73,123	77,803	82,483
Total Capital Investment	$ 83,407	$ 95,681	$ 96,711	$102,867	$109,023

Exhibit 3—Continued

B. Cash expenses:					
1. Computer carrying charges	$ 21,000	$ 16,440	$ 11,760	$ 7,080	$ 2,400
2. Core carrying charges		5,172	3,696	2,220	744
3. Regular maintenance contract	43,596	43,596	43,596	43,596	43,596
4. Overtime maintenance (3 hrs./day 1962, 7 hrs./day other years)	17,500	7,500	17,500	17,500	17,500
5. Insurance	300	300	300	300	300
Total Cash Expenses	$ 82,396	$ 73,008	$ 76,852	$ 70,696	$ 64,540
C. Depreciation: (Same as 4-Year Plan)	$ 88,715	$122,891	$122,891	$122,891	
D. Total expenses	$171,111	$195,899	$199,743	$193,587	$ 64,540
Tax credit (50% expenses)	85,555	97,949	99,871	96,793	32,270
E. Calculation cash flow:					
1. Capital investment plus	$ 83,407	$ 95,681	$ 96,711	$102,867	$109,023
2. Cash expenses equals	82,396	73,008	76,852	70,696	64,540
3. Total cash outflow minus	$165,803	$168,689	$173,563	$173,563	$173,563
4. Tax credit equals	85,555	97,949	99,871	96,793	32,270
5. Cash drain	$ 80,248	$ 70,740	$ 73,692	$ 76,770	$141,293

Univac Rental Plan

1. Basic rent (12 × 16,740)	$200,880	$200,880	$200,880	$200,880	$200,880
2. Overtime (3 hrs./day 1962, 7 hrs./day other years)	87,880	32,960	87,880	87,880	87,880
Total Expenses	$288,760	$233,840	$288,760	$288,760	$288,760
3. Tax credit	144,380	116,920	144,380	144,380	144,380
4. Total cash flow	$144,380	$116,920	$144,380	$144,380	$144,380

IBM Proposal	*1961*	*1962*	*1963*	*1964*	*1965*
A. Capital investment 1410 central processor			$ 46,104	$ 46,104	$ 46,104
B. Cash expenses:					
1. Univac file rental	$259,680	$259,680			
2. 1410 rental as proposed by IBM 1410			89,760	89,760	89,760
3. Maintenance on 1410 central processor			1,236	1,236	1,236
4. Extra features			14,700	14,700	14,700
Total Cash Expenses	$259,680	$259,680	$105,696	$105,696	$105,696
C. Depreciation			$ 46,104	$ 46,104	$ 46,104
D. Total expenses	$259,680	$259,680	$151,800	$151,800	$151,800
Tax credit (50% expenses)	129,840	129,840	75,900	75,900	75,900
E. Calculation cash flow:					
1. Capital investment plus			$ 46,104	$ 46,104	$ 46,104
2. Cash expenses equals	$259,680	$259,680	105,696	105,696	105,696
3. Total cash outflow minus	$259,680	$259,680	$151,800	$151,800	$151,800
4. Tax credit equals	129,840	129,840	75,900	75,900	75,900
5. Cash drain	$129,840	$129,840	$ 75,900	$ 75,900	$ 75,900

In each of the purchase contracts, the machine would be depreciated on a straight-line basis during the period 1961–64 down to scrap value equal to 3 percent of its original purchase price. The magnetic core memory would be depreciated during the period 1962–64 in a similar manner. Carter would be obliged to cover the insurance on the machine as well as to pay for a maintenance contract. Exhibit 3 summarizes the relevant cash flows stemming from the several alternatives.

In presenting the case for acquisition of the cores, the Remington Rand salesman made the following points, which seemed particularly relevant to Mr. Marzo.

Further benefits will accrue as follows:
1. Present successful systems concepts can be retained.
2. Present programming can be retained.
3. The investment in the installation of equipment and the training of personnel will be protected.
4. Continued operation of the file computer will result in additional management benefits in the shortest possible time.

There are further benefits to be gained by retaining your present equipment during the development phases of your production scheduling application. When your complete requirements are clearly defined, you may then take advantage of technical developments in the computer art by writing your requirements in COBOL (common oriented business language) and selecting equipment on the basis of actual performance of your data processing problem. Since COBOL is a common language, it is applicable to equipment of vendors participating in this program.

In November, 1960, the assistant manager of the production department unexpectedly left the company. Mr. Marzo was quick to feel his loss, because he had been the man in the production area who was really behind the automation of production scheduling and had handled all the liaison work with the data processing department. At approximately the same time, the more experienced of the two programmers working on the production scheduling project left Carter's to take another job. Mr. Marzo was still looking for a suitable replacement.

QUESTION

If you were president of The William Carter Company, would you acquire an IBM 1410 or would you add memory capacity to your Univac file computer?

Case 11-3

Curwen Electronics Company

On January 2, 1964, James Phillips, manager of the Curwen Electronics Company's data processing center, was reviewing the procedures used to evaluate and control overall performance of the data processing center (DPC) and its individual employees. He wondered whether the present procedures provided the most useful measures of performance or whether some other scheme of evaluation would be more meaningful.

BACKGROUND

The Curwen Electronics Company was a wholly owned subsidiary of the Porter Corporation, a nationwide manufacturer and distributor of electronic components and assemblies. The Curwen Electronics Company manufactured and distributed Porter Corporation products exclusively in the southern states. The Curwen Electronics Company had eight manufacturing plants at various locations throughout the South and a central office located in Atlanta, Georgia. At each plant, also, was a warehouse from which products were distributed. The Curwen company had annual sales of about $300 million and employed about 15,000 people.

The data processing requirements of the company were extensive. Payroll preparation, customer billings and collections, and disbursements to suppliers were the major large-volume EDP tasks. Curwen Electronics had nine data processing units; eight of these units (one at each plant location) were responsible for the routine, repetitive, high-volume tasks described above. Their work was carried out satisfactorily with a small staff and machine operators who had little or no previous training or experience. No programming was done at these units.

THE DATA PROCESSING CENTER

The ninth unit, the data processing center (DPC), was located in the central office at Atlanta, and its work was quite different from that of the other eight units. This work consisted principally of many small, difficult, one-time jobs rather than high-volume, repetitive jobs. The unit was primarily concerned with providing management information reports requested by various departments of Curwen Electronics. Some of this work, however, was routine, because some jobs were required by the customer departments on either a monthly or quarterly basis. At any given time during the year, the center was responsible for nearly 300 projects.

Organizationally, the DPC was evaluated as a separate cost center and reported as a line group to the accounting department. Although job costs were compiled, the DPC did not charge customer departments for its services. To make sure, however, that only those jobs in the company's best interests were undertaken, Curwen Electronics had established a headquarters staff group called the mechanized procedures staff group (MPS). Its function was to examine all proposals, to evaluate their usefulness from the company's viewpoint, and to correlate them with the present schedule of the DPC. If the MPS group felt that a job was to the overall advantage of Curwen Electronics, it was discussed with the DPC, and a joint agreement was reached on whether or not to run the job in the center.

A company spokesman noted:

> It is a real advantage to have someone with a knowledge of operating conditions, coupled with knowledge of Curwen Electronics' other data processing units throughout the country, examine each job to insure that Curwen Electronics' best interests are met. For example, a number of small jobs require a great deal of programming and debugging time, with little resultant machine time. Under the present system of internal evaluation, it is clearly not in the DPC's best interests to take these jobs, even though the company as a whole might be benefited.

The MPS staff also helped to arbitrate situations where the DPC, because of timing or scheduling problems, was unable to handle all the work expected of it. The staff negotiated with the center so that a mutually satisfactory agreement could be reached between the DPC and the customer department.

Organization of the DPC

The DPC, which had about 50 employees, was headed by Robert Phillips. Reporting directly to him were Peter Black (line) and William Mitchell (staff). Mr. Black had responsibility for the machine operators and their supervisors, together with the control section. Mr. Mitchell supervised the activities of the programmers and analysts. Line operations were currently on a two-shift basis. An organization chart of the DPC is presented as Exhibit 1.

Most of the machine operators were women, either married and middle-aged or recent high school graduates. Turnover was high (33 percent a year) particularly in the recent graduate group. The operators were unionized, and company–union relations were excellent; little, if any, trouble had occurred in the past or was expected in the future.

Exhibit 1

DATA PROCESSING CENTER CONDENSED ORGANIZATION CHART

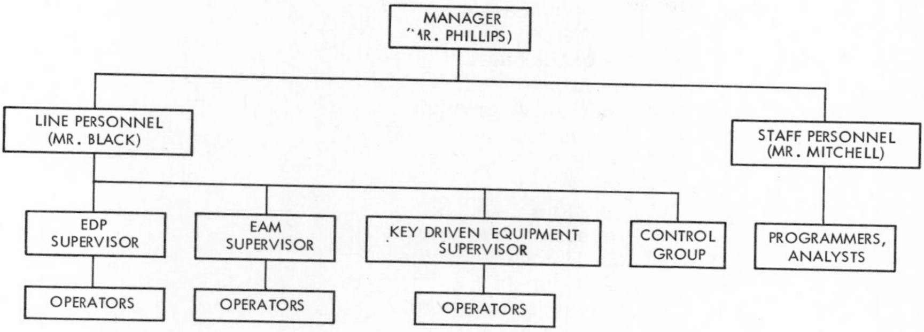

During the training period, operators were moved from one machine to another (see Exhibit 2 for a list of the DPC's equipment) so that they could run all machines effectively, from the key punch to the 1401 computer. It was believed that operators' versatility was necessary if the center was to meet the changing work load composition. In general, each operator followed a job through from beginning to end. This policy was modified to the extent that one operator was assigned full time to the 1401 and two operators to key punches. Operators were not required to perform any machine maintenance, although through experience they often were able to prevent machine stoppages and to correct minor breakdowns.

The control group was responsible for scheduling work through the machines and insuring that accurate instructions were available to the line people. Either the staff group or the customer departments made available to the control group sufficient information to enable detailed instructions to be given to the operators. Detailed instructions included such things as what switches to turn on a particular machine, the cards to place in the primary feed, or the columns to sort. Members of the group also made frequent spot checks to confirm that the correct operations were being carried out.

The staff function at the DPC was very important and required the most highly trained and skilled people in the department. Most of these individuals were men, and their pay range was considerably above that of the line level. Their function was to plan and develop procedures for each approved job. First, they met with the customer departments to determine the exact requirements of the job. Then, they selected an approach to the problem that would provide an acceptable solution and developed the necessary machine procedure. This function included flow charting the job, writing a program, wiring panels for the appropriate machines, and debugging. They also had to prepare instructions for the program's implementation before turning the job over to the control group. When necessary, they worked with the machine operators during the initial production runs.

Exhibit 2

DATA PROCESSING EQUIPMENT

Key Punches and Verifiers:			
5	IBM	024	key punches
5	IBM	056	verifiers
Electronic Accounting Machines:			
1	IBM	519	reproducer
1	IBM	407	accounting machine
1	IBM	557	interpreter
1	IBM	083	sorter
1	IBM	084	sorter
2	IBM	088	collators
Electronic Data Processing Machines:			
1	IBM	108	card proving machine
1	IBM	534	card punch
1	IBM	867	numerical typewriter
2	IBM	7330	tape units
1	IBM	1401	central processor and 4,000 units core storage
1	IBM	1402	card read punch
1	IBM	1403	printer
1	IBM	1406	extra 4,000 units core storage

Data Collection

A number of management reports were used to evaluate performance of departments and individual employees. The basic data for many of these reports came from the "Record of Machine and Employee Time" (see Exhibit 3), which was prepared every day by each machine operator. This sheet provided the following information about each employee:

1. The number of hours she spent actually running each machine (indicated by a time meter on the machine).
2. The number of hours she spent working with a machine. (Because of card jams, machine setup, and a variety of other reasons, an operator usually spent more time working on a machine than was recorded on the machine's time meter.)
3. The number of machine and operator hours spent on each job.
4. A detailed breakdown of how the operator spent her time when she was not working on a particular job.

The day following preparation of these sheets, the information was transferred to punched cards. At various intervals during the month, these cards were processed by the 1401 to produce the necessary management reports.

EVALUATION OF DPC PERFORMANCE

Four principal reports were used in the formal evaluation of the DPC's performance. These were the 937 report, the 937–1 report, the EDP–42 report, and the performance against budget report. Each of these is described below.

Exhibit 3

RECORD OF MACHINE AND EMPLOYEE TIME

DATE ____________ EMP. NO. ____________ EMPLOYEE NAME ____________

MACHINE TIME AND VOLUME

MACH Type	MACH No.	JOB No.	JOB Step	Mach. No.	Batch No.	Exchange Location	CLOCK TIME From	CLOCK TIME To	CLOCK TIME Elap. Hrs.	METER TIME From	METER TIME To	METER TIME Elap. Hrs.	CARD COUNT	CYCLE RATE	APPORT. OP. TIME
						TOTAL Clock Hrs.				TOTAL Meter Hrs.			TOTAL OP. CODES 100 & 200		

EMPLOYEE TIME

Clock	Hours	Emp. No.	Job No.	Job Step	Op. Codes	EMPLOYEE OPERATION	Total Hrs. By Op. Codes
					100	OPERATOR KEY PUNCH & VERIFY	
					200	OPERATOR AUTOMATIC MACHINES	
					510	NONMANAGEMENT TRAINING & DEMONSTRATION WORK	
					520	NONMANAGEMENT STAFF TIME	
					530	CONFERENCE TIME	
					590	ALL OTHER NONMANAGEMENT TIME	
					700	UNMEASURED WORK	
					910	VACATIONS AND HOLIDAYS	
					921	PERSONAL ILLNESS (PD.)	
					922	PERSONAL ACCOMMODATION (PD.)	
					923	OFFICE ACTIVITIES (PD.)	
					924	GENERAL EMPLOYEE WELFARE (PD.)	
					925	FEDERATION WORK (PD.)	
					926	LOST TIME - OTHER (PD.)	
					931	PERSONAL ILLNESS (NOT PD.)	
					932	PERSONAL ACCOMMODATION (NOT PD.)	
					935	FEDERATION WORK (NOT PD.)	
					936	LOST TIME - OTHER (NOT PD.)	
					937	FURLOUGHS (NOT PD.)	
	Total				938	DISABILITY ABSENCE (NOT PD.)	
						TOTAL TIME	
						OVERTIME WORK	

*MACHINE OPERATION CODES
Production
Technical Panel Development
Oper. or Machine Trouble Reruns
Procedure Change Reruns
Training

937 Report

This report was prepared monthly and sent to the corporate offices of the Porter Corporation in New York. On a quarterly basis, the Porter Corporation staff summarized the data received from the data processing installations for all subsidiaries throughout the country, and it sent the results to their managers. Each manager could then compare his performance with that of the installations in other subsidiaries. To facilitate comparisons, the results from each installation were gathered into one of five groups, depending on the type of work done at the installation.

The two key figures generated by this report were an equipment processing index and an operator ratio. The development of these indices is explained below.

Equipment Processing Index.

1. An "office standard total available hours" figure was computed for the installation. This indicated the normal number of working hours for the month in the installation. This figure varied from installation to installation, depending on local customs, and also from one type of equipment to another. For example, for an office with a 7½-hour day, which worked 22 days a month, the figure was 165 hours (one shift) for EAM equipment and 330 hours (two shifts) for an EDP system.

2. The number of hours each machine in the installation was run in the month was determined from the machine's time meter. This figure was called the "actual processing hours."

3. Different EDP machines had different data handling times. The result was that, whereas it might be economically justifiable to have certain machines, in normal circumstances they were not fully utilized. On the basis of historical data for the entire Porter Corporation system, a series of "Systems Standard Equipment Use Factors" was developed (see Exhibit 4). These factors represented the normal percentage of office standard total available hours that the machines were used. The following calculation was then performed:

(SYSTEM STANDARD EQUIPMENT USE FACTOR) × (OFFICE STANDARD TOTAL AVAILABLE HOURS)

= OFFICE STANDARD TOTAL AVAILABLE PROCESSING HOURS

This office standard total available processing hours figure represented the number of meter hours necessary to achieve an index of 100 on a particular machine. (An index of 100 indicated that the machine was fully utilized.)

4. The standard monthly rental for the machine was divided by the office standard total available processing hours to develop a "standard processing rate per hour."

5. The standard processing rate per hour was then multiplied by the actual processing hours indicated by the meter. The result of this computation was then divided by the actual rental figure paid during the month to give the "equipment processing index" for the machine. Samples of this computation are shown in Exhibit 5.

The equipment processing indices for the several machines in the installation were then averaged together to provide an equipment processing index for the installation as a whole.

Operator Ratio. The operator ratio was calculated for each of the main groupings of machines and for the installation as a whole. The main group-

Exhibit 4

SYSTEMS STANDARD EQUIPMENT USE FACTORS

	Standard Equipment Use Factor	Standard Operator Factor	Systems Standard Processing Conversion Factor
Key Driven Equipment			
Class 10		98.0	
024 card punch	68.5		
026 printing punch	68.5		
027 card proof punch	68.5		
056 verifier/punch	68.5		
EAM Equipment, Except Key Driven			
Class 20		82.0	
075 sorter	43.0		
077 collator	41.0		
082 sorter	43.0		
083 sorter	43.0		
084 sorter	43.0		
085 collator	41.0		
087 collator	41.0		
088 collator	41.0		
108 elec. stat. tabulator	48.0		
402 accounting machine	63.5		
407 accounting machine	63.5		
419 accounting machine	63.5		
514 reproducing punch	55.5		
519 reproducing summary punch	55.5		
523 gang summary punch	55.5		
552 interpreter	58.0		
557 interpreter	58.0		
607 calculator	48.0		
609 calculator	65.0		
EDP Main Frames and Off-Line Devices			
Class 50		95.0	
1401T processing unit	90.0		115.0
1401C processing unit	70.0		115.0
7070 data processing unit	75.0		115.0
7074 data processing unit	75.0		115.0
Class 60			
1402T read punch	90.0		115.0
1402C read punch	70.0		115.0
1403T printer	65.0		115.0
1403C printer	51.0		115.0

ings of machines were the key-driven machines, EAM equipment, and EDP equipment. The ratio was designed to measure the efficiency of the installation operators. Its calculation took three factors into consideration:

1. Meter hours—the number of hours the machine was operated in the month.
2. Operator hours—the number of hours in the month that operators were working on the machine.

Exhibit 5

CALCULATIONS FOR COMPUTATION OF PROCESSING VALUE AND EQUIPMENT PROCESSING INDEX

Items	*EAM*		*EDP*
1. Machine type	407		1401
2. Number of machines	1		1
3. Available hours (office) (7.5 × 22 days)	165	(7.5 × 2 × 22 days)	330
4. Equipment use factor (system)	63.5		70.0
5. Available processing hours (3 × 4) (office standard)	105		231
6. Actual processing hours (production and development)	181		266
7. Standard processing conversion factor	—		115.0
8. Standard equipment use hours (5 × 7)	—		266
9. Basic use hours (by contract)	—		176
10. Standard additional use hours (8 — 9)	—		90
11. Basic rental	$1,200		$6,000
12. Standard additional use rental	—	(11 ÷ 9 × 10 × .40)	$1,228
13. Standard base rental (11 + 12)	$1,200		$7,228
14. Standard processing rate per hour (13 ÷ 5)	11.428		31.290
15. Processing value (14 × 6)	$2,068		$8,323
16. Actual rental	$2,200		$9,834
17. Equipment processing index (15 ÷ 16)	94		85

3. Standard operator factor—A factor reflecting the fact that an operator had to spend a certain amount of time getting the machine set up and handling the data (see Exhibit 4). There was a different one for each machine. The factor was used in the calculation of an operator index, according to the following formula:

$$\text{Operator Index} = \frac{\text{Meter Hours}}{(\text{Standard Operator Factor}) \times (\text{Operator Hours})}$$

937-1 Report

This report was prepared monthly and sent to the executives of Curwen Electronics and the staff officers of the Porter Corporation. It was concerned solely with the computer operation. It analyzed in detail how the computer was used during the month.

EDP-42 Report

This report was prepared weekly and submitted only to the executives of Curwen Electronics. It was concerned with the computer operation and presented the following three calculations for each job run during the week:

1. $\text{Machine Rate/Hour} = \frac{\text{Card Volume}}{\text{Meter Time}}$
2. $\text{Overall Rate/Hour} = \frac{\text{Card Volume}}{\text{Elapsed Time}}$
3. $\%\ \text{Meter to Elapsed Time} = \frac{\text{Meter Time}}{\text{Elapsed Time}}$

In addition, a space designated for comments could be used to explain unusual operating results.

Budget

As one of Curwen Electronics' cost centers, the DPC each year submitted a budget which covered rentals, salaries, and sundry other expenses. The budget for the coming year was initially prepared by Mr. Phillips in October. Its preparation reflected the best estimates that he and the MPS could make concerning the DPC's work load for the coming year. This estimated work load was then used to predict probable levels for the various expense categories. Mr. Phillips then sent his budget forward to the budget committee for approval. If they thought that any changes were required, a joint meeting was arranged to resolve the points in contention. The finished product then became his budget for the coming year. Each month, Mr. Phillips had an opportunity to revise his budget for the rest of the year on the basis of the most recent information.

Each month, the actual departmental expenses were collected and were used to develop the following five ratios:

1. Ratio of actual monthly expenses to most recently prepared budget for the month.

2. Ratio of actual monthly expenses to amount budgeted at the beginning of the year for the month.

3. Ratio of actual monthly expenses to actual expenses incurred for the same month in the previous year.

4. Ratio of cumulative, year-to-year expenditures to amount budgeted for the period at the beginning of the year.

5. Ratio of cumulative, year-to-date expenditures to amount incurred for the same period in the previous year.

These ratios consolidated all the performance factors in the other reports. Such things as poor machine indices, bad operator performance, weak scheduling, and poor programming all manifested themselves in actual costs that were greater than estimated.

EVALUATION OF NONMANAGEMENT PERSONNEL

Mr. Phillips believed that it was very important to maintain close control over hourly payroll personnel. He felt that the high turnover among the women operating the data processing equipment necessitated a formal reporting system for their evaluation. Two complementary reporting systems were currently being used by the DPC. The first involved the preparation of two reports, the 601–12H and the 601–180. They were developed by the DPC to evaluate quantitatively each operator's performance. The second system consisted of completing the standard Curwen Electronics' nonmanagement appraisal form.

Quantitative Evaluation

During preparation of a report, a machine operator spent about 25 percent of her time actually running a machine. She spent the rest of her time on such operations as checking output, getting materials together, and waiting for machine time. The portion of her time that she spent on the machines was subject to relatively objective quantitative evaluation. The two reports developed by the DPC for this purpose were the 601–12H and the 601–180.

601–12H was a monthly report used to measure the performance of workers on EAM equipment only, exclusive of the key punch and the key verifier machines. A copy of the report is included as Exhibit 6. The report provided the following information for each operator:

1. The number of hours during the month that the operator was assigned to particular machines (column *B*).

2. The number of hours that the machines to which the operator was assigned were actually processing data (column *C*).

3. Productive hours are the same as operator hours except for small differences outside the control of the operator, e.g., relief time (column *D*).

4. The number of calculations or cycles performed by the operator's machine during the month (column *E*).

Exhibit 6

601-12H OPERATOR REPORT

	Month	Operator Number	Operator Hours	Meter Hours	Production Hours	Number of Cycles	Number of Cards	Operator Index (C ÷ B)	
		(A)	(B)	(C)	(D)	(E)	(F)	(G)	
	09	222	39.6	32.3	31.4	468612	11833	.82	
	09	417	62.6	50.4	59.9	1434728	22918	.81	
	09	524	65.3	49.5	65.9	19617691	70424	.76	
	09	317	41.1	31.1	35.8	1252076	30464	.76	
	09	353	50.0	36.3	48.1	3100317	62006	.73	
Totals			*534.0*	*358.3*	*519.1*			.67	*Average*
	09	215	16.3	10.3	17.0	748542	45922	.63	
	09	372	84.6	50.2	86.2	9940924	11220	.59	
	09	443	56.9	32.5	56.7	3175767	55813	.57	
	09	328	58.2	32.8	59.7	4622029	79416	.56	
	09	501	59.4	32.9	58.4	3353339	56543	.55	

5. The number of cards processed by the operator's machines during the month (column F).

6. The operator index (column G). This was calculated by the formula:

$$\text{Operator Index} = \frac{\text{Meter Hours}}{\text{Operator Hours}}$$

The operator index was the most important figure on the report. The operators were listed according to the size of their indices in descending order from the top of the report. The average index for all operators also was placed in the ranking and thus divided the list into above-average and below-average operators. The figures for number of cycles and number of cards provided an indication as to whether an employee's index was affected by a job with an unusual number of cards or an unusual number of calculations.

601–180 report was a monthly report that provided a detailed breakdown on how each operator performed on each type of EAM equipment. (Key-punch machines were again excluded here.) The report listed each operator and provided the employee's operator index for each EAM machine she used during the month. The office average index for each type of equipment was given on the top line of the report. A sample report is shown as Exhibit 7. Mr. Phillips was concerned as to the usefulness of the form of the report. For example, an operator's reported performance on a particular machine was considerably affected by the amount of time that she used the machine during the month. This sharply limited the extent to which reasonable vertical comparison of operator indices could be made. It was also difficult to make horizontal comparisons on the operator's performance on several machines, since the indices did not take into account differences in such things as the setup time and card-handling time for the several machines.

Nonquantitative Evaluation

At least once a year, each employee was formally appraised in seven categories by his immediate supervisor. This appraisal was reviewed by a committee consisting of the appraiser, one or two other people of the same rank who knew the appraised individual, and the appraiser's own supervisor. Once the appraisal had been made, reviewed, concurred in, and signed by the appraiser and supervisor, the appraiser discussed it with the appraisee with the objective of helping him to improve himself. A description of the criteria used in filling out each of the seven categories is provided below.

1. *Work Produced.* As described earlier, each operator followed a whole job through all its stages from the key punching to the final output on the 1401 or 407. Although, since February, this technique had been modified slightly by having a girl work full time on the 1401 and two girls specialize on the key punch and key verifiers, the overall policy remained the same. Basically, work produced was considered as the total number of reports produced in a day, week, or month. Since these reports varied in work content from one to several hundred hours, the

Exhibit 7

601–180 OPERATOR REPORT
INDIVIDUAL EFFICIENCY RATIOS BY MACHINE TYPE

MO	EMP NO	077	082	083	087	088	407	519	523	557	607
05	Average	.57	.55	.59	.69		.63	.65	.69	.77	.66
05	202	.48	.37	.50	.75		.69	.79	.41	.81	
05	206	.52		.59	.75		.65	.67	.67	.75	.67
05	208	.43		.68	.80		.55	.56		.82	.50
05	209	.55	.61	.47	.33		.63	.36	.87	1.00	
05	211	.67		.67	.71		.68	.82		.78	1.00
05	212						.33				
05	214			.73	.72		.74			.87	
05	216										
05	219	.70		.42	.47		.67	.68		1.00	.70
05	401	.44	.33	.36			.34	.37		.25	.67
05	402	.60		.68	1.25		.72				
05	403	.67	.25	.64	.67		.74	.96		.80	.74
05	404	.50	.67	.45	.56		.68	.77			.67
05	405	.55		.55			.52	.40		.83	.50
05	406	.62		.59	.57		.59	.70		.71	
05	407	.83		.68	1.00		.75	.83		1.00	
05	411	.66		.64	.63		.57	.60			
05	412	.72		.83	.76		.73	.46		.67	
05	419	.41	.40	.35			.41	.53	.64	.76	

supervisors took into account the length and difficulty of the reports. Then, the operator was qualitatively evaluated on both her operator indices and the overall production of reports. Control group operators were rated on their output of reports prepared for the machines; however, no indices were available to evaluate this output. Key punch girls and others who did regular key punching from time to time were evaluated quantitatively by their strokes per hour, 5,000 being the expected average. The 1401 operators were evaluated by reference to meter time standards and by how well they kept the machine running. In all cases, the operator's experience and her working conditions were taken into account.

2. *Quality.* Accuracy of work, neatness, and initiative in preparing reports were considered. Special emphases, however, existed for different groups of operators. The quality of output for a control group employee was measured by the ease with which the machine operators could interpret her instructions. If a control girl regularly had her work questioned, she was not producing at quality levels.

The standard quality for key punchers was the number of mispunches; the allowable range was between .5 and 1 percent. Since all key-punch output was verified, errors were detected and counted. Because of the problems of correcting errors, employees were encouraged to go relatively slowly and to make fewer errors.

On the EAM machines (except for the 407) the standard of quality depended partly on the number of errors traceable to the operator. These included such things as lost or damaged cards, or failure to check the sequence of cards soon after the start of the sorting or collating process. The number of errors expected was very small—on the order of two or three a week, varying with the experience of the girl. Quality also referred to the operator's overall method of working. If the operator did all the right things and made all the right checks in her work, and still made errors, she was evaluated less harshly than if she did not.

The 407 and 1401 operators' quality was a measure of their neatness in working and the quality and ingenuity of their ways of saving machine time. Also, neatness of output and minimization of paper waste were taken into account.

3. *Ease of Learning.* This was considered very important, because most operators had to learn to operate all the machines, and because the labor turnover was 33 percent a year. Similarly, control group people had to learn all the peculiarities of the other jobs, so that they could schedule and instruct each job optimally.

4. *Application to Work.* The ability of an operator to work well with little supervision was considered. This was less important in the EDP service center, where supervision was closer than elsewhere. Also, the jobs were largely machine time controlled, and the programs had built-in quality checks. It was more important in the control and key punch groups.

5. *Cooperation.* The employee's attitude toward her work, her supervisors, her associates, and her union were rated. Cooperation was particularly important for those operators handling the bottleneck machines, such as the 407 and 1401, which required very close scheduling. The operator was evaluated on her ability to coordinate well with those around her, so as to optimize output efficiency.

6. *Dependability.* Responsibility for the job well done and the reliability of her estimates and promises were most important. Again, operators of bottleneck machines were scrutinized most closely.

7. *Attendance.* An operator's tendency to take off extra days and to arrive late to work were evaluated here. Strict policing of attendance and lateness was carried out.

EVALUATION OF MANAGEMENT PERSONNEL

The Curwen Electronics Company had a well-developed system of evaluation that applied to all management personnel. Consequently, each person in the DPC department who was above the level of machine operator was formally evaluated by his supervision at least once a year. An evaluation was made specifically of 15 characteristics that were believed to be important. These characteristics included such things as performance, obtaining results, and development of subordinates. The purpose of this evaluation was threefold:

1. To encourage and help the individual improve his performance.
2. To determine the individual's potential for promotion.
3. To provide information that would assist in determining salary treatment.

In most respects, the supervisors within the DPC department were evaluated in the same way that all managers in Curwen Electronics were evaluated. The following factors were considered to be of particular importance in their case, however.

1. Good scheduling. This was the one factor that could do most to improve the department's performance, because it reduced costs, improved speed of output, enabled delivery dates to be met, and minimized friction among the department members.

2. Cost control. Given the large rental value of the machines, it became very important that they be utilized efficiently so as to minimize overtime costs.

3. Development of subordinates. This was crucial because this center was the only one of its type in Curwen. Thus, Mr. Phillips very rarely acquired "qualified" personnel. Nearly all the new entrants to the department needed to be trained in the skills of handling (*a*) a highly flexible job shop and (*b*) tape and computer equipment. Also, the managerial skills of the subordinates had to be developed in order to maximize their abilities and to produce promotable individuals.

EVALUATION OF PROGRAMMERS AND SYSTEMS ANALYSTS

Programmers and systems analysts were appraised in the same way as the supervisors in DPC, with most of the same criteria being used. In addition, however, heavy emphasis was placed on their technical abilities. Important factors in evaluation of a programmer included these:

1. His overall output of workable programs.
2. The degree of optimization of time and cost in his programs.
3. The freedom from bugs and errors in his programs.

Curwen Electronics had not set up quantitative standards to answer these questions. Rather, Mr. Mitchell examined each program, whenever possible, both before and after debugging. He evaluated it and, when appropriate, suggested changes. Records were kept of the systems analysis and programming hours put into each program. Although these records were not subjected to a formal analysis, they were frequently consulted by Mr. Mitchell to get a rough measure of a programmer's efficiency. Other special evaluation factors were ingenuity in planning programs, foresight in preparing the most useful forms of output, and ease with which programs could be run under current conditions in the department.

QUESTIONS

1. What do you think of Curwen's system for evaluating its EDP group?
2. What kind of a system would you develop to evaluate the EDP operation in this company?

Case 11-4

Harmony Life of Hartford*

Harmony Life of Hartford, one of the large insurance companies, had more than 8,800,000 policyholders—350,000 new holders in 1960. New life insurance sold by Harmony Life in 1960—$70 million above 1959 sales—totaled $2.758 billion, of which individual insurance contributed $1.946 billion. Premium income in individual insurance, annuities, and health insurance totaled $354 million, of which $13.888 million was on policies written in 1960.

DATA PROCESSING AT HARMONY LIFE

Since 1953, electronic computers had played an ever-increasing role in the operation of Harmony Life. The nature of the company's business involved the handling of vast amounts of data. The functions performed in connection with each policy were divided among sales, underwriting, issuance, billing, collection of commission payments, dividend calculations and apportionment, valuation of reserves, claims handling, termination operations (on maturity, death, lapse, or surrender), and the preparation of general operating reports. Each of these functions included a variety of processing activities, which were handled by various types of data processing equipment.

Functions performed by the data processing department of Harmony Life are presented in Exhibit 1. Projects being developed and projects under study also are listed in that exhibit.

ESTABLISHMENT OF THE DATA PROCESSING DEPARTMENT

Machine equipment had been used by various departments in Harmony Life for many years. The actuarial department (see Exhibit 2 for a partial

Exhibit 1

DATA PROCESSING IN HARMONY LIFE OF HARTFORD IN 1961

	*Premium Notice Business**			*Debit Business†*			*Group Business‡*		
Activity	*Ordinary*	*Annuity*	*Personal Health*	*MDO§*	*MPI‖*	*Ind.¶*	*A & H***	*Life & DD††*	*Annuity‡‡*
Sales	D	D	D	D		S	S	S	S
Underwriting				S		D			
Issue	P			P		D			
Premium billing	P	P	P	P	S	S	D	D	S
Premium accounting	P	P	P	P	S	S	P	P	S
Dividend calculation	P	P		P			P	P	
Valuation	P	P	P	P	P	P			S
Claims		P		S	S	S	P	D	P
Statistics	P	D	D	D			D	D	D

Legend: P—being performed; D—being developed; S—under study.

* Policies billed by mail (mostly large-size policies).

† Policies on which premiums were collected at the home of the insured.

‡ Large combination policies covering whole factories or businesses.

§ Monthly debit ordinary insurance (intermediate-size policies).

‖ Monthly premium industrial insurance (no longer issued).

¶ Industrial insurance (small-size policies).

** Accident and health coverages.

†† Life and accidental death and dismemberment.

‡‡ Retirement income coverages.

Exhibit 2

ABBREVIATED ORGANIZATION CHART

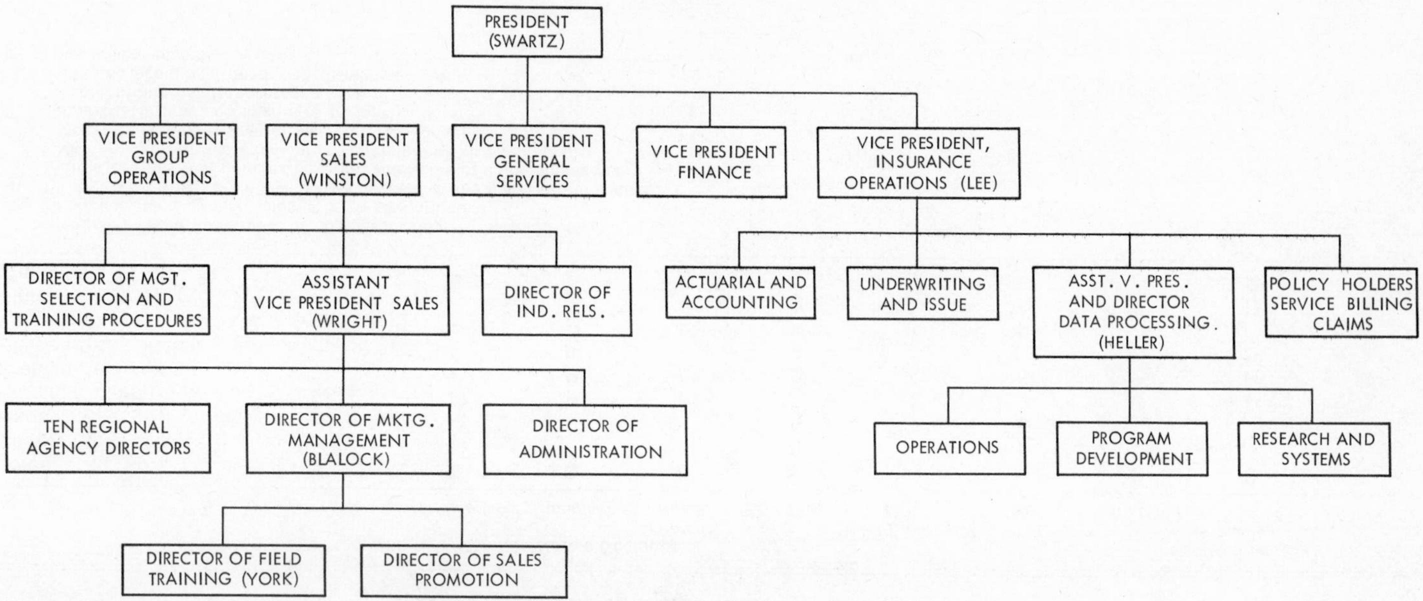

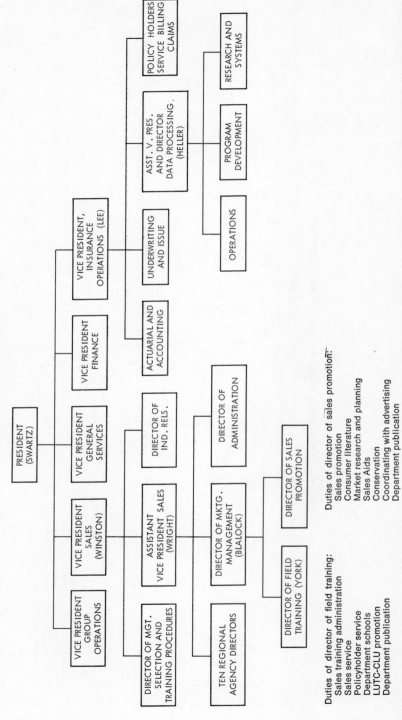

Duties of director of field training:
- Sales training administration
- Sales service
- Policyholder service
- Department schools
- LUTC-CLU promotion
- Department publication

Duties of director of sales promotion:
- Sales promotion
- Consumer literature
- Market research and planning
- Sales Aids
- Conservation
- Coordinating with advertising
- Department publication

organization chart) had used various types of machines since 1916. When the accounting department needed equipment in 1942, the actuarial department was reluctant to share its equipment because of anticipated problems in scheduling work from two departments on the same machines. The accounting department therefore obtained its own equipment. During the next few years, a large number of other functional groups obtained either mechanized or electronic data processing equipment.

By 1958, the large investment in equipment had led top management to appoint a committee to study the entire data processing function. An outside consultant also was employed. Based on the recommendations contained in the two reports, President John Swartz issued an order to begin centralizing responsibility for all data processing activities into one department and to provide for the gradual merger of the existing equipment of all departments.

O. D. Heller was appointed assistant vice-president and director of data processing to administer the new department. Mr. Heller had previously been manager of the data processing section in the policy department. In this department, he had had experience with both major types of data processing equipment used by Harmony Life—i.e., mechanized punch-card machines and medium- and large-size electronic computers. Mr. Heller had been with the company since 1946. His prior training and experience included a degree in business administration and 15 years' practice in systems and procedures work with a large manufacturer of data processing equipment.

The physical merging of equipment and data processing activities began in 1959, when two departments were brought under the new centralized control. In 1961, merger of the data processing facilities of the remaining departments was completed.

The equipment available to the new department was as follows:

3 large-scale, electronic tube-type computers (plus input and output equipment)	company owned
5 medium-size, tube-type computers (plus input and output equipment)	company owned
80 mechanized data processing machines (plus auxiliary equipment of key punch, sorters, and printers)	rented

In 1961, a new, large solid-state[1] computer (7070) and four auxiliary computers (1401) were purchased at a cost of more than $1.5 million. Three of the 1401's were to be delivered at a future date. These machines were intended to replace the five medium-size computers and, in addition, would take over most of the work performed on the mechanized data processing equipment. It also was planned to use the new equipment to service one

[1] This equipment used transistors instead of vacuum tubes, and required less servicing and air conditioning.

functional group (monthly debit ordinary), which previously had not been mechanized.

One medium-size computer, a 1620, was permitted to remain in the actuarial department for research purposes, although general responsibility for the equipment was retained by the data processing department. This equipment had considerable processing capacity, but the limited input and output equipment made it more adaptable to scientific or problem-type applications than to general business applications. Auxiliary input and output equipment could be purchased, but the irregularly occurring needs of the actuarial department made it difficult to integrate the 1620 with the computers being scheduled for regular business applications, so auxiliary equipment was not a part of the present installation.

PROBLEMS ARISING FROM THE UNIFICATION

The manager of the new data processing department was confronted not only with the technical problems inherent in the physical merger of data processing activities but also with the human relations problems that arose from centralizing responsibility and equipment outside the functional areas. Managers of these functional areas frequently made requests to the central data processing department for services considered by the manager of the new department to be uneconomical or unsuited for handling by a computer. The manager frequently rejected such requests and felt that these refusals were resulting in a reputation that the new department was often uncooperative.

Mr. Heller expressed the problem by saying, "How can we control these excessive uneconomical requests for work on the new computer so that we can live within our budget and still keep good relations with the management of the functional departments we serve?"

Reasons for this problem, as viewed by Mr. Heller, were as follows:

1. Widespread publicity in the press about the capabilities of computers without explanations of their limitations, costs, and proper role.
2. Lack of rudimentary understanding by functional managers about business uses of computers.
3. Overenthusiastic reports from earlier advisory committees on results that might be expected from the new installation.
4. Presentation of vague service requests that had not been thoroughly analyzed before presentation.

ORGANIZATION AND OPERATION OF THE NEW DEPARTMENT

To carry out his new responsibilities, Mr. Heller organized the new department into three sections: (1) operations, (2) program development, and (3) research and systems. The operations section was the largest of the three and employed about 250 persons. This section was responsible for routine production. Only work that had previously been approved and programmed by the other two sections was handled by operations.

The program development section consisted of 62 persons, chiefly programmers, who did the coding, debugging, and preparing of program tapes for new applications. Only programs approved by the research and systems section were handled by the program development section.

Requests for new computer applications or variations of existing applications were received first by the research and systems section. If the request appeared to the staff of the section to have merit and indicated to them that the person making the request had rather thoroughly thought through the need, the research and systems section made an advisability study. During the study process, requests were often modified in line with suggestions from the research and systems section. This study served as a guide to the department manager in making a decision to approve or reject the request. It also served as a basis for the requesting official to determine whether he wanted to adopt the new procedure.

An advisability study was sometimes called a feasibility study, but the term advisability was considered by personnel in the research and systems section as more accurate, since a request might be feasible but not advisable because of cost, anticipated change in operation, or other reasons. These studies usually covered the following topics:

1. Statement of the problem.
2. Description of the present system, including schedules, volumes, personnel requirements, and costs.
3. Findings and recommendations, including the suggested approach and equipment, systems and programming development, time and manpower requirements, estimated computer production time, and costs and suggested conversion schedules.
4. Advantages and limitations of the suggested approach.
5. Net savings or costs.
6. Alternative approaches.

The cost of an advisability study was usually charged to the department making the request. The cost varied greatly according to the nature and complexity of the problem. The written report was often 20 to 25 pages in length.

COSTS OF PROCESSING DATA

The advisability study suggested probable costs of machine time and programming. The actual costs, however, might vary considerably from the estimate, since they were computed at the time of performance. An internal costing group outside the data processing department allocated costs according to a current rate schedule.

Rate schedules for machine usage were difficult to formalize and publish in advance. The first computer obtained by Harmony Life was rented, and the cost figure of $300 an hour was widely discussed in the company. Later, when other computers were purchased, no general rate was quoted, since costs would obviously be affected by many factors, such as the rate of depreciation, number of shifts being operated, idle machine time, and amount of setup time in relation to running time.

Although the figures were subject to frequent change, the expense analysis and controls unit was currently using the following rates for actual running time on the new solid-state computer:

Number of Units	*Type of Equipment*	*Rate per Hour (Each Unit)*
1	7070 central processor	$110.50
5	729 II tape unit	3.50
4	724 IV tape unit	4.50
1	1401 central processor	18.50
1	1402 card reading punch unit	2.50
1	1403 high-speed printer	3.25
2	729 IIA tape unit	2.75

Hourly rates were total costs, including both direct and indirect costs of labor, depreciation of equipment, and general overhead.

All the equipment listed would be needed simultaneously on most types of computer processing, since input and output data for the central processor (7070) were transmitted through the 1401 and its related equipment. The number of tape units required would vary considerably according to the nature of the job. Since the 1401 was also a self-contained computer with a limited memory capacity, some jobs requiring a limited number of variables and limited memory storage could be performed using only the 1401, 1402, 1403, and 729 IIA. Single-problem computations on the 7070 using 20 variables could be processed in approximately 30 seconds.

Before any project could be placed on the computer, a program (machine instruction tapes) had to be prepared by the program development section. Costs of programming varied greatly according to the nature of the job. A simple program using a "canned" routine could be prepared for as little as $50. Programs for major applications, such as setting up premium billing on the machine, might require the services of six programmers for two years at a cost of approximately $84,000. Program costs generally ranged from $12,000 to $50,000.

In addition to the cost for running time on the machine and for the initial programming costs, the user was charged for setup time each time the machine was used. This preparation usually included the following steps:

1. Putting on the master instruction tape.
2. Clearing the memory drum.

3. Reading new instructions into the machine.
4. Setting the console instruction buttons.
5. Mounting the input and output tapes, and possibly others, such as error tapes, and factor tapes.
6. Inserting necessary forms in the high-speed printer.

These steps usually required five minutes but sometimes took ten minutes, and they were required whether the anticipated machine running time was five seconds or five hours. Costs for setup time were calculated at the same rate as that for running time.

Because of the nature of the machine operation, Mr. Heller was strongly convinced that computers should be devoted to large-volume, continuous-operation types of jobs, and that small-volume, infrequent, or sporadically occurring jobs could not be economically handled on the large computers because of the setup costs for short runs.

These sporadically occurring jobs also created scheduling problems, since it was difficult to schedule the machine usage in advance if there was no way of knowing whether the job would require three minutes or three hours on a specified day. In order to keep costs down, the new solid-state computer was being carefully scheduled several weeks in advance.

A REQUEST FROM THE SALES DEPARTMENT

In July of 1961, W. A. York, CLU, training director for the 5,200 agents of Harmony Life, read an article in *National Underwriter* magazine briefly describing a new service being introduced by the sales division of the Mutual Benefit Life Insurance Company, a competitive insurance firm. This service was to prepare an individualized proposal setting forth the insurance program that a prospective customer should be carrying. Pertinent facts were obtained from the customer and were fed into the computer, which promptly computed a recommended insurance program based on the individual's specific needs.

Insurance programs prepared for individual prospects were currently used in the insurance industry. These were of two types. One was a rather simple form that assisted a salesman to compare a customer's stated insurance needs with his present insurance program and to recommend additional coverage if needed. The form could be completed by the salesman within a few minutes in the presence of the prospect, but it was based upon the prospect's judgment of his personal insurance needs rather than upon an objective analysis of the facts.

A second type of program planning was done by analysts in the home office. There were comprehensive proposals based upon facts obtained from the prospect by the salesman and included such items as age, income, number and status of dependents, indebtedness, social security status, retirement plan, insurance in force, veteran's benefits, and total assets. These comprehensive proposals required from two to six hours to prepare. All proposals in the past had been manually prepared, and the announcement from Mutual Benefit was the first indication to Mr. York that such a comprehensive personalized proposal might be prepared by an electronic computer.

Mr. York had discouraged the use of comprehensive program planning because of the time required either by salesmen or by the home office, as many computations were necessary with this technique. He felt that salesmen could more profitably spend their time in contacting prospective policyholders and selling them insurance than in spending time doing "paper work." Manual preparation by analysts in the home office was expensive and was generally discouraged. In spite of this discouragement, salesmen occasionally requested the service. Forty proposals of this type had been prepared by Harmony Life during 1960. Of the proposals prepared, one out of every three resulted in a sale, whereas the average of completed sales without use of the device was one out of every four or five sales presentations. The average policy value in these cases was $24,453. The average annual premium income of the 40 prepared proposals was $1,281, of which the agent received approximately 43 percent the first year and 9 percent during each of the following 4 years, plus additional benefits in succeeding years which totaled approximately 3 percent. Commission rates varied on different types of policies, but the above schedule was representative of typical returns to the salesmen on the premium-notice type of business. This type of business represented 63 percent of the dollar volume of individual life, annuity, and health sales, and 10 percent of the total number of policies annually issued by the company.

Mr. York strongly favored the use of the planned program technique if machines could do the detail work at a reasonable cost. Among the benefits he could see from this new plan were these:

1. It would help the salesman to establish a professional counselor–client relationship with the prospect.
2. The prospect who provided the detailed information would be more likely to make a favorable decision.
3. Repeat sales to present policyholders would be easier.
4. The salesmen would not be required to learn any new sales techniques, since the principle was already generally understood.
5. The prospect would receive a valuable service by having an answer to the question: How much insurance is enough for me?

The average number of sales annually per agent in 1960 was 56.4. It was Mr. York's opinion that this average was too low and that some technique, such as the proposed program planning, would help increase this average.

Mr. York attempted to obtain information on how the new plan had worked in the competitor's operation. He learned it was used primarily by one general agent who was a large producer, but he could not obtain other details. The competitor reported that he believed the new technique had given his firm a competitive advantage and stated that the new service was being advertised in *The New Yorker* magazine. This information further strengthened Mr. York's conviction that the plan had genuine merit. Because of the availability of the new and superior computer, the 7070, at Harmony Life, he believed it would be possible to provide a more comprehensive sales proposal, using a few more variables than those pioneered by the competitor.

Mr. York asked the data processing department for general estimates of cost for the proposal. He was informed that costs could not be quoted, as they were dependent on the nature of the project and the amount of estimated input and output expected. Mr. York at that time was not able to furnish specific items which should be included in the analysis. He had, however, heard that Mutual Benefit Life used 19 variables in preparing each program. He also was unable to estimate precisely the amount of expected usage, as he felt this was dependent on probable costs and the amount of encouragement given the agents by the home office. He attempted to determine whether the cost would be $5,000 or $500,000, since the cost would determine whether or not he wished to pursue the matter further. But he could obtain no general estimate from the data processing department. He was informed that the project as presented did not appear to be acceptable for scheduling on the new computer.

In explaining his position concerning cost and usage figures, Mr. York stated:

> The home office should provide service to the field agents and to the public. In sales work we can never actually tell whether a sales tool will pay out or not. We spend money on a sales brochure, but how can we tell what the return will be? A sales meeting costs money, but we can't measure the direct returns in relation to costs. Indirect sales resulting from the expenditures can't be computed.
>
> Why then must the computer people have definite figures on the usage before accepting a sales idea? I want to be practical about the matter, but I can't be too concerned over internal costs until we've had an opportunity to try out the new procedure to see how it works. Some things must be taken on faith when your judgment tells you it is a good idea. Obviously, acquisition cost of new business can't exceed a reasonable figure, but often we can't definitely evaluate this until we try it.
>
> Sales are the lifeblood of our business, and we must move ahead when we are convinced a new idea is a good one.

RESPONSE OF THE DATA PROCESSING DEPARTMENT

When Mr. York made his initial request, Mr. Heller attempted to determine what would be expected in the form of programming and anticipated output if the new idea were approved. Mr. Heller received the general impression that the project would result in a low-volume, irregularly occurring operation, so he informed Mr. York that he would be unable to set it up on the new computer. When Mr. York pressed for a general estimate of probable costs, Mr. Heller told him that such an estimate was impossible without extensive study of the proposal, and this study could not be undertaken unless Mr. York could provide more definite information. Mr. Heller also informed him that the new computer would soon be heavily scheduled with other types of work that were clearly adapted to it.

Mr. York inquired if the job might be set up on one of the 650 computers, since Mutual Benefit Life had used this type of equipment. Mr. Heller replied that a decision had been made to dispose of these machines to help defray the costs of the new solid-state computer installation. He explained that if one of the 650 computers, valued at $120,000, were retained for Mr. York, the air-conditioning, space, and other costs might bring the total costs to one-half million dollars. These costs would, of course, be charged to the sales department. The possibility of keeping a 650 for the sole purpose of service to the sales department was not acceptable to Mr. York.

Mr. Heller analyzed the case as being typical of the type of request he had to refuse. His analysis was as follows.

This is a low-volume job and isn't suited for a large-scale computer. The only low-volume jobs we should consider are the "by-products" requests that can be taken off existing information already in our basic file of stored information. This is not such a request.

Furthermore, we have no way of determining how many emergency or quickie requests we are likely to receive if the plan were adopted. Will people be calling in all the time and saying, "I need this bit of information right away," or "I've promised to get this one piece of information out in a hurry"? They forget that the setup time is the same for one case or a thousand.

This case sounds more like a gimmick than a real computer problem. We don't even know if the other personnel of the sales department support this request. Only the training director has requested it, and we don't know if the sales vice-president and the field agents really want this plan. It is true that Mr. York is a good, old-line salesman who knows how to teach men to sell insurance instead of policies, but we don't have any way of knowing if the rest of the sales department will support this idea if we approve his request. Anyway, I doubt whether Mr. York has really thought through this request. Any computer installation works on a decreasing scale of costs after the setup has been completed, and he hasn't any information as to whether there might be one case or a thousand cases per week. It sounds as though he's acting primarily on a whim based on the report of a sales gimmick at Mutual Benefit.

We have to say no to such requests as these, because the big computer can be operated only 24 hours a day—not 25 hours—and we can't always be bringing in a new computer, for computers are not like punched-card equipment where small components can be added at will. It hasn't sunk in on the managers of the other departments that I can't justify asking for another one- and one-half million-dollar computer just to be of service on every whim they get. We ought to avoid as many of these requests as possible.

It is true that we may nip in the bud some ideas that would save or make money for the company, but we can't cost them all out, so we are bound to make some mistakes. We don't have the staff or the time to make detailed advisability studies of every vague idea that comes to us, and we can't give general estimates of costs without careful study of what is involved. If we did, this would lead to all sorts of trouble. Costs can vary too greatly, depending on what is included in the request. Unless the person has taken time to sit down for a day or two to crystalize what he expects in the form of output, it is usually just a whim, so we say no.

In this business can you afford to be a good fellow? If I said yes to all service requests, I wouldn't ever get our main job done. Costs would go up. Then, top management would think I was doing a poor job. I don't mind being called a slob by lower management as long as top management feels I am doing a good job. After all, this is a selfish world. If by being "uncooperative" we save the company thousands of dollars, then it would seem irresponsible for us to use less than extreme care in scrutinizing requests. People used to come in on Friday afternoon and say, "Put this on the punch-card machines. We want the answers on Monday." We stopped that foolishness. Now they usually have to request service in a written memorandum unless we have real confidence in their sincerity and genuine need. Our attitude is caused by the way people come to us. It is amazing the requests we get. Historically, machine people have been considered low skilled by others in the company. Now that we have grown up that impression hasn't changed much, yet we no longer can cater to every whim when a great deal of money is involved in programming costs.

Of course, we often provide a real service to a department that has a problem suitable for computers, such as mailing a confirmation notice on the anniversary date of a policy—a service suggested by our public accounting firm. But the volume in that case was two million. We did a smaller job for payroll recently, and they wrote a letter of appreciation for our service.

But we take on only those jobs we feel are worthwhile projects for the company as a whole. Even though the department requesting the service will be charged for it, it is our responsibility to try to keep off the computer things that have no business being on it.

We've given 40-minute talks in the various departments to inform management about the use and misuse of computers. If they know anything about computers, they don't come in with foolish requests, stating, "I want it set up so I can get the information I need in one minute," when it takes much longer than that just to set up the machine. I believe that a general knowledge of computers should be a part of the training of all managers. We have a couple of good examples of men who worked for a while in this department and are now managers in functional departments. Our relations with these departments are excellent.

MANAGEMENT'S CONSIDERATION

In October, 1961, President Swartz was presented with a formal request from David Winston, vice-president in charge of sales. This request contained a proposal that Harmony Life adopt a sales technique similar to that of Mutual Benefit Life, and that the data processing department be directed to provide the necessary service on the new electronic computer.

This request originated with Mr. York, and had been approved by Mr. Blalock, director of marketing management, and Mr. Wright, assistant vice-president for sales. Mr. Winston reported that he had previously discussed the matter with Mr. Lee, vice-president of operations, who had rejected the proposal on the advice of Mr. Heller.

In attempting to arrive at a decision on the request, Mr. Swartz weighed the following possibilities:

1. If he approved the request, this might set a precedent so that other requests of this nature would be directed to him rather than to the newly established data processing department, which was technically qualified to make decisions in such matters.
2. The data processing department might use this approved request from top management as leverage to obtain approval for additional computers.
3. Disapproval of the request might be used by the sales department to shift blame to top management in case sales quotas were not reached in the coming years.

Mr. Swartz was aware that regardless of his decision on the present request, some action was needed to prevent similar cases from arising in the future. He had pointed out to the board of directors when the new equipment was purchased that the centralization of equipment and responsibility would reduce costs and improve efficiency in data processing. Excessive demands on the new equipment might jeopardize the basic objective of cost reduction, but he was aware that data processing efficiency required that functional departments have service available when their requests could be economically justified.

Chapter Twelve

CONCLUSION

The readings and cases in this chapter are intended to be a capstone to the course. The readings include a description of the Du Pont system, which has had a greater influence on American practice than that of any other company, and a pair of articles by leading practitioners, Messrs. Rickard and Laing. As an antidote to possible euphoria, a list of unresolved problems also is given.

The cases provide an opportunity to apply concepts and techniques developed in earlier chapters.

Reading 12-1

Return-on-Operative-Investment—The Du Pont Approach

By Wm. Travers Jerome III*

The intent of this chapter is to consider how E. I. du Pont de Nemours & Company uses return-on-operative-investment as a key device for guiding corporate destinies. Return-on-investment is one of the most successful yet simple techniques ever conceived to aid both decision making and performance evaluation.

As practiced by Du Pont Company executives, return-on-investment has become a symbol for the company's system of management control. As such, return-on-investment is a way of approaching the problems of top-level control rather than a magic formula for solving these problems. Indeed, the deceptive simplicity of this return-on-investment concept can lead the unwary to make poor decisions and to create an unsettled climate for control. The reasoning behind these assertions is at the heart of this chapter.

Return-on-investment is often a loosely used term with many shades of meaning. In this chapter, however, it is used in only one sense. In simplest terms it is the percentage figure that results from a comparison of operating profits (either before or after taxes) with the total of working capital, plant, and equipment used to make such profits.

The diagram† shows the relationship of the operating factors that affect return-on-investment. The significance of these factors can perhaps be best

* President, Bowling Green University. From *Executive Control—The Catalyst* (New York: John Wiley & Sons, Inc., 1961). Chap. 13.

† Source: The charts reproduced in this chapter are from the Du Pont publication, "Executive Committee Control Charts."

understood in terms of the question: "How can management increase the return received from its investment?" A study of the diagram suggests four ways to do this.

First, cost of sales can be reduced. This will increase operative earnings and thus return-on-investment.

Second, selling prices can be increased. Assuming that the price increase will not result in a proportionate drop in sales volume, this will increase operative earnings. It will also have the effect of increasing the turnover of total investment with a consequent rise in operative return.

Third, the volume of sales can be increased. This will have the same effect on return-on-investment as will increasing the sales price. The proviso here, of course, is that the increase in sales volume is not the result of a disproportionate increase in promotional or manufacturing costs.

Fourth, both working capital and permanent investment can be reduced. A decrease in either means a smaller investment base and therefore a higher operative return on that investment.

Return-on-investment is thus calculated in terms of the money invested in plant and working capital rather than on stockholder invested capital. There are, of course, times when the return on stockholder capital provides useful information. However, such information is largely related to financial matters rather than to the effectiveness of operations.

Our interest here is how well management uses the property of a company to generate profits. The fact that some of this property is financed by stockholders, some by bondholders, and some by banks or trade creditors is irrelevant. How effectively, however, are the resources a company has acquired being used? This, in brief, is the question that the return-on-operative-investment test seeks to answer.

The importance of return-on-investment is evident in the increased number of articles and conferences devoted to this subject. An official publication of the Du Pont Company recognizes this importance in the following statement: "In one operating principle, Du Pont methods differ from those of many U. S. companies: it chooses to measure performance in terms of the return on investment, rather than the more familiar percentage on sales." The now classic discussion of the company's use of return-on-investment is described in "Executive Committee Control Charts," prepared by the treasurer's department.

A more recent statement indicating the significance attributed to return-on-investment is that of an officer of the Armstrong Cork Company:

> Our company adopted the return-on-investment measurement in 1950. Today it is our basic working tool in planning and striving for the best results possible. All other working tools and controls in our business, such as those provided by production and inventory planning, engineering of all kinds, accounting, purchasing, and sales promotion, are designed to improve the return on investment. Since they are so designed, we would stand to lose a major part of their effective-

Formula Chart

RELATIONSHIP OF FACTORS AFFECTING RETURN ON INVESTMENT

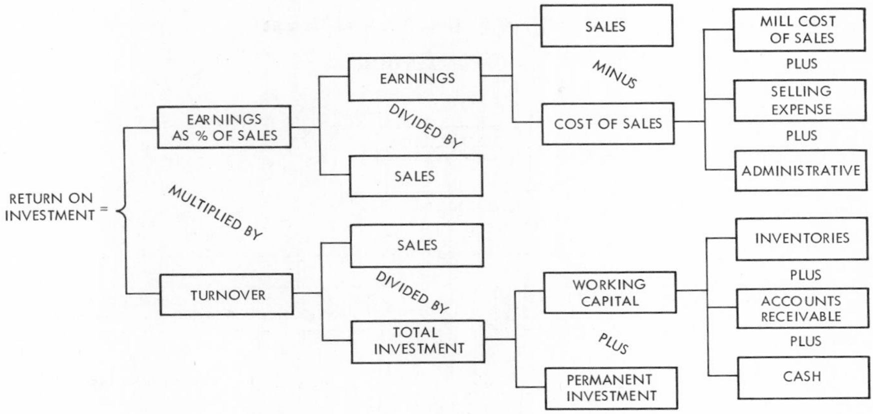

ness if objectives were to be stated in terms of growth, share of markets, or well-rounded lines, or in any other terms rather than return on investment.

The preceding perhaps represents an extreme claim for the merits of return-on-investment. It does suggest, however, the importance attributed to this concept and why managers must understand how it can be used to best advantage.

THE DU PONT ORGANIZATION—THE COMMITTEE SYSTEM

To understand how return-on-investment fits into the Du Pont picture, it is first necessary to describe the company's organization and its underlying philosophy. The organizational plan under which Du Pont now operates was put into effect in 1921, when Irénée du Pont was president. The bare outlines of this organizational scheme are shown on the diagram. Despite the active interest that the 32-man Board of Directors takes in the company, the Board does much of its work through committees made up of its own members. The principal committee, in the day-to-day management of the company, is the Executive Committee. The Executive Committee consists of eight vice presidents plus the president of the company, who acts as chairman. The members of this committee have all come up through the company. They are technically trained men with considerable operating experience behind them.

The members of the Executive Committee have only two primary functions. The first function is to establish the overall operating policies of the company and to review the activities of the industrial and auxiliary departments, particularly to see that balanced company growth is being insured.

The second function of the members of the Executive Committee takes place in their individual, rather than committee, capacity. This function is that of giving technical advice in their particular fields of competence, such as sales, engineering, public relations, or finance.

E. I. du Pont de Nemours and Company

ORGANIZATION

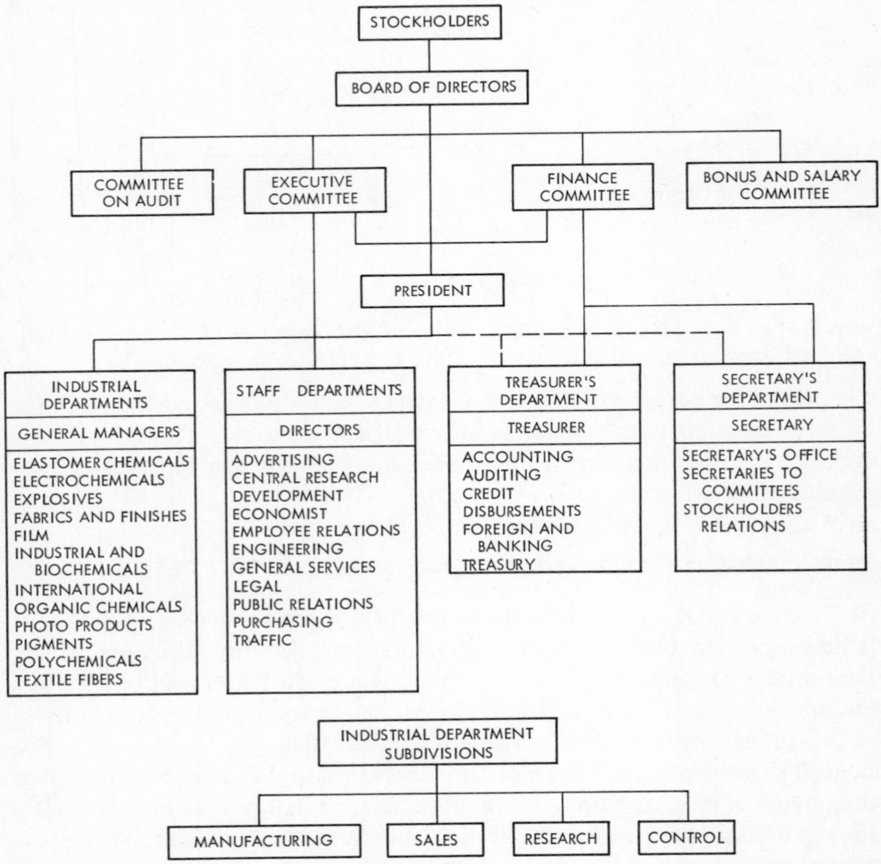

The members of the Executive Committee, in other words, have absolutely no operating authority or operating responsibility. As the supervisory body for all operations, however, the committee establishes all major policies and passes on important projects before they are undertaken by any of the departments. Specific projects are reviewed for their return-on-investment. If such projects involve the expenditure of sums beyond specified amounts, these projects are in turn referred to the Finance Committee for its approval.

The Finance Committee, like the Executive Committee, is a subcommittee of the Board. Its membership of eight includes the president, but he does not serve as chairman.

The function of the Finance Committee is considerably more limited in scope than that of the Executive Committee. Its concern is with the financial affairs of the company, as well as with expenditures beyond a given limit. As the organization chart shows, both the treasurer's department and the secretary's department are directly responsible to the Finance Committee. The treasurer's department does, however, have very close relationships with the industrial and auxiliary departments, as well as with the Executive Committee. Thus, it is the treasurer's department which is responsible for devising the accounting, budgeting, costing, and other controls used throughout the company.

The return-on-investment charts also are the responsibility of the treasurer's department. These are the charts, as will be discussed, that are used by the Executive Committee in its review of the industrial departments. These charts, although the responsibility of the treasurer's department, are nonetheless designed largely according to the dictates of the Executive Committee. This fact is mentioned in order to stress the high degree of liaison that must exist between the financial and operating activities of a company like Du Pont if effective control is to exist.

It is also suggestive to note how these two committees act as a check and balance, one on the other. The importance of the Finance Committee, and correspondingly of the treasurer's department, no doubt lies in the company's traditional policy to keep out of debt. This policy, along with the desire of the company to take advantage of profitable investment opportunities, demands careful husbandry of cash resources. The attention given to return-on-investment and to the forecasting done by the industrial departments all bear on this problem of cash management. The financial controls, as will be pointed out, thus blend beautifully with the operational controls used by the Executive Committee.

The Role of the General Managers

To understand the way in which return-on-investment enables the Executive Committee to exercise supervisory control over operations, it is necessary to look further at the twelve industrial, and thirteen auxiliary departments. The industrial departments simply represent a division of the company by the Executive Committee into operating investments along logically related product lines. As of January 1960, Du Pont employed some 86,000 persons, maintained nearly 100 laboratories and manufactured more than 1,200 chemical products and product lines in some 78 plant locations.

These twelve industrial departments act like independent companies in almost every respect. Each is under the direction of a general manager appointed by the Executive Committee. These departments buy and sell among themselves and often compete with each other. The general manager has full responsibility for all the activities of his particular department. His is the responsibility for improving manufacturing processes, for developing new products, or for setting prices. Except in his selection of the assistant general manager, who must be approved by the Executive Committee, the general manager has complete authority and control over his own organization. Although this organization ordinarily varies in some degree from department to department, in general it consists of four main subdivisions. These subdivisions, each headed by a manager, or director, who reports to the general manager, consist of production, sales, research, and control. This decentralization of research is particularly significant, because it is a further indication of the degree of responsibility given to these general managers.

The role of the general manager was colorfully suggested in an article in *Business Week*. "A du Pont General Manager Runs Kingdom in an Empire." This is an apt description. Both to maintain a venturesome spirit and to encourage the development of personnel, decentralization is essential in the Du Pont scheme. In this scheme, the Executive Committee thus becomes, in effect, a Board of Directors for each of the twelve industrial departments. The trick in maintaining this relationship between the Executive Committee and the general managers is to see that communication is maintained and undue home office direction is restrained. The communication is maintained through monthly reports submitted by each of the general managers, through an analysis of return-on-investment before the entire committee once every three months, through a discussion of departmental forecasts with the Executive Committee at the same time that return-on-investment is analyzed, and, finally, through the periodic visits that a general manager may have with individual members of the Executive Committee in soliciting their expert advice on particular problems or projects.

For the Executive Committee to maintain true autonomy in these twelve departments demands a high degree of skill. It would be a simple matter for supervision of operations to become direction of operations. To avoid any such direction which would tend only to discourage initiative and new ideas, the Executive Committee is extremely sensitive to a general manager's proposals. The committee must be willing to accept such proposals even when it may believe that the proposal has doubtful merit. As one vice president put it: "We err on the side of letting the general managers run their businesses according to their own lights. When I was a general manager, they let me spend half a million dollars playing around with superpressures without getting any results."

Another member of the Executive Committee expressed the same idea as follows: "Sometimes we don't agree with a general manager but it is better to let a mistake be made than to order a general manager to act against his judgment—unless too many people would be hurt." Similarly, a general manager tells of his first trip before the Executive Committee to justify a new project that involved dealing with an outside company. To his surprise, he was asked but one question: "Is it fair to the other fellow?"

Clearly, when the relationship of the Executive Committee and the industrial department is carried on in this sort of environment, departmental autonomy can, and will, exist. Anything else would make the Du Pont committee system self-defeating. In other words, if the Executive Committee attempted to do the directing of operations, the burden and complexity of the work would soon sap the company of its vitality and venturesomeness.

The thirteen auxiliary departments have the same tradition of service as the Executive and Finance Committees do. These departments perform staff services. They comprise highly trained specialists who are available for counsel to operating management. Each of these departments, like the industrial departments, is headed by a director and an assistant director. The actual organization of these departments varies considerably, since the organization structure is a responsibility of each individual director. The auxiliary departments, like the manufacturing departments, answer to the Executive Committee. The treasurer's and secretary's departments answer also to the Finance Committee. The appearance of the directors of any of the auxiliary departments before the Executive Committee is somewhat less common than for the industrial departments, since the auxiliary departments are not entrusted with operating investments on which a return must be earned. The auxiliary departments submit annually for committee approval a proposed budget under which they operate. Provided the portion of this budget charged to administrative expense is not exceeded by 5 percent, or underspent by 10 percent, no additional approvals are required of the Executive Committee.

A Report-Writing Organization

Thus far, our review of the Du Pont organization has been fairly general. Now, let us look with considerably more detail at the work of the Executive Committee, which is the nerve center of company operations. The importance of return-on-investment as a measure of performance becomes understandable only in terms of the delicate relationships that this committee has established with the operating departments. The Executive Committee, as has already been pointed out, consists of eight vice presidents and the president of the company as committee chairman. There is nothing particularly magical in the number nine, as the size of the committee has varied in the past. On the other hand, this number seems to be approximately right in making workable the deliberations and at all times insuring representation of such key functions as manufacturing, engineering, sales, financial, or technical. Decisions are by majority vote, although an affirmative vote of four is necessary before any resolution can be adopted.

The preponderance of the day-to-day work of the individual committee member is spent in reading reports. The weekly quota of reports is approximately five inches high when stacked one on the other. "We are a report-writing organization," is how one executive expressed it. Certainly a major function of the Executive Committee is to see that these reports lead to purposeful effort. This means that these reports must be used as a basis for communication, as a means for evaluating performance, as a device for planning, and as an aid in policy making. It is difficult to imagine a more ingenious, yet simple, way of making a system of executive control meaningful than by giving a group of respected, senior executives time to read and to evaluate reports covering the work of the firm. The reason for this assertion should become clearer as we progress in this analysis.

To understand clearly the work of the Executive Committee, however, it is essential to emphasize again that the principal job of the individual committee members is to read reports. The advisory function on technical matters, previously mentioned, is definitely incidental in terms of time consumption as compared with the job of reading and studying reports. These reports take various forms. The key report, however, which indicates more than anything else the approach of the Executive Committee to this problem of control, is the report known as the Executive Committee Chart Series. This particular Chart Series is designed to put primary emphasis on return-on-investment. In particular, its intent is to bring to the attention of the committee the various factors contributing to the return-on-investment.

The Chart System

It is important to understand that this all-important operative return-on-investment figure does not stand in solitary splendor at Du Pont. This figure is backed up by a series of charts designed to show: (1) the trend of costs and their effects on profits, and (2) the trend of the various investment components and their turnover. These charts are always presented in a way that relates present operations to forecasted operations as well as to past accomplishments.

Illustrative of how this chart series is presented is the hypothetical ABC Department shown. The two top segments of this chart show the result of the department's operations to date, namely, the operative return-on-investment both before and after taxes. The two essential elements contributing to this return, namely, operative earnings as a percentage of sales and sales as a percentage of total investment (i.e., the turnover) are shown in the lower two-thirds of the chart.

This is the first in the chart series shown to Du Pont's Executive Committee in its periodic reviews of the twelve industrial departments. Other charts follow this key one. They are designed to help the committee analyze the various sales, expense, and investment factors contributing to the reported investment return.

The mechanical details of these charts need not concern us now. Both their mode of presentation and their use, however, are important to understand because here lies much of their symbolic significance to the company.

ABC Department

OPERATING RATIOS

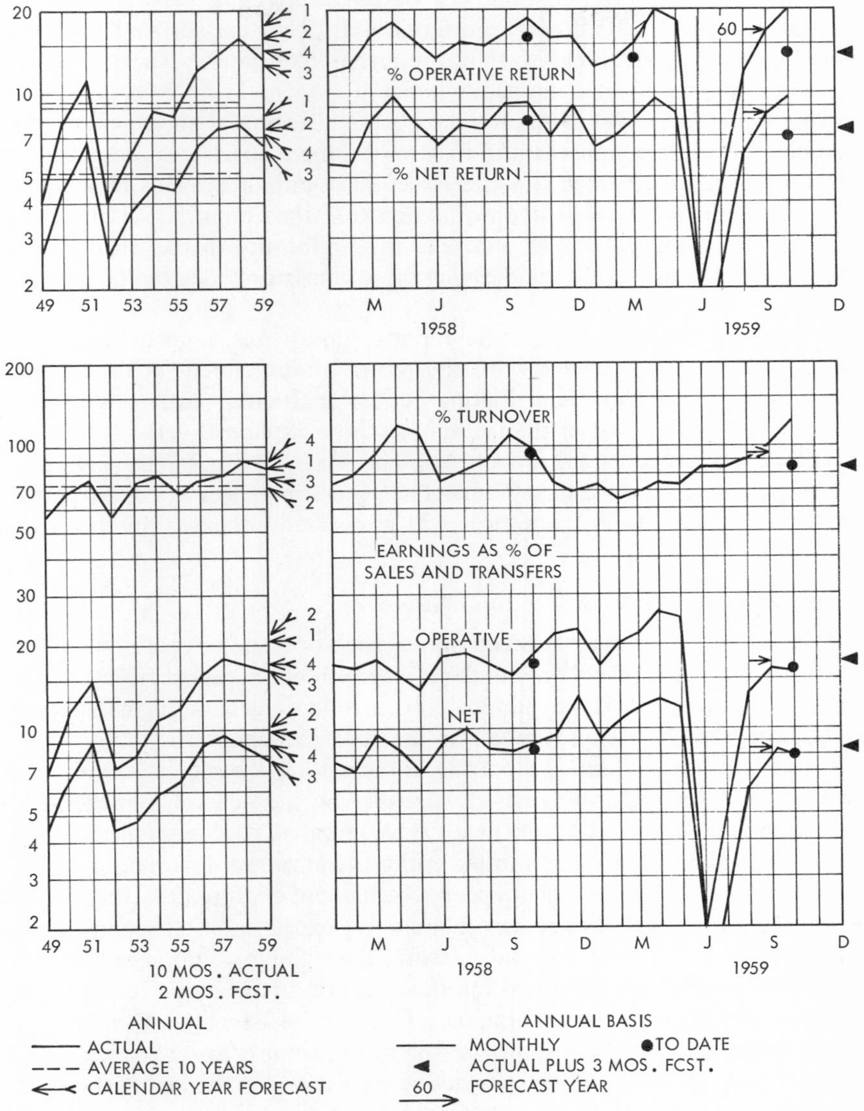

The Executive Committee meets for an all-day session every Wednesday. Most of the time spent between these meetings is consumed in reading reports preparatory to the next meeting. Regularly each month a portion of one of these Wednesday meetings is given over to a review of the charts for four of the twelve departments and for the total company operations. Accordingly, not less than once every three months each department comes under Executive Committee scrutiny. The general manager is present for this review which is held in a specially designed chart room in Wilmington. The charts are hand-prepared on cardboard and are approximately two and one-half feet by three and one-third feet in size. They are suspended from a network of overhead tracks so that any given chart can be wheeled before the committee's view at a moment's notice.

This visual form of presentation directs the attention of all the committee members toward the same data. Furthermore, these charts are presented on the basis of rules developed by the Executive Committee. This means that the charts portray the sort of information that the committee itself wants to further its deliberation. In addition, the uniformity in the presentation and preparation of the data underlying these charts provides rapid and easy committee consideration.

It deserves emphasis that these reports show *what* happened, but not *why*. Attention is directed toward the return-on-investment achieved, and also toward the factors contributing to that particular return. The *why* accounting for the trend of the factors has to be explained verbally. This is done by the chart room supervisor, who has responsibility for the presentation before the Executive Committee. The general manager of the particular department under review, however, will answer any detailed questions regarding operating matters.

Emphasis on Forecasting and Review

In addition to this chart presentation of each operating department's performance, the Executive Committee reviews a monthly report from each of the general managers. These monthly reports follow a general format and are usually prepared by a staff assistant to the general manager.

In the Du Pont system of reporting, forecasts are a basic and continuing factor. These forecasts are revised quarterly by the general manager and are continually projected for the next twelve months. To this extent, it might be said that planning is built into the entire organization. Planning, in other words, is not a one-shot, once-a-year job that can be forgotten for the remainder of the period. As one general manager expressed it, "I spend a good part of my time thinking about the future. Everything we do is based on a forecast, and that forecast is tied into a system of financial controls."

These forecasts also play an important role in the Executive Committee's use of the chart series. As shown in the sample chart, arrows are used to indicate the projected position expected to be attained at the end of the year. An arrow is used for each quarterly forecast. In this way, anticipated changes in the original forecast submitted to the Executive Committee are readily seen. In addition, these periodic forecasts aid not only in forward planning but also in measuring progress toward stated objectives.

These quarterly forecasts, which use in effect a "rolling year," are by no means the only report employed to plan activities. A longer, ten-year look into the future is taken in so-called "Whither-Du Pont" reports. These reports may be about operating departments or even about particular products still to be commercially developed. They help to point up future need for construction and also for working capital.

Another type of report is called the "Report on Accomplishment." This is used for every capital project that has been approved on the basis of a projected return-on-investment. If a project performs with the success anticipated in the original proposal, no further reports on accomplishment are required. If such success is not obtained, however, the Executive Committee may request that reports continue until they are satisfied with the performance of the facilities. A member of the Executive Committee, accordingly, sometimes has to listen to a series of reports on a project that he promoted in his operating days.

Another type of report, called "Low-Return Investments," grows out of studies by the treasurer's department. These reports are designed to help focus attention on potential trouble spots. The people responsible for these studies include engineers, chemists, and other technically trained personnel. Each of the twelve industrial departments has its own "control group" which also acts as liaison with the corporate treasurer's department.

In addition to the reports mentioned, there are commonplace periodic reports and nonrecurring reports on special problems like leasing, inventory levels, and purchase commitments.

There are also the usual financial statements. These statements are prepared by the treasurer's department. Perhaps the most important of these statements is the overall company financial forecasts entitled "Forecast of Net Income and Cash Position." This statement comprises a forecast of: (1) sales and operative earnings, from which net income is derived, (2) working capital requirements, and (3) construction authorizations and expenditures. This coordinated forecast is based on the individual forecasts that the treasurer's department receives from the various industrial and auxiliary departments.

The Climate for Control

The various reports discussed here are all for the Executive Committee. Similar reports are used in each of the industrial departments. Return-on-investment on particular projects is carefully watched. Thus profit consciousness and planning awareness are pushed down into the organization. In other words, in order for the general manager to build up his forecasts for the Executive Committee, he must in turn require forecasts of his plant managers and staff heads.

Consequently the attitude of the Executive Committee toward return-on-investment, planning, and reporting and communication necessarily sets the pattern for overall company behavior. This pattern of behavior is made real and meaningful because the Executive Committee actually has time to analyze the reports with the intent of seeing that prompt corrective action is taken by the responsible general managers. Continuous attention is thereby focused on profits, planning, and the exercise of initiative.

A perhaps small, but, to me, significant feature in this pattern of control established by the Executive Committee is the company attitude toward forecasts. In all my discussions with officials of the company, the term "forecast" was invariably used rather than the term "budget." The staff, or auxiliary, activities operate within budgets, but not the industrial departments. Except for advertising and research expenditures, which are budgeted, the industrial departments operate under forecasts, with all the open-endedness that this term conveys. *The job of the operating department is thus to make a projected return-on-investment, not to live within a budget. The overall forecast is simply a useful means for seeing that the resources are available for the operating departments to perform profitably.*

To reiterate, appraisal of the organizational performance of the twelve industrial departments is based on the return-on-investment achieved, not on compliance with budgets, or with any forecast other than the return-on-investment projected. Even capital budgets as such are nonexistent. A general manager, in his various reports to the Executive Committee, is expected to indicate his capital needs from time to time. These, again, are in the nature of forecasts. Quarterly, the Executive Committee receives a summary of construction authorizations and expenditures anticipated for the entire company for the ensuing twelve months. Ultimate approval for any investment project is given only when the particular project is submitted to the Committee for its specific approval. Even if it is approved by the Executive Committee, a major project still needs the authorization of the Finance Committee. Approval by the Finance Committee after a project has been reviewed by the Executive Committee is almost wholly contingent on the availability of funds.

Generally speaking, except for the formal reporting requirements, the controls used by Du Pont seem broad and flexible. Such flexibility tends to exist even in the operating departments themselves. In analyzing the company, *Business Week* expressed this thought as follows:

> It's apparent that no one man can make all the decisions for so large a business empire. Du Pont's answer: decentralization of authority to the general managers. It's also apparent that a corporation with the propensity to expand that du Pont has cannot be bound by a rigid operating procedure. The answer: flexibility, made possible by a few broad rules, as opposed to—Roman-fashion—a rule for everything.

The control manager of one of the industrial departments explained his philosophy of control to me in this way:

> Whenever the need arises either to change or to introduce a new production-

planning or inventory-control system in one of the plants of our department, the responsibility belongs to the plant's own personnel. My men on the control staff will give all the help necessary. It is up to the operating people in the plant, however, to indicate the system wanted and then to implement it.

The absence of formal control or operating procedures in this particular industrial department led one of the members of the control staff to say, "Some people don't understand how our controller operates." And yet it did seem to me that the controller of this particular department, as well as his own general manager, was acting within the same pattern of control in his domain as that pattern established by the Executive Committee for the company as a whole.

It is easy to mistake the form of control for the spirit of control. Du Pont, by minimizing some of the conventional outward forms, nevertheless has a very strictly controlled system. Indeed a high degree of "disciplined individualism" is required of Du Pont executives to make this system work. Forecasts, return-on-investment, periodic cost studies are all inexorable taskmasters which require the highest exercise of the art of self-discipline and self-control.

The climate for the Du Pont system of management control is also abetted by the fact that all twelve general managers, and their key staff members, are domiciled in the same building in Wilmington, Delaware. This makes possible many informal meetings both with the staff people in the auxiliary departments and with Executive Committee members. Such close working relationships make it easier to formulate policies, to try out ideas, and to detect any possible imbalance before undesirable events become reflected in unfavorable return-on-investment results.

A similar climate of understanding based on close working relationships is also being created at lower echelons of management. Thus future executive talent is usually tagged after ten years of service. The men in their early thirties so tagged are moved about frequently. They not only cross functional lines but also may be transferred from one department to another. The purpose is to achieve a good exchange of new ideas as well as to develop well-rounded executives. An intimate knowledge of company policies and practices inevitably results from such experience. The net effect is a form of self-control or disciplined individualism of the highest order.

Return-on-Investment—Some Problems

Despite the basic simplicity of the return-on-investment concept, difficulties do exist in its computation and use. These difficulties should not be bypassed, even in a general chapter like this, without some mention. Thus the section that follows is in the nature of a brief technical note which might well be skipped over by those who have neither interest in the mechanics of this interesting control device nor the need to avoid possible pitfalls in its use.

The first mechanical difficulty that arises in developing a return-on-investment figure concerns the selection and valuation of the assets comprising the investment base. Specifically, should the calculation of plant and eqiupment be on a gross basis or net of depreciation?

In calculating return-on-investment, Du Pont uses the gross value of plant and working capital. Management's reasoning on this particular issue is as follows:

> Return on Investment as presented in the chart series is based upon *gross* operating investment and earnings *net* of depreciation.
>
> Gross operating investment represents all the plant, tools, equipment and working capital made available to operating management for its use; no deduction is made for current or other liabilities or for the reserve for depreciation. Since plant facilities are maintained in virtually top productive order during their working life, the depreciation reserve being considered primarily to provide for obsolescence, it would be inappropriate to consider that operating management was responsible for earning a return on only the net operating investment. Furthermore, if depreciable assets were stated at net depreciated values, earnings in each succeeding period would be related to an ever-decreasing investment; even with stable earnings, Return on Investment would continually rise, so that comparative Return on Investment ratios would fail to reveal the extent or trend of management performance. Relating earnings to investment that is stable and uniformly compiled provides a sound basis for comparing the "profitability of assets employed" as between years and between investments.
>
> In the case of any commitment of capital—e.g., an investment in a security—it is the expectation that in addition to producing earnings while committed, the principal will eventually be recovered. Likewise, in the case of funds invested in a project, it is expected that in addition to the return earned while invested, the working capital will be recovered through liquidation at the end of the project's useful life and the plant investment will be recovered through depreciation accruals. Since earnings must allow for this recovery of plant investment, they are stated net of depreciation.
>
> There are, of course, many different viewpoints among businessmen as to how Return on Investment should be computed for different purposes. It is the purpose of the Du Pont chart series to seek to present as clearly as possible the results produced by operating management. The capital, liability and reserve positions of an enterprise are largely a reflection of the philosophy of top management as to how the business should be financed. The Du Pont Company believes that operating management should be responsible for turning in a profit on capital assigned to that management, regardless of how the capital was raised.

The use of a gross assets base, without taking into account such reductions as depreciation, has greatly agitated some writers. One of these, for example, calls the use of a gross assets base "heresy."

On the other hand, Du Pont's reasoning is practically sound if not accounting pure. In the technologically progressive chemical business, plant and equipment that fail to show satisfactory productivity as measured by return-on-investment will usually be scrapped before the expiration of useful life.

Du Pont does give some recognition to depreciation charged to each industrial department. This recognition comes from the committee-approved formula used by the treasurer to assign cash to each of the twelve industrial departments. Thus, the cash allotted each quarter to a department for purposes of determining its gross assets base is one and a half times that department's forecasted average monthly cost of sales less the depreciation taken on that department's plant. To this degree the depreciation charge reduces the working capital on which a return must be earned.

A second mechanical problem in the calculation of return-on-investment concerns the changing value of the dollar. Thus the sales of today usually are inflated in dollar value when contrasted with the dollars tied up in the plant and equipment of other years. As the cheaper dollar inflates the prices charged by the firm, reported return should increase year by year, even without changes in operating efficiency and despite the use of a gross assets base. This results simply from having more sales or profit dollars despite the same volume of output or gross asset base.

Or put another way, in today's economy the maintenance of a fairly stable rate of return on any established grouping of assets is unwise. Such stability suggests a deterioration in a company's profit-making ability, unless prices are either reduced or held constant as a matter of conscious policy. Although deteriorating dollar values do not necessarily lessen the validity of return-on-investment as a control, they require added discrimination in its use.

A final mechanical difficulty in the use of the return-on-investment formula concerns the proper allocation of plant and working capital to some responsible level of management. Also involved is the collection of costs and revenues at the same level of management that is given responsibility for this investment. In other words, one of top management's major objectives in using return-on-investment is to make possible the delegation of authority and responsibility (and actual control) for the furtherance of overall company profits. The manager responsible for making such profits must have identifiable property over which he has control. Further, he also must have control over the marketing and production activities that use the property generating the costs and revenues. Lacking such control, he cannot be held responsible for the return-on-investment earned.

Many companies have stressed these practical difficulties of identifying such clusters of assets and then of giving managers the requisite authority as a reason for not using return-on-investment. For management to develop the needed organization, product divisions, production facilities, and reporting systems in order to use return-on-investment effectively admittedly can be a most difficult task. On the other hand, it is possible to adopt too puristic an approach to these problems. Take, for example, the allocation of investment and expenses in a plant that is perhaps producing items for two managers, each of whom is being held responsible for a "profit center." If the reported return is used to help management analyze its operations in order to improve overall performance, the matter of allocation is not too serious. If, on the contrary, the reported return is used to evaluate each of the managements or to serve as a basis for incentive pay, such joint tenancy can become an excuse to discredit this and perhaps other company controls.

Other shortcomings in using return-on-investment are essentially conceptual rather than mechanical. In other words, failure to understand some of the implications of this particular device can lead to bad decisions. The following are representative of some of these shortcomings:

1. Emphasis is placed on improvement of ratios rather than improvement of dollar profits, which may deprive stockholders of maximum returns through increased dollar profits. Highly profitable segments of the business also may have less incentive than less profitable segments to grow and to expand because of the difficulty for the profitable segments to maintain their high return ratio.

2. Emphasis on return-on-investment also tends to cultivate short-range thinking and to de-emphasize matters of overall corporate concern. For example, to increase the return ratio in the short run, management may be tempted to defer training programs or needed upkeep and maintenance. Leasing and subcontracting also became particularly attractive as ways for improving showing. Perhaps another way of saying all this is that the short-run emphasis is on immediate cost savings rather than on investment for the future.

3. Return-on-investment tends to be a poor measure of performance because many extraneous and noncontrollable factors enter the picture. A competitor's action may determine prices, a shift in economic climate can effect volume, a new product may make plant obsolete, or a strike in a customer's plant can ruin sales. Often, too, present returns are the result of the wisdom or unwisdom of past managers rather than of the incumbents. Older buildings constructed at lower price levels tend to contribute to a better showing than newer buildings or equipment with no marked productivity benefits to show for the higher construction costs.

4. The climate for control is detrimentally affected by the tendency toward conservatism which the return-on-investment measure breeds. Taking risks, in other words, is discouraged rather than encouraged. Also, organizational conflicts grow out of the favored position of those responsible for earning return-on-investment. The idea here seems to be that staff people in particular lose much of their influence. The managers who are given responsibility for the return are the ones who call the tune.

5. Return-on-investment gives undue significance to capital resources. In the past, capital may have been the scarce factor limiting corporate growth. In the future, however, is not management know-how the factor that must be husbanded? If so, does return-on-investment provide an adequate guide for allocating managerial skills? Especially on government contracts where facilities are government furnished, are adequate criteria being developed to recompense industry (or universities) for both the technical and managerial man-hours expended?

The preceding criticisms of return-on-investment, as well as the various practical problems connected with its use, do not necessarily limit its value as a control device. Actually, one of the principal values of return-on-investment lies in its forcing management to give due consideration to just such factors as those discussed. The final investment return figure is seldom the most critical matter anyway. Of far greater significance is the overall approach to executive control cultivated by management's knowing emphasis on this figure.

Summary Remarks

In summary, the Du Pont Company serves as an outstanding illustration of how a system of executive control can be designed. The basic ingredient of this or any other successful system is continuous and systematic planning, programming, and follow-up or review. The primary function of Du Pont's Executive Committee is to see that just such planning, programming, and review is being performed. Return-on-investment is simply the particular technique that top management finds useful in helping it see that operations are properly conducted.

Specifically, return-on-investment accomplishes the following objectives: (1) it spells out responsibility for profits, (2) it provides a way of evaluating the job being done by departmental managers, (3) it gets away from the gross sales or volume phobia, (4) it indicates the need for getting rid of unprofitable items when the return falls below prescribed minimums, (5) it provides a way of deciding on alternative uses of scarce funds in the sense of giving priority to high return items, and (6) it provides a common goal, or measure, which all can agree on.

The difficulties in using the return-on-investment measure have been pointed out but not stressed, simply because for Du Pont these have proved quite surmountable. Thus Du Pont has been able to divide operating investment into twelve industrial departments plus subdivisions of these. Common backgrounds and experience have also enabled the Executive Committee to use return-on-investment as an invaluable focal point for its information system. Since the charts and related reports only serve as a basis for planning and for analysis of departmental operations, return-on-investment is not the heavy-handed control that it might first appear. Thus the Executive Committee, through its staff or auxiliary department reports, keeps in close touch with other important matters such as executive development, employee relations, safety, research, and public relations. Share of the market or well-rounded product lines are other considerations that cannot be minimized. However, these mean relatively little unless the actual return on the overall investment is satisfactory.

The importance of return-on-investment in accounting for the successful working of Du Pont's system of executive control cannot be denied. Nonetheless, without both the Executive and Finance Committees this tool would not be as effective as it is. The importance of the Executive Committee lies primarily in the fact that the members of this committee have no operating responsibilities; they have time to think. They are in a position to develop an overall point of view, and to take a detached, judicious look at company operations.

The Executive Committee also provides a degree of stability to management that seldom exists when most of the authority is vested in a single president. The fact, too, that the Executive Committee has time to read and to study reports means that these reports in turn are taken seriously by lower echelons of management. It also means that since the Executive Committee takes time to plan, the departmental managers must do likewise; otherwise they will show up poorly in the periodic chart room reviews. The pattern of behavior, then, set by the members of the Executive Committee serves as an example for the entire organization and thereby sets the climate for control.

The importance of reports in the Du Pont system of control needs continual re-emphasis, too. At Du Pont these reports are read and used. Accordingly they become an excellent medium for planning, for communication, and for measuring performance and are not just symbolic of red tape as such reports often are. To achieve such a balanced state of affairs is extremely difficult to accomplish and further points up the need for providing top managers with time to devote to such matters.

One final point needs additional emphasis. The Du Pont system of executive control works because the chief officers of the company clearly recognize the difference between direction and control. They recognize that in a company as complex as Du Pont considerable responsibility and authority must be given to the department managers. This degree of authority and responsibility must be given to encourage a venturesome spirit. It must also be given because no single man is capable of directing in any detail an organization as complex as Du Pont. This means that lower echelons of management must be allowed to go ahead on some projects even if the likelihood of mistakes is great. After all, mistakes are the stuff of experience, the price that has to be paid for progress and creativity.

Despite the unquestioned success of the Du Pont system of management control, this system is not equally applicable to all companies. Few companies, for example, have the depth in manpower to make a committee system like Du Pont's work; nor can they afford to be as selective in their choice of investment opportunities as Du Pont is. But more to the point, any effective system of control is a matter of trial and growth. It is a mistake to think that a system effective in one company can be transplanted in full bloom to another company. The most that we can hope for from this analysis of the operation of the Du Pont Company is to see ways in which each company's system of control may be strengthened and improved.

Reading 12-2

The Past Is History . . .
The Future Is Planning

By E. B. Rickard*

If a management control system is to operate effectively, it must be placed in the hands of imaginative, creative people with sound business judgment who, in fact, have the capacity to develop farsighted solutions to the problems, risks, and changing environment that confront the patricular enterprise. How to recognize such people in the first place, and assure their promotion in the business organization in the second place, is a subject of the greatest importance—but it is not a subject with which we shall be concerned here.

A second essential ingredient in an effective management control system is the existence of a set of organizational responsibilities which have been defined with reasonable clarity and which allow individual members of the organization to define with reasonable precision the contribution they are expected to make to the welfare of the enterprise, and the manner in which their contribution relates to, or is affected by, other individuals who are working toward the common goals of the enterprise.

There is a third essential aspect of a management control system—the one we will discuss in this article. It relates to this question: *Given an able, imaginative and farsighted management group possessed of good business judgment and with clearly defined responsibilities, what can be done to harness and direct the energies of that group to achieve the optimum results for the business enterprise?*

---

* Formerly controller, now general parts and service manager, Ford division, Ford Motor Company. From *The Controller*, October, 1962. Reproduced by permission of Financial Executives Institute.

It is obvious that some companies should rank higher than others in managerial effectiveness, based on historical results. Organizations such as General Motors, du Pont, and Standard Oil of New Jersey, have shown an extraordinary ability to achieve excellent results in spite of complete changes in their executive roster over a period of years.

On the other hand, we are all acquainted with companies which have been organized around the business genius of one man—or which have been organized to exploit the advantages that have accrued from a particular invention or a particular technological development unique to that company—or which have been favored with some fortunate accident of locational advantage that has conferred on the company a competitive headstart. However, the advantages enjoyed by these latter companies are transient and temporary. In time the genius passes on, the invention becomes obsolete or locational advantages give way to less favorable developments or new competitors.

What we should be seeking in our quest for the essential ingredient of an effective management system are those elements which tend to assure perennial success for a business enterprise in the face of technological changes, in spite of changes in management personnel, and regardless of the elimination of some temporary advantages which the company may have enjoyed.

If you read the literature of business management you find countless discussions of the individual tools of the control technician, such as, budgeting, forecasting, profit-planning, cash management, performance-reporting, and so on. However, you do not find these separate tools exposited as part of an integrated general management philosophy which lends itself to application in different companies in different industries with different kinds of business problems. Too often the discussion describes how a particular company in a particular situation dealt with a particular control problem.

The recent past has seen, however, a considerable amount of introspection on this subject. As competition becomes keener, as decisions become more complex, and as the problem of survival becomes more acute, the premium placed on effective management action becomes increasingly high. The cost-price squeeze in which industry has found itself in the past few years and the increasing competition from foreign sources have made it mandatory for businessmen to seek more effective means of organizing and directing the collective efforts of the individuals who contribute to the business process.

There was a time when we could excel foreign competitors in the automotive industry because of superior production methods. While we paid higher wage rates in this country, we overcame that disadvantage with superior productivity. However, such advantages are rapidly disappearing and our reliance in the future, it seems, will have to be placed increasingly on superior and more responsive management controls.

Electronic data processing has been touted as a part of the answer to this fundamental problem. Others have emphasized the contributions to be made through the mathematical techniques of operations research. In the curricula of the business schools of the country, you find increasing attention being given to a subject described as "Managerial Accounting." All these different approaches profess to improve a manager's ability to deal more effectively with his complicated environment. They all are provincial in their approach, however, and tend to deal in the language of technicians—a language that does not lend itself to general management consumption or motivation.

This article will discuss some concepts which appear to have validity in the area of managerial effectiveness. To some extent these views have been formed as a result of participation in the research project of Financial Executives Research Foundation on the subject of management planning and control. They have also been influenced by my intimate association with the financial control system of the Ford Motor Company.

MANAGEMENT'S RESPONSIBILITIES

Before we can talk about management controls we must define management's job more precisely. Unless we can agree on the essential responsibilities of management, it is obviously impossible to agree on the systems, methods, procedures or approaches by which management shall discharge its responsibilities.

We probably would all agree that managerial responsibility is epitomized by decision-making—that is, choosing among a number of alternative courses of action. The alternatives may involve such fundamental considerations as basic corporate policies, future products or facility programs, or other major plans or proposals that will have an important long-run influence on the future profits and asset requirements of the enterprise. In addition, management must make decisions relative to the near-term or shorter-run operating problems of the enterprise, and must devise the plans or programs which should be adopted within the confines of the fundamental policies and programs which have been adopted. Moreover, management must determine whether or not the performance of the several operating segments of the business is satisfactory, and what shall be done in those instances where performance is not satisfactory.

THE DECISION-MAKER

The role of decision-maker, which is the essential role of management, is obviously a complicated one. Management is seldom asked to choose between two alternatives of which only one is acceptable. On the contrary, an endless and overwhelming array of alternatives usually exists. The number of alternatives is limited only by the imagination and creativeness which management can bring to bear on its problems. In addition, the degree of risk that each alternative entails may vary as greatly as the potential rewards.

It is not enough to recognize that decision-making is the essence of management's task. We must also agree on the criteria which management should use in reaching its decisions. *What are the standards that should govern when one alternative is selected in preference to another?*

There are only two criteria that should guide management: The first of these criteria is that management should seek to maximize its profits in the long run with the resources and assets that are at its disposal; and second, management should seek opportunities for the employment of additional capital or additional resources on which it can earn a satisfactory rate of return.

There really is no other course of action open to management in the long run. You may find a business enterprise that is sufficiently well off and so strong financially that it can enjoy the luxury of making decisions on a basis that is not profit-oriented. This, however, cannot be a constant way of life in a competitive business situation. If management pursues such an approach to decision-making, it sooner or later will find itself compelled either to retrace its steps and begin making decisions on a sound profit basis, or it will be forced out of business by its competitors.

You will note that I have not suggested that management attempt to maximize profits in the *short run*. Short-run profits can be realized by disregarding high-quality standards, price-gouging, or other practices which will, in time, alienate the customer by giving him less for his money. The only way to maximize profits *in the long run* is to adopt a consumer-oriented approach to your business. You must cultivate your customers with care and supply value with quality, or they will spend their money elsewhere. The ability to please the public, while earning over a long period of time a rate of return as good as, or better than your competitor, is the only hallmark of a successful company. It should also be noted that giving more people improved products at lower cost is the essence of social responsibility and Christian endeavor.

LOOK AHEAD—NOT BACK

If you accept the premise that management, in its decision-making role, must be primarily concerned with profit maximization, there are some important corollary propositions that follow.

One of these corollaries is that management is, or at least should be, primarily interested in the future not in the past. That, perhaps, is a trite statement. Yet it appears not to be trite to many people, including controllers, academicians, and members of the accounting fraternity. There is a considerable feeling afoot that historical accounting information is a pretty useful tool, along with historical production, sales, and operating statistics, if you have to make an important decision.

I couldn't disagree more fully. Such data are helpful in deciding what your problems are, but they don't help a bit in choosing among alternative ways of solving those problems. They form a basis upon which you can erect the data or the analyses which you need if you are to make a decision. However, taken alone, accounting information relates to the past and there isn't a confounded thing you can do about the past. The accounting data are historical and they are recorded. But they are also irrevocable. Management must seek to order the corporate affairs of the months and years ahead so that the profit and loss statement and the balance sheet will be pleasing to look at in the future. It cannot do that by paying attention primarily to historical information.

Obviously, it is necessary for a business management to know the current and past levels of profits, or the quality of historic cost or sales performance, so that it can be aware of its present position and can determine better the magnitude and priority of the tasks that lie ahead of it. But management's decisions relate to the months and years ahead for which no financial statement, budget performance reports and sales statistics are yet available.

Looking back over my experience in Ford Motor Company, I cannot think of any significant management decision which relied on historical accounting data in choosing among alternative courses of action. Such data are simply not responsive to the needs of the situation. I do not mean to suggest that accountants do not render an important service in corporate affairs. We would not employ as many as we do in industry if that were so. It does seem clear, however, that the historical reporting function is slanted in directions which are not related to the main stream of management responsibility.

There are some additional corollaries which follow if you accept the premise that management's basic responsibility is to maximize profits in the long run. Rather than deal with these corollaries as abstract philosophical concepts, it may be more useful to develop their nature and meaning by using selected aspects of the financial control system of the Ford Division to illustrate the points I have in mind.

While I shall use the Ford Division as a vehicle to illustrate an approach to the development of a management control system, the basic propositions which we shall be discussing are not only applicable to the automotive industry but, in my opinion, are generally applicable to other companies in other industries, whether they may be manufacturers of plastic products, retailers of soft goods, or sellers of a service.

ELEMENTS OF PLANNING AND CONTROL

Our discussion of the elements of an effective management planning and control system can be divided into three broad sections. They are:

1. The decision-making process;
2. The manner in which a business enterprise accumulates the effect of operating decisions to form a total operating plan; and

3. The methods or techniques used in evaluating the effectiveness with which individuals execute the plans and programs of the enterprise.

In dealing with the first area, the decision-making process, I would like to discuss the method by which decisions are reached in an area which is of major importance to an automotive manufacturer, that is, an annual model-change program.

For many companies one of the most difficult, complex and risk-laden areas of decision-making relates to the introduction of new products or services. In this area the automobile industry not only faces the unique problem of attempting to determine whether a proposed product will meet the demands of the public three to five years in the future, but it also must recognize that any such decision will be a major determinant of our future profits, first because of the large investment required by new product programs, and also because of the heavy financial penalties which result if the product does not appeal to the public when it is introduced.

Before describing this aspect of our control system, it might be useful to review the timing and planning strategy required to bring a new product to the market.

PRODUCT-PLANNING CYCLE

Exhibit 1 traces the product-planning cycle of a typical model change which we shall assume is the 1964 Ford Galaxie.

The first several years of the cycle are basically a conceptual period that ends with the approval of the product program. This phase would include the market research and planning which may begin three to five years before the eventual introduction of the product. The product decision we make will be shaped, to an important degree, by the results of this research as to probably future automotive demand and, particularly, the anticipated wishes of the public.

The next two steps will be the development of alternative product specifications and cost and product objectives.

After evaluation of alternative plans, a specific program for the 1964 Ford car is recommended, usually about two and a half years prior to the scheduled production of the particular model. Following this "paper" program proposal, a full-sized clay version of the proposed vehicle is prepared to permit a more detailed and precise review of the particular features of the new model in terms of sheet metal contours, ornamentation and interior trim.

When the clay model has been approved, a little less than two years prior to the first regular production, we enter a phase which we might call the pre-production section of the cycle in which the detailed engineering is completed, facilities plans are prepared, tooling is fabricated, and finally, intro-

Exhibit 1

PRODUCT PLANNING CYCLE OF THE 1964 GALAXIE

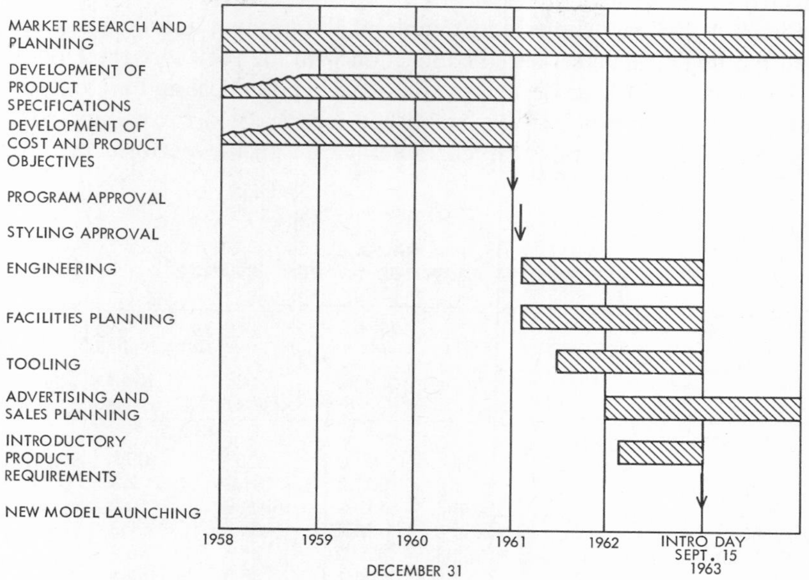

ductory advertising and sales programs are developed and vehicle-pricing plans are reviewed and approved.

When all these steps have been completed, we are ready for the final steps leading to the production of the new model and shortly thereafter its introduction to the public by our dealers. It is important to recognize that prior to the time the vehicle is introduced to the public, we have made decisions that will, for the most part, determine the cost and price position of the vehicle, its acceptability in the market place and, hence, the financial success or lack of success we will experience with the particular model. It should also be noted that the pattern of our planning is not unlike the planning cycle which many companies should follow when faced with a major product decision. Therefore, the way we approach such a problem would seem to have application beyond the automotive industry.

CONTROL SYSTEM

We shall now describe the way in which our control system operates to assist the planning and execution of this typical product program from its inception to the introduction of the model to the public, and the way in which we attempt to assure that our plans and programs will be financially sound.

When management reviews the 1964 Galaxie product program, it is given first a full statement of the product and merchandising considerations that have dictated the design recommendations on which that program is based. As an integral part of such a review, a summary of product and financial objectives is presented.

Figure 1 (below) shows an example of the product and financial objectives that might be presented in connection with the review of the Division's plans for the 1964 Galaxie. All the data are hypothetical and are only illustrative. The product objectives established for the 1964 car will include details of the vehicle's physical characteristics, specific performance goals,

Figure 1

1964 GALAXIE
REVIEW OF A PROPOSED PRODUCT CHANGE

	1964 Galaxie	*Comparative Data*		
	Original Objective	*1960 Falcon*	*1962 Galaxie*	*1962 Competitor A*
Package Size				
Weight	3670	2387	3771	3702
Length overall	209.9	181.2	209.3	209.6
Wheelbase	119.0	109.5	119.0	119.0
Height	55.0	54.5	54.8	55.0
Headroom—front	39.0	38.8	38.1	37.9
Legroom—front	44.1	43.0	44.1	43.4
Performance				
Acceleration (feet travelled in 10 seconds)	452	387	443	429
Passing time at 50 M.P.H. (sec.)	10.4	14.2	11.2	11.0
Average miles per gallon	15.3	24.0	14.9	14.9
Volumes and Timing				
Initial production date	9-1-63	9-1-59	9-1-61	
Planning volume (units)	700,000	500,000	700,000	
Maximum capacity (units)	1,200,000	750,000	1,200,000	
Variable Costs				
Material	$1420	$1163	$1424	
Labor and overhead	151	146	155	
Total Variable Costs	$1571	$1309	$1579	
Fixed Expenditures (Millions)				
Styling	$ 2.3	$ 1.9	$ 2.1	
Engineering	10.9	9.6	11.2	
Tooling	55.4	44.2	36.0	
Launching	11.7	9.8	8.7	
Facilities	8.9	6.9	6.2	
Total Fixed Expenditures	$ 89.2	$ 72.4	$ 64.2	
Ford Division Profits (At financial planning volume)				
Profits—economic—per unit	xxx	xxx	xxx	
—accounted—per unit	xxx	xxx	xxx	
—accounted—millions	73.8	xxx	xxx	
Return on assets (after taxes)	xx.x%	xx.x%	xx.x%	

including acceleration, passing performance, and a specific gasoline-economy objective. These product objectives are developed in recognition of the characteristics of prior model Ford cars, competitive products, and whatever our marketing research studies have told us about probable future consumers' desires.

In addition to detailed product objectives on package size and performance, the product presentation includes the product's related volume characteristics, including planning volume and maximum capacity, as well as the initial production date.

Next, the variable costs of the new model are compared with the costs of prior models and other car lines. In addition to the variable cost objectives, the major fixed expenditures that are directly associated with the program are shown. These include the expenditures that will be required for styling, engineering, tooling, launching and facilities.

In addition to detailed product and cost objectives, the presentation includes detailed profit objectives. You will note that the Ford Division profit objectives have been stated at a so-called "financial planning volume." It is necessary to take a moment to discuss the volume concept that we use in developing our future financial projections in an industry beset by wide swings in consumer demand.

Obviously, vehicle sales volumes can and do vary greatly from year to year. We have no way of determining the probable level of industry volume in each of the next three or four years, nor can we be sure of the share of industry volume which will be secured by the Galaxie. To solve this volume problem, we attempt to estimate the probable average annual sales volume of the Galaxie and all Ford cars over the next five years and use that vehicle volume as the basis for our planning. Under this approach we are willing to accept the penalty of low volume and low profits in certain years in the expectation that it will be offset by higher profits in those years when sales volume is above average. We call this assumed volume "financial planning volume." The use of financial planning volume as a planning base provides an essential continuity to our pricing, product planning and cost planning. We do not expect to raise our prices or cheapen our products in years when volumes are below average and, conversely, we do not cut our prices or increase our product costs when volumes are above average. As we look further into our system of financial planning and control, you will see that financial planning volume is the basis on which we make all our financial projections.

The financial summary of program objectives, shown at the bottom of Figure 1, includes the estimated Ford Division profits, both before and after the assignment of fixed costs, shown on a per-unit basis and in total millions of dollars. We use the term "economic profit" to refer to profits excluding fixed expenses, while the term "accounted profits" includes all costs that are properly assignable to the Galaxie in 1964. We also determine the assets properly assignable to the Galaxie product line and establish a return on assets objective.

The cost, profit and expenditure information shown in Figure 1 does not represent a set of financial projections which have been developed in the Controller's Office of the Division; rather, each operating activity which is affected by the future program (especially, manufacturing, purchasing and engineering) is furnished with a detailed description of the product program so that it is in a position to evaluate the probable effect of the program on its operations and enters into a commitment to the effect that it will be able to carry out its share of such a program for the amount shown as its responsibility.

Each of the financial figures is backed up in considerable detail. One of the lessons you learn rather early in the game when you are involved in controlling the results of future programs is that you can not control in any greater detail than the detail with which you developed your initial plan. If you plan on spending $10 million (with no detail) for tooling, and actual expenditures turn out to be $11 million, you have no means of determining what went wrong or why the $1 million overrun occurred. You can only determine the reason for the overrun and take appropriate corrective action if you have developed your initial estimates in sufficient detail so that you can isolate the specific tools that have caused the overrun and can determine why the initial estimate was less than the actual cost. Only then can you truly understand the overrun. The same is true of other expenditure figures as well as the profit estimates.

An effective control system must begin with the development of objectives in detail rather than in aggregates. If you don't plan in detail, you can't control in detail. If you don't control in detail, you don't control effectively. How much detail is required is, of course, a matter of judgment which must be determined in the light of the specific problems which face the company and the seriousness or urgency with which those problems are viewed.

PROFIT PICTURE IN ADVANCE

Returning to our hypothetical 1964 Galaxie program, it is quite possible that when the initial analysis is completed, we may find that the planned program is not a particularly attractive venture. It may involve cost increases or asset investments which cannot be contained within our established objectives. If this is the case, the product assumptions are changed or other modifications are made to be sure that the plan, in its initial conception, is a financially attractive venture. The key point is that management is told precisely what the expenditures and profits are going to be before they are asked to make a decision. Stated differently, our objective is to have management aware of the full financial impact of future programs before a decision is made, not after.

In presenting the 1964 Galaxie proposal, we also summarize the effect of the decision on the profit position of the Galaxie, the Ford Division, and the company. Figure 2 shows how we would describe the effect of a product decision on company profits. We have shown at the top an estimate of profits, assets and returns for the model years 1962 through 1965. We have then shown the effect on profits, assets and returns of the 1964 Galaxie program decision. In the years 1962 and 1963, the program will reduce profits $2.4 million and $3.0 million, respectively. However, in 1964 and 1965, the program will improve profits $10.0 million and $20.0 million. In the bottom section we have shown the current estimate of profits, assets and returns, assuming the proposed 1964 Galaxie program is approved.

Figure 2

EFFECT OF 1964 GALAXIE PROGRAM
GALAXIE PROFITS, ASSETS AND RETURNS
(At Financial Planning Volume)

	Model Years			
	1962	*1963*	*1964*	*1965*
Prior Estimate				
Profits before taxes (millions)	$ 71.0	$ 63.0	$ 63.8	$ 66.8
Assets (millions)	xxx.x	xxx.x	xxx.x	xxx.x
Return after taxes (percent)	xx.x%	xx.x%	xx.x%	xx.x%
Effect of Proposed Program				
Profits before taxes (millions)	$ (2.4)	$ (3.0)	$ 10.0	$ 20.0
Assets (millions)	(0.5)	(5.0)	(20.0)	(10.0)
Return after taxes (percent)	(0.4)%	(0.9)%	0.6%	2.9%
Current Estimate				
Profits before taxes (millions)	$ 68.6	$ 60.0	$ 73.8	$ 86.8
Assets (millions)	xxx.x	xxx.x	xxx.x	xxx.x
Return after taxes (percent)	xx.x%	xx.x%	xx.x%	xx.x%

As indicated before, this kind of summary is shown for the individual product line, for the Ford Division, and for the total company, and permits the management of the Division and the company to see their over-all profit position at the time a major product decision is made and to examine this information *before* a decision is made.

The objective of our control system as it relates to decision-making is to determine the profit effect and the degree of financial risk involved, evaluate the attractiveness of available alternatives, assure that all the reasonable alternatives have been explored, that the representations made by the supporting offices are appropriate, attainable, and are recorded as commitments which those offices will be expected to achieve. Such detailed analyses are not only undertaken in the product area but are a part of every significant decision which management makes. Such matters as major facility changes, sales contests, major changes in advertising and sales promotion programs, quality programs, pricing actions, cost-reduction programs, reliability and durability programs, and so forth, are ordinarily subjected to a careful financial evaluation as part of the management approval process.

PERIODIC EVALUATIONS

Thus far we have indicated that an effective control system must provide management with evaluations and analyses that assist in decision-making. However, it must also provide management with periodic summaries or evaluations of the total profit and investment position of the business. In other words, we must synthesize the total effect of the operating plans and programs that have been approved into a consistent and coordinated control program for the entire business. The vehicle through which this synthesis is accomplished at Ford is the profit plan or profit budget. The profit plan is not a financial forecast but is a synthesis of the collective effect on profits of all the approved plans and programs of operating activities of the business. We take the same decisions we've just been talking about plus those that can be reasonably foreseen at that point in time, bundle them up and take a financial reading, crosscut through all of them, and produce a statement of the profits, assets, and returns that will be realized in future years if everyone meets his commitments. We try to be realistic in the sense that if somebody will obviously fail to meet his commitments and management has in effect agreed that the deviation is unavoidable, we modify our plans accordingly. However, we try to assure that the decision to depart from the plan gets proper review and approval. We don't cavalierly disregard the commitments that people have made. We try to hold their feet to the fire if it appears at all reasonable.

FUTURE PROFITS

Exhibit 2 shows a chart from the annual presentation of our profit plan to corporate management. In the course of this review we discuss historical profits but the major emphasis is on our profit plans for the future. As shown by the two lines, profits are stated on two bases: First, at actual volume which varies with industry volume changes and Ford market penetration; second, at the Division's financial planning volume which is constant volume. Future profits are shown only at financial planning volume. We also show, in this presentation, the profit projection which was included in last year's review. This provides management with an opportunity to review the organization's total profit performance versus the commitments we made a year ago.

It should be emphasized again that the projections for future years in our profit plan are not mere forecasts of profit results. They are the cumulative result of specific detailed commitments which have been received from each operating activity in the Division. Consequently, our projections represent a financial expression of the specific contributions each office has agreed to make to the profits of the Division in future years.

Exhibit 2

ACCOUNTED PROFITS BEFORE TAXES

(Hypothetical)

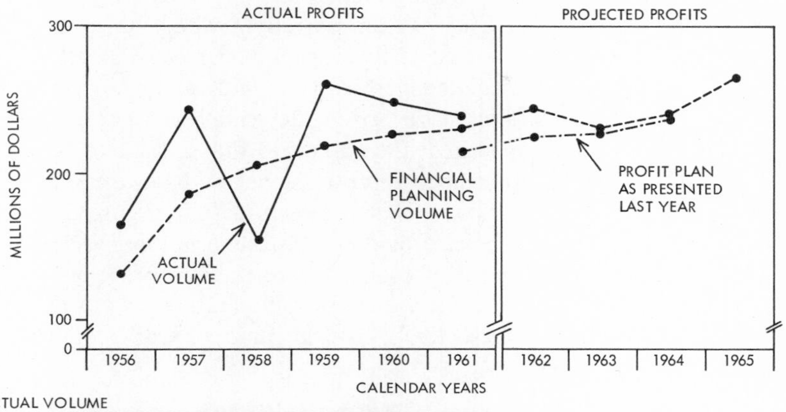

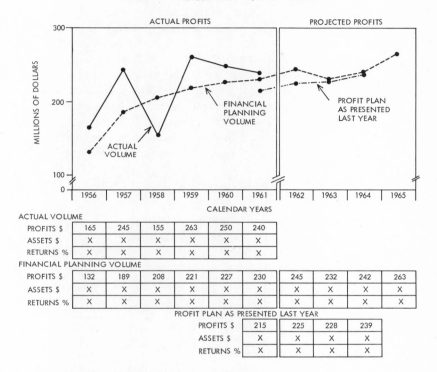

ACTUAL VOLUME

	1956	1957	1958	1959	1960	1961
PROFITS $	165	245	155	263	250	240
ASSETS $	X	X	X	X	X	X
RETURNS %	X	X	X	X	X	X

FINANCIAL PLANNING VOLUME

	1956	1957	1958	1959	1960	1961	1962	1963	1964	1965
PROFITS $	132	189	208	221	227	230	245	232	242	263
ASSETS $	X	X	X	X	X	X	X	X	X	X
RETURNS %	X	X	X	X	X	X	X	X	X	X

PROFIT PLAN AS PRESENTED LAST YEAR

	1961	1962	1963	1964
PROFITS $	215	225	228	239
ASSETS $	X	X	X	X
RETURNS %	X	X	X	X

The remainder of the profit plan presentation to corporate management describes in some detail these future operating plans both in financial and nonfinancial terms.

The question which frequently arises in this connection is how far the profit plans of an enterprise should be carried into the future. *Should we seek to project profits for one year, five years, or some other period of time*? It seems apparent that the answer to this question will vary among companies—there is no simple pat answer that can be given. A company should extend its planning far enough into the future to be able to anticipate and adapt itself to developments that may have a potential effect on its future operations. The objective of a control system is to avoid the possibility of the company being suddenly confronted with adverse developments which have not been foreseen and for which no provision has been made in the operating plans and programs of the enterprise. It would appear that most companies should be developing their future plans in detail for at least four or five years in the future, while in some instances, five to ten years might not be an unreasonable period.

MEASURING EFFECTIVENESS

The third and final element in the Ford Division's control system is the measurement of how effectively individuals and the total Division execute the plans and programs in line with the objectives which have been established. The essential characteristic of this aspect of our control system is that we compare actual or anticipated performance with planned performance. We isolate the variances that have arisen, determine the cause, and take whatever action we can to correct the situations that appear to be unsatisfactory. Some of our performance reports, however, have a unique flavor which deserves special mention. This is illustrated in Figure 3 which is taken from a monthly report we provide for the general management of the Division. It describes the status of each forward product program.

As shown at the top of the report, the objective (referred to as the "Product Planning Committee Objective") is the same objective approved by

Figure 3

STATUS OF 1964 GALAXIE PROGRAM
CURRENT ESTIMATE VERSUS PRODUCT PLANNING COMMITTEE OBJECTIVE

	Profits Per Unit	*Assets Per Unit*	*Return After Taxes*	*Fixed Expenditures (Millions)*
Product Planning Committee Objective	$xxx	$xxx	x.x%	$89.2
Current Estimate	xxx	xxx	x.x	88.3
Current Estimate Favorable/(Unfavorable) versus P.P.C. Objective	$ 5	$ 2	0.5%	$ 0.9
Explanation of Variance				
Design Changes:				
Improved hood release mechanism	$(1)			
Added floor pan reinforcement	(2)			
Seat belt attaching hardware to all models	(1)			
Tooling:				
Reduced cost of rear doors due to styling change	1	1		0.4
Projected reduction in tooling cost due to change in vendor	1	1		0.5
Freight:				
Increased usage of multilevel rail cars...	5			(0.1)
Launching and Overhead Costs:				
Closing of Chester Assembly Plant	1			0.3
Added cost of redesigning front suspension				(0.2)
Final estimate of the effect on labor costs of the U.A.W. contract	1			
Total Variance	$ 5	$ 2	0.5%	$ 0.9

management for the original program. This is the base with which the current position is compared. All product changes, revisions in cost estimates, and projected expenditure overruns or underruns are summarized monthly and presented to management with concise explanations as to why the program is ahead or behind objective.

If this report were to indicate, for example, that the program was lagging behind its financial objectives, management attention would be directed to the unfavorable areas and attempts would be made to correct the specific problem that caused the overrun. Failing this, all aspects of the program would be subjected to an intensive review to offset the unfavorable variance by taking action in other areas of the program.

The point that warrants emphasis in connection with this discussion of performance reporting is that we seek to determine far enough in advance what our performance will be so that we can change our thinking if we do not like what we see. If a program has been reviewed and approved, we do not necessarily wait until that approval has been translated into actual profits or actual costs and is, therefore, beyond repair.

MANAGEMENT CONTROL PATTERN

In addition to reports for each product line, we also prepare a monthly financial summary that brings together the effect of all future product programs and all other operating programs. We compare this to our position as planned in the annual operating plan discussed earlier.

In Exhibit 3 I have attempted to portray grapically the cyclical or circular pattern of an effective management control system. Each step bears a direct relationship to the next succeeding step. We have placed "Performance Evaluations" at the top of the circle. These evaluations, when combined

Exhibit 3

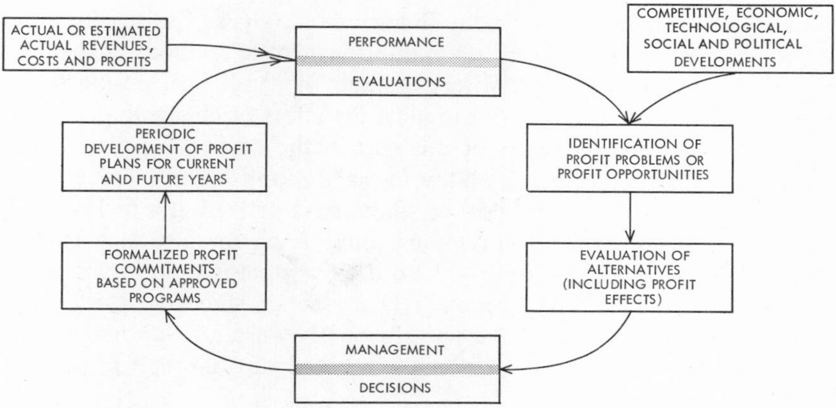

with the impact of competitive, economic, technological, social and political developments, lead management to the identification of profit problems or profit opportunities which confront the business. In turn, the identification of such problems or opportunities requires that management evaluate the acceptability of alternative courses of action for dealing with each such situation. Out of such deliberations flow specific management decisions.

The profit commitments which are implicit in those decisions must be formalized and recorded. They must also periodically be accumulated into a profit plan, or financial plan, that summarizes the profit effect in current and future years of the approved plans and programs of the enterprise. These profit plans or profit budgets, when compared with actual or estimated actual revenues, cost and profits, represent the basic tool of performance evaluation. Thus, we return to the beginning of the cycle we have been describing.

PROOF OF THE PUDDING

One of the notable successes in the automobile business in recent years is the Ford Falcon, which outsold all other compact cars within three months after it had been introduced. It is a product of the management control system we have been discussing. Not only did the Falcon turn out to be a success in the market place but it was priced from $70 to $90 below comparable vehicles of our competitors brought out at the same time. Notwithstanding its low price, the Falcon has been a financial success for the company as well. This is probably less true of our competitors who introduced similar products at the same time. They had to cut prices substantially in order to stay in the competitive race. Our management control system can take an important part of the credit for the success of the Falcon.

You will note from this description of our control system that our management does not rely on accounting information or historical reports of costs or profits as a tool of control. It seems to me that there is a moral here that has not been grasped by many financial executives. The success of our system has not been contingent upon improvement in methods of allocating costs or the use of so-called "direct costing" in handling fixed charges, or the re-evaluation of fixed assets to reflect the effect of changing price levels on the economy. Refinements of this sort in the accounting process have little to do with management's ability to make sound future plans.

Accountants, after a great deal of study, have arrived at a highly refined approach to the problem of developing sound and generally accepted rules of accounting practices. They have also done a great deal in improving the systems of internal control that protect the presently owned assets of the company. Financial executives have not always shown a similar zeal for protecting the future financial position of the company through a system of forward-looking controls.

There is little solace in the knowledge that we have accurately recorded all the events that have pushed a company into bankruptcy. It is much more useful and satisfying to devote our energies to the development of a system of controls which prevents bankruptcy.

SUMMARY

Further refinements in the accounting process are not necessary to meet management's need for useful control tools. Historical accounting information is one subject management should not pay attention to in decision-making. What management *should* pay attention to, and this cannot be overemphasized, is the development of a control system which has three essential characteristics:

1. The system must provide management with adequate information on the probable financial consequences of a decision *before* the decision is made—not after.
2. The financial results on which a decision is based must be analyzed in enough detail so that the responsible persons in the organization can be assigned a clearly defined financial task in carrying out the decision. Only by so doing can we accept and meet the financial commitments which are implicit in the particular decision.
3. A system must exist under which you know well in advance whether each operating activity will meet its commitments so that appropriate and *timely* action may be taken if it appears that a particular program is not on target.

If we compare these criteria with the usual published description of the type of information that management should receive from a controller's office, it is apparent that they have very little in common. It is easy to place too much emphasis on the value to management of budget performance reports, comparative cost reports, and similar analyses of past performance. It is true that financial data have to be the universal language of business management, since they are the only common denominator which allows management to deal with such unrelated factors as units of output, square feet of floor space, quality of production, number of hourly employes, and so on. While you must control a business enterprise in terms of revenues, costs and profits, it is essential to recognize that an effective control system must be able to determine the factors that will affect costs and profits in the years ahead rather than analyze the factors that have influenced costs and profits in the months or years that have gone by.

Reading 12-3

MPC—Key to Profit Growth

By R. Stanley Laing*

I can assure you at the outset that we in the business equipment industry have not developed a new electronic computer which has either solved or eliminated the problem of achieving effective management control. I will say, however, that our industry is intensely interested in this subject because our business, like our product line, is highly complex and the decision-making processes are highly involved.

Every year our industry develops hundreds of new pieces of equipment designed to improve the efficiency of business everywhere and yet every year the total number of clerical workers rises sharply. As Werner Von Braun, the eminent missile scientist, said recently, "We face only two obstacles in the battle for space—gravity and paper work."

Although much has been written about management planning and control systems, it has almost universally been based on the experience of our larger decentralized companies—companies which have intentionally designed their organizations to provide more effective control. These companies have generally decentralized by-product line so that responsibility could be placed for engineering, product development, manufacturing and sale of a single product group to more clearly measure profit results and return on investment.

Little has been written on planning and control in those innumerable corporations, including my own, which, for a multitude of valid reasons, have not chosen to decentralize. The need for effective management control is every bit as acute, but product profit or return on investment targets cannot be nearly so easily assigned. For instance, the vice president in charge of all production is clearly not responsible for the profit of any specific

---

* President, National Cash Register Company. From *Financial Executive,* February, 1963. Used by permission of Financial Executives Institute.

line. The measurement of his contribution to profit is much more difficult to assess.

I submit, however, that the basic principles of management planning and control are just as applicable and just as potentially rewarding in a centralized organization as they are to General Motors, Westinghouse, or Du Pont. I venture to say that the majority of financial executives must face the challenge of improving the control of the profitability of their companies in the context of centralized management. Consequently, one of the purposes of this presentation will be to point out that effective control is possible in a centralized organization.

WHAT ARE THE OBJECTIVES?

Now a few fundamentals upon which we must agree before we can dwell more definitely on specific plans or concepts.

In the first place, we must agree that the objectives of a competitive enterprise are two.

First—to maximize long run profits (and I emphasize the long run) from the use of the resources under a control.

Second—to seek investment opportunities for the profitable employment of additional resources.

It is vital to the discussion of control of the actions of an enterprise to continue to focus attention on long range profit as the ultimate objective. It is *not* the objective of a business enterprise to have the largest sales volume, the most new products, the greatest number of employees, the best looking buildings or the most attractive advertisements, except to the degree that they tend to maximize long range profits.

Given these two objectives, the principal responsibility of business management is to choose between alternative courses of action so as to maximize the profit and investment opportunities of the business. This decision-making responsibility is an intensely difficult and involved one. It is never a case of choosing between an alternative which is clearly the right course of action and one which is obviously not. The alternatives offer varying rewards or penalties and may involve substantially different amounts or risks. Management cannot evaluate the various alternatives by itself. There must be some organizational procedure within the company to provide management with the analysis and evaluations required to discharge its basic planning and control responsibility. The means by which the management of a particular company is able to meet this fundamental challenge is the system of management planning and control for that company. Every company has such a system. The system may be good or poor and it may operate under clearly defined ground rules or it may be ill-defined and not well understood, but every management has some method by which it carries on the affairs of the business in order to realize profit and investment objectives.

There are at least three essential ingredients of a management planning and control system:

First—The system must provide management, before a decision is made, with all the information available with respect to the matter under review. This must include not only the short and long range consequences of the principal alternatives in terms of profit and investment. It must also include the nonfinancial aspects of each alternative.

Second—With respect to the selected alternative, the system must clearly define the responsibility of each operating activity in sufficient detail to measure actual results against the original plan, and to fix responsibility for variances.

Third—There must be a reporting system to inform management of the progress of important programs and to report variances in time to take corrective action.

SETTING UP A SYSTEM

The nagging fear of every manager is that he does not have the business under control—that it has become too large for him to keep his finger on—that important decisions are being made "out of control." He wants to keep hold of the reins, but he recognizes the absolute need to delegate. The problem is, "How to organize to do this job." This need is one of the reasons why we have such a vast maze of accounting statements, reports, schedules, analyses, budgets, forecasts, etc. But these tools fall far short of the mark since they generally report deviations from past performance or from certain norms or standards. A real system must report deviations from objectives.

The system of management control which we use at NCR is called "The Profit Plan" and if there is a single word which typifies the Profit Plan at NCR, it is the word "Objectives."

We begin with a top management outline of broad corporate objectives, for we believe that an essential of profit planning is top management participation and support. These broad corporate objectives embrace both short and long term targets and financial and nonfinancial goals. Most important, they represent the considered judgment of top management as to the course the business should take.

At the beginning of each year, our Chief Executive Officer calls together the entire management group and presents, in a detailed set of charts, the Company's Objectives for the year. These objectives cover every major phase of our business and are tied in directly with the approved Profit Plan. This meeting sets the Company's course for the year and provides specific direction to the entire management team.

Consistent with these overriding objectives, each operating division, with the assistance of the financial division, develops its own set of objectives for each year's operation. These division objectives are tied specifically into the

Company's Profit Plan for that year. For example, in our 1963 Profit Plan, if we expect to bill fifteen million dollars of new Product "A," the Marketing Vice President assumes responsibility for this result, including the attainment, let us say, of new orders totalling twenty-one million dollars in sales. He also formulates specific supporting plans such as the completion of sales and service training by a definite date within a specific expense budget; the release of the product for sale by a certain date and the attainment of a predetermined rate of incoming orders. These supporting commitments are essential in providing check points against which to measure progress towards the accomplishment of the primary objective.

Nor do we stop here since our Marketing Division can obviously not do this job alone. Our Manufacturing Vice President, for example, must include in his 1963 objectives the production of these units in accordance with a precalculated schedule. This, of course, again contemplates many subsidiary objectives such as the completion of tooling by a certain date for a specific investment, the required factory rearrangement and training, the completion of production models for test purposes, and the attainment of a target production rate by a definite date.

Finally, our Vice President in charge of R&D commits himself in advance to complete the final design and to release drawings to the Manufacturing Division by a specific date as well as to complete prototype models within a budgeted model-making allocation.

These objectives are established by each of the responsible divisions and become their goals. The Vice Presidents sign their names to documents setting forth these objectives in specific terms. Psychologically we find that this practice materially increases the attention given to the achievement of these results. On a non-psychological basis, year end bonuses are also affected by the achievement of these objectives.

COORDINATING THE PROGRAM

The coordination of this program to achieve consistency is the task of the financial planning department. But we believe that objectives must be established by the man responsible for the results since he knows best the significance of the assignment, the meaning of deviations and ways to correct them. Let me emphasize that the figures entered in the profit plan for the marketing, manufacturing, and R&D divisions do not represent estimates of the financial division. Rather, each expenditure, each cost, each projection represents the considered judgment of the division responsible for carrying out the program.

Division managers are required to be specific in these objectives. It is not enough to say "we must reduce costs." He must say "we will reduce costs on product 'X' by so much." It is not enough to say "we must increase volume." It must be "we will increase volume of product 'Y' by 'Z' units."

It is not enough to say "we will tool product 'A.'" We must have a commitment to "complete the tooling of product 'A' by a specific date and for so many dollars."

At this juncture, I should emphasize our experience that we cannot control in any greater degree than we plan. For example, if our sales budget for a period is fifty million dollars and we only achieve forty million dollars, we will be unable to clearly analyze the variances if we have not planned the sale of individual products and recorded the actual results in the same detail.

Once management approves a profit plan and the detailed programs making it up, the financial data becomes an approved budget and an approved target for the operating divisions against which actual results will be measured.

CONTROL BY EXCEPTION

During the year the financial planning department must provide control reports to measure results and report progress towards the established objectives. Our reports of variance are prompt—they are available before the financial statements. The reports are designed for the managers involved—they do not follow the format of regular accounting statements. The reports include a covering analysis of deviations. Our reports at this level do not go to top management. As we detect variations we either must agree on corrective action or we must, as a management team, make other adjustments to our profit plan. We stress control by exception—we deal with variances from the objectives making up the profit plan.

We do not depend completely on variance reports to identify deviations from our Profit Plan. The responsible parties must report when they know that they are going to miss a particular target for no one knows sooner than they. A variation at this point may cause some unpleasantness with the front office but it is nothing compared to that which occurs if they fail to point out the variance until it is too late to do something about it.

We believe, of course, that tight financial supervision is a key to the Profit Plan. It puts realism, measurability and consistency into the entire Plan. This includes the challenge of putting measurability into the nonfinancial objectives of the Plan. The purpose of our reporting system is to throw the spotlight on problems as soon as they develop so that the decision-making attention of management may be focused on the specific item causing a major deviation from the profit objective.

Let us now take a specific example of NCR's "Profit Plan" in action in the area of new product development. Nowhere in the business machines industry is an effective system of planning and control more critical to the long-range profitability of a Company than in the area of research, engineering and product development.

Not only do we realize that future sales volume is at stake, but, equally as important, it is our conviction that the profit margins of the future depend on the engineering of today.

Satisfactory profit margins are produced on the drawing board and an adequate control system must insure that the planned margins justify the investment and that these margins are not allowed to shrink during the development cycle. Once a product is tooled and production begins, margin improvement is then confined to the relatively limited area of manufacturing cost reduction.

THE KEY TO EFFECTIVE PLANNING

At NCR, we establish, for each major product development, a Planning Blueprint on which we set forth, in specific terms, the parameters which justify the investment in this project. We analyze the market potential and the competitive situation, the features desired, the total investment required, the desired timing of each step in the cycle, and the cost-price-margin relationships.

It is our objective to determine the full financial impact of a new product program before a decision on that project is made. Assuming that these factors produce the kind of an answer we seek, the project is started but the planning and control process has just begun. Without adequate control, it is perfectly possible—in fact likely—that during the long development period the parameters which originally justified the investment will have changed so appreciably that, in the absence of a control system, we may find ourselves tooling and producing a product which no longer is attractive either in terms of margin or return on investment.

We believe that the key to effective control of R&D projects is the establishment of clearly defined check points. We further believe in a regimented review of all aspects of the program to identify variances from the plan and to insure that corrective action is taken to re-adjust the plan to produce a satisfactory end-result.

For example, let us say, in a hypothetical case, that in June 1962—a year after the start of the program—our regular project review indicates that Competitor "C" has released a new product with improved features at an attractive price. To meet this new situation, we must institute a complete review of the features now required of our product, the additional engineering and tooling investment, the lengthening of our timetable, the effect on MLB, on margin and on price and finally the ultimate effect on our project market volume and the return on investment.

Based on this detailed review, we must, as a management team, decide on a course of action—either we go ahead with a modified program, assuming that we like the results of the analysis, or we drop the project or replace it with another.

This R&D project review is tied in directly with our "Profit Plan." When we first approved the project we did so based on a favorable impact on our long-range profit objectives. At each check-point, we must go through the same procedure. We must determine, before we move forward with additional investment commitments on this project, that it will have a sufficiently favorable impact on our long-range "Profit Plan."

If you are tired of tooling for products which don't sell or which produce unsatisfactory margins, I recommend heartily the "Product Blueprint" approach with regular review and regular correlation with your own "Profit Plan."

If you were to ask me whether NCR is 10 percent, 25 percent, 50 percent or 90 percent along the way to achieving a completely effective system of management planning and control, I am sure that I could not give you the answer. I do know that we have made much progress; I know, too, that we have far to go. Every day we see evidence that our system needs improvement or modification consistent with changes in our business.

Two additional thoughts for your consideration.

First, top management itself must be willing to plan carefully, and must insist that the organization do likewise. Top management must continue to demonstrate its emphasis on planning and on the results obtained by constant review and by instituting a system of motivation; in other words, compensation and recognition must follow performance under the plan.

Top management must refrain from making decisions without exploring thoroughly the impact on the profit plan, decisions which, if made unilaterally may drastically upset the ability of one or more divisions to achieve their own assigned objectives.

Second, we are convinced that in moving toward the objective of more effective control of a business, it is vital not to damage the spirit of the organization and the freedom of communication which may have been largely responsible for the Company's success. There is no substitute in a business organization for the esprit de corps which make people work together, as a team, often far beyond the time and effort norms for the job in the interests of a business which has come to mean far more to the individual than merely an inanimate corporate entity.

NO SUBSTITUTE FOR SALESMANSHIP

In this regard, let me give you a personal observation which may be considered heresy, but I shall risk it. And that is, that at every step of the way—salesmanship has been more important than accountingmanship. How many times during the development of our profit plans have I heard the words, which I am sure ring through the corridors of business offices all over the country:

. . . "That profit plan is a bunch of—"

. . . "Those miserable objectives again"
. . . "A five year plan—I cannot even find out about next September"
. . . "Another brain child of those Harvard boys"

There is a striking similarity between the salesman who is trying to get an order for his product and the financial officer who is seeking to "sell" a corporate organization on installing and using an effective system of profit control.

I don't believe that there has been anything with which I have been more impressed, during my association with NCR, than the extent to which selling principles and methods have been developed ever since the days of John H. Patterson, who has often been referred to as "The Father of American Salesmanship." I am convinced that these selling fundamentals are sound and that they have a practical usefulness to those of us in financial management.

I know of no finer product than an effective system of management planning and control but I submit that those of you who endeavor to promote it within your own business have a selling problem. How many times have you seen a sound plan or recommendation fail to see the light of day because it was not properly sold?

We believe at NCR that to sell creatively (and that is what we are talking about here) you must sell with a Plan.

In passing from a "cold" to a "sold" attitude, there are five fundamental states of mind.

The selling plan is based on these mental steps:

Mental Steps	*Selling Plan*
Curiosity	The approach—obtain favorable attention
Interest	Arouse interest—secure information
Conviction	Prove the need
Desire	Demonstrate the benefits
Action	Close the sale

Every good salesman must lead his prospect from step to step towards the desired goal which is action on the proposal.

We must be prepared to find our prospect in this mental attitude at the outset. Believe me, this fellow is no setup to work on—even at this tender age. You may, however, recognize a similarity to certain prospects in your own organization.

Our problem is to lead the prospect from this frigid state to one of curiosity. "Well, I don't think I am interested, but I will take a look." The first step in the selling plan, therefore, is to obtain favorable attention.

From here we want to lead our prospect to a state of interest. "Well, now, tell me more about that." So the second step in the selling plan is to arouse or create interest.

And now, our task as salesmen is to take our prospect another step down the road by convincing him that our plan is needed. "Ah, that I need." So that the third step in the selling plan is to prove the need.

The next logical step is to create desire. "Oh boy, I must have that." Thus the fourth step in the selling plan is to demonstrate the benefits of our proposition.

If we have done our job well up to this point, we are not far away from our goal which is to secure favorable action. "Okay, let's play ball." So the last step in the selling plan is to close the order.

There is no substitute for a carefully planned sales campaign—a campaign designed to sell your ideas of an effective management planning and control system not only to your top management, but also to the key man in your organization without whose cooperation the plan will just not work.

And don't short cut the steps in your own selling plan.

Let me summarize briefly again what we consider to be the essence of an effective control system. The system must be:

Future oriented:

Timely—with information available *before* a decision is reached.

Responsibility oriented—with personal commitments as integral parts of the profit plan.

Tied in with motivation—recognition and compensation.

Capable of reportability—far enough in advance for corrective action.

Tailor-made to the requirements of the company.

The system must constitute a detailed Plan of Corporate Action aimed at specific profit goals against which all important decisions must be weighed.

With growing competition, the intensified squeeze on profits resulting from rising costs, and the increasing complexity of business decisions, the premium placed on effective management planning and control as a means of profit growth becomes steadily greater.

In this area, you have a great opportunity for service to your companies.

Reading 12-4

Basic Considerations in Management Control

By Robert N. Anthony

Following is a list of considerations that are relevant in the design and use of a management control system. No solution is suggested for most of these problems. Admittedly, a list of problems without solutions is not so useful as solutions would be. Nevertheless, such a catalog is available as a checklist of matters that must be resolved in a specific situation. Failure to take account of these problems is one of the major sources of weakness in management control systems.

Several of these problems are examples of the phenomenon that President Lowell called "conjugate principles," namely, a pair of principles mutually contradictory or inconsistent, yet each of which is partially, or under some conditions, true. (See A. Lawrence Lowell, *Conflicts of Principle*, Harvard University Press, 1932).

1. *Balance between Measured and Unmeasured Elements.* The very act of measuring and reporting on an aspect of performance tends to focus attention on this aspect; yet no measurement system encompasses all aspects of performance. It is difficult to focus adequate attention on unmeasured aspects of performance; yet these may be more significant than the measured aspects (e.g., the *quality* of legal service is much more important than the ability of the head of the law department to reduce his expenses). In particular, the formal system in a business usually centers on a number labeled "profit," but this number does not measure all the elements that determine true profit; and even if it did, profit is not a complete measure of performance.

2. *Goal Conflict: Balance between Current and Future Considerations.* All measures of profitability tend to show *current* (i.e., this year's) profits; yet top management presumably is interested in long-run profitability. Man-

agers can make many decisions that increase current profitability but that hurt the company in the long run. (Cutting research expenditures is an obvious example.) The stronger the emphasis on current profitability, the greater the temptation to ignore the long run. Yet, emphasis on long-run considerations is by no means a valid excuse for poor current profits in many situations.

3. *Balance between Competition and Cooperation.* The spur of competition is a powerful motivating force. The stronger the emphasis on an individual division's profitability, the more vigorously it will compete with other divisions. There are many situations, however, in which a division should sacrifice its own reported performance for the overall good of the whole organization (e.g., giving advice and assistance). Cooperation between divisions is, therefore, essential, but the greater the emphasis on divisional profitability, the less likely the necessary degree of cooperation will be achieved. Yet, too much emphasis on cooperation leads to a soft-headed attitude and to inadequate attention to profits.

4. *Balance between Effectiveness and Efficiency.* Especially in non-profit organizations, it is difficult to decide on and to communicate the right balance between effectiveness and efficiency. Everyone agrees, in the abstract, that both are important and that neither should be given undue emphasis, but it is difficult to make this feeling operational. When the emphasis on the budgeting process is strong, efficiency is often given undue weight.

5. *Defining Goals.* The management control system should be goal congruent; yet managements rarely are able to state their goals accurately and completely. Their own attitudes and actions are inconsistent with their words. We must try to infer the real goals, and not rely on the verbalizations.

There is an unfortunate, but widespread, tendency to draw an analogy between a business and a sporting event, and thus obscure the fact that a business has multiple, conflicting, and ill-defined goals. In a business, success is not measured so simply as the fastest, the highest, the longest, the most runs, the least strokes, etc.

6. *Control of Managed Costs.* (See Notes in Chapter 5.)

7. *Transfer Pricing.* (See Notes in Chapter 6.)

8. *Measurement of Assets Employed.* There are many individual, technical problems here for which solutions are not now known, but generalizations for at least some of these probably will be developed in the fairly near future.

9. *Long-Range Planning.* We do not know in what circumstances formal, systematic, long-range planning is warranted, nor the best way to do it.

10. *Capital Budgeting.* Although a conceptual framework exists, there are holes in it, especially with respect to the right discount rate and the allowance for risk and uncertainty.

11. *Planning Data versus Control Data.* The system should produce information that is useful both for planning and for control. In order to pro-

vide a valid basis for decision-making, planning data should essentially be neutral—show what is most likely—whereas control data should essentially lead to desired actions.

12. *Strength of Motivation.* Various devices, ranging in strength from a word of praise to a bonus, exist for inducing desired behavior. We do not know how strong each of these is, nor the right mix to use in a given situation.

13. *Differences among Individuals.* The system is *designed* on certain assumptions about the knowledge, skill, and personality of a typical manager. The only personality specifically considered is that of the man at the top. In *using* the system, one must adapt it to the individuals involved, allowing for such differences as the pessimist and the optimist, the tough and the timid, the quantitatively oriented and the socially oriented, and so on.

14. *Systems Cost versus Systems Benefits.* Beyond the obvious fact that the benefits derived from a system should be worth more than they cost, we do not know how to balance costs and benefits. Nevertheless, this is a problem that should not be overlooked. Costs include not only data handling costs, but also executive time and annoyance.

Case 12–1

Wallace Box Company

In May, 1961, Milton Purcell, a Boston management consultant, paid a visit to Fall River, Massachusetts, to meet William Barrett, president of the Wallace Box Company. Mr. Barrett had asked Mr. Purcell to help him, he said, "to take a look at where my company is right now, and help me make any necessary plans."

As Mr. Barrett explained the situation to Mr. Purcell, "The company is making satisfactory profits, and I expect it to continue to do so.[1] But although I am not concerned about current profitability, I do want to be sure that nothing has been overlooked in making the business as efficient as is feasible." He went on to suggest that Mr. Purcell might start his review by looking at the company's accounting and control system, simply because this particular aspect had not been studied by an outsider for some time; he reiterated that he was not dissatisfied with the present setup. Major elements in the system were a complete budget, a standard cost system for all elements of manufacturing costs, and a regular reporting procedure that produced monthly financial statements by the middle of each succeeding month. Mr. Purcell agreed to follow the approach suggested by Mr. Barrett. His investigations revealed the information that follows.

COMPANY HISTORY

The company had had its beginnings in 1850, when George Wallace, a Scottish papermaker, settled in Fall River and started a small paper mill. In 1897, control passed to a local converter who had previously taken the bulk of the mill's output. From that time on, the company operated as an integrated manufacturer of folding boxes.

Mr. Barrett had acquired a majority interest in the company in 1921, after several years of unprofitable operations had taken it to the verge

---

[1] Five-year financial statements are reproduced in Exhibits 1 and 2.

Exhibit 1

BALANCE SHEETS, DECEMBER 31, 1956–60

(000)

	1960	*1959*	*1958*	*1957*	*1956*
ASSETS					
Cash	$ 216	$ 407	$ 641	$ 392	$ 684
State and municipal bonds	475	604	467	618	577
Accounts receivable (net)	581	609	610	383	337
Inventories	1,183	1,033	822	863	764
Total Current Assets	$2,455	$2,653	$2,540	$2,256	$2,362
Cash value of life insurance	419	418	408	322	310
Securities and cash held for plant and equipment replacement	985	985	485	485	485
Plant and equipment (net)	1,914	1,529	1,576	1,575	1,176
	$5,773	$5,585	$5,009	$4,638	$4,333
LIABILITIES					
Accounts payable	$ 312	$ 355	$ 442	$ 326	$ 312
Accrued liabilities	56	89	31	88	85
Income taxes	316	419	331	359	423
Total Current Liabilities	$ 684	$ 863	$ 804	$ 773	$ 820
Replacement reserve, plant and equipment	985	985	485	485	485
Capital stock:					
Common	900	900	900	900	900
6% preferred	600	600	600	600	600
Earned surplus	2,604	2,237	2,220	1,880	1,528
	$5,773	$5,585	$5,009	$4,638	$4,333

Exhibit 2

CONDENSED INCOME STATEMENTS, 1956–60

(000)

	1960	*1959*	*1958*	*1957*	*1956*
Sales	$7,478	$7,344	$6,086	$6,170	$5,374
Manufacturing expenses	5,228	4,795	4,302	4,464	3,780
Gross profit	$2,250	$2,549	$1,784	$1,706	$1,594
Selling, administrative, and general expenses	906	954	649	586	496
Profit-sharing and retirement plan contributions	171	179	155	151	132
Income before taxes	$1,173	$1,416	$ 980	$ 969	$ 966
Income taxes	608	740	511	509	515
Net income	$ 565	$ 676	$ 469	$ 460	$ 451
Dividends paid	198	162	126	108	108
Balance to surplus	$ 367	$ 514	$ 343	$ 352	$ 343
Note: Depreciation	$ 201	$ 177	$ 174	$ 153	$ 138

of bankruptcy. Under Mr. Barrett's management, annual losses were reduced, and the company showed a profit in 1925. It had not lost money in any year since that time, although it had not covered its preferred dividend in 1932. Mr. Barrett and his family owned or controlled 75 percent of the company's stock; the remainder was held by executives or retired executives who had obtained it under an incentive compensation plan that Mr. Barrett had instituted soon after he had taken over the company.

In describing those early years to Mr. Purcell, Mr. Barrett said, "I'll never forget the hard times we went through. The company was in urgent need of refinancing, and there just seemed to be no money available for a small, unprofitable company. I made up my mind there and then that if I succeeded in putting Wallace back on the road to recovery (which I did), I would take all possible steps to build up its financial strength to a level that would almost guarantee that we would never again be short of funds at a crucial moment. You see as a small company we've never had the flexibility that larger companies have, but we find ourselves needing money just the same way that they do. They can always fall back on their banking relationships, or on their big financiers. But in a crisis, we don't have access to those sources of funds. We have to look after ourselves. Call it New England conservatism, if you like. I regard it as prudent business management."

Wallace manufactured paperboard cartons for a wide variety of uses, primarily as packages for consumer products. The box factory used paperboard made in the firm's adjoining mill. Mill production was geared to the needs of the box factory, according to the production manager. "In general, we produce paperboard only for immediate use in production. We keep very little paperboard in inventory." The plant complex also included a 60,000-square-foot warehouse (built at a cost of $300,000 in 1960), where finished orders were stored pending delivery. The warehouse was currently about 60 percent full; it had been built large enough to provide for the company's needs until 1966. The company had approximately 425 employees in 1961.

MARKETING SITUATION

The company's marketing area included the New England states (primarily Massachusetts and Connecticut), New York, New Jersey, and eastern Pennsylvania. There were seven sales engineers who were compensated on the basis of a nominal salary plus commission. Three of them operated from the Fall River plant; the other four were based in a sales office in New York City.

Mr. Barrett told Mr. Purcell "One of our major assets is our excellent reputation for product quality and customer service. We control our product quality to a far greater degree than do many of our competitors, because we control practically all the elements that go into our final product. In addition to the normal operations of making our own paperboard and doing the various printing, cutting and creasing, folding, and gluing operations, we even make our own dies and grind and mix our own inks."

Mr. Barrett emphasized that the industry was characterized by strong competition. Wallace met this by fulfilling special design requests, by actively catering to all customer requirements, and by strict adherence to promised delivery dates. Whereas all cartons were manufactured to order, some finished goods were kept in storage at customers' requests. The rate charged for such storage was .75 percent per month, covering interest and storage costs; Mr. Barrett thought that this was adequate. In May, 1961, finished orders priced at approximately $250,000 were overdue for delivery; i.e., customers had postponed acceptance of thes orders beyond scheduled delivery dates. Mr. Barrett was not disturbed about this, however, as he had reassured himself that the bulk of these orders were from good customers whose financial integrity was unquestioned. "Anyway, this isn't too big a part of our finished goods inventory, and we have confirmed orders for all of it—overdue or not."

Mr. Purcell inquired whether Mr. Barrett could give him the reasons for his statement that the industry was highly competitive. "This," Mr. Barrett said, "is basically the fault of the potential overcapacity that exists in most plants. The production process requires that paperboard mills run a continuous three-shift operation, but the typical industry box plant usually operates only one and one-half shifts per day. Because of this overcapacity, competition for high-volume orders is particularly vicious, and price-cutting is common, especially among the larger producers. On the other hand, we have avoided the temptation of going after the high-volume, low-margin business of some of the large national companies for whom we manufacture specialty cartons. If you get big enough, you find that you have to do high-volume work to keep your plant busy, and that often goes at break-even prices, unlike specialty work. We've managed to keep our size down to the point where we do a large volume of specialty business—we're good at it—and we don't have to bother with high-volume work."

Mr. Barrett told Mr. Purcell that pricing was a crucial element in marketing. Prices were prepared by the company's estimators for each bid or order, on the basis of sales specifications and the appropriate standard cost elements according to tables the company had developed for this purpose. Total costs, as calculated, were then increased by certain percentages for selling and administrative expenses, profit, sales commissions, and cash discounts. These percentages were determined annually when the company's budget was drawn up. A record of the percentages used from 1956 to 1961 is shown in Exhibit 3, and a representative price estimate is reproduced in Exhibit 4. Mr. Barrett remarked, however, that the price calculated in the estimate was often adjusted, for quotation purposes, to meet competitive conditions, to reimburse the company for additional costs not included in the estimate, or to pick up some of the savings, if any, known to be realized

Exhibit 3

ADD-ON PERCENTAGES USED IN PRICE ESTIMATING

	1961	1960	1959	1958	1957	1956
Administrative and selling expenses* (percent of manufacturing cost, excluding material)	45%	47%	46%	39%	46%	42%
Profit (percent of total delivered cost)	20	20	20	20	20	20
Commission and discount† (3% and 1%, respectively, of the total of delivered cost plus profit)	4	4	4	4	4	4

* Including factory overhead, amounting generally to one-half of the percentage added on.
† A provision against expenses incurred as percentages of sales.

by the customer through the special design or service provided by the company.

Mr. Purcell was interested to hear from Mr. Barrett that it was customary for estimators in the trade to meet regularly under the auspices of a trade association to price sample boxes according to their own formulas. The price of the paperboard would be given, for the purpose of these comparisons; Wallace normally priced paperboard, in its own estimates, at 10 percent over mill cost, which, Mr. Barrett was sure, was less than nonintegrated manufacturers would normally have to pay. It seemed that Wallace's prices were usually in the lowest tenth in these comparisons, a fact that gave Mr. Barrett not inconsiderable pleasure. In practice, he said, most producers probably varied from their formulas in quoting to customers. But, he pointed out, whereas most of his competitors were shaving prices below formula, Wallace's quoted prices were higher than the calculated estimate about 65 percent of the time, identical about 20 percent of the time, and lower 15 percent of the time. "It all depends on the competition, and on your assessment of the whole situation."

ACCOUNTING AND BUDGETING

The paperboard mill, headed by its own superintendent, was treated as a single cost center. The box factory, also under a superintendent, had 10 principal cost centers, each consisting of a press or a group of similar presses and associated equipment, and each headed by a foreman. Minor operations such as ink manufacture, quality control, and the storage warehouse also were treated as separate cost centers. The paperboard mill was operated 24 hours a day, and the presses were operated 16 hours a day, either 5 or 6 days a week, depending on demand. Considerable variation was possible in the output per hour, and for this reason the foremen were paid partly on an incentive plan, which was based largely on the comparison of their actual

Exhibit 4

PRICE ESTIMATE

ITEM: 1 million boxes 6⅙ × 2¾ × 1½, printed 2 colors and varnish, on .024 caliber white patent coated, news backed.

PREPARATORY COST	Production Per Hour	Rate	/MM Unit	/MM Material Cost	/MM Mfg. Cost	M Unit	M Material Cost	M Mfg. Cost	M Unit	M Material Cost	M Mfg. Cost
Original Plates	F. or E.										
Electros 9¾ x 9¼ (91)		18.94	28	530 32							
Wood				15 99							
Rule				34 09							
Composing											
Die Making	③	4.85	41.8		202 73						
Make Ready - ptg.	2X	12.80	30.0		384 00						
Make Ready - C. & C.	11.55	11.25	15.8		177 75						
44¼ Total Preparatory Cost				580 40	764 48						
QUANTITY COST											
Board 65,005 (3¾)	171.00 +25			5557 93							
Board (32.5025)				25 00							
Ink		.37	300	111 00							
Ink 30"		.75	300								
		.45	231	328 95							
Cases Corrugated	700	.30	1429	428 70							
Cellulose Material											
Board, Storage & Handling		1.87			60 78						
Cutting Stock											
Printing		22.766									
Cut and Crease					813 09						
Stripping	.933-4	.178+120			391 60						
Cellulose											
Auto Gluing		.562	466 +11	24	477 24						
Hand Gluing											
Wrapping or Packing		6.503			92 93						
Inspection											
Total Quantity Cost				6451 58	1835 64						
Total Preparatory Cost				580 40	764 48						
Total Cost to Make				7031 98	2600 12						
Selling & Commercial		45+8	(% + $)		1178 05						
Material Forward					7031 98						
77' Shipping 56+		7.25+2	60,287		220 54						
Freight and Cartage		.40			241 15						
Total Cost					11271 84						
Profit		20%			2254 37						
Total Selling Price					13526 21						
Finished Stock St'g											
Commission & Dis.		4%			541 05						
Total Selling Price					14067 26						
Selling Price per M - Calculated					14 07						
Selling Price per M - Quoted					15 30						
Form 40											

hourly output with predetermined standards for different types of paperboard or cartons.

The annual budget was drawn up under the direction of James Lewis, the treasurer. The budget was synthesized from estimates of sales prepared by the sales staff and from corresponding activity rates and cost expectations developed by manufacturing personnel. The manufacturing people participated in discussion of the relevant portions of the budget. Mr. Lewis used his experience with past budgets to combine the separate elements into a meaningful whole. The budget was stated in terms of a specified dollar amount per month for each major expense item in each manufacturing cost center. Separate schedules listed budget allowances for selling, administrative, and general expenses. This scheme made possible the annual determination of the selling and commercial expense percentage to be used in price estimates. (See Exhibit 3.) While no formal capital rationing system was used, all capital expenditures were reviewed both before and after being incurred, on an annual basis for an overall review and on an individual basis as specific projects were undertaken. The annual budget also facilitated the development of standard costs for use in price estimating and inventory valuation. For the inventory purpose, all costs were included through factory overhead; i.e., costs such as selling and other administrative were excluded from inventory and charged off as incurred.

REPORTS—INTERNAL

Mr. Barrett received a variety of internal and trade association reports on a regular basis. The internally generated reports were as follows.

1. Balance sheet.
2. Profit and loss statement, monthly (Exhibit 5).
3. Cost center spending report, monthly (Exhibit 6).
4. Selling, general, and administrative expense statement, monthly.
5. Overdue accounts receivable, monthly (usually aggregated between $60,000 and $100,000).
6. Overdue shipments, monthly.
7. Inventory breakdown, monthly. Typical percentages were: finished goods, 50 percent; work in process, 35 percent; and raw materials, 15 percent.
8. Raw material shrinkage report, monthly.
9. Cash and securities listing, monthly.
10. Sales, weekly.
11. Sales recapitulation, monthly. This analyzed sales against budgets, and included profit and expense estimates.
12. Salesmen's report, monthly.
13. Carton shop production, monthly. This included operating hours statistics and efficiency percentages.
14. Foremen's bonus report, monthly.
15. Outstanding orders, weekly.
16. Progress schedule, weekly.
17. Machine production report, daily.
18. Quality control report, monthly.
19. Other special reports, prepared as the need arose.

Exhibit 5

PROFIT AND LOSS STATEMENTS*
(Abbreviated)

	November 1960	*December 1960*	*12 Months 1960*
Board Mill			
Net sales of board	$ 12,427	$ 12,842	$ 144,797
Transfers to carton factory	167,885	140,973	1,969,599
Total sales and transfers	$180,312	$153,815	$2,114,396
Cost of sales and transfers	162,830	139,401	1,895,581
Standard profit or (loss)	$ 17,482	$ 14,414	$ 218,815
Burden variance†	1,417	5,552	18,609
Over or (under) earned burden†	(2,600)	(6,539)	18,343
Inventory adjustment	—	(2,370)	(2,370)
Profit or (loss) board mill	$ 16,299	$ 11,057	$ 253,397
Carton Factory			
Net sales of cartons	$628,259	$626,463	$7,068,025
Cost of sales:			
Materials	273,144	275,196	3,038,625
Scrap and cuttings sales	(1,657)	(1,978)	(24,427)
Manufacturing	142,265	141,712	1,693,488
Remakes	5,427	350	23,207
Miscellaneous charges	24,907	8,983	20,301
Selling and commercial	31,457	31,283	374,326
Shipping and storage	19,366	17,782	207,603
Leased machines	2,607	(309)	24,126
Salesmen's commissions	18,192	19,216	197,684
Total cost of sales	$515,708	$492,235	$5,554,933
Standard profit, cartons	$112,551	$134,228	$1,513,092
Burden variance†	32,856	41,501	320,712
Over or (under) earned burden†	(52,793)	(52,853)	(575,221)
Inventory adjustment	(323)	17,215	535
Profit, carton factory	$ 92,291	$140,091	$1,259,118
Miscellaneous income and costs	$ 675	$ (4,393)	$ (49,156)
Total profit from carton and board sales	108,590	151,148	1,512,515
Gain for period	$109,265	$146,755	$1,463,359
Less: Bonus and profit sharing	15,771	16,501	324,956
Net gain for period	$ 93,494	$130,254	$1,138,403
Less: Reserve for income taxes	48,332	66,058	590,175
Net income after taxes	$ 45,162	$ 64,196	$ 548,228

* These statements are those produced internally for management use (see text). Differences between the 12-month statement and the figures in Exhibit 2 are accounted for by year-end and audit adjustments not determined when the above were compiled.

† Explained in more detail in the structure of and notes to Exhibit 6.

Mr. Barrett said he usually reviewed the first four reports carefully, although he sometimes put off for several months the cost center spending review. These reports were distributed to executive and operating personnel, as

Exhibit 6

SPENDING REPORT
COST CENTER #014
(Five Two-Color Miehle Printing Presses)

	1960 Standards		November 1960 (5 Weeks)		December 1960 (4 Weeks)		Year 1960 (52 Weeks)		
	(5 Weeks)	(4 Weeks)	Actual	Variance	Actual	Variance	Standards	Actual	Variance: Gain or (Loss)
Fixed charges	$ 4,190	$ 3,352	$ 4,190		$ 3,352		$ 43,576	$ 43,576	
General press, fixed overhead	2,701	2,426	2,701		2,426		30,212	30,212	
General press, variable overhead	10,909	8,749	9,399	$1,510	8,721	$ 28	113,628	103,541	$10,087
Press supplies	274	219	135	139	373	(154)	2,849	3,279	(430)
Repairs	1,009	808	1,754	(745)	1,472	(664)	10,500	16,560	(6,060)
Power	900	720	666	234	484	236	9,360	6,369	2,991
Labor, pressmen	10,032	8,025	7,502	2,530	5,315	2,710	104,328	73,957	30,371
Labor, press helpers	3,688	2,950	2,984	704	2,074	877	38,352	28,978	9,374
Liability insurance and payroll taxes	1,029	823	825	204	580	243	10,700	8,107	2,593
Total Cost	$34,732	$28,072	$30,156	$4,576	$24,797	$3,276	$363,505	$314,579	$48,926
Standard credit			(28,463)		(19,266)			(267,585)	
Burden variance			4,577		3,274			48,927	
Over or (under) earned burden			(6,270)		(8,805)			(95,921)	
Gain or (loss)			(1,693)		(5,531)			(46,994)	
Number hours makeready			668		389			6,390	
Number hours machine time			1,441		1,047			13,783	
Number hours total	2,600	2,080	2,109		1,436		27,040	20,173	
Production units per hour			2,984		3,036			3,049	
Fixed cost per hour	$ 2.65	$ 2.78	$ 3.27		$ 4.02			$ 3.66	
Variable cost per hour	10.71	10.72	11.03		13.25			11.93	
Total cost per hour	13.36	13.50	14.30		17.27			15.59	

NOTES:
1. Standard credit = Actual hours worked × Standard hourly costs.
2. Over or (under) earned burden = Standard credit — Standard costs.
3. Gain or (loss) = Actual costs — Standard credit = Over or (under) earned burden — Burden variance.

appropriate, for information and action when necessary, such as the production manager's review, with the departmental foreman, of cost center spending statements. Most of the other internally generated reports were prepared primarily for other executives and were sent to Mr. Barrett for his information.

REPORTS—EXTERNAL

Mr. Barrett paid close attention to several reports he received regularly from the Folding Paper Box Association of America, the industry trade association. These were as follows:

1. Quarterly Economic Report. This 16-page report was prepared by a consulting economist. The first half dealt with current economic trends, and the second half went into specifics in analyzing the probable effects of these trends on different segments of the paperboard carton industry.
2. Industry Statistics. This was a monthly report, by month and cumulative, in dollars and tons, quoting sales, new orders, and other related statistics. Figures were quoted by company code number. Because of his many years of experience in the industry, Mr. Barrett thought that he could identify some of the companies from the characteristics of the data they reported. Sample sheets are summarized in Exhibit 7. Wallace's code number in the exhibit is 617.
3. Industry Operating Results. This annual booklet summarized percentage operating results and ratios, by types and sizes of company. An excerpt from the 1960 report is shown in Exhibit 8. The report was usually issued in the early part of the summer.

Each following Tuesday, Mr. Barrett also received several weekly reports from the National Paperboard Association. He studied these reports carefully in order to keep currently informed on important industry data. These reports covered nearly 90 percent of the paperboard manufacturing industry, and quoted data by company name. They included:

4. Paperboard Production and Operating Summary. This stated paperboard production tonnage by type, activity percentage (relative to a 144-hour week), and percentage of industry production, all on a previous-week and cumulative basis.
5. Orders Received, Manufactured and Unfilled. This covered paperboard tonnage, by type, on a previous-week and cumulative basis.
6. Paperboard Stock Report. The information was stated in tons, by type, at the end of the week.

ORGANIZATION

An abbreviated organization chart for the company is shown in Exhibit 9.

Exhibit 7

INDUSTRY STATISTICS, JANUARY 1–APRIL 30, 1961*

(Issued May 9, 1961)

Folding Paper Boxes
Shipments and Orders Entered

		Dollars							*Tonnage*						
		Per Cent of Industry							*Per Cent of Industry*						
	Company Code	*Entire Year 1958*	*Entire Year 1959*	*Entire Year 1960*	*Year To-Date 1961*	*Total Shipments This Year To-Date*	*Percent This Year Over or Under Last Year*	*Total Orders Entered This Year To-Date*	*Entire Year 1958*	*Entire Year 1959*	*Entire Year 1960*	*Year To-Date 1961*	*Total Shipments This Year To-Date*	*Percent This Year Over or Under Last Year*	*Total Orders Entered This Year To-Date*
Eastern Area	213	.26	.26	.31	.29	863,574	0.3	952,382	.30	.32	.42	.41	3,008.1	13.9	3,337.0
	215	.28	.30	.32	.28	835,513	—14.1	1,150,489	.16	.18	.17	.14	1,047.9	—18.2	1,575.0
	224	.26	.30	.39	.35	1,017,501	— 2.0	972,453	.12	.13	.16	.14	1,001.3	—13.5	1,339.5
	225	.14	.18	.18	.21	624,651	4.1	642,276	.09	.10	.10	.12	843.7	— 2.6	1,064.1
	226	.30	.32	.29	.29	859,072	—16.2	842,015	.29	.34	.31	.33	2,368.0	—18.1	2,238.2
	227	.03	.03	.04	.04	113,246	0.4	107,767	.06	.06	.07	.08	547.8	1.7	528.3
	248	.12	.12	.12	.17	494,562	12.6	426,458	.09	.08	.09	.12	863.0	9.4	1,082.1
	259	.31	.32	.36	.37	1,089,287	— 3.6	976,258	.19	.18	.20	.18	1,311.3	— 8.4	1,424.6
	318	.11	.13	.14	.14	409,557	— 6.3	505,507	.09	.10	.11	.10	736.4	— 9.5	961.5
	351	.83	.79	.76	.73	2,134,350	— 0.8	2,073,000	.80	.76	.70	.65	4,707.5	— 4.2	4,468.1
	352	1.85	1.86	1.87	1.68	4,969,802	13.4	5,342,981	1.79	1.74	1.82	1.68	12,214.8	12.7	13,742.4
	423	.61	.68	.61	.61	1,798,319	— 2.9	2,196,793	.59	.66	.59	.62	4,551.6	5.3	5,167.1
	451	2.64	2.61	2.37	2.21	6,504,923	—15.7	6,940,605	2.70	2.73	2.34	2.17	15,776.4	—21.7	20,660.4
	519	.61	.59	.58	.58	1,717,143	— 5.9	1,799,074	.58	.58	.57	.56	4,094.1	— 8.7	4,515.0
	521	.37	.41	.38	.42	1,222,353	—14.3	1,095,846							
	540	.10	.10	.10	.11	314,435	9.4	275,550	.11	.11	.11	.12	845.8	6.9	861.1
	553	1.49	1.20	1.14	1.12	3,288,523	—13.0	4,525,314	1.47	1.18	1.10	1.13	8,259.5	— 8.8	10,936.1
	554	.72	.63	.60	.40	1,185,394	—29.8	901,286	.85	.77	.74	.55	3,972.6	—21.7	3,127.5
	616	.20	.22	.23	.23	664,342	—23.2	506,889	.18	.19	.21	.21	1,528.1	—24.0	1,068.6
	617	.64	.75	.77	.85	2,502,532	— 7.2	2,455,316	.49	.55	.58	.67	4,907.4	1.7	4,764.3
	618	.17	.17	.16	.19	545,417	— 8.1	511,141	.16	.15	.15	.17	1,242.9	— 6.7	1,284.7
	643	.31	.31	.30	.30	872,382	— 9.3	861,063	.25	.27	.26	.26	1,886.5	— 6.2	1,838.0

	647	.16	.17	.18	.20	575,843	9.8	514,102	.12	.13	.15	.15	1,109.7	3.8	1,026.6
	652	1.70	1.67	1.63	1.72	5,063,439	6.9	4,797,477	2.11	2.08	1.96	1.98	14,373.2	3.5	13,316.2
	660	.37	.41	.36	.38	1,115,315	— 1.1	438,412	.32	.34	.31	.33	2,415.0	— 7.3	824.9
	714	.05	.06	.06	.06	166,697	—13.8	181,909	.05	.05	.06	.07	533.5	—12.8	584.1
	720	.12	.12	.09	.08	236,850	—32.0	292,959	.08	.07	.06	.05	353.6	—34.7	553.5
	721	.35	.28	.31	.30	872,417	— 7.7	800,290	.27	.22	.27	.21	1,561.8	—31.8	1,636.6
	723	.06	.06	.06	.07	220,259	21.4	139,406	.03	.03	.03	.03	24.7	24.0	172.4
	726	.49	.42	.37	.36	1,066,132	—14.2	1,106,131	.55	.48	.40	.39	2,833.1	—13.7	3,186.7
	733	.60	.55	.61	.62	1,813,079	— 7.8	1,703,650	.68	.64	.66	.69	5,034.1	— 6.2	4,824.6
	742	.09	.09	.08	.08	236,499	— 3.9	199,949	.09	.09	.08	.08	566.2	—11.1	457.8
	751	.20	.21	.22	.24	693,850	— 4.2	797,763	.20	.20	.22	.22	1,621.6	— 9.7	2,002.3
	752	.14	.15	.16	.16	457,815	— 5.5	510,369	.15	.18	.18	.18	1,323.0	— 3.6	1,513.3
	753	.21	.22	.21	.23	669,736	3.5	580,067	.24	.27	.29	.31	2,267.9	7.3	2,135.4
	834	.26	.29	.35	.37	1,079,598	— 8.9	1,023,624	.17	.18	.21	.21	1,541.0	—14.5	1,558.0
	836	.21	.18	.21	.20	574,114	—16.5	558,642	.16	.13	.16	.16	1,129.8	—14.2	1,289.9
Eastern	917	.09	.09	.09	.10	292,897	— 4.1	291,796	.06	.06	.06	.07	476.3	— 3.5	596.8
Area Total		17.45	17.25	17.01	16.74	49,161,418		49,997,009	16.75	16.45	16.01	15.66	113,994.3		122,623.0
Southern Area Total		3.74	3.83	4.06	4.05	11,947,931		12,620,050	4.09	4.15	4.27	4.26	31.145.0		33,585.5
North Central Area Total		23.94	24.21	24.43	24.49	72,127,835		75,533,636	24.22	24.54	25.10	25.31	184,354.3		204,601.2
Pacific Area Total		2.94	3.05	2.99	3.01	8,905,238		10,081,433	3.04	3.24	3.12	3.09	22,500.9		25,792.9
Reporting Companies Total		48.07	48.34	48.49	48.29	142,142,422		148,232,128	48.10	48.38	48.50	48.32	351,994.5		386,602.6
Balance of Industry		51.93	51.66	51.51	51.71	152,209,249			51.90	51.62	51.50	51.68	376,467.8		
(Millions) Total Industry		909	944	940	294				2.314	2.367	2.313	0.728			

* Copyright, Folding Paper Box Association of America. Reproduced by permission. Information by paperboard type, and in distant areas, omitted here.

Exhibit 8

COMPARATIVE INDUSTRY OPERATING RESULTS, 1960*

STATEMENT OF OPERATION FOR THE YEAR 1960

	Integrated Box Manufacturers with Sales Volume over $4 Million†		*Wallace Box Company*
	Median	*Range of Middle 50%*	
Net sales	100.00%	—	100.00%
Total materials used	56.16	50.42% to 62.34%	43.48
Manufacturing wages and salaries	21.63	18.29 to 23.90	21.61
All other manufacturing expense	10.15	7.17 to 11.76	6.69
Total cost of goods sold	86.49%	82.24% to 92.08%	71.78
Gross profit on sales	13.51%	7.93% to 17.77%	28.22
Total administrative expense	4.61	3.44 to 6.17	7.57
Total selling expense	7.38	6.04 to 8.93	8.17
Total administrative and selling expense	11.99	9.29 to 14.78	15.74
Net profit from operations	1.52%	(2.05%) to 6.01%	12.48
Total income credits	.26	.17 to .50	1.98
Total	1.78	(1.96) to 6.55	14.46
Total income charges	.48	.20 to 2.17	2.58
Net profit before federal and state income taxes	1.30%	(3.76%) to 6.55%	11.88
Net profit after federal and state income taxes	.80%	(3.76%) to 3.14%	4.81

BREAKDOWN OF MATERIALS USED

As a Percentage of Net Sales

Paperboard	46.58%	41.47% to 54.15%	34.86
Ink	2.28	2.09 to 2.83	1.68
Corrugated containers	2.66	2.11 to 3.18	2.78
Other materials	5.27	2.38 to 6.60	4.16
Total	56.79%‡	49.37% to 61.08%	43.48

Exhibit 8—Continued

OTHER FINANCIAL RATIOS§

	Integrated Box Manufacturers with Sales Volume over $4 Million†	
	Median	*Range of Middle 50%*
Current ratio	4.0	2.57 to 5.43
Number of weeks' sales in:		
Finished goods inventory	6.0	4.56 to 7.17
Total inventory	8.7	8.31 to 9.06
Sales per dollar of:		
Net worth	$ 2.57	$ 2.52 to $ 2.75
Working capital	4.89	4.76 to 5.01
Inventory as a per cent of:		
Sales	16.79%	15.98% to 17.42%
Working capital	82.99	69.45 to 96.53
Net worth	41.17	36.16 to 46.18
Current assets to net worth	75.20	72.35 to 78.05
Fixed assets to net worth	41.02	34.11 to 47.93
Total assets to net worth	131.26	113.32 to 149.19
Return on investment, basis of:		
Net worth	(3.10%)	(8.68%) to 2.49%
Total assets	(1.82%)	(7.96%) to 4.53%

† The published data broke down integrated manufacturers into two groups—sales below and above $4 million.

‡ Varies from the median reported for total materials in the Operating Statement because not all the companies submitting figures were able to break down their material costs into the categories listed above.

§ Wallace's figures were not inserted by Mr. Lewis, because he said the company's financial situation was sufficiently different from the average company's to make these comparisons of dubious value.

Exhibit 9

PARTIAL ORGANIZATION CHART

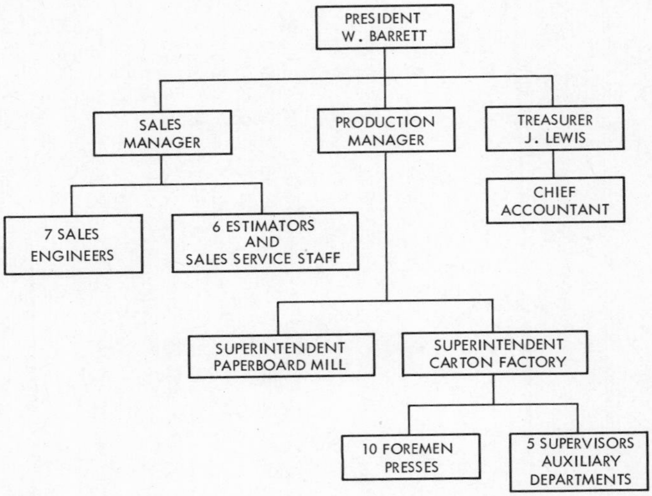

QUESTION

You are asked to appraise the planning and control system of this company. What are the *important* points you think should be made to Mr. Barrett? Include suggestions for any changes that you think should be considered.

Case 12–2

Olympian Oil Company

In 1954, the marketing department of the Olympian Oil Company submitted to the president a 17-page memorandum relating to the company's marketing expansion program. The main problem giving rise to this memorandum was the unsatisfactory outcome of an expansion program that had been launched seven years before. Most of the expansion was in service station outlets. From an initial commitment of $1.9 million in 1948, the annual expenditure on the program grew to just over $4.3 million in 1951, and approximately this amount was spent each year through 1954. Nine service stations were added or rebuilt in 1948; approximately 80 stations each year in 1949, 1950, and 1951; and approximately 100 stations each year in 1952, 1953, and 1954. At the end of 1954, the total number of Olympian service stations was well over 700.

The results of the expansion program had not been satisfactory, however. The gasoline sales volume per station had been below expectations, and, particularly, the sales volume of the more recently built stations was below that of the stations built in the initial stages of the program. (See Exhibit 1.) The dollar return also had been unsatisfactory, as evidenced by the comparison of Cumulative Commitments and Cumulative Cash Income, shown in Exhibit 2. This exhibit was part of a yearly report presented to the president by the controller. Following is the controller's comment accompanying the exhibit:

> For the six-year period 1949–1954, cash income from bulk plants and service stations has been $12.2 million less than the capital commitments of $24.8 million for marketing facilities. It should, of course, be anticipated that cash income would build up more slowly than capital commitments, particularly in view of the fact that our investment in marketing properties was relatively small at the beginning of the six-year period. On the other hand, it should be noted that the cash income figures used in the exhibit *include* the new income attributable to manufacturing as well as marketing operations. Moreover, the upward trend in

Exhibit 1

GASOLINE STATION SALES RECORDS

Five 12-Month Periods Ending September 30, 1950–54

*Station Groups**	*1950*	*1951*	*1952*	*1953*	*1954*
A. Average Sales per Station per Year in Thousands of Gallons					
1949	243	245	245	232	220
1950		188	197	188	188
1951			183	179	176
1952				150	149
1953					146
B. Average Percent of "Normal"† Volume					
1949	89.6	91.3	95.6	89.4	82.9
1950		77.5	83.4	80.2	80.2
1951			84.6	81.8	81.0
1952				72.8	72.4
1953					74.0
C. Total Sales for All Postwar Stations Built Since September 30, 1948 (thousands of gallons)					
	4,411	16,266	27,883	40,764	50,187

* Stations built in the 12 months preceding September 30 of the stated years, 1949–53, not including stations sold and leased back.

† The volume a station was expected to achieve after the five-year lead-in period.

Exhibit 2

CUMULATIVE COMMITMENTS AND INCOME

1949 to 1954

(000,000)

	Cumulative Commitments, All Marketing Facilities	*Cumulative Cash Income after Taxes, Bulk Plant Service Station Channel*
1949	$ 4.7	$ 1.4
1950	8.3	2.9
1951	12.6	4.5
1952	17.0	7.0
1953	21.4	9.6
1954 (estimate)	24.8	12.6

cumulative cash income has been so slow relative to that in cumulative capital commitments that it may be some years before cash income can catch up with capital commitments.

The marketing department believed that an improvement in this situation would require not only a more realistic appraisal of new investment opportunities from a volume and profit standpoint, but also an adequate review of results from established stations and the elimination of unprofitable, low-gallonage outlets.

CURRENT PROPOSAL PROCEDURES

The three common types of service station arrangements, involving various means of financing land, building, and equipment, were (1) company-owned stations, (2) ground-lease stations, and (3) three-party lease stations. In company-owned stations, all assets were owned by the company; in ground-lease stations, the company leased land from an outsider, but owned the building and equipment; in three-party lease stations, the company leased the land and building, but owned the equipment. Each service station, however acquired, was ordinarily leased to an operator, who paid Olympian rent, generally based on the monthly sales volume of the station.

In considering new service station proposals, the company followed the basic approach of relating estimated cash income to total investment on the basis of a calculation of the discounted cash flow return on investment. Cash income was the after-tax cash flow expected to be generated by the station. Total investment was Olympian's required cash outlay for the assets purchased. For company-owned station proposals, the total investment included land, building, and equipment; for ground-lease stations, it included building and equipment; for three-party lease proposals, it included equipment only. In brief, the total investment was the value of the assets that appeared on the company's books.

An illustration of the calculation made for a company-owned station is shown in Exhibit 3. The economic life of company-owned and ground-lease outlets was considered to be 25 years; and for three-party lease outlets, 10 years. In the first instance, the economic life was the period after which it was estimated that a station would have to be either sold as obsolete property or rebuilt. In the second instance, it was the period after which a station would have to be reequipped.

A "normal" gallonage volume of gasoline sales was projected on the basis of station location, traffic, and street or highway frontage. The company assumed that on the average only 70 percent of normal gallonage would be sold in each of the first five years and that the normal would be maintained thereafter. Thus, two periods of different income levels were used in calculating the return. The net market spread used in calculating estimated income was detailed by products and was the difference between the tank wagon price (price at which products were sold to the service station operator) and the estimated bulk market price (based on published refinery-gate prices), plus a marketing differential (estimated selling expense that would have been incurred had the refinery sold the products to outside customers), and less (*a*) a current freight adjustment in many areas and (*b*) estimated commis-

Exhibit 3

APPRAISAL OF PROPOSED NEW RETAIL OUTLET
COMPANY OWNED, LESSEE OPERATED—CURRENT METHOD

(1) Total investment
Capitalized outlay

(*a*) Cost of plant and equipment	$38,000
(*b*) Cost of land	22,000
Total	$60,000

(2) *First 5 Years*

Gasoline Sales	*Gallons*
1st Year	100,000
2d Year	130,000
3d Year	150,000
4th Year	180,000
5th Year	200,000

(3) *Normal* annual net income before depreciation and income taxes

Product	*5th Year Sales Gallons*	*Per Gallon: Market Spread*	*Frt. or Frt. Adj.*	*Com-missions*	*Net Spread*	*Total Net Spread*
Regular Gasoline	130,000	$ .05175	$ —	$ .005	$ .04675	$ 6,078
Premium Gasoline	70,000	.06175	—	.005	.05675	3,973
Motor Oil	3,500	.40000	.0519	.066	.28210	987

(4) Gross profit after commissions	$11,038
(5) Add profit on TBA sales ($3.00 per 1,000 gal. gasoline)	600
(6) Add rent received ($.012 per gal. gasoline)	2,400
(7) Total income before expenses	$14,038
(8) Less expenses ($1,250 plus 1% of investment)	1,850
(9) Net income before indirect gain	$12,188
(10) Indirect gain 10% of line (9)	1,219
(11) Normal net income before depreciation and income taxes	$13,407

	1st Period 70% Normal	*End Period 100% Normal*	*Total*
(12) Economic life (years)	5	20	25
Average Annual			
(13) Net income before depreciation and income taxes	$ 9,385	$13,407	
(14) Less taxable depreciation on P&E (at 3.6%)	1,368	1,368	
(15) Taxable net income	$ 8,017	$12,039	
(16) Income taxes at 50%	4,009	6,020	
(17) Cash income after income taxes	$ 5,376	$ 7,387	
(18) Year to pay out (*9.5*)			
(19) Discount factors (*10*% return)	3.79	5.29	
(20) Present values (line 19 times line 17)	$20,375	$39,077	$59,452
Add land value 25th year (Project return discount factor 25th year — 10% = 0.01)			220
Total Present Value			$59,672

sions expense. For example: if the tank wagon price was 15.0 cents; the estimated bulk market price, 11.0 cents; the marketing differential, 0.1 cents; the current freight adjustment, 0.2 cents; and commissions, 0.5 cents; then the estimated net market spread was 3.4 cents. The tank wagon price was a long-run (up to 20-year) average of past prices in principally statewide or larger areas, and the bulk market price was similarly an average of historical refinery-gate prices. (In actual practice, Olympian stations were supplied by company-owned bulk plants or directly from company or exchange terminals.)

A Normal Net Income before Depreciation and Income Taxes was next calculated by subtracting direct cash costs (other than commissions) and estimated variable indirect costs from the estimate of total gross profit after commissions. Three income items were included as credits in figuring the costs: rent income from the service station lessee-operator, income from TBA (tires, batteries, and accessories) sales, both based on the gallonage estimate and a theoretical indirect gain to all stations in the market of 10 percent of the net income before indirect gain. The taxable net income was calculated by subtracting depreciation (at 3.6 percent on owned and ground-lease stations, and 9 percent on three-party lease stations), and then by applying a 50 percent income tax rate, the cash income after income taxes was found. Since the annual income in the first five years was different from that for the remaining years, a trial-and-error method was used to find the discount rate that would provide a present value (including the end value of land in owned station proposals, found by discounting the land investment at the projected rate of return) equal to the total investment. This rate was the indicated return on investment. The minimum acceptable return on investment was set at 10 percent after tax.

CURRENT PROCEDURES FOR EVALUATING PERFORMANCE

The current system of evaluating the actual performance consisted of (1) a comparison for each station of actual gallonage sales with gallonage sales anticipated at the time of the proposal and (2) an analysis of the profit and loss statement for each bulk plant, including the service stations in the bulk plant territory, whether or not they were supplied by the bulk plant. The primary measure of performance at new or rebuilt stations was gallonage sales, which were reported quarterly for each station open one year or more (see Exhibit 4). The quarterly report showed number of months open, normal annual volume of sales, actual volume in the preceding 12-month period, and difference between normal and actual. Failure of a station to attain its anticipated gallonage was called to the attention of the local manager for corrective action.

Also available in appraising service station performance was the Bulk Plant Manufacturing–Marketing Joint Income Statement (see Exhibit 5), an annual summary of pretax earnings for each bulk plant territory, ordinarily one or two counties. The bulk plant served four classes of trade: company service stations (company-owned, ground-lease, three-party lease), Olympian dealer outlets, farmers, and commercial or industrial consumers. The

Exhibit 4

POSTWAR SERVICE STATION CONSTRUCTION
NEW AND REBUILT STATIONS OPEN ONE YEAR OR MORE

Comparison of Fifth Year Estimated Gallonage with Last 12 Months' Gallonage

One Year's Sales Ending December 31, 1953

			Thousands of Gallons			
City	*Station Number*	*Number of Months Opened*	*Fifth Year Estimated Sales of Gasoline*	*Actual Sales of Gasoline*	*Over or (Under) Fifth Year Estimate*	*Actual as Percentage of Fifth Year Estimate*
A	2	13	156	82	(74)	53
B	52	32	156	197	41	126
B	50	12	210	91	(119)	43
B	39	17	330	169	(161)	51
C	1	39	192	103	(89)	54
D	6	45	180	149	(31)	83
E	1	35	168	18	(150)	11
F	2	60	252	169	(83)	67
G	1	34	180	69	(111)	38
H	1	43	180	85	(95)	47
I	1	56	216	267	51	124
J	1	34	210	125	(85)	60
K	5	17	144	75	(69)	52
L	1	64	180	164	(16)	91
M	2	48	240	178	(62)	74
N	2	59	180	298	118	166
O	6	38	240	84	(156)	35
P	1	35	240	100	(140)	42
P	1	49	180	—	(180)	—
Q	1	33	192	44	(148)	23
R	1	44	240	16	(224)	7
S	1	50	180	65	(115)	36
T	6	71	300	147	(153)	49
T	7	72	300	125	(175)	42
T	8	42	180	99	(81)	55
T	9	45	180	162	(18)	90
T	11	41	240	91	(149)	38
T	12	48	240	91	(149)	38
T	13	37	192	226	34	118
T	14	19	240	155	(85)	65
T	15	35	180	118	(62)	66
T	16	35	180	88	(92)	49
T	17	37	198	90	(108)	45
U	1	34	192	192	—	—
V	1	36	240	123	(117)	51
V	1	74	240	54	(186)	23
X	1	34	150	83	(67)	55
Y	1	77	240	131	(109)	55
Z	1	36	216	91	(125)	42

statement indicated for the four classes combined total sales and pretax earnings before and after direct and allocated indirect expenses. It was called manufacturing–marketing joint income statement because no effort was

Exhibit 5

JOINT MANUFACTURING–MARKETING INCOME STATEMENT
January 1, 1953 to December 31, 1953

	Service Station* Amount	Service Station* Unit§	Bulk Plant† Amount	Bulk Plant† Unit§	Total‡ Amount	Total‡ Unit§
Gross margin before commissions					$130,268	$.0614
Direct expenses:						
Rent	$ 2,198		$ 217		2,415	
Net three-party lease rental	4,374		—		4,374	
Three-party depreciation	188		—		188	
Property taxes	2,268		605		2,873	
Depreciation and retirements	5,508		497		6,005	
Rent income (deduct)	(15,292)		—		(15,292)	
Total Real Estate and Plant	$ (756)	($.0004)	$1,319	$.0047	$ 563	.0003
Commissions or bulk plant salaries					19,397	.0091
Salary and travel	$ 4,873	.0026	905	.0033	5,778	.0027
Net two-party lease rentals	—		266	.0034‖	266	
Stock (over) and short	—		2,151		2,151	.0010
Loaned equipment	—		610	.0022	610	
Loaned equipment depreciation	—		146	.0005	146	
Advertising	—				16,311	.0077
Operating supplies	374	.0002	613		987	
Rebuilds, repairs and maintenance	3,646	.0020	300	.0011	3,946	.0019
Station auditing clearance			262		262	
TBA income (deduct)			(1,130)		(1,130)	(.0005)
Miscellaneous	1,169		114		1,283	
Total direct expenses					$ 50,570	$.0238
Profit before indirect expenses					79,698	.0376
Indirect expenses					23,530	.0111
Profit after indirect expenses					$ 56,168	$.0265

FINANCIAL INVESTMENT

	Real Estate	Buildings and Equipment	Total
Bulk plant	—	$ 15,000	$ 15,000
Service stations(s)	$ 70,689	133,047	203,736
Loaned equipment	—		
Three-party	—	3,157	3,157
Farmers	—	5,009	5,009
Other consumers	—	710	710
Surplus	—	27	27
Truck tanks	—	3,301	3,301
Total Investment	$ 70,689	$160,251	$230,940

Rate of return on total investment.... 24.32%

Unit Basis:
* Total service station gasoline volume.
† Total all products bulk plant ex-service station gasoline volume, 277,932.
‡ Total bulk plant and service station volume.
§ Dollars per gallon.
‖ Total two-party lease gasoline volume, 77,170.
Number of company service stations, 8.

made to apportion the income to manufacturing and marketing activities, as was done in the calculation of return on investment for the purpose of investment selection. The statement also showed a pretax percentage return on investment, based on gross financial investment and earnings after allocated indirect expenses. No statement was prepared for service stations or bulk plants individually.

RECOMMENDED CHANGES IN PROCEDURES FOR PROPOSAL SELECTION

The marketing department proposed that the minimum acceptable appraisal return on investment be lowered to 8 percent, and suggested several procedural changes for appraising new investment proposals in order (1) to improve forecasting gallonage sales and (2) to provide economic comparability in alternative financing proposals. The following is a summary of the procedural recommendations contained in the department's memorandum.

1. Inasmuch as the cash income used in the calculation of return on investment was dependent on the forecast normal sales volume, a carefully thought-out forecast was essential. The experience of the past seven years, however, indicated a continuing optimistic bias in the forecast of gallonage sales. This was largely due to the eagerness of local managers to originate under the expansion program a sufficient number of investment proposals which would be accepted by top management. Two things were therefore recommended in order to improve the forecasting accuracy: First, the regional manager could give final approval only to proposals showing estimated gallonage sales no higher than the highest volume attained in the most recent calendar year by an already existing station of the same type and size in the same market. Second, when new service stations in any region failed to realize their first full calendar year estimates of gallonage by more than 10 percent, the authority for new project approval by regional managers concerned should be rescinded. In such cases, new projects would thereafter require the approval of the marketing headquarters.

2. Under present procedures, the three types of proposals were not comparable. Since the impact of fixed rent commitments on the company's cash or credit position was not fully recognized, the order of desirability of the three different types of proposals from a return-on-investment standpoint was always (1) three-party lease, (2) ground lease, and (3) owned. It was therefore proposed that annual fixed rent commitments be capitalized and thus considered as a component of the total investment. The capitalized amount would be the present value of the annual rent payments, found by discounting these payments over the life of the lease at 5 percent, the company's approximate pretax borrowing rate on long-term debt. To afford further comparability between lease and purchase proposals, the same economic life would be used in the appraisal of all projects, provided in lease deals the company had the necessary options. Twenty years, rather than 25, would be the maximum life assumed, in light of company experience on obsolescence and building replacement. The end value of land in com-

pany-owned outlets would be deducted from the total investment to get appraisal investment. This value was to be found by discounting the land investment at a 6 percent after-tax rate, (i.e., the company's long-run average cost of capital adjusted for an assumed average increase in value of land of approximately 20 percent). These changes would allow the development of an appraisal format that provided practical comparison of a purchase proposal versus a groundlease versus a three-party lease. Exhibit 6 illustrates the recommended methods of calculating the returns on investment for the three types of projects.

Exhibit 6

APPRAISAL OF NEW RETAIL OUTLET—PROPOSED METHOD

(20 Years of Life)

		Purchase Proposal	*Ground Lease*	*3-Party Lease*
(1) Appraisal investment:				
(*a*) Land		$ 22,000	$ —	$ —
(*b*) Equipment		13,000	13,000	13,000
(*c*) Building and other		25,000	25,000	—
(*d*) Rent commitment (present value—5% discount factor)		—	19,687*	45,479†
(*e*) Total		$ 60,000	$ 57,687	$ 58,479
(*f*) Less end value of land (6% discount factor)		6,820	—	—
(*g*) Appraisal investment		$ 53,180	$ 57,687	$ 58,479
(2) Estimated gasoline sales gals. (all years)		200,000	200,000	200,000
(3) Gross margin:				
(*a*) Gasoline	5.78	$ 11,560	$ 11,560	$ 11,560
(*b*) Other products at 10%	.58	1,156	1,156	1,156
(*c*) Total	6.36	$ 12,716	$ 12,716	$ 12,716
(4) Direct cash costs:				
(*a*) Commission or salaried B/P expense	.60	$ 1,200	$ 1,200	$ 1,200
(*b*) Operating supplies		100	100	100
(*c*) Repairs and maintenance:				
Equipment at 4%		520	520	520
Building and other at 1%		250	250	250
(*d*) Property taxes		380	380	380
(*e*) Rent income	(1.25)	(2,500)	(2,500)	(2,500)
(*f*) TBA income	(.15)	(300)	(300)	(300)
(*g*) Total		$ (350)	$ (350)	$ (350)
(5) Cash contribution, including manufacturing		$ 13,066	$ 13,066	$ 13,066
(6) Estimated manufacturing profit	.75	1,500	1,500	1,500
(7) Cash contribution, excluding manufacturing		$ 11,566	$ 11,566	$ 11,566
(8) Depreciation at 4.5%		1,710	1,710	585
(9) Amortization		—	984	2,274
(10) Taxable cash contribution		$ 9,856	$ 8,872	$ 8,707
(11) Income taxes at 54%		5,322	4,791	4,702
(12) After-tax appraisal cash contribution		$ 6,244	$ 6,775	$ 6,864
(13) Discount factor		8.52	8.51	8.52
(14) After-tax DCF return on appraisal investment		10%	10%	10%

* Rent $1,580/yr.
† Rent $3,650/yr.

3. Recent company studies indicated that it could be assumed that most stations would attain their maximum volume during the first full calendar year. Therefore, it was recommended that a uniform cash contribution be used for the full life of the project. This change would also eliminate the need for a trial-and-error method of calculation.

4. In the absence of figures for strictly service station channels, gasoline gross margins used should be the most recent three-year average bulk plant and service station margin per gallon as taken from the detailed annual income statement for the market involved. These margins were intended to reflect actual market conditions and to distinguish the variations from market to market. The three-year average would give reasonable weight to price disturbances caused by market pressures. Gross margins on other products were to be calculated at 10 percent of gasoline gross margin, which recent analyses indicated to be more in line with actual results than the amount currently used in appraisals.

5. Only direct cash costs, excluding estimated variable indirect costs, should be considered. Direct costs for supplies should be $100. Repairs and maintenance should be 4 percent of equipment cost plus 1 percent of other depreciable assets per year. These amounts reflected actual operating data more closely than those currently used.

6. Rent income from station operators should be calculated at the actual rate proposed for the outlet involved, rather than at the average of the 10 highest rent income stations in the region. TBA income of 15 cents per gallon was a more realistic expectation than 30 cents, according to the most recent income studies. Indirect gain should not be included.

7. The cash contribution calculated from the estimated operating data appears to be the gross profit from marketing operations. In effect, however, the manufacturing profit from refinery operations was included in the gross margin rate. Consequently, in order to appraise the marketing-only return on investment, it would be necessary to deduct an estimated refinery profit from the cash contribution. Analysis of 1953 data indicated that $.0075 per gallon of gasoline sold approximated the profit on the manufacture of gasoline and all other products sold through a service station.

8. The taxable cash contribution from marketing-only would then be calculated by deducting depreciation (at 4.5 percent) on those portions of the appraisal investment that appeared as assets on the company's books, based on a 20-year economic life. In the case of lease proposals, the present value of the rent commitments would be amortized over 20 years and the annual amount taken as another tax deduction. Next, application of the correct 54 percent income tax rate to the taxable cash contribution would give the after-tax appraisal cash contribution. Finally, the discount factor would be found by dividing the appraisal cash contribution into the appraisal investment. The appraisal rate of return corresponding to the discount factor would be easily read from published discount tables.

RECOMMENDED CHANGES IN PROCEDURES FOR PERFORMANCE EVALUATION

According to the memorandum of the marketing department, no matter how carefully and intelligently the original decision to build a new service station had been made, many unpredictable circumstances could cause a poor showing by a particular station. For example, one station was built next to a new housing development with only one competitive station in the area. After a year of satisfactory sales, two other stations were built by competitors within a block of the Olympian location, and thereafter Olympian's station sold only about two-thirds of its predicted volume. Other instances occurred in which in-town stations suffered from the population movement to the suburbs. This was a continuing problem, not easily solved. On one occasion, in order to take advantage of this shift, the company traded an in-town station for two sites on the edge of town, and though this increased the total gasoline sales in the area, neither of the new stations sold as much gasoline as had the one in-town station. Thus, it was clear that a constant after-the-fact evaluation of the performance of service stations was necessary. Should a service station perform below expectations, the cause for the unsatisfactory performance ought to be determined and corrective actions taken. If necessary, the service station could be disposed of.

The memorandum stated that the current system of evaluation was inadequate. The quarterly gallonage variance report failed to give consideration to the effect on earnings of gross margins and expenses. The manufacturing–marketing joint income statement hid instances of poor profit performance at individual stations. In addition, it did not permit individual station comparison of actual returns with forecast returns on investment.

In order to overcome these shortcomings, it was recommended that a Performance Return Analysis be made for individual stations at the time of approval of investment, and that the Bulk Plant Manufacturing–Marketing Joint Income Statement be changed to an annual Profitability Analysis Statement, showing a similar return individually for each bulk plant and each service station. Calculation of the performance return is illustrated in Exhibit 7. The estimated manufacturing profit of 0.75 cents per gallon was added back to obtain manufacturing–marketing joint cash flow; before-tax rather than after-tax figures were used; only assets appearing on the books were included as investment; and annual lease-payments in cases of ground leases and three-party leases were deducted from the cash flow. In summary, the performance return was the discounted cash flow manufacturing–marketing joint return before taxes on booked investment. These adjustments were necessary because company accounting practices neither capitalized lease payments nor readily yielded estimated marketing-only incomes.

In order to determine the relationship between appraisal return and performance return, a study made in 1954 calculated the two kinds of returns for about 400 new, owned service stations which had been built since 1949. The analysis indicated that the performance return was generally about double the appraisal return when the appraisal return was above 7 percent. When the appraisal return was below 7 percent, the relationship widened. This presented no problem, however, since such low returns on either basis

Exhibit 7

PROPOSED METHOD OF CALCULATING PERFORMANCE RETURN

	Purchase Proposal	*Ground Lease*	*3-Party Lease*
(1) Booked investment (Exhibit 6)			
Land	$22,000	—	—
Equipment	13,000	$13,000	$13,000
Building and other	25,000	25,000	—
Total	$60,000	$38,000	$13,000
(2) Cash contribution, including manufacturing profit (Exhibit 6, line (5))	$13,066	$13,066	$13,066
(3) Less: Annual rental (Exhibit 6, footnote)	—	$ 1,580	$ 3,650
(4) Cash contribution, including manufacturing profit, less annual rental	$13,066	$11,486	$ 9,416
(5) Discount factor	4.59	2.43	1.38
(6) Pretax DCF return (20 years)	21%	41%	72%

indicated unsatisfactory results. Exhibit 8 is a summary of these comparative return calculations.

Another study of performance and appraisal returns for all three kinds of stations (owned, ground lease and three-party) determined that, on the average, where the performance return was less than 15 percent for an owned station, less than 20 percent for a ground-lease station, and less than 50 percent for a three-party lease station the appraisal return was less than 7 percent.

CONCLUSION

The memorandum concluded that implementation of the 8-percent return-on-investment goal and of the recommended procedures would result in more effective selection of new service station outlets and more meaningful measurement of performance, thus enabling the company to take positive action with regard to performance improvement and the disposition of unprofitable low-gallonage outlets.

QUESTIONS

1. Should the recommended changes in procedures for evaluating proposals for new stations be adopted?
2. Should the recommended changes in procedures for evaluating the performance of stations be adopted?
3. What do you think of the coupling between these two procedural areas —proposal evaluation (i.e., capital expenditure analysis) and performance evaluation?

Exhibit 8

RETURN ON INVESTMENT ON 411 NEW OWNED SERVICE STATIONS IN OPERATION THE FULL CALENDAR YEAR, 1953

	Average Appraisal Return Percentage*	Average Performance Return Percentage†
District A	6%	14%
District B	7	15
District C	10	20
Region 1 total	7%	16%
District D	6%	14%
District E	9	19
District F	4	11
Region 2 total	7%	16%
District G	11%	21%
District H	13	27
District I	9	19
Region 3 total	11%	22%
District J	8%	18%
District K	9	19
Region 4 total	8%	18%
District L	11%	23%
District M	7	16
Region 5 total	9%	19%
All regions	9%	18%

* Twenty-year DCF marketing-only return (after taxes) on marketing investment, including capitalized rent commitment.

† Twenty-year DCF manufacturing–marketing return (before taxes) on book value marketing investment only.

Case 12-3

Petroleum Supply Company*

On December 20, 1958, the Petroleum Supply Company, with headquarters in Houston, Texas, mailed out its usual Christmas bonus checks to all of its more than 400 employees. This bonus averaged a week's salary for each employee and totaled something in excess of $40,000.

When the financial statements for the month were reviewed by the chairman of the board, who was also the majority stockholder, he immediately spotted this annual disbursement figure classified as "bonus." He had never liked the idea of paying a Christmas bonus. It was not that he had any basic objection to paying a bonus to his employees, but he had an ingrained philosophy about a bonus. He felt that as long as it was an outright gift with no implications of reward for superior performance, it not only was not appreciated by the employees who received it, but it was costly to the company with no reciprocating benefits. He decided to do something about it.

He called in the president and general manager of the company and made known his views. In fact, he said that he would no longer authorize the payment of employees' bonuses until the management presented to him a plan which would embody the following essential elements:

1. It would reward performance that resulted in improving the company's profit position and would provide an incentive to employees to achieve this goal.
2. It would not be paid to everyone. First, the plan would extend only to those employees whose positions were such that they could substantially affect the company's profit position. Among this group of employees, the plan would have to provide that in order to receive a bonus one must earn it. This meant that some would receive a bonus and some would not.
3. The formula for figuring the bonus must provide for an amount large enough to furnish an incentive for superior performance; no niggardly amounts would be paid.

* Although not previously copyrighted, this case was written by Professor E. L. Swearingen, Oklahoma State University, published by Intercollegiate Case House (ICH 7G42), Soldiers Field, Boston, and reproduced here with the permission of the author.

4. The amount to be disbursed should be roughly the same as in previous years; but because of the rearrangement in distribution, the amounts received by individuals who qualified would be substantially increased.

The chairman reviewed with the president the sales and profit figures for the year just completed and compared them with previous years. He stated that the profit figures for the past year had been disappointing. The facts reviewed in this session included the following:

1. Of more than 40 retail outlets, over 20 percent had sales amounting to less than the break-even point.
2. The assets of the company totaled something more than $14 million, of which about $5 million was invested in inventory, $8 million in receivables, and $1 million in fixed assets, including over $300,000 in automobiles and trucks.
3. Sales for the past year had declined somewhat from the previous year's total of almost $50 million, but operating expenses had continued to rise steadily.
4. A net profit (before taxes) of only $1 million in 1957 had produced a return on investment of a little under 11 percent, which he considered less than satisfactory. The situation had worsened in 1958.

The chairman told the president that he wanted this situation improved and it was his belief that a well-administered incentive bonus plan could be an important aid in improvement.

Needless to say, the president was concerned over the chairman's straightforward mandates, nor did he doubt that the chairman meant every word he said. When he returned to his office, he called a staff meeting of the principal officers, and they talked over the assignment that lay before them. There was some sentiment in the group for seeking the services of an outside management consultant, but the consensus was that at least a first effort should be made with the talent at hand, thus saving the consultant's fee and perhaps discovering a formula better adapted to this company's needs than one an outsider could devise.

The president appointed a committee to devise a draft of a bonus plan. This committee included the controller, who was to serve as chairman; the general sales manager; and the director of purchases. The first problem they tackled was identification of the areas of operation where improvement would have a direct bearing on the return on investment percentage to which the chairman had obviously attached considerable significance. These areas were not hard to identify. They were broken down into three general categories:

1. Sales and/or gross profit ratios.
2. Purchasing.
3. Management of the company's assets and employees.

The next step was to identify an individual employee's contribution to, or responsibility for, improved performance in these areas. The sales manager foresaw great difficulties in identifying improved sales volume with an individual salesman, principally because of the nature of the supply industry. He made three points:

1. Many of the company's best customers placed their orders with the company because of financial ties through credit.
2. Personal friendships existed between the top officers of some companies that were good customers and the top officers of Petroleum Supply Company.
3. Many of the major customers apportioned their business among suppliers in an area.

All these conditions made it relatively unimportant which salesman called on and serviced an account; the volume of business from these customers would remain virtually unchanged.

The sales manager recognized a further problem. In the supply industry, it was customary for a field salesman to call on and service the tool pusher or drilling superintendent at a field location; but orders were placed at the city where the customer's headquarters were located. The city salesman felt that his receipt of the order was a reward for the service he had rendered the purchasing department of the customer; whereas the field salesman was equally sure that except for his superb service and efforts with the field staff of the customer, the order would never have been placed. The sales manager believed that to have the various salesmen in competition with one another to receive credit for orders was a detriment to the company's overall sales effort.

The director of purchases also foresaw problems in attempting to recognize and reward individual buyers. He believed that discounts obtained on an order were related to factors over which the buyer's control was so small that it was not a valid basis for a bonus award.

The controller viewed as somewhat easier the task of identifying and measuring performance within the area of management of the company's assets and its employees. He pointed out that the overwhelming preponderance of the company's assets were concentrated in inventory and receivables, and that good management of either one of these assets involved maximum turnover and minimum loss, both of which were easy to identify through accounting records. Expense control also was a direct result of good management of employees; and since the greatest items of expense, other than payroll, were operation of the company's fleet of automobiles and trucks, long-distance telephone expense, and entertainment and travel expense, improvement in any of these areas would be easy to measure from accounting records. By the same token, gross revenue at any given field store in relation to expenses incurred was a natural for measuring improvement. It would be easy to exactly identify the investment at any field store, including, of course, investment in inventory, receivables, cash, and fixed assets. Taking the lead furnished by the chairman, the controller decided that the return on investment should be measured at the stores, where income had to be generated.

He believed the managers of the stores held the key to improved management of assets and people that was necessary for a better return on investment. He also believed that store managers were largely sales-oriented and had never really given much consideration to the idea that they had capital invested or entrusted to their custody on which a satisfactory rate of return had to be earned. They therefore constituted an ideal target for an incentive program for better management.

Most of the store managers had a high school education or less, and since all accounting work was performed in the headquarters office the managers understood very little of the relationship between their performance and the return on investment at their stores. It was the controller's view that a concentrated management training program for store managers, supplemented by a bonus plan, would make them conscious of the necessity of increasing profits through better management and would furnish them the incentive to put better practices into effect.

Of course, the controller recognized that obstacles had to be met, such as identifying sales allocated to a store because of delivery into its territory even though the store really could lay no claim for credit. The biggest single item involved was oil country pipe, which historically had been in short supply and had been allocated to customers.

On the basis of the above considerations, the committee recommended to the president that the controller prepare a bonus plan embodying the elements he thought would satisfy the chairman's mandate. Shortly thereafter, the controller submitted to the president the bonus plan described in the appendix.

The president observed that it was drawn to include only store managers and district managers. He said, "You can bet your bottom dollar that the salesmen on the road aren't going to be happy when they hear about a bonus plan for store managers. What does the general sales manager have to say about the proposed plan?"

The general sales manager had had his say all right, and in brief he did not think well of it. His views were these:

1. The plan was discriminatory against salesmen.

2. The plan tended to overemphasize the importance of the management function at store locations, whereas the really important key to improved performance lay in increased sales volume.

3. Any bonus paid purely on application of a formula based upon accounting records would result in some inequities, i.e.,
   a) Payments to those who did not deserve them.
   b) Failure to pay some who were deserving, without regard to what the figures showed.

In spite of the misgivings of the general sales manager, the draft of the plan was submitted to the chairman, who approved it, and it was put into effect.

One final obstacle had to be overcome before the matter could be considered concluded—namely, how to announce to the employees that their Christmas bonus would be discontinued and that a limited bonus plan, open only to managers, would be substituted. A gratuitous circumstance contributed very substantially to the solution of this potentially serious problem. A wage survey conducted by the office of personnel had disclosed that the Petroleum Supply Company had not kept pace with the industry in its basic salaries and that an adjustment was needed to correct this condition; whereupon, an overall wage increase was authorized and placed in effect.

The announcement of discontinuance of the Christmas bonus was made to coincide with the announcement of the overall wage increase, which was slightly in excess of the Christmas bonus. It was therefore possible to announce that in lieu of the Christmas bonus an amount in excess of this was now being added to the regular compensation.

QUESTIONS

1. What changes would you propose to the bonus plan outlined in the appendix?
2. Even with these changes, would you, as the president, approve this plan?

Appendix

A Bonus Plan for Store Managers and District Managers to Provide an Incentive for Better Management

I. General Statement of Plan.
This bonus plan is designed to provide store and district managers with an opportunity to earn additional compensation for improved performance as reflected by an increased return on the company's investment at the stores under their management.

II. Prerequisites of the Plan.
In order for the plan to work fairly, both to the company and to the managers involved, it is necessary that the manager at each location:

A. Be given sufficient authority over the management of his assets, personnel, and the sales program within his assigned territory to give him substantial control over his performance.

B. Be charged with accountability and responsibility for the performance of his store or stores.

C. Be furnished with adequate yardsticks to measure his performance, the information used to measure performance being based upon highly accurate reports of achievement.

III. Definition of Terms.
Following are definitions of terms used:

A. *Investment.* Investment at each location will include the annual average of the following items.

1. Cost of month-end inventory maintained at the store, excluding:

a) Casing, tubing, and drill pipe.

b) Used machinery which the machinery department determines should be charged against the general office inventory account.

c) Central stocks placed at a given location at the direction of the purchasing department.

2. Investment in automobiles and trucks assigned to the location.
3. Investment in furniture and fixtures (including shelving, air conditioners, typewriters, counters, desks, chairs, file cases, adding machines, etc.).
4. Amounts invested in receivables growing out of bonusable sales credited to the location.
5. Funds maintained in agents' bank account at each location.

NOTE: Company-owned real estate, such as store buildings and lots, is not classified as an investment. Rental will be charged for the use of these facilities and will be included in the monthly store expenses.

B. *Bonusable Sales.* Bonusable sales are those for which a manager will receive credit in computing his bonus. They will include the following:

1. Allocated direct sales of machinery, supplies, and aluminum, plastic, and line pipe, except those sales that result exclusively from the activities of general office or sales office personnel.
2. Stock shipments out of a store's inventory, except casing, tubing, and drill pipe.
3. Allocated sales accomplished through emergency order buy-outs.

The omission of casing, tubing, and drill pipe from bonusable sales requires further comment. It is felt that in today's market no appreciable efforts or expense on the part of store personnel are required to sell casing, tubing, and drill pipe. All available pipe of this type could be easily disposed of through the general office by allocation to a few customers. On the other hand, such pipe allocated to a store, either by way of direct sales or to its inventory, constitutes a lead item that, properly used, can be a device for generating sales of supplies and equipment classified as bonusable sales.

The cost of casing, tubing, and drill pipe in a store's inventory is not to be charged as an investment at the store when computing return on investment.

The exclusion of casing, tubing, and drill pipe from the bonusable sales and investment is based upon today's market conditions. This determination is subject to change at any time, if and when conditions change so that the sale of casing, tubing, and drill pipe becomes competitive and the market changes from a seller's to a buyer's market.

The theory on which stock shipments are identified as bonusable sales rather than allocated stock sales is: a store that maintains an inventory and has the cost of such inventory included in the investment on which it must make a profit return in order to enjoy a bonus is the store whose management has foreseen the requirements for the material and has stocked its inventory to meet such requirements, even though it may be sold by another store in another location.

C. *Bonusable Gross Profit.* Bonusable gross profit is the balance remaining after deducting cost of sales from bonusable sales.

D. *Bonusable Net Profit.* Bonusable net profit is the profit left after subtracting expenses from bonusable gross profit.

E. *Expenses.* Expenses are those operating costs, in addition to cost of sales, that will be deducted from bonusable gross profit determining bonusable net profit. Such expenses shall include:

1. Regular monthly direct store expense.
2. The pro rata share of total district office expense.

   The pro rata share of total district expense of the district office, divided by the number of stores in the district.
3. Cost of routine general office services which apply to bonusable sales.

   Every sale involves, over and above those incurred at a store or district, certain direct expenses arising because certain routine services necessary to consummate the sale are performed at the general office, where by the use of skilled specialists and modern machines and equipment they can be handled more economically than if performed individually at each store point. For example:

   a) Processing of orders, including pricing, costing, invoicing, recording, collection, and maintenance of customers' accounts.
   b) Purchasing of materials for inventory and direct shipments.
   c) Maintaining and servicing accounts payable.
   d) Credit investigations and issuing lines of credit.
4. Actual cost of special general office services.

   This includes:

   a) Making quotations at managers' request.
   b) Repossession or special collection efforts involving employment of a collection agency or prosecution of a claim in the courts.
   c) Sales assistance. Special assistance from the general office staff is available on request to complete a sale. Most often, this applies to the sale of a rig or other heavy machinery. For example, when a store determines that a customer within its territory is in the market for the purchase of a rig or other heavy machinery items, such sales can ofttimes be expedited

by calling on the machinery sales division to furnish a machinery specialist who can appraise machinery or work out the details of sales and terms of payment. The services of such specialists are available to a store, but their services require incurring expenses of travel, entertainment, communications, and the time of personnel. The expenses incurred will be charged directly against the store on an actual cost basis, whether the sale for which the services were requested is consummated or not. Money is wasted each year within the company by requesting such services when the opportunity for consummating the sale is extremely remote. A store or district manager must share the responsibility for incurring such expenses and share the risk involved in incurring needless expense.

5. Operating losses incurred as a result of the following will be charged directly against the responsible store as an expense when determination is made by the bonus committee that the loss resulted from negligence, bad judgment, or failure to adhere to prescribed company policy or procedure by store personnel:
   a) Inventory shortages.
   b) Loss of cost of repairs to damaged property.
   c) Loss on sale of assets.
   d) Bad debt losses.

F. *Return on Investment.* Return on investment at any given location may be computed in terms of percentage by dividing the total of all investment items (A, above) into the bonusable net profit (D, above).

G. *Bonus Committee.* The bonus committee is a committee of three company executives appointed by the general manager to review facts and circumstances of any questions arising out of administration of the bonus plan which are not specifically covered in this statement of the plan, and to render decisions which will resolve such questions.

IV. Earning a Bonus.

The purpose of this bonus plan is to create an incentive for managers to improve the return on the company's investment at the stores under control of the respective store managers and district managers. It would be highly desirable to outline at this point a specific formula that would permit a manager to know in advance the exact amount of bonus he would be able to earn if he achieved certain specific improvements in his operation. Unfortunately, it has not been possible to reconstruct information on past performance at the various store locations which would permit a completely accurate measure of past performance in those areas of management held to be subject to improvement. In order to establish such a measure with the degree of accuracy believed to be necessary, it is going to be essential that additional information be recorded over a period of at least one year.

In lieu of a precise formula for computing a bonus based on improvement, the entire matter of awarding a bonus to district and store managers for the year 1959 is going to be left in the hands of a bonus committee appointed by the general manager. At the end of the current year, this committee will review the achievements of each store and will make an independent determination of whether a bonus shall be awarded. This committee admittedly will not be able to arrive at a conclusion as to the achievement at each store on a basis of mathematical certainty. It will, however, take into account all known factors of measurement and will base its determinations of bonus awards on its best judgment of improved return on investment in 1959 over the 1958 performance. It is possible to state at this time the general basis upon which bonus award determinations will be made.

A. *Bonus Will Be Based on Improved Return on Investment in 1959 over 1958.* The 1958 company-wide average return on investment from bonusable sales is tentatively accepted as "satisfactory." It follows that there are a number of stores and districts whose return on investment during the year 1958 was less than average. There are also a number of stores and districts whose return for the year 1958 was better than average. Since the whole purpose of this bonus plan is to provide an incentive for every manager to improve his performance, bonus awards will be made to managers for improvement over 1958 performance, whether this performance was above or below average.

B. *A Reward for Holding Your Own.* There will undoubtedly be cases in which a store achieves a 1959 return on investment that is the same as the 1958 return. In such cases, recognition for holding your own will be given by awarding a bonus. It is probable, however, that the bonus awarded in these circumstances will not be so generous as that made to those managers whose stores have shown an increased return on investment. It is also probable that the award made to a manager whose store earned a satisfactory or better return on investment in 1958 and who held his own in 1959 will be more generous than that to the manager whose return in 1958 was less than satisfactory and who held his own in 1959.

C. *A Premium for Achieving a Satisfactory Return.* It is probable that the manager of a store that earned less than a satisfactory return on investment in 1958 but was able to improve his return on investment in 1959 to a point that reached or exceeded the company-wide average will receive special consideration in the form of a premium bonus over and above one which would have been earned solely on the basis of improvement from previous year's performance.

D. *Some Will Earn No Bonus.* It probably is inevitable that there will be stores whose 1959 performance measured in terms of return on investment will not be so good as their 1958 performance. At those stores where the 1958 performance was less than satisfactory and the 1959 performance was worse, it is highly probable that no bonuses will be paid to the managers. In those cases where even though the 1959 performance was not so good as 1958 but the return on investment in 1959 is still considered satisfactory, a bonus will be awarded to the store manager involved, although the amounts will be less than those awarded to managers who held their own or showed improvement.

V. Computing Bonuses for District Managers.

A district manager's bonus will be determined by the return on total investment in the district from all bonusable net profit earned by the stores in his district. In general, in determining the bonus awards to be made to district managers the same considerations as those outlined above will be given, except that the performance of all stores in the district will be taken into account in measuring the district manager's achievements.

VI. What will be the amounts of bonus awards?

It is not possible at this time to state with any degree of certainty the exact amount of bonus awards. First, the amount available for distribution will be directly related to the profit earned for the year 1959; second, it is going to be necessary to have at least one year's experience in determining the profits that will be generated by the improved performance which justifies bonus awards and the distribution of bonus funds available. Until such experience has been acquired, it will be necessary to call on managers to rely on the fairness of the bonus committee and its expressed intention to reward as generously as possible those employees whose management efforts and profit results have contributed the most to the company's profit position. About the only guide that can be given at this time is that it is believed the minimum bonus should be $300, and for superior performance bonuses may reach a high that will approximate 10 percent of the manager's annual salary.

[Sections VII, VIII, IX of the report are omitted. They describe the details of monthly performance reports and of how bonuses will be figured for new managers, managers transferred, and terminated managers; amendments to the plan; and so on.]